ELIZABETHAN RECUSANT PROSE
1559-1582

WILLIAM, CARDINAL ALLEN

From the contemporary (?) portrait at Ushaw College

Elizabethan Recusant Prose

1559-1582

A historical and critical account of the books of the Catholic Refugees printed and published abroad and at secret presses in England together with an annotated bibliography of the same

by

A. C. SOUTHERN, PH.D.(LOND.)

with a Foreword by

H. O. EVENNETT

Fellow of Trinity College (Cambridge) and University Lecturer in History in the University of Cambridge

SANDS & CO. (PUBLISHERS), LIMITED

15 KING STREET, LONDON, W.C.2

and

76 CAMBRIDGE STREET, GLASGOW

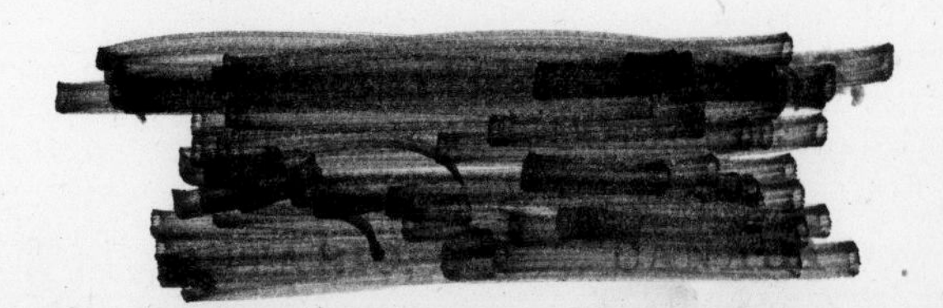

Made and printed in England by
STAPLES PRESS LIMITED
at their Rochester, Kent, establishment

It is wel knowne . . . that in the realme of Ingland at this day, there are three different and opposite bodies of religion, that are of most bulk, and that do carry most sway, and power, which three bodies, are knowne commonly in Ingland by the names of Protestants, Puritanes, and Papistes, though the later two, do not acknowledge these names, and for the same cause would not I vse them neither, if it were not only for cleernes and breuities sake, for that as often I haue protested, my meaning is not to giue offence to any side or partye.

R. Doleman. *A Conference about the Next Succession to the Crowne* (1594).

To

My Mother

R.I.P.

FOREWORD

The Catholic Recusants of Elizabeth's reign are not of sentimental or picturesque interest merely. They are men and women profoundly significant in our national history. Without their sacrifices and heroism English Catholicism would not exist to-day, except perhaps as a wholly foreign import from Ireland or France. Nor is this their only importance. The writers whom Dr. Southern studies in this book were drawn from the front rank of early Elizabethan England's men of learning and letters, and their part in the development of English prose can no longer be regarded as a backwater. It is therefore in more senses than one not only a denominational but also a general historical interest that is served by Dr. Southern's book, the fruit of long labours which have won for him the Ph.D. degree of London University. With equal learning and discernment he has set out systematically before us the nature and scope of the Recusant prose of the first twenty-three years of Elizabeth's reign, in a manner that will make his work indispensable for any further study, either bibliographical or literary, of the subject-matter. Perhaps it is a matter of reproach to Catholic scholarship that no such general treatment of the writings of the Recusants has been attempted before. It is much to be hoped, therefore, that Dr. Southern will find not only readers but also emulators, for there is a great harvest waiting to be reaped in the literary and other aspects of Recusant history – and, indeed, in the whole story of Catholicism in modern England.

H. O. Evennett.

Trinity College,
Cambridge.

11th January, 1950.

AUTHOR'S PREFACE

This book presents in an abridged form a thesis which was originally submitted and approved for the degree of Ph.D. of the University of London. As its title indicates, it deals with a select group of prose writings covering roughly the first half of the reign of Queen Elizabeth. It was nearly thirty years ago that the present Provincial of the Society of Jesus, the Very Rev. M. C. D'Arcy, suggested to the writer that a study of these Catholic authors would be a rewarding piece of work, and it was in consequence of that suggestion that some ten years later he approached the Quain Professor of English in University College, London (the late Dr. R. W. Chambers), with a view to a thesis on the subject for the degree of Ph.D. It was under Professor Chambers's supervision that most of the work for this thesis was done. What the writer owes to his enthusiasm and inspiration and care he cannot adequately express. However imperfect the result of his labours may be, the profit which he has derived from working under so outstanding a scholar as Chambers is something 'out of all count', as all know who have had the like privilege.

It is a noteworthy fact that all the Catholic authors (with one notable exception) to whom reference is made in the chapters of this book either have been entirely ignored in our histories of English literature, or have been given such scant reference as amounts to the same thing. It is significant that such treatment has not been meted out to those whom we may regard as their opposite numbers. Such names as Jewel, Fulke, Sandys and John Rainolds are all at least remotely familiar to the student of Elizabethan literature; but how many know of Allen or Harding or Sander or William (the brother of John) Rainolds? *The Cambridge History of English Literature* will tell the reader much about Donne and Browne and Jeremy Taylor, but it will tell him little or nothing of the devotional works of Persons and Brinkley and Hopkins. And yet these Catholic writers, as we hope this book may show, are not a whit behind their Protestant countertypes either in seriousness, or scholarship, or in the finish of their prose.

What, then, we may ask, are the reasons for this strange neglect?

There can be little doubt that one, perhaps the chief, of the contributory causes is the fact that, owing to printing and other difficulties, the books of these Recusant writers were from the outset exceedingly hard to come by, and things did not become easier as the ban imposed upon the books came to be more rigorously applied by the authorities. Perhaps, too, since in the religious division of the kingdom the Catholics were of the weaker side, it was to some extent inevitable that the literary merits of their works should go unrecognized. Again, the subject-matter of many of their books – stern theological stuff as it is – however interesting it may have been to contemporary Elizabethans, is not such as to invite investigation by the modern literary student. But this is not all. Catholic scholars themselves must shoulder some of the responsibility for the prevailing ignorance of these Elizabethan authors. The Protestant reformers have never been without their editors. Learned societies like the Parker Society have made available for the modern reader the works of Coverdale, Cranmer, Grindal, Hooper, Latimer, etc. Jewel has been edited three times over. Whereas, if we except the Scottish Recusants, whose works, owing to the careful diligence of Scottish scholars, have for long had adequate recognition, not one of the major writers dealt with in this book has so far been given the treatment which is his due. And yet Harding was reckoned the equal of Jewel in his own day, and Cardinal Allen's English prose style has been described by a later writer, who was certainly not prejudiced in favour of the Catholic outlook, as incomparable (see below, Chapter III). And the sixteenth-century Protestants, at any rate, thought the devotional works of Hopkins and Persons worth pirating.

The establishing of a Catholic counterpart to the Protestant Parker Society is surely long overdue. Such a society, undertaking to reprint *in toto* outstanding Recusant works, would seem the natural complement to the Catholic Record Society, whose excellent transcripts of old registers and personal and genealogical records of the Faith are so well known.

It will be observed that our investigation in this work has, with one or two notable exceptions, been limited to the printed books of the Catholic Recusants. The preliminary nature of our examination necessarily imposed this limit upon the field of our research and so far narrowed its scope. It is important, therefore, to bear in mind that manuscript sources, as yet untapped, may very well provide fruitful material for further investigation in this field and may help to elucidate some of the unsolved problems connected with the books. It is well, too, to remind ourselves that there may be some additional volumes not recorded in our bibliography lurking in the great national and monastic and university and college libraries of the Continent. The feeling of the present writer, however, in respect of these latter is that they are more likely to provide *desiderata* for a later period than for that with which this book is concerned. This is certainly true of the library of the English College in Rome, a library which one might have expected to be particularly rich in Recusant books of our period. A careful examination, very kindly undertaken by Monsignor R. L. Smith, when he was Vice-Rector of the College, revealed a surprising paucity of exemplars in the library; though it should be stated that, in this particular case, as Mgr. Smith pointed out to the writer, the lack can be traced to the special circumstances which prevailed in the College and in Rome in the seventeenth and eighteenth centuries, circumstances which led at one time to some indiscriminate marketing of the books by those in authority.

Our aim in this book may be described as twofold. It has first been our endeavour to put at the disposal of the scholar an *apparatus criticus* which may enable him, if he so will, to pursue further the subject of our discourse. Secondly, we have tried to suggest the value of such further pursuit by copious quotations from our authors, indicating thereby that they hold a not unimportant place in the history of our English prose. The purport of this, our second end or aim, will, we hope, become abundantly clear as this book proceeds. Meanwhile, it may help if we outline, in a preliminary way, what we conceive to be their chief contribution to the preservation and development of our English tongue.

And first it is to be observed that in using English as a medium of expression for learned subjects, these Catholic Recusant writers were helping materially to extend the art and the scope of the language. They were not, of course, pioneers in this. Discussion of philosophical and theological subjects in the vernacular had been going on since the beginning of the century. They were not, therefore, without models. But the spreading influence of their own practice, both in critical method and in cultivating good sense, at a time when the language of philosophy and criticism was still in a fluid state, may justly be remarked, and this certainly calls for investigation in any serious study of our English prose tradition.

Following upon this we note that the chief characteristic of these writers is their insistence upon logic in expounding an argument or in arranging a pleading, and, correlatively, the importance they attach to *construction* as a primary element in prose composition. In this matter they were reviving the earlier tradition of the schools of rhetoric, where composition (Invention and Disposition) was regarded as at least of equal importance with elocution or ornament. The growing tendency on the part of professors of rhetoric in the sixteenth century to discard, in favour of elocution, those parts of rhetoric which dealt with composition is almost a commonplace. It finds its principal exponents in the courtly writers of Elizabeth, for whom ornament is the hall-mark of distinguished writing. Now, it may be argued that this emphasis on elocution, as practised by these writers, tended to change the character of English prose and, while it contributed to the development of both vocabulary and rhythm, tended to create an instrument unsuited to the various uses to which a vernacular prose must be put. If this is so, the practice of our Recusant authors is of some importance in our literary history. This is not to suggest, of course, that they deliberately set out to oppose this tendency, or that they were inspired by any idea of restoring English prose to its proper function of constructive expression. Primarily, as must be evident, they were not concerned with literature as an accomplishment at all. Their business was to combat what they believed to be error and to expose the truth, not to produce literary masterpieces, and their writing is altogether directed towards this end. But they are not unstudied in their manner of composition. It is clear that they aimed at a simple and straightforward exposition of their themes, such as would appeal to the unlearned or at least to those not versed in the technicalities of theological nicety. As a rule, therefore, they preferred the plain style while at the same time insisting upon the dictates of reason. In short, they aimed at good sense in plain language.

But we must not infer from this that their prose is a colourless and flat affair. Our writers, as trained rhetoricians, knew the value of metaphor and its kindred imagery for aiding thought or for stirring emotion, and they understood, and indeed shared, the taste of their generation for the use of proverbs, proverbial similes, and wise sayings as a means to emphasis or vivid simile. They have, therefore, constant recourse to these modes of expression in their writings – not after the manner of the new rhetoric, however, with its tendency to mere verbal exaggeration of feeling or thought in order to obtain a vague impressiveness, but in the style of the old vernacular type of composition in which imagery is duly proportioned to the meaning or intended effect. Generally speaking, their aim – that is to say, in their use of imagery – is either to give clearness and precision to their language or to give to the expression of their thought colour, vigour, intensity. To this end, following the Augustinian precept which demands in preaching and exposition unmistakable clearness combined with popular expressions and appeal, they draw their similitudes, for the most part, from the everyday life of the people, and garnish their sentences with the saws that were upon everyone's lips. By thus rendering their meaning easily intelligible, they may be said to effect that economy in the reader's attention which is perhaps the most important use of figurative language; at the same time by the undoubted sincerity of their inward feeling they give momentum to the truth which they wish to express. The general absence of affectation or grandiloquence or floridness may be taken as the measure of their practice; the fact that they do not sacrifice thought to the figure, truth to the image, will indicate their integrity of purpose.

It may seem strange to the reader, at first, that we should here be offering as a subject for literary research the writings of a number of men who were avowedly concerned in their books and pamphlets principally (though not entirely, as we shall see) with the defence and dissemination of Catholic faith and practice. It would, no doubt, have appeared strange to the authors themselves. But we must remember, for our own profit, that they wrote at a time when, to borrow a recent statement, 'theology was more literary and literature more theological than the modern mind can conveniently imagine', and the fact that in practice these two elements, the theological and the literary, were seldom separated in their minds and are often to be found inseparably combined should be sufficient to put us on our guard against rejecting even the most technical of their treatises as matter for literary investigation. This was the view held by Professor Chambers (cf. *Continuity of English Prose*, p. clxiii), whose judgement in such matters must always carry very great weight, and we believe a perusal of the later pages of this book will amply justify our own acceptance of it. The reader may be encouraged, therefore, to proceed with us in our examination of the works of these Recusant authors; and, if we may adapt some words originally applied to one who is, perhaps, the supreme master in this kind of writing – we mean, of course, Richard Hooker – 'such who will patiently attend and give them credit all the reading and hearing of their sentences, will have their expectation most surely paid at the close thereof'.

* * *

It is a grateful task, indeed, as I look back over the years in which I have been engaged upon this work, to call to mind the numberless kindnesses and unstinted help which I have received from so many and such diverse quarters. Chiefest, I recall a series of happy visits to our great Catholic colleges, to Stonyhurst, Oscott, Ushaw and Ware, where, in each case, every facility was given me for consulting the books and manuscripts in the magnificent college libraries and where, invariably, I was most hospitably entertained during my stay. Then it was also my good fortune to have access to certain other private libraries. These included the London Oratory library, by invitation of the Rev. John Talbot; the library at Arundel Castle, by permission of His Grace the Duke of Norfolk; the library of Foxcote Hall, the seat of the Howards, now dispersed; the Gillow library; and the library of the late Sir Leicester Harmsworth, which was particularly rich in rare specimens of Recusant books which he generously put at my disposal. Also, by the courtesy of the Lady Abbess, a full inventory of the Recusant books in the library of Syon Abbey, South Brent, was prepared and made available for me.

It is a pleasure to express my gratitude to Archdeacon Claude Jenkins for many profitable hours spent in the Lambeth Palace library; also to the librarian of Sion College and to the librarian of Dr. Williams's library for the loan of books. Nor do I forget the kindness of the late Canon Christopher Wordsworth and of Canon W. H. Kynaston in helping me in my researches in the cathedral libraries at Salisbury and Lincoln respectively.

One can never cease to be grateful to the directors and officials of the Reading and Manuscript Rooms of the British Museum and to those of the Public Record Office for their courtesy and attention and help over many years. No less am I grateful to the librarians and staffs of the Bodleian Library and of the Library of the University of Cambridge, where I have worked from time to time.

To the late Mgr. P. Hallett I owe much, both for a number of corrections and for many useful suggestions in the revising of this work for publication. Also to Professor C. J. Sisson of University College, London, for his kindly help and criticism after he had undertaken my supervision at the eleventh hour. But they are in no way responsible for any opinions which I may have expressed in this book.

With the late Fr. C. A. Newdigate, S.J., and Fr. Leo Hicks, S.J., I have often discussed the bibliographical problems arising out of this work, and it is a pleasure to record the fact that I seldom came away from such discussions empty-handed.

But perhaps one of the greatest debts I owe is to my friend and colleague, the late Major George Balls, who typed the whole of the difficult manuscript of my original thesis, some pages many times over, and never spared himself, not even when on active service, on my behalf.

To my cousin, Mrs. G. C. Maughan, of Yardley Grange, Tonbridge, and to the late Mrs. M. Case, of Park Hill, Frome, I am deeply grateful. Had it not been for their generous hospitality during two of the war years the task of finishing this book might have been immeasurably delayed.

Finally, I should like to thank both publishers and printers for their close and kindly co-operation at every stage in the publishing of this book.

A. C. S.

Tunbridge Wells.

August 1949.

CONTENTS

ILLUSTRATIONS

The portrait of Allen is reproduced by the kind permission of the Rt. Rev. Mgr. C. Corbishley, President of Ushaw College

The remaining plates are reproduced by the courtesy of the Trustees of the British Museum

PRINCIPAL SOURCES AND WORKS CONSULTED

For the Recusant and kindred works with which this study is immediately concerned the reader is directed to the Bibliography which forms the second part of this book.

Manuscript Sources

Additional MSS. British Museum.
Cotton MSS. British Museum.
Harleian MSS. British Museum.
Lansdowne MSS. British Museum.
State Papers, Eliz. Dom. Public Record Office. (Cited *P.R.O.*)

Publications of Learned Societies

Analecta Bollandiana.
Publications of the Bannatyne Club.
Transactions of the Bibliographical Society.
Publications of the Camden Society.
Publications of the Catholic Record Society. (Cited *C.R.S.*)
Chetham Miscellanies. Vol. V.
The Library (transactions of Bibl. Soc. as above).
Publications of the Maitland Club.
Publications of the Oxford Historical Society.
Publications of the Parker Society.
Publications of the Scottish Text Society.

Published Catalogues of Libraries

Catalogue of the Arundel MSS. in the Library of the College of Arms. W. H. Black.
Catalogue of the Bible Society. Darlow and Moule.
Catalogus Librorum Impressorum Bibliothecae Bodleianae in Academia Oxoniensi. 4 Vols.
Catalogue of the Books in the Library of the British Museum, printed in England, Scotland and Ireland, and of books in English printed abroad to the year 1640. C. Sayle.
Catalogue of Early English Printed Books in the University Library, Cambridge, 1475–1640. C. Sayle.
An Index of such English Books, printed before the year MDC, as are now in the Archiepiscopal Library at Lambeth. S. R. Maitland.
Bibliothecae Cleri Londinensis in Collegio Sionensi Catalogus.

Periodicals

The Academy. Vol. IX (for June 1876).
The Dublin Review. Vol. CLIII (for July 1913).
The Gentleman's Magazine (for November 1865).

The Month (for July 1889, 1894; January 1905; January 1910, etc.).
Notes and Queries. Tenth Series. Vols. IV and V.
The Rambler. New Series. Vol. VII.
The Tatler (for September 1710).

GENERAL

Calendar of State Papers, Domestic Series, Elizabeth.
Calendar of State Papers, Domestic Series, Elizabeth. Addenda, 1566–79.
Calendar of State Papers, Foreign Series, Elizabeth.
Calendar of State Papers, Simancas.
The Cambridge History of English Literature (1918). Vols. II, III, IV, V, VII.
The Catholic Encyclopedia. (Cited *Cath. Encyc.*)
The Dictionary of National Biography. (Cited *D.N.B.*)
The Encyclopedia Britannica.
Essays and Studies by Members of the English Association. (Cited *Essays and Studies.*)
Grenville Proclamations. British Museum.
The Harleian Miscellany. Ed. T. Park.
Historical Register of the University of Oxford (1900).
The Year's Work in English Studies.

ALEGAMBE, P. Bibliotheca Scriptorum Societatis Iesu. (See Sotuello.)
ALLEN, H. E. English Writings of Richard Rolle. 1931.
AMES, J. Typographical Antiquities; or an Historical Account of the Origin and Progress of Printing in Great Britain and Ireland . . . considerably augmented by William Herbert. 1785–90.
ANDERSON, J. Collections Relating to the History of Mary Queen of Scotland. 4 vols. 1727.
ANON. The Life and end of Thomas Awfuld (Alfield). n.d.
ANSTEY, H. Munimenta Academica, or Documents illustrative of Academical life and studies at Oxford. (Rolls Series.) 2 vols. 1868.
ARBER, E. A Transcript of the Register of the Company of Stationers of London, 1554–1640. 5 vols. 1875–94.
ASCHAM, R. The Whole Works of Roger Ascham, now first collected and revised, with a life of the author; by the Rev. Dr. Giles. 3 vols. 1865.
ASCHAM, R. English Works of Roger Ascham. Ed. by William Aldis Wright. (Cambr. Eng. Classics.) 1904.
ATKINS, J. W. H. English Literary Criticism: the Medieval Phase. 1943.
BACON, F. Works. Ed. Spedding, Ellis and Heath. 14 vols. 1857–74.
BACON (or SOUTHWELL), N. Bibliotheca Scriptorum Societatis Jesu. 1676.

BAGSTER, S. The English Hexapla. 1841.

BAILLET, A. Jugemens des Savans. 1722.

BALDWIN, C. S. Ancient Rhetoric and Poetic. New York. 1924.
–Medieval Rhetoric and Poetic (to 1400). Interpreted from Representative Works. New York. 1928.

BALE, J. The laboryouse Iourney & serche of Iohan Leylande, for Englandes Antiquitees, geuen of hym as a newe yeares gyfte to Kynge Henry the viij. in the. xxxvij. yeare of his Reygne, with declaracyons enlarged: by Iohan Bale. 1542.

BAYLE, P. Dictionnaire Historique et Critique. 1820.

BAYNE, C. G. Anglo-Roman Relations. 1558–65. (Oxford Historical and Literary Studies, Vol. II.) 1913.

BERNERS, LORD. The Chronicle of Froissart translated out of French by Sir John Bourchier Lord Berners Annis 1523–25. Ed. by W. P. Ker. (The Tudor Translations.) 1901.

BIRT, DOM H. N. The Elizabethan Religious Settlement. 1907.

BOLTON, E. Hypercritica. Ed. by Anthony Hall. 1722.

BOMBINUS, P. Vita et Martyrium E. Campiani. Martyris Angli e Societate Iesu. 1620.

BOSWELL, A. Heir followeth the coppie of the ressoning which was betuix the Abbote of Crosraguell and Iohn Knox. 1812.

BOURCHIER, T. Historia Ecclesiastica de Martyrio Fratrum Ordinis Minorum Divi Francisci. Paris. 1582.

BRIDGETT, T. E. Blunders and Forgeries. 1890.

BRIDGEWATER, J. (AQUAPONTANUS). Concertatio Ecclesiae Catholicae in Anglia adversus Calvino-Papistas et Puritanos sub Elizabetha Regina. (Cited *Concertatio.*) Treves. 1588. (The original edition of 1583 was edited by J. Gibbons and J. Fen.)

BRIGHTMAN, F. E. The English Rite. 2 vols. 1921.

BROWN, S. J. The World of Imagery. 1927.

BROWN, T. A ritch Storehouse or Treasurie for Nobilitye and Gentlemen, which in Latine is called Nobilitas Literata, written by a famous and excellent man, Iohn Sturmius, and translated into English by T. B. Gent. 1570.

BURNET, G. The History of the Reformation of the Church of England. Revised by N. Pocock. 7 vols. 1865.

CAMDEN, W. Annals. Translated into English by R. N. 3rd edition. 1635.

CAMM, DOM BEDE. William, Cardinal Allen, Founder of the Seminaries. 1908.

CAMPION, E. Description of a copy of 'Rationes decem Campiani'. 1581. (Miscell. of Philobiblon Soc. 9.)
–Ten Reasons. (Cath. Library 6.) 1914.

CANISIUS, P. Opus Catechisticum. 1577.

CARLETON, J. G. The Part of Rheims in the Making of the English Bible. 1902.

CARPENTER, F. I. Arte or Crafte of Rhetoryke. By Leonard Cox. (English Studies 5 of the University of Chicago.) Chicago. 1899.

CASSAN, S. H. Lives of the Bishops of Bath and Wells. 2 vols. 1830.

CATANAEO, J. M. Continentur Hoc Volumine Georgii Trapezuntii Rhetoricorum libri V. Consulti Chirii Fortunatiani libri III. Aquilae Romani de figuris sententiarum, & elocutionis liber. P. Rutilii lupi eaurendem [sic] figurarum è Gorgia liber. Aristotelis Rhetoricorum ad Theodecten Georgio Trapezuntio interprete libri III. Eiusdem Rhetorices ad Alexandrum à Francisco Philelpho in latinum uersae liber. Paraphrasis Rhetoricae Hermogenis ex Hilarionis monachi Veronensis traductione. Priscianus de Rhetoricae praeexercitamentis ex Hermogene. Aphthonii declamatoris rhetorica progymnasmata Io. Maria Cantanaeo tralatore. Venice. 1523.

CAXTON, W. Eneydos. 1490.

–The myrrour: & dyscrypcyon of the worlde with many meruaylles. & the. vii. scyences As Gramayre Rethorike wyth the arte of memorye Logyke Geometrye wyth the standarde of mesure & weyght and the knowlege how a man sholde mesure londe borde & tymber and than Arsmetryke wyth the maner of accoũtes and rekenynges by cyfres and than Musyke and Astrnomye with many other profytable and plesant cõmodytes. 1527?

(cp. also Caxton's Mirrour of the World. Ed. by Oliver H. Prior. E.E.T.S. 1913.)

CHAMBERS, R. W. England before the Norman Conquest. (Univ. of London Intermediate Source-Books of History. No. VII.) 1926.

–Introduction to the Life and Works of Nicholas Harpsfield. (E.E.T.S. – Harpsfield's Life of More.) 1932.

–The Continuity of English Prose from Alfred to More and his School. (As in the foregoing. Cited *Continuity of English Prose*.)

–Thomas More. 1935.

CHAUCER, G. The workes of Geffray Chaucer newly printed. 1532. (Contains William Thynne's Preface to Henry VIII.)

–Poetical Works. Ed. by Robert Bell. 8 vols. 1854–6.

CHAYTOR, H. J. From Script to Print. An Introduction to Medieval Literature. 1945. (A valuable publication, but too recent to receive notice in the text of this thesis.)

CLAY, W. K. Liturgies and Occasional Forms of Prayer set forth in the Reign of Queen Elizabeth. (Parker Soc.) 1847.

CODE, J. B. Queen Elizabeth and the English Catholic Historians. Louvain. 1935.

COLLETE, C. H. The Authorized Version of the Bible as compared with the Douay and Rhemish Versions vindicated from the charge of corruption. 1891.

COLLIER, J. P. The Egerton Papers. (Camden Soc.) 1840.

COLSON, F. H. Quintilian, De Institutione Oratoria. Ed. by F. H. Colson. 1924.

COOPER, C. H. Annals of Cambridge. 5 vols. 1842–1908.

COOPER, C. H. and T. Athenae Cantabrigienses, 1500–1609. 3 vols. 1858–1913. (Cited *Athen. Cantab.*)

Cotton, H. Rhemes and Doway. An attempt to shew what has been done by Roman Catholics for the diffusion of the Holy Scriptures in English. 1855.

Courthope, W. J. A History of English Poetry. 6 vols. 1895–1910.

Coverdale, M. The Newe Testament both in Latine and Englyshe. 1538.

Craik, G. L. A compendious history of English Literature. 2 vols. 1861.

Craik, H. English Prose. 5 vols. 1893–6.

Cranstoun, J. Satirical Poems of the time of the Reformation. 2 vols. (Scottish Text Soc.) 1891.

Crowley, R. The Select Works of R. C. Ed. by J. M. Cowper. 1872.

Daiches, D. The King James Version of the English Bible. Chicago. 1941.

Dasent, J. R. Acts of the Privy Council. New series. Ed. by J. R. Dasent. 1907.

De Backer, A. Bibliothèque des Écrivains de la Compagnie de Jésus ou Notices Bibliographiques . . . par Augustin de Backer de la Compagnie de Jésus avec la collaboration d'Alois de Backer et de Charles Sommervogel de la même Compagnie. Nouvelle Édition refondue et considérablement augmentée. Liége & Paris. 3 vols. 1869.

De Lacaille, J. Histoire de L'Imprimerie et de la Librairie. Paris. 1689.

Dickson, R. and Edmond, J. P. Annals of Scottish Printing from the introduction of the Art in 1507 to the beginning of the seventeenth century. 1890.

Dinsmore, C. A. The English Bible as Literature. 1931.

A discourse touching the pretended match betwene the Duke of Norfolke and the Queene of Scottes. 1571? (Contains the *pagella* of Pope Pius V to Dr. Harding, granted 14 August 1567.)

Dodd, C. Certamen utriusque Ecclesiae: or, A List of all the Eminent Writers of Controversy, Catholics and Protestants, since the Reformation. 1724.

–The Church History of England, from the Year 1500, to the Year 1688. 3 vols. Brussels. 1737–42.

[Drant, T.] Impii cuiusdam epigrammatis quod edidit R. Shaklochus in mortem C. Scoti . . . 1565.

Durrant, C. S. A Link between Flemish Mystics and English Martyrs. 1925.

Duthilloeul, H. R. Bibliographie Douaisienne, ou Catalogue Historique et Raisonné des Livres Imprimés à Douai, depuis l'année 1563 jusqu'à nos jours, avec des notes bibliographiques et littéraires. Douai. 1842.

Dyson, H. A Booke containing all such Proclamations, as were published during the Raigne of the late Queene Elizabeth. 1618.

Early Typography, being fragments of books published at different periods, in several languages, and by various Printers, English and Continental, but chiefly the latter. s.l., n.d.

Edwards, R. The Paradyse of daynty deuises . . . Deuised and written for the most part, by M. Edwardes . . . the rest by . . . Iasper Heywood etc. 1578 etc.

Einstein, L. The Italian Renaissance in England. New York. 1902.

–Tudor Ideals. 1921.

Eliot, T. S. Selected Essays, 1917–32. 1932.

Elyot, Sir T. The Castel of Helth corrected and in some places augmented, by the fyrste authour therof, syr Thomas Elyot knyght, the yere of oure lord 1541.

–The Boke named The Gouernour Deuised by Sir Thomas Elyot, Knight. Ed. by H. H. S. Croft. 2 vols. 1880.

Evans, L. The Castle of Christianitie. 1568.

–The Hatefull Hypocrisie and rebellion of the Romish prelacie. 1570.

Faral, E. Les Arts Poétiques de XIIe et du XIIIe Siècle. Paris. 1924.

Farr, E. Select Poetry Chiefly Devotional of the Reign of Queen Elizabeth. (Parker Soc.) 2 vols. 1845.

Fitzherbert, N. De antiquitate, et continuatione, Catholicae Religionis in Anglia, et De Alani Cardinalis vita, libellus. Rome. 1608.

Fletcher, J. R. The Story of the English Bridgettines of Syon Abbey. 1933.

Flores Cleri Anglo-Catholici, or An account of All the eminent clergymen, who, by their Virtue, Learning and Deaths, have supported the cause of the Church of *Rome*, in England since 1500. (A quarto of about the year 1720, and printed abroad. At Oscott College.)

Foley, H. Records of the English Province of the Society of Jesus. 7 vols. 1877–83.

Forbes-Leith, W. Narrative of Scottish Catholics under Mary Stuart and James VI. 1885.

Foxe, J. Actes and Monuments. 1563, 1570 etc.

Frère, E. De l'Imprimerie et de la Librairie à Rouen, dans les XVe et XVIe siècles, et de Martin Morin, célèbre imprimeur rouennais. Rouen. 1843.

–Des Livres de liturgie des Eglises d'Angleterre (Salisbury, York, Hereford), imprimés à Rouen dans les XVe et XVIe siècles. Etude suivie du catalogue de ces impressions, de m.cccc.xcii à m.d.lvii, avec des notes bibliographiques. Rouen. 1847.

Fuller, T. The History of the Worthies of England. 3 vols. 1840. (Cited *Worthies*.)

–The Church History of Britain: from the birth of Jesus Christ until the year 1628. 3 vols. 1842.

Gairdner, J Lollardy and the Reformation in England. 3 vols. 1908–13.

GARDINER, J. H. The Bible as English Literature. 1906.
GARVIN, K. The Great Tudors. Ed. by Katharine Garvin. 1935.
GASCOIGNE, G. Certayne notes of Instruction concerning the making of verse or ryme in English, written at the request of Master Edouardo Donati. 1575.
–The Spoyle of Antwerpe. Faithfully reported, by a true Englishman, who was present at the same. 1576.
–Complete Works. Ed. by J. W. Cunliffe. 2 vols. 1907–10.
GASQUET, CARDINAL F. A. The Old English Bible and other Essays. 1897.
–The Eve of the Reformation. 1927.
GASQUET and BISHOP, E. Edward VI and the Book of Common Prayer. 1890.
GEBERT, C. L. An Anthology of Elizabethan Dedications and Prefaces. 1933.
GEE, J. The Foot out of the Snare: with a Detection of sundry late practices & impostures of the Priests & Jesuites in England. 1624.
GIBSON, S. Statuta Antiqua Universitatis Oxoniensis. 1931.
GILLOW, J. The Haydock Papers: a glimpse into English Catholic life. 1888.
–A Literary and Biographical History, or Bibliographical Dictionary of English Catholics, from the breach with Rome . . . 1534 to the present time. 5 vols. 1898. (Cited *Bibl. Dict.*)
–The Origin and History of the Manual. 1910.
GODWIN, H. The Psalter of Jesus. From a manuscript of the fifteenth century; with variations from some late copies. 1885.
GRAESSE, J. G. T. Orbis Latinus. Berlin. 1909.
GREENE, R. The Repentance of Robert Greene. 1592.
GREG, W. W. English Literary Autographs. Part III. 1932.
GREG and BOSWELL, E. Records of the Court of the Stationers' Company, 1576–1602, from Register B. 1930.
GRIERSON, H. J. C. Metaphysical Lyrics and Poems of the Seventeenth Century. Donne to Butler. 1921.
GUILDAY, P. The English Catholic Refugees on the Continent, 1558–1795. 1914.
GUINEY, L. I. Recusant Poets . . . With a Selection from their Work. I. Saint Thomas More to Ben Jonson. 1938.
H., D.L. The Douay Bible; being remarks on what is said by authority in regard to it. [1931].
HAGEDORN, M. Reformation und Spanische Andachtsliteratur. Luis de Granada in England. Leipzig. 1934.
HAILE, M. An Elizabethan Cardinal, William Allen. 1914.
HALES, J. D. Romish Versions of the Bible. 1856.
HALLAM, H. Introduction to the Literature of Europe in the fifteenth, sixteenth, and seventeenth centuries. 3 vols. 1847.
HARPSFIELD, N. Dialogi Sex contra summi Pontificatus, Monasticae vitae, Sanctorum, sacrarum imaginum, oppugnatores, et Pseudomartyres . . . Nunc primum ad Dei Optimi Maximi gloriam, &

HARPSFIELD, N.
Catholicae religionis confirmationem ab Alano Copo Anglo editi. Antwerp. 1566.
–Historia Anglicana Ecclesiastica, a primis gentis susceptae fidei incunabulis ad nostra fere tempora deducta, et in quindecim centurias distributa . . . Nunc primum in lucem producta studio et opera R.P. Richardi Gibboni Angli Societatis Iesu Theologi. Douay. 1622.
–Harpsfield's Narrative of the Divorce. Ed. by Lord Acton. [1880?].

HARVEY, G. G. Harveii Ciceronianus. 1577.

HAWES, S. The History of Graund Amoure and La Bel Pucell, called The Pastime of Pleasure, Conteynyng the knowledge of the Seven Sciences, and the Course of Mans Life in this Worlde. Invented by Stephen Hawes, Grome of Kyng Henry the Seventh his chamber. 1555. Ed. by Thomas Wright for the Percy Society. 1845.

HAWKES, A. J. Lancashire Printed Books, a Bibliography. Wigan. 1925.
–The Birchley Hall Secret Press. (Bibl. Soc.) 1926.

HEARNE, T. J. de Trokelowe's Annales Eduardi II. 1729.

HEBEL, J. W. and HUDSON, H. H. Poetry of the English Renaissance, 1509–1660. New York. 1929.

HEREFORD, P. The Ecclesiastical History of the English People, By the Venerable Bede. Ed. by Philip Hereford. With an Introduction by the late Father Bede Jarrett, O.P. 1935.

HERFORD, C. H. Studies in the Literary Relations of England and Germany in the Sixteenth Century. 1886.

HEYLYN, P. Ecclesia restaurata or the history of the Reformation of the Church of England. 1661.

HEYWOOD, J. Collection of Statutes for the University and Colleges of Cambridge. 1855.

HITCHCOCK, E. V. The Lyfe of Sir Thomas Moore, knighte, written by William Roper. Ed. by E. V. Hitchcock. (E.E.T.S.) 1935.

HILTON, W. The Scale of Perfection. Ed. by an Oblate of Solesmes. (The Orchard Books.) 1927.

HOBY, SIR T. The Book of the Courtier from the Italian of Count Baldassare Castiglione: done into English by Sir Thomas Hoby, Anno 1561. With an Introduction by Walter Raleigh. (Tudor Translations.) 1900.

HOLINSHED, R. The Chronicles of England, Scotlande & Irelande. 2 vols. 1577.
–The Chronicles of England, Scotlande & Irelande newlie augmented & continued . . . to the yeare 1586. By John Hooker. 2 vols. 1587.

HOLLAND, H. T. Stapletoni . . . Opera quae extant omnia, nonnulla auctius et emendatius, quaedam iam antea Anglice scripta, nunc primum studio doctorum virorum Anglorum Latine reddita. 4 vols. Paris. 1620.

HOOKER, R. The Works. 2 vols. 1865.

HOSKINS, E. Horae Beatae Mariae Virginis or Sarum and York Primers with kindred books and Primers of the Reformed Roman Use together with an Introduction. 1901. (Cited *Horae.*)

HUDSON, H. H. Directions for Speech and Style, by John Hoskins. Ed. with an introduction and notes by Hoyt H. Hudson. (Princeton Studies in English.) Princeton. 1935.

HUMPHREY, L. I. Iuelli . . . Episcopi Sarisburiensis Vita. 1573. (Includes Whitaker's translation of Jewel's works from English into Latin for the larger European audience.)

JANELLE, P. Robert Southwell the Writer. 1935.

JEBB, S. De vita et rebus gestis Mariae Scotorum Reginae. 2 vols. 1725.

JELF, R. W. The Works of John Jewel. 4 vols. 1848.

JESSOPP, A. Letters of Fa. Henry Walpole, S.J., from the original MSS. at Stonyhurst College. 1873.

–One Generation of a Norfolk House. 1878.

KEITH, R. History of the Affairs of Church and State in Scotland. 1734.

KEMP, W. Education of Children. 1588.

KENNEDY, J., SMITH, W. A. and JOHNSON, A. F. Dictionary of Anonymous and Pseudonymous English Literature. 1926.

KER, W. P. Essays of John Dryden. 2 vols. 1926.

KNOX, T. F. First and Second Diaries of the English College, Douay, and an Appendix of Unpublished Documents, edited by Fathers of the Congregation of the London Oratory, with an Historical Introduction by Thomas Francis Knox, D.D. 2 vols. 1878. (Cited *Douay Diaries* or *D.D.*)

–The Letters and Memorials of William Cardinal Allen (1532–94). Ed. by Fathers of the Congregation of the London Oratory. With an Historical Introduction by Thomas Francis Knox, D.D. 1882. (Cited *Letters and Memorials.*)

KRAPP, G. P. The Rise of English Literary Prose. 1915.

LAING, D. The Miscellany of the Wodrow Society. 1844.

LAW, T. G. A Catechisme or Christian Doctrine by Laurence Vaux, B.D., Canon Regular and Sub-prior of St. Martin's Monastery, Louvain, sometime Warden of the Collegiate Church, Manchester. Reprinted from an Edition of 1583; with an introductory memoir of the author. (Chetham Soc.) 1885.

–Historical Sketch of the Jesuits and Seculars in the Reign of Elizabeth. 1889.

–Catholic Tractates of the Sixteenth Century, 1573–1600. (Scottish Text Soc.) 1901.

LEE, S. The French Renaissance in England. 1910.

LE LONG. Bibliothèque Historique de la France. Paris. 1769.

LEWIS, C. S. Rehabilitations and Other Essays. 1939.

–A Preface to Paradise Lost. 1942.

LEWIS, D. Rise and Growth of the Anglican Schism. By Nicolas

Sander, D.D. . . . Published A.D. 1585 with a continuation of the History, by the Rev. Edward Rishton, B.A. . . . Translated, with Introduction and Notes, by David Lewis, M.A. 1877.

LINGARD, J. History of England. Vol. VI. A.D. 1555–1603. Dublin. 1878.

LLANEZA, M. Bibliographia del V.P.M. Fr. Luis de Granada de la Orden de Predicadores. 4 vols. Salamanca. 1926.

LODGE, E. Portraits of Illustrious Personages of Great Britain. 12 vols. 1825.

LYTE, H. C. M. A History of the University of Oxford from the earliest times to the year 1530. 1886.

MACRAY, W. D. The Pilgrimage to Parnassus with the two parts of the Return from Parnassus . . . Ed. from MSS. by the Rev. W. D. Macray. 1886.

MAGEE, B. The English Recusants. 1938.

MAITLAND, J. Apologie for Maitland of Lethington. Ed. by Andrew Lang. (Scottish History Soc. 44.) 1904.

MALLETT, C. E. A History of the University of Oxford. 3 vols. 1924.

MANLY, J. M. Chaucer and the Rhetoricians. (Warton Lecture on English Poetry.) 1926.

MATTHIESSEN, F. O. Translation: an Elizabethan art. 1931.

MAUNSELL, A. The First Part of the Catalogue of English printed Bookes: which concerneth such matters of Diuinitie, as haue bin either written in our owne Tongue, or translated out of anie other language: And haue bin published, to the glory of God, and edification of the Church of Christ in England. 1595.

MAYOR, J. E. B. The Scholemaster by Roger Ascham, edited from the texts of the first two editions. By John E. B. Mayor . . . With a memoir of Ascham by Hartley Coleridge. 1884.

MCCANN, DOM J. The Cloud of Unknowing. Ed. by Dom Justin McCann. (The Orchard Books.) 1936.

MCKERROW, R. B. A Dictionary of Printers and Booksellers in England, Scotland and Ireland, and of Foreign Printers of English Books, 1557–1640. (Bibl. Soc.) 1910.

–Printers' and Publishers' Devices in England and Scotland, 1485–1640. (Bibl. Soc.) 1913.

–An Introduction to Bibliography for Literary Students. 1928.

MESSENGER, E. C. History of Mediaeval Philosophy, by Maurice de Wulf. Trans. by E. C. Messenger. Vol. I. 1926.

MEYER, A. O. England and the Catholic Church under Queen Elizabeth. Trans. by J. R. Mckee. 1916.

MORE, H. Historia missionis Anglicanae Societatis Jesu. St. Omer. 1660.

MORE, SIR T. The Workes of Sir Thomas More. 1557.

MORRIS, J. The Troubles of our Catholic Forefathers. 3 vols. 1872–7.

MORTON, J. The Nun's Rule being the Ancren Riwle modernised by James Morton. (The King's Classics.) 1905.

MULCASTER, R. Positions wherin those primitiue circumstances be examined, which are necessarie for the training vp of children, either for skill in their booke, or health in their bodie. 1581.

MULLINGER, J. B. The University of Cambridge from the earliest times to the Royal Injunctions of 1535. 3 vols. 1873–1911.

–The University of Cambridge from the Royal Injunctions of 1535 to the Accession of Charles the First. 1884.

MUNDAY, A. The English Romayne Lyfe. 1582.

MURRAY, D. Some Old Scots Authors whose books were printed abroad. 1921.

MURRY, J. M. The Problem of Style. 1922.

NICHOLS, J. G. Machyn's Diary. (Camden Soc.) 1848.

NORTH, SIR T. Plutarch's Lives of the Noble Grecians and Romans Englished by Sir Thomas North. Anno 1579. Ed. by George Wyndham. (Tudor Translations.) 1895.

–The Diall of Princes. Ed. by K. N. Colville. (The Scholars' Library.) 1919.

OLIVER, G. Collections towards illustrating the biography of the Scotch, English, and Irish members of the S.J. 1845.

OLTHOFF, F. De Boekdrukkers, boekverkoopers en uitgevers in Antwerpen. Antwerp. 1891.

–Ordinancie, statuyt ende gebot provisionnael . . . aengaaende de Printers, Boeckvercoopers ende Schoelmeesters. Brussels. 1570.

OWEN, L. The Running Register, recording a true relation of the State of the English Colledges, seminaries, and cloysters in all forraine parts. 1626.

OWST, G. R. Preaching in Medieval England. 1926.

–Literature and Pulpit in Medieval England. 1933.

PAQUOT, J. N. Mémoires pour servir à l'Histoire Littéraire des dix-sept provinces des Pays-Bas, de la Principauté de Liége, et de quelques contrées voisines. Louvain. 3 vols. 1765–70.

PEEL, A. The Seconde Parte of a Register. 2 vols. 1915.

PEERS, E. A. Spanish Mysticism. 1924.

PITS, J. Ioannis Pitsei Angli, S. Theologiae Doctoris, Liverduni in Lotharingia, Decani, Relationum Historicarum de Rebus Anglicis. Paris. 1619. (Cited *De Illustribus Angliae Scriptoribus.*)

PLIMPTON, G. A. The Education of Chaucer. New York. 1935.

POLLARD, A. W. Records of the English Bible. 1911.

POLLARD and REDGRAVE, G. R. A Short-Title Catalogue of Books printed in England, Scotland and Ireland, and of English Books printed abroad, 1475–1640. 1926. (Cited *Pollard and Redgrave.*)

POLLEN, J. H. Acts of English Martyrs. 1891.

–Biographical Sketch (of N. Sander). 1891.

–A Briefe Historie of the Glorious Martyrdom of Twelve Reverend Priests, Father Edmund Campion & his Companions. By William Cardinal Allen. With Contemporary Verses by the Venerable Henry Walpole, & the Earliest Engravings of the Martyrdom. Reprinted from the (probably unique) copy in the British Museum. 1908.

POLLEN, J. H. Ten Years' Work of the Catholic Record Society. 1914.
–Campion's Ten Reasons. 1914.
–The English Catholics in the Reign of Queen Elizabeth. 1920.
PONTANUS, J. Poeticae Institutiones. Ingolstadt. 1594.
PYNE, H. List of English Books printed not later than the year 1600. 1876.
QUILLER-COUCH, A. On the Art of Writing. 1921.
RAINOLDS, W. Caluino-Turcismus. Antwerp. 1597.
RASHDALL, H. The Universities of Europe in the Middle Ages. 2 vols. 1895.
RASHDALL and RAIT, R. S. New College. (College Histories Series.) 1901.
RASTELL, J. A new interlude and a mery of the nature of the iiij. elementes . . . [1520?]
RAVAISSON. Catalogue Général des MSS. des Bibliothèques publiques des Departements. Vol. I. 1849.
READ, H. English Prose Style. 1928.
REED, A. W. Early Tudor Drama. 1926.
RENOUARD, P. Imprimeurs parisiens. Paris. 1898.
RENWICK, W. L. Edmund Spenser. 1933.
REYNER, C. Apostolatus Benedictinorum in Anglia siue disceptatio historica, de antiquitate ordinis congregationisque monachorum nigrorum S. Benedicti in regno Angliae. Douay. 1626.
RIBADENEIRA, P. Bibliotheca Scriptorum Societatis Iesu. (See Sotuello.)
RITSON, J. Bibliographica Poetica. 1802.
ROBERTS, M. Elizabethan Prose. 1933.
ROMBAUTS, E. Richard Verstegen, Een Polemist der Contra-Reformatie. Brussels. 1933.
RONAN, M. V. The Reformation in Ireland under Elizabeth, 1558–80. 1930.
ROUSSELLE, H. Annales de L'Imprimerie à Mons. 1858.
ROWSE, A. L. Tudor Cornwall. 1943.
SAINTSBURY, G. Specimens of English Prose Style from Malory to Macaulay. 1885.
–A History of Elizabethan Literature. 1887.
–Historical Manual of English Prosody. 1910.
–A History of English Prose Rhythm. 1912.
SANDER, N. De visibili monarchia ecclesiae. Libri Octo . . . Auctore Nicolao Sandero, Sacrae Theologiae Professore. Louvain. 1571.
–Doctissimi Viri Nicolai Sanderi, De Origine ac Progressu Schismatis Anglicani, Liber . . . Editus et auctus per Edouardum Rishtonum. Rhemes. 1585. (See also LEWIS, D.)
SANDYS, E. Europae Speculum. The Hague. 1629.
SCOTT, J. A Bibliography of Works relating to Mary, Queen of Scots. 1544–1700. (Edinburgh Bibl. Soc.) 1896.
SCOTT, M. A. Elizabethan Translations from the Italian. Cambridge, Mass. 1916.

SEEBOHM, F. The Oxford Reformers of 1498. 1869.

SIBBALD, J. Chronicle of Scottish Poetry; from the thirteenth century, to the union of the crowns. 4 vols. 1802.

SILVESTRE, M. L.-C. Marques Typographiques ou Recueil des Monogrammes, Chiffres, Enseignes, Emblèmes, Devises, Rèbus et Fleurons des Libraires et Imprimeurs qui ont exercé en France, depuis l'introduction de l'Imprimerie, en 1470, jusqu'à la fin du seizième siècle: à ces marques sont jointes celles des Libraires et Imprimeurs qui pendant la même période ont publié, hors de France, des livres en langue française. Paris. 1867.

SIMPSON, R. Edmund Campion. A Biography. 1896.

SKELTON, J. Poetical Works. Ed. by A. Dyce. 2 vols. 1843.

SMITH, G. Elizabethan Critical Essays. 2 vols. 1904.

SOLE, S. H. Jesu's Psalter. 1888.

SOMERS, BARON J. A fourth Collection of scarce . . . Tracts. Vol. I. 1752.

SOTUELLO, N. Bibliotheca Scriptorum Societatis Iesu opus inchoatum a R.P. Petro Ribadeneira eiusdem Societatis Theologo, anno salutis 1602. Continuatum a R.P. Philippo Alegambe ex eadem Societate, vsque ad annum 1642. Recognitum, & productum ad annum Iubilaei M.DC.LXXV. A Nathanaele Sotuello eiusdem Societatis Presbytero. Rome. 1676.

SPENSER, E. View of the State of Ireland. 1596.

SPINGARN, J. E. A History of Literary Criticism in the Renaissance. New York. 1912.

STAPLETON, T. Apologia pro rege Catholico Philippo II. 1592.

STOW, J. A Survey of the Cities of London and Westminster . . . Written at first in the Year MDXCVIII. By John Stow . . . Corrected, Improved, and very much enlarged: And the Survey and History brought down from the Year 1633 . . . to the present Time; By John Strype. 2 vols. 1720.

STOWE, A. M. English Grammar Schools in the Reign of Queen Elizabeth. New York. 1908.

STRICKLAND, A. Letters of Mary, Queen of Scots. 2 vols. 1864.

STRYPE, J. The Life of the learned Sir Thomas Smith. 1820.

–Historical Collections of the Life and Acts of the Right Reverend Father in God, John Aylmer. 1821. (Cited *Life and Acts of Aylmer.*)

–The Life of Sir John Cheke. 1821.

–The History of the Life and Acts of the Most Reverend Father in God, Edmund Grindal. 1821. (Cited *Life and Acts of Grindal.*)

–The Life and Acts of Matthew Parker, the first archbishop of Canterbury in the reign of Elizabeth. 3 vols. 1821. (Cited *Life and Acts of Parker.*)

–The Life and Acts of John Whitgift. 1822. (Cited *Life and Acts of Whitgift.*)

–Annales of the Reformation and Establishment of Religion, and other various Occurrences in the Church of England, during Queen Elizabeth's happy Reign: together with an Appendix of original Papers of State, Record, and Letters. 7 vols. 1824. (Cited *Annals.*)

STURMIUS, J. I.S. de amissa dicendi ratione . . . Libri duo. 1538.

SYMONDS, J. A. Renaissance in Italy. The Revival of Learning. 1897.

–Shakespere's Predecessors in the English Drama. 1900.

TANNER, T. Bibliotheca Britannico-Hibernica. 1748.

TAWNEY, R. N. Religion and the Rise of Capitalism. 1929.

TAWNEY and POWER, E. Tudor Economic Documents. 1924.

THEUX DE MONTJARDIN, X. DE. Bibliographie Liégoise. Liége. 1885.

THIRIOT, G. Oeuvres Mystiques du Bienheureux Henri Suso de L'Ordre des Frères Precheurs. 2 vols. 1899.

This prymer of Salysbery vse bothe in Englyshe and in Laten is set out a longe without any serchyng etc. 1536. (Perhaps the most complete of the several editions of the Salisbury Primer published in the sixteenth century.)

TIERNEY, M. A. Dodd's Church History of England. 5 vols. 1839–43.

TILLYARD, E. M. W. The Elizabethan World Picture. 1943.

TONSON, L. An Answere to certein Assertions of M. Fecknam. 1570.

TURBERVILE, G. Tragical Tales. 1587.

TURNER, C. Anthony Mundy, an Elizabethan Man of Letters. 1928.

UNDERHILL, J. G. Spanish Literature in the England of the Tudors. 1899.

VANDERHAEGHEN, F. Bibliographie Gantoise. 7 vols. Gand. 1858, etc.

–Livres et Brochures imprimés à Gand. 1865.

VAN HAVRE, G. Marques Typographiques des imprimeurs et libraires anversois recueillies par le Chev. G. van Havre. 2 vols. 1883.

VEECH, T. McN. Dr. Nicholas Sanders and the English Reformation, 1530–81. Louvain. 1935.

VEREPAEUS, S. Precationum Piarum Enchiridion. Antwerp. 1565.

WARRACK, G. Revelations of Divine Love Recorded by Julian, Anchoress at Norwich Anno Domini 1373. Ed. by Grace Warrack. 1901.

WATSON, F. Elyot's Gouernour. Introduction and Glossary by Foster Watson. (Everyman Series.) 1907.

–The English Grammar Schools to 1660; their Curriculum and Practice. 1908.

WAUGH, E. Edmund Campion. 1935.

WELDON, B. Chronological Notes . . . of the English Congregation of the Order of St. Benedict. 1882.

WENKENBACH, E. Studien zur Geschichte der Medezin John Clement ein englischer Humanist und Arzt des sechzehnten Jahrhunderts. Leipzig. 1925.

WESTCOTT, B. F. A General View of the History of the English Bible. Revised by W. A. Wright. 1905.

WHITE, H. C. English Devotional Literature, 1600–40. Madison. 1931.

WHITE, W. A. Catalogue of Early English Books chiefly of the Elizabethan period. 1926.

WHITFIELD, J. H. Petrarch and the Renascence. 1943.

WHYTFORD, R. The Following of Christ translated out of Latin into English A.D. 1556 . . . by R. Whytford. Ed. by W. Raynal. 1872.

WILKINS, A. S. Cicero's De Oratore, Book I. 1895.

WILLCOCK, G. D. and WALKER, A. Puttenham's Arte of English Poesie. 1936.

WILLIS, W. Mancuniensis; or, An History of the Towne of Manchester, and what is most memorable concerning it. By R. Hollingworth. Ed. by W. Willis. 1839.

WILSON, T. The Rule of Reason, conteinyng the Art of Logic. 1552, etc.

–The Arte of Rhetorique. Ed. by G. H. Mair. (Tudor and Stuart Library.) 1909.

–A Discourse upon Usury. Ed. by R. H. Tawney. 1925.

WOOD, A. à. The History and Antiquities of the University of Oxford. Ed. by J. Gutch. 2 vols. 1792.

–Athenae Oxonienses. Ed. by P. Bliss. 3 vols. 1813.

WOOD, N. The Reformation and English Education. 1931.

WOODWARD, W. H. Studies in Education during the age of the Renaissance, 1400–1600. 1905.

PART I

CHAPTER I

INTRODUCTORY

BETWEEN the years 1559 and 1603 more than two hundred English works were written and published by the Catholics who were exiles for their religion. The great majority of these are prose works, sometimes of great length, on controversial, historical and devotional topics. The writers, as we shall see in the next chapter, were for the most part men of considerable intellectual standing, and, in some cases, men of European reputation for learning. A glance at the bibliography at the end of this book, which is, of course, concerned only with about half of these works, will enable the reader to estimate for himself what a very large body of work this Recusant prose constitutes. Its importance will, we hope, be unfolded in the pages which follow. But its size is impressive, and it is a remarkable thing that up to the present no attempt at a systematic handling of these books as a whole has taken place. And let us state here that we do not forget Joseph Gillow's heroic attempt to provide a bibliography. Every student of the works of Catholic writers must owe something to his *Bibliographical Dictionary*. Unfortunately, Gillow worked on far too large a scale to ensure completeness and accuracy, and his method of classification, according to names and names only, left no room for a fairly large body of anonymous publications; consequently, his *Dictionary*, which includes Catholic writers of all periods, is, for the Elizabethan period at any rate, in many respects imperfect.* With the exception, then, of a small group of Scottish Recusant writers, most of whose works have been edited by learned societies, and perhaps half a dozen studies of individual English Recusant writers (all recent), there is nothing at all to guide the ordinary student of literature in respect of Elizabethan Recusant prose.†

* It will be noted that Gillow's *Dictionary* presents a somewhat lop-sided appearance. The writers are arranged in alphabetical order, the first four volumes covering the letters A to MET, and the fifth, which is not the largest, completing the alphabet. It is only fair to point out that after the printing of the fourth volume it was found necessary to cut down the remaining entries as the work had grown too unwieldy. This accounts for the absence of many well-known names in the latter part of the work.

† I do not, of course, include in these studies such books as Simpson's *Life of Campion*, the purpose of which is not primarily literary.

To provide materials for the critical study of these books is the object of this thesis. The need for such a study seems now beyond question. Indubitably, there have been of recent years signs of a new and growing literary interest in the writings of the Catholics of the sixteenth century, and in this revival of interest the work of R. W. Chambers and A. W. Reed is outstanding. The influence of Thomas More and his circle on Tudor drama is the special contribution of Dr. Reed to this revival and Dr. Chambers has argued convincingly on More as 'the great restorer of English prose'. The *return to More* inevitably must lead to an examination of the works of 'the inheritors of More', a title which has been applied (justly, as we think) to the principal Recusant authors of our period. Chambers has the distinction of being the first in a work of any importance to refer to this need for such a valuation. Speaking of the way in which the *Anglo-Saxon Chronicle* of the reigns of William I, William II and Henry I has been ignored by the teachers of the history of English literature, he writes:

> In a very similar way the Roman Catholic prose of the Reformation period has been ignored. In some measure this was the inevitable result of the difficulty of printing it in Elizabethan times. But this neglect has continued far too long.*

It is owing to this neglect that this present work is so largely of an introductory nature. The business of collecting materials has been very great, and the lengthy bibliography will itself bear witness to the many problems connected with some of the books. No more than a preliminary survey of the ground has therefore been possible, and no attempt has been made to pass a final judgement on any writer.

Before we proceed to our main task of putting before the reader such material as goes to make up the body of this Recusant literature, it will be advisable to say something on the general subject of Modern English prose in the earlier phases of its growth, for the importance we attach to these Recusant writers will depend upon our understanding and, consequently, our interpretation of what we commonly call the English literary tradition. Our remarks must, of necessity, be brief and may seem 'a little too positive'; but this will hardly matter, since a

* *Introduction on the Continuity of English Prose*, p. clxxi, in the Early English Text Society's edition of *Harpsfield's Life of More* (1932).

full and masterly exposition of the theme is available in Chambers's work on the *Continuity of English Prose* already referred to above.

The subject can be most conveniently introduced here by referring to a statement made many years ago by the late Professor J. S. Phillimore in an article in *The Dublin Review*. Phillimore believed that English prose writing ceased to progress after More until we come to Dryden. 'Whatever the language was when More found it', he writes, 'where he left it, there it remained until Dryden definitely civilized it.' And then, in pursuance of this theme, he adds the following note:

> Let me suggest a theory of the literary history of English for this epoch [i.e. the Elizabethan]: namely, that there was a bifurcation: a main-stream dammed, and a new cut opened; and after the new cut had carried off most of the water, the old stream reopened. Dryden is the meeting-point of the two channels. The true main-stream of English tradition in prose was in the line of Parsons, Campion, Allen and the translators of the Douai and Rheims Bible. These are the inheritors of More. But these admirable writings, proscribed and destroyed by the Government of Elizabeth, have remained (such is the obscurantist force of ancient prejudice) unknown not merely to the blinkered schoolboy but even to many professors and students of literature in our own time. A critical comparison of the prose rhythms in the Catholic and the Government Bible would be a most interesting study.*

The implication of these words should be clear. The writer suggests that what has passed for traditional in English prose of the Elizabethan epoch must be regarded as in the nature of a sport, out of the main tradition, and that if we wish to trace correctly the history of that prose tradition we must fix our attention on the prose of the Catholic exiles. '*The true main-stream of English tradition in prose was in the line of Parsons, Campion, Allen and the translators of the Douai and Rheims Bible. These are the inheritors of More*.' We may find it necessary to qualify this statement before we have done, nevertheless it contains, as I

* *The Dublin Review*, Vol. CLIII (July 1913), p. 8, footnote. The passage is cited by R. W. Chambers in his *Continuity of English Prose* at p. cxlvi. Perhaps I may be allowed to supplement the above passage with some words from a personal letter of Phillimore's: 'My *feeling* is that you will find that the main stream of scholarship and culture was in the Catholic exiles (this is why learning was so low in England during the time of Eliz. and James); that the commonsense unaffected English Prose that reappeared in Dryden was the English Catholic tradition revived.' The letter is dated August 26, 1921.

believe, sufficient truth to warrant some re-examination of the nature of sixteenth-century English prose. We cannot do better, then, in this matter than follow up Phillimore's lead and ask ourselves: in what sense, if any, is it possible to speak of 'a bifurcation: a main-stream dammed, and a new cut opened' in respect of the literary history of the period in question.

Probably one of the most remarkable things in the literary history of sixteenth-century England is the number of English treatises on rhetoric (to say nothing of the various poetics) which were published in that period. Altogether some seventeen separate titles are extant, and, in addition, there were something like twenty reprints of two or three of the more important of these during the reign of Elizabeth alone.* Now, 'rhetoric' may be rightly considered as embodying the principles of literary composition, and it is these principles as commonly understood which will naturally be reflected in and, in their turn, will reflect the literary productions of any particular period. It is pertinent, then, to enquire as to the nature and contents of these treatises, for they should throw considerable light upon our English prose as it was practised in the epoch which we are considering. Actually, the very titles of many of the treatises are significant enough. We begin with the *Arte or Crafte of Rhethoryke* written by Leonard Cox about 1530, and this is followed by a whole series of rhetorics intended as a guide to eloquent and ornamental writing under such titles as *A treatise of Schemes and Tropes* (Richard Sherry – [1550]), *A Treatise of the Figures of Grammar and Rhetorike* (same author – [1555]), *The Garden of Eloquence Conteyning the Figures of Grammer and Rhetorick, from whence maye bee gathered all manner of Flowers, Coulours, Ornaments, Exornations, Formes and Fashions of speech*, etc. (Henry Peacham – 1577), *The Arcadian Rhetorike: Or the Praecepts of Rhetorike made plaine by examples, Greeke, Latin, English, Italian, French, Spanish, out of Homers Ilias, and Odissea, Virgils Aeglogs, Georgikes, and Aeneis, Sir Philip Sydneis Arcadia, Songs and Sonets, Torquato Tassoes Goffredo, Aminta, Torrismondo, Salust his Iudith, and both his Semaines, Boscan and Garcillassoes Sonets and Aeglogs* (Abraham Fraunce – [1588]), and so on. The point is

* We may add to this fact, though we cannot pursue the subject further here despite its relevance, that an almost undue importance seems to have been given to the subject of rhetoric as it figures in the curriculum both of the school and of the university in the latter half of the century.

that almost invariably these treatises occupy themselves with setting forth all the appurtenances reckoned as necessary for fine writing or for imitation with a view to fine writing. Following the 'sophistic' tradition, that is to say, not the rhetoric conceived by Aristotle and expounded by Cicero, according to his larger meaning, with its roots firmly grounded in logic and its emphasis upon composition (*inventio* and *dispositio*), but that rhetoric of style and decoration which came later to be associated with declamation (*declamatio*) and which confines itself to the practice of elocution (*elocutio*),* their authors – and none of them is entirely exempt from the charge – sought first to inculcate a fashion of writing which could only result in the unnatural and affected sort of prose which we find practised in varying degrees by nearly all the well-known writers of the second half of the century and which finds its apogee in the Euphuism of Lyly and the Arcadianism of Sidney;† and second, by their insistence upon the following of classical and foreign models (and here let the reader glance again at the explanatory title of Fraunce's work above) and, above all, of Cicero, they sought to foster a habit of imitation which inevitably led to a purely mechanical conception of literary composition and which resulted in the kind of inelegancies and obscurities which are to be found even in such sober prose writers as Hooker and Jonson.

Contemporary witnesses are not wanting to these aberrations of Elizabethan prose. Shakespeare, Ben Jonson, *even Sidney himself* (in the sonnet – 'Let dainty wits cry on the Sisters nine') all cry out upon the rhetoricians in one way or another. And Francis Bacon, whose shaft was aimed specifically at the Ciceronians and the Cambridge School of rhetoricians, in a notable passage in *The Advancement of Learning* roundly censures the literary affectations and extravagances of the age. His words are worth quoting. Pronouncing upon 'the affectionate‡ study of eloquence and copie§ of speech' of the Elizabethan epoch he writes:

This grew speedily to an excess; for men began to hunt more

* These, together with *memoria* (memorizing), made up the fivefold division of the ancient rhetoric.

† Even Berners and North bear witness to the rhetorical vogue, the former in his translations of *The Golden Boke of Marcus Aurelius* (1532) and *The Castell of Love*, the latter in his *The Diall of Princes* (1557).

‡ *Unduly affected.* § *Copiousness.*

after words than matter; and more after the choiceness of the phrase, and the round and clean composition of the sentence, and the sweet falling of the clauses, and the varying and illustration of their works with tropes and figures, than after the weight of matter, worth of subject, soundness of argument, life of invention, or depth of judgement. Then grew the flowing and watery vein of Osorius, the Portugal bishop, to be in price. Then did Sturmius* spend such infinite and curious pains upon Cicero the orator and Hermogenes the rhetorician,† besides his own books of periods and imitation and the like. Then did Car of Cambridge, and Ascham,‡ with their lectures and writings, almost deify Cicero and Demosthenes, and allure all young men that were studious unto that delicate and polished kind of learning. Then did Erasmus take occasion to make the scoffing echo: *Decem annos consumpsi in legendo Cicerone*, and the echo answered in Greek, *One*, *Asine*. Then grew the learning of the schoolmen to be utterly despised as barbarous. In sum, the whole inclination and bent of those times was rather towards copie than weight.§

Such criticism as this may seem excessive, and before we proceed it is only just to remind ourselves that it would be incorrect to conclude that English prose derived no advantage from the study and practice of rhetoric. Rhetoric has its uses and, in calling attention to the arrangement of words and the need for variety in expression and in opening up new possibilities of rhythmic effect, it may be said to have brought about something of permanent value for English prose during the period under review. No one will doubt this who has read his Hooker – or his Shakespeare for that matter, for Shakespeare was also master of that 'other harmony of prose'; and the eloquence and majesty of cadence of the sixteenth-century versions of the Scriptures are a sure witness to its powerful aid as a means to expression. Yet the fact remains that if it is not used judiciously it may very easily prove itself a snare and a delusion and may even render itself absurd. This is the burden of Bacon's charge against the sixteenty-century 'makers' of our prose, and modern

* John Sturm, the Strasburg humanist: a close friend, correspondent and inspirer of Roger Ascham.

† The works of Hermogenes of Tarsus, a Greek rhetorician of the time of Marcus Aurelius, were one of the principal sources of the sophistic tradition (see above), as it was handed down through the Middle Ages.

‡ The leading lights of the Cambridge school of rhetoricians were Nicholas Carre (1524–68), Sir Thomas Smith (1513–77), Sir John Cheke (1514–57), Roger Ascham (1515–68) and Thomas Wilson (1525?–81).

§ *Works of Francis Bacon* (*Advancement*), ed. J. Spedding (1857), Vol. III, pp. 283–4.

scholarship, speaking generally, may be said to confirm his view. Here, for instance, is Henry Hallam. Writing of the later years of Queen Elizabeth he says:

> In these later years of the queen, when almost everyone was eager to be distinguished for sharp wit or ready learning, the want of good models of writing in our own language gave rise to some perversion of the public taste. Thoughts and words began to be valued, not as they were just and natural, but as they were removed from common apprehension, and most exclusively the original property of those who employed them. This in poetry showed itself in affected conceits, and in prose led to the pedantry of recondite mythological allusion, and of a Latinised phraseology.*

More recent scholars, with their wider knowledge of the history of English literature, are even more explicit, and the researches of such students of our English prose as W. P. Ker, R. W. Chambers, A. W. Reed and G. R. Owst, to name only a few, would point to the continuity of an English tradition in prose, which is very far removed from the affected and ornate and Latinized style of writing so popular in the second half of the sixteenth century.

This Elizabethan predilection for what has been variously described as an aureate, Euphuistic, Ciceronian, or even Gorgianic manner of writing has its roots, as we have already indicated above, in the medieval cult of rhetoric, as applied to composition in the Latin tongue, commonly called 'sophistic'. More specifically it can be related to the prevailing influence of the Italian Renaissance on Western learning and literature. This is not the place, of course, for a detailed discussion of this subject in its more general aspect: that must be left to our literary historians of the movement; though it is worth recalling, in passing, that the significance and importance attached to fine writing, which is so characteristic of English literary theory throughout the sixteenth century, reflects unmistakably the dominant and perhaps unique preoccupation with style of the *savants* of the new humanism, such as da Feltre, Valla, and, above all, Cardinal Bembo, and the growing cult of Ciceronianism, largely initiated by the last named.† There is, however,

* *Introduction to the Literature of Europe* (1847), Vol. II, p. 194.

† For a careful and well-balanced statement in respect of the rhetorical nature of humanism the reader may be referred to J. H. Whitfield's recent study of the early Renaissance – *Petrarch and the Renascence* (1943).

one particular phase of Renaissance literary history which has a very close bearing upon our present subject, and to this we shall for a moment turn.

The near coincidence of the revival of learning with the rise of the vernacular in this country in the fourteenth century must have gone some way towards helping to establish the rhetorical tendencies in later English prose. Since for some three hundred years prior to 1350 native literary prose had suffered an eclipse, Latin meanwhile having taken its place as the natural literary prose medium, a Latin, it should be remembered, subject to the neo-classical rules of composition, what more natural, when men turned once again to employ English for serious writing in prose, than to compose according to the Latin manner. Nor should we omit to recall that alongside this cultivation of the neo-classic style there was a growing tendency on the part of English writers to emulate the foreign and learned tongues, with the consequent reference to models of alien origin, and this, too, must have assisted in fostering the rhetorical impulse. It cannot be a matter of surprise, therefore, in the circumstances, that there should have been no general resurgence of the native tradition in prose during this period, but that rhetorical influences should have continued to dominate literary practice, both verse and prose, throughout the fourteenth and fifteenth centuries. And this is true, if we make due allowance for individual traits of style, of such diverse and representative writers as Pecock, Fortescue, Caxton and Malory.*

That the native tradition still persisted, however, in spite of its apparent eclipse, there can be no question. 'The old prose of Alfred and Aelfric, despite evil days, had nevertheless lived on', writes Chambers.† And again, 'Obviously the English *Language* is continuous – it lived from generation to generation on the mouths of men.'‡ For us it survives mainly in sermons and in such devotional treatises, written usually for recluses in English prose, as the *Ancren Riwle*, the prose tracts of Richard Rolle, *The Cloud of Unknowing*, Walter Hilton's *Scale of Perfection*, and, we may add with Chambers, in the numerous copies of the books of Old English writers which were transcribed during

* Fortescue is a possible exception, but rather of the kind which proves the rule. His English works were not printed until the eighteenth century.

† *Continuity*, as before, p. xc.

‡ ibid.

this period in the scriptoria of the religious houses.* Here, then, is the evidence for the persistence of the native tradition in the fourteenth and fifteenth centuries and the principal link, as the same writer points out, which binds the later work of More and Tyndale to our earlier prose writings.

But it is not the only evidence we have. Despite the general acceptance of alien rules and standards as a measure of excellence for writing in the vernacular during the period in question, it is important to remember that the neo-classical theories had not gone entirely unchallenged, and some fairly striking evidence of this is to be found in certain contemporary critical opinions put forward by names well known in the history of our literature. This expression of critical opinion contrarying the false rhetoric of the Schools must also have played its part, even if only a minor one, in keeping the native tradition alive.

The reference is to the attempt at the end of the fourteenth century on the part of such writers as Wiclif and Trevisa to devise a more efficient English prose which should be suitable for general purposes, for both religious and secular writings. A recent writer, Professor J. W. H. Atkins, in his *English Literary Criticism: the Medieval Phase*,† has called especial attention to this movement, and cites in addition to the two names already mentioned Thomas Usk, John Purvis and Chaucer as having also contributed each in his own degree to making English prose 'a more effective instrument of expression'.‡ Trevisa, he submits, argues for prose in translating on the grounds of clearness and that it is easier to understand than verse, 'comynlich prose is more clere than ryme, more esy and more pleyn to knowe and understonde';§ Purvis for a free and idiomatic rendering of Scripture, for a translation 'aftir the sentence (i.e. meaning) and not oneli aftir the wordes, so that the sentence be as opin, either openere, in English as in Latyn';|| Thomas Usk (in spite

* 'The books of Aelfric and other Old English writers continued to be copied assiduously. A large body of extant manuscripts testifies to this; and we must allow for the very much larger number now lost.' *Continuity*, p. xci.

† C.U.P., 1943. Professor Atkins's important and compendious little volume touches upon a number of points advanced in this introductory chapter, though from a rather different angle.

‡ For this and following references, see especially pp. 147 et seq. of Atkins's book.

§ Preface to *Polychronicon*.

|| Prologue to his revision of the 'Wiclifite' Bible.

of his own pretentious and inefficient prose) for plain writing.*
But it was Wiclif who 'gave direction and impetus to the movement, by his deliberate choice of English as a means of exposition and persuasion; and in his Latin *Sermones*, collected probably in retirement during the last five years of his life, he set forth his ideas on the art of preaching, and, indirectly, of prose writing in general'. His theories are described by Atkins as a direct attack upon the false rhetoric of the New Sophistic, for in insisting upon 'plain and simple utterance in accordance with both speaker and hearer, as well as on the avoidance of all artificial emotional devices whether rhetorical or rhythmical, he was essentially at one with Aristotle in his opposition to Gorgianic prose, when the latter declared clearness and propriety to be the two fundamental virtues of good speaking and writing'. Wiclif's immediate influence was slight, the writer adds, but 'he had revealed the secret of all good prose, and the foundations on which later masters of English were to build'.

Chaucer's contribution to this movement is, of course, well known and need not be detailed afresh here. In a number of places, sometimes by precept, more generally by practice, he advocates a simple and realistic style as opposed to medieval rhetoric and poetic. The quixotic *Tale of Sir Thopas* and the *Nun's Priest's Tale*, each of them burlesquing current poetic practices, provide unmistakable evidence of his attitude towards the prevailing literary customs of his day, and such oblique criticism as that afforded by the Franklin in his Prologue, who knows no rhetoric, is a stranger to Mount Parnassus and Ciceronian methods, and who further decries the ingeniosity of the rhetorical 'colours', is an illuminating sidelight upon his own poetic intention.

Finally, a hundred years later, there is Caxton, who, reverting to Wiclif and Chaucer, questions the use of aureate diction and resolves to make use of an English 'not ouer rude ne curyous, but in suche termes as shall be understanden'.† And there is More.

And this brings us back to our original question, propounded earlier in this chapter, which perhaps we may now be allowed to restate in some such terms as – How far may the old native

* *Testament of Love.*

† *Eneydos* (1490), Preface.

prose tradition, the spirit of which was to be recaptured later by the seventeenth-century masters of English prose, how far may this tradition be said to have survived in Elizabethan times, and where best may we look for it? It is with this question in mind that we come to our examination of the Recusant prose of Elizabeth published between the years 1559 and 1582.

CHAPTER II

THE MOVEMENT AND THE MEN

A. THE MOVEMENT

IN the early years of Elizabeth three groups of Catholics may be distinguished: (*a*) the refugees, (*b*) those who for one reason and another never left the country but refused to conform, and (*c*) those who conformed in some sort outwardly and who were variously known to their Catholic brethren as demi-catholics, catholic-like protestants, external protestants and internal catholics, church papists, &c.* With these last we are only indirectly concerned here. They had no real part in the movement to which I am about to refer. They were certainly not officially regarded as Recusants, a term which implies refusal to attend the public services of the parish churches.† The Catholic writers who are to engage our attention belong exclusively to the first two of the groups, and they may be described as being *openly* antagonistic to the religious changes which had taken place in the homeland, their efforts being wholly directed towards restoring the Catholic culture and worship of their ancestors. They represent an important 'spiritual, cultural and educational movement which', it is held, 'they succeeded in firmly establishing on English soil'.‡

1. RECUSANT LOYALTY

It has been not uncommon in the past to picture the Catholic Recusants as a number of bigoted clergymen and laymen who, for some ends not very clearly defined, either engaged in treasonable practices at home or fled from their country, proving disloyal to their sovereign in that action and in all subsequent

* cf. *The Disposition or Garnishmente of the Soule* (1596), at sig. C8v &c., by T. N.

† A Recusant was 'simply one who refused to be present at the public services in the parish churches. This is the only meaning which the word has in official documents of the period' – Card. Gasquet, *The Old English Bible and other Essays* (1897), p. 282. cf. Robert Crowley: '. . . all such papists as do refuse to ioyne with vs in the profession and exercise of religion' – *A Deliberat answere made to a rash offer* (1588), at sig. A2. The term began to be applied especially to Catholics after the Bull *Regnans in Excelsis* was published in 1570 (see J. H. Pollen, *The English Catholics in the Reign of Queen Elizabeth* (1920), pp. 156, 365), though it was occasionally applied to the Puritans subsequent to that date (see *The Seconde Parte of a Register*, ed. by A. Peel (1915), Vol. I, pp. 210, 244).

‡ P. Janelle, *Robert Southwell the Writer* (1935), p. 2.

actions. Such is the view of many of our English historians, who have seen only in the Catholic Recusants the apparent treachery of Englishmen leaguing themselves with their country's bitter enemies, but who have failed to note, not always from any deliberate unfairness, their sincerity, virtue and even patriotic aims.* It is a view which we must get out of our minds if we are to understand what the Recusant movement really meant.

Admittedly the charge of disloyalty is one which is not easy to disprove. We cannot deny the existence of certain intemperate and ambitious spirits among Elizabeth's Catholic subjects, those who did 'seake unnaturallie to disturbe and chaunge the estate by joininge or consentinge to forrayners to the subversion of hir Majesties estate . . . withoute any regarde of religion, makinge thatt onelie a colour of the accomplishinge of theare ambitious desires', as Dr. William Gifford writes.† Again, the fact that the Queen united in her own person the religious and political supremacy made it impossible even for those who wished to deny only her spiritual powers to escape the charge of seeming disloyalty towards their country and their sovereign. On the other hand, we cannot pass over the many strong assertions of loyalty which are to be found in the writings of Allen, Persons and others,‡ and we must allow to the Catholic Recusants what we should be equally ready to grant to the Protestant exiles of Queen Mary's reign, the 'necessity' of conscience – 'there are some things which the state cannot command'§ – if we would judge the matter fairly. The following passage from Cardinal Allen's *Apologie* puts the Catholic standpoint clearly and comprehensively:

> The vniuersal lacke then of the soueraine Sacrifice and Sacraments catholikely ministred, without which the soule of man dieth, as the body doth without corporal foode: this cōstrainte to the contrarie seruices, whereby men perish euerlastingly: this intolerable othe repugnāt to God, the Church, her Ma.ties

* cf. T. McN. Veech, *Dr. Nicholas Sanders and the English Reformation, 1530–1581* (1935), p. 199.

† In a letter to Sir Francis Walsingham, pleading for toleration, dated from Rhemes, 18 April 1586. The letter is quoted in *The Letters and Memorials of William Cardinal Allen* (1882), no. 145.

‡ cf. Allen, *A True Sincere and Modest Defence* (1584), *passim*. Persons, *A Brief Discours* (1580), sig. I5, and *A Discouerie of I. Nicols* (1581), sig. F2. Again Allen, in a letter to Richard Hopkins (Rome, 14 August 1593), quoted in *Letters and Memorials*, as before, no. 212, &c.

§ R. W. Chambers, *Thomas More* (1935), p. 396.

honour, and al mens cōsciences: and the daily dangers, disgraces, vexations, feares, imprisonments, empouerishments, despites, which they must suffer: and the railings and blasphemies against Gods Sacraments, Saincts, Ministers, and al holies, which they are forced to heare in our Countrie: are the onely causes, most deere Sirs, or (if we may be so bold and if our Lord permitte this declaration to come to her M.ties reading) most gratious Soueraine, why so many of vs are departed out of our natural Countrie, and do absent our selues so long from that place where we had our being, birth, and bringing vp through God, and which we desire to serue with al the offices of our life and death: onely crauing correspondence of the same, as true and natural children of their parents.

From which we are not fugitiues, as sometimes vncourteously we are called, nor are fled for folowing any factions or differences of noble families, nor for any crimes or disloyalties done against the Prince or Commonwealth, nor for any disorder in our liues, or worldly discontentment or disagrement with the present ciuil state and politie, or for mislike of any her Ma.ties ministers, whose persons, wisedoms, moderation and prudence in gouernement, and manifold graces, we do honour with al our hart in al things: excepting matters incident to Religion, wherein their honours can not be offended, if we preferre the iudgemēt of Gods Church before their humane counsel. Acknow-ledging that her Ma.ties reigne and their regiment had been most glorious and renowmed to the world abrode, and most secure and happie to the subiectes at home, if it had not been contaminated by the fatal calamities (so to call Gods prouident iustice for our sinnes) of alteration in Religion and the things thereon depending. Which not consisting (as we haue declared) with any Christian Catholike mans cōscience, such as we professe our selues to be, nor with libertie of mind, nor saftie of bodie, we were constrained to flee and forsake our Countrie, parents, frendes, and what so euer by nature is there deere vnto vs, by the warrant and exāple of Christ, his Apostles, S. Athanasius, S. Hilarie, and other our forefathers in faith, in the like persecutions.*

The fact is that the majority of the Elizabethan Recusants acted from much the same compelling motives as those which guided Thomas More a generation earlier. They were the Queen's good and loyal servants, but God's first.† This is always their attitude when they had to face the supreme test.

* *An Apologie and true declaration of the institution and endeuours of the two English Colleges* (1581), sigs. B3v – 5. Thomas Stapleton expresses similar views in his *Apologia pro rege Catholico Philippo II* (1592).

† For the full implication of this statement the reader is invited to refer to the work of R. W. Chambers just cited.

Indeed, the example of More must have been constantly before their minds supporting and sustaining them in exile and revolt. For this there is ample evidence. His memory was cherished and kept alive among them by members of his own family and household and by his friends – by John Clement and his wife Margaret, by Judge William Rastell, by John Harris, his secretary, and his wife Dorothy, to name only the principal; his prayers were frequently printed in the Catholic books of devotion published abroad; Nicholas Harpsfield, William Rastell* and Thomas Stapleton, each wrote his life; his *Dialogue of Cumfort against Tribulation* was printed abroad by John Fowler† in a handy edition for the convenience of the average reader. Nor was his influence confined within the limits of a select circle. It was an ever-widening influence. It is the same spirit, the spirit of More, which moved such men as Thomas Hoghton to endure that common experience of many a Catholic exile which he relates in *The Blessed Conscience*, a ballad which, in itself, should afford a sufficient reply to any general charge of contumacy.‡

To lovelie Lea then I mee hied,
And Hoghton bade fayrwell:
Ytt was more tyme for mee to ryde,
Than longer ther to dwel.
I durst not trustt my dearest frende,
Butt secretlie stole hence,
To take ye fortune God shulde sende,
And kepe my conscyènce.

* * *

Thus took I ther my leave, alas!
And rode to ye sea-syde;
Ynto ye shipp I hied apace,
Wich dyd for mee abyde.
With syghs I sail'd from merrie Englande,
I asked of none lycènce:
Wherfor my estate fell from my hande,
And was forfeitt to my Prynce.

* The date of Rastell's *Life of More* is, however, uncertain.

† The only reprint in Elizabeth's reign. See bibl. ent. 42.

‡ The ballad is without date, but was probably written between 1573 and 1580, the date of Hoghton's death. It describes the author's departure from his seat called the Lea, by the Ribble, and his subsequent exile. There are twenty-three stanzas in all. See *The Haydock Papers* (1888) by Joseph Gillow, pp. 10–15.

Men do not seek voluntary exile, forsaking home, family and fortune, for trivial causes.

2. AIMS OF THE MOVEMENT

It is not the purpose of this thesis to trace the history of the Recusant movement in any great detail, but rather to provide material for an examination of that movement in its literary aspect. Nevertheless, for the sake of clearness something must be said of a general nature concerning the circumstances out of which the movement arose and its early development at home and abroad. The aim of the movement has been described as threefold: spiritual, cultural and educational,* and it will be well, before we pass on, to state precisely what is meant by that description. We shall refer directly, in this connexion, to two important statements by the Recusants themselves, showing that by the year 1568, the date of the foundation of Douay College, their aims were becoming very clearly defined; we may preface those statements by pointing out that the three aims were fundamentally one – that, first and foremost, the Recusants had in view the spiritual regeneration of their country, which they believed could only be brought about by the re-establishing of the Holy, Catholic and Roman Church on British soil, and to that spiritual end all else was subordinate. The cultural and educational sides of the movement, that is to say, were secondary to that end and could not exist apart from it. In the passage from Allen which follows this seems to be quite clear, and Allen may be regarded as the spokesman of the whole movement. It will be observed that he is concerned chiefly with its educational aspect. He sets out the meaning and purpose of the institution of the seminaries abroad as follows:

> This is a cleere case, that the persons which first put them selues together in the Vniuersitie of Duay the yere 1568, yelding to Collegial forme of studie and discipline vnder one President (which after some yeres and good proofe of their profitable endeuours, by Gods goodnes obtained his Holines protection and monethly exhibition) had these intentions: first, to draw diuers youths, who then for their conscience liued in the low Coũtries, from sole, seueral, and voluntarie studie, to a more exact methode and course of cõmon conferẽce and publike exercise, to be pursued by their Superiors appointmẽt rather

* Above, p. 14.

then their owne choise: that they might be more apt to serue their Countrie, when it should please God mercifully to reduce thē home againe. Secondly, doubting the time of our chastisement might be so long as to weare out either by age, emprisonmēt, or other miseries, the elder sort of the learned Catholikes both at home and abrode, it was thought a necessarie duety for the posteritie, to prouide for a perpetual feede and supply of Catholikes, namely of the Clergie: nothing mistrusting but the times and opportunities would come (were they neere, were they far of) whē they might take aduātage for restitutiō of religiō, no Sect euer being liked lōg, nor permanēt without enterchāge, as we see in Arianisme the paterne of al other . . .

Thirdly, their purpose was, for their better furnishing of meete men to the end aforesaid, and for disaduantaging the aduersarie part therein, to draw into this College the best wittes out of England, that were either Catholikly bent, or desirous of more exact education then is these daies in either of the Vniuersities (where, through the delicacie of that Sect, there is no art, holy or prophane, throughly studied, and some not touched at all:) or that had scruple of conscience to take the othe of the Queenes Supremacie in causes Ecclesiastical, (which gaue vs diuers, not onely Catholikes but others, out of both the Vniuersities, where it is specially exacted, and tormēteth the consciences of many that seeme pure Protestants:) or that misliked to be forced to the Ministerie, as the vse is in diuers Colleges, a calling cōtemptible euen in their owne conceit, and very dānable in the iudgmēt of others, (the due consideratiō wherof hath yelded to vs many, yea some scores, partly before, and partly after their enterāce to that trade:) or that were doubtful whether of the two religiōs were true, wherein to take trial of none but the one which the sway of the Countrie forcibly driueth vnto, when they might haue proofe of the other so neere at hand in a College of their owne, without great cost or trauail, seemed to many much shame and inexcusable negligence in cause of saluation, which is the iustest cause to trauail (as S. Augustine telleth Honoratus) in the world. Which hath driuen diuers ouer, to their great satisfaction and admiration of the euidence of our part.

Grammar Schooles also from al partes of the Realme haue yelded vs many youthes, which hauing their whole and ful trayning in Catholike Colleges here, proue no lesse seruiceable for their Countrie then the others.

And the rest brought vp in the Vniuersities there, do easily here by comparison perceiue the great corruption in the same, specially of life and maners: sinne, libertie, and licentiousnes daily more and more shewing them selues to be companiōs of this new doctrine. Which doctrine who so euer attempteth to amend, let him know by our experience, that the place affected

> is custom and pleasure in sinne, and shame and lothsomnes to cōfesse and amend: Which being cured, there remaineth no difficultie.*

An earlier statement by Richard Shacklock emphasizes rather the cultural side of the movement. Speaking of his fidelity, loyalty and humble obedience to the Queen, he writes:

> The which, because I was not able to wytnesse vnto the world, ether by famouse feates of armes, for lack of experience: ether in bryngyng golden gyftes, for lack of abilitie, ether in writyng workes of nue inuention, for fault peraduenture of learnyng and knowledge, I thought, I myght declare no small token of a true subiectes harte towarde your gracyouse hyghenes, in trauaylyng to trāslate some godly worke of some worthy wryter: and when I had translated it, to dedicate it to youre excellent Maiestie: specyally seing your hyghnes euen from your tender age, hath bene trayned vp in the treasure howse of learnyng, not so muche bewtyfyed with byllementes and precyouse pearles, as garnyshed with maruaylouse gyftes of grace and godlynes, and euen with the increase of yeares, hathe had an increasyng desyre of true science and knowledge: in so much that I here it reported credibly, and beleue it verily, that euery nyght callyng your selfe to an accompt accordyng to Pythagoras councell, howe you haue spent the day, if by reason of consulting and caryng for youre commonwealth, any day scape withoute learnyng of one lesson oute of some godly authour, you be wont to saye vnto them, which be aboute youre noble grace: Frendes, this day haue I loste, for I haue learned neuer a lesson. O sentence worthy to be pronounced of so excellent a Prynce, O saying worthie to be translated in to all languages, and to be written in letters of golde.
>
> Truly (moste noble Quene) thys one saying, dothe encorage many of your graces faythfull and learned subiectes on this syde of the sea to wrytyng: some to make nue workes neuer sene before, some to translate bokes, which haue bene made of other. Some to wryte in Latē, some in Englyshe, some in verse, and other some in prose. All whose diligence and studye intendeth nothyng lesse, then to wryte one worde wyllingly, whiche myght displease youre Maiestie, which may sowe any sedes of sedition, which may disquyet the peace of oure natyue countrie (as in your graces deare systers dayes dyuerse sedityouse sectaryes dyd) but only to further and to preferre as muche as is possible, thys pryncely desyre of knowing the truthe, which we heare with greate ioy to be reported of youre Maiestie.†

* Allen, op. cit., sigs. C5^{v} – 8.

† Richard Shacklock, *A most excellent treatise of the begynnyng of heresyes in oure tyme* (1565), sigs. a3 et seq.

The emphasis on learning in both these passages is to be noted. The conjunction of sound scholarship and letters is distinctive, as I believe, of the movement we are considering. It may be held, on the other hand, that the divorce of these two was the greatest handicap to English letters on this side of the Channel during the latter part of the sixteenth century. 'It is possible', writes R. W. Chambers, 'to represent English prose and English scholarship as checked by Tudor despotism, surviving only among the exiles on the Continent, but handicapped on this side of the Channel, so that humanism only achieves its fulfilment three generations later than it had promised to do when Erasmus visited England.'*

3. ORIGIN OF THE MOVEMENT: THE REFUGEES

We may take it as a general statement of the position that Elizabethan policy was the subjugation of every element within the realm to the Protestant ideal. The basis of this policy is to be found in the Acts of Supremacy and Uniformity of 1559, two Acts which were buttressed by the further Act of 1563, 'which required all holding, or taking, public office to subscribe to an oath forswearing the Catholic religion and denying the papal authority over the Church in England'.† The origin of the Recusant movement is to be found in these Acts, which no self-respecting and conscientious Catholic could possibly subscribe to. The immediate effect of the Acts was to bring about the voluntary resignation or deprivation of many of the most prominent figures in Church and university life,‡ and to drive into exile a number of both clergy and laity.§

The process of achieving complete conformity within the realm was gradual. To begin with, the Statutes of Supremacy and Uniformity were not altogether rigidly enforced. This seems to have been notably the case at Oxford. Even down to the year 1588 Catholics were still taking degrees there,|| which means they were managing to evade the oath, and the anti-Protestant bias of such colleges as New College, throughout

* *Continuity of English Prose*, as before, p. cxli; cf. the words of J. S. Phillimore cited at p. 5 above, footnote.

† Norman Wood, *The Reformation and English Education* (1931), p. 267.

‡ Including the entire episcopate with the exception of Kitchen of Llandaff.

§ How many went into exile at the commencement of the reign cannot be rightly determined. The number was considerable before the end of the century.

|| Wood, as before, p. 122; cf. Pollen, op. cit., pp. 252–4.

the early part of the reign, was notorious.* At Cambridge, also, the presence of Catholics in the university even as late as 1591 would seem to point to the same thing.† The fact seems to have been that the authorities were aware of the danger of driving out the best brains in the country and, at any rate for a time, acted accordingly. This is the view expressed in a passage of Bridgewater's *Concertatio*, of which the following is a paraphrase:

> Since the Queen's Councillors were informed that very many Oxonians, and those the young men of best ability, altogether refused the oath concerning the Queen's supremacy, and therefore that there was a danger of their giving up their studies altogether and seeking another mode of life; in order that Oxford might not be deprived of some of its best brains and so be reduced bit by bit to a state of barbarity, they decided that the oath should not be proposed to any of those who were likely in due course to succeed.‡

Nevertheless, the exodus abroad of many of the best wits in the realm was not stayed, and there is some foundation for Edward Rishton's statement that as a consequence of the Act of Uniformity 'the very flower of the two universities, Oxford and Cambridge, was carried away, as it were, by a storm, and scattered in foreign lands'.§ Later in this chapter will be found detailed reference to some of the most notable of the Recusant writers, meanwhile the following supplementary account of

* See *New College* (*College Histories*), by Hastings Rashdall and Robert S. Rait (1901), pp. 114, 124, 129, 131, &c.; cf. also Cardinal Allen to Fr. Agazzari (16 March 1583): 'Great complaints are made to the Queen's councillors about the university of Oxford, because of the numbers who from time to time leave their colleges and are supposed to pass over to us.' Cited by T. F. Knox in *Douay Diaries*, introd., p. lxx. Knox also cites from the State Papers similar references with regard to Trinity and Balliol; ibid., pp. 362, 363.

† 'In 1591 the Privy Council ordered that an enquiry should be made with regard to papists in the universities. The answer of the Heads of the Colleges at Cambridge was that, after enquiry, they found that recusants were "more in number and more dangerous than comenly is thought".' Wood, op. cit., p. 279.

‡ *Concertatio* (1589), p. 144. The original runs: Sed consiliarii Reginae, cum certiores fierent, esse Oxoniae complures eosque maximae spei adolescentes, qui hoc de primatu Reginae iuramentum omnino respuerent, eoque timendum esse, ne illi, relictis plane bonarum literarum studiis, alias vitae rationes suscipere cogerentur; quo fieret, ut Oxoniensis Academia praeclarissimis quibusque ingeniis destituta, ad quandam paulatim barbariem redigeretur: statuerunt, ut iuramentum istud nemini eorum, qui deinceps promovendi erant, (ad aliquot saltem annos) proponeretur.

§ *Rise and Growth of the Anglican Schism. By Nicolas Sander, D.D. . . . Published A.D. 1585 with a continuation of the History, by the Rev. Edward Rishton, B.A. . . . Translated, with Introduction and Notes, by David Lewis, M.A.* (1877), p. 261. The numbers from Cambridge were much less than those from Oxford.

some eminent Recusants will indicate the force of Rishton's remark.*

Of the more important deprivations we note that RICHARD SMITH, the regius professor of divinity at Oxford, eventually became Chancellor of Douay University. WILLIAM SOONE, the regius professor of civil law at Cambridge, went on to profess law at Louvain and later acted as assistant to Abraham Ortelius, the geographer, in Cologne. FRANCIS BABINGTON, the distinguished Vice-Chancellor of Oxford, retired abroad in 1565, as also did JOHN BAVANT, one of the first fellows of St. John's, Oxford, and the first reader in Greek in that college, about 1560. Of some twenty-five fellows ejected from New College, Oxford, OWEN LEWIS, after holding a number of important appointments abroad, which included that of Vicar-General of the diocese of Milan, was consecrated Bishop of Cassano; and RICHARD WHITE, after a long term as professor of canon and civil law in the University of Douay, was made by order of the Pope 'magnificus rector' of the university. JOHN PITS, also of New College, the author of the *De Illustribus Angliae Scriptoribus*, who left Oxford for Rhemes in 1581, was appointed after a distinguished academic career to the deanery of Liverdun. RICHARD BARRETT, of Oriel College, Oxford, and proctor in the university, entered the English College at Rome in 1576 and was afterwards President of Douay College. GEORGE BLACKWELL, who resigned his fellowship at Trinity College, Oxford, in 1574, later made history as the first of the Archpriests in this country. ALAN COPE, fellow of Magdalen College, Oxford, the learned editor of Nicholas Harpsfield's *Dialogi Sex*, became Canon of St. Peter's, Rome. THOMAS DARBYSHIRE, of Pembroke College, Oxford, a doctor of canon and civil law, became a distinguished Jesuit. JOHN GIBBONS, of Lincoln College, Oxford, a man of great learning, was eminent in Germany as a controversialist. WILLIAM GIFFORD, of the same college, after a distinguished career in the Church (he was one of the greatest English Benedictines of his time), was appointed finally Archbishop of Rhemes. WILLIAM GOOD, fellow of Corpus Christi College, Oxford, became a prominent member of the Society of Jesus, and played an important part in the early history of the English

* It is to be observed that no connected account of the Elizabethan ejections from Oxford and Cambridge has yet been attempted.

College in Rome. RICHARD HALL, fellow of Pembroke College, Cambridge, for long reputed the author of the anonymous *Life of Fisher*, held important appointments at Douay University and at the English College in Douay. He was finally made Canon of St. Omer. A number of learned works stand to his credit. EDMUND HOLLINGS, of Queen's College, Oxford, who proceeded abroad in 1579, was a substantial author on medical topics. WILLIAM HOLT, S.J., of Brasenose and Oriel Colleges, Oxford, a talented and forceful character, exercised an important influence upon English Catholic events on the Continent. THOMAS WORTHINGTON, also of Brasenose, who held the presidency of Douay College from 1599 to 1613, has both devotional and doctrinal works to his credit. DAVID HYDE, fellow of Merton College, Oxford, classicist, mathematician and antiquarian, was, according to Wood, the author of a number of works printed in Ireland, whither he fled in 1560, or abroad. JOHN SANDERSON, fellow of Trinity College, Cambridge, and reader in logic to the university, professed theology at Rhemes and later was appointed Canon of Cambray. JOHN SETON, the distinguished dialectician of St. John's College, Cambridge, after a term of imprisonment in this country, also sought refuge abroad.

This list is by no means exhaustive. Such distinguished names as THOMAS BAILEY, Master of Clare Hall, Cambridge, JOHN BRIDGEWATER (Aquapontanus), Rector of Lincoln College, Oxford, and GEORGE BULLOCK, Master of St. John's College, Cambridge, all three refugees, might have found place in it. Again, account might have been taken of those Recusants who were lost to the universities, but who actually remained in the country. These would include such men as GEORGE ETHERIDGE, regius professor of Greek at Oxford, and THOMAS SEDGWICK, regius professor of divinity at Cambridge. Even so, if taken in conjunction with the later biographical references of this chapter, it is fairly formidable, and gives substance to the claim made earlier in the chapter as to the importance of the movement we are considering. Reversely, we may find in it one of the causes for that decay in learning in the universities which Whitgift called attention to in the year 1589,* and which is attributed by Bass Mullinger to the fact that 'the ancient and Catholic conception of their functions as great schools of all

* Strype, *The Life and Acts of John Whitgift* (1822), pp. 610 et seq.

sciences and of all learning, had narrowed to one whereby they came to be regarded as little more than seminaries for the education of the clergy of the Established Church', a view which is confirmed by the bishops' declaration of 1584 that Oxford and Cambridge were 'founded principally for the study of divinity and increase of the number of learned preachers and ministers'.* A remarkable confirmation, be it noted, of Cardinal Allen's contention cited above (p. 19), that 'there is no art, holy or prophane, thoroughly studied, and some not touched at all' in the universities.

4. EARLY SETTLEMENTS ABROAD: LOUVAIN

The story of the early Recusant settlements abroad has been often told.† Groups of exiles were to be found in all the principal university towns of the Continent and in those towns of the Spanish Netherlands and of northern France, which, owing to their geographical position, provided an easy means of access from this country. Such centres as Brussels, Antwerp, Mechlin, Douay, Dunkirk, Rouen and Rhemes all afforded protection to the Elizabethan refugees, clerical and lay. Of the various religious foundations which were driven to flight, the Carthusians of Sheen settled, to begin with, at Bruges, and the Bridgettines of Syon began life anew at Termonde. But it was Louvain which was the principal asylum for English refugee scholars in the early years of the dispersion, and thither the greater number of the exiles from Oxford and Cambridge flocked. One of the attractions of the old university town for the Elizabethan Recusants was, no doubt, its close association with the circle of Thomas More, for it was there that in 1549 Antony Bonvyse, the wealthy London merchant of Crosby Hall and the life-long friend of More, had formed a colony of English exiles, which included the Clements and the Rastells.‡ More important than this, however, were the very definite advantages of its nearness to England and its reputation for theological learning. And so 'the more learned sort repaired unto the Universitie of Lovaine', as Fr. Persons writes, 'and there for

* Citations from Wood, as before, p. 108; cf. also the statement to the same effect by A. W. Ward in the important fourteenth chapter of Vol. V of *The Cambridge History of English Literature*.

† Most recently by Peter Guilday, who gives a very complete account in his *The English Catholic Refugees on the Continent, 1558–1795*, published in 1914.

‡ cf. A. W. Reed, *Early Tudor Drama* (1926), p. 87. P. Guilday, op. cit., p. 378.

that they had byn brought up partely in the University of Oxford partly in Cambridge, they began two houses under the names of the foresaid Universities, calling the one Oxford house and the other Cambridge house'.* The leader of the exiles of Louvain was NICOLAS SANDER, and to him must be attributed the founding of what has been called the Louvain School of Apologetics.† The English apologetical works which were the product of this school will be discussed in the next chapter. We will only note in passing that Sander's chief assistants were JOHN MARTIALL, THOMAS STAPLETON, THOMAS HARDING, THOMAS DORMAN, JOHN RASTELL, RICHARD SHACKLOCK, THOMAS HESKYNS, ROBERT POINTZ and WILLIAM ALLEN, and that the methods of controversy adopted by these writers was of deep interest to Bellarmine, who acknowledges his own debt to them in his later works.‡ Altogether some forty publications were issued from Louvain between the years 1564 and 1568, no small achievement considering the great difficulties in printing the books. In 1568 the output from Louvain ceased, partly owing to the religious disturbances in the Low Countries, partly also owing to the fact that the centre of the Recusant movement shifted with the founding of Douay College by Cardinal Allen. For the next twenty-five years from 1568 to 1593 Douay (Rhemes after 1578) became the focus point of English Catholic intellectual life on the Continent, and to Douay and Allen's foundation we must now turn.

5. DOUAY AND ITS DEPENDENT FOUNDATIONS

The foundation of the English College at Douay in the Michaelmas term of 1568 marks the 'commencement of the Seminary movement, which, from very humble beginnings, grew to be the source of a powerful and permanent Catholic renaissance'.§ To trace the growth of that movement in detail would occupy many more pages than we can allow ourselves in this book, nor is it necessary, since it has not lacked historians both English and foreign.|| We may content ourselves, therefore, with calling attention to a few outstanding facts. Allen's intentions in founding the college have already been set out

* *Memoir II*. Catholic Record Society, *Miscellanea II*, p. 62.
† P. Guilday, op. cit., p. 9.
‡ cf. below, p. 44. Dr. R. Smith (see above) also assisted.
§ J. H. Pollen, op. cit., p. 244.
|| cf. P. Guilday, op. cit., p. 63, where some of the principal are listed.

above (p. 18), and it seems clear from the words of the *Apology* quoted there, that from the beginning he had in mind the idea of missionary activity. This appears, too, in his words to Dr. Vendeville, cited by Pollen: 'We thought it would be an excellent thing to have men of learning always ready outside the realm to restore religion, when the proper moment should arrive, although it seemed hopeless to attempt anything while the heretics were masters there.'* But this idea was not at first prominent. Primarily he hoped the college would preserve that spiritual and cultural tradition which he believed was the hallmark of Catholic life and which was slowly disappearing in the universities at home. Thus it was his endeavour 'to draw into this College the best wittes out of England, that were either Catholikly bent, or desirous of more exact education then is these daies in either of the Vniuersities'.† He hoped to establish and maintain a tradition of English university life in the college by means of college tutors drawn from Oxford and Cambridge.

Among the earliest members of the college we note the names of RICHARD BRISTOW, fellow of Exeter College, Oxford; JOHN MARTIALL, fellow of New College, Oxford, and second master at Winchester; and MORGAN PHILLIPS, who had been Principal of St. Mary's Hall and Allen's tutor at Oxford. The year 1569 brought THOMAS STAPLETON, fellow of New College, Oxford, and THOMAS DORMAN, fellow of All Souls. Among those who entered in 1570–1 were JOHN HAWLET, fellow of Exeter College, Oxford; JOHN SANDERSON, fellow of Trinity College, Cambridge; THOMAS FORD, fellow of Trinity College, Oxford; and those two distinguished *alumni* of St. John's College, Oxford, GREGORY MARTIN and EDMUND CAMPION. Rather later, Dr. RICHARD HALL, fellow of Pembroke College, Cambridge, Dr. THOMAS BAILEY, Master of Clare Hall, Cambridge, and his friend Dr. LAURENCE WEBB, also of Cambridge, joined the college. All these men gave to the rising seminary the advantage of their brilliant learning, and they left an ineradicable stamp upon the college life. It is thus reasonable to suppose that many of the traditions of Catholic Oxford were perpetuated

* J. H. Pollen, as before, p. 245. Jean Vendeville was at the time regius professor of canon law at Douay. Allen consulted him closely in connexion with the founding of the college.

† As above, p. 19.

at Douay, just as the presence of such noted Wykehamists as John Martiall and Thomas Stapleton, as John Pits attests, helped to keep alive in the college the spirit of Winchester.

The twenty years of Allen's presidency were among the most fruitful and the most intellectual of the whole two centuries and a half of the college's existence.* The numbers in the college were high – they reached 150 a few years after its foundation – in spite of grave pecuniary difficulties;† the course of studies was both exacting and liberal; and the spiritual zeal of professors and students alike was exceptional. A steady stream of controversial and other works issued from the college during this period. The Douay Bible, one of the chief undertakings, was complete by 1582. The vitality engendered by Allen and his colleagues was such as to enable the college to survive the shock of the expulsion. The latter event happened on 22 March 1578, and was caused by the treaty of 7 January 1578 between the Prince of Orange, Elizabeth, and the Spanish Low Countries.‡ Fr. Persons' account of the flight is as follows:

> The occasion then of this niew benefit was that the state of England, having procured by those that took arms ag^{t} ye K. of Spain in Flanders that the citty of Douay bowing somewhat to their bent they should first of all dissolve & expell ye Engl. seminary & apprehend Mr Allen that was their President – they did so & gave vere few hours of flight as wel to ye Jesuits as to them. And as for Dr Allen, he being privily advertised of such a design, fled privily by secret meanes to Rheims in France, wch was ye next citty & university of any security unto Douay. And thither also followed him his children & schollers flying by other ways; from whence also when the state of England by their Embassador in Paris would have procured ye K. to expulse them as not confident to France they remained by entreaty of Pope Gregory ye 13 and by ye compassion wch the Card^{l} & Duke of Guise chief governors there at y^{t} time had of them.§

* cf. P. Guilday, op. cit., p. 66.

† Allen was at first almost entirely dependent upon the alms of the faithful for support. Later, pensions from Rome and Spain helped to resolve these difficulties, and, to an extent, the sale of books.

‡ P. Guilday, op. cit., p. 19, footnote.

§ *Memoirs III.* Catholic Record Society, *Miscellanea II,* p. 192. Marlowe comments on the same event thus:

> Did he [the Duke of Guise] not draw a sort of English priests
> From Douay to the seminary at Rheims,
> To hatch forth treason 'gainst their natural queen?

The Massacre at Paris, sc. xviii, 102.

With the Rhemes period (1578–93)* we reach the high-water mark in the annals of the college. It stands to the credit of English Catholicism that at this time Allen's foundation became a model for similar foundations. 'Bishops in other parts of Europe wishing to begin the constructive work of training their young clergy according to the new regulations of Trent wrote to the Rector at Rheims for a description of the work done in the College. When Philip II began the foundation of two Seminaries in Belgium, he ordered that they be modelled upon the system at Rheims. John Leslie, the exiled Bishop of Ross and the ambassador of Mary Stuart, desiring to do for Scotland what Allen was doing for England, erected on the Rheims model the Scottish Seminaries of Paris, Rouen, and Douay.'† What the system of training was we may read in a long letter of Allen's to Dr. Vendeville written about this time.‡ It is enough here that we record this notable fact.

The danger which had brought about the migration to Rhemes led also to a new foundation in Rome.§ The idea of a house of studies in the capital of Christendom seems to have been mooted as far back as 1568, probably by Dr. Maurice Clenock, its first rector. But the idea did not materialize until 1576, when Allen sent ten students from Douay thither under the care of Gregory Martin. From that date there was a continual stream of students from Rhemes and Douay to Rome, with great advantage to the seminary movement in general, as we learn, and to the missionary activity of the exiles in particular. 'Very real as were the trials incident to this retreat from Douay,' writes J. H. Pollen, 'they were well compensated by the establishment of the English College at Rome; for the high-water mark of Catholic missionary zeal came with the first mission sent out from that college.'|| Other foundations which witness to the strength of the seminary movement were – Valladolid and Seville in Spain, founded by Fr. Persons in the years 1589 and 1592; Eu in Normandy, also founded by Persons in 1582 for English boys and later removed to St. Omer; and the Scots colleges already referred to. Altogether between 1568 and

* The college returned to Douay in 1593 under the presidency of Dr. Richard Barrett.

† P. Guilday, op. cit., pp. 78–9.

‡ See *Letters and Memorials*, as before, no. 25.

§ It was occasioned by the heretics' persecution, writes Fr. Persons. *Memoirs*, loc. cit.

|| op. cit., p. 271.

the end of the century many thousands of English youths must have passed through the Catholic colleges and 'there can be no doubt', to quote the words of Norman Wood, 'that the recusant movement was revived, given new life and turned into an important national problem chiefly because of the seminaries'.*

6. BOOKS: PRODUCTION

Side by side with the growth of the seminary movement went the further production of Recusant books, and it must be our next business to offer some general remarks on this most interesting topic.† Cardinal Allen attached great importance to this side of Recusant activity from the beginning. A paper is extant, written about 1576, in reference to London and especially to the students of the Inns of Court, in which he states: '. . . our men have, these last years, made wonderful headway, both by personal intercourse – for nowhere do men lie hid more safely than in London – and still more by books in the vulgar tongue, written in Belgium and imported'.‡ Writing to Dr. Vendeville on 16 September (1580?) he says:

> To bring about this change of mind certain books of our men in English concerning almost all matters of controversy, formerly made and printed in Flanders, had done much; in which, for the comprehension of the people, with a wonderful clarity almost all the deceits of the heretics and their consequences, their disputes, blasphemies, contradictions, absurdities, falsifyings both of the Scriptures and the Doctors of the Church were exposed; so that in every matter not only in the judgement of the wise but also of the people we were superior, nor at any point were our adversaries equal to us save only in the power of their prince and in arms and in the orders of the laws.§

Again, in the *Apologie of the English Seminaries* (1581) he states his belief that it was the books which opened the way for the great Catholic revival of the 1580's. The output was certainly

* op. cit., p. 302.

† A detailed account of the publishers and the persons employed in the publication of these books will be found at Chapter VI.

‡ Cited by J. H. Pollen, as before, p. 259.

§ Original: Ad hanc animorum mutationem multum fecerant libri quidam a nostris hominibus lingua Anglica de omnibus rebus pene controversis, antea in Flandri facti et impressi, quibus ad populi captum mira claritate omnes pene haereticorum fraudes, fructus, contentiones, blasphemiae, contradictiones, absurditates, falsationes tam Scripturarum quam Doctorum sunt patefactae, ut in omni genere non modo sapientum sed etiam populi iudicio essemus superiores, nec ullo essent loco nobis pares adversarii nisi principis potentia ac armis legumque praescriptis. Cited *Letters and Memorials*, as before, no. 25.

considerable. Roughly, we may estimate that between 1559 and 1570 (the date of the Bull) fifty-eight English books and pamphlets were published; between 1570 and 1582 (the date of the Rhemes Testament) forty-seven books were published; between 1582 and 1594 twenty-one books; and during the last ten years of the reign about eighty, these latter including a number of works arising out of the Archpriest controversy.* During the period with which this book deals, that is between 1559 and 1582–3, there were then altogether some 105 books and editions printed, the most active period being that of the great controversy (1564–8), when forty-four books were published, after which there was a falling off, the numbers in creasing again with the coming of the Jesuits in 1580.

When we consider the difficulties which had to be faced by these writers in producing their books, their achievement is the more remarkable. Printing difficulties are referred to again and again in the books themselves and in letters of the period, with special reference to the difficulty for foreign compositors of composing in an unknown tongue.† The state of unrest in the Low Countries tended to hold up production. Allen and Bristow, for instance, both complain of this. And there was, above all, the question of costs. So Allen writes to George Gilbert in a letter concerning money affairs: 'All that is yet gathered, for any that I know, will not pay for the printing of our bookes this yeare past.'‡ Gregory Martin writes to Campion that Allen and Bristow were unable at the time of writing to publish their replies to Fulke 'on account of the troubles and our lack of means'.§ And in another letter to Campion he states that he himself has written a treatise on the fruit and theologic use of Greek and Hebrew, mainly against the heretics, which is to be printed *if the cost of printing can be met.*‖ It is indeed a standing marvel that Allen was able to raise the necessary money – 1,500 crowns (over £3,000 of our money today) – for the printing of the Rhemes New Testament in 1582. Some of the money undoubtedly came from the home country. William Roper

* The numbers here do not include certain reprints. There were, of course, numerous Latin works besides during the period.

† References will be found in the bibliography to this book.

‡ From Rhemes, 12 May 1582. Cited *Letters and Memorials*, no. 63.

§ From Rhemes, 22 August 1578. Cited *D.D.*, p. 318.

‖ From Rhemes, 13 February 1579; ibid., p. 319.

seems to have come under the suspicion of the authorities on this score for one.* George Gilbert also, as I have stated elsewhere, supplied some money for this purpose. But largely the money must have come out of the pockets of the exiles, and the sacrifice that this must have entailed further testifies to the importance attached to these publications.

The books were printed at various Continental centres, except for a very few which were printed surreptitiously in England,† and up to the year 1568 usually bore on the title-page their place of origin, with the name of the author. In some cases these earlier publications were even dedicated to Elizabeth herself and bore on the reverse of the title the royal arms – a signal mark of the writer's loyalty. After that date, however, owing to the activities of the English authorities abroad, it became necessary to conceal the place of origin and very often counterfeit imprints were used instead. That the subterfuges adopted by the printers and publishers for putting the English authorities off the scent were largely successful is not surprising to the writer of this book, who has spent many laborious and often unsuccessful hours in endeavouring to trace some of these anonymous publications.

The following story, recorded by Kervyn de Lettenhove, while it also describes one of the difficulties experienced by the refugees in getting their books printed, is illustrative of the methods employed for discovering the origin of the print of these Recusant works. Some years after the printing of Sander's *De visibili monarchia ecclesiae* (1571), Wilson, the English ambassador at Brussels, related to Burghley how he had become friendly with Montano, the Spanish humanist,‡ who at the time of the printing of this work held the position of royal censor, a post introduced by the Duke of Alva in 1569 to supervise the printing establishments of the Low Countries in order to prevent the publication of seditious and heretical literature. He thus hoped to discover the authors and printers of the tracts which flooded England. Montano told him, on one occasion, that Dr. Sander approached him, as was required by law, to obtain permission for the printing of the book. Montano per-

* See *The Lyfe of Sir Thomas Moore*, ed. by E. V. Hitchcock. E.E.T.S. (1935). Introduction, p. xxxviii.

† See Chapter VI.

‡ Benito Arias Montano, orientalist and humanist, was associated with the religious policy of Philip II. He left Flanders in 1576.

ceived that the seventh book would offend Elizabeth, and as Philip's policy towards England was outwardly one of strict neutrality he refused the required permission within the dominions of the King. Fowler, therefore, printed Books I–VI and Book VIII which the censor had passed, and had Book VII last of all printed at Cologne.* In like manner, about the year 1585, we find Walsingham's spy, Nicholas Berden, making friends with Richard, servant to Cardinal Allen, in order to find out 'what bookes are in pryntinge, whoe is the prynter, and whoe did wryte them'.† We may note also that a special inquiry was set on foot to discover the author of Bishop Leslie's *Treatise of Treasons* (1572) by means of the printer,‡ and the fact that Richard Verstegan, the well-known Catholic writer and publisher, was imprisoned in Paris in 1584 at the representation of the English ambassador, Sir Edward Stafford, not for printing, but because he was engaged in writing a book which was unsavoury to the English authorities, points to the searching nature of such enquiries.§ However, the information gleaned in these and similar ways seems on the whole to have been of little use to the home government, for the printing continued to go on almost uninterruptedly throughout the Queen's reign.

7. BOOKS: DISTRIBUTION

The difficulties of publishing were, of course, not over when the printing was done. The difficulty of disseminating the books remained. The effect of the various Royal Proclamations against the importation, circulation, even the reading or possession of the Catholic books was to make distribution a dangerous and costly business.‖ As Allen writes to Agazzari, the Rector of the English College in Rome, there was not only the expense of shipping the books to England, but there was the further expense of distributing them up and down the land, and added to this the impossibility of selling or buying them

* *Relations politiques des Pays-Bas et de l'Angleterre sous la règne de Philippe II*, Vol. VII, pp. 469–70, cited by T. McN. Veech, op. cit., pp. 90–1. It can, however, be clearly established on bibliographical grounds that Sander's seventh book came from the same press as the other seven.

† See Catholic Record Society, Vol. XXI, pp. 72 et seq.

‡ cf. Strype, *Annals* (1824), Vol. II, pt. 1, pp. 264–5.

§ See below, Chapter VI.

‖ These were promulgated almost yearly between 1565 and 1575.

owing to the danger attending such transactions.* The resultant measures taken by the Government to suppress publication in England were indeed elaborate and far-reaching. They included the appointment of special customs officials to the port of London for the examination of all books that came into the custom-house;† careful watch at other principal ports and creeks by hired 'promoters' and 'waiters', who searched all incoming vessels;‡ an order to all booksellers who sold foreign books in England to supply the Commissioners with a list of such books before any sales were effected;§ munificent rewards for informers or, for any who should turn Queen's evidence, pardon and reward;|| systematic search of the houses of known Recusants, as also of those suspected of leanings towards recusancy; and, finally, the careful examination of all those in custody on charges of recusancy. In the face of such measures, with their attendant penalties, the utmost precaution was necessary on the part of the Catholics in spreading the books.

And first with regard to their shipment to England. The busy trade between Antwerp and the English ports without doubt afforded the best opportunities of sending them across the sea, and throughout the Queen's reign it was the principal port used by the Catholic agents for this purpose. A good many of the books were also secretly shipped from Dunkirk. There is a special note to this effect in the Douay Diaries under date 1576, which states that a certain Dunkirk man arranged the safe dispatch of books, letters and other necessities from the port of Dunkirk to England.¶ Dieppe and Rouen are also referred to in contemporary documents as centres of distribution, and it is pretty certain that a fair number found their way into the country by way of Calais and Boulogne. Less obvious routes must also have been used, for, rather later in the period, Fr. Persons writes (in Italian): 'B. Ralph Emerson

* Nunc accingimus nos ad alia scribenda; et omnia ista fiunt magnis sumptibus, et tales libri propter pericula vendi aut emi non possunt in Anglia, sed praeter expensas vecturae per tot terras et maria debent spargi in vicos civitatum per totam Angliam. – From Rhemes, 16 August 1582. Cited *Letters and Memorials*, as before, no. 74.

† See Elizabeth's letter to the Bishop of London, under date 1566, cited by Strype, *Annals* (1824), Vol. I, pt. 2, pp. 529–30.

‡ cf. Thomas Harding, *A Detection of sundrie foule errours* (1568), 'Preface to the Reader', sig. *****3. § Strype, *Life and Acts of Parker* (1821), Vol. II, p. 172.

|| Proclamation of 1 July 1570. Dyson, *Proclamations*, fol. 133.

¶ *Douay Diaries*, p. 105.

... has now come back from the sea where he has done wonders, having arranged two new routes, along which he has sent four priests and 810 books; but that has cost him a lot.'* The methods employed for transport varied according to the circumstances. Very often the books were smuggled into England concealed in goods destined for the friends of the cause. Sometimes a friendly merchant would include a sack of books in his baggage. The copies of Richard Bristow's *Motives* (1574) were carried in this way.† Sometimes, again, they were brought over by priests bound for the English mission or by other undaunted companions in the Faith. Whatever the methods, one thing only guided those who were responsible for their dispatch, namely the grave difficulties which had to be faced on the other side of the sea.

We may indicate broadly the nature and extent of the Government's watchfulness for this line of contraband by reference to some contemporary records. William Carr was searched for books at Berwick on 3 July 1572. He had come into the country by way of Leith and 'had a great cloak bag in Tweedmouth', wherein was found 'a great sort of English books, with English litanies'.‡ A list of 'trayterous and popish bookes intercepted' dated 1574 includes twenty copies of Bishop Leslie's *Treatise of Treasons* (1572), which Charles Baillie probably brought over.§ It also includes nearly the whole of the 1574 edition of Richard Bristow's *Motives*, which was brought across by a merchant friendly to the cause.|| Ralph Emerson, a Jesuit lay-brother, who brought over the first consignment of 'Leicester's Commonwealth' in 1584, seems to have been taken at Scarborough, books and all.¶ Thomas Alfield lost his life at Tyburn, 6 July 1585, for bringing in and distributing copies

* Cited *Letters and Memorials*, as before, p. 241. † *Douay Diaries*, p. 102.

‡ *Calendar of State Papers, Dom. Eliz. Add., 1566–1579*, p. 416.

§ Charles Baillie was twice taken for distributing Bishop Leslie's books and was 'diuers waies afflicted' therefor. See Brit. Mus. Lansd. MSS., Vol. 42, no. 78, and Leslie, *Treatise of Treasons* (1572), sig. E4v.

|| See above. The list, which also includes 700 pamphlets and forty-three other works, will be found in Brit. Mus. Lansd. MSS., loc. cit. The entry is misdated 1584; cf. Strype, *Life and Acts of Parker* (1821), Vol. II, p. 382.

¶ See below. *The Copie of a Leter, wryten by a Master of Arte of Cambrige, to his friend in London* (1584), known as 'Leicester's Commonwealth', was probably written by Charles Arundel. See Catholic Record Society, Vol. XXI, for evidence of authorship. A note in C.R.S., Vol. V, from P.R.O. Dom. Eliz., 181, no. 78, refers to books against Leicester being found on 'one' at Scarborough, in the early part of 1585.

of Allen's *True Sincere and Modest Defence* (1584). He admitted at his trial that he had brought five or six hundred copies of the book in and had managed to distribute a few of them before he was apprehended.* In a secret document Nicholas Berden informs his master, Walsingham, that the priests

> moste commonly do come over in French boates that come to Newcastell for Coales, whoe do lande the sayd Preists either at Newcastell, or in some Creeke nere to the same. They make Choyse of that place the Rather for that Robert Higheclyf her Mats officer at Newcastell is a papiste in harte & made acquaynted with there comynge, & that his wyef is and hathe bynne a papiste this iii or iiii yeres, and that by her Directions the sayd preists with there bookes do passe in Securitie.†

In a prison list of Recusants under the year 1588 William Bray is described as 'a common conveyer of priests and recusants, and of naughty books over the seas'.‡ And, to pass on to the end of the reign, we may note the information and precise instructions contained in a letter addressed by the authorities to the 'Maior of Plymouth, the preacher of that towne and the officers of the Custome', which reads:

> Whereas wee understande that divers tymes there are brought into the porte of Plymouth and other the Westerne portes many lewde and seditious bookes and other superstitious reliques dangerous and unfit to be dispersed, both in regarde of the State and common peace of the Churche . . . wee . . . do authorize you or any three of you, whereof the Maior, preacher or customer beinge one, to view all kinde of bookes and reliques or whatsoever you finde tending to idolatrie or superstition, or contrary to her Majesty's lawes and quiett peace of this kingdomme, which you shall staye and safely keepe in your custodie untill further direccion from us . . .'§

And yet, in spite of the dangers and difficulties, we learn that before the year 1580 'not less than 20,000 of these books were imported into England and secretly sold'.||

* He was assisted in the distribution of the books by Thomas Weblie, who also lost his life. See *The Life and end of Thomas Awfuld*, London, no name or date. (Lambeth Palace Library 30.viii.17.)

† Catholic Record Society, Vol. XXI, pp. 72 et seq., as before, citing P.R.O. Dom. Eliz. 177, no. 19. The document is endorsed 13 April 1585.

‡ Strype, *Annals* (1824), Vol. III, pt. 2, p. 600. The ubiquitous Berden made Bray's acquaintance in 1585 and, 'fayninge to bye some of his bookes yf he had any to sell', managed to get some useful information out of him. C.R.S., as before.

§ Cited by Helen C. White, *English Devotional Literature, 1600–1640* (1931), p. 136, from *Acts of the Privy Council, New Series, XXXII*, ed. by John Roche Dasent (1907).

|| N. Sander, *De Schismate*, cited by J. H. Pollen, as before, p. 111.

A letter from some English priest to Father Agazzari, dated July 1581, gives us some account of their subsequent distribution in England.

> So much for the books (he writes), which are as difficult and dangerous to publish as to print. The way is, all of them are taken to London before any is published, and then they are distributed by hundreds or fifties to the priests, so that they may be published all together in all parts of the realm. And the next day, when the pursuivants usually begin to search the Catholics' houses, it is too late; for during the night the young gentlemen have introduced copies into the houses, shops, and mansions of the heretics, and even into the court, and the stalls in the streets, so that the Catholics alone cannot be accused of possessing them.*

There appear to have been regular agents for carrying out this work. Thus Richard Lacey of Brodishe in Norfolk, when examined on 13 March 1583, confessed 'thatt one Mr Godshale and one Mr Moore and one Marshm[an] ar common cariers of papisticall bookes and letters from one papist to an other'.† Bryan Lacey, Richard's brother, seems to have been in similar case, for he told Richard that he had left certain books at one Anthony Bourne's house of Brome 'in a Cloke bagge, which bookes he said came from beyonde the seas since Hallow-masse last'.‡ Again, John Barber, it would seem, was also a 'common carrier'. When examined he said, 'That he received a tronke with certayne bookes therin directed unto him by a superscription, as he thinks from Mr Awlfeild,§ to be conveyed to Gloucester, and that he opened the same Tronke, and saw therin one booke agaynst the execucon,|| and shutt the Tronke agayne . . . and so it was sent (as he thinkethe) to Gloucester . . . and that his wyffe opened the Chest as she wrytes and conveyed the bookes into a Privye wheare by the sayd vice-chancellor's meanes they weare fownd,¶ and after burned in the open strete'.** A certain Peter Lowson, who had in his possession some packs of books, is referred to in the examination in 1583 of John Nutter, with whom he was arrested. The

* Cited by R. Simpson, *Edmund Campion*, pp. 289–90.
† Catholic Record Society, Vol. V, p. 73, from P.R.O. Dom. Eliz., 169, no. 19.
‡ C.R.S., as before, p. 72.
§ Thomas Alfield, referred to below.
|| Allen's *True, Sincere and Modest Defence* (1585).
¶ The examination was taken by Dr. Underhill, Vice-Chancellor of the University of Oxford.
** Catholic Record Society, Vol. V, p. 109, from P.R.O. Dom. Eliz., 178, no. 36.

examiners recorded 'a note of suche thyngs as remayne in dyverse packs of Peter Lowson' –

> In primis in the fyrste packe IIII[er] C Catechisms. Item in a nother pack oon C Catechisms and certen other boks and XXX[ti] lattyn premers. Item in a nother packe XV latten testaments and XLV medytacions.*

Nicholas Berden reports to Walsingham in his 'secret advertisements' that a certain Tremayne had ninety unsold copies of the Rhemes *New Testament* in his possession, and that William Hartley, 'the late banyshed preiste whoe is presently in London', had brought over some store of Persons' *Christian Directory*.† Ralph Emerson, Edward Shelley and Thomas Weblie are also referred to as 'dispersers of traiterous bookes' in their examination at the instance of Topcliffe and others on 18 March 1585,‡ and both Edward Cooke, servant to proctor Smythe in Paternoster Row, in whose desk were found forty books, and one Norwood of Symons Inn are described as publishers of these books.§ We may add as an interesting sidelight upon this particular form of Recusant activity that, as a result of a memorandum of 14 April 1565 from de Silva, the Spanish ambassador in London, to Philip concerning the influence of the Louvain writings, the latter replied (6 June 1565) that the ambassador was to do all that was possible to further the distribution of the books in as wide a circle as possible, but not to compromise Spain with the Queen over the affair.||

The campaign to keep the books of the exiles from the English Catholics was, as has already been suggested, only partially successful. Despite the fact that the reading or possession of such books by private individuals was a punishable offence¶

* J. H. Pollen, *Unpublished Documents* in C.R.S., Vol. V, p. 38, cited by N. Wood, as before, p. 289.

† Catholic Record Society, Vol. XXI, as above.

‡ Catholic Record Society, Vol. V, p. 105, from Brit. Mus. Lansd. MSS., 157, fol. 167.

§ ibid., p. 27, from P.R.O., Dom. Eliz., 152, no. 54 (February 1582?).

|| *Calendar of State Papers, Simancas*, Vol. I, p. 432. Cited by T. McN. Veech, as before, footnote, p. 100.

¶ cf. Proclamation of 1 March 1569 – 'her Maiestie . . . wylleth and earnestlye chargeth all manner of persons, to forbeare vtterly from the vse or dealing with any such seditious bookes . . . and that such as alredy haue any of the sayde bookes, shall present, or cause to be presented the sayde bookes, within twentie and eyght dayes after the publishing of this proclamation, to the byshop of the diocesse . . . not to kepe or reade any seditious bookes, vpon payne of her Maiesties greeuous indignation, and to be punished seuerely, as the qualitie and circum-

and in spite of the high prices, they were read in all parts of the kingdom and were in constant demand.* This we may learn from the records of the searchers and from the Government examinations. For instance, John Stow,† 'the laborious collector of the Historical Antiquities of London and England', was reputed to be a great collector of popish books, 'under the pretence of making collections for his History'. An order was therefore given by the Lords of the Council to search his house and examine his books. In the inventory which was made 'of such books as had been lately set forth in the realm, or beyond sea, for defence of Papistry' we find:

A Parliament of Christ, made by Thomas Heskins.
The Hatchet of Heresies; set out by Shacklock.
A Discourse of the Troubles in France, in print. Translated by Thomas Jeney, Gent.
Bede: translated by Stapleton.
A Proof of certain Articles in Religion, denied by Mr. Juel &c. by Thomas Dorman.
Two Homilies, upon the first, second, and third Articles of the Creed, made by Dr. Feckenham.
A brief Shew of false Wares &c., by Rastal.
Testimonies of the real Presence of Christ's Body and Blood in the Sacrament of the Altar: set forth by Poiner [Pointz?], Student in Divinity.
A Copy of a Challenge taken out of the Confutation of Mr. Juell's Sermon, by John Rastal.

All of which, said Archdeacon Wattes, 'declared him to be a great fautor of Papistry'.‡ In 1570 Robert Seede, of Blackburn, was ordered to give up into the hands of the vicar of the parish a copy of Vaux's *Catechisme* which he possessed.§ Northumberland, under examination 24 June 1572, confessed to the influence of the works of Harding, Sander, Stapleton and

staunces of the offence shall require and deserue'. Dyson, *Proclamations*, fol. 114. The works of Harding, Dorman, Allen, Sander, Stapleton, Martial, Bristow and Rastell were specially singled out in this connexion. So Strype, *Annals*, *Acts of Parker*, *Acts of Grindal*.

* cf. J. B. Code, *Queen Elizabeth and the English Catholic Historians* (1935), p. 7, citing H. Thurston.

† Stow was not, of course, a Recusant. We may assume that he belonged to that group described above as 'demi-catholics': hence the suspicion of the authorities.

‡ Strype, *Life and Acts of Grindal* (1821), pp. 184 and 516 et seq. The inventory is dated 24 February 1568. It has also been reprinted by Arber, *Stat. Regist.* (1875), I, p. 181, from Brit. Mus. Lansd. MSS. All the items listed here are referred to in the bibliography at the end of this book.

§ T. G. Law, introduction to Chetham Society reprint of Vaux's *Catechisme*, p. lxxx.

others in reference to the Northern Rebellion.* One John Lee, a Catholic, in examination, confessed to having read the works of Harding and Jewel.† Sir Thomas Metham, 'a most wilful papist', is described as using 'the corrupt Louvaine books'.‡ A list of books taken from Sir Thomas Tresham's house at Hoggesdon contains:

> the Jesuit's Testament in English:
> a Manual of Prayers, dedicated to the gentlemen of inns of court:
> Vaux's Catechism:
> the first book of the Christian Exercise:
> a book of prayers and meditations.§

A similar list of those taken from Mr. Thomas Wilford's house, also in Hoggesdon, includes G.T.'s *An Epistle of the Persecution of Catholickes in Englande* with its Latin original, and John Fowler's *An Oration Against the Unlawfull Insurrections of the Protestantes.*|| A British Museum Lansdowne manuscript (MSS., Vol. 50, no. 76) furnishes us with 'The catalogue of the supersticious bookes and reliques founde in the lodgeinge and studie of George Brome and in the lodgeinge of Elizabeth and Briget Brome sisters to the said George and lodged in Borstall house where the said George doth lodge vppon searche there made by comaundent from her ma^ties most honorable priuie counsell the xxvij^th of August in the xxviij^th yere of her Maties most happie raigne'. In the lodging and study of George Brome were found amongst a number of foreign works:

> (1) A discourse conteininge reasons whie Catholiques refuse to come to churche.
> (4) Campions booke of decem rationes as it was set forthe by himselfe with a supersticious figure printed in the first Leafe.
> (19) A replie against the false named [Defence] of the truthe.
> (20) A Treatise of christian peregrinacōn and of Pilgrimage and reliques.¶

* *Calendar of State Papers, Dom. Eliz., Addenda*, 1566–79, p. 414.

† ibid., p. 448.

‡ ibid., p. 224.

§ Strype, *Annals* (1824), Vol. II, pt. 2, p. 346, citing from State Papers of 27 August 1584. The first book in this list is the Rhemes *New Testament*; two and five are by Richard Hopkins; four is Persons' well-known work. Sir Thomas appears as William in Strype's citation.

|| ibid. The Latin original is Persons' *De Persecutione Anglicana Epistola*.

¶ The numeration is from the original. No. (1) is by Persons; (19) by John Rastell; and (20) by Gregory Martin.

The books in the lodging of Elizabeth and Briget Brome include:

(1) A booke entituled A manuell of praiers wth a Iesus psalter in the end imprinted 1586.
(5) The exercise of a xtian written by Iasper Loart of the Societie of Gesus translated into Englishe by E. S.
(6) A Cathechisme in English compiled by Lawrence Vaux with an addicōn of Informatiō of the lawdible Ceremonyes vsed in the Catholique Churche.
(7) The booke of resolucōn.
(8) A treatise in englyshe of confession & pennāce imprynted at Lovayne.
(9) An induction to devocōn for Ladies and gentlemen shewinge the significations of the masse and implements to it.
(10) A treatise made by Lewis de granado prouinciall of the holy order of preachers in the prouince of Portugale translated out of Spanishe into Englishe.*

In 'an Inventorie of such superstitious thinges as were founde in Sir John Sothworthe his howse at Samlesburie,† by Richard Brereton, esquier, one of her Maties Justices of the Peace, at a Searche made there by the said Richard Brereton' we find:

A Rhemes Testamente.
An apologie of the Englishe Seminaryes.
A defence of the censure given upon two bookes written against Edmund Campyon, prieste.
A treatise of Schisme, shewinge that all Catholickes must absent theymselves from hereticall conventicles, to witt, prayer and sermons.
A discoverie of John Nichols.‡

Contemporary sources point also to the fact that the Catholic books must often have found their way into unofficial Protestant hands. Robert Greene in his *Repentance* attributes his deathbed conversion to reading Persons' *Resolution.*§ References to the works of Harding, Persons and Robert Southwell may be found in the controversial pamphlets of Gabriel Harvey against

* Numeration from original. No. (1) was a favourite Catholic book of devotion, first printed in 1583; (5) translated by Stephen Brinkley. The initials should be I.S., i.e. James Sancer, Brinkley's pseudonym; (6) may be either the 1574 or the 1583 edition of Vaux's *Catechisme*; (7) Persons' *Christian Exercise*, commonly called *The Resolution*; (8) may possibly refer to John Fowler's treatise; (9) I have been unable to trace; (10) *Memoriall of a Christian Life*, translated by Richard Hopkins.

† Samlesbury Hall, in Lancashire. The Southworths were one of the finest Catholic families in the county.

‡ J. P. Collier, *The Egerton Papers* (Camden Society, 1840), p. 164. The *Apologie* is Allen's; the *Defence of the Censure* and the *Discoverie* are Persons'; the *Treatise of Schisme*, Gregory Martin's. The inventory is dated 21 November 1592.

§ *The Repentance of Robert Greene* (1592), sig. B2^{v} et seq.

Thomas Nash.* Roger Ascham also, indirectly, points to the same fact when he writes, 'Mo Papistes be made by your mery bookes of Italie than by your earnest bookes of Louain',† and again, 'when the busie and open Papistes abroad could not, by their contentious bookes, turne men in England fast enough from troth and right iudgement in doctrine, than the sutle and secrete Papistes at home procured bawdie bookes to be translated out of the Italian tonge'.‡ But perhaps most interesting of all in this connexion is Edmund Bunny's address to the Archbishop of Canterbury, prefixed to the 1584 edition of the Protestant version of Persons' *Resolution*, in which he writes:

> May it please your Grace to understand that wheras at first by a fri[e]nd of mine, and after mine own experience, I perceived, that the booke insuing was willingly read by divers, for the persuasion that it hath for godlines of life, which notwithstanding in manie points was corruptly set downe: I thought good in the end, to get the same published againe in some better manner than now it is come foorth among them; that so the good, that the reading therof might otherwise do, might carrie no hurt or danger withal, so far as by me might be praevented.§

From the evidence we may justly conclude, then, that the influence of the Catholic books was both widespread and diverse. There are also strong presumptive grounds for this view. A very large proportion of the books was concerned with the burning questions of the day, and if in recalling the Elizabethan appetite for controversy we remember that little satisfaction can be gained from reading one side only of such questions we shall better understand the interest the books aroused. In the earlier part of the reign, when religious controversy was one of the principal topics of the day, both Catholic and Protestant controversialists recognized the nature of the demand. It was usual, therefore, when replying to a religious opposite, to incorporate the text of his work, very often in full, in the reply. A further counter might mean the incorporation of three books in a single text. The enormous tomes which resulted from this practice are an eloquent tribute to the Elizabethan reading public. Incidentally, too, they were a further means of disseminating the Catholic books, as the Bishop of

* Gregory Smith, *Elizabethan Critical Essays* (1904), Vol. II, pp. 247 and 280.
† ibid., Vol. I, p. 3 – from *The Scholemaster*. ‡ ibid.
§ *A Booke of Christian exercise, appertaining to Resolution* (1584), sig. *2.

Norwich seems to have recognized when, in reply to Archbishop Parker's advice to set up Jewel's answer to Harding in the churches of the diocese of Norwich, he wrote:

> That as he had singular cause to allow well of the author of that work [Jewel], so he did conjecture, that the placing of controversies in open churches might be a great occasion to confirm the adversaries in their opinions. For they having not wherewith to buy Harding's book, should find the same already provided for them; and were like unto the spider, sucking only that might serve their purposes.*

We may take it for granted, then, that even the theological treatises of the Recusants had a much wider vogue than has generally been supposed, and we would maintain (as it is the purpose of this book to show) that we cannot neglect these treatises if we are to gain a right perspective of Elizabethan literature and life. And what is true of the theological treatises is no less true of the political tracts of the later part of the reign. But it is pre-eminently true of the Recusant devotional works. The popularity of these works in England in the sixteenth and seventeenth centuries can only be described as exceptional, and, as has been pointed out recently in two notable books on the subject,† their influence upon English religious thought and expression cannot be ignored.

B. THE MEN

We have already referred in this chapter to the many eminent names which may be found among the Elizabethan Recusants.‡ It remains for us now to say something of the principal Recusant authors whose books and pamphlets find a place in the bibliography to this work. Our object will be, in the main, to call attention to the intellectual characteristics of the writers only, though occasionally some additional details have been furnished where it was felt that they would assist in building up for the reader the general background of the movement which we have been describing. Biographical notices of most of our writers are to be found in the *Catholic Encyclopedia*, in the *D.N.B.*, and in Gillow's *Bibliographical Dictionary*. Other sources of information are referred to in the footnotes.

* The letter is cited by Strype, *Life and Acts of Parker* (1821), Vol. II, p. 153.

† *English Devotional Literature, 1600–1640* (1931), by Helen C. White, and *Reformation und Spanische Andachtsliteratur* (1934), by Maria Hagedorn.

‡ Above, pp. 23–4.

The 'Louvainists', as they have been called, must be the first to occupy our attention,* and first among these was Dr. NICOLAS SANDER (1530?–81), the most eminent of that early group of Wykehamists who so faithfully served the Catholic cause.† Sander became fellow of New College, Oxford, in 1548 and five years later was appointed regius professor of canon law. In 1558 he followed the learned Dr. Peter Sotho in the reading of the Hebrew lecture in the university. Shortly after the accession of Elizabeth he left England for good and, travelling to Rome, he was ordained priest by Bishop Goldwell of St. Asaph. He was also created D.D. in Rome about this time. He next attended the Council of Trent as theologian to Cardinal Hosius and subsequently he accompanied the Cardinal on a tour through Poland, Prussia and Lithuania with the object of holding synods and attempting to put into force the decrees of the Council. It was during this tour that he was inspired by John Francis Commendone, the papal nuncio, to undertake the writing of what was in his own day regarded as one of the most outstanding examples of books dealing with the history of the Church, the *De Visibili Monarchia Ecclesiae*, published by John Fowler in 1571.

We have already alluded to Sander's leadership among the English scholars of Louvain:‡ we have only to add here that so great was his reputation for learning§ that St. Pius V appointed him in 1566 to be the second of five theologians to assist Cardinal Commendone, the papal legate at the Diet of Augsburg, and that in 1572 he summoned him to Rome to assist in the controversy with the Magdeburg Centuriators. It is generally thought that but for the death of St. Pius, shortly after Sander's arrival in Rome, he would have been nominated cardinal at this time. After a period at the court of Philip II (1573–9) he sailed as papal agent on the ill-fated expedition to Ireland which was to result in his death in 1581 among the lonely hills of Clonlish.

* Above, p. 26.

† The most complete account of Sander's life and works will be found in the recently published volume *Dr. Nicholas Sanders and the English Reformation, 1530–1581. By Thomas McNevin Veech*. Louvain, 1935. Shorter studies will be found in Fr. J. H. Pollen's *Biographical Sketch* (1891) and in David Lewis's *Rise and Growth of the Anglican Schism* (1877).

‡ Above, p. 26.

§ Bellarmine himself acknowledges his debt to Sander and the English theologians of Louvain. See Veech, op. cit., p. 70.

Closely associated with Sander in Louvain were his six fellow Wykehamists, Thomas Dorman, Thomas Harding, John Martiall, Robert Pointz, John Rastell and Thomas Stapleton. Most redoubtable of these in controversy was THOMAS HARDING (1516–72) who, like Sander, had been a fellow of New College, Oxford, and also had been appointed in 1542 to read the Hebrew lecture in the university. His eminence as a scholar was recognized both at home and in learned circles on the Continent, and he, too, was honoured by St. Pius V in his appointment (along with Sander) as apostolic delegate to give faculties to priests in England for absolving from heresy and schism, etc. As President of Oxford House* he was clearly a great source of inspiration both to his fellow controversialists and to others of the exiles.

Of the remaining five THOMAS STAPLETON (1535–98) is likely to be the most familiar name to the reader as the translator of Bede's *Ecclesiastical History*. It is a remarkable fact that Stapleton's life has still to be written.† One of the most learned men of his time, and a considerable writer in the Latin and English tongues, his works were early 'collected' on the Continent into four large folio volumes (in 1620) by Henry Holland. But his own country has so completely ignored him that it is only as recently as 1930 that his great version of Bede was republished for the first time,‡ and it is a fact that the *Cambridge History of English Literature* mentions him once and only once, and that in a completely irrelevant context.§

After leaving Winchester Stapleton proceeded to New College, Oxford, where he was elected fellow in 1554. On taking orders in 1558 he was appointed to the prebend of Woodhouse in Chichester Cathedral, but was subsequently deprived in 1563. He was closely associated with Cardinal Allen in the founding of the English College at Douay, where he taught for some twenty years. Meantime he professed divinity at Douay

* Above, p. 26.

† The Rev. E. J. McDermott, S.J., is now engaged upon this work.

‡ In the noble edition of the Shakespeare Head Press, edited by Philip Hereford.

§ In the following passage: 'The remark of Clement VIII on hearing the first book [of Hooker's *Of the Laws of Ecclesiastical Polity*] translated at sight into Latin by Stapleton, related by Walton, is as creditable to the judgment of the pontiff as to "the poor obscure English priest who had writ . . . such books"' (ed. 1918, Vol. III, p. 415). There is no evidence that Stapleton was ever in personal contact with Clement VIII. In fact, the evidence points distinctly the other way.

University and also held the canonry of Saint-Amé there. Philip II later conferred on him the chair of Holy Scripture at Louvain (13 July 1590), together with the canonry of St. Peter, which was annexed to the professorship. Finally, in January 1597, Clement VIII honoured him by making him a protonotary apostolic and by inviting him to Rome.*

Stapleton's great learning has been justly commended by such writers as Dr. Owen Lewis, Dr. William Whitaker and Anthony à Wood. Lewis writes of him: '. . . doctissimus et pientissimus et utile membrum sanctae matris ecclesiae, quam contra haereticos saepe et cum magno fructu defendit'.† Wood states that he was 'the most learned R. Catholic of all his time'.‡ Thomas Fuller quotes Whitaker as saying 'that Bellarmine was the *fairer* and Stapleton the *shrewder* adversary', and himself pungently adds: 'His preferment (in mine eye) was not proportionable to his merit, being no more than canon and master of a college in Louvain. Many more admired that Stapleton missed, than that Allen got, a cardinal's cap, equalling him in strictness of life, exceeding him in gentility of birth, and painfulness of writing for the Romish cause. Such consider not that Stapleton's *ability* was drowned with Allen's activity; and one grain of the statesman is too heavy for a *pound* of the student; practical policy, in all ages, beating pen-pains out of distance in the race of preferment.'§

THOMAS DORMAN (1532?–77), JOHN MARTIALL (1534–97), ROBERT POINTZ (fl. 1566) and JOHN RASTELL (1527–77) were all distinguished fellows of New College, Oxford. Dorman, it is true, held a probationary fellowship only, which he resigned in King Edward's reign, as he tells us, for conscience' sake. But he was later elected fellow of All Souls in 1554, where he resided until 1562–3, when he joined his patron, Dr. Harding, at Louvain. Martiall, after graduating Bachelor of Canon and Civil Law, returned to his old school as second master under the celebrated Dr. Hide.|| In 1560, following Hide's example, he, too, went into exile. Pointz, who lost his fellowship shortly after the accession of Elizabeth, is reported as studying divinity in

* The journey to Rome was never accomplished.

† Letter to Cardinal Sirleto of 30 March 1577. Cited in *D.D.*, p. 307.

‡ *Ath. Oxon.* (1813), Vol. I, p. 609.

§ *Worthies* (1840), Vol. III, pp. 261–2.

|| See below.

Louvain in 1566. Rastell,* who was the most brilliant controversialist of these four, retired abroad about the same time as Pointz and a few years later, in 1568, entered the Jesuit novitiate in Rome. Dorman and Martiall were both later associated with Allen in the founding of Douay College. Martiall was subsequently created D.D. of Douay University and was appointed Canon of St. Peter's Cathedral, Lille. Rastell finally became Vice-Rector of the College at Ingolstadt. Strype classes him among 'wilful scholars, and learned in divinity'.†

THOMAS HIDE (d. 1597), fellow of New College (1543) and Canon of Winchester (1551), already referred to above as Headmaster of Winchester College, is described in a contemporary document as 'one very stiff and perverse' in papistry;‡ and undoubtedly it was the lead which he gave by his uncompromising attitude which caused the boys of the college to refuse attendance at the new services.§ After his resignation Hide resided partly at Douay and partly at Louvain. Fuller, quoting Pits, writes: 'This Hide is charactered by one of his own persuasion "to be a man of upright life, of great gravity and severity".'||

Two further names will complete our list of writers who at this time hailed from Winchester and New College, Oxford.¶ These are JOHN FEN (d. 1615), who established a great reputation for himself in Queen Mary's reign as headmaster of the free grammar school of Bury St. Edmund, and JOHN FOWLER (1537–79), who as publisher and editor of Catholic books abroad performed a unique service for the Catholic cause and perhaps, too, for our English tongue. For the greater part of his life abroad Fen was Chaplain to St. Ursula's Convent of Austin Canonesses in Louvain, and a number of his works,

* It is to be observed that our Rastell here has no connexion with the famous John Rastell, the printer, brother-in-law of St. Thomas More. See A. W. Reed, *Early Tudor Drama* (1926), p. 1.

† *Annals* (1824), Vol. I, pt. i, p. 412.

‡ cf. N. Wood, *The Reformation and English Education* (1931), p. 271.

§ A brief account of the troubles at Winchester will be found in Wood, op. cit., pp. 44 et seq.; cf. also J. H. Pollen, *The English Catholics in the Reign of Queen Elizabeth* (1920), p. 43.

|| *Worthies* (1840), Vol. I, p. 135.

¶ The New College group of fellows who either resigned or were expelled from the college shortly after Elizabeth's accession included also William Knott, Dr. John Catagre, Dr. Thomas Butler, Robert Fen (brother of John above), John Hardy, John Noble, Thomas Daryll, Richard White, Edward Astlow, and Owen Lewis. See *New College* (*College Histories*), by Hastings Rashdall and Robert S. Rait.

which were translations from Latin and Italian ascetical treatises, were written for the direction of the English nuns of the convent. In 1583 he published, in collaboration with Fr. John Gibbon, S.J., the *Concertatio Ecclesiae Catholicae*, a very reliable source book for the lives of the Recusant martyrs of the period, which was later, in 1588, to be expanded into Dr. John Bridgewater's (Aquapontanus) valuable *Concertatio.** Nicolas Sander, in a letter to the Countess of Northumberland of January 1572, refers to him and William Knott (see footnote above) as 'the flower of Louvain'.† A special notice of Fowler's activity as publisher will be found in Chapter VI of this book. Meantime let us record two statements concerning him which suggest the esteem in which he was held by Catholic and Protestant alike. Cardinal Allen, in a letter to Fr. Agazzari, dated 18 November 1583, refers to him as *catholicissimus et doctissimus librorum impressor.*‡ Anthony à Wood says: 'He was well skill'd in the Greek and Latin tongues, a tolerable poet and orator, and a theologist not to be contemn'd. So learned he was also in criticisms, and other polite learning, that he might have passed for another Robert, or Henry, Stephens, printers.'§

Two Cambridge graduates only seem to have shared at this time in contributing to the many English works of controversy which were emanating from Louvain. They were THOMAS HESKYNS (fl. 1565) and RICHARD SHACKLOCK (fl. 1575). According to Dr. William Fulke, Heskyns shares with Sander and Rastell the distinction of being accounted (among their faction) one of the 'three pillers and Archpatriarches of the Popish Synagogue'.‖ That he was a man of great learning we may gather from his career and from his single surviving work, *The Parliament of Chryste* (1566). After twelve years at Oxford (1528–40?) he removed to Cambridge, where he became fellow at Clare Hall. There he proceeded M.A. in 1540, and later (in the years 1548 and 1557) was granted the degrees of B.D. and D.D. At the time of his deprivation in August 1559 he was Vicar of Brixworth and Chancellor of the diocese of Salisbury. Some

* *Concertatio Ecclesiae Catholicae in Anglia adversus Calvino-Papistas et Puritanos sub Elizabetha Regina*, etc. *Augustae Trevirorum.* 1588.

† Cited C.R.S., Vol. XXVI. 'Some Letters and Papers of Nicolas Sander, 1562–1580.'

‡ *Letters and Memorials*, p. 216.

§ *Ath. Oxon.* (ed. Bliss, 1813), Vol. I, col. 441.

‖ See title to his answer to *The Parliament of Chryste* of 1579.

time before 1566 he entered the Order of St. Dominic. Shacklock had been elected a fellow of Trinity College in 1559, but shortly after, being deprived of his fellowship, he retired to Louvain, where he devoted himself to the study of civil law.

The part played by HENRY COLE (d. 1580), JOHN FECKENHAM (1518?–84) and NICHOLAS HARPSFIELD (1519–75) in the controversies which are the theme of our early Recusant prose will be unfolded in the course of the next chapter. The names of these three divines are well known to students of the period and they have always been recognized by historians as among the most distinguished churchmen of their day. Needless to say their presence in the mother country (for none of them sought refuge abroad, probably owing to reasons of age or health) was a perpetual source of anxiety to the Elizabethan authorities, and all three were kept under fairly close restraint until their deaths: Cole and Harpsfield in and out of the Fleet, and Feckenham first in the Tower and later at Wisbech Castle. Cole's reputation for learning in his own day is voiced in the words of a letter addressed to him by Roger Ascham: 'I have heard so much by common report of your erudition, and by Mr. Morysin of your humanity, that I must renounce all pretensions to learning if I did not esteem you, and be altogether inhuman if I did not love you.'* Pits thus sums up the character of Feckenham: *Erat in eo insignio pietas in Deum, mira charitas in proximos, singularis observantia in majores, mitis affabilitas in inferiores, dulcis humanitas in omnes, multiplex doctrina, redundans facundia, incredibilis religionis catholicae zelus.*† With the recent publication of Harpsfield's *Life of More* by the Early English Text Society,‡ which includes a scholarly review of his Life and Works by the late R. W. Chambers, Harpsfield's reputation as a scholar and as a writer of English prose is assuredly secure.

WILLIAM ALLEN (1532–94) has a special claim upon our attention in this brief survey of our Recusant authors.§ He was shortly to become by far the most important figure of that band of exiles which gathered at Louvain in the early 1560's, and

* Cited by Thompson Cooper in the *D.N.B.*

† *De illustribus Angliae scriptoribus* (1619), p. 786. ‡ Original Series, no. 186, 1932.

§ Full-length portraits of Allen will be found in Dom Bede Camm's *William, Cardinal Allen, Founder of the Semininaries*, London, 1908, and M. Haile's *An Elizabethan Cardinal, William Allen*, London, 1914. The Introduction to *The Letters and Memorials of William Cardinal Allen* by T. F. Knox (1882) deals mainly with Allen's political life.

his general influence upon the course of the movement which we have described earlier in this chapter was paramount. 'Allen', wrote Father Persons in 1583, 'possesses the hearts of all . . . all the exiles bear him such reverence that at a mere word from him there is nothing they would not do.'*

At Elizabeth's accession Allen was Principal of St. Mary Hall, Oxford, and proctor in the university. Although still a layman he also held a canonry at York. In 1560 he resigned his preferments and a year later he sought refuge abroad in Louvain. Owing to ill health he returned to his native Lancashire towards the end of 1562, and he remained (for the most part in hiding) in the home country for the next two years. On his return to Flanders in 1565 he was ordained priest at Mechlin and later in the year began to lecture on theology at the Benedictine College there. Two years later came that noteworthy journey with his friend, Dr. Vendeville, to Rome, which resulted in the founding of the English College at Douay in 1568.

In 1570 Allen was appointed regius professor of divinity at Douay University, where he commenced D.D. in 1571. A second visit to Rome resulted in the founding of the English College there in 1576, and in 1579, on a third visit to the Holy City, he was able to arrange, on the request of Fr. Persons, for the Jesuits to take part in the English mission. Meanwhile the college at Douay had been removed to Rhemes owing to the hostility of the Orange faction, Allen's own life being threatened by assassins. He finally left Rhemes for good in 1585 for Rome, whither he had been summoned by the new Pope, Sixtus V, to assist in carrying out the reforms which he contemplated. Sixtus created him Cardinal Priest of St. Martinus in Montibus in 1587. Two years later Philip II nominated him Archbishop of Mechlin, but the appointment for some unknown reason was never confirmed. In 1591 he was made Apostolic Librarian by Gregory XIV, and appointed with others to revise the Vulgate of Sixtus V and also to undertake the correction of the text of St. Augustine's works. This task was unfinished when he died on 16 October 1594.

That, in brief, is a summary of Allen's career as a churchman. The facts speak for themselves. They lead one to realize

* Cited by Bede Camm, as above, p. 151.

afresh the relevance of Rishton's statement cited earlier in this chapter, that as a consequence of the Act of Uniformity 'the very flower of the two universities, Oxford and Cambridge, was carried away, as it were, by a storm, and scattered in foreign lands'.*

Among Allen's principal coadjutors in those early and fruitful years of the English College at Douay and Rhemes were the three well-known scholars and writers RICHARD BRISTOW (1538–81), GREGORY MARTIN (d. 1582) and WILLIAM RAINOLDS (1544?–94). All three were distinguished sons of Oxford University. Bristow had been a fellow of Exeter and was selected to dispute before the Queen and Leicester on the Queen's visit to the university in 1566. He crossed the seas in 1569 in order to join Allen at Douay, where he was exceedingly active in every branch of the college life, and during Allen's absences deputized for him as rector. The Douay records state, with perhaps forgivable enthusiasm, 'that he might rival Allen in prudence, Stapleton in acumen, Campion in eloquence, Wright in theology, and Martin in languages'.† Martin had been nominated one of the original scholars of St. John's College by its founder, Sir Thomas White, in 1557, and like Edmund Campion, his college companion for thirteen years, 'whom he rivalled in every branch of academical learning',‡ he was a man of mark in Oxford – 'the Hebraist, the Grecian, the poet, the honour and glory' of St. John's.§ He arrived at the English College in 1570 and was one of the first priests to be ordained from that place. Except for a period of about two years (1576–8), when he was engaged in assisting to direct Allen's new foundation at Rome, he lectured at Douay and Rhemes continuously up to his death in 1582 in Hebrew, Greek and Holy Scripture. His translation of the Scriptures has been described as 'the greatest glory of the English College at this time',|| and A. W. Pollard rightly assigns to Martin a due share with Tyndale, Coverdale, Whittingham and Parker in the building of the English authorized version of the Bible.¶ Rainolds, yet another Wykehamist, was, like his younger brother John, the Puritan divine, probably one of the most brilliant Oxford

* Above, p. 22.
† cf. Gillow, op. cit., s. v. *Bristow*.
‡ Wood, *Ath. Oxon.* (1813), Vol. I, col. 487.
§ R. Simpson, *Edmund Campion* (1896), p. 30.
|| P. Guilday, *English Catholic Refugees on the Continent* (1914), p. 79.
¶ *Records of the English Bible* (1911), by A. W. Pollard, p. 36.

scholars of his day. He was admitted perpetual fellow of New College in 1562 and later became Rector of Lavenham in Sussex. On his conversion he crossed over to Louvain and then passed by way of Douay on to Rome, where he made public recantation in 1575. After ordination at Châlons-sur-Marne (31 March 1580) he was appointed professor of divinity and Hebrew at Rhemes and became one of Martin's assistants in the preparation of his version of the English Bible. His *Calvino-Turcismus*, that 'distillation of the spirits of Turcism out of the books of Calvin' in something more than 1,000 octavo pages of closely printed Latin, provides a mighty monument to his industry and his learning.*

There is a letter of Martin's written to his sisters about the year 1578 and printed in *A Treatyse of Christian Peregrination* (1583),† a part of which it will not be inappropriate to insert in our account of these Recusant scholars and writers at this point. His words bring vividly before us the situation as it must have presented itself to many of those who, rather than compromise in the matter of religion, sought refuge abroad.

> Sisters geue me leaue to tell you some-what of my selfe (he writes), not for anye bragge, but the more to moue you and to geue God all the praise for his great goodnes towardes me. It pleased my parentes to bring me vp in learning as you know, as I was not the best, so I was at al times not compted the worst among my felowes and companions: some small estimation I had in *Oxforde* aboue my desert, more afterwards whē it pleased the *Duke* to make me though vnworthy, Tutor to the *Erle* his sonne:‡ as long as his grace did prosper, I liued in his howse to my conscience without trouble: when he was in the Tower, & other men ruled his howse, I was willed to receaue the Communion, or to depart: if I would haue yeelded, I had verye large offers which I neede not tell. It pleased God to staye me so with his grace, that I chose rather to forsake all then to doe agaynst my beleefe, against my knowledge, agaynst my conscience, agaynst the law of almightie God. For a time I lay secretly in England, afterwards I came beyond the seas into these catholicke Countries, out of schisme and heresie: for the which I do thāke almighty God much more, then for all the estimation that I had or mighte haue had in Englande. Whatsoeuer my estate is here, I doe more esteeme it, then all the riches of England as it now standeth!

* Completed and published by his friend, the learned Dr. William Gifford, in 1597.

† Bibl. ent. 88.

‡ The reference is to Thomas Howard, the fourth Duke of Norfolk.

Before we pass on to the small group of writers connected with the English Jesuit mission of 1580, four further names remain to be recorded of writers closely associated with the scholars of Douay and Louvain. They are Thomas Alfield, Roger Baynes, Thomas Butler and Richard Hopkins.

THOMAS ALFIELD (d. 1585)* was educated at Eton and King's College, Cambridge, where he was elected fellow in 1568. In 1576 he entered Allen's college at Douay and was ordained priest on 4 March 1581. He was active on the English mission between 1581 and 1585, when he suffered martyrdom for distributing Catholic books as recorded above (p. 35).†

ROGER BAYNES (1546–1623), who appears to have belonged to that earlier Elizabethan group of writers which included George Gascoigne, George Turbervile and Nicholas Roscarrock, arrived at the English College at Rhemes on 4 July 1579. Thenceforth he was closely associated with Cardinal Allen, becoming in 1585, when Allen settled in Rome, his secretary and major-domo of his household. Strype refers to him as at this period 'a gentleman of some forty years of age, or rather upward, well languaged, and otherwise very well qualified, discreet, secret, and inclined to high matters. He is a cardinal's secretary of outlandish languages'.‡

THOMAS BUTLER (fl. 1570) graduated B.A. at Cambridge in 1543, and later, probably at Louvain, proceeded Doctor of Canon and Civil Law. He accompanied Sander to Rome in the spring of 1559, and Cardinal Morone, the Protector of England, procured him a position in the judiciary of the States of the Church.§

RICHARD HOPKINS (d. 1594), who occupies an important place in the history of English devotional literature, was a commoner of St. Alban's Hall, Oxford, about the year 1563, but owing to religious scruples he left the university for the Middle Temple. In 1566 or 1567 he left England for Louvain and proceeded from there to Spain, where he appears to have spent some years in perfecting himself in the Spanish tongue.

* There is a short monograph of Alfield in *The Rambler* (New Series, Vol. VII, pp. 420–31) entitled *Life and Martyrdom of Thomas Alfield.*

† A detailed account of his trial will be found in Strype, *Annals* (1824), Vol. III, pt. i, pp. 448–52.

‡ *Annals* (1824), Vol. IV, p. 386.

§ cf. Veech, *Dr. Nicholas Sanders and the English Reformation, 1530–1581* (1935), p. 23.

Of his divers translations from Lewis de Granada, only the two recorded in the bibliography of this book seem to have survived.

The two Jesuit writers, EDMUND CAMPION (1540–81) and ROBERT PERSONS (1546–1610), can need no introduction to readers of this volume. Even the proverbial schoolboy (if schoolboys still read *Westward Ho!*) will know something of these two distinguished agents of the Counter-Reformation. Their fame is secure, though Persons, for good reasons, has not yet found a biographer.* It will be enough, therefore, for our present purpose to recall only that both these Oxford dons (Campion of St. John's, Persons of Balliol) were scholars of the first order: Campion the more brilliant perhaps, Persons the more profound; that both held high office in college or university; and that both subsequent to their conversion continued to wield a powerful influence over the minds of their contemporaries. It is regrettable that Campion left behind only two English prose pieces. It is astonishing, on the other hand, that Persons, who was so continuously and actively engaged throughout his life in the practical affairs of religion, should have found time to compose and publish nearly thirty books and pamphlets in English, Latin, Spanish and Italian, and, when occasion demanded, to supervise the actual printing of his volumes.

Closely associated with Campion and Persons in the English Jesuit mission were the two law students THOMAS POUNDE (1539–1613)† and STEPHEN BRINKLEY (fl. 1584). Pounde, who was a kinsman of the Earl of Southampton, was for a time in high favour with Queen Elizabeth, but, abandoning the court

* Four Memoirs of Fr. Persons have been published by the Catholic Record Society in *Miscellanea*, II, pp. 12–201 and *Miscellanea*, IV, pp. 1–161. Recently has come from the same source the first volume of Fr. L. Hicks's important *Letters and Memorials of Father Robert Persons* (London, 1942). The Introduction to this volume, to quote Fr. Hicks's own words, 'is taken up with a chronological account of Persons' life [up to 1588] . . . together with such a concise indication of the political background as should suffice for the better understanding of the letters. No estimate of the man will be found there; rather has it been my aim to get at the facts, often disputed, upon which such an estimate must eventually be based. In any case such an estimate must wait until the edition of the letters is completed'. (Preface, p. vi.)

The standard biography of Campion is Richard Simpson's *Edmund Campion* (1896). A 'short popular life' has recently come from the brilliant pen of Mr. Evelyn Waugh (*Edmund Campion*, 1935).

† Important biographical material for Pounde will be found in Henry Foley's *Records of the English Province of the Society of Jesus* (1877–83), Vol. III, and in *Notes and Queries* (10th series), Vols. IV and V.

and court life about the year 1570, he began to devote himself wholeheartedly to the Catholic cause, with the result that, the Queen turning against him, from the year 1574 to the end of the reign he was almost continuously in prison. During his imprisonment he was admitted to the Society of Jesus – the Father General of the order taking his imprisonment in lieu of novitiate, since there was no chance of his going abroad to take his religious vows, as he would have liked to do. J. H. Pollen describes him as 'of tried faith, witty, generous, with considerable literary powers and respectable abilities as a controversialist'.* Brinkley, as we shall see in a later chapter of this book, played a major part in connexion with Persons' secret press, and continued to assist in the printing of Recusant works after his flight abroad in 1583.

Alban Langdale (fl. 1580) concerns us on account of his short controversy with Fr. Persons, described in our next chapter. He was a distinguished son of Cambridge University, having been admitted fellow of St. John's in 1534 and having served as proctor of the university in 1539. He was a D.D. of both Cambridge and Oxford.† Like his friend, Henry Cole, he held a number of important Church appointments and was one of the eight who 'disputed' on the Catholic side at Westminster (31 March 1559). After being deprived of his preferments he was placed under 'house arrest' in the dwelling of Viscount Montague, whose chaplain he had been. Here he probably remained until his death.‡

To the remaining writers whose English works are listed in the second part of this volume we can allow ourselves only the briefest of references. The three most outstanding are John Leslie, Bishop of Ross (1527–96), Richard Stanyhurst (1547–1618) and Richard Verstegan (1548?–1641). Two of these are well known. Leslie, as the ambassador of Mary Queen of Scots to the English court from September 1568 to March 1572, figures naturally in all histories which are concerned with the relations of England and Scotland at this period. The notoriety which Stanyhurst achieved in his own day because

* *The English Catholics in the Reign of Queen Elizabeth* (1920), p. 347.

† Incorporated D.D. of Oxford on the occasion of the disputation with Cranmer, Ridley and Latimer (April 1554).

‡ There is no evidence to support the statement in the *D.N.B.* that he withdrew to the Continent.

of his prosodic theory and his metrical experiments and his connexion with so important a work as Holinshed's *Chronicles*, have given him an assured place in all histories of English literature. Verstegan, however, who still awaits an English biographer, has not yet had his due.* He entered Christ Church, Oxford, in 1565, but took no degree on account of the religious tests. Having removed to London he set up a press for the printing of Catholic books. We show elsewhere (Chapter VI below) how this press was seized and how Verstegan had to flee the country. Abroad, he was one of the most active of the Recusants. Not only was he a considerable writer himself, but he also assisted others in the preparation of books; he aided the missionaries on their way to and from England; he was agent for the transmission of Catholic books; and he was also for a time corresponding agent for Cardinal Allen at Rome, the Catholics in England, and especially for the Jesuits. His last published work in English, *A Restitution of Decayed Intelligence* (Antwerp, 1605), shows the author to have been well in advance of his age in his special predilection for Anglo-Saxon remains: language, customs and laws.

JASPER HEYWOOD (1535–98),† son of old John Heywood and a great-nephew of St. Thomas More, we should expect to find among the Recusant exiles. He had been a fellow of Merton College, Oxford (1553), and later of All Souls (1558), but had relinquished this latter appointment on the accession of Elizabeth, and soon after departed abroad. He was admitted to the Society of Jesus on 21 May 1562 and was for seventeen years professor of moral theology in the Jesuit college at Dillingen in Bavaria. Having returned to England as missionary in 1581, he managed to evade the authorities for some three years, but was finally expelled the country 21 January 1585. LAURENCE VAUX (1519–85),‡ at one time fellow of Corpus Christi College, Oxford, and later Warden of St. Mary's Collegiate Church of

* An important study of Verstegan's life and writings, with a complete bibliography, has recently been published by Dr. Edward Rombauts, viz. *Richard Verstegen, Een Polemist der Contra-Reformatie*, Brussels, 1933. There is also a short *résumé* of his writings in J. B. Code's *Queen Elizabeth and the English Catholic Historians*, Louvain, 1935.

† For a scholarly study of the Heywoods, see A. W. Reed, *Early Tudor Drama* (1926).

‡ There is an excellent notice of Vaux's life in T. G. Law's reprint of *A Catechisme or Christian Doctrine by Laurence Vaux* (1885). See also *Mancuniensis*; or, *An History of the Towne of Manchester, and what is most memorable concerning it*, by R. Hollingworth (ed. by W. Willis, 1839), for a contemporary account.

Manchester, is the author and compiler of the very popular Catholic Catechism which bears his name. Having joined the Canons-Regular of St. Augustine in the monastery of St. Martin, Louvain (1572), he was appointed sub-prior about 1578. He later took part in the Jesuit mission to England (1580), but was almost immediately apprehended, and spent the remainder of his life in the Gatehouse and the Clink. THOMAS COPLEY (1514–84), a kinsman of Queen Elizabeth, is probably less known for his translations than for the fact that he was the father of Anthony, the author of works both in verse and prose, and uncle of Robert Southwell, the Elizabethan poet. He left England without licence about 1570, his estates having been confiscated, and spent the remainder of his life abroad. JOHN MORWEN (1518?–68?), at one time fellow of Corpus Christi College, Oxford, was a Greek scholar of some repute. During Queen Mary's reign he had been secretary to Bishop Bonner and in 1558 had been appointed a prebendary of St. Paul's, of which office he was deprived in the following year for preaching in favour of the mass. He is described in a State Paper of 1561 as wandering in Cheshire, Staffordshire and Lancashire, very seditiously.* It is a point of interest that he was the instructor in the Latin and Greek tongues of Mary Bassett, granddaughter of St. Thomas More.†

C. THE SCOTS WRITERS

The inclusion of the names of half a dozen Scots writers in a study which is concerned with English literature needs no apology here. On the other hand, the works of the Scots Recusants have perhaps a more particular interest for the student of the Scots language, since the writers attempt to preserve the purity of the Middle Scots dialect, the literary Scots of the day, seriously preferring the charge against their Protestant opponents of writing after the southern manner in contempt of their native language.‡ So John Hamilton writes: 'Giff King Iames the fyft var alyue, quha hering ane of his subiectis knap suddrone, declarit him [ane] trateur: quhidder vald he declaire zou triple traitoris, quha not onlie knappis suddrone in zour

* Strype, *Annals* (1824), Vol. I, pt. i, p. 416.

† Wood, *Athen. Oxon.* (ed. Bliss, 1813), Vol. I, col. 196.

‡ John Leslie, who writes in the standard English of the southern kingdom, is an exception.

negatiue confession, bot also hes causit it be imprentit at London in contempt of our natiue langage.'* And Ninian Winzet somewhat sarcastically remarks of Knox's southern speech: 'Gif ze, throw curiositie of nouationis, hes forzet our auld plane Scottis, quhilk zour mother lerit zou: in tymes cuming I sall wryte to zou my mynd in Latin: for I am nocht acquyntit with zour Southeroū.'† The charge of the 'knapping' of 'suddrone' is, of course, somewhat naïve, since the dialect in which they wrote was already strongly interfused with southern forms, both ancient and modern. Nevertheless, the attempt, made at a time when the vernacular literature was becoming rapidly anglicized, has clearly a linguistic interest and on that score deserves notice.

It is to the credit of their Scottish editors that these Recusant writers have received far ampler treatment than has been accorded to their English contemporaries. Notices of their lives and reprints of their works have for some time now been available in the publications of the various Scottish learned societies. For the reader in search of information as to the standing of these men in the learned and literary circles of their own day these publications are, of course, invaluable. Full references to them will be found under the various titles listed in the bibliography which forms the second part of this volume.

* *Ane Catholik and Facile Traictise* (1581), sig. V viij^v^.

† *The Buke of Four Scoir Thre Questions* (1563), sig. H4.

CHAPTER III

APOLOGETICAL WORKS

The earliest expression of the movement which we considered in the previous chapter is to be found in the works, both Latin and English, of the Catholic apologists. The Latin productions are, of course, not our particular concern. With regard to the English works, since they are largely (though not entirely) controversial in character, it will be convenient to group them as far as possible according to their subject matter, while at the same time keeping in view their historical setting. This, we may hope, will give the reader some sort of perspective and will the better enable him to understand and appraise the passages which will be quoted by way of illustration. The following sectional arrangement will therefore be followed in this present chapter:

(1) The controversy which originated in Bishop Jewel's 'challenge' sermon and in his *Apology of the Church of England.* This we shall name The Great Controversy.

(2) The Osorius-Haddon controversy – the result of the letter of Osorius to Queen Elizabeth concerning the change of religion.

(3) The Feckenham-Horne controversy – arising out of Abbot Feckenham's refusal of the Oath of Supremacy.

(4) The controversy concerning attendance at the Protestant service.

(5) Allen's Scroll of Articles.

(6) The controversy which resulted from Campion's *Letter to the Lords of the Council.*

(7) The affair of John Nichols.

(8) Miscellaneous controversial and doctrinal works.

As we proceed to refer in detail to the controversial works we shall in each case outline the nature and the history of the particular controversy to which they are related. No attempt, however, will be made to pronounce judgement on the relative merits of the opposing contestants, either in respect of literary ability or strength of argument, since we are concerned solely with the works of the one side.

1. THE GREAT CONTROVERSY

Note: Details of all the works in the tables of this chapter may be found in the bibliography. Latin titles are included only where they have a direct bearing upon the English works. The labels (*P*) or (*C*) indicate the source of the various items, Protestant or Catholic.

The 'Challenge' sermon of Bishop John Jewel was first delivered at Paul's Cross on 26 November 1559. Taking as his text I Corinthians xi. 23 (on the institution of the Blessed Sacrament), Jewel used words somewhat (as he says) as follows:

> If any learned man of all oure aduersaryes, or if all the learned mē that be aliue be hable to brīg, any one sufficient sentence, oute of any olde catholique doctour, or father: Or oute of any olde generall counsell: Or out of the holye scriptures of God: Or ani one example of the primitiue Churche, wherby it may be clearly & plainly proued, that there was ani priuate masse in the whole world at that tyme, for the space of sixe hūdred yeares after Christ: Or that there was then ani Communion ministred vnto the people vnder one kind: Or that, the people had theire commen prayers then in a straunge tonge that they vnderstoode not: Or that the Bishop of Rome was then called, an vniuersall Byshop, or the head of the vnyuersall Churche: Or that, the people was then taught to beleue that Christes body is really, substantially, corporally, carnally or naturally in the sacramente . . .

and so on through twenty-seven Articles, concluding:

> If any man alyue were hable to proue, any of these articles, by ani one clear, or playne clause, or sētence, eyther of the scriptures: or of the olde doctours: or of ani olde generall Counsell: or by any exāple of the primitiue church: I promised then yͭ I would geue ouer and subscribe vnto hym.*

The sermon was repeated at Court on 17 March 1560 (N.S.), and was again delivered at Paul's Cross a fortnight later (31 March).

The challenge was taken up by Dr. Henry Cole, who wrote Jewel an adroit letter, telling him of certain points in his sermon which had been reported to him and asking for substantiation of them. The points Cole raises are four:

(1) Whether there remaine any substance of Bread and Wine after the consecration done as the Churche appointeth.

(2) Whether it be tolerable that yͤ people should receaue vnder one kind or no.

(3) Whether it be any offēce before God that the common

* *The Copie of a letter sente from D. Cole to the Bishop of Sarum*, 1560, sigs. F5ᵛ et seq. A shortened form of the declaration will be found in Strype, *Annals* (1824), Vol. I, pt. i, pp. 300–1.

Seruice shoulde be saide in a tonge that the people vnderstandeth not.

(4) Whether it be any offēce before God a Prieste to saye Masse, onles one or other receaue with him.*

A short correspondence ensued in which Cole, while inviting Jewel to prove the essentials of his creed, pointed out that such differences as existed between the primitive and medieval Church were the result of growth but not of change in the underlying doctrines of the Church. Meanwhile a more elaborate answer to the Challenge was being prepared by John Rastell for private circulation in manuscript among his friends – a common practice of the time. This was eventually printed four years later (1564).

The stage was finally set for the opposing disputants with the publication in 1562 of Jewel's *Apologia Ecclesiae Anglicanae*, both in Latin and English.

> It was written (writes Strype) upon a state account by the common advice and consultation, no doubt, of the college of divines that were then met about the reformation of the Church. And so the reverend author himself shewed in his epistle to queen Elizabeth before his Defence, viz. that it contained the whole substance of the catholic faith, then professed and freely preached throughout all the queen's dominions: that thereby all foreign nations might understand the considerations and causes of her doings in that behalf.†

The following table sets out the course of the controversy:

(1) Challenge Sermon delivered by Bishop Jewel at Paul's Cross, 26 November 1559.
(2) Challenge Sermon repeated at Court, 17 March 1560 (N.S.).
(3) Dr. Cole's first letter, dated 18 March 1560 (N.S.).
(4) Jewel's reply to (3), dated 20 March 1560 (N.S.).
(5) Cole's second letter to Jewel, dated 24 March 1560.
(6) Jewel's reply to (5), dated 29 March 1560.
(7) Challenge Sermon repeated at Paul's Cross, 31 March 1560.
(8) Cole's reply to Jewel's second letter (no. 6 above), privately circulated in an abridged form; the original being withheld from Jewel – 8 April 1560.

* *The Copie of a letter*, sig. A4.

† *Annals*, as before, Vol. I, pt. i, p. 426.

(9) Jewel's reply to Cole's abridged reply (8), 18 May 1560.

(10) Jewel's letter to Cole asking for Cole's 'owne copie full and large' of (8), so that he may reply fully to it. He has 'caused the print to staie' upon Cole's answer – 22 July 1560.

(11) No reply from Cole being forthcoming, Challenge Sermon and correspondence printed September (?) 1560.*

(12) Jewel's *Apologia Ecclesiae Anglicanae* published early in 1562. According to Fr. Persons the occasion of this work was Harding's Answer to Jewel's Challenge (see below, no. 16).† (*P*)

(13) Translation into English of Jewel's *Apologia*, under the direction of Archbishop Parker, 1562. (*P*)

(14) The anonymous *Apologie of priuate Masse* (1562), replying to a part of Jewel's Challenge. (*C*)

(15) The answer to (14) by Bishop T. Cooper. This was printed with the *Apologie*, November 1562. (*P*)

(16) Thomas Harding's *An Answere to Maister Iuelles Chalenge.* Printed in 1564, but written some two or three years earlier for private circulation. Each of the twenty-seven articles is discussed in turn. (*C*)

(17) Dean Nowell's sermon on the Fourth Sunday after Easter, 1564, at Paul's Cross, against Harding's *Answere* (16). (*P*)

(18) Lady Bacon's translation of Jewel's *Apologia*, published with Parker's approval, 1564. This may be regarded as the official translation of Jewel's work. (*P*)

(19) Thomas Dorman's *A Proufe of Certeyne Articles in Religion, denied by M. Iuell,* 1564 [July]. Four articles are dealt with: one concerning the primacy of the Pope, and three concerning the Sacrament. (*C*)

(20) John Martiall's *A Treatyse of the Crosse,* 1564 [October]. (*C*)

(21) John Rastell's *A confutation of a sermon, pronoũced by M. Iuell, at Paules crosse.* Printed November 1564, but written four years earlier. (*C*)
(William Fulke replied to (21) in his *Refutation of Rastell's Confutation,* 1579.)

(22) Harding's enlarged edition of his *Answere* (no. 16

* Entry in Sta. Reg. reads 26 Sept. 1560.
† Persons, *A Relation of the Triall* (1604), at sig. D3v.

above), 1565 [January]. Edited by John Martiall. (*C*)

(23) Rastell's *A Copie of a challenge*, January 1565. A reprint of pp. 160–76 of (21). (*C*)

(24) Rastell's *A Replie against an answer (falslie intitled) in Defence of the truth*, 10 March 1565. Replies to Bishop Cooper's answer (15 above). (*C*)

(25) William Allen's *A Defence and Declaration of the Catholike Churchies Doctrine, touching Purgatory*, 1565 [March]. Especially aimed at Jewel's Challenge on this subject. (Fulke replied to (25) in *Two Treatises written against the Papistes*, 1577. Bristow replied to Fulke in 1580. See below, no. 64.) (*C*)

(26) Stapleton's translation of *The Apologie of Fridericus Staphylus*, 1565. (*C*)

(27) Harding's *A Confutation of a Booke intituled An Apologie of the Church of England*, 1565 [April]. (*C*)

(28) Jewel's sermon at Paul's Cross criticising Harding's *Confutation*, 27 May 1565. (*P*)

(29) Nowell's *A Reproufe*, 30 May 1565. Answers Dorman's *Proufe* (19 above). A second issue appeared in July following. (*P*)

(30) Harding's printed letter to Jewel requiring a copy of the sermon preached at Paul's Cross the previous May (28 above), dated 12 June 1565. (*C*)

(31) Lewys Evans's translation of *Certaine Tables*, 1565 [June]. (*C*)

(32) Jewel's second sermon at Paul's Cross criticising Harding, 8 July 1565. This sermon is a forerunner of the *Replie* (35 below). (*P*)

(33) Harding's *A Briefe Answere* to Jewel's second sermon (32), 26 July 1565. (*C*)

(34) Richard Shacklock's *The Hatchet of Heresies*, 10 August 1565. Translated from Hosius's treatise. (*C*)

(35) Jewel's *A Replie vnto M. Hardinges Answeare* (16 and 22 above), August 1565. (*P*)

(36) Thomas Stapleton's translation of Bede's *The History of the Church of Englande* and his *A Fortresse of the Faith*, 1565 [October]. (*C*)
(Fulke rejoined with *T. Stapleton and Martiall (two Popish Heretikes) confuted*, 1580.)

(37) Dorman's *A Disproufe of M. Nowelles Reproufe*, 3 December 1565. Answers (29) above. (*C*)

(38) Nicolas Sander's *The supper of our Lord*, 1565 [December]. Answers Jewel's *Apologia*. A second issue appeared January 1566. (*C*)
(Fulke replied to (38) in 1581 in his *A Reioynder to Bristow's Replie*. See also Nowell's answer under (60) below.)

(39) Evans's *A brieue Admonition*, 1565. (*C*)

(40) J. Calfhill's *An Answere to the Treatise of the Crosse*, 1565. Answers (20) above. (*P*)

(41) Nowell's *The Reproufe of M. Dorman his proufe*, 1566. A continuation of (29) above. (*P*)

(42) Robert Pointz's *Testimonies of the Real Presence*, 1566. Answers Jewel's Challenge on the Mass. (*C*)

(43) Thomas Heskyns's *The Parliament of Chryste*, 1566. A further answer to Jewel's Challenge with regard to the Mass. (*C*)

(44) Rastell's *A Treatise intitled, Beware of M. Iewel*, 1566 [May]. Replies to (35) above. (*C*)

(45) John Fowler's translation of *An Oration Against the Vnlawfull Insurrections of the Protestantes of our time*, 1566 [May]. (*C*)
(Fulke replied to (45) in *An Apologie of the Professors of the Gospel*, 1585.)

(46) Martiall's *A Replie to M. Calfhills blasphemous Answer made against the Treatise of the Crosse* (40 above), 1566 [June]. (*C*)
(Fulke rejoined with *T. Stapleton and Martiall (two popish Heretikes) confuted*, 1580.)

(47) Stapleton's *A Returne of Vntruthes upon M. Iewels Replie*, 1566 [July]. Answers (35) above, with special reference to Articles 3 and 4. (*C*)

(48) Harding's *A Reioindre to M. Iewels Replie*, 1566 [August]. Answers Article 1 of (35) above. (*C*)

(49) Rastell's *The Third Booke, Declaring . . . that it is time to Beware of M. Iewel*, 1566 [November]. Continues (44) above. (*C*)

(50) John Barthlet's *The Pedegrewe of Heretiques*, 1566. Answers Shacklock (34) above. (*P*)

(51) Stapleton's translation from Hosius, *Of the Expresse Worde of God*, 1567 [January]. (*C*)
(Fulke replied to Hosius in a *Responsio* in Latin, 1578.)

(52) Sander's *The Rocke of the Church*, 1567 [February]. Answers Jewel and others on the primacy of St. Peter. (*C*)
(Fulke replied to (52) in 1580 in his *A Retentiue to stay good christians &c.*)

(53) Allen's *A Treatise made in defence of the lauful power and authoritie of Priesthod to remitte sinnes*, 1567 [April]. (*C*)
(Fulke replied in 1586 in *A Confutation of a Treatise made by William Allen.*)

(54) Jewel's protestation sermon at Paul's Cross, 15 June 1567. In defence of his truthfulness. (*P*)

(55) Dorman's *A Request to M. Iewell*, 1567 [September] – To keep his promise uttered in his sermon (54 above). He refers especially to Stapleton's *Returne of Vntruthes* (47 above). (*C*)

(56) Rastell's *A Briefe Shew of the false Wares*, 1567 [August]. Attacks Jewel's *Apologia* and looks ahead to the coming *Defence* by Jewel (58 below). (*C*)

(57) Harding's *A Reioindre to M. Iewels Replie against the Sacrifice of the Masse*, 1567 [September]. Continues his *Reioindre* (48), and answers three further articles of the Challenge. (*C*)

(58) Jewel's *A Defence of the Apologie of the Churche of Englande*, October 1567. Replies to Harding's *Confutation* (27 above). (*P*)

(59) Sander's *A Treatise of the Images of Christ*, 1567. Refers especially to Jewel in his *Replie vnto M. Hardinges Answeare* (35 above). (*C*)
(Fulke rejoined with *D. Heskins, D. Sanders, and M. Rastel* (*accounted among their faction*) *three pillers*, 1579.)

(60) Nowell's *A Confutation as wel of M. Dormans last boke entituled A disproufe &c. as also of D. Sander his causes of transubstantiation*, November 1567. Answers (37) and (38) above. (*P*)

(61) Edward Dering's *A Sparing Restraint* [April 1568]. Replies to Harding's *Reioindre* of 1566 (48 above). (*P*)

(62) Harding's *A Detection of sundrie foule errours*, 1568 [May]. Replies to Jewel's *Defence of the Apologie* (58 above). (*C*)

(63) Jewel's second and enlarged edition of the *Defence of the Apologie* (58 above). Contains, in addition, an answer to Harding's *Detection* (62 above), 1570 [June]. (*P*)

(64) Richard Bristow's *A Reply to Fulke*, 1580. Against his *Two Treatises* (1577), and in defence of Allen's *A Defence* (1565). See (25) above. (*C*)

The magnitude of this controversy is surely one of the most remarkable things in the history of English writing, and it would be strange indeed if it had been without influence or significance in the development of English prose. Professor R. W. Chambers has called attention to the danger of ignoring the theological treatises of the sixteenth century in determining the course of this development,* and when we remember the important part that religion and theology played in men's lives in that century and the evident enjoyment that controversy and long theological discussion evoked, we can hardly resist the conclusion that these works provide something which is vital to the understanding of the Elizabethan habit of mind and expression. We shall, in fact, find in these treatises and pamphlets many pages devoted to purely academic questions, the niceties of logic, the interpretation of scriptural and patristic texts, and so forth; we shall also find pages as lively as any that are to be found in, say, Foxe's *Book of Martyrs*, and occasionally as violently partisan; what we shall not find is the preciosity of thought and language, the affected conceits, and the classical pedantry of the 'polite' writers of the period. We may conceive these writings, therefore, to have a twofold bearing upon the study of our literary development. First, as providing a considerable body of prose work, the outstanding marks of which are, as we shall find, clarity and naturalness of expression (to deal in controversy is itself a wholesome stimulus in this direction), it may be held that they fill or help to fill a significant gap in the general history of our English prose; and second, since their appeal was not only to men's religious nature but also to their sense of excitement and drama, it is possible that here is one of 'the very places where the art of dramatic representation was feeling its way, till it bursts out later on the Elizabethan stage'.†

* *Continuity of English Prose*, as before, p. clxiii. † ibid.

Contemporary opinion singles out Harding and Jewel as the two leaders in this long controversy.

> Harding and Iewell were our Eschines and Demosthenes (writes Gabriel Harvey); and scarsely any language in the Christian world hath affoorded a payre of aduersaries equivalent to Harding and Iewell, two thundring and lightning Oratours in diuinity.*

Therefore with Harding let us begin.

THOMAS HARDING

Fr. J. H. Pollen, in his *English Catholics in the Reign of Queen Elizabeth*, remarks on the literary value of these controversial works that the 'literary effect is confused by the handling numerous objections in scholastic form', and again that 'both sides were too grimly in earnest to take thought for the amenities of literature – for style, illustration, ornament'.† It is quite true that sustained literary effect is barely possible in treatises in which the writer sets out his opponents' arguments and, in the manner of debate, proceeds forthwith to demolish them. It is also true (as Pollen points out) that in such case the writer will appear to be arguing with himself, and that the general effect will be unconvincing. On the other hand, to say that the writers of these controversial works 'were too grimly in earnest to take thought for the amenities of literature' is to confuse the issue. That they did not intend their works to be finished literary products hardly needs stating; they were usually written under such conditions of stress as to make that impossible, even if it had been desirable. But that they consciously endeavour to write plainly and openly, and, more than this, that they seek to temper their style to the matter in hand, is manifest from the writings themselves and is, furthermore, in clear accordance with their own statements. Though we may therefore meet with long stretches of unimaginative writing in many of the works, yet we shall find, on the whole, not only that they are adequate to their purpose, but we shall also find many passages which, in respect of language and idiom, are in the best tradition of English prose.

* Gregory Smith, *Elizabethan Critical Essays* (1904), Vol. II, p. 247: from *Pierces Supererogation*; cf. also p. 238. Also, Hooker, *Ecclesiastical Polity*, II, 4, &c.

† As before, p. 110.

Before turning to such passages in his works we may first observe what was Harding's own judgement as to his aim and method of writing, and we must not forget that his words have a special importance owing to his position as the leading figure among the Catholic apologists. His aim is set forth in the following lines:

> To make harde thinges easy to be vnderstanded, and to geue light to thinges, that of them selfe be darke, and not to swarue from the exact rule of truth, it is a point of great witte and cunning: neither is it lightly perfourmed, but of suche as God hath endewed with special giftes –*

and, in a passage, wherein he takes Jewel to task for obscurantism, he disclaims any intention in his manner of writing save that of procuring the truth:

> As for my selfe, how so euer it please you to charge me with *Vetus Comoedia*, verely I seme to men of right good discretion, rather to offende in lenitie and softenes: and many do wish I had tempered the Incke wherewith I wrote my Answer, with sharper ingredience then I haue. Albeit I sought not to please the homours [*sic*] of men, but rather to serue yͤ wil of God, & as I might, to defend yͤ truth, and discharge my conscience. wherein touching the order of my stile, I though[t] good, to doo rather what became the cause, then what belonged to your deserte.
>
> But with what face could you M. Iewel reproue me for the vse of wordes, that might offend? Is it not reason, who blameth an other, that in the thing he blameth, he be not founde faulty him selfe? A man would thinke to finde you softe and sweete, yͭ thus haue rebuked me for being rough and sowre. But whosoeuer wil come neare you & feele you, & pluck of your fruites, & taste of thē: shal soone perceiue what a pricking vrchin you are, & what Crabbes you beare. Verely of al yͤ writers yͭ I haue read, I neuer foūde any, yͭ vseth yͭ lothsō māner of scoffing & mocking, so much as you do, when reason faileth, a scoffe is at hande when an argument presseth, a mocke serueth for answer, when the mater goeth plaine on the contrarie side, then Hickescornes bestirreth him, and with ieasting pulleth away the minde of the reader to an other light thought: that so al might be laughed out, and the chief point let passe.†

As for his method, he adopts a 'meeke, sober and cold demeanour of writing' because (amongst other reasons) it is 'fitting for such kynde of argument':

* *A Reioindre to M. Iewels Replie* (1567), sig. I4^{v}.
† *A Reioindre to M. Iewels Replie* (1566), Address to Jewel.

> If any man that shall reade this (he writes), be of that humour, as shall mislike it as being colde, lowe, flatte ād dull, ād requyre rather such verder of writing, as is hote, lofty, sharp ād quycke, which pleaseth best the tast of our tyme: vnderstand he, that before I intended to put this forth in printe, I thus tempered my stile for these cōsyderatiōs. First, where as a certaine exercise of a learned mā of fiue or six sheetes of paper spredde abroade in the Realme in defence of some of these Articles by M. Iuell denyed, was fathered vpō me, which in dede I neuer made sentēce of, and therefore a storme imminent was mystrusted:* that by chaūging the hew, which many know me by, that know me familiarly, in case it shuld come to the handes of many, as it was likely, I myght escape the dāger of beīg charged with it, and neuer the lesse satisfye my frendes request, and in some parte also my conscience, and doo good. Secōdly, that I thought meeke, sober and cold demeanour of writing to be most fitting for such kynde of argument. Thirdly and specially that my hart serued me not to deal with M. Iuel myne old acquaīted, felow ād coūtreymā other wise, thē swetly, gētilly ād courteouslye. And in dede here I protest, that I loue M. Iuell, ād detest his heresies.†

Finally, the stylistic principle which animates his work is summed up, in words reminiscent of the poet Horace, as *prodesse* rather than *delectare*, 'to profite holesomely, not to please delicately':‡

> Now this much haue I thought good here to warne the of, that where as at the first, I appointed this to my priuate frend only, and not to all in common, (though in sundry places I folow the maner of such as mynde to publish their writings): I haue so both ordered the matter and tempered the style, as I iudge it might haue ben liked of my frend at home, and doubte whether it may beare the light abroade. I see mennes stomakes of oure time to be very delicate and diuerse. Some require swete iunkettes, some sower and sharpe sawces, some esteme the curiositie of cookerye, more then the holesomnes of viandes, some can like no dishe, be it neuer so well dighte. In this diuersitie no man can please all. Who so euer seeketh it, shal fynde him selfe deceiued. I wene the best waye is, if a man herein mynde to doo ought, to make his prouision of the thinges only, wich be holesome. So shal he displease many, hurte none, and please al the good. Who so euer in doing this directeth his whole purpose and endeuour to this ende, that he may

* The reference is to *An Apologie of priuate Masse* (1562), no. (14) above. The meaning is that he had purposely written in an unfamiliar style in order to avoid the suspicion of having written the *Apologie*. Which he denies.

† *An Answere to Maister Iuelles chalenge* (1565), Preface to Jewel.

‡ *Ars Poetica*, 333.

> profite and helpe all: in my iudgement, he doth the dutie of an honest and a good man. Verely in this treatise this hath ben myne onely purpose, and the meane to bring the same to effecte, hath ben such, as whereby I studied to profite holesomely, not to please delicately. How much good I haue performed, I know not, my conscience (which is ynough) beareth me witnes of good will. What the Apostles haue plãted, in this great barraynesse and drouth of faith, I haue desyred againe to water. God geue encreace.*

Lucidity, truthfulness and propriety, these, then, constitute for Harding the marks of faithful expression, and, if we may add a certain quality of reserve which is to be found in his writing and which was a natural characteristic of the man, they may be said to indicate fairly accurately his literary practice. The truth of this may be tested by reference to his Articles on 'substance' and 'accident' (Articles 22–26 of his *An Answere to Maister Iuelles Chalenge*) – too long to quote here – which he describes as 'scoole pointes' and which illustrate excellently his talent for making 'harde thinges easy to be vnderstanded' and for giving 'light to thinges, that of them selfe be darke'.

In view of what has been already said the reader will not be surprised to learn that the most important constructive element in Harding's prose is the syllogism, a characteristic which we meet with continually in these Recusant writings. It is a highly significant fact. In an age which had come to rely largely upon an elaborate metaphorical apparatus upon which to base its prose style, with its consequent tendency to darken meaning, here is a group of authors, who, deeply engaged in argument and 'grimly in earnest', eschew all showiness and expressly seek to determine their style in accordance with the dry light of logic. For Harding this is the theme of themes. It is the ground of his principal complaint against Jewel. And he returns to attack him again and again for darkening the issues by substituting rhetorical device for logical precept. Such passages as the following indicate the tenor of his attack, together with his own method of exposition:

> To confute any parte of the Replie, it is easy. by due examination to stay at euery Untruth, it is paineful. He doth not so much wring vs with fastnesse of close argumentes, as he encombreth vs with heape of loose sayinges. He presseth not with weighte, but troubleth with number. His blowes come thicke,

* *Answere*, as before, Address to the Reader.

but his weapōs lacke edge. Some in olde time likened Logique to the hand closed together, Rhetorique to the hand stretched abrode. Thereof it may be cōceiued, how much we feare this Rhetoriciā. wel may he swepe duste frō of our coates with flap of hand: he cānot hurte our boanes ỽ stroke of fiste. The onset of such an ennemie cānot fray vs, the chasing of him may put vs to some labour.*

Item, The Fathers speake muche of the spiritual Aulters of our harte, and of mere spiritual sacrifices: *Ergo*, they denie, that there be any material Aulters, and that thereon the real and external Sacrifice of Christes body and bloude is offered.

Logique is good cheape, where these Argumentes be allowed. But he that lacketh a Recorder, may yet pype with an oten reede. If Logique can not handsomly be applyed, to mainteine M. Iewels glorious Chalenge, yet Rhetorique wil do good seruice. And yet in Rhetorique it selfe these Argumentes be but childish. As wel might one proue, there is none other heauen, besides our hartes, bicause S. Augustine saith, in a Sermon. *Corda fidelium coelum sunt.* The hartes of the faithful be heauen. *Ergo*, heauen that is said to be out of this worlde, is but a tale. As wel one might say, Christe is not the Sonne of God, bicause he is the sonne of man. And in a mater of lesse weight, as wel, and by like Logique, one shrewde boy might say to an other, Iacke, I will proue thou hast no nose. Thou hast great lolling eares, *Ergo*, thou hast no nose. Of such Argumentes we haue great stoare in M. Iewels writinges, and in manner none other. For which cause to any graue and learned man, he semeth rather worthy of contempte, then of Answer. Who so euer cōsidereth, not the number of his wordes, but the weight of his sentences, not the multitude of his patched and peeced allegations, but the force of the mater by the same auouched: shal iudge no lesse. God be thanked, that heresie hath so weake a defence.†

Christe offereth vp vs vnto God, Item, Through Christe we haue accesse to the throne of Grace: Ergo, a Priest hath no auctoritie to offer vp Christe vnto God in the Sacrament.

O profounde Logique, O sharpe witte, O inuincible Disputer. Here your owne skoffing Rhetorique might wel be returned vpon you. It were harde to tel vs, how this Antecedent, and Consequent came together. No man hath auctoritie thus to mince his Logique, but M. Iewel. Why Sir, must it needes folowe, that if Christe (who is the head of his Churche, vnder which name both he, and the Churche be oftentimes conteined) haue offered vp vs vnto God, that we may not offer vp Christe vnto God?‡

* *Reioindre* (1566), Address to Reader. † *Reioindre* (1567), sig. NNN1v.
‡ ibid., sig. SSS2.

Conformable to this insistence upon the need for logical propriety in the mode of handling a theme, Harding's usage may be observed even in such a rhetorical passage as the following, taken from his confutation of Jewel's *Apologie of the Church of England*:

> The comparison which ye make betwen your selues and Sophocles, gladly we admitte. Yet we acknowledge that as in many respectes ye are like, so in some vnlike. Sophocles was a poet, that is to saye, a fainer, and deuiser of thinges that be not true, but fabulous. Ye also are fainers, and deuisers of nouelties, and folowers of newe deuises, that be false. Sophocles was a tragicall poet, ye are tragicall diuines. A tragedie setteth forth thouerthrowes of kingdomes, murder of noble personages, and other great troubles, and endeth in wofull lamentations. Your gospel inuadeth Christes heauenly kingdome the church, it murdereth soules bought with a most dere price, it causeth a hellish garboile in mennes consciences, in the end it bringeth to euerlasting weping and gnashing of teeth. Sophocles was accused of his vnkinde sonnes, ye are accused of your fathers, of your brethren, of your mother, who loue you most tenderly and with vnspeakeable griefe of hart bemone your case. Sophocles in his olde dayes, ye in your young dayes. For your english church hath not yet fulfilled the age, or number of those yeres, which we call the yeres of discretion. He for a doting and a sottish man, ye for making infinite numbers of men to dote and to be sottes. He for wasting his owne substance, ye both for spoiling of others outward substance, and robbing of their spirituall treasures. He rehersed his cunning tragedie for proufe that he doted not, before the laufull iudges of his countrie. Ye flye from al lauful iudgement, ye shewe not your faces where ye ought, and hauing written in a corner this inuective or famous libell, geuing it name of an Apologie: without due order cast the same abrode, offering your cause to be examined and iudged by the temeritie of the common multitude.*

The syllogistic turn of the earlier part of this paragraph is the more significant owing to the intentional rhetoric, which, let us add, is, here as elsewhere, always carefully controlled by the writer.

We may conclude this short survey of Harding's prose by referring to some further characteristic features of his style. And first we may note his habit of varying his theme by numerous illustrations drawn sometimes from history, sometimes from the

* *A Confutation of a Booke intituled An Apologie of the Church of England* (1565), sig. K1.

more homely incidents of everyday life. In the following passage the pointedness of the illustration will be appreciated:

> The thinges worthy to be most wondered at in M. Iewel, be these. His impudencie in lying, his falshed in corrupting the Doctours, his continual scoffing, his common running from the present mater into common places that be impertinent, his immoderate bragging, his common thrusting away of one truth by an other truth, his deepe dissembling where he is pressed with truth, his often ieasting and railing at the Pope and Cardinals, his vile, spiteful and blasphemous talke against our holy Mysteries.* These in his Replie he vseth with so great excesse, as no man euer more.
>
> Many haue thought, and so reported, this Replie to be such a peece of worke, as neither could, nor would be euer answered. But wilt thou knowe myne opiniō Reader, and what I thinke of it? Verely I iudge of it in much like sorte as Annibal did of Antiochus Armie. King Antiochus mynding to warre vpon the Romains, had caused a great Armie to moustre before him in sight of Captaine Annibal, who fled vnto him after he had ben ouerthrowen by the Romains. whē al had shewed them seules, as them semed best, the foote men braue in their colours, yͤ horsemen sumptuous in their gilted harnesse, the Captaines al clad in golde and pearle passing rich: the king reioising hereat, how like you this Sir Annibal, quod he. Here is ynough, quod Anibal, for the Romains, if they be not insatiable. Antiochus looked for an other answere, thinking so wel an appointed Armie of so skilful a Captaine should haue ben praised. But Annibal, who had wel tried the Romains power, knewe al should be but a praye for them.†

And here are two illustrations of the more homely kind. The first will strike a familiar note even for the modern reader:

> Thou knowest Reader, the maner of Pearemongers is, the rather to allure byers vnto them, to set their best peares for shew in the vpper part of their Paniers, and when any byer commeth to geue him for a taste of the better sorte. The like policie here vseth M. Iewel. He bringeth forth the proufes of his doctrine, as it were summer fruit to a market, that is soone ripe, soone roten. And here setting forth to the eye his chiefe store, he geueth thee a taste of his best dish that he is able to make. Other fooisty and rotten fruite he semeth to haue, whereof he would make shew, were not for feare it should offende, and marre the whole sale.‡

* 'He wrote in good temper and avoided personalities', says the *D.N.B.*, s.v. *Jewel.*

† *Reioindre* (1566), Address to Reader.

‡ ibid., sig. HHh3v.

No less familiar and equally suggestive will be the following:

> Whereas against this Sacrifice, [the sacrifice of the mass] by many men many wordes haue ben said, many villanies haue ben wrought, many blasphemous bookes haue ben written (as is before mẽcioned) according to the sprite, that Satan the enemie of the sacrifice hath enspired into their wretched breastes: Out of al M. Iewel, like a spyder, hath suckte the most venemous iouice, and in his Replie hath vttered it, as it were spitting forth his poison. Which Replie, as perhaps it poisoneth the lighter sorte, who haue delite to feede thereon: so to the wise, and those that be stedfast in the Catholique Faith, al the stuffe of his great booke appeareth, as it were but Cobwebbes. For in dede as with Cobwebbes nothing is holden, but light motes, and weake flees: euen so of a light witte, and feeble Faith he sheweth him selfe to be, whom that Replie catcheth, and holdeth.*

Spiders, cobwebs and street vendors are everyday matters, as, indeed, are hedgehogs (urchins), crab apples and junkets,† and we may note in passing that in introducing such 'homespun images' into serious writing Harding is simply following the tradition of much of the best English prose of the preceding ages. The passages cited, for directness and vividness of touch, might easily have come from the pen of Thomas More.

In the two short extracts which follow, Harding shows himself, in his fondness for playing with a word or an expression, a true child of his own age:

> Where say I, that ye haue no manner Oblation in your Communion? Looke vpon my wordes againe, reade them diligently, and if I say so, then your Replie standeth in force against me. If I say it not, what shal I then say, but all is false that you say? But what els should you say, being determined rather than to subscribe, to gainsay me, though you damne your soule for it, but that which is false?‡

> Who is now to be asked, whether he haue the chynecoffe, which in a place of your Reply with out cause you twite me of? What kinde of coffe I shal cal this, I wote not, I feare me the il mater of it lyeth not in your chyne, a place so farre from the harte, but in the harte it selfe. For were not the same by Satans worke festred with the corruption of heresie, you had not ben letted, as with a coffe, from bringing forth the

* *Reioindre* (1567), sig. I2.

† See above.

‡ *Reioindre* (1566), sig. Y2.

later parte of S. Cyprians saying, whose beginning you falsly abuse to obscure the cleare truthe. Who so euer thus coffeth, I wil not say, he hath the chynecoffe, as you ieast, but verely (sauing my charitie) that he coffeth as like an heretique, as a rotten yew coffeth like a sheepe.*

In loftier vein we get such a passage as the following:

Ye haue searched al stuffe, as Iacob said to Laban, ye haue examined our doctrine, and what haue ye founde? Ye haue examined vs, ye haue depriued vs, ye haue condemned vs, some to prisons, some to certaine places, ye haue debarred vs of libertie to see our deare frendes, to enioye our swete Countrie, ye haue taken from vs great summes of money, ye haue thirsted our bloude, ye haue oftetimes called for the Princes sword to be drawen against vs, ye haue geuen the cause of the losse of many of our liues. This and much more, haue ye done touching our parte.

But as touching Gods parte, what iniurie, what dishonour, what pillages, what robberies, what Sacrileges, what spoiles, what prophane and Turkish saggages of Churches, what contempte, what despite, what villanies, ye and your brethren, haue done in sundry places of Christendome, what needeth it any man to speake, the secretes of hartes do speake, the sighing of Gods people speaketh, the Earth, the Heauen, God him selfe by his brute and dumme Creatures speaketh. But what auaileth it to make complaint vnto them, that be not onely farre from al griefe of their euil doing, and from remorse of conscience, but also reioyse, and glorie in malice?†

The sincerity and feeling here, no less than the reserve, call to mind the noble eloquence of that passage in the Authorized Version of the Bible where St. Paul, too, speaks of his sufferings in the service of Christ.‡ Finally, in a passage which rises to a notable eloquence, we may perceive the dramatic instinct at work even in a theological treatise:

But sir, sith you require me to be so courteous in my writinges against you, why did not you your selfe in yours against me, vse more courtesie? Is that commendable in you, whiche is reproueable in me? Or els, what, haue you a special dispensation to say what you liste, and to require al others to adore you, and say, Aue Rabbi? Shal it be lawful for you, to crie out vpon vs, *tolle*, *tolle*, *crucifige*: and must we sing vnto you, *Sanctus*, *Sanctus*, *Sanctus*? Whiles ye barke and bite, must we caste a disshe of fragmentes vnto you? Whiles ye play the Beare

* *Reioindre* (1567), sig. EE4v. † ibid., sig. I1.
‡ *II Corinthians* xi. 21–30.

with vs, must we throw honny vnto you? Whiles ye play the parte of Satan, must we light a candle before you?

S. Paule the chosen vessel of Christe, teaching Titus, how to demeane himselfe towardes such as you are, said, *Increpa illos durè*, rebuke them sharpely. But what soeuer you say, or doo, must we needes sothe you, and smoothe you? Must we, stroke you and cooxe you, as men doo curst boyes, after they haue done shrewd turnes? If you passe al men that euer wrote, in number of lyes, in vanitie of boasting, in the common custom of scoffing, as now it hath benne prooued against you: shal we feare, that we seeme not to lacke the ciuilitie you speake of, to cal you a lyer, a boaster, a scoffer? What is the matter, that doing so il, you require to be spoken of so wel?

Perhaps whereas the Rentes of the Bishoprike of Sarisburie cause men al to belorde you, your eares being of long tyme accustomed to suche honorable greetinges, you looke to be honoured at our handes, as you are of your poore hungry Craftesmen, that hauing learned to reade Englishe pretily, sue vnto you for Ministerships. And then whereas you lye impudently, folowing them we muste saie, were it not, that your good Lordship saith so, verely we should haue thought otherwise. And whereas you falsifie your testimonies, we must put the fault in your Spectacles. When you hew and mangle the Doctours so fowly, that al the worlde may see it: we must beare you in hande, that when your Lordship wrote so, the booke was not at hande. When you serue vs with a point of Scurrilitie, we muste saye: O howe it becommeth your L. to be meary? When you shoote at randon, diuerting altogether from the special point that is to be answered, vnto impertinent matter: we must say, your L. shooteth faire, though somewhat wide of the marke. When by no witte, nor cunning, you are hable to make good your Chalenge: yet then we must say, that your L. lacketh no woordes, and hath geuen a good Push towardes it. To be shorte (for these be the special pointes for whiche you accuse my vtterance of vncourtesie) when you speake big, and Goliathlike vpbraid al the hoste of God, to witte, the whole Catholique Churche of these laste thousand yeres: what must we doo, but to shew token of feare, as the Israelites vnder king Saul did, and geue backe, that you may boast, and crake alone?*

Surely the trenchant irony of this passage is of the very same nature as that later magnificent outburst in which Shylock vindicates the essential equality of Jew and Christian, and justifies his purpose of revenge by Christian example.†

* *A Detection of sundrie foule errours* (1568), sig. K1^{v}.
† *Merchant of Venice*, III, i.

JOHN MARTIALL

The two volumes on the Cross, which John Martiall, editor of the second edition of Harding's *Answere*, contributed to the Catholic side of this controversy, constitute a more general attack upon the Protestant dispensation than that of Harding, and from a literary point of view they are of much less interest. Martiall was still comparatively young when the two books were written, and this perhaps will account for his showing a less-controlled fervour than his older colleague. There is the same appeal to logic that we find in Harding, and on occasion he can be equally terse and antithetical, yet he is much more inclined to 'infarce' (to use his own word) his writing with rhetorical device than Harding is, and as a rule his rhetoric is not so well managed. That he had some gift for narrative and a sound sense of rhythm the following excerpt will show:

> At what tyme the vertuous lady Helena willed as the story mentioneth by reuelation from god to seeke the crosse of Christ in *Hierusalē*, founde after lōg digging in the mounte of Caluary thre crosses so confuse that nether by the title which Pilate set vp in Hebreue, greke, and latyn, nether by any other meanes they could discerne which was the crosse that bore oure sauiour Christ, a noble woman of the citie consumed and spent with long sicknesse did lie at deathes doore. *Macarius* then bishop of Hierusalem seing the good lady Helena staggring at the matter, and al her trayne discomforted, saied vnto them, bring hether the thre crosses which are founde, and god shal open and reuele vnto vs, which is the crosse that caried oure sauiour Christ. They did so: and when the crosses were brought, *Macarius* went with *Helena* into the chamber where the foresaied noble woman lay, and being there, fel downe vppon his knees, and prayed in this sorte. O lord who by thy only begotten sonne vouchsauffidest to geue saluation to al mankinde, by his death vppon the crosse, and hast inspired the harte of thy hand maydē in these later dayes to seeke that blessed wood in which oure saluation did hange, shewe I beseek the, wich of thes thre crosses serued to the glory of god, and which to the seruile punishement of the theafes, that this ladye which lieth here half dead, may be brought from death to liff agayne, as sone as the wood of saluation hath touched her. And when he had ended his prayer, he put vnto the sick woman one of the thre crosses, it auayled nothing: he put vnto her the second, no help came: he put vnto her the third, and as sone as euer it touched her, she opened her eies, rose out of her bed, and receuing strenght agayne, was more lustier and lyuelier then

> when she was in her best health, and wēt vp and downe the house, and magnified the greate mercy, and mighty pouer of god.*

A further short passage may well suggest that, as regards the sixteenth century at any rate, even a theological treatise, as a contemporary document, may have a far wider interest and significance than one would be led to expect:

> Be not lordes heastes, na scribes fantasies, parasites pleasures, Macheuelianes policies holden and folloed for lawes? Are not many matters hudled vp in corners? examined in chambres? and determined without ordinary processe of the law? haue not some bene borne with al because they were protestantes? some ouerborne because they were papistes? some of late put to open paenaunce, pryson, and furder trouble for speaking of a sprite walking vnder a nutte tree in W parke. And he that broke downe the pale, hunted without his Ladies warrant, imbossed the white doe, and made the Cockrel crack, neur touched? but by his holy brother adiudged innocent? I appeale here to the publick fame, and their consciences who beare the sway (if they haue any cōsciences at al) and complainctes of them who haue felt the smarte of it, the more is the pitie. And for al this we may thanke haeresie: who to cloke her deare dearlinges trechery, and help her frendes and promoters at a pynche, hath no reuerence to publick ordinaunces, and common lawes.†

Is the 'sprite walking vnder a nutte tree in W[indsor?] parke' Herne the Hunter's ghost? If so, Shakespeare is no longer our sole authority for that phenomenon. And what of the later reference?

THOMAS DORMAN

Besides Harding and Martiall, the group of Wykehamists who took part in The Great Controversy includes Thomas Dorman, John Rastell, Thomas Stapleton, Nicolas Sander, Robert Pointz and John Fowler. We may consider these writers in that order.

As a polemist of the more popular kind, Harding's *protégé*, Thomas Dorman, deserves to rank high. The strong feeling which had moved him to write, as he himself confesses,‡ together with his obvious sincerity, gives his writing a distinction which commands both our respect and attention. He can, of

* *A Treatyse of the Crosse* (1564), sig. N4. † ibid., sig. S2.
‡ cf. *A Proufe of Certeyne Articles in Religion* (1564), sig. E1v.

course, indulge himself in quips and he can strike home when he thinks it necessary, but one never feels that he passes the bounds of decency and charity, and he clearly *enjoys* girding at his opponents. His long and somewhat involved sentences, the result of his unrestrained ardour, sometimes make rather heavy demands upon the average reader; at the same time they give a buoyancy and swiftness to his writing which saves it from turgidity. An added robustness of expression and directness of attack, by means of frequent address to the reader and of appeal to common experience, give vivacity to a type of discourse which might easily have been dead and dull.

The following quotation illustrates comprehensively Dorman's method and style. He is attacking Jewel on the subject of transubstantiation:

> Truelie good readers this man semeth to me, to be like a makeshifte that falling into a companie of others making merie, braggeth and boasteth of his purse wherein is neuer a crosse, that he hath to spende as largelie as the best, and will beare his part as franckelie as the proudest what so euer he be, and yeat for all his high lookes and greate bragges made before, when it cometh to the gathering of the shotte he slippeth faire and well awaie, and leaueth the honest companie to paye for all. Euen so, I praie yowe marcke, when it commeth to the reconing of this heauenlie bancket, where is prepared for vs the moste pretiouse bodie and bloude of oure sauiour Christe, where is required of vs for the shotte that faithe as saithe holie S. Basil that Christes wordes (This is my bodie) teache vs: let vs I saie marcke howe well for all his bragges he paieth his parte. Forsothe yowe shall see. If Christe had made his bodie in the sacrament to appeare like a bodie, and his bloud to taste and showe like bloude, if he might haue sene it with his eyes, as the people of Israel sawe the rodde, as theie tasted of the water: if Christe had euer done anie such miracle before as this is, that is to saie if he had turned the substance of one thing in to an other, and left still vnchanged the qualities of th' other thing that it was before, that it might not haue semed a iuggling, if finally he had had anie necessitie to constreine him to worcke anie suche change, then he woulde haue beleued as we doe notwithstanding all the apparence of impossibilitie to the contrarie.
>
> These be the conditions requisite to the faith of this protestant. But here it is a worlde to see, while he would seme humblie to graunte the omnipotencie of god, and to deliuer him selfe and his companions, from that note of infamie, whereinto by long struggling ageinst the same theie ar runne with all men,

while he patcheth and cobbleth with his rottē lingells a nombre of clouted ifs, and is like the false tineker that mendeth one hole and maketh two newe, or craftie Couper that to fasten one whoope looseth three: he tumbleth hedlōg in to a greate heape of absurdities, whereof euerie one is as greate as that which he thought to haue auoided, and wherein yeat he sticketh notwithstanding. For if thow beleuedest man (as thowe vainelie braggest that thowe doest) that god wer omnipotent, wouldest thow so limite and restreine his power, that he shoulde not change the nature and substance of a thinge, onlesse he change the accidentes thereof withall? Wilt thow first see blood and taste it as did the children of Israel the water, and then after beleue? O notable faithe to be cōpared with the grayne of a musterd seede, whose guydes the eyes and other fallible senses be. *Quid memorabile facis si videas & credas?* what great act doest thow to beleue after thowe hast seene I may say to yow, as *Theophilus* the B. of Alexandria sayd vnto one *Autolicus* to whome he wrote. Thus saide the Iues of Christ our sauiour hanging apon the Crosse. *Descendat nunc de cruce vt videamus & credamus.* Let him come downe now from the crosse that we maye see and thē beleue. And except you may see fleshe and bloud, is it iuggling? What yow meane herebie I knowe not, of this suer I am, that greate blasphemie it is so to terme the miraculouse worcking of almightie god, besides the horrible presumption to apointe god in what sorte he shall doe his miracles, and last of all extreme folly to saie that he rather iuggleth, that turning the substance of one thing in to an other leaueth yeat vnchanged the olde forme (which no iuggler is able to doe) then he that altereth the fourme although he can not the substance, which dailie experience telleth vs that euerie iuggler to our sight doeth. So that almightie goddes worcking is moste vnlike to iugglers iuggling, and rather might yow haue saide, that Moses wand was a iuggling sticke for that that commonlie iugglers seme to doe as Moses did, then that in this high misterie consisting all in faithe, anie such false dealing should take place. Yow that call this iuggling, so far vnlike theretoe, if Christe I feare me had turned in this sacrament in dede the accidentes and outewarde forme, which euery Iuggler promiseth and semeth to doe in his trickes: your false faithe is such, that yowe woulde not haue letten to haue called that plaine iuggling, besides other pretie termes that yowe kepe in store.*

The popular appeal of such a passage as this will at once be evident. The point about the juggler is well made and helps to simplify a difficult subject. The images serve to fix the attention.

* ibid., sigs. V1–2.

And how easily we may travel back with Dorman into sixteenth-century England. The 'makeshifte' or rogue, who leaves others to foot the bill, is still with us, and the false tinker and the crafty cooper, they, too, have their modern counterparts.

Here is another picture, this time of the precocious schoolboy. It is taken from the writings of More and is used to emphasize Alexander Nowell's methods of controversy:

> My maister plaieth here with me, as S. Thomas More writeth that a poet of Cambridge did once with his boye whome (plaing with him being a yong Sophister on a time for his pleasure) he offred to proue an asse: which when the boye denied, well quoth the poet thow wilt graunte me this first, that euery thing that hath two eares is an asse. Nay mary maister will I not quoth the boye. No wilt thow quoth the poete? Ah wyly boye there thow wentest beyond me. For and thow wouldest haue graunted me that, I woulde haue proued the an asse anon. Mary maister quoth the boye ye might well, and so might euery foole toe. Well quoth the poet I will goe now an other waye to worcke with the. Thow wilt graunt me that euerie asse hath two eares. Naye marie will I not maister quoth the boye. Why so boye quóth he. Mary maister quoth he, some asse maie happē to haue neuer a one, for they maie be cut of bothe. Naye then quoth the poet I giue the ouer, thow arte to forwarde a boye for me.*

More must, of course, be given some credit for this story, though I imagine it has lost nothing in the retelling. But it is the fact that Dorman has recourse to More for an illustration which we would specially wish to stress here. Not only does this suggest that More's writings continued to be studied by the Catholic exiles, thus affording further proof of the statement we have made earlier in this work that his memory and influence lived on amongst them,† but it suggests also that Dorman was particularly beholden to More for what is a constituent element in his style, the graphic image. In this there is a close similarity between the two writers, and it is this which makes Dorman's books so much more than mere apologetical treatises.

* *A Disproufe of M. Nowelles Reproufe* (1565), sig. N1.

† Elsewhere Dorman refers to Fisher and More as 'those two most worthy pearles of Englande'; ibid., sig. Oo1.

JOHN RASTELL

The works of John Rastell are a further tribute to Harding's influence as the leader of the Louvainists. Like John Martiall, he edited one of Harding's books, under the title of *A Briefe Shew Of the false Wares* . . . (1567), and there are repeated references to Harding in his pages. He, too, insists upon the absence of right reasoning in his opponents' arguments and his own writing is distinguished by its logical structure. He makes no claim to profundity, however; rather, he says: 'I thinke it no fault with a breth onlie (if I could) to dryue backe an enemye. And if with a penknyfe I diminishe his lustie bloude. lett other vse the great swordes, and pickes, which shall kyll his heresie.'* His aim is to write 'intelligiblie and familiarlie'.† If he lacks something of Harding's lucidity, this is due in part to his greater use of subordination in the sentence, and in part to a tendency to crowd his canvas with images. For this reason his expression occasionally becomes somewhat involved, though the general sense will usually remain clear.

In the two passages which follow, the logical character of Rastell's expression should be abundantly clear. In the first, the writer argues that the preservation of the Christian faith depends solely upon such authority and order as is exercised by the Church:

> It semeth that now at length, the long since intended Purposes of the Dyuel, are almost come to theyr perfection: And there lacketh no more nowe, but that, by Open Apostasie, he make the faith of Christe to be forsaken: and that, not so much as the name thereof, shal be suffered in the world.
>
> Speake I this without cause? Let any Indifferent man be Iudge. For take the fundations awaye frome an howse, and can it contynue any space together? Take all credite awaye, betwixte man and man in this trade of life, and will there be left any Occupying to and fro? If no Authoritie and law be in a Common wealthe, can the state thereof endure? What is that among Christians which hath brought them vnto the Faith, and Staied, and Gouerned them in it? Is it not the Authority of the Churche, Commending the Doctrine of Christ vnto vs, By Fathers, By Councels, By Custome and Tradition, And by Succession of Bishoppes euen from S. Peter hitherto? Emong all which, if no one, may safely be leaned vnto, what remaineth in all the world worthye of credite? And except there be an

* *A confutation of a sermon* (1564), Preface to the Reader. † ibid.

> Authoritye and Order, which we may and must folow, what Faith can we haue at all?
>
> But who is he, that prepareth suche waies for the Antichrist? Or who shaketh the Hartes and Consciencies of Christians, euen from the very botome and foundations of them? Mary, except you BEWARE of him, M. Iewel emonge other, is he.*

In our second passage the writer is aiming at the contentious reasoning of Bishop Cooper, in claiming for the Protestant religion the marks of the true Church.

> [*Defence*]. The right church therfore, as the fold of Christ, hath the true worde of God and vse of his sacramentes, according vnto the same, for the due markes therof.
>
> [*Reply*]. After this maner, you shall haue some tymes the symple idiotes of the countrey to make answer vnto straingers asking the right waye vnto this or that place, which they would come vnto. For, (saye they) you must goe by my grandsyres close, and then keepe the straytwaye, and you shall neuer mysse. Or else, lyke as a man would sende his seruant to London for a cupp of pure and cleane wyne, and tell hym that he shall be sure to haue it there, where he seeth an Iuye garland to hang at the dore, or the drawer of the wyne to vse no deceptfull bruyng of it, (wheras the Iuye garland is no certayne tokē of good wine ready to be solde, and euery tapster will easily saie for his owne truth and honestye) so you haue tolde vs such markes to know the true church by, that as the true church hath them in deede, so yet euery mysbegotten congregatiō, will chalendge them vnto herselfe.†

The interesting feature of this extract is the way in which the rhetoric is made to subserve the writer's logical purpose. The implication of Cooper's conclusion is gradually unfolded by means of a series of analogies drawn from everyday life, the logic giving rise to and supporting these, and they in their turn enforcing the logic. The result is a thoroughly well-controlled piece of rhetoric.

To turn to lighter matters, let us now examine some of the commoner features of Rastell's style. And, first, we may note the pithy familiarity of many of his passages. Such a paragraph, for instance, as the following is not infrequent in his works:

> And so, like as bells do sound in diuers mens eares diuersly, and diuersly in one selfe same eare, as the mind is affected: so Scripture and custome are made to sound in these mens fancy,

* *A Treatise intitled, Beware of M. Iewel* (1566), sig. P6.

† *A Replie against an answer (falslie intitled) in Defence of the truth* (1565), sig. Z8.

> euen as their mind is to haue this or that opinion to goe forward. When it pleaseth them: all the bells shall goe, *With customes of primatiue churche, examples of good men, testimonies of blessed Doctors.* And when so great a sound doth troble their studie, then loe it pleaseth them to haue *one bell onely to ring, With nothing is to be beleued without expresse worde of Scripture.**

And here is a like passage, where the use of dialogue gives an added dramatic touch to the writing:

> For they haue forsaken the high way, and what by breaking of ceremonies, what by ouerturning of monasteries, what by false libertie of conscience, that they may doe what they will, vnder the name of the crosse of Christ and his passion: they haue so crossed the wayes, and broken down so many hedgis, and troden downe so much good corn, & so many faire pastures of all pietie and deuotion: that, except they com back to the beginning againe, they can neuer com to good end. Whither be you posting Sir, and please you? vnto heauen? you must ride then a pase for company bycause by your owne confession, these nine hundred yeres and more, none did euer take this way which you doe folow. But, where will you bayt by the way? At the signe of the booke with seuen claspes, which is the Ghospell. Sir, then I besech you, what call you the city where that signe is? Mary, Geneua where Caluin readeth. What, if Geneua be destroied, and Caluin burned? . . .†

Variety is obtained in a number of ways – by irony, the occasional use of verse, proverbial sayings, &c. – but in none more effectively than by graphic little sketches taken from contemporary life. There are a number of these of varying length. The one which we now quote refers to the common quack and with its pointed application is one of the most striking pieces that we have so far met with in these writings. It comes from the Preface to the Reader of Rastell's *The Third Booke, Declaring by Examples out of Auncient Councels, Fathers, and Later writers, that it is time to Beware of M. Iewel* (1566):

> But I may wel compare, the seeing and suffering of false and blind Teachers that now take cure of Soules, to the permitting & honouring of Mountebanks, that goe abroad with diuerse thinges for mens Bodies.
>
> These Mountebanks, are a free kind of wanderers, Pedlars, Surgeans, Physitians, Historiographers, Poetes, or what so euer name besides you wil geue vnto them, men altogether for the penie, which is the cause that they professe so many thinges.

* *A confutation of a sermon*, as before, sig. C7v. † ibid., sig. D3v.

They take vp their standing in Market places, or void roomes meete for the cōcourse of people, there they set a stoole to stand vpon, or make a litle scaffold for the purpose, from which they play their part.

Their Greatest Grace is in the Countenance & Tongue, through which, they looke so Saddely, and speake so eloquētly, that a man would sweare upō a booke for them, that they thinke as they speake, & speak nomore, than they wil do.

What so euer thing they haue to sel, as *Newes out of India*, Or *The Original of the Turkishe Empire*, Or *Mery Tales*, Or *Songes and Ballets*, Or *a Pouder to kil wormes*, Or *A Preseruatiue againste the Plague*, Or *A Water to make the skynne faire and white*, Or *Pinnes*, *Pointes*, *Laces*, *Whistles*, & other such ware, whatsoeuer it be, they commend it and praise it before. But they doe it with such a Grace, with such a Constancie, with such Copie of words, with such mouing of Affections, that it is wonderful.

If it be a water, a Pouder, an Oyntmente, a Confection not worth twentie pence, he wil make such a doe about it, as though it could scarse be bought for halfe a Kinges raunsome. And standing first vp like a worshipful man, Arayed in his silkes and veluettes, And al to be rayed with braslettes & bowed peeces of golde, And chained about the neck with a great thing (of copper and gylt, as many iudge, but) of pure and fine gold, as farre as the eye seeth, he wil tel his Audience: That he is come vnto them for good wils sake, moued in him by the Fame and worthines of them and theyr Citie or Toune: He will tell them, that he can not tarie long, & that, before he depart, he would faine bestow vpon them some token of his good affection: Then wil he bring furth that water or pouder, or conceipt, which he would vtter, and say, That it was brought from beyonde Calecut, or the Red Sea: and then wil he point with his finger towardes Calecut, and make a like disgressiō, to declare how far that is of, from their Countrie, as M. Iewel doth to praise (after his maner) ye Popes of Rome: after this, he wil shew the vertue and strength of his Pouder: And further declare, how much thereof hath been bought in greate Cities, and of noble Personages which he wil name: and further yet, he wil make them think, that it is al that he hath leaft, that which he offereth to be bought of them: He wil also disgrace other Mountebankes that goe abroad the Countrie, and say, That their wares are but counterfeit, but that his are fine, and pure, and fresh. For why he seeketh not after gaines, as the couetous and beggarly knaues doe, but as it becommeth a good Gentleman, he trauaileth farre and wide vpon his owne Charges to get such geare, as may bring Commodities to whole Countries. In Cōclusion, when he hath spoken as much as he can, then he prouoketh the hearers againe and againe to bye. And if it be a water which he commended, he putteth in Glasses, made for the purpose, halfe a skore or a skore of droppes thereof: If it be a pouder, he putteth as much as he can hold betwen his Thombe and Forefinger, in seueral papers, and beginneth to make merchandise. And that which as it should seeme by his tale, should be wel worth a Croune a droppe, he wil sel, with good gaines, for a myte or two, of which, twelue do make but a penie.

* * *

A Mountebank then, may crake, and lie, and outface his Aduersarie, and make somewhat of nothing, and mingle sporte with sadnesse, and play what part he wil in the sight of the people, and hundreds wil gase vpon him, but none wil reproue him.

Like vnto these, in an other kinde, there be other Mountebankes, men so free, that they be lawlesse, So ful of faire promises, that they sel, for one comming vnto them, euerlasting life, So louing & kind harted, that they forsake their owne Countrie, and without asking of licence, or directly against commaundment, bye and sel within other mens Iurisdiction.

Yet, in Faith, they doe it somewhat manerly, they rush not into Cities and Townes at the first, but, without the Towne walles, they choose out a place in the open fielde, or in some wodde, and xx. or xxx, turues being cut & set one vpō the other, there straitewaies is a place for the Preacher, and there straitwaies doth the Mountebanke beginne to open.

But what stuffe it is, that he there openeth, it can not be declared in a short time and Preface. the Sōme yet is this: That he commeth vnto them with comfortable wares: That he commeth from farre Countries: That except they wil be thankeful and receiue the Grace that he bringeth, he wil depart againe: That he wil aske nothing for his labor: That he deliuereth them quite, from feare of Purgatorie, and Hel also (for Purgatorie there is none at al, and to hel he wil warrant them neuer to come) That thei shal haue no more bonde of fasting, watching, praying, performing of lawfull vowes, &c: That they shal haue no more Signe of Crosse, or Christ, or our Lady, or any Sainct in their eye, nor any memorie of them in their hart, & y^t they shal haue al peace & cōfort, if they wil bye but one dram of the doctrine y^t he bringeth.

And so the passage continues until finally Jewel himself is attacked in the words:

But what speake I of other? Is M. Iewel him selfe any better than a Mōtebanke? Consider by that only which I haue proued against him, how faire spoken he is, how much corrupt stuffe he hath, how highly he setteth by it, how loudely he craketh of it, how singularly he auanceth him self by it. For

> when he prouoketh *al the learned men that be aliue*, And asketh for no more than *One sufficient sentence*, And requireth to haue that brought out *of any Olde Catholique Doctour or Father, or any Olde General Councel, &c*: What other thing is this, but a Mountebankes Preface, to commend his wares vnto the Audience? As if he should say in plainer woordes vnto them:
>
> Deerely beloued in the Lorde, you may take me perchaunce for a Benchwhistler, or a man of litle knowledge and practise, and altogeather vnhable to reproue the General and Catholique Doctrine of the whole world, and to draw you from those Maisters and Teachers which alwaies hitherto, ye haue ben ruled by. But I shal tel you (deere brethren) I haue seene and readen as much as any man, yea – as *all the learned men aliue*: I haue trauailed vnto the very *Primitiue Church* it selfe: I haue bene conuersant with *Old Catholique Doctors, and Fathers, and old General Councels*. As for these Priests, Cardinals and Popes, whom you folowe, they bring nothing, but Conclusions of Scholemen, and deuises of Later Doctours, and Ceremonies of their owne making, &c. But I will bring you no other thing, but that which is Auncient.

In reading this passage one is immediately put in mind of the stylized character sketches which were popular in the next century, and we shall probably agree that Rastell's mountebank, in spite of the restriction imposed by the emblematic nature of his figure, loses nothing in the comparison.

Let us conclude this notice with a passage written in the more elevated style, a passage which, in some respects, anticipates the eloquence of Hooker:

> But, I tell yow, ascend in yowr myndes, dilate yowre hartes, and enlarge yowre thowghtes. This is his bodye, in deed, as he hath spoken hymself the word, which can not be false, and this ys his bloude. But whose body and bloud? lyft vp yowr hartes now, The body of the second person in trinite, the onlye begotten of the Father, the maker of the world, the wisedome of God, the ouerlooker of all creatures, good and badd, angells and diuells, men, and beastes, the sercher of owre hartes, the disposer of tymes, the iudge of the worlde, the felicytie and ioye of the good, the terror and feare of the condempned. Lyft vpp yowr hartes I saye. Thinke you that here ys present, a bodye or flessh onlye? And that, as in diseases some whott meates doe cumfort the bodye, so that yow haue but a lyuely peece of his flessh onlye? Or els, doe you conceaue the matter after this sort, that as one frinde sendeth to an other a morsell of good meate, which the other had not: that so Christ in this banket geueth vnto euery man a tast, or els a portion onlye of his pretious bodye, as it were a most excellent gyft, but yet

> baser, then his sowle and diuinitie? O, lift vpp your hartes. You must not seeke Christ so grosselye, looke not to haue hym so vpon the earth. Christ ys one perfect person, God and man, maker of all tymes, and borne according to flesh in tyme, euerlasting lyfe, and yet putt to most shamefull death, reignyng at the right hand of God his father, and present among men vpon the altar. Stick not therefor I say vnto the body, lett not your thoughtes and desires rest in the flessh onlye: but goe hyer by your faith, and cõsider that blessed sowle of his, so chast, patient, wise, charitable, bright, glorious, and yet hyer and hyer, in to the very heauens, and aboue all heauens, beholding and wondering, how the maker of them all, whom thowsand thowsandes, and ten hundred thousand thousandes do wayte vpon: ys present here for vs, to be receaued of vs, and to incorporate vs in to hym selue.*

THOMAS STAPLETON

Stapleton's English works consist of three translations from Latin originals, viz. *The Apologie of Fridericus Staphylus* (1565), *The History of the Church of Englande* (1565), and *Of the Expresse Worde of God* (1567); two original controversial tracts, viz. *A Fortresse of the Faith* (1565), and *A Returne of Vntruthes vpon M. Iewelles Replie* (1566); and his *A Counterblast to M. Hornes vayne blaste* (1567), written in collaboration with Nicholas Harpsfield. Altogether these works cover the equivalent of more than 3,000 quarto pages, and we would suggest that they can hardly be excluded from any serious study of the Elizabethan epoch, whether theological, historical or literary. But they are of especial importance to the literary student. Stapleton was a man of wide learning and of considerable power of mind, and if we add to this his undoubted command of the English language we shall perhaps begin to understand the truth of this. That he is essentially a stylist we may gather from his statement in the translator's preface to *The Apologie of Fridericus Staphylus*, where he writes:

> I wil here breake of, and after the ende of the Authors whole discourse, put for conclusion the rest of my meaning, aduertising in the meane season the reader of this one thing, that this our labour being an interpretation and bound to the inuentiõ of the Author, we haue not, ne coulde not vse the like eloquence as the free stile geueth: beseching the notwithstanding, gentle Reader, to take our paines in good part.†

* *A confutation*, as before, sig. L1.

† sig. C4.

DR. THOMAS STAPLETON
From the engraving in the fourth volume of the *Opera* (Paris, 1620)

We may distinguish, then, between Stapleton's original works and his translations. In these works, where he can 'vse the like eloquence as the free stile geueth', he is able to employ his favourite device of doubling the expression 'to amplify and vary his argument' to the full, and to expand his theme, apart from continual reference to Holy Scripture, the Fathers, and the martyrology, by frequent resort to the use of the Figures, more especially to metaphor and simile. There is thus a fulness of expression in them which is, to an extent at any rate, absent from his translations. His vocabulary also is more lively, and the absence of restraint very often gives a piquancy to his utterance which we do not find when he is tied to an original text. In a following section, when we come to deal with the *Counterblast*, we hope to give the reader, by means of illustration, a full and comprehensive view of this aspect of his genius. Meanwhile his work as a translator is our immediate concern, and since his translation of Bede, *The History of the Church of Englande*, is by far the most important of his works and has a literary distinction which neither *The Apologie* nor *Of the Expresse Worde of God* can claim, we cannot do better than give our attention to a passage from that work, a passage which for the general appeal of its subject and for the intrinsic interest of the presentation must surely be judged as equal to anything of a like nature written during the period.*

How King Edwine was prouoked to receiue the faith, by a vision appearing to him in bannishment.

The. 12. Chap.

Thus much did Pope Boniface by his letters, for the conuerting of king Edwine, and all his countrie, which king was also well holpen, and almost forced to receaue the faithe, and marke diligently the holesome preceptes of Christian doctrine by an oracle, and vision from heauen. Which the goodnes of God vowchesafed to shewe him, while he laye bannished in kinge Redwaldes courte, king of the east Englishmen. For when bishop Pauline had well perceaued that the princes haughty courage could hardly be brought to the lowly humblenes of Christianite, and that it would styfly be bowed and bent to beare the mysterie, and burden of Christes crosse: when he remembred also, how he had nowe laboured a longe tyme bothe with

* For other outstanding passages we would refer the reader especially to the account of Caedmon (IV, xxiv), the excellent chapter on a cure by St. John of Beverley (V, vi), the vivid account of purgatory and hell mouth (V, xiii), and the lovely vision concerning St. Chad (IV, iii).

preaching to the people, and with praying to God's mercie for the saluation of king Edwine, and all his subiectes: at the lenght hauing lerned in sprite (for so it is most lykest to be,) what was that vision, which had longe before ben shewed to the kinge from heauen, he made no delayes at all, but came spedely to the kinge, and warned him to fulfill and accomplishe his vowe, whiche in the vision that appeared to him he had promised to doe in case he were deliuered from his present miseries and restored againe to his raygne, and kingdome. Nowe was this vision suche, as foloweth: At what time king Edelfryde Edwines predecessour with greuouse pursuing put Edwine to flight, and made him lye pryue, and lurke in diuers places of other realmes for manie yeres space as a bannished man: at the lenghth Edwine came to king Redwald, besechinge him, that he would saue him, and defend his life from the traynes, and ernest serche of this his dedly ennemie. Who gladly entertained hym, and promised to fullfill this his requeste, and petitiō. But after that king Edelfride had heard say that Edwine was seene in that prouince, and vnderstood that he liued ther, and dwelled familiarly with all his cōpany, forthwith he sent out his Embassadours to king Redwald, with a greate somme of monie, to procure Edwines deathe. But it preuailed nothing. Thē sent he the second tyme, and the thyrd tyme also offring greater gyftes, and more plentifully bothe gold and syluer thretning him at the laste warres, yf his request were [not] accomplished. Then king Redwald other dreading the threts or corrupted with the brybes graunted his request, and promised that he would put Edwyne to death himselfe, or els yealde him vp to thimbassadeurs. Which thing when a certayne faythfull frend of Edwynes had marked and well vnderstoode, he entred incontinent to the chamber where Edwyne purposed to take his rest. For it was now an houre within nyght and calling him forth, told him what the king had promised to doe against him: sayeng in the end this muche: I shall therfore (yf it so please yowe) leade yowe owt of this prouince, and bryng yow into suche a place, that nother king Redwald, nor yet king Edelfryde shalbe able to fynde yowe. To whome Edwyne answered in this maner: Sir, I thanke yow most hartely for this your greate gentlenes. But I can not folowe your counsell herin. For first, I must not breake my promesse, which I haue made to so greate and mightie a Prince as is king Redwald, especially wheras he hath done me no harme, ne wronge, nor hath as yet shewed anie hatred, or displeasure towardes me. And truly if I must of necessite dye thus, I had rather he shuld put me to deathe, then anie baser man or person of lesse nobilite. Agayne whether I pray yow shuld I flee nowe, who haue so many yeares, and so long tyme walked lyke a vagabounde through all prouinces of this yle of Britannie, only to auoyd and eschewe myne enemies snares, and assaultes? Now when this his frend was gone, Edwyne remained without alone and sytting sadly before the palace begane to be troubled with manie stormes, and vexations of thoughts, as a man not witting what to doe or whither to goe in this so ruefull case. After he had ben longe vexed with inwarde, and priuie troubles of mynde, burning inwardly with close fyre of secret sorowe, behold, in the greate sylence, and quyet of the mydde nyght he sawe a man vtterly vnknowen to him bothe for visage and countenaunce, and also for his aray and apparell to approche and drawe toward him. Whome bycause he had espyed thus at a blushe, and so straungely desguised, he was not a lytle a frayde. The straunger cometh euen vnto him, greteth him and asketh him, wherfore he sate so soroufull on the stone abrode watching, and all alone at that howre especially when other men were within at rest, and in their depe sleape: Then Edwyne lykewise demaundyd of him, what he had to doe therwith, yf he passed ouer the nyght within dore, or els without. To whome this mā answered, and sayde: Thinke ye not but that I know the cause of your heauynes, and watche. And also of this your solitarie syttinge with out dores. For I know certainly who ye be, and wherfore you are so sad, and soroufull. And also what myscheffe yow feare shortly shall befall you. But tell me of fryndshippe, what reward would you geaue him, that shuld now rydde yowe quyte out of all these sorowes, and trowbles and persuade king Redwald, that neyther he himself shuld hurte yowe, nor yealde yowe vp to your enemies, that they myght slaye yow? When Edwyne answered that he would geaue all that he possible could to anie suche a one for reward of so good a turne, this mā added moreouer and sayde: But what if besyde this, he do warrant you, that ye shalbe a kinge, and all your enemies vanquished, yea and that in suche sorte that you shall not only excell all your auncient progenitours, but also far passe in powre all the kinges of Englishemen, which haue euer ben in this coūtrie. Here Edwyne being made more firme, and constant by ofte questioning doubted not to promis, that in all pointes, and at all tymes he wold be answerable with worthie thankes geauing to the man that shuld bestowe on him such greate benefites. Then this man spake the thyrd tyme and sayde: But tell me againe, what yf besyde all this, the same man, which sheweth yow now before, truly, and vnfaynedly, that yow shall hereafter surely, and vndoubtedly haue suche and so greate benefites, can geaue yowe also better coūsell, and more profitable for your sowles health, and saluation, then euer any your parentes, and auncesters heard of, could ye then consent, and obey him, and harken to his holsome sayenges? Here Edwyne promised owt of hand without anie lenger delaye, that he would altogether followe his lerning, and doctrine which both could, and would deliuer him presently from so manie miseries, and so greate daungers as he was in, and exalte him afterward to the raygne and souerantie of his countrie. Which his answer was heard, and taken. Then this man straightwaye, which had so long talked with him, layde his right hande vpon Edwines head, and said: when these thinges therfore shall happen herafter in suche sorte to yowe, remember well this tyme, and this our talke. And differ not at that time to fulfil and accomplishe this, that yow do nowe promesse me. Which being sayde, by and by he vanished awaye. To the entent that Edwine might vnderstand and perceaue, that it was no man, but a ghoste which appeared to him. Now when this younge prince was lefte alone, and sate there solitarie, reioysing with himselfe for this gentle consolation, and good comforte, but yet very careful, and muche counting with himselfe who it shuld be or whence he shuld come which had thus spoken, and talked familiarly with him: beholde his forsayd frende came againe, and greating him cherfully, Arise Edwine (sayde he) and come in. Let passe this your carke and cares. Set your harte at rest, and take your quiet sleape. For the kinges minde is chaunged. Neither dothe he purpose nowe, or intend to doe yow any wronge, but rather to defend yowe, and accomplishe his promised fayth vnto yowe. For after he had shewed the Quene in secret that his purpose, which I told yowe of before, she dehorted him moste ernestly, and withdrew him from so euill, and so deadly an intention, saying: that it was in no wise mete for suche a king, of so greate prowe[ss]e, and honour, as he was, to sell his best, and derest frend, being now browght into straightes and miserie, for a litle gold. Nor that he should breake his faith, and promesse, which owght to be more estemed then al treasures, or not bide by his word for the coueit, and loue of monie. But to be shorte the king did euen as his Ladie had counselled him to doe. For he not only not betrayed, and yelded to thembassadours this his banished man Edwine: but helped him rather to the kingdome. For as sone as these embassadours were thus with deniall departed home againe, he gathered incontinētly a myghtie armie to conquer king Edelfrede. Whome he slewe without difficultie (bicause he marched forth against him hastely and with a weake and vnordred oste) in the borders of the Marchland men, at the Este syde of the riuer called Idle. For in deade kinge Edelfride had not time, and space enowgh grawnted him to gather all his force together, and to ioygne his powre with well disposing his hoste, and sowldiers in order. In this skirmishe Renier king Redwalds sonne was slayne. And thus Edwin according to the oracle which he had receiued, not only auoyded the dawnger of his most dedly enemie, but also by his death succeeded in thonor of his Souerainte, and kingdome. Now therfore to returne againe vnto my purpose, thowgh Bishop Pawline seriously preched the word of God, yet kinge Edwine slacked and lengered to beleaue him. Vsing yet for a certaine space, at diuers competent howres to sitte solitarie, (as I haue sayde before) and diligently to compte with himselfe, what were best to be donne and what religion was best to be folowed. At which solitary meditation of the prince this good and godly bishoppe Pawline entred on a daye in to the palace, and cominge to the kinge, laied his right hand on his heade and asked hym, whether he remembred that sygne, or no? The king sodenly trembled therat for feare. And when he wold haue fallen downe at Paulinus feate, the bishoppe lyfted him vppe, and spake after a familiar sorte thus vnto him: Behold o Soueraine Prince, by the bountifull hand and powre of our Lorde, and God, you haue eskaped the hande and vengeance of your moste hated, and dredfull enemie. Behold also, by his most gratiouse goodnes you haue obtained the Soueraintie of raigne, and rule of the kingdome. Remember now therfore the third thinge, which yowe promised him, and differ no lenger to performe, and accomplishe the same, by receauing his faithe, and keaping his commaundements, who hath deliuered you from your temporall aduersities, and exalted you to the honour, and maieste of a king. Whose holy will yf you will hereafter obey and euer more doe his pleasure, which by me he preacheth, and declareth to yowe, he will also deliuer you from the perpetuall tormente of hell, and make you partakener with him in heauen of eternall kingdome, and blesse without end.*

The character of such writing as this is unmistakeable, and it is difficult to see why Stapleton's translation should have been so generally neglected.† The familiar ease and picturesqueness of the prose invites comparison with North's translation of Plutarch: the description of Edwin, for example, sitting solitary outside the palace, inevitably reminds one of the similar description of Coriolanus at the hearth of Aufidius, one of the most telling passages in the *Life of Coriolanus*. Again, the lyrical phrases ('burning inwardly with close fyre of secret sorowe', 'in the greate sylence, and quyet of the mydde nyght', 'when other men were within at rest, and in their depe sleape', and so on),

* sig. Q3 et seq.

† A notable exception to this general neglect is provided by R. W. Chambers's *England before the Norman Conquest* (*University of London Intermediate Source-Books of History*, no. VII, Longmans, 1926). Citations from Stapleton's *Bede* cover about fifty pages of this work and include the entire passage I have quoted. The passages cited are chosen, of course, for their historical interest and they do not profess to reproduce Stapleton's version exactly, though Chambers notes that 'Bede, the first great scholar of the English Church, can best be rendered in the language of the time which gave us the Prayer Book and the English Bible'. Introduction, p. xxiv.

introduced to heighten the feeling at the appropriate moment, are admirably expressive. And then there is the drawing of the character of Edwin – his inwardness, pride, fidelity and courage – largely, of course, the work of Bede, but suitably emphasized by Stapleton, which gives to the passage, as the reader will himself judge, a concreteness and actuality which is none too common in historical writing. The book is, indeed, to use an expression of Saintsbury's, at least a quasi-classic. Yet it was not reprinted until 1930.* It has since been made available for the general reader by Philip Hereford in an edition which reproduces the exact text of the original, but in modern spelling.†

NICOLAS SANDER

The three English works of Nicolas Sander which are our present concern are *The Supper of our Lord* (1565), *The Rocke of the Church* (1567), and *A Treatise of the Images of Christ* (1567). The first of these is an exceedingly long book and can hardly be said to make exciting reading. The author's learning is beyond dispute, and, since he is engaged for the most part in closely reasoned argument, there is little room for what are sometimes called the amenities of literature. The style is necessarily plain and depends for its effect upon eloquence of the idea rather than of the word. As we should expect, therefore, the emphasis (here, as elsewhere, in fact) is upon 'invention' and 'disposition' rather than upon 'elocution'. In spite of a rigid economy of expression, practised even in the more rhetorical passages, the prose is marked by an exceptional clarity, and this is helped out by a natural, easy rhythm, which, in its turn, is determined by the even tenor of the thought. The two passages which follow must not be taken as characteristic of the whole work, except in so far as they are free from inflation or diffusion. They are intended, primarily, to illustrate the means which Sander employs to obtain variety within the limits of a style where verbal eloquence is of secondary importance. In the first, the directness and objectivity of the writing will be remarked:

> But on the other side, if Christ call one of them before him, who denieth his reall presence, & aske him why he did not

* See above, p. 45.

† *The Ecclesiastical History of the English People, by the Venerable Bede. Edited by Philip Hereford. With an Introduction by the late Father Bede Jarrett, O.P.* (1935).

beleue the Sacrament of the altar to be the body of Christe: what will he answer for him selfe?

Will he say? Syr I beleued your body to sit at the right hand of God, the Father, and therefore that your body was not in the Priestes hand? Why then thinkest thou, that I am not able to make the same, which is at the right hand of my father, to be also present vnder the form of bread? Sir whether you be able or no, I can not say, but I haue hard many preachers tel, ꝧ one body cā not be at one time in diuerse places. O howe dreadfully would Christ answere in this case? Did not those preachers, whom thou pretēdest to folow, say alwaies: they preached to thee the sincere word of God? Did they not by that colour ouerthrow monasteries, Churches, altars, images of Saintes, and mine owne image and crosse? Did they not denie the sacrifice of the Masse, praing for the dead, and such like auncient vsages, only for pretence of the word of God? And now see, how inexcusable they and thou art. I said, *Take, eate, this is my body*. I said this to twelue men, I gaue eche of them my body, & bad them make that thing, as it is written in the Gospel. I shewed at Capharnaum, that I was signed of my Father, and equall with him in power. they them selues beleue that I made al creatures, places, times, of nothing: and now is it doubted how I am able to make my body present vnder the form of bread in diuerse places?

Yea to maintaine the better ẏͤ argument against my allmighty power, they say, I entred not into my disciples, the dores being shut: But eyther preuented the shutting of them contrary to the wordes of my Gospell, or came in by the window (as theues do) or by some hole (as crepers doe) yea any thing is soner beleued then my diuine strength and working. Thou hypocrite, seing the word of God hath it written foure tymes in the new testament, *This is my body*: how comest thou to talke with me of my sittīg in heauen, as though one of my workes were contrary to the other. If in dede thou haddest bene humbly perswaded, that I were God, thou wouldest not measure my allmightie power by thy simple wit. Thou art twise condemned: first, for deniall of a truth, and againe for denying it against my expresse word: which thou pretendest to esteme, and yet pronōucest it false.*

In the next passage, which deals with 'what the supper of Christ is', we would call attention especially to the *pattern* of the style. The reader will observe how a single theme informs the whole passage, viz. the supernatural character of the Eucharist under the image of a banquet, and how the argument, representing successively the *idea* of the Last Supper, its

* *The Supper of our Lord*, sig. PPpp1^{v}.

Institution, its Matter and Form, and finally its Effect, is fashioned in accordance with this theme. The passage is cited in a slightly shortened form:

> When a man departeth from his frends taking his leaue with a banket, it is lyke that his banket shalbe, according to his habilitie, full of deinty dishes and costly cates, specially if it be published before and long time looked for, as Christes banket was . . .
>
> Christ in a parable describing the great supper made at the mariage of the kinges sonne which him self was, telleth of oxen and other fatlings kylled and made readie for that purpose. And now shal we suppose, that the sonne of the king of heauen making a parting supper vnto his best beloued and the pillours of all his Church, doth geue them outwardly at his farewel none other deynties besides common bread and wine sanctified in vse only, and not consecrated in substance?
>
> A litle before, he had eaten with the same Apostles the paschall lambe, and rising from that table (as being the table of Moyses rather than of Christ) he wasshed his Apostles feete to make them meete for a greater mysterie. And sitting doune againe he toke bread and wine, not as the dishes of his banket, but as matter and stuff wherof he wold make his owne supper. For it is to be well weighed, that this banket is called our Lords supper, that is to say, made, and ministred, and fornished by Christ himselfe. He now did not send S. Iohn & S. Peter to prepare his supper (as he sent them to make ready the Paschall lambe) Christ in his owne supper is the prouider and maker of it. He taketh bread and wine into his holy handes, intēding lyke a most conning workeman, of simple and litle stuff to make the greatest and finest feast that euer was hard of.
>
> It is a great glorie in the profession of cookery, to be able to make of one kind of stuff (as for example of egs alone) sixtene or twenty diuerse dishes. But to doe that feate, much labour many spices and sauces, great compositions and mixtures are required. Christ in stede of all those shyfts vsed blessing, & working words of thankes geuing, which were so sure to worke their intent, that some men haue doubted, whether he gaue thanks first, because he forsaw the whole purpose out of hand should be obtained as him selfe wished, or else (which is more probable) whether the very working of the feate were not the selfe thankes geuing for the worke. For his blessing and thankes geuing was the sayng ouer the bread, *This is my body*: and ouer the wine, *This is my blood* . . . The which body and blood his Apostles eating and drinking were made partakers of ye greatest bāket, that euer was made in earth.
>
> For the better vnderstanding wherof it maye please the

reader to repete in his minde, how God in the beginning adorned this world, first with angels and heauenly spirits. Secondly with the heauens them selues. Thirdly with the elements of fyer, ayer, water and earth. And as the angels occupie the highest place, so doe the heauens with the lights and starres in them occupie the second place, & the foure elements are beneth them. When things were come after this sorte from the highest order of Seraphins to the earth, which is the lowest element of all, then it pleased the wysedome of God to make as it were a reuolt of all things, and to returne his creatures from the bottom of the earth vpward againe towards him selfe. He therefore made the earth to bring forth grene grasse with all such kind of things as haue *animam vegetatiuam*, that is to saye, as liue and are quick by the strength which they haue in them selues to grow and encreace, of which kinde all herbes, springs and trees be. Aboue those in a higher degre were byrdes, fishes & beasts, which haue a life sensitiue, being able (those that be perfit) to moue from place to place.

Last of all God made man, who hath not only the vegetatiue power and sensitiue in his soule, but also reason and vnderstanding. In whose body are the vertues of the foure elements, with the influēce of the heauens, in whose soule is free will and power to gouern, agreable to the nature of angels and of heauenly spirits. For which cause this creature hath bene worthely called, euen of the Christen Philosophers, Microcosmos, a lytle world . . .

Now when the sonne of God taking pitie, that this litle world the worke of his great power was by the deuyll seduced, came doune and toke flesh of the virgyn Mary, being true God and true man in one person. At that tyme were all things briefly brought again to God, whence they first were created & brought forth. Christ aboue is all in one. In his Godhed, he is all that is aboue the heauens, and that fylleth the world. In his manhod which is the footestole of God, he is all that is in, or vnder the heauens. In this manhod are all creatures most perfectly compiled, without all blemmysh of nature, of mynd or of body. So that seing this body of Christ, (wherein also the fullness of Godhead dwelleth) is geuen and eaten at a banket, there is no doubt but the same is such a banket, as can not be made with all the creatures of heauen and earth gathered together. In this one dysh is a composition most delicate of angels, heauens, elements, of herbes, fysshes, byrds, beasts, of reasonable men, and of God hym selfe. No kind of salit, meate, sauce, fruyts, confection, no kynde of wyne, aqua vite, aqua composita, liquors, syrops can be found in nature, made by arte, deuysed by wyt, but it is all set vppon this table, and that in a small rome, where it cloyeth not with the abundance, ne annoyeth with the vncleane handling, it fylleth without lothsomnes, it prouoketh the appetite without daunger of surfeating. To be shorte, were it not a banket prouided by the sonne of God, no man wold think it possible, to haue any such feast made in the desert of this wycked world.*

The characteristic simplicity, literalness and economy of expression of the foregoing passages will again be observed in the following context from *The Rocke of the Churche*, which records the death of St. Peter. It will be noted how ease is sacrificed for the sake of compression in the second sentence:

> Neither did S. Peter only come to Rome, and preache at Rome for a tyme, but he also died there, ād so died there, that it appered euidently God would haue him die no where els. For whereas (according to the duty of the chiefe pastour) he came to Rome chiefely to saue his flocke there from the raging furie of Simon Magus the capitaine of al heretiks (who began to be worshipped for a God in Rome) whē by his praier he had caused the deuils who caryed Simon Magus along in the ayer, to let him fall (whereupon his death insued shortlie after) the Emperour Nero (who toke no small delight in the sorcerie of Simon Magus) being sore offended with S. Peters dede, sought straight waies his apprehension and destruction.
>
> At that tyme the Christians being verie loth to be depriued of so good a pastour as S. Peter was, with much intreating and many teares praied him to goe out of the way, and to saue himselfe. At whose requeste Saint Peter (otherwise vnwilling therevnto) beganne to take his iourney out of the citie.
>
> But when he was come to the gate, he seeth Christ comming toward him, whome he adoring said, *Domine quo vadis*, O Lord, whether goest thow? Christ said vnto him, *venio Romam iterum crucifigi*. I come to Rome to be crucified againe. Peter vnderstoode thereby, that Christ would suffer in him at Rome, who suffereth in euery of his members, not by paine of bodie, but by compassion of pitie, or rather by the greatenes of glorie which is gotten to him by the victoriouse death which his Saints are put vnto.
>
> Vpon this vision Peter returned againe into the Citie of Rome, and being taken, he was putte to death vppon the crosse with his head downward: so that Christ himselfe appointed Rome to be the place, where S. Peter should rest.†

Finally, *A Treatise of the Images of Christ* provides a model of lucid exposition, which is worth the closest scrutiny. Again, we give the passage in a somewhat shortened form:

> Here it is to be noted, that euery real thing which is in this worlde, hath both a nature of his owne, and also a seueral

* ibid., sig. F1–2.

† sig. V3.

subsistence, or being, the which subsistence in reasonable substaunce, is called *a person*. For example: My nature is to be a reasonable Creature, which hath life and sense. My person is that kinde of being, wherein my nature is so limited, and fitted, or made apt for me alone, that it semeth none other creature beside me, in al the worlde.

As therefore euery man, yea euery thing hath a Nature, and a Person, or a seueral Subsistence: so eche of them may haue an Image of it selfe, but not after one sorte.

For a mans nature may onely be represented by a natural Image, that is to say, by an other thing which taketh of him the same nature, which him selfe hath. For euery thing begetteth an other thing like vnto it selfe, as when the sonne is naturally begotten of his Father, then he is made the natural Image of his Father.

In so much that if the Father be God by nature, the Sonne begotten of him must needes be God by nature. If the Father be man, the sonne also must haue mans nature, and thereby he is the natural Image of his Father.

But although a mans nature can by no means be expressed by art, yet his person, or at the least wise his outwarde shape may be right wel expressed, and represented, by grauing, painting, or otherwise by fashioning ye same in wax, earth, or like matter. The cause why the shape of our Persons may be represented by arte, and not our natures, is, for that, the Artificer who worketh by his own knoledge, is able to conceiue in his vnderstanding, and afterward to foorme outwardly that proper shape of euery thing which he perceiueth by his senses that it hath. But the inward nature which he neuer saw, nor was able to see naked, & as it is in it self, that nature he is not able to conceiue in his owne Imagination, & therefore he can draw foorth no resemblance thereof.

And that al artificial Images do represent the shape of our persons, and not our natures, the very experiēce & cōmon vse of speaking fully declareth. For if wee come where an Image of *Cicero* standeth, a right wise man may, and sometimes doth say, *Here is Cicero*, or *this is a man*, taking the word *man*, for a thing which beareth and signifieth the person, and not the nature of a man. For albeit that be no propre speach, to say of the Image of S. Paule, *This is S. Paule*: yet it is vsed, because the names of the thinges them selues are often times in common speach geuen to their signes and Images.

But certainely no meane wise man comming to the same Image of S. Paul or of Cicero, did, wil, or can iustly say, *This is a liuing or a reasonable creature.*

* * *

The brief summe is, that a natural Image expresseth and imitateth the verie substance of that thing, whose Image it is: the artificial Image expresseth onlie the shape of the person and propriety of anie thing, according to ỷ foorm, which the artificer doth iustly conceaue thereof.

Seing then an Image made by art is not able to expresse the natural substāce of any thing, and yet the personal proprietie that is resembled, can not be sette before our eyes without some substance or other: *the artificial Image must borrow an other substance*, wherein it may shew his own representation.

That other substance, whether it be wood, stone, gold, paper, or any like stuffe is not anie essential part of an Image in it self, although it be the material part of this, or of that Image, as the which can not be shewed to our eyes, without some like matter.

* * *

If then the Image may be separated by our vnderstanding from the material substance wherein it is shewed, as sone as we haue printed the said Image in our own head and mind: either it hath no truth at al to be referred vnto (and thē it is a vaine Idol, and onlie a phantastical thing) or if it be an Image of a truth, it hath none other real person or proprietie to stay in, besyde that truthe whereof it is the Image, & therunto it is straight waies referred by him, that vnderstādeth whose Image it is. For he saith or thinketh immediatlie, *this is Christ*, or, *this is S. Peter*, or, *this is our Lady*, ioyning the Image to that truth, where vnto it belongeth.

So that, if we see the Image of Christ crucified, we straight lay aside the brasse, yron, or wood where vpon that Image was drawen or made, and we apprehend Christ himself, to whose person that Image doth leade vs.*

There is nothing obsolete about *this* writing. Like the style of the Brobdingnagians, it is 'clear, masculine, and smooth', multiplying no unnecessary words and paying careful attention to the organization of the period and the paragraph. It is not the prose of formal periods. The sentences run on easily, clause being added to clause to enlarge and complete the argument. The words are ordered so that the stress falls where the sense requires it. In short, the emphasis is upon structure and not upon ornament, and the result is a piece of writing of sustained perspicuity and even tenor, the thought seeming to mould the style and the style reacting to mould the thought.

* sig. $H5^v$ et seq.

ROBERT POINTZ

A direct answer was given to Jewel's challenge – that the first six hundred years after Christ could furnish no witness to the Catholic doctrine of the Eucharist – by Robert Pointz's *Testimonies for the Real Presence* (1566). The reply takes the form of a number of translated passages from SS. Chrysostom, Cyril, Cyprian, Hilary, Augustine and Ambrose with a following exposition. Pointz is, perhaps, the most urbane of the Recusant writers (William Allen resembles him in this), and, eschewing all rhetorical tricks, relies almost entirely in this, his one work, upon the power of reason to persuade his reader. The single passage quoted, from one of his 'simple notes', has been taken, more or less, at random. It is, however, an average example of Pointz's method. The English is simple, clear and exact; the rhythm natural and easy. The argument, which, it will be observed, is informed and animated by a single idea, moves grave and unhurried to its appointed close, its cogency not a little dependent upon the felicitous spacing. The general manner of the expression is marked by the due proportion of reason and discourse.

> To begin now with the sixth Chapiter of S. Jhon, that you may more plainly conceaue of what force that place is to proue the real presence of Christes flesh and blood in the blessed Sacrament, and also howe S. Chrysostoms words here doe come in: You shal first vnderstand, that the Iewes of Capharnaum (whiche thereof are commonly called Capharnites) after they had ben miraculously fede of Christ with fiue barly loues & two fishes being them selues in nomber about fyue thousand, retorned vnto Christ again, looking for some other like banket: and to prouoke him the more as they thought, began to bragge how their fathers dyd eate Manna in the desert, doing him to vnderstād thereby if he would get credite amōgst them, he should in like sort feed thē. Whereuppon our sauiur tooke occasion to declare vnto them before hand, that miraculous & heauēly foode which he minded afterward to ordein in his last supper & which should not only aunswere their Manna: but so far passe the same as a true body passeth a shadow. And therefore he saied vnto them, the bread which I shall geue is my flesh. & that he ment by those wordes to leaue his true flesh in dede to be eatē in stede of their Mañа: it appereth by that which foloweth most euidently. For whereas the Capharnite Iewes gruged strait way saying: how cā this man geue vs his flesh to eat? imagininge suche a grosse and homly eatynge

of Christes fleashe as of other common fleshe which is bought in the shābles, he did not take away that scruple as our Protestātes do now a dayes with saying ỷ it should be a bare figure ouly [*sic*], or that they should eate bread only and not fleshe, and feed on hym only spiritually by fayth. He sayde none of all these thinges but cleane contrary to confound their gruging infidelity & to cōfirme his former words added ther vnto other of more vehemēce saying: *verely, verely, I say vnto you, but if ye eate the flesh of the sōne of man and drinke his bloode, ye shall not haue lyfe in you*, with many moe of lyke perspicuity and playnesse. Nowe if Christ had mente by these first wordes a figure or tokē only of his fleshe, how easely might he haue satisfied the Iewes, who coulde so well away with figures beinge allwayes vsed therunto in Moyses Law. And what likelyhood is there, ỷ he being so merciful a Sauiour vnto al men, and bearing such a special affection to hys countrimen, that he neuer departed from them, but witnessed that he was chiefly sent vnto the lost shepe of I[s]rael, would not only not appease their grudging, but more increase ẏͤ same? In so muche that in the ende they quite forsoke him saying: this is an hard talke, who can heare him? whereas if he hadde ment a bare signe or figure, by telling the truth only, he might haue kept them continually in his company. Truely no man (I suppose) that thinketh wel of God, can imagine any such vnmercifulnes to haue bene in Christ. And therefore seing he made no such interpretation, but cōtrariwise immediatly after their grudging, threatned thē, that onlesse they did eat his flesh and drinke his blood they should not haue life, & confirmed the same with his accustomed othe *verily, verily*: it seemeth vnto me a very strong argument, ỷ his meaning was to promise thē his true naturall flesh, & not a figure thereof only.*

JOHN FOWLER

The literary interest of John Fowler's translation of Peter Frarin's *An Oration Against the Vnlawfull Insurrections of the Protestantes of our time* (1566) is slight. The work was intended as a refutation of those who asserted that Catholics desired to disturb the Commonwealth, and it endeavours to show that in various countries that was the very object of the Reformers rather than the Catholics. In this way it forms part of the frontal attack upon the position of the Protestant Reformers in our country. It alludes to most of the well-known names connected with the Reformation and reproduces in particular the popular scandals about Luther, Calvin and Beza. The

* sig. C1v.

stories of the martyrdoms of the Catholics are told sometimes in revolting detail, and the greater number of the woodcuts of the Table refer to these. Each of these woodcuts (thirty-six in all) is accompanied by some lines of doggerel by way of explanation. They were introduced, we are given to understand, for the benefit of those who could not read. The translation is vigorous and is usually couched in highly rhetorical language, suitable to the character of the original, but it is hardly worth quoting here.

WILLIAM ALLEN

The most considerable writer who took part in The Great Controversy outside the group of Wykehamists we have just been discussing was William Allen. And we would first call attention to a remarkable judgement passed on Allen's style by a writer, who could hardly be accused of partisanship, more than a hundred years ago, a judgement which subscribes in a quite unusual way to the statement of J. S. Phillimore quoted at the beginning of this book.* We refer to the following:

> His English style was incomparable. At once dignified and simple; clear and concise; choice in terms without the slightest affectation; and full of an impassioned liveliness which rivetted the attention even to his gravest disquisitions; it stood then wholly unrivalled, and would even now furnish no unworthy model. Such however is the weakness, and it is almost blameless, of human prejudice, that the merits of the writer were condemned to share in the abomination of his doctrines, and that *an example which might have anticipated the gradual progress of nearly a century in the improvement of English prose* was rejected because he who set it was a rebel and a Papist.†

This statement has reference, of course, to the whole of Allen's works, and since we are here concerned with only two of these, viz. *A Defense and Declaration of the Catholike Churchies Doctrine, touching Purgatory* (1565) and *A Treatise made in defence of the lauful power and authoritie of Priesthod to remitte sinnes* (1567), it will be readily understood that we shall not be in a position fairly to judge its applicability to Allen's writings until, in the later pages of this book, we shall have completed our survey

* See p. 5.

† Memoir of Cardinal Allen from *Portraits of Illustrious Personages of Great Britain*, Vol. III, p. 6, by Edmund Lodge, London, 1825. The italics are mine.

of this author. For the present, therefore, while bearing it carefully in mind, let us turn to some statements by Allen himself on the question of his style.

The first comes from the preface to the second book of *A Defense and Declaration*. After alluding, in reference to Book I, to 'a certaine bitter taediousnesse bothe in the writer, and the reader', he then goes on to say:

> But the wearinesse of that roughe part, which might bothe by the weight of the matter, and allso by my rude handeling, quickely arise to the studious reader, I shall in this booke wholy wype away: not by arte or pleasaunt fall of wordes, which in plaine dealing is not much requisite, but by the singulare comforte of oure cause.

In other words, he intends to pursue the method of the plain style as being most suitable to the seriousness of the subject he has in hand, and (so we gather) he means to rely upon his own enthusiasm and fervour and the strong appeal of the subject to keep the interest of the reader going.

In a second passage from the preface to *A Treatise*, which affirms his deep sincerity and his singleness of aim, he promises

> yͭ I wil deal sincerly in al poynts & faythfully: I wil not couer my selfe nor yͤ light of yͤ cause in cloud of words, neither by any artificial sleight (as new doctours now a daies oftē doo) circūuēt yͤ sense of him yͭ is most simple, such indifferēcy shalbe vsed euery where in trial of yͤ truth, yͭ I wil seme for his sak, to doubt of yͤ matter my selfe.

Further statements, also from *A Treatise*, relative to his aim in exposition, point to his desire to enlighten the unlearned ('the simple, whō I would most helpe in these matters', i.e. in the matter of binding and loosing; 'the simple and the sinful . . . that can not in their lacke of intelligence, compare reason to reason, nor gather one trueth of an other, and therefore to their mouthes we must chewe all meates verie small'), and notably the following:

> I wil studie first, clearly to open the meaning of that, whereon we stande, and then to go through the whole question with as much light and breuitie as I can: tempering my self, as much as I may, from al such subteltie, as the depth of so grounded a conclusion, and the learned disputatiōs of Schoolmen might driue me vnto. Wherein, I am content, rather to followe the desire & contentation of the Reader, then to satisfie my owne appetite, which I feele in my selfe, to be somwhat more greedie

of matter sometimes, then ẏͤ common people, whome I study moste to helpe, can wel beare . . . yet . . . they must learne to abide the orderlie methode.*

In short, Allen's aims were precisely those which were set forth by Dr. Harding, and which have been described above as lucidity, truthfulness and propriety.† Added to this, there is the same reliance upon logical precept in his method of exposition (indicated in such words as 'the orderlie methode' above) as we find in Harding and his fellow Wykehamists, with the same frequent recourse to the syllogism as the final court of appeal.

The following context will serve to illustrate Allen's 'orderlie methode' in presenting an argument. Starting with the idea that Sin is Debt and that we are all, therefore, the debtors of Almighty God, he proceeds to enunciate the necessity for liquidating the debt hereafter according to the principles of justice, and cites St. Jerome, the ancient hermits, the monastic institutions, etc., as witnesses to this necessity:

She [Paula] well considered (for it was the doctrine of that holy tyme) that euery sinne be it neuer so small or common, doth indebt the offender vnto God: and therfore the iustest person that liueth (excepting Christe, and for his honour his moother) as S. Augustine saith must confesse debte, and crye for pardon by oure maisters praier: *Dimitte nobis debita nostra:* forgiue vs oure debts. the whiche, because they be debt, must ether be pardoned by praier, or paide by paine. And therfore being not here remitted, or not satisfied by worthy poonishment in this liefe, they must of iustice be purged after oure departure, according to the numbre of theime and the negligence of the offender. And this faithe of Purgatory and respecte of Goddes iudgements to come, feared the holyest persons that euer were in goddes Churche. This droue many a blessed man to perpetuall paenaunce: this broght Hierom him sellfe in to the wildernesse of *Syria*, there to lament the lapse of his fraile youthe, euer in expectation of this call: *Exi foras Hieronime* Coom out Hierom: this filled the desertes with many a noble heremite, this raysed vppe the cloisters and all the holy houses of mowrning and praiers in the whole worlde, and hathe in all agyes appeared bothe in the wordes and woorkes of all Christen people, as we shal better a none declare.‡

A second passage introduces us to an element in Allen's style

* *A Treatise*, sigs. E2v, H1, R2v. † p. 70.
‡ *A Defense and Declaration*, sig. G4.

which must not be overlooked. The passage is intended to meet a difficulty that some may feel in regard to the practice of Confession and to evoke a response. In spite of the three paragraph divisions it depends neither upon structural arrangement nor the progress of the thought to achieve this end; indeed, it appears to be quite haphazard in structure and certainly defies ordinary analysis, its appeal lying rather in a happy balance of thought and feeling which finds expression in an unquestioned appropriateness of word and rhythm. Here is the passage:

> Harde it semeth, I knowe to the wordlinges and to the weake, (and so harde, yͭ neuer man could haue brought it into the Churche, much lesse to haue continued it so long, if it had not proceded from the precept of Christes own mouth) to open the whole harte and minde to man. And it can not but be ioyned with some naturall bashefullnesse, in this oure frailtie, to vtter that to an other, whiche in it selfe, of what sorte of sinne so euer it be, is most filthie and lothsome. But knowing and feeling vndoubtedly, that the continual close keping thereof in the couert of oure conscience, is much more great and greuous tormente, and therwith conceiuing Christes ordinaunce to be suche, that no consideration of oure imbecillitie, nor contrarie liking of oure phātasie, may or ought to withdrawe vs from that thing, which for vs all, is accompted moste conuenient, and necessarie, let vs neuer by oure disobedient willes, striue a gainste Goddes wisdome.
>
> If the burden therefore, of confession seeme to any man intolerable, as in deede it is not, but verie pleasaunt to all suche as haue tasted howe swete Christe is, lette him ease it with earnest consideration, that it is exceding commodious to breake the pride of mans harte, & to make him knowe him self. And, if that any burdē of shamfastnesse appeare in yͤ vttering of his sinnes, he maye learne to take it gladly as some worthie payne for his offences, and some peece of recompence and satisfaction for the same. It pleased God at the first fall of oure fathers, to ioyne shame and some confusion to sinne, by which they were bashful at the voice of God, & of their owne nakednes. Seing that of his infinite wisdome, it pleased him to make yt the first punishment for sinne, and to laye it upō his own Sonnes most innocent person, in his contemptible death and manifold rebukes sufferred for oure sinnes and sakes, lette vs not disdaine to bear some portion therof in this sacrament of confession, for the release of oure owne sinnes. That verie shamefastnes so much abhorred and so much respected shal often preserue man from further offending, whereof he knoweth after, he muste againe so soone before God and his minister be rebuked.

> But what shoulde we talke of so smal a lette, wher the cōfort of opening oure sores and woundes to a mā, ẏᵗ by nature is a like sinner, and by vse of hearing manie faultes, can not muche marueile at oures, and by office there is moste secret, tender, and carefull ouer vs, what should we talke of other impedimentes, where this comfortable motion is so great? What comforte can be more, thē to haue suche a frend, who, for that I ioyne with him, yea euen my owne soule to his, after the dearest maner and moste secret sorte, must needes be to me as a ful staye in al doubtes of conscience, a witnesse of my sorowfull harte, an intercessour for my sinnes, a suerty before God for my amending, a minister in my reconciliation, and one that vnder Christ (as S. Clement also saieth) shal both beare my sinnes vpon him selfe, and take charge of me to saluation? In which case me thinke surely, man is after a sorte set in merueilous quietnesse, and almost discharged euen of him selfe, & his owne custody, whiles he giueth ouer his owne aduise & iudgement, and wholly hangeth in earth vpon him, whome God hath appoynted to be his pastour, and gouernoure of his soule.*

Let us repeat, the attractiveness and the appeal of such writing is not to be found in the structural arrangement of the matter nor in the progress of the thought, but rather in the mind of the writer. Allen's own words would lead us to some such conclusion, where he asserts, in the contexts quoted above, his 'indifferency', and his desire to *temper himself* 'from al such subteltie, as the depth of so grounded a conclusion, and the learned disputatiōs of Schoolmen' might drive him to, etc. Systematical arrangement, indeed, is not really necessary (it might definitely be out of place) in this style of writing, and the same thing is true of organized thinking; in fact, we will go so far as to suggest that the equivocation in the use of the *idea* of contemptuous, as it is applied first to Adam and Eve in the sense of 'appeared contemptuous in their own eyes' (shamefastness) and then to Christ in the sense of 'contemptuous in the eyes of others' (contemptible), in the above passage, adds to the attractiveness of such writing rather than detracts from it. If we may use a rather general term we should describe this style as *personal*, and it is this personal element in Allen's style which has called forth such approving epithets as 'princely', 'grave' (Edmund Bolton, *Hypercritica*), 'dignified', 'choice', etc. (Edmund Lodge, above), and which we shall refer to again

* *A Treatise*, sigs. Q3ᵛ–5.

when we come to consider his later writings. Meanwhile, let us very briefly allude to certain other elements in Allen's prose which contribute to the 'liveliness' of his writing.

We may note first his use of the common device of antithesis, occasionally reinforced by alliteration. This device he employs more frequently than any other, but it is always used with discretion and is never tedious. It may be observed in such phrases as 'pardoned by praier, or paide by paine' (cited in the 'Paula' passage above) or in such a context as the following:

> This socyety is called in oure crede, *communio sanctorum*, the communion of Sanctes . . . This happy socyety, is not inpared by any distance of place, by diuersity off goddes giftes, by inequalyty off estates, nor by chaunge of liefe: so farre as the vnity of goddes spirit reacheth, so farr this fellowship extendethe, this city is as large, as the benefite of Christes deathe takethe place. Yea withein all the compasse of his kingdom, this felloweship is fownde. The soules and sanctes in heauen, the faithful people in earth, the chosen childrē that suffer chastisement in Purgatorye, are, by the perfect bond of this vnity, as one abundeth, redy to serue the other, as one lacketh, to craue of the other. The soules happely promoted to the ioye of Christes blessed kyngdom, in this vnitye and knotte of loue, perpetually praye for the doubtfull state, of theyre owne fellowes benethe: the carefull condition of the membres belowe, contynually criethe for helpe at theire hādes in heauen a boue. Nowe the mēbres of Christes Church here yet trauelling in earthe, they pray together, they faste together, they desire together, they deserue together . . .*

His occasional use of a form of *paronomasia* appears in such expressions (all from *A Defense*) as 'paide by paine' (above); 'they desire together, they deserue together' (above); 'the streames of his holy blodde and beames off his grace'. And here is an example of one of the stock figures of rhetoric of the controversialist, named in the manuals *ecphronesis* (outcry):

> O oure cursed time. O corrupte conditions: this beaste [Calvin] writeth thus ageinst oure blessed sauiours death, and ageinst the sufficiency of the abundant price of our redemption: and yet he lieueth in mannes memory, yea his bookes be greedely redde, redde? Nay by suche as woulde be counted the chiefe of the cleargie, and beare bishops names, they are commaunded to be redde: and the very booke wherein this and all other detestable doctrine is vttered, especially by theire authoritie commendid to the simple curates study: that they might there

* *A Defense*, sig. R4.

THE PARLIAMENT OF CHRYSTE

From T. Heskyns's book of that title, printed by William Silvius (Antwerp, 1566)

> lerne closely in deuilishe bookes, such wicked haeresies as the preachers theimeselues dare not yet in the light of the worlde vtter nor maintaine.*

On the whole, however, such devices are used sparingly in the two works we have been considering, and nowhere are they allowed to overrun their proper function. It is his racy locutions and picturesque expressions rather than his use of the Figures which contribute most certainly to Allen's liveliness of style. Some of these we have already met ('cloud of words', 'to their mouthes we must chewe all meates verie small', 'in the couert of oure conscience'); further examples are: 'wrething or wraesting' (an Elizabethan commonplace for 'pervert the meaning of'), 'setting not a butten by theyme all', 'mighte haue wonne of all the worlde, two games at a clappe', 'how fast they will tennesse one to another in taulke' (i.e. 'toss to and fro like a ball at tennis'), 'owle light or mooneshyne I trowe, or mirke midnight were more fit for theyre darke workes and doctrine, oure way is ouer muche trodden for theues'.

THOMAS HESKYNS

In spite of its immense length and the enormous number of references to the Bible, the Fathers, and the Doctors of the Church, *The Parliament of Chryste* (1566), which was Thomas Heskyns's sole contribution to the Recusant attack on Jewel, is by no means a dull book, and it deserves the very careful consideration of the student of English prose. The writer himself points out that it was intended for the general reader –

> wishinge that this my laboure might be profitable to the simple and vnlearned, for whose helpe I haue most speciallie taken yt, I haue framed my writing, as neare as the matter will suffre, to their capacities –†

and in a particularly pertinent context he tells us that he writes in the 'plain' style as most suitable for setting out the plain truth:

> Nowe yowe vnderstand, M. Iuell, what I haue here doen, to the whiche yf either yowe or anie other for yowe shall by railing Rethorike make a pretended answer, I do yowe to witte, that I will not vouchsafe to putt my penne to the papire for that kinde of answer. For I haue begonne with yowe in an other sort, and like a diuine, railing I haue left to ruffins and skoldes, and coolours of persuasions to rethoricians, directlie according

* ibid., sig. E6.

† The Prologue to the Gentle Reader.

to my profession with all plain trueth haue I proceaded. Yf answere therefor shall be made, let yt be either a direct answere or none. Direct answer ys soche as I make to yow, where yowe abuse the vnderstāding of the scripture, or doctour, to proue the same vnto yowe: where yowe falsilie [falsifie], to alleage the place truely: where yowe corrupt, to shewe the right saing, when yowe adde and put to, to declare what yowe adde and put to: whē yowe leaue oute, to expresse the woordes so by yowe left oute.*

The book is a model of execution – the theme of 'Christes Parliament house' is never lost sight of and the unity of the thesis is carefully preserved by the constructional arrangement.

We will confine our attention to two short passages only from this work, which illustrate some of the more interesting features of Heskyns's style. The first, which deals with the question of the open Bible, is as follows:

Howe little incitament of vertue appeareth to be in the Ballettes of Salomon? Yea raitheir howe vngodlie and wanton seme they to be? raither in the outwarde face teaching, and prouoking wantonnesse, then godlynesse of life. In the first chapiter ye reade thus: O howe faire arte thowe my loue, howe fair arte thowe. Thowe hauest doues eies, O howe fair arte thowe, my beloued, howe well fawoured arte thowe. Owre bed ys deckt with flowres, the syllinges of oure house are Cedre tree. And again: O stand vppe my loue my beautifull and come. For lo, the wynter ys nowe past, the rain ys awaie and gone. The flowres are comed vppe in the feldes, the tyme of the birdes syngynge ys comed, and the voice of the Turtle doue ys heard in oure lande. The figge tree bringeth furthe her figges, and the Vines beare blossomes, and haue a good smell. O stande vppe my loue, my beautyfull, and come my doue oute of the caues of the Rockke, oute of the holls of the walls. O let me see thy coũtenāce, and heare thy voice. For swete ys thie voice, and fair ys thie face, &c. Like vnto this ys all that booke. What can the vnlearned finde, or vnderstande here? any thinge to edificacion of godlie life? or rather (as ys saied) a prouocation to wanton life?

Yet Iesus Sonne of Syrac semeth to haue more vnsemelie woordes then theise, yea so vnsemelie, as an honest mē wolde be ashamed to speake them, as I also wolde be ashamed to wryte thē, yf they were not scripture. He speaking of an harlotte, writeth thus: Like as one that goeth by the waie, and ys thriftie, so shall she open her mouth, and drynke of euerie next water, that she maie gette. By euerie hedge shall she sitte her downe, and open her quoiuer to euerie arrowe.

* Address to Jewel.

What trifeling, what iestyng, what pastime, I haue heard and seen vpon the reading, and rehersall of this texte, and what vnseemlie, and vnchaist woordes haue fallen oute by occasiō of the same, yt ys vnmeete in this place to be rehersed. But this I will reporte, for that trulie as God liueth, I know yt to be true. This texte was spoken in the presence of a good vertueouse gentlewoman, and one that feared God, and she misliking the same, yt was auouched to her to be scripture. The booke was turned, the place was red, she exclamed, and saied: that yf the scripture had soche bawdie woordes, she wolde no more beleue the scripture. for yt was naught. with mo soche like woordes, which nowe memorie reteyneth not.

Maye not this grieue a christian heart, that the scriptures Gods holie woorde shoulde be thus blasphemed? And what ys the cause of yt? verilie bicause they be made common to their handes, that vnderstande them not. That this place was not vnderstanded of them that handeled the same, as ys afore saied, yt ys more manifest then I nede reporte. For the effecte well proueth yt.*

'We have forgotten', writes R. W. Chambers, 'how many people in the Sixteenth Century had the power of writing a glorious prose style – straightforward, vivid, simple in the best sense, essentially dramatic.† The subject of the second extract is the inconsistency (as the writer feels) of the Protestants in respect of the Order of the Blessed Sacrament. It is little more than a short sketch, but it is worth attention on account of the careful arrangement of the material.

I remembe[r] the Somer before I wrote this rude woorke, I was nere vnto this man (whom I terme the Proclamer) [Jewel] within whose iurisdictiō one of his ministres ministring the communion to a woman, gaue her to drinke a cuppe of ale in stead of wine. Whiche when this man vnderstoode, no entreatie, no desire, no letters of mē of woorshippe of the Same contrie might appease his displeasure, nor obtein pardon for the offender, but open penance must he do in diuerse places. And certen I am that he was so inioined, and did parte er I departed the contrie. I mislike not that an offender was punished, but I moche mislike that they so straietlie punishe the breach of their disordre, and they them selues breake the ordre of the catholique Churche. When I heard of this correction, ther came to my minde the straunge conscience of the high preistes of the Iewes, who made no conscience in the compasing of the death of Chryst, and yet when Iudas brought the

* sig. B5v–6. The Scripture references are *Canticles* i. 15–17, ii. 10–14, and *Ecclesiasticus* xxvi. 12.

† *Continuity of English Prose*, as before, p. clxxii.

moneie again to them whiche they gaue him to betraie his master, here their consciences were spiced, and they saied, those pence might not be cast in the Threasurie, bycause yt ys the price of bloode. Their consciences suffred them to make awaie Chryste, whiche was incomparablie a more heinouse offence, and yet their consciences grudged that those plates shoulde be put in to the treasurie, whiche was but a small matter.

So to impugne the trueth of Chryst, to take awaie his bodie and bloode from vs in the Sacrament, and as yt were, to make Chryst awaie, to transgresse the order of the catholique Churche, yt ys easie ynough to their cōsciences. But when they haue taken the fatte and swete of the Sacrament awaie, and left nothing but lean bread, and bare wine, yf then wine be not ministred howe greate an offence ys committed?

Thus ye streign oute a gnatte, and swallowe (as Chryste saied) a Cammel. And as the prouerbe ys, ye stomble at a strawe, and leape ouer a blocke. Ye are curiouse in tithing minte, anise and commin, but ye omitte the weightier matters of the lawe: ye are busie in bread and wine and leaue oute the bodie and bloode of Chryst, the weightier matters of the lawe of the Gospell. Ye cast awaie the kernell, and fight for the shale. And thus ye transgresse the commaundement of God for your traditions.*

RICHARD SHACKLOCK

In his earlier translation of the Epistle of Osorius to Queen Elizabeth,† Shacklock tells us why he has played the 'inferior' *rôle* of translator rather than produced some original work of his own. He writes:

> I thought it to apperteine to me, which am (I trust) a membre of Chryst hys Catholyke churche, to doo as muche as in me lyeth, that the broken and battred walles of it may be reedified. And where as it passed my strengthe, to bryng any principall beames, any corner stones, by wrytyng newe workes of myne owne inuention, rather then I would be an ydle loker on, I thought it my part to be an inferior laborer, to bryng morter, to carry sand, and as it were beare baskettes, by translatyng some worthy worke of some other wryter.‡

In his dedication of *The Hachet of Heresyes*§ he apologizes for using the more barbarous English tongue instead of 'fyner forren language', but argues 'that no man is so wel indued with

* sig. M5. † See below, p. 120.
‡ *A Pearle for a Prynce*, Address to the Reader.
§ Running title of his translation of Hosius's *De origine haeresium nostri temporis*.

the knowledge of forren tonges, but when a matter of greate importaunce is tolde hym, the truthe of the which he is desyrouse to knowe certaynly, and to the which he is mynded to make an aunswer wysely, had rather haue it declared in his natural and mother tonge be it neuer so barbarouse, then in a straunge language be it neuer so eloquēt'.*

There is no doubt that Shacklock is more successful as a translator than as an original writer, as the original parts of his two works testify. As for his attitude towards the English language and the question of style, we may clearly recognize in the second quotation above an echo of the *dicta* of the Cambridge Ciceronians (after all, he was a Cambridge man himself), and his own practice would confirm the suspicion that he regarded 'elocution' as the proper means to cultured expression.† We must not, however, expect to find in his books anything in the nature of a formal style. His sole endeavour is to give an intelligible and vigorous translation of his Latin originals, and this he accomplishes by means of a pithy familiarity of word and phrase which makes the books a regular storehouse of Tudor expression. The scattered fragments here appended from *The Hachet* are intended to illustrate this predominant feature of Shacklock's prose.

And first, some random excerpts taken from Hosius's dedication to Prince Sigismund and referring to Petrus Paulus Vergerius, who had dared to dedicate a 'heretical' book to that prince:

> that he had the face to dedicate it to you – this sckyppe Iacke – his blynde and beastly boldness – do not these thynges differ as muche as chalcke and chese – he was all together patched and clouted of guyle – but that dyd nypp me nearer the hart, that the saucy face syr durst presume, etc.

From the body of the treatise we offer the following specimens:

> in stede of that which he sayde, This is my body, they haue made no bones at it to say, this is my bread [B6v].

> wycked wretches wyll take vpon thē either to clyppe, or ells to ouer hyppe‡ Christ his owne wordes [B7].

> & if they se theire fautes corrected, which they love beyond home – [B7v].§

* Address to the Queen.

† See above, pp. 7–8.

‡ To pass over.

§ To the uttermost.

> But hercken with in a lyttell whyle after, how farr he raungeth at ryot in a rage, as though he had a familiar spyrit of fury (sayd reuerence) in his tayle [B8v].*

> Yet Baltasar lept on lyne lenghte farther – [H6].†

> al other synnes compared to it, serue but a mote weyghing in balaunce with a myll poste [H7v].

> As for Bernard, often tyme he turneth the cat in the pan [I1].‡

> they toke the matter so in the snuffe, that they were not farr from raysing an vpp rore [I7v].

> they do so bycker among them selues, not aboute the mone shyne in the water (as the common saying is) but . . . aboute the cheife article of Christian doctrine [K3].

> euen they, be they neuer so lapped in shepe skynnes, yet euery one of them hathe theyr hand on theyr halffe penye,§ not regarding the thinges appertayning to Iesu Christ [K4].

> did he [the Emperor] grudge or complayne, that he was put to foyle|| of his seruaunt? [L6].

> Therefore arre we so wone with courte holy water, that is, fayre and flattring wordes [M1v].

> Alexander King of the Macedonians, when he obtained not his request . . . storming and stomakyng at the matter [M4v].

Let us add, in conclusion, two short quotations which will illustrate more openly the expressiveness of Shacklock's English and, at the same time perhaps, give the reader some better general notion of the style of his translation. The first deals with one of the principal bones of contention between the sectaries themselves.

> But lest any man sholde be deceaued with this false rumor, I think it good to folde vpp in a few wordes, what I knowe certaynly of this matter. I haue already opened, what heauyng & shoueing was betwene Luther, who affirmed the breade to be the body of Christ substantially and really, and Oecolampadius and Zuinglius, which sayde, that it was but a signe & bare figure only. The which contention so sone as it begā to be made hotte, in cōtinuance of tyme, it grewe to suche a

* Range at ryot=to shoot wildly (here used figuratively). 'Sayd reuerence' is a misprint for 'save reverence'=with all due respect.

† Went further still.

‡ Turns words so as to give their opposite sense.

§ So engrossed in their own petty view.

|| Was repulsed.

> greate flame, yͭ they tossed the fyar brandes of this controuersie one at an others heade, about the space of fyften yeares, because (as Calvyn wryteth) they coulde not abyde to heare one an other quietlye to speake theyre myndes: For (sayth he) althoughe they met once together to discusse thys matter, yet they so helde one an other at the staffes end, that they brake of, and left the matter in as euell a pyckell as they found it [C6v].

The second has reference to Calvin's attack upon the Lutherans in 'The laste admonition of Ihon Caluin to Ioachimus Westphalus'.

> He [Calvin] saythe, yͭ these beastely men [the Lutherans] neuer tasted what vertue is in the supper of the Lorde, or what it ment, that they be past all shame, that nothing cometh from them but shouelles full of slaunders and false reportes: whilst they tell for truthe Luther his lowde lyes, so that they may make theyre blynde brotherhode and the ignorant sort beleue that the mone is made of grene chese, being cōtented only to be praysed of yͤ people, they feare neither the iudgement of God, neither of hys Aungelles. He casteth in theyr tethe theire bedlem boldnes, flyrtyng, and folishe lightnes, blynde dronckennes, doggishe and currishe curstenes, Lucifers loftynes, saying that pryde is to them in stede of Godlynes, that madnes hathe spoyled them of all manly & ciuile manners, that stubbornnes hathe left no light of reason or discretion in them. He calleth thē brayne sycke noddies, Cyclopes, a prowde rablement takyng part with those Gyauntes which the Poetes fayne to haue interprysed to pull Iuppiter oute of heauen, barkars and bawlers, phrantyke, beastes, peuishe, prowde as peckockes, styf as stakes, & with suche other coloures he paynteth them . . . These be the wordes of Caluin in hys forsayde boke, by yͤ which it is gyuē vs playnely to vnderstand, that it is but a tale of a tub, which is reported of the agrement of the Lutherās and the Zwinglians, seyng all yͤ Churches of Saxonie for yͤ most parte, haue condemned yͤ doctryne of yͤ Sacramentaries. Although in yͤ meane season, that is not to be dissembled, howe he dothe make hys bragge in the same boke, that yͤ two eyes of Saxonie, Wittenberge, and Lipsia, dyd not decree any suche thyng agaynst his doctryne, neither Philipp Melancthon, whome he saythe, can no more be pulled from agreing with hym in this one poynte, then he can be pulled from his owne bowelles. But it followeth not by and by that it is true, because Caluin wryteth so: & we do conceaue a better opinion of Philipp Melancthon then so [D2v].

LEWYS EVANS

Lewys Evans, who wrote on both sides of this controversy, can hardly be regarded as a serious controversialist. Just as in his later tracts his main object seems to have been to prove the licentiousness of the Catholic clergy, their bishops, and the popes, so the two tracts which he contributed to the Catholic side are little more than personal attacks upon the lives of the 'new-made Ministers of England'. In spite of a highly rhetorical style and the employment of the usual polemical vocabulary and idiom of his day, we must allow him a certain naturalness and spontaneity of expression which is not altogether unattractive. But there is too much of the bitter taunt and too little of the merry scoff in his writing to give it that distinction which we find in such similar productions as, shall we say, the best of the Marprelate tracts, with their boisterous humour and biting satire. The two passages which follow are quite characteristic of the writer, and in their abundance of common rhetorical device exhibit the trained rhetorician.

Evans's first tract, *Certaine Tables* (1565), translated from the *Tabulae Grassantium passim Haereseôn anasceuasticae, atque analyticae* of William Lindanus of Dordrecht (Bishop of Rurimund), is accompanied with disquisitions from the translator's pen, of which the following is a sample:

> But wylte thowe (good Reader) weyghe, what men they bee, and of what authorytie they are? they be (to speake the beste of theym) the beastlyest part of al the people, they be the most loytering lecherous laddes of the whole Realme, & for an example, beholde him, who, hauing his priuate whoore in hys owne howse (whom he calleth wyf) durst neuertheles, betraye the treasure of his deare and faythful freande, durst (ah las, ah las) most lewdelie abuse the virginitie of his freandes doughter, and durst, fy, fy, deflowre so yong a thing. Yf thou wylte aske me now, what kynd of man this was, which cōmitted thys vyle facte, yea, thys vyllanie, and whether that he had any thing to doe with this dreaming diuelish doctrine. I must then say, that he was the pratyng pyller of this pelting newe founde faithe. I must say, that he buselie wrought for a Bushopryke, & I must say, that his good Lordes, the false named Bushopes of this tyme, haue thought him wel worthie therof. & now (as I heare) he begynneth to preache vpon *Miserere*, O Huntingtō, this leasson was wel looked for, this saued the neckes of manie of thy neare breatherne these newe

made Ministers.* and yf you will not beleue me, looke then vpon the hande of your neare neyghebour [marg. Norbr[oo]ke], and thou shalt fynd there the note & signe of thaefte & infamie. Exeter Gayle can testifye yt, & there the Bushopes pryson must needes wytnes yt.†

His second tract is an abusive little pamphlet entitled *A brieue Admonition vnto the nowe made Ministers of Englande* (1565), and is mainly concerned with references both direct and indirect ('by pronouncing of some doubtful phrase') to the private lives of the English clergy. The following will serve as a specimen:

Yowe your selfes (o Ministers) doe knowe, that the most parte of youe be onlie throughe meere pouertie thus compelled to putt your selfes so rashelie in these disordered orders, & youe which haue consumed and riotouselie wasted your welthe and goodes, are nowe glad to professe a peruerse doctrine, thereby to drawe into some abilitie for to wade with the worlde agayne. Yf that in anie paryshe (a pietiefull thing to heare) there was any pastthrifte and rashe mate‡ which colde but reade, such an vnrulie runneagate is nowe, not onlye, in the churche a reader, but also (which thing passeth all impudencie) a preacher and a pulpitte possessor in the holye howse of God . . . I knowe my selfe suche as, hauing forsaken theyr handieworke and former trade of lyuing, haue afterwardes laboured to reade, that then they might be Ministers, & readers. I know theym who, hauing some skyll in reading, haue rashelie forsaken their maisters seruices, & so that haue not onelye sought thus vnorderlie for orders, but also which haue obtayned the same. I know theym who, (being delyuered out of the Bushoppes pryson, and whose handes, before the temporall Iudge, of the yron and fyre haue sufficientlye fealte.) haue notwithstanding strayght passed into the next Diocesse, and there desyryng orders, were furthe with there charged with the cure & charge of soules.

Agayne, yf you marke the yong sorte of newe made Ministers, you shall fynde in theym suche follye and pryde, suche wilfullnes and wantonnes, that woefull yt is to heare yt. they be in theyr attyre and apparaill so rooffed, welted, iagged and stytched,§ as meeter to be ministrels then of the ministery.

* The reference is to Psalm 50 (Vulgate), commonly known as the neck-psalm, by reading the first few verses of which one claiming benefit of clergy might save his neck. John Huntington was a Protestant preacher and Canon of Exeter. His near neighbour, Norbrooke, may possibly be a reference to John Northbrooke, the Puritan divine. See *D.N.B.*

† sig. E2v.

‡ A derisive phrase, meaning 'beggarly and unruly fellow'.

§ Rooffed = having ruffs (?); welted = adorned with welts or borders; jagged = slashed; stitched = embroidered.

These doe no sooner attayne this one newe onelye order, but then busylie seeke they for some bassing* gyrle to make vpp theyr newe godlynes: they labour so hardelie to gett theym a huswife, as be she good or bad, vertous or a varlat: they passe not, this is the ende of theyr studie, this is it which they seeke, and this is theyr *summum bonum*, theyr chiefe felicitie. Seeke further, what your grauest fathers and newe named Bushoppes haue bene, and you shall fynde, that they were the inferiour sorte of the whole cleargie, that they were for theyr learning meater to be compared with the laitie, then with the learned: that they were the most wantonne lyuers (as by theyr light, vnaduised, and vnluckie made maraiges appeareth) amōgest the spiritualtie: that they were those, for whō the whole cleargie were accused of incontinencie, that they were but the riffe raffe amongest the religious: that they were but truantes in comparison of the true Catholyke teachers: that they were the verye worste of all those which professed Priesthoode & sanctitie, and that they were but the verye Dregges of the Diuines and Doctors of our dayes. Beholde of them some, who hauing lyued this long tyme without anie matching in mariage, doe nowe in theyr olde age fall to suche follye and doting, as theyr meere madde doinges must well declare, what kinde of fayth they seeke to maintayne, and also what maner of lyfe they heretofore haue leadde. These be not of theyr simple sortes, for they be of theyr Bushopes, and they be of theyr newe godlie, deuoute, and (as the Protestantes can call theym) most graue fathers. But is it grauitie for a Bushop with a graye bearde in his extreme age to waxe wantōne, and to wade in loue with a light mayde of his hoaste his kytchynne,† with whom he hathe made suche hast to marye? I shall not neede to trouble your [*sic*] with hys name, for the cyttie and countrey doe well knowe yt. Yet, yf anye farre dweller hereof doe dowbte, let hym truste, that it is as true: as that BATHE and WELLES be within one Bushopryke. Is it grauitie agayn for a man in yeares more thē fowr score, a man being a Preacher, and once aswell as the best a mocke Bushoppe, after the buryeng of his late bedfellowe & wyfe, to fall to *lasciuire* of freshe, to seeke a yong woman to woe, and to marye one who for her yeares, were meter to be hys niece or mayde, then wyfe and mate?‡

* A probable misprint for 'bussing'; cf. Herrick – 'we buss our wantons but our wives we kiss'.

† His host's kitchen (?).

‡ sigs. A7ᵛ–B2. Is the reference in the passage to Bath and Wells to Gilbert Berkeley, the holder of that see from 1559 to 1581? S. H. Cassan, in his *Lives of the Bishops of Bath and Wells* (1830), Vol. II, quoting from Sir John Harington's *Nugae Antiquae*, says of him: 'He was a good Justicer, saving that sometimes being ruled by his wife, by her importunity he swerved from the rule of justice and sincerity, especially in persecuting the kindred of Bourne his predecessor.'

2. THE OSORIUS-HADDON CONTROVERSY

Jeronymo Osorio da Fonseca (1506–80), Bishop of Silves, the originator of this part of the general controversy arising out of the Elizabethan religious settlement, was a Portuguese scholar of European reputation. As a writer he appears to have been well known in this country: Roger Ascham praises his Latin style;* Gabriel Harvey refers to him several times in his *Ciceronianus* and his *Rhetor*; and Elizabeth herself, we may understand, was a reader of his works.

> I was, [he writes] I assure you (moste noble Princesse) here to fore sufficientlie prouoked to the loue of youre Maiestie and highnes, when I herd say howe muche you did preuaile in witte, how greately you had profited in Greke and Latten, and howe you did ioyne youre Princely dignity with liberalle learning and knowledge: But after that certaine men brought me worde, that you willingly did reade my workes, [marg. 'Hys booke intituled De vera nobilitate.] my former good will was so much increased towarde you, as in wordes I am not able to vtter . . . I mistruste not, but with the same fauoure with which you reade my workes (if it be true, that you be not a littell delighted in reading them) you will interteine these my letters.†

Respect for 'the Portuguese Cicero', as he was styled by his contemporaries, is shown by the duration of the controversy, which lasted altogether thirty-five years.‡ It is set out fully in Strype's *Annals of the Reformation.*§ Here is briefly a table of its progress as far as the year 1581:

(1) Osorius writes *Epistola ad Elizabetham Angliae Reginam de Religione* (Louvain, 1563) – described by Strype as 'a malicious libel against England, and the reformation of religion here, by way of letter to the queen; intending to persuade her to return to the Roman Catholic faith'. (*C*)

(2) Walter Haddon replies in Latin in *Gualtheri Haddoni pro Reformatione Anglicana Epistola Apologetica ad Hier. Osorium. Lusitanum* (Paris, 1563). Sir Thomas Smith, the

* cf. Letter to William Petrees in the *Familiar Letters*.
† The *Epistle to Elizabeth*, as below, sig. A6.
‡ See J. G. Underhill, *Spanish Literature in the England of the Tudors* (1899), p. 143.
§ ed. 1824, Vol. I, pt. 2, pp. 69 et seq. Further references will also be found in Vol. I, pt. 1 and Vol. III, pt. 1 of the same work.

Queen's ambassador in Paris, made corrections and additions, and was responsible for getting the book printed. (*P*)

(3) Richard Shacklock translates Osorius's Letter (1) in *An Epistle of the Reuerend Father in God* . . . (John Latius, 1565)='A Pearle for a Prynce'. (*C*)

(4) Second issue of Shacklock's translation published in the same year by Aegidius Diest. (*C*)

(5) Shacklock's translation (3) countered by Abraham Hartwell's translation of Haddon (2) in *A sight of the Portugall Pearle* (1565). (*P*)

(6) Osorius replies to Haddon (2) in *Amplissimi atque Doctissimi Viri. D. Hieronymi Osorii, Episcopi Syluensis, in Gualterum Haddonum . . . libri tres* (1567). (*C*)

(7) John Fen translates Osorius's reply (6) in *A Learned and very Eloquent Treatie* (1568). (*C*)

(8) Meanwhile Haddon had been engaged upon an answer in Latin to Osorius's book (6 above). He died in 1572, having completed the answer to Book I and part of Book II.

(9) A second answer to Shacklock (3 above) appeared in 1570, entitled *An answer in action to a Portingale Pearle, called a Pearle for a Prince.* [By D. Emilie?] (*P*)

(10) John Foxe completes Haddon's answer (8 above), which was published in 1577 under the title of *Contra Hieron. Osorium, eiusque odiosas insectationes pro Euangelicae veritatis necessaria Defensione, Responsio Apologetica.* (*P*)

(11) James Bell translates (10) into English under the title *Against Ierome Osorius Byshopp of Siluane in Portingall and against his slaunderous Inuectiues* (1581). (*P*)

RICHARD SHACKLOCK

The *Pearle for a Prynce* further exemplifies those marks of Shacklock's style to which we have already alluded above (p. 113). We may note the same pithy familiarity of expression, the same predilection for picturesque language, and the same rhetorical manner as we observed in *The Hachet of Heresyes*. And in this connexion the reader will not miss the *naïveté* of the protestation in the following passage:

I was not ignorant (he writes) that our base tounge coulde not

> atteine to the maiestie of Osorius his Laten, for I regarde not so much the fynes of wordes, as the diuynenes of the matter: notwithstanding this epistle of Osorius is after a sorte answered *à quodā osore veritatis*, who shall be nameles, for all the world can wytness that the answer osoris illius is no more to be compared to the epistle of Osorius, then the light of a lampe to the light of a lynck, then the light of a lynck to the light of the Sonne. Allthough being compared with other of his owne sect, I confess hym to be as he is taken a man of handsome eloquence.* But compare hym to the glistryng starres, which are this daye in the catholike church, and namely to Osorius, against whome he setteth hymselfe, he is but a candle vnder a bushell.†

A little later, by way of pleasantry, he adds, of his 'nameless' opponent: 'I almost *had don* his name to be vnderstanded against my will.'

His genius for the expressive word and phrase to give colour and vigour to his writing may be further judged from the following examples taken more or less at random from our text:

> Suche a mynde . . . that it will be kept in awe at the commaundment of one, that it will suffer it self as it were to be tyed short‡ with the lawes and procedinges of one [A7].

> Counterfet fynes of lying, and deceaueable lickersomnes§ of flatterie [B5].

> Riches closed and chested vp, may ether be caried away of theues, or be lasht oute|| and made hauock of, through the falshode of the kepers. But the remembraunce of a good turne, is rooted for euer in thākfull myndes, & can not be plucked out by any mans pilfrie [B7].

> Partly because thei mistrust not his goodnes, and stand not in dought that he wil forget publike profit, whilst he licketh his owne fyngers, they willingly obey hym [C6].

> There is nothing of more powre then the feare of God . . . to cutt the combe¶ of bragging and lightnes [C7v].

> Doth not euery mā see that they shoote all at this marke, that Princes being dispatched oute of the way, there might none be left which shold once say, black is theyr eye?** Therefore we

* Haddon had a reputation for a Ciceronian style in Latinity in his own day.
† sig. A4.
‡ Restrained under strict discipline.
§ Sweetness.
|| Squandered.
¶ Lower the pride.
** The meaning of these last words may be gathered from the original: *impunitam flagitiorum omnium licentiam consequantur*.

haue cōmaunded all those which beleue in Christ, to set cocke on hoope, & crye care away* [F6v].

But oure men, which crake that they came oute of God his bosome, and knowe all hys secretes, doo plye the box busyly, that they may seale Christian men a Quitāce from al feare of God, and so make them lyke blynde bayardes boldely to leape in to the myar of al mischefe† [F8].

Their deadlye hatredes, theire contentions, theire scamblyng by the eares,‡ theire tauntynges and rybauldry raylinges [I1].

. . . mocke those thinges, which be wryten of God hys iudgemētes, as thoughe they were but Caunterbury tales and grym vysardes only deuysed to fray younge chyldren [I2v].

JOHN FEN

We observe much the same characteristics in John Fen's translation of Osorius's reply to Haddon (nos. 6 and 7 above) as we observed in Shacklock's work. The translator allows himself considerable liberty in the way he turns his Latin original into the vernacular idiom, and just as Shacklock will convert such an expression as *nescio quo amentia vexati* into 'being verbes actiue I knowe not of what mad moode', or will enlarge a mere *quod autem* into 'and that it is no God a mercye to them', so Fen, following the same method, transforms his original into something which is purely English, with the result that we hardly feel we are reading a translation at all. The reader may judge the truth of this statement for himself by comparing the Latin and English versions of the following short extract:

Te vero, si quemadmodum ego scriptis, ita coràm verbis vrgerem, & argumētis huc & illuc contorquerem, num tibi constare posses? Non profecto. Sed varias & instabiles causae tuae defensiones excogitares, & in omnes latebras te frustra conijceres, vt facile appareret, tibi neque linguam, neque mentem vlla ratione consistere.

Thinke you, M. Haddon, if, as I doe now reason with you in writing, so I mighte be presente wyth you, and presse you with

* To cast off all restraint, and cry care begone. (Orig. *sine cura esse.*)

† . . . take the greatest care that they may grant Christian men a quittance from all fear of God and so make them recklessly leap &c. (Orig.: *Isti, qui se diuinae mentis interpretes esse iactant, operam obnixe dant, vt homines Christianos omni Dei metu soluant, & ita in omne facinus sanè cōfidenter impellant.*)

‡ Contentiousness.

> wordes, and wind you to and fro by the force of argumentes, that you were able to stande to your tackelinges? No without dowbt. But you woulde deuise a hundred diuers shiftes of descant* to face out the matter, and seeke out all the starting holes and blind corners in the world: in such sort, that it might easily appeare, that neither your tongue, neither yet your wit were in perfecte good plight.†

Fen's writing is also no less rich in colloquialisms than Shacklock's. Plentifully scattered throughout his pages may be found such expressions as: 'to gallowe his chariot horses' (to frighten); 'thy vnsetled fantasie and mad gare' (sudden and transient fit of passion); 'weied downe with the peise of synne' (weight of); 'to escape out of your clammes' (clutches); 'take it in snuffe' (take offence at); 'huggermugger' (secret); 'an odde man' (distinguished); 'pricked and yearked forth' (spurred on and driven forth); 'drawlatches' (lazy laggards); 'harishness' (foolishness); and so forth. The vigour which such expressions impart to his writing and the general level of excellence he maintains, both in the management of the sentence and in rhythmic effect, may be gathered from the two following passages which may be taken as a fair specimen of the whole:

> There are two kind of men within the folde of Christes church. The one is of them, which liuing a cōmon life, cōtent them selues with the commendable exercise of meane vertue and godlines. The other is of such, as endeuour them selfe to excell in the folowing of heauenly life and discipline. Now for so much as the ende, whiche euery Christian man ought to set before his eyes, is the likenes of the perfection and iustice of God, the which they atteine muche sooner, which are prōpter and redier to behold the beautie of the wil of God: the which beautie no man can wel cōceiue in his hart, so long as he is as it were tied downe with the bandes of streight frindship and familiaritie of the bodie: it came to passe, that suche as had an earnst and feruent desire to ioyne them selues vnto God, called away their mindes (as much as was possible) from the familiar acqueintance of the body, to the intent they mighte the better fasten the eyes of their hearts in the cleerenes‡ of God. These are they, which (as our Lord saith) haue ghelded them selues for the loue and earnest desire of the kingdome of heauen. For the pleasure of the bodie weyeth downe the heart euen to the earth, and with her importunitie carieth away the

* Changes of tune.

† Osorius at sig. S1; Fen at sig. GG6v. The extract is a fair sample of the whole translation.

‡ Beauty, fairness.

minde from the contēplation of the brightnes of God. The which thing is so true, that, although Mariage be honorable, and the bed vndefiled, and he that defraudeth his wife of the right of Mariage, committeth no small sinne, yet it is sometimes necessarie for such as do minde to receiue this cleerenesse of God within them selues to absteine from their owne wiues [H7ᵛ–8].

You dalied with me, Sir pleasaunce, you dalied: and the ladie Venus, in the honour of whome you haue prophaned and vnhalowed the tēples of chastitie, hath besprinkled you with her comelie and pleasaunt graces. Howbeit I thinke this very much to be misliked in this your pleasauntnes, that it can not be well perceiued, when you speake in earnest, and when you sport. But peraduenture you thinke it a cōmendation of a sharpe witte, to speake darkly, and therefore you vse it in disputation also. But howe often you caste me in the teeth with the name of Cicero? As though I shoulde be ashamed of hym, or els thought my selfe hable to expresse in my writinges anie parte of his witte, vehemencie, and copie: as though I had studied Cicero only, and had not spent verie muche time in other the highest pointes of learning. But you like a foxie lawier and wilie proctour, haue made a verie good prouiso, that no man maie wel laie the name of Cicero to your charge. For you speake nothing in cleane speach, nothing plainly, nothing distinctely, nothing orderly, nothing grauely, nothing eloquently. What so euer liketh you, you put it in: and then you prooue it, not by argument and reason, but by railing and shameles talke. At the length as though you had wonne the field, you pricke me with the bristles of your reprocheful tongue, you presse me with a numbre of apish questions, you triumph like a noddie before the victorie. Whervpon you saie thus?

What saie you good sir? And then? *S. Paul detesteth it: Ierome Osorius is not afraied to auouch it.* As though I affirmed that thing, whiche you there denied, or els meaned to dispute with S. Paul, and not with Luther. And again. *What saieth, Ierome Osorius?* And again. *Doe I make anie thing? Doe I chaunge anie thing?* And with these woordes forsooth, you would haue seemed to be a vehement speaker. Learne this of me, M. Haddon, if you can (bicause your euyl lucke was to chaunce vpon such a maister, which brought you vp so foolishly and so ignorātly) that these questions are then both graue and vehement in deede, when the aduersarie is cōuinced by some firme and sure argument. For otherwise they are verie folish and to be laughed at: for so much as they haue no vehemēcie or strength in the worlde, but only a declaration of a certaine pitifull pang or heat of the stomake. So God healpe me, as I could not sometime (although your talke seemed vnto me verie much to be pitied) hold my selfe frō laughing. And so I am fully discharged of my promise, whiche I made you, that, in case you could driue me either by grownded reasons, or els by true exāples to geaue my assent vnto you, I would not refuse it. For neither haue you brought anie argument, neither alleaged any example, that was to the pourpose: and yet, as though you had borne your self like a pretie* man, you rage and reuel in wordes, and keepe a meruelous pitifull and frantique stirre. I can not deuise, what wicked sprite it should be, that put you in mind to take this charge of writing vpon you. Yet I meane not, but that you maie doe, as you thinke good: neither wil I limite you in suche sorte, that you maie not in writing shew your selfe to be as foolish, as you list. And to put you in good comfort, take this of my worde, that no man, which is of anie iudgement, wil find fault with you, for being to much a Ciceronian [AA8–BB1v].

3. THE FECKENHAM-HORNE CONTROVERSY

The full story of this controversy will be found in Strype's *Annals of the Reformation* and in his *Life and Acts of Grindal.*† Very briefly we may summarise it as follows:

When the Abbot of Westminster was 'borrowed' (to use one of Feckenham's own expressions) of the Tower by Bishop Horne in October 1563, it was in the nature of things that some argument would arise over the question on account of which he had been committed, viz. his refusal to take the Oath of the Queen's Supremacy. Daily conferences, we are told, were held at Horne's residence at Waltham, touching religion, during the winter of 1563–4, in the presence of picked audiences, but so acrimonious did the disputing become that Horne, for his peace of mind, had the Abbot once more removed to the Tower. While still in his custody Horne had invited Feckenham to put his views into writing, and it was then that he had handed Horne a treatise he had composed the previous year while still in the Tower, which he had intended to deliver 'to the Commissioners (if any came) as the staie of his conscience, concerning the refusall of the foresaid othe'.‡ This treatise was called

(1) *The Answere made by M. Iohn Fekenham, Priest and Prisoner in the Tower, to the Queenes highnes Commissioners, touching the othe of the Supremacie.* (*C*)

* Clever, skilful, ingenious.
† cf. *Annals* (1824), Vol. I, pt. 2, pp. 178–87. *Grindal* (1821), p. 117.
‡ *Counterblast*, as below, 'Answer to the Preface'.

It was afterwards enlarged and secretly spread abroad as

(2) *The Declaration of suche Scruples, and staies of Conscience, touchinge the Othe of the Supremacy, as M. Iohn Fekenham, by wrytinge did deliuer vnto the L. Bishop of Winchester, with his Resolutions made thereunto* (1564).* (*C*)

In April 1565 Horne managed to get hold of a copy of this book, and, to quote Strype, the Bishop 'was fain to write a book in his own vindication against Feckenham'. This was entitled

(3) *An Answeare Made by Rob. Bishoppe of Wynchester, to a Booke entituled, The Declaration of suche Scruples* . . . (1566). (*P*)

The reply to this came from the pen of Thomas Stapleton, who, from notes supplied by Nicholas Harpsfield (see Appendix III), produced in the following year

(4) *A Counterblast to M. Hornes vayne blaste against M. Fekenham* (1567). (*C*)

Finally, John Bridges contributed the last item to the controversy in his publication

(5) *The Supremacie of Christian Princes, ouer all persons throughout their dominions, in all causes so wel Ecclesiastical as temporall, both against the Counterblast of Thomas Stapleton, replying on the Reuerend father in Christe, Robert Bishop of Winchester: and also Against Nicolas Sanders his Visible Monarchie of the Romaine Church. touching this controuersie of the Princes Supremacie* (1573). (*P*)

Only the first book of the *Counterblast* is dealt with in this treatise. Sander's book is the well-known *De Visibli Monarchia Ecclesiae* (1571). In it he refers to Stapleton's *Counterblast* as a book, 'quem omni & eloquentia, & doctrina refertum contra Hornum Pseudoëpiscopum Vintoniensem, edidit'.†

STAPLETON'S *Counterblast*

Although he originated this particular disputation, Feckenham's own slender contribution to it hardly calls for notice here. On the other hand, Stapleton's work, which runs into more than a thousand pages, is one of the most comprehensive documents of Elizabethan controversy and deserves the careful

* I cite the title from Horne's *Answeare*. The book was probably circulated in manuscript only.

† sig. r2v.

consideration both of the literary student and of the student of ecclesiastical history. Touching the Oath of Supremacy, it claims to be (to quote from the title-page) 'a Chronicle of the Continual Practise of Christes Churche in al ages and Countries, frō the time of Constantin the Great, vntil our daies: Prouing the Popes and Bisshops Supremacy in Ecclesiastical causes: and Desprouing the Princes Supremacy in the same Causes'. What this means may be gathered from a perusal of Books II and III (there are four Books altogether), the contents of which include sections on: Constantine the Great–Athanasius–the Nicene Council–the sons of Constantine–Theodosius the Great–the sons of Theodosius–Eutyches–Pope Leo the Great–the Council of Chalcedon–the sixth, seventh and eighth General Councils–Hildebrande–Spain–France–Italy–Germany–pre-Conquest England–William the Conqueror–William Rufus–Henry I–Stephen–Henry II–Richard I–John–Henry III–Edward I–Edward III–Richard II–and Henry VIII.

We have referred above to Harpsfield's having supplied Stapleton with the notes for this volume. Stapleton's acknowledgement of his debt to this unnamed creditor is contained in his Preface to the Reader, wherein, after calling attention to his insufficiency for the task he has undertaken, 'first, for that many things in this booke pertaine to certaine priuat doinges betwixt M. Feckenham and M. Horne, of the which I had no skil. Secōdely, for that a number of such priuate matters touching the state of the Realme occurred, as to them without farder aduise, I could not throughly shape any answer', he goes on to declare – 'afterward it so happened, that by suche as I haue good cause to credit, there came to my knowledge such Instructions, as well for the one as for the other, that I was the better willing to employ some study and paines in this behalfe . . . I haue therefore by such helpes [he continues], as is aboue saied, added my poore labour thereto, and with some diligence in the reste, shaped to the whole booke, a whole and a full Reply. Wherein I rather feare I haue saied to much, then to litle. But I thought good in a matter of suche Importance, to be rather tedious to make al perfitte, then shorte and compendious, to leaue ought vnperfecte'. What exactly may have been the extent and nature of these 'Instructions' must be left to some future student of this work. Provisionally, at any rate, we may treat

Stapleton as solely responsible for its ordering and style, and (while retaining our opinion as to Feckenham's authorship of the notes) may accept Henry Holland's account of the matter which I here paraphrase:

> When Robert Horne, Superintendent of Winchester, (into whose custody John Feckenham, the most Reverend Abbot of Westminster, had been committed) came to demand the oath of the Queen's primacy in ecclesiastical causes from Feckenham, and the latter had set forth in a choice book excellent reasons why he should not take such an oath: Horne then seized the opportunity of writing a book on the sovereign's primacy in such causes, full of historical references to the Kings and Emperors, and these with amazing boldness and impudency he falsified most foully. For which reason Horne deserved to be mortified with a mordant and sharp reply, that he might learn to be more prudent in future. The style of the young Stapleton was particularly pleasing to the aged Feckenham, as being lively and caustic, *his word burning as it were like a torch.* Therefore the venerable old man dispatched to Stapleton the notes of his reply against Horne, in order that he might arrange them, and embellish them with his own style, and enrich them from other sources, and publish them in his own name, so that the publication might not bring any new penalties upon him in prison. And this Stapleton accomplished in a very fine and learned manner; proving that Horne in this single pamphlet of his concerning the primacy had very impudently blabbed out six hundred lies.*

Many examples of Stapleton's 'lively and caustic' style might be adduced from this volume. Two notable instances are the following. Addressing Horne, he writes:

> Ye keep now your said Madge in the face of al the worlde without shame, whiche in King Henries daies ye kepte in hucker mucker and lusky lanes† as many other did of your sort: especially M. Cranmer that occupied the See of Cāterburie: who caried about with him his pretie conie in a chest full of holes, that his nobs‡ might take the ayer.
>
> You wil perchance stande in defence of your pretensed mariage, and also of your other heresies, and say they are no heresies at all, and turne lecherie into wedlock as some of your sorte haue of late daies turned vppon good fridaie, a Pigge into a Pike, putting the said pigge in the water and saying: goe in pigge, and come out pike.§

* Introduction to *T. Stapletoni . . . Opera quae extant omnia* (1620), Vol. I, sig. ā6v. The original passage is cited at Appendix III.

† Secret and hidden byways. ‡ Darling. § sig. B4v.

Speaking of one of Foxe's 'Martyrs', he says:

> But nowe is it worth the hearing to know, how handsomly M. Foxe hath conceyued his matters: wherein he plaieth in dede the wily Foxe and springleth with his false wily tayle, his fylthy stale not into the doggs, but into his readers eies. And as the Foxe, as some hūters say, when he is sore driuen, wil craftely mount from the earth and kepe himself a while vpon the eather* of a hedge, only to cause the howndes that drawe after him to leese the sente of the tracte: euen so for all the worlde hath our Foxe plaied with his reader. But I trust I shal trace him, and smel him out wel inoughe.
>
> First then, though M. Foxes authority be very large and ample in this his canonisation, and such as neuer any Pope durste take vpon him, yea and though he hath authority to make martyrs, yet I dowbte whether he hath authority to make knights to: for this Sir Roger Onley is neither a Sir, but of M. Foxes making, nor Onley neither: But M. Roger Bolinbroke only: put to death for the treason before specified, as not onely his owne authours Fabian and Harding, whome he doth alleage for the story of Dame Elleanour, but al other also doe testifie. Truthe it is that Harding writing in English meeter and speaking of this M. Bolinbroke endeth one of his staues with this worde *Only*, which is there to signifie no name, but to better and sweate the meeter, and is as much to say, as chiefly and principally, meaning that Maister Roger was the principal worker in this nigromancy. The meeters of Harding are these.
>
> *He waxed then strange eche day vnto the King,*
> *For cause she was foreiudged for sorcery,*
> *For enchantments that she was in working*
> *Against the Church and the King cursedly,*
> *By helpe of one M. Roger, only.*
>
> Whiche last woorde, some ignorant or Protestant Printer hath made Oonly. And then hath M. Fox added a Syr, and a Martyr too, and adorned him with no common inke, to set foorth and beutify his Martyr withal. And so of M. Roger Bolinbroke, sorcerer and traitour, by a cunning Metamorphosis he hath made, Syr Roger Onlye Knight and Martyr.†

* Top (the top of a hedge being bound with edders or osiers).

† sig. P4ᵛ. Roger 'Onley' is referred to in the first edition of Foxe's *Acts and Monuments* (20 March 1562–3) as 'a knight of . . . nobility and order'. Alan Cope (i.e. Nicholas Harpsfield) in his *Dialogi Sex* (1566) takes Foxe to task for thus creating Roger Bolinbroke knight and martyr. Foxe in his second edition (1570) corrects 'knight' to 'priest', but criticizes Alan Cope for not having read John Harding, where he will find, he says, these words:

> Again, the church and the king cursedly,
> By help of one Master Roger Only, etc.

This criticism persists in the third and fourth editions of the *Acts* (1576 and 1583), without any reference to this passage in the *Counterblast*. One must therefore suppose that Foxe had not read the latter work.

It is, perhaps, dangerous to separate short extracts of this nature from their contexts. It is possible that they will be misunderstood and may be regarded as simply scurrilous. However, if we remember that in both extracts Stapleton is emphasizing the state of topsy-turvydom produced by the new Lay Supremacy in religion, and that it is this leading idea which 'orders' the expression of his theme, we shall, I think, judge correctly the real effectiveness of the irony and the sincerity of the writer.

Stapleton is, above all, an eloquent writer, and his eloquence, like all true eloquence, springs from a sincere mind. Intellectual rectitude and integrity of purpose give to his writing a stamp of genuineness and exactness even when he is most 'free, loose and bold'. Thus, even in his most impassioned periods, feeling is never allowed to get the upper hand, but is controlled and organized. Here is a characteristic passage in which he accuses Horne of recklessness in attacking the Papacy:

> With the like discretiō you cal blessed S. Augustin of whome we Englishmen first receyued our Christendome, in contempt and derision, *the Popes Apostle*, maligning in him the name of the Apostle of Englande, and calling him beside, together with the blessed Apostle of Germany and Martyr, Bonifacius, *blinde guides and blind bussardes*. But who so bolde as blind bayarde? or who can see lesse in other men, then such as can see nothing in them selues? And what doe you els herein, but like a furious Aiax, thinking to deface the Pope, fall a whipping and rayling at his shepe, (such shepe, I say as Christ committed to Peter, whose successour the Pope is) as Aiax in his fury whipped the shepe of Vlisses, thinking he had whipped Vlisses him selfe? But as the fury of Aiax reached not to Vlysses person, but onely encreased his owne misery and madnes: so your Turkish talke M. Horne, blemisheth not the See Apostolike, or hurteth it the valewe of one rushe, but only expresseth the Turkish sprit that lurketh within you. Therefore bluster and blowe, fume and frete, raue ād raile, as lowdely as lewdely, as bestly as boldly, do what you can, you must heare, as the Donatists hearde of S. Augustine: *Ipsa est Sedes, quam superbae non vincūt inferorum portae*. That See of Peter, is the See, which the proude gates of hel doe not ouercome. The more you kick against that Rocke, the more your [*sic*] break your shinne.*

The style of this, which is both vehement and piercing, is to be measured by the principle of selection which has clearly been

* sig. **4^{v}.

at work in the passage, together with the appropriateness of the rhythmical structure.

If we turn to Stapleton's use of imagery we shall find further evidence of this same 'faithfully authentic note'. In the two following examples it will be observed that, as the image is unfolded or developed, in no way is the thought sacrificed to the figure; rather is the outward form of the expression strictly commensurate with the inner structure of the thought. The argument of the first passage may be set out as follows: 'I have detected your mis-statements, Mr. Horne, which are as far as they can be from the truth. Your arguments and the marshalling of them are feeble in the extreme. Better give up using the Old Testament to prove your case and try some other grounds of argument. We give you a last chance to deal openly with this question of Lay Supremacy in religion. So far you have proved nothing.' Here is Stapleton:

> O M. Horne, your manifolde vntruthes are disciphired and vnbuckled, ye are espied, ye are espied, I say, well enough, that ye come not by a thousande yardes and more nigh the marke. Your bowe is to weake, your armes to feable, to shoot with any your cōmendation at this marke: yea if ye were as good an archer, as were that famous Robin Hood, or Litle Iohn. Wel shift your bowe, or at the least wise your string. Let the olde Testament goe, and procede to your other proufes, wherein we will nowe see if ye can shoote any streighter. For hitherto ye haue shotten al awrye, and as a man may saye, like a blinde man. See now to your selfe from henseforth that ye open your eies, and that ye haue a good eye and a good aime to the marke we haue set before you. If not, be ye assured we wil make no curtesie eftsones to put you in remembrance. For hitherto ye haue nothing proued that Princes ought, which ye promised to proue, or that they may take vppon them such gouernment, as I haue laid before you, and such as ye must in euery parte iustifie, if either ye will M. Fekenham shal take the Othe, or that ye entende to proue your selfe a true man of your worde.*

The same precision in the working out of an analogy is to be remarked in our second example:

> The shepeherd M. Horne doth not onely feede his sheepe, and carefully choseth owte suche grownde and pastour, as is most conueniente and holsome for them: but besides that, sondreth the whole and sownde, from the infected and rottē: he greaceth

* sig. O3.

> and tarreth them, he byndeth, he cutteth them, he hath a staf with a hooke to draw thē in when they stray: he hath a staf to beat away the wolfe: he hath a folde to close and shutte them vp saufe from the incursiōs of the woulf, ād other rauening beasts. And what doth all this, but resemble and expresse vnto vs the pastorall office of Bishops and prelates?*

In other words, it is the office of a bishop to instil true doctrine, to prevent the contagion of heresy, to administer spiritual consolation, to dispense the sacrament of penance,† and to reconcile those who go astray from the Church, which is the sure means of salvation.

But it is in the historical sections of this book that Stapleton's sincerity of mind is most evident. And in this connexion we would invite the reader to note something which is almost unique in sixteenth-century writings. In addition to the usual prefatory matter in his book Stapleton has a special *Advertisement to the Learned Reader* calling attention to his use of certain manuscript copies of ancient writers, no printed copies being available save in one case where a special reference is made in the margin.‡ A prefatory statement of this nature speaks volumes for Stapleton's candour, and there can be no doubt that much controversial ink would have been saved if writers had followed his example and had been more exact about their sources.

We propose, then, to cite one last passage from Stapleton's chronicle 'Of King Richarde the first, and King Iohn, Kings of England'.§ He is examining John Foxe's assertion that King John was poisoned by a monk of Swinstead Abbey, who gave the King poison in a cup of ale. Foxe bases his story on the evidence of a chronicle which he attributes to Caxton.

> But this is your, and your fellowes trade, (he writes) especiallie Maister Foxes in the setting forth of this Kinges storie, to lye extremely, to bring thereby the clergie into hatred and enuie: as in thys storie among other thinges he hath done, touching the poisoning of this King by a monke of Swinstead abbey . . .

* sig. lll 1v.

† The image here is perhaps least plain. The word 'bind' has the meaning of 'restrain', and to cut is probably to set free, though it might possibly mean to shear. I take it that the idea of binding and loosing was in Stapleton's mind, probably as it occurs in Matthew xviii. 12–18.

‡ Nicholas Harpsfield has a similar, but much more elaborate, bibliographical note in his *Dialogi Sex*, indicating the editions of the authors which he has used.

§ Book III, chapter 23. Another passage from this same book will be found at Appendix III.

First then, this is a manifest lie, that ye say M. Foxe, *the chroniclers moste agree in this, that he was poysoned by the monke at Swinstead.* Which thing I could easely proue, by reciting specially, what euery authour writeth concerning the maner of his death: But M. Foxe himself hath, we thank him, prouided that we neade not trauayle so farre: for lo, he bringeth in Polidorus, saying he died of sorowe and heuines of harte: Radulphus Niger, saying he died, of surfeting in the night: *Roger Houeden*, saying he died of a bluddie flixe: *Matheus Parisiensis*, saying that by heuines of minde, he fel into a feruente agewe, at the abbey of Swinstead, which he encreased with surfeting, and nawghty diet: by eating peaches and drinkinge of newe Ciser, or sydar. Then adde ye farder Maister Foxe that some saye he died of a colde sweate: some of eatinge apples: some of eating peares: and some of eating plummes. So haue ye here good reader, fowre chroniclers by name, and at the least fowre other vnnamed, that make no mention of any poyson. Now could I bring the Polichronicon, and Fabian which reciting the sayed Polychronicon, saieth that the King died of the fluxe. Here also could I bring in, that those that write of his poysoning, write very diuersly, nothing agreing with your authour in the kind of poyson. And also that they rehearse it rather as a common tale, then for any assured storie or truthe. Many other thinges could I bring in, but what needeth yt, when we haue by hys owne tale store ynoughe of witnesses agaynst him? Yet will I adde one more, but such a one, as ought to be to M. Foxe in steade of a greate sorte: that one I say, of whome by all that I can iudge (for he hath not vouchsafed ones to name him) M. Foxe hath taken all his declaration, concerning the election of Stephen Langton, and of all the greate busines that issued thereof: yea the writyng obligatorie, touching the resigning of the crowne into the Popes handes. Whiche lyeth in our authour worde for worde, as M. Foxe hath translated it.

This our authour sheweth, that as the Kyng was going northwarde, the grounde opened and swallowed vp hys cartes and caryage, that yt coulde neuer be recouered. Wherevppon the Kyng fell into a greate griefe and heauinesse, and fetched many sighes from the very bottome of hys harte. And beyng at Swinstead surfeated with peaches and other fruite, and there fell sicke. And so beynge sicke departed, and being not able to continue on horsebacke, came in an horselytter to Leadforde castle: and afterwarde to Newemarket, where perceiuyng him selfe to be paste all cure and remedie, he sent for the Abbatte of Crokestone that was skylfull in physicke, of whome he was confessed, and receiued the Sacrament of the holye *Eucharistia*. And by and by he endeth this storie of King Iohn, saying that because this king was hated of many, partly for the death of his nephewe Arthur, partly for his adultrie, partly for hys tyranny, partlye for the tribute, by the whiche he browght England into a perpetuall bondage, partly for the warres that hys doinges sturred vppe, he was scarslie worthie to be bemoned and lamented for, of anye man. Here haue we now M. Foxe fyue authors by name, and more aunciente thē your Caxtō, and of an other iudgemente, towching this Kinges death, then your Caxton is: beside fowre some sayes at the leaste.

And now let vs weighe with a word or two the creditte of this yowr owne Authour. I passe ouer, that ye call yt the chronicle of William Caxton, he being neither the maker, neither the translatour, sauing he hath adioyned out of Polichronicō the description of Englande and Irelande, of Treuisa his translation, and added as they say, certayn other thinges to his vnknowen Author. Belyke ye thowght to wynne some credite to your authour clothing hym with the name of this Caxton, a man of late remembraunce, because he hath no name of his owne. And so a mete worke for you, in the darke to lurke and lie withall, and in dede vnworthy to haue the name of the chronicles of England, or to be called *Fructus temporum*: being as vnfruytful as any booke that was made many a.100. yeres. Onlesse we may call him beinge barrē of al good truthe and choise of good matter, fitte for a story of any credit or fruytful, being only fruytful ād plētiful of wōderful vntruths, and opē lewde lies. I report me (for his truth) to his fable of the xxxiij. Daughters of king Diocletiā king of Syria, that after they had slain their husbands, stole away by shippe into our Ilelād of Britannie whiche was then vnhabited and vnpeopled, and afterwarde beinge conceyued by deuilles browght forth gyantes whiche inhabited the lande, vntill the commynge of Brute that slewe them. And that our Ilelande was called Albion of the eldest dawghter Albine: as afterward Britānie by the name of the foresayd Brute. Againe of king Arthure, that being not able to kepe the possessiō of his owne realme from the Saxons, caried an armie of one hundred thousande and more into farre countries, hauing vnder his conducte a nomber of kinges, and there slewe the Emperour of Rome, ād discomfited his huge army, wherin were aboue.5. or 6. hundred thousande armed men. Make now M. Foxe the citezens of Rochester beleue, that in the olde tyme, by the prayer of S. Augustyne, theyre forefathers were borne with tayles: or any wise man to belieue, that king Ethelbertus ioyning with his frend Elfride the king of Northumberlād (who yet was an heathen, the other being christened) leuied an army, and set vppō the Britaines, because they would not receyue and obey the sayd S. Augustine. Make vs, if you can beleue this, with the vaine fabler Galfride (a sadde Author with your felowe Iewel) against the approued

> history of venerable Bede, and of all other sence his time. Make vs, I say, M. Fox, by any good or probable demōstratiō, believe this and an hundred suche other fables, for the which your *Fructus temporum*, is vnfruitfull to his wise ād discrete reader: and then tel vs and spare not, of this mōk of Swīstead. Otherwise he wer a very swyneshead that would be lightly and rashly perswaded, by suche swynish fables. Paynt ād picture thē as fast ād fayre as ye wil to make fooles fayn withal: I say not this because I wil excuse hym, or any other yll monke, of theyre nawghty doinges. I do require but cōuenient proufe namely of you M. Foxe, and your fellowes, that are so precise with the Catholikes for their proufes.

There are many things to which one might refer in such a passage as this: the skilful marshalling of the facts, for example; or the change of style as the writer passes from the argumentative to the narrative in the account of the King's last hours; or again the effective word-play, the natural and unaffected language, the vigour of the periods, the free movement of the rhythm. But it is *the careful weighing of the evidence* which we judge to be especially important in the extract: the insistence, in referring to the point at issue, upon discussion of actual fact. This shows Stapleton to be one of our early scientific historians. It also reminds us that Stapleton was here following a tradition, the tradition of More, who is described by R. W. Chambers as 'the originator and master of a school of historical writing'.* More's 'School', says Chambers, included those who actually came under his personal influence and 'those who felt More's influence rather through his writings than through personal contact'. Of these latter 'Harpsfield is the chief'.† Stapleton may also claim to hold an honoured position in this school. His devotion to More is common knowledge. His contact with living members of More's circle, which finds expression in his Latin *Life of More*, is historical fact. And if we add to this the fact that he has given his name to a work which exhibits just that historical attitude to questions of religious controversy which Lord Acton claims for Harpsfield,‡ and which the latter inherits from his master, More, then surely here are grounds enough for this claim and for classing the *Counterblast* as a second important memorial of More's school.§

* *Continuity of English Prose*, as before, p. liii. † ibid. footnote.

‡ *The Academy*, 24 June 1876, p. 609.

§ 'Harpsfield's *Life* [of More] is the chief extant memorial of this school.' Chambers, as before.

4. ATTENDANCE AT THE PROTESTANT SERVICE

Note: By the Act of Uniformity of 1559 all Elizabeth's subjects were obliged to assist at the Anglican service. The quandary of the Catholics as the result of this Act and its bearing upon the history of English Catholicism is fully discussed in such works as J. H. Pollen's *The English Catholics in the Reign of Queen Elizabeth* (1920).

Throughout the early years of Elizabeth's reign there was considerable diversity of opinion among Catholics in the matter of the vexed question whether they might or might not be present at the Anglican services. Indeed, to the minds of some, the question seems to have remained an open one right down to the closing years of the century. A ruling had been sought from the Council of Trent in 1562, and a committee of thirteen was set up in order to consider the matter, with Cardinal Hosius at its head. This committee, which included in its number Bishop Goldwell and Dr. Sander, decided that such attendance was not permissible. At the same time the matter had been laid before the Pope, Pius IV, who referred it to the Congregation of the Holy Office. From here, too, came an emphatic negative. There is nothing, however, to show that Pius issued any orders to English Catholics directing them to obey the ruling of the Trent Committee.* In the summer of 1566, we are told, Pope Pius V 'spoke strongly in Consistory against the toleration of such a practice, and Laurence Vaux, one of the foremost of the English clergy, was afterwards admitted to audience, at which the Pope ordered him to convey to Doctors Sander and Harding the substance of what he had said'.† The two doctors invited Vaux to carry the Pope's message to England. This he did, carrying with him a Pastoral Letter from Sander (since lost) the contents of which may be gathered from a longish letter written by him for general circulation among his Lancashire friends and dated 2 November 1566. In it he writes: 'Concerning M. Doctor Sander's letter I am charged to make a definitive sentence, that all such as offer children to the baptism now used, or be present at the communion of service now used in churches in England, as well the laity as the clergy, Do not walk in the state of Salvation; Neither we may not communicate or sociate our selfes in company with schismatic or heretic in divine things; there is no

* cf. C. G. Bayne, *Anglo-Roman Relations, 1558–1565* (Vol. II of *Oxford Historical and Literary Studies*, 1913), cap. 8. Bayne has a fully documented account of the early stages of this controversy.

† Pollen, as above, p. 104.

exception or dispensation can be had for any of the laity, if they will stand in the state of salvation'.* Vaux's authority, however, was unacceptable to a number of Catholics, and on the appeal of Thomas Wilson who, together with Thomas Peacock, shared the powers of absolution granted to Harding and Sander, the two latter again appealed to Rome and obtained an official declaration (August 1567) confirming the bishoply power granted them.† The difficulty of promulgating this document no doubt accounts for the fact that the question continued to be regarded as unsettled by some Catholics.

With the coming of the Jesuits into England in 1580 it was once more revived, and at the Synod of Southwark (see section 6 f.), where the matter came up for discussion, it was concluded that 'a Catholic cannot without great impiety bind himself to be present at those acts' etc., and this was to be 'the sum of that which all priests should teach and insinuate unto Catholics in all places, as hitherto they had done'.‡ Subsequently Fr. Persons published his *Reasons of Refusal* (see below), partly in order to confirm the faithful in face of the new laws which were threatened against the non-conformists, partly to show that conscience and not obstinacy was the true cause of Catholics refusing to go to the Anglican services. This called forth the pamphlet of Alban Langdale (below) and the reply of Persons and Blackwell.§ Some temporizing, however, still went on, and Fr. Garnet's two works, *The Declaration of the Fathers of the Councell of Trent, Concerning the Going vnto Churches at such time as hereticall seruice is saied, or heresy preached* and *A Treatise of Christian Renunciation . . . Wherunto is added a shorte discourse against going to Hereticall Churches with a Protestation*, published between 1590 and 1600, certainly seem to show that doubts were still felt about the question at that time. We may surmise that the dic-

* S.P.O. Dom. Eliz., Vol. 41, no. 1. Cited by T. G. Law in his reprint of Vaux's *Catechisme* (1885), p. xxxiii. Spelling modernized.

† A copy of this declaration was found by the Government after the Northern Rising and 'was printed by the English Government with a fiercely Calvinistic Declaration by Thomas Norton', the rack-master, in June 1570 as *A Bull graunted by the Pope to Doctor Harding and other by reconcilement and assoyling of English Papists to undermyne faith and allegiance to the Quene* . . . Pollen, as above, p. 105. Fr. Pollen goes on to point out that 'the document printed is not a Bull, but a petition to the Holy Office', made up of quotations from Harding's and Sander's appeal and the answer of the congregation.

‡ Pollen, op. cit., p. 335, citing Persons, *Life of Campion*.

§ Persons' account of this part of the controversy will be found in the bibliography to this work. Entry 92.

tates of charity prevented undue pressure being brought to bear upon recalcitrant Catholics and the matter was allowed more or less to resolve itself, which it did towards the end of the century. This would seem to be the view of Fr. Persons, who, writing some time after 1598, says: '. . . whether it were lawful to go to hereticall churches, where hereticall and schismaticall service was used in the Englishe tongue or noe, wherin divers even of the greater sort in respect of the troubles and losses that might come to them that should refuse, and not considering the greevous spirituall inconveniences that might and would ensue upon Catholiks frequenting hereticall churches, were very indulgent in this behalfe at the beginninge, judginge it no greate offence to goe; but others of more fervour and more forecast also in these deceitfull practises of heretickes and of there alluringe flattery, held altogeather the contrary, which contention indured many yeares and the matter was consulted at Rome and Paris with learned men, and never ended, untill by time and by practise, zeale and authority of priests comminge from the Seminaries beyond the seas and by good Catholike men at home, the matter hath byn cleared and the negative parte fully established to the confusion of heresy and edification of all forrayne nations.'*

We may trace the course of the paper debate down to the year 1581 as follows:

(1) Nicolas Sander's *A Treatise of the Images of Christ* (1567). In this work, already referred to in 'The Great Controversy' above (no. 59), Sander expressly denounces attendance at the Protestant services. In the Preface he speaks of a 'rumour spread by certain men, that this going to schismatical service is, or may be winked at, or dispensed in the Catholics' and replies – 'of certainty it is not so. But rather by this key-cold demeanour of

* Catholic Record Society, *Miscellanea II*, p. 61. Cited from Archives S.J., *Anglia IX*. A footnote suggests that the Roman decision to which Persons refers was probably a later one than that of either 1562 or 1566 (see above). William Allen obtained a *viva voce* condemnation of the practice from the Pope, about the same time as the formal opinion given by Father (afterwards Cardinal) Toledo, dated 14 June 1581. Writing from Rhemes to the Cardinal of Como, 8 August 1581, Allen says: 'Resolutionem de non adeundis haereticorum ecclesiis, quam non ita pridem Roma accepimus et in Angliam misimus, pro oraculo habent, ac quidvis patientur potius quam hac specie mali se contaminent.' (*Letters and Memorials*, as before, p. 100.) The consultation at Paris was presumably that held at the Sorbonne, probably early in 1581.

the Catholics, we may perceive how just God was in punishing them with heresy in whom he saw so little true and hearty faith, that for fear of a small temporal loss, they can be content to put in hasard their everlasting salvation'. (*C*)

(2) Gregory Martin's *A Treatise of Schisme. Shewing, that al Catholikes ought in any wise to abstaine altogether from heretical Conuenticles, to witt, their prayers, sermons, &c.* (1578). (*C*)

(3) Robert Persons' *A Brief Discours contayning certayne reasons why Catholiques refuse to goe to Church* (1580). The work generally known as *Reasons of Refusal*. (*C*)

(4) Alban Langdale's pamphlet ('secretly spread abroad in wrytten hand'), *A treatise to prove that attendance at the Protestant church was in itself no sin, and therefore might be lawfully submitted to for the purpose of avoiding a persecution so intolerable at present, and threatening to grow so much more so* [1580].* This was intended as a reply to Persons (no. 3). (*C*)

(5) Persons' answer to Langdale. Written in collaboration with George Blackwell and disseminated in manuscript. No copy of the writing has survived. (*C*)

(6) William Fulke's *A briefe Confutation of a Popish Discourse* (1581). Answers Persons' *Brief Discours* (3) above. (*P*)

(7) John Fielde's *A Caueat for Parsons Howlet* [1581]. A second answer to Persons. (*P*)

(8) Perceval Wiburn's *A Checke or reproofe of M. Howlets vntimely schreeching* (1581). A third answer to Persons. (*P*)

(9) Sometime before 1584 Richard White put Fr. Persons' *Reasons of Refusal* (no. 3 above) into Welsh verse. (*C*)

Later Catholic contributions to the debate, in addition to the two works of Fr. Garnet already mentioned, were H. B.'s *A Consolatory Letter to all the afflicted Catholikes in England*, and George Cotton's (?) *An answer to a comfortable advertisement with it addition written of late to afflicted Catholykes concerninge goinge to*

* Title according to Joseph Gillow's *Bibliographical Dictionary*, s.v. *Alban Langdale*.

churche with protestantes, both written about the year 1588.* Persons has a final word to say on the question in his *Quaestiones duae de sacris alienis non adeundis*, published at St. Omer in 1607.

LANGDALE, MARTIN, PERSONS

Both Gregory Martin and Robert Persons may justly claim the close attention of all students of Elizabethan prose. Each was eminent in his own sphere as a writer: Martin as the translator of the Bible, and Persons, among other works, as the author of one of the best-known books of devotion of the age.† Both these writers will receive full treatment in the later pages of this book, and we shall therefore reserve any serious consideration of their style for those pages. Alban Langdale, on the other hand, can only be regarded as a very minor contributor to Catholic Recusant literature. His short pamphlet on the question of attendance at the Protestant service (never printed) is his only known work, and is not remarkable in any way for its literary style. Since its interest is largely academic, it hardly calls for detailed examination here. We may confine ourselves, therefore, to a brief reference to the substance of the three pamphlets of these writers and a short quotation or two, which will perhaps give the reader some idea as to the points at issue and the process of following them up.

Gregory Martin's little book, which has a special interest for both the bibliographer and the historian,‡ was intended to stiffen the waverers, and endeavours to meet the arguments of the Catholics which were commonly put forward in support of attending the Anglican services. Its substance is set out on the title-page (see facsimile), and its four chapter-headings are as follows: (1) 'Reasons that Catholikes ought in any wise to absteine from heretical Conuenticles'; (2) 'Examples out of Scripture'; (3) 'Examples out of ecclesiastical Histories'; (4) 'Aunsweres to the chiefe obiections' – these include six objections and a section headed 'Of carnal affection to wife and children'. The fourth chapter is, perhaps, the most enlightening. For example:

* The second of these is preserved in a quarto paper MS. at Oscott College and is initialled G.C.; cf. C. G. Bayne, op. cit., Appendix 43, p. 289. The 'addition written of late to afflicted Catholykes' would appear to be a transcript of H.B.'s pamphlet.

† *The Christian Exercise* (1582).

‡ See the note on William Carter's printing press in Chapter VI; cf. also bibl. ent. 84.

A TREATISE OF SCHISME.

Shewing, that al Catholikes ought in any wise to abstaine altogether from heretical Conuenticles, to witt, their prayers, sermons, &c. deuided into foure Chapters, whereof

1. Conteineth sundry reasons to that purpose, grounded for the most part vpon Scriptures and Fathers.
2. Examples out of holy Scripture.
3. Examples out of ecclesiastical histories.
4. Answeres to the chiefe obiections.

By Gregorie Martin Licentiate in Diuinitie.

DVACI.
Apud Iohannem Foulerum.
1578.

TITLE-PAGE OF
G. MARTIN'S *TREATISE OF SCHISME*
Printed at a secret press in London by William Carter

> The fift Obiection.
>
> There be many good men of them, godly prayers, Psalmes, Scriptures, although somewhat be lacking, yet that which they haue is good, and agreing with the Catholikes.
>
> The Aunswere.
>
> Many good men? Are they better then Angels? *Si Angelus de coelo euangelizet vobis: Si quis vobis euangelizauerit praeter id quod accepistis, Anathema sit.* If an Angel from heauen preache vnto you, if any whosoeuer he be shal preach otherwise then that you haue receaued, be he accursed: Any man or Angel whatsoeuer he be. And because many folowe their good vicar, which before said Masse, and now preacheth the contrary for aduantage, and saith the cōmunion, S. Paule addeth of him selfe, *licet nos.* If we our selues, and the rest Apostles come and preache contrary to that we first preached, *Anathema sit.* Be he accursed. But are they gentle persons, sweete men? no meruaile: *Eiusmodi pseudo-apostoli* . . . Suche false Apostles are craftie woorkers, transforming them selues into the Apostles of Christ, and no meruaile, for Satan himselfe transformeth him-selfe into an Angel of light, and therefore it is no great matter, if his ministers be misshapen as the ministers of Iustice or righteousnes. Such common places are infinite.*

The style of the writing is, on the whole, compact, but the continual appeal to authority, backed up by numerous quotations, makes somewhat tedious reading.

Persons' *Reasons of Refusal*, published under the pseudonym of John Howlet and dedicated to the Queen, is a piece of good workmanlike argumentative prose. The style is much more vigorous than that of Martin and there is greater readiness to enlarge the theme where it is deemed necessary. The treatment of the subject is both systematic and thorough, the argument being presented in the form of nine reasons 'why I being a Catholicke in minde, may not goe to the Churches or seruice of the contrarie relygion'. These reasons are: (1) 'Perill of infection'; (2) 'Scandal'; (3) 'A signe distinctive betwixt religion and religion'; (4) 'Schisme'; (5) 'Participation'; (6) 'Dissimulation'; (7) 'Noughty seruice'; (8) 'Loosing the benefit of Catholique religion'; (9) 'Examples of infidels and hereticks'. Each of these is particularized under a series of sub-headings. Thus the seventh reason, 'noughty seruice', develops into six short paragraphs explaining 'Where in the Protestants seruice is euil, in particuler': (1) 'Deuysed by them selues different from the

* *Treatise of Schisme*, sig. I4.

rest'; (2) 'Condemned by the Puritains'; (3) 'False translations of scripture'; (4) [Services &c.] 'Sayd by laymen'; (5) 'Falsehoode & blasphemie in their seruice'; (6) 'Lacke of necessarye thinges which it should haue in it' [notably six of the sacraments and ceremonies].

The tone of Langdale's pamphlet is that of counsel for the defendant in a case of law, and his pleading takes the form of interpreting anew the evidence supplied by Persons, the prosecutor, in the light of his unnamed client's case, and of supplying fresh evidence for the defence mainly from Scriptural sources. His pleading, that is to say, is special rather than general, and is drawn with particular reference to the circumstances of time and place, 'for good menn and martirs', he says, 'in tyme of persecution haue gon amongest Protestants and Idolators and some tymes to their churches and temples without grudg of conscence & were not defiled with theire woorkes of Protestantism or Idolatry and thus they did as circumstances moved them, for circumstances do alter cases'.

We offer as a sample of the fashion of this debate a short passage from Persons' third reason ('a signe distinctive betwixt religion and religion') with Langdale's reply. Here is Persons:

> For when a Catholick doth come before the Commissioners, there is nothing asked of him, but when he was at Church, and if he wil promise to goe to Church, commonly they account him a sufficient conformable man, (yͭ is to haue yelded sufficiētly vnto them.) Furthermore, the multitude of thē, which haue of long tyme abydden imprisonment, and nowe in greter nūber doe for this only thing, in the sight and knowledge, not only of Ingland, but also of al Christendome, and of the enemies of the same in the world besids, doth make this abstayninge from Churche to be a proper and peculier signe of a true Catholique, nowe, if it were not before: and the yealding in the same, (especially if a man be called to publique tryal about it) to be a flat and euident denyinge of God and of his faith . . . I wil put an example of the Primatiue Church, wherin the wearing of a garland was lawful for al souldiers, vntil the Emperours, and the common opinion of men, had abrydged it onelye to infidel souldiers, to distinguish them thereby, in honour, from Christian souldiers. And then, after that (as Tertullian prouethe) it was noe longer lawful for Christian souldiers to weare them, for that the wearing thereof, was a denyal of the Christian faith. Wherevpon, we reade that a certayne Christian souldier offered him selfe rather to suffer

> death, then to weare one of them: as appeareth in the same booke of Tertullian. But now, much more is the thing vnlawful in our case. For that the going to the Protestants Churches (which a Catholicke must presume to be heretical) was neuer a thing of it self lawful, (as I wil hereafter proue) which the wearing of a garland was: and therfore much lesse now to be tollerated, seeing besides this, it is also made a sign distinctiue as I haue alredye proued.

And here is Langdale:

> The goinge and not goinge is not made a signe distinctiue betwene. C. & P. for puritans refuse to go to the churches of. P. againe yͨ. P. do not account yt a speciall marke, for they know that ther be many cath. wͨh goe to the churche of. P. and many cath. ther be wͨh wold be so accepted & reddy to dye for theire faithe wͨh neuertheles go to the churche of. P. and make yt not a speciall marke further in the case sett dowen there be speciall markes anoughe and a plaine profession, yf I pray not wͭh them, if I sett whan they knele, if I refuse theire [communion] &c be not these signa distinctiua and do not these factes shewe a dissent as well as express woordes but it is not to be neglected that this is made signū distinctiuū betwene a trew subiect and a rebbell and therfore if the bare goinge be but in his owen nature a thinge indifferent, lett euery wise man weighe his owen case, And for thexample of the garland marke that they did yett beare the garland in theire hande though not on their heddes, and so they did weare the garland thoughe not to the honnor of the Idoll.

Richard White's versifying of Persons' nine reasons must be one of the curiosities of Welsh literature. For the benefit of the English reader we append a translation of the first four as given in the *Publications of the Catholic Record Society*, Vol. V (p. 93):

> Hear a song, a great thought,
> Which has been made by a pilgrim.
> I know one who will go to a deep prison,
> Sooner than go to the church of Calvin.
>
> And reasons nine has he,
> And these will be witness,
> To show you why
> He will not go to a wrong service.
>
> [Perill of Infection]
> The first reason is the infection to a man,
> Like a canker in the bone, their naughtiness

Will infest thy mind as a deceit,
To steal thy reason and to cheat thee.

[Scandale]

The second is scandal, or injury,
And woe to every land which is infected with it!
This is the great cause of thy fault,
Which makes another man to fall.

[Goynge or not goeynge to Church . . .]

The third is – a special point,
That thou art of the Catholic Faith.
From their church keep thyself wisely away,
Lest thou walk into a pitfall.

If thou goest amongst them,
To hear the teaching of thy foes,
That is a sign clear enough,
That thou art not a true Christian.

[Schisme]

The fourth – a matter for grave debate –
Against going into an alien church,
Is Schism, chiefest whore
That came from the Tower of Babylon.

5. ALLEN'S SCROLL OF ARTICLES

The importance attached by the Protestant authorities to the pamphlets which gave rise to the attack upon Allen's 'Scroll of Articles' may be gathered both from their action in trying to suppress them entirely and from the use to which they were subsequently put in the examination of the Catholic martyrs. Evidence for these facts will be found in the bibliography to this book (entry 21). The connexion of the pamphlets with Allen's 'Articles' is examined in detail at Appendix I. It concerns us only to state here that these Articles were never published by Allen himself, but found their way into print in the following three Catholic versions:

(1) Richard Bristow's *A Briefe Treatise of diuerse plaine and sure wayes to finde out the truthe in this doubtful and dangerous time of Heresie: conteyning sundry worthy Motiues vnto the Catholike faith* (1574).

(2) The anonymous *Offer made by a Catholike to a learned Protestant, wherin shall appere the difference betwixte the open knowen Church of the Catholikes, from the hid and vnknowen Congregation of the Protestantes* (1575). This forms the second part of *A notable Discourse* (see section 8 of this chapter) and was once known as Rishton's 'Challenge'.

(3) *Bristow's Demaundes to bee proponed of Catholickes to the Heretickes* (1576) – an epitome of (1).

The following Replies came from the Protestants:

(4) William Fulke's *Two Treatises written against the Papistes the one being an answere of the Christian Protestant to the proud challenge of a Popish Catholicke* (1577). This was not a direct answer to any of the above, but to some manuscript version of Allen's Articles. It was reprinted in the same year under the title of *An Answer of a true christian to the proude challenge of a counterfet Catholike.*

(5) Oliver Carter's *An Answere made by Oliuer Carter, Bacheler of Diuinitie: Unto certaine Popish Questions and Demaundes* (1579). Answers no. (3) above).*

(6) Fulke's *A Retentiue, to stay good christians, in true faith and religion, against the motiues of Richard Bristow* (1580). Answers no. (1) above.

These were followed by:

(7) Bristow's *A Reply to Fulke. In defense of M. D. Allens scroll of Articles, and booke of Purgatorie* (1580). Answers no. (4) above.

(8) Fulke's retort to this – *A Reioynder to Bristows Replie in defence of Allens scroll of Articles and Booke of Purgatorie* (1581).

And finally Robert Crowley answered the anonymous 'Offer' (no. 2 above) in

(9) *A Deliberat answere made to a rash offer, which a popish Antichristian Catholique, made to a learned protestant (as he saieth) and caused to be publyshed in printe: Anno. Do. 1575* (1588).

* For two later Replies to Bristow's *Demaundes*, one from the pen of Dr. John Rainolds, see bibliography.

RICHARD BRISTOW

There is little in particular to remark upon in the three works listed above which bear Bristow's name. We have already referred to their author's indebtedness to Allen's Articles for his *Motives* and *Demands*: we should perhaps add here, in reference to this, that a comparison of these two works with what is probably a near original version of the Articles, as cited by Fulke in his *Two Treatises written against the Papistes* (no. 4 above), shows the presentation of those Articles to have been entirely his own. With regard to that presentation Bristow's own words should be noted. 'My purpose & studie', he writes, 'is here and in al this Treatise [i.e. the *Motives*], rather how to make short, then how to make long: & not to heape togeather so much as may be said, but to take out so much as is sufficient.'* His aim, that is to say, was to compass much in a little space, and this was to be achieved by conciseness of the expression and a careful selection of his material. This leads him to use somewhat long and, sometimes, involved sentences, and since the subject-matter of both the *Motives* and the *Demands* is serious theological stuff it might seem that there was some ground for Fulke's gibe at 'those wodden workes'.† Certainly Bristow makes no attempt at being merely graceful and, though he finds room for an occasional illustration, he seldom departs from the strait and narrow way of strict argument. Yet his works are not without eloquence, and there is much to interest even the modern reader in their topical allusions.

The *Reply to Fulke* is a much longer book than the *Motiues* and its chief interest for the modern reader will probably be its many allusions to contemporary events. These include references to Catholic studies at Rhemes [sig. O2], the disputation at Westminster [P1ᵛ], the invitation of English divines to the Council of Trent [P1ᵛ], the coming Rhemes version of the Scriptures – an important statement concerning the relative value of Hebrew, Greek and Latin texts – [P2ᵛ], English Grammar Schools and the Universities [Yy2], and Roundheads and religion [Ww4ᵛ], on which last topic Bristow writes as follows:

> *Of the Messalians or Martyrians, you lerned* (saith he) *to shaue your beardes, and to let your lockes grow long, Comas muliebres producunt,*

* *Motiues*, sig. O3ᵛ.

† *A reioynder to Bristows Replie*, sig. A2ᵛ.

*They kepe their heare long, like women.** Do we so? Be our heades like womens long heades? womens heades bylike are rounded heades: or S. Paule did meane that men should poll their heades, *Ita ad pressum tondentes vt rasorum similes videantur*, *Cutting them so neare the skin that they should be like to shauen heades*. Or do not some Protestantes weare round heads and shaue their beardes, as well as some Catholikes: and some Catholikes, euen also the Cleargie in Italie and Spayne, weare beardes and polled heades, as well as some Protestantes?†

The two following further short excerpts from this work with which we shall conclude this notice will illustrate the characteristic harmony and movement of Bristow's prose:

This is your goodly substantiall stuffe that you haue against the Popish Church: which may seeme [serue] you well amongest the blinde, that will needes follow such blinde guides. But vs that haue eyes, how can you alienate from it with such geare? yea could you more confirme vs in our liking of it, then after this sort to bewray your selues, that you haue no matter, no substance, yea no shadow of any thing, agaynst it? Well, in the name of God bethinke your selues in time, and humble your selues to your louing Mother, this one onely Church of God. In olde time it was the true Church, as your selfe confesse, and therefore if you had liued then, you would not haue spurned agaynst it, you would haue bene a good childe of it, yea also though you thought it to erre. How much more, considering now you see that it erred not, as you thought it did? Proue therefore that your heart meaneth, as your tongue speaketh: Proue it (I say) by yeelding to the same Church now, which you see nowe no lesse, yea muche more cleared from all errors, in this answere to eche error that you haue charged it withall. Or at leastwise let all other men, as they loue their soules, forethinke thē selues, and ponder wel, whether these obiections are like to be admitted of their Iudge, the head & husband of this Church, for good pleas, in that generall and most terrible Court day [sig. L3v].

When you here in the laste Chapter, and your Masters and Scholefelowes commonly in their writinges feare not to open your mouthes thus against Gods holy Tabernacle in earth: I that am nothing, and in very deede nothing, and lesse then nothing, may not disdaine the like opening at me by the foresaide Vnlearned, but contenting me with mine owne conscience, and the conscience of God him selfe and his Angels, and all

* The reference is to Fulke's *Two Treatises*, p. 22.
† This significant use of 'round head' predates the earliest reference in the N.E.D. to the same by some sixty years.

his Seruauntes that knowe me by my person, or by my writings, beeing moste certaine how alwayes in heart and worde I haue honored the most holy Scriptures, euen as gods owne liuely and infallible worde, I submit my selfe with Dauid in an humble and contrite heart, to all that Semei hath or shall vtter against me,* if peraduenture my Lorde God most mercifull will accept it to forgeuenes of my manifold and heynous sinnes: desiring of him no other reuenge, but the parties conuersion and reconciliation to him and his sweete spouse my lieue Mother the Catholike Church. And so muche in this place to that man [sig. N2].

6. EDMUND CAMPION'S LETTER TO THE LORDS OF THE COUNCIL

(Commonly called Campion's 'Challenge')

The events which led to the publication of this great *Apologia* have been recorded often enough by Catholic historians of our period, and we have nothing to add to what is already well known to students of the Counter-Reformation in England. In setting forth briefly again, therefore, the circumstances out of which Campion's Letter arose, while at the same time acknowledging our debt to those writers from whose books we have drawn our facts,† we must apologize for repeating what has been already well said. It will be generally agreed, however, that it is impossible to separate such a document as this from its historical context if we would get a full understanding of its purport.

Let us recall, then, the principal details of the Jesuit mission to England prior to the setting out of Persons and Campion on their missionary journeys through the country. The two Jesuits had arrived in London in June 1580 and almost at once (probably early in July) they called together a meeting of the leading Catholic clergy and laity, partly in order to introduce themselves to their friends and colleagues and partly to settle certain outstanding questions. The Synod of Southwark, as it has been called, sat secretly in a small house on the south side of the river near St. Mary Ovaries (now St. Saviour's), Southwark. Four principal topics came up for consideration:

* II Samuel xii. 5 et seq.

† Richard Simpson (*Edmund Campion*, 1896), Evelyn Waugh (*Edmund Campion*, 1935), and, above all, Fr. J. H. Pollen, S.J. (*The English Catholics in the Reign of Queen Elizabeth*, 1920).

BLESSED EDMUND CAMPION, S.J.
From the engraving in Cornelius Hazart's *Kerckelycke Historie van de Gheheele Werelt* (Antwerp, 1669)

(1) The aims of the mission, concerning which Fr. Persons 'read out the instructions the missionaries had received against taking any part whatever in politics' (Pollen, p. 335).

(2) Lawfulness of attendance at the Protestant services. Here a strong negative verdict was returned.*

(3) Rules of fasting. An ecclesiastical question concerning the diversity of practice up and down the country.

(4) Certain smaller matters concerning particular persons. Pollen mentions Thomas Cottam, John Hart and James Bosgrave (p. 337).

As soon as the Synod was over the Fathers decided to leave London for the shires – a sudden recrudescence of penal activity no doubt hastened this resolve – and, having been magnificently equipped by George Gilbert, one of the leaders of the group of Catholic laymen who had pledged themselves to support them, they set forth with Gilbert and Gervase Pierrepoint as guides for Hoxton, where they were to spend the first night before finally parting for their different destinations. There, early on the morning of 19 July, Thomas Pounde, another and somewhat eccentric member of the Catholic group, found them as they were about to set out once again. Pounde was actually a prisoner in the Marshalsea at this time, but, having managed to bribe his keepers, not a difficult thing to do in the Marshalsea, he had ridden post-haste after the Fathers in order to put a certain proposal before them. He explained his sudden visit by saying that he and his fellow prisoners had come to the conclusion that the missionaries ought to take an important precaution. They were under grave risk of capture, and 'once captured they would be buried in seclusion, then examined, and malignant reports would be spread abroad about their confessions, which no one would be able to answer. Therefore prepare now, he said, some protest or declaration, which may be published by your friends as soon as you are taken' (Pollen, p. 348). Pounde's advice was clearly sound, and both Fathers forthwith prepared documents the general lines of which are very similar.† And here is Persons' own account of Campion's

* See section 4 above.

† Persons' *Confessio Fidei ad Magistratus Londini* survives only in a Latin translation, so that any exact comparison with Campion's paper is not possible. See Pollen, p. 354, for a brief *résumé* of it.

writing, according to Simpson. 'Campion', says Persons, 'being a man of singular good-nature, and easy to be persuaded to whatever religion or piety inclined towards, rose from the company, took a pen, and seated himself at the end of the table, where in less than half an hour he wrote the declaration which was soon to be so famous. It was written without preparation, and in the hurry of a journey; yet it was so "pithy in substance and style" that it was a triumph to one party and poison to the other' (p. 225).

Copies of the two documents having been made, these were committed to Pounde's keeping, it being understood that they were not to be divulged until necessity demanded it. Persons had taken the precaution of sealing his paper before he gave it to Pounde; Campion, however, left his open. The result was that Pounde read the paper that evening at the Marshalsea. 'The effect', and here I am quoting Waugh, 'upon his own somewhat volatile nature was instantaneous. There and then he set about the composition of a challenge on his own account, modelled upon Campion's; in the first instance, a brief thesis giving three reasons why Scripture should not be taken as the sole grounds of faith, which he followed, shortly afterwards, with an appeal for a formal dispute before the Bishops and Council' (p. 127). The three reasons eventually became six, and were duly answered early in the next year by Robert Crowley and Henry Trippe, two Puritan ministers who had been commissioned by the authorities to confer with the prisoners of the Marshalsea.*

Meanwhile Pounde had begun to pass on Campion's *Letter* or *Challenge*, and during the months of September and October it acquired a wide circulation for those days.† There can be no doubt that it was a 'bright literary success'. Campion writes in November:‡ 'A certain matter fell out these days unlooked for. I had set down in writing by several articles the causes of my coming in and made certain demands most reasonable . . . One copy of this writing I determined to keep with me,

* See bibl. ent. 119.

† It should be noted that it was this early publication of the document which gave such emphasis to the idea of a challenge, which was originally quite a subordinate issue.

‡ To the General of the Jesuits. Probably 17 November 1580. See note in Simpson, p. 525. The translator appears to be unknown.

that if I should fall into the officers' hands, it might go with me; another copy I laid in a friend's hand that when myself with the other should be seized, another might thereupon straight be dispersed. But my said friend kept it not close long, but divulged it, and it was read greedily; whereat the adversaries were mad, answering out of the pulpit, that themselves certesse would not refuse to dispute, but the queen's pleasure was not that matters should be called in question being already established. In the mean while they tear and sting us with their venomous tongues, calling us seditious, hypocrites, yes, heretics too, which is much laughed at. The people hereupon is ours, and that error of spreading abroad this writing hath much advanced the cause' (Simpson, p. 249). Before the year was out the first printed reply had come from the pen of William Charke, and thus the battle of the books began. The controversy can hardly be said to have come to an end before the year 1586, by which time 'no less than twenty works had appeared, dealing either with the *Brag*, the *Ten Reasons*, or the Disputes in the Tower, which were their direct consequence' (Waugh, p. 149). We may table the principal items of the controversy as follows:

(1) Campion's *Challenge* (1580). (*C*)

(2) Thomas Pounde's *Sixe Reasons* (1580). These may be regarded as an offshoot of Campion's *Challenge*, from which they are derived. (*C*)

(3) William Charke's *An answere to a seditious pamphlet* (1580). Answers (1). (*P*)

(4) Robert Crowley's *An Aunswer to sixe Reasons* (1581). Pounde's pamphlet is printed for the first time in this work. Appended to Crowley's *Aunswer* is Henry Trippe's *A breefe Aunswer to Maister Pounds six Reasons*. (*P*)

(5) Meredith Hanmer's *The Great bragge and challenge of M. Champion a Iesuite* (1581). Campion's *Challenge* is printed for the first time in this work. (*P*)

(6) Robert Persons' *A Brief Censure vppon two bookes written in answere to M. Edmonde Campions offer of disputation* (1581). Answers Charke and Hanmer (3 and 5 above). (*C*)

(7) Charke's *A Replie to a Censure written against the two answers to a Iesuites seditious Pamphlet* (1581). Replies to Persons (6 above). (*P*)

(8) Hanmer's *The Iesuites Banner* (1581). A further reply to Persons. (*P*)

(9) Campion's *Rationes Decem* (1581). Written by Campion, to quote Simpson, in order to 'meet the charge of overweening pride which Charke and Hanmer had made against him, because he had challenged to dispute single-handed with all the learning of a whole realm; a charge which had become so general, that every pulpit was ringing with his impudence, and with the frauds and sedition of the Jesuits. Hence he was forced to show that his trust was not in his own power, but solely in the strength of his cause, which he exhibited in ten reasons, relying on which, *quibus fretus*, he offered to dispute with any or all of the ministers of the Established Church' (p. 265). The *Rationes Decem* gave rise to a short separate controversy conducted in Latin, the items of which (six in all) are listed by Simpson (p. 492). (*C*)

(10) Persons' *A Defence of the Censure, gyuen vpon two bookes of william Charke and Meredith Hanmer* (1582). Replies to (7) and (8) above. (*C*)

(11) *An Answeare for the time, vnto that foule, and wicked Defence of the Censure* (1583). Replies to (10) above. The *Short Title Catalogue* attributes this to Charke. (*P*)

(12) Charke's *A Treatise against the Defence of the Censure, giuen vpon the Bookes of W. Charke, and Meredith Hanmer, by an vnknowne Popish Traytor* . . . (1586). Another reply to (10). (Adjoined to this are two treatises of William Fulke's against Allen and Fowler.) (*P*)

To these we may add:

(13) *A true report of the Disputation or rather priuate Conference had in the Tower of London, with Ed. Campion Iesuite, the last of August, 1581. Set downe by the Reurend learned men them seules that dealt therein. Whereunto is ioyned also a true report of the other three dayes conferences had there with the same Iesuite. Which nowe are thought meete to be published in print by authoritie.* January 1583 (O.S.). (*P*)

CAMPION'S *Challenge*

Campion's *Letter to the Council* is the only piece of his English written during his golden period which has survived. It deserves to rank with the greatest of the short Apologies of the language. Indeed, in its kind, it is doubtful whether as a piece of prose writing it has ever been surpassed. We make no apology, therefore, for printing it in full.

TO THE RIGHT HONOURABLE LORDS OF HER MAJESTIE'S PRIVY COUNCIL*

Right Honourable,

Whereas I have come out of Germanie and Boëmeland, being sent by my Superiours, and adventured myself into this noble Realm, my deare Countrie, for the glorie of God and benefit of souls, I thought it like enough that, in this busie, watchful and suspicious worlde, I should either sooner or later be intercepted and stopped of my course. Wherefore, providing for all events, and uncertaine what may become of me, when God shall haply deliver my body into durance, I supposed it needful to put this writing in a readiness, desiringe your good Lordships to give it ye reading, for to know my cause. This doing, I trust I shall ease you of some labour. For that which otherwise you must have sought for by practice of wit, I do now lay into your hands by plaine confession. And to ye intent that the whole matter may be conceived in order, and so the better both understood and remembered, I make thereof these ix points or articles, directly, truly and resolutely opening my full enterprise and purpose.

1. I confesse that I am (albeit unworthie) a priest of ye Catholike Church, and through ye great mercie of God vowed now these viii years into the Religion of the Societie of Jhesus. Hereby I have taken upon me a special kind of warfare under the banner of obedience, and eke resigned all my interest or possibilitie of wealth, honour, pleasure, and other worldlie felicitie.

2. At the voice of our General Provost, which is to me a warrant from heaven and Oracle of Christ, I tooke my voyage from Prage to Rome (where our said General Father is always resident) and from Rome to England, as I might and would

* The text followed is that of Pollen (pp. 349–52) in this reprint. Other modern reprints are those of Simpson (pp. 225–28), Waugh (Appendix, pp. 219–23), and *The Month* for January 1910. A footnote in the last (p. 62) says: 'The text of this document has never been satisfactorily settled by a collation of the principal texts, e.g. R.O. Dom. Eliz., 142, 20; Harleian 422, 12 and 422, 13; Stonyhurst *Coll.* P., ii, 583, etc.; the editions of Charke, Hanmer, etc.'

have done joyously into any part of Christendome or Heathenesse, had I been thereto assigned.

3. My charge is, of free cost to preach the Gospel, to minister the Sacraments, to instruct the simple, to reforme sinners, to confute errors – in brief, to crie alarme spiritual against foul vice and proud ignorance wherewith many my dear Countrymen are abused.

4. I never had mind, and am strictly forbidden by our Father that sent me, to deal in any respect with matter of State or Policy of this realm, as things which appertain not to my vocation, and from which I do gladly restrain and sequester my thoughts.

5. I do ask, to the glory of God, with all humility, and under your correction, iii sortes of indifferent and quiet audiences: *the first* before your Honours, wherein I will discourse of religion, so far as it toucheth the common weale and your nobilities; *the second*, whereof I make more account, before the Doctors and Masters and chosen men of both Universities, wherein I undertake to avow the faith of our Catholike Church by proofs innumerable, Scriptures, Councils, Fathers, History, natural and moral reasons; *the third* before the lawyers, spiritual and temporal, wherein I will justify the said faith by the common wisdom of the laws standing yet in force and practice.

6. I would be loth to speak anything that might sound of any insolent brag or challenge, especially being now as a dead man to this world and willing to put my head under every man's foot, and to kiss the ground they tread upon. Yet have I such a courage in avouching the Majesty of Jhesus my King, and such affiance in His gracious favour, and such assurance in my quarrel, and my evidence so impregnable, and because I know perfectly that no one Protestant, nor all the Protestants living, nor any sect of our adversaries (howsoever they face men down in pulpits and overrule us in their kingdom of grammarians and unlearned ears) can maintain their doctrine in disputation. I am to sue most humbly and instantly for the combat with all and every of them, and the most principal that may be found: protesting that in this trial the better furnished they come, the better welcome they shall be.

7. And because it hath pleased God to enrich the Queen my Sovereigne Ladye with notable gifts of nature, learning and princely education, I do verily trust that – if her Highness would vouchsafe her royal person and good attention to such a conference as, in the ii part of my fifth article I have motioned, or to a few sermons, which in her or your hearing I am to utter, – such manifest and fair light by good method and plain dealing may be cast upon these controversies, that possibly her

zeal of truth and love of her people shall incline her noble Grace to disfavour some proceedings hurtful to the Realm, and procure towards us oppressed more equitie.

8. Moreover I doubt not but you her Highness' Council, being of such wisdom and discreet in cases most important, when you shall have heard these questions of religion opened faithfully, which many times by our adversaries are huddled up and confounded, will see upon what substantial grounds our Catholike Faith is builded, how feeble that side is which by sway of the time prevaileth against us, and so at last for your own souls, and for many thousand souls that depend upon your government, will discountenance error when it is bewrayed, and hearken to those who would spend the best blood in their bodies for your salvation. Many innocent hands are lifted up to heaven for you daily by those English students, whose posteritie shall never die, which beyond seas, gathering virtue and sufficient knowledge for the purpose, are determined never to give you over, but either to win you heaven, or to die upon your pikes. And touching our Societie, be it known to you that we have made a league – all the Jesuits in the world, whose succession and multitude must overreach all the practices of England – cheerfully to carry the cross you shall lay upon us, and never to despair your recovery, while we have a man left to enjoy your Tyburn, or to be racked with your torments, or consumed with your prisons. The expense is reckoned, the enterprise is begun; it is of God, it cannot be withstood. So the faith was planted, so it must be restored.

9. If these my offers be refused, and my endeavours can take no place, and I, having run thousands of miles to do you good, shall be rewarded with rigour, I have no more to say but to recommend your case and mine to Almightie God, the Searcher of Hearts, who send us His grace, and set us at accord before the day of payment, to the end we may at last be friends in heaven, when all injuries shall be forgotten.

There is no call here for minute analysis. The method follows roughly (but only roughly) the order of the rhetoricians, with its *exordium*, *narratio*, *contentio*, and *peroratio*;* the theme, 'that the Faith is absolutely satisfactory to the mind, enlisting all knowledge and all reason in its cause: that it is completely compelling to any who give it an "indifferent and quiet audience" '(Waugh, p. 126), is clear and open. This much further may be said. The force, and indeed the charm, of the writing lies in the extreme simplicity of the structure and vocabulary.

* It would be classed as an 'oration deliberative'.

Though the style is not epigrammatic, yet everything is brief and to the point. Its sureness is reflected in the words, which are those which men then used in their daily talk, and where emphasis is sought it is by the position and weight of the word in the sentence only. The absence of parallelism or antithesis of clause or word gives freedom to the expression, as it does also to the rhythm. Yet there is a fitting reserve; but it is the reserve of neither the indifferent nor the self-complacent. The writing is, indeed, aglow with the writer's own keen spirit, and from this springs its consistency and luminosity, and on this depends the vigorous march of the elocution.

ROBERT PERSONS

The two controversial works in which Persons replied to the animadversions of Charke and Hanmer upon Campion were both written under unusual stress and bear eloquent witness not only to the author's resource, but also to the readiness of his pen. William Fleetwood, the pursuivant, we are told, on finding a copy of the *Brief Censure* outside his door ten days after the publication of Hanmer's *The Great Bragge*, was amazed at the size of the book and the shortness of the time in which it was produced.* Persons himself says of *A Defence of the Censure:*

> In generall, euery one can imagine by hym selfe, how difficult a thing yt is in England at this daye, for a Catholique man to write any book: where nether libertie, nor rest, nor librarie, nor conference, nor beinge is permitted hym. And in particular, thus muche I must adde, whiche you alredie in part doe knowe: that soone after the publishinge of your reply to the Censure, the Author therof addressed hym selfe to a defence, and had in greate part dispatched the same, redie for the printe, in suche sort as the rigorous tyme of your persecution permitted hym. But God sufferinge at that verie instāt, that the sayd print so long sought, and muche feared by you, should be taken: there was taken, lost, and dispersed ther-withall, not onelie all furniture there redy for this booke, but also for sundry other thinges, partlie printed, and partlie in printing, concerning our defence of trueth and equitie, against your falsehood and violent oppressions.†
>
> This disturbance, and losse beinge fallen owt by gods most holy and fatherlie permission: and the Author of the Censure hauing nether tyme, nor place, nor bookes, nor leysure to

* *Douay Diaries*, under 20 March 1581.

† For the seizure of this private press, see Chapter VI.

> begynne agayne, nor any hope of print when he should haue done the same: being also necessarilie called awaye at that verye tyme, to a place somewhat farof, vppon vrgent businesse: he resolued vtterlie to gyue ouer the sayd attempt of defence.

And he adds that it was only on account of Campion's unfair treatment when on his defence that he finally resolved 'to take in hand agayne the Answer of your booke'.*

Propriety demanded of Persons seriousness and solidity rather than the graces of an artful literary style, and the situation in which he found himself compelled him to be brief. Yet there is no doubt that he must be counted as one of the most effective of the English controversialists of his day. The strict and succinct manner of his writing, combined as it is with a rich expressiveness (he has always an illustration or an analogy to hand), gives to his prose a lucidity and forcefulness which serves to distinguish it from much of the controversial literature of the period. Whether he is engaged in the close analysis of his opponent's argument or in expanding his theme by means of illustration, always we may note the same simplicity of utterance 'following the normal custom of English speech' and the same brevity which, as he himself in one place avows, was his conscious endeavour,† and which renders his prose both sure and swift. The following three examples will illustrate sufficiently well a style which was commended by Swift for its clearness and intelligibility.‡ The first two of the quotations taken respectively from the *Brief Censure* and the *Defence*, exhibit Persons' manner in close argument:

> Mary (saythe he) Christe delyuerethe a contrarie note. Math. 22. *Yee erre not knowing the Scriptures, nor the power of God:* whereof he would inferre, that all men must read the Scriptures. A stronge argumente the circumstances considered: for first, the men to whome Christe spake these woordes, were noe ignorante people, but learned Saduces, which came prepared to pose Christe, about the resurrection. This appeareth by the subtile question which they put forthe, of seuen brethren which had al one wife, groũded vppon the lawe of Moyses, wherby they thought to ouerthrow the doctrine of resurrection. But Christe hauing heard their question, toulde them, that they erred, not vnderstanding the Scriptures touching that poynte of resurrec-

* Epistle to Charke, in *A Defence of the Censure*, sig. A2.

† op. cit., sig. Aaa4. 'I meane to vse as great breuitie, as my poore wytt can reache vnto.'

‡ *The Tatler*, no. 230.

N

tion, which Scriptures he interpreted to them presentlye out of the iij. chapter of Exodus. Also he sayde, they erred, not vnderstanding the power of God, wherby he is able to rayse againe the self same bodye in nomber, whiche is dead, though it be vnpossible (as it is) in all natural reason. Soe that Christ spake not here to vnlearned men, nor of all Scriptures, nor of readinge, but of vnderstanding. What maketh therfore this to your purpose M. Charke? forsoothe as much as if you should reason thus: my Lorde Chaunceller sayd to certayne Doctors of the Arches, pleading a case vnskilfully before him: you erre, not vnderstandinge the common lawe in this case, nor the Princesse authoritie. Ergo, by these woordes he meanethe, that al the clownes of Englande, shall fall to readinge of the common lawe, albeit they vnderstand neuer a woorde therof [sig. C4v].

Lastlie, he chargeth me with alteration of the text of scripture, for translating *omnis qui facit peccatum* euerie one that sinneth, where I should haue translated (sayth he) euery one that doeth sinne. This is a charge woorthie of M. Charke, that will playe small game rather than sytt owt. I praye you sir, what difference is there in the two phrases, *your wyfe spinneth, and your wyfe doeth spinne*? But you cōfesse in deede there is litle holde in this, and therefore freendlie you doe pardon me, for it, and doe conclude, sayeing: *you think perhaps to serue the Lorde in your opinion, and I know I serue the Lorde*. You are happie that haue so certaine knowlege of your good estate M. Charke, though to vtter it in this place I doe not see what occasion you had. But I praye you let me learne how you came to this knowlege: Not by Aristotles demōstrations (I am sure) which yett are the onelie means of certaine science properlie. How then? by fayth? but you know, that faith can assure nothing, whiche is not reuealed by the woorde of God. What parte of gods woorde then, teacheth vs that william Charke in particular serueth the Lorde a-right? but you will saye perhappes. Your spirit within you telleth you soe. And my spirit (M. Charke) telleth me the contrarie. One of them must needes be a lyeing spirit: and whie not yours as well as myne? These are fansies (gentle syr william) proper to hereticall braynes, to assure them selues such knowlege aboue other men. Luther sayde many yeres after he was a protestant. *ego credo fortiter, imo ausim dicere, scio purgatorium esse*: I beleeue stowtelie, yea I dare auowe that I know there is a purgatorie. Yet he denied it after. Martin Bucer whē he was a Zuinglian knew (as he sayd) that doctrine to be deliuered from heauen: but yet afterward comming backe to be a Lutheran he protested openlie that he knew it was moste false. And againe returninge to be a Zuinglian: he knew it was true againe, and the other false: and yet all this while certaine knowlege can not be false. Yf a man should aske all the sectaries now lyuing, they wold say the same that you doe of theyr certaine knowlege. Wherefore me think you might haue spared these woordes *of your certayne knowlege*, whiche nether helpe your cause, nor hurt ours, any further than the credit reacheth of your owne bare woorde, & that also in your owne commendation [sig. H8].

Our third quotation, from the *Brief Censure*, illustrates Persons' power of presenting events, within a brief compass, in a vivid and expressive manner. By means of two short and contrasted sketches he points to the first-fruits of the reformed religion. We are thus invited to look first on this picture:

Ignatius de Loyola, was a gentleman of a Noble house in Spayne, which yet remayneth, who being cheefe captayne of Pompeiopolis, and defending it, against the frenchmen in the year 1536 was hurte and taken prisoner by the same. But afterward beinge perfectly healed, and curteously restored to libertie agayne, and now in great possibilitie of honour and prefermente in his countrye, resolued him selfe, to serue God onelye for the time to come, and to take paynes for the gayning of Heauen. Wherupon leauing al his frends, and distributinge al that he had to the poore: stale away from the Courte, and betooke himselfe to a maruelous straite lyfe, and after he had with contynuall labour of many yeares, gotten learninge, and gayened manye soules from sinne, vnto vertue, and from the Deuill vnto Allmyghtye God, by his example of auster lyfe and godly persuasions: there adioyned them selues vnto him, nyne other of diuers nations in the Vniuersitie of Paris, to the like trauelsome lyfe for gayning of soules. Which kinde of lyfe was afterward (after diuers examinations and probations of their spirit and purpose) alowed and confirmed by Pope Paulus tertius, and soe consequently (dyuers worthye men leauing the worlde and taking vppon them that order of lyfe) was made a distincte order of religious men, in the which this Ignatius bothe liued and dyed with singuler example of al humilytie, vertue and holynes, but espetially in zeale of gayninge of soules and recalling men from sinne, and his posteritie after him hath by imitatiō of the same vertues, broght forth infinit frute vnto the world.

and then on this:

Martin Luther, walking in his youth in a certayne medowe, was stroken with a thunderbolt, and ther vpon sodaynlye for very feare made him selfe an Austen fryer, where after in the Abbaye of Erford, seruinge in the Church vpon the third sunday in Lent, when the ghospel was read of the deafe and dumme deuil throwē out by Christ, he sodenly fel doune on the pauemente, and the deuil cried horriblye out of his mouthe sayinge: *I am* *not, I am not dūme, I wil speake yet vnto the world.* After this, vpon a certayne emulation and contention, betwixt him and the fryers of S. Dominiks order, he lefte his religion, cast away his habite, broke his vowes, married a nonne, and by litle and litle began to preache straunge new doctrines, especiallye tending to al libertie and carnalitie.*

7. THE AFFAIR OF JOHN NICHOLS

The affair of John Nichols relates to one of those unsavoury episodes which are only too common when a people or a section of a people is subject to a settled policy of persecution by its rulers. A Welshman by birth, Nichols had begun life as a minister in the west country, and at the outset of his career had shown himself to belong to that class of 'crafty conscienceless men' who are always ready, for their own ends, to perjure themselves with 'a hundred false tales and forged devices'. 'Him selfe vsed often to declare', writes Fr. Persons,† 'how that he preached commonlie certaine sermons of one Norbrooke‡ as his owne, and thereby gathered opinion of very good and sufficient learning. Also, that he procured himselfe two benefices by Simonie, and that M. deane of Powles and he coulde neuer agree.' His difficulties with the authorities eventually compelled him to leave the country, and, to continue with Persons' account, 'he passed ouer to Flaunders, and there applyinge him selfe to the religion and manners of the place, plaied some time the souldier and some times the minister, vntill beinge werie of both, he departed thence, and passing by Cambraie, (being holpen by the liberality of English men there) he tooke his walke towardes Italie'. There for a time he was in the service of some bishop until 'attired ridiculouslie in an old cast purple cassoke doune to the groūd' he finally made his way to Rome in 1577.

At Rome he gave himself up to the Holy Office, and after some difficulty and delay owing to his apparent insufficiency he was admitted to the English College and 'deliuered ouer (as the manner is) to the posers to trie what studdie he was fit for, who found him verie raw in the latine tonge, and therefore determined him to the studie of Rethorike and Humanitie: wherein hauinge spente some time, he was aduaunced to the

* *A Brief Censure*, sig. A8.

† *A Discouerie of I. Nicols*, sig. A5 – as also the further references to Nichols's life in this notice.

‡ See above, p. 117.

studie of Logique, but not beinge able to wade in so greate matters, he was remoued againe thēce, as *non proficiens*, and shifted of to the studdie of certaine cases of conscience more easie for his capacitie, wherein, notwithstanding, he profitinge litle or nothing, the Colledge began to be werie of him'. The rector of the College seems to have finally persuaded him to move on to Rhemes, for Persons tells us that it was while he was journeying thither (in 1580) he suddenly resolved to return to England, and so going 'neere vnto a citie called Fuligno in Vmbria or the Dukedome of Spoleto [he] came directlie into Englande, where in shorte space he mett with Sir Owen Hopton, whoe conuerted him soone after in the tower of London'. There followed in due course from his pen, in the year 1581, the *Declaration* of his recantation, the *Pilgrimage*, and the *Oration*, listed below, to which Fr. Persons replied with his *Discouerie*, Thomas Lupton and Dudley Fenner contributing counter-replies.

Meanwhile, after his release from the Tower, Nichols had again taken up his work as a preacher and, to quote Strype, 'his condition being needy . . . such was the kindness of the court, that the lord chancellor Bromley, and the lord treasurer Burghley, and others of the council, sent to the archbishop in his behalf, that some collection might be made for him. And a contribution was accordingly made for him by the bishops of the province'.* The Council also ordered the Archbishop of Canterbury to present him to a vacant living. He soon, however, fell into discredit with the authorities, apparently after the publication of the *Pilgrimage*, which was regarded even by the Protestants as an offence against religion,† and, probably during the ensuing year, he again sought refuge abroad. The reasons which he himself gave for this second flight are recorded in Allen's *True Report* (see below) as follows: '. . . al came of deepe remors of mind and conscience for the death of the innocents, which he knew came by his false accusation, wherewith he was inwardly so vexed in England, though he continued as he dooth yet in his peruerse pretēded religion, that he both confessed his foule dealing to one of the cōdemned persons and to some in office and authoritie there: and also

* *Annals*, as before, Vol. III, pt. 1, p. 61.
† See Dasent, *Acts of the Privy Council*, xiii, p. 199.

in fine left the Realme therefore specially, and partly, as he saith him self, because the Bishops who were cōmaunded and had promised him euery one of them a yerely pension for recompence of that his seruice, would not keepe touch with him. but shaked him of with a *Tu videris*, like as the iewes did their copesmā Iudas.'* Having reached the Low Countries in company with his friend Laurence Caddey, who had also been at one time a student of the English College in Rome, it seems that he first set out to journey to Turkey, but thinking better of it he returned to his friend who, early in 1583, 'procured his apprehension, not for hatred or hurt of his person, as God dooth know, but for desire of sauing his soule'.† From his prison at Rouen he was in communication with Cardinal Allen, who at one time had some hopes of his conversion. Allen writes to Fr. Agazzari from Rhemes, 2 March 1583: 'With regard to John Nicols, whom (as I wrote) we have taken care to imprison at Rouen, I know not what will happen; here the laws against heresies are inactive. The evil fellow has confessed that he invented all the charges which he brought forward either in the assembly [at the trial] or in his book against those who lately suffered martyrdom, at the order of certain of the Queen's Ministers and Councillors and under threat of the rack. Even so, he says that he has said many things concerning religion against the Catholics from private conviction, although he does not go all the way with the Protestants; but now he wants to talk things over with the Catholics. I sent the letter which he wrote to me, after he had turned back from his journey into Turkey which he was contemplating, from Paris, where I left his comrade Caddey, a man about as constant as himself and equally crazy. So God rewards these wretched turncoats.'‡ And again on 14 March 1583: 'I hope very shortly to inform you of the penitence of Laurence Caddey and John Nicols.'§ Early in the following month Nichols was liberated from prison at the command of Philip, through the intercession of Elizabeth. Though he withdrew all his accusations against Rome and Roman institutions it is very doubtful whether he was ever reconciled to the Church. What was his subsequent history is not known.

* sig. A4^{v}. † *True Report*, sig. D4^{v}.

‡ From the Latin original cited in *Letters and Memorials*, as before, p. 177.

§ ibid., p. 182.

The following list of works which relate to Nichols's attack upon the Catholic Church gives the various items in chronological order:

(1) *A declaration of the recantation of Iohn Nichols (for the space almost of two yeeres the Popes Scholer in the English Seminarie or Colledge at Rome) which desireth to be reconciled, and receiued as a member into the true Church of Christ in England* (1581). (*P*)

(2) *The Oration and Sermon made at Rome by commaundement of the fowre Cardinalles, and the Dominican Inquisitour, vpon paine of death. By Iohn Nichols, latelie the Popes Scholler, Which Sermon and Oration was presented before the Pope and his Cardinalles in his Consistorie, the xxvij day of Maie. 1578. and remaineth there registred. Now by him brought into the English tongue, for the great comfort and commoditie of all faithfull Christians. Heerin also is aunswered an infamous Libell, maliciouslie written and cast abroad, against the saide Iohn Nichols, with a sufficient discharge of himselfe from all the Papists lying reports, and his owne life both largelie and amplie discouered* (1581).* (*P*)

(3) *Iohn Niccols Pilgrimage, wherein is displaied the liues of the proude Popes, ambitious Cardinals, lecherous Bishops, fat-bellied Monkes, and hypocriticall Iesuites* (1581). (*P*)

(4) Robert Persons' *A Discouerie of I. Nicols minister, misreported a Iesuite, latelye recanted in the Tower of London. Wherin besides the declaration of the man, is contayned a ful answere to his recantation. with a confutation of his slaunders, and proofe of the contraries, in the Pope, Cardinals, Clergie, Studentes, and priuate men of Rome. There is also added a reproofe of an oration and sermon, falsely pretended by the sayd Nicols to be made in Rome, and presented to the Pope in his Consistorye. Wherto is annexed a late information from Rome touching the autētical copie of Nicols recantation* (1581). (*C*)

(5) *The Christian against the Iesuite. Wherein the secrete or namelesse writer of a pernitious booke, intituled A Discouerie of I. Nicols Minister &c. priuily printed, couertly cast abrod, and secretely solde, is not only iustly reprooued: But also a booke,*

* The 'Libel' referred to in this title I have been unable to trace.

dedicated to the Queenes Maiestie, called A persuasion from papistrie, therein derided and falsified, is defended by Thomas Lupton the author thereof (1582). (*P*)

(6) *An Answere vnto the Confutation of Iohn Nichols his Recantation, in all pointes of any weight conteyned in the same: Especially in the matters of Doctrine, of Purgatorie, Images, the Popes honor, and the question of the Church. By Dudley Fenner, Minister of Gods word* (1583). (*P*)

(7) William Allen's *A true report of the late apprehension and imprisonment of Iohn Nicols Minister, at Roan, and his confession and answers made in the time of his durance there. Whereunto is added the satisfaction of certaine, that of feare or frailtie haue latly fallen in England* (1583). (*C*)

PERSONS' *Discouerie of I. Nicols*

In the previous notice of the controversial works of Robert Persons we referred to the unusual lucidity and vigour of his prose, which we suggested was due to a direct simplicity of utterance and conciseness of expression combined with a rich expressiveness of image and locution. We offer here a passage from the *Discouerie of I. Nicols* which further illustrates these points of style and which also throws additional light upon Persons' method of writing. The passage has reference to the 'seuen kindes of men vppon whom ye Romans vse principallye their charitie', and takes up the challenge of William Fulke in *Two Treatises written against the Papistes* (1577): 'Shew me M. Allen, if thou canst for thy gutts, or name me any city in the world, where popery preuayleth, that hath made such prouision for the fatherlesse children and widowes and all other kind of poore, as is in the noble city of London.' Here is Persons:

> *And* first for children, the company of the holye Ghoste receaueth as many Infantes as come, and because many are ashamed to bring their infantes thyther openly, there is a secret place wher they may lay them downe and not be seene, so that the multitude of infantes which are brought, is very greate, and commonlye neuer lesse then 200. and the number of Nurces there continually mayntained, is neuer fewer than 100. Besides this societie, there is another howse appointed for Orphan boyes, in Antonines bathes, and another for Orphan maydes, in another place named *gli quattro Coronati*, and ech howse re-

ceaueth 100. All which children cominge to ripe age, are distributed into two sortes, the boyes, some to learninge, and some to handie craftes: the maydes, some chuse to enter into Monasteries, and the rest haue portions allotted them to be married away, as shalbe shewed more hereafter.

For sicke men, the prouision of Rome is maruelous. For besids the hospitalls which ech Nation hath there, seuerally, the Romanes haue made great prouision for all sicke men by their hospitalls, which in number are many, but fower doe excell aboue the reste. If a man haue an ague, then he may goe to the hospitall of S. Spirite, if he haue a freshe woonde or hurt, he may goe to the hospital of our Lady, if he haue an ache, then he may goe to the hospitall of S. John: if he haue a festered sore or incurable desease, he may repayre to S. Iames his hospitall. In al which places he shal finde as good prouision, of meate, drincke, cleane beddinge, phiscike, surgerie, and dilligente attendance, for nothing, as commōlie he could haue for his monie in the citie, or rather better, for which cause, many gentlemen doe remoue from their owne howses, to the hospitall of S. Spirite, for recouerie of their health: which hospital of S. Spirite hath commonlie noe lesse then 300. sicke persons in it, with goodlie partitions for men and women, gentlemen, and of the porer sorte. S. Iames his hospital receaueth in number 155. men, and 45. women: the other two hospitals receaue fewe lesse: all thinges are kept so sweete and cleane in these hospitals, that many noble women, Ladies and gentlewomen doe repaier often thither, to comefort the sicke, as also verie manie gentlemen, especiallie the holie daies, bringinge with them some what or other to present vnto the sicke people for their comefortes. These hospitals are thought to spende aboue 150. thowsande crownes by the yeere, which depende for the most parte vpon the almes of the Romanes.

Towching straungers the liberalitie of the Romans is very great, for besids the particuler hospitalls which are in Rome, for euerie countrie, there are diuers hospitals of the Romanes, appointed out for the receite and releefe of poore straungers. But the hospital of the Trinitie excelleth all the reste, which, all the whole yeere of Iubilee *Anno 1575.* was neuer emptie of great numbers of straūgers: and some dayes they receaued 14. thowsande together, with aboundance notwithstanding, of meate and lodging, and with so good entreatie, as diuers noble & gentlemē of Rome, would repaire thither to serue ye saied Pilgrimes and to washe their feete for loue and deuotion.

For Prisoners, the care of ye Romans is singuler, aboue al other nations in the worlde. For they haue amongst them a companie named the companie of charity: which company, by licēce of the Pope doth chuse euery yeere, two officers for the releefe of the prisoners, the one a protectour, who hath to defend yͤ poore prisoners yͭ are wrōged, by law or otherwise. The other a procter, whose office is, to make sufficiēt prouisiō for meat, drincke & other necessities for thē. Thes mē also doe see, yͭ al things passe orderly in yͤ prisōs, & yͭ all yͤ prisōers haue diuine seruice said before thē daily: & yͭ ther come euery weeke once or twise, preachers, to preache vnto the sayed prisoners. Lastelye, that there be conuenient bookes of pietie and deuotion in euery prison, tyed with chaynes for all to reade: and that al books of scurrilitie and dishonestie, be remoued thēce, by which good meanes, and other vsed by them, many profite more in pietie by one monethes imprisonment, then they had done before, in many yeeres libertie.

For men indebted, the Romanes take very charitable order. For firste, they haue a greate bancke of monye, *called mons pietatis*, out of the which al banckrupts or other poore people may borrow mony without intrest, bringing a paune or sufficient sureties. Secondly, the company of charitie, by helpe of other Romanes do deliuer out 80. euery yeere, which are imprisoned for debt. Thirdly, the societie of S. Apostle, vseth to goe aboute the citie, and to enquire of poore gentlemen or gentlewomen whoe are behinde hand, and are ashamed to aske helpe, and if their debtes be not very excessiue, they seeke meanes to discharge them.

Towchinge those that liue in sinne, & lewde lyfe, or are in daunger to fall into the same, the Romanes do practise great pietie. For first, towching maydes destitute of frendes, which for neede mighte fall vnto an euill trade of lyfe, they marrye euerie yeere of their owne charges aboue 500. as after shall appeare more in particuler. Other they place in monasteries, and 140. they maintaine from time to time in a howse named S. Catharins besides those which I named before. Secondly, for them that be married and can not agree with their husbandes, and by that meanes are in daunger to turne to dishonest lyfe, the Romanes haue builte a goodly monastery dedicated to S. Martha, and named it *Delle Mal Maritate*, in which howse such yonge women may liue vertuously, vnder the gouernmēt of certaine graue Noones, vntil they be reconciled to their husbāds againe. Thirdlie, for them that are now dishonest and will be conuerted, they haue a howse to maintaine them in, as I noted before, called the howse of Conuertites. Lastly, because, they which once enter into this howse, of Conuertites, maye not turne back, or go fourth againe, but must perseuer there al their life, (which manie of these dishonest womē can not at the first resolue them selues to doe.) Therfore haue the noble matrones of Rome procured another howse, called *Casa pia*, behind *Pantheō*, where these women may come for a time, to proue what they will resolue vppon, in which time, the sayed matrones, doe omitt no meanes to perswade them from all dishonestie for the time to come, and do offer to prouide for them by good seruices with vertuous gẽtle women, if they can not resolue them selues to enter into the monasterie of Conuertites, & by this meanes also many be reclaimed from wikednes & sinne.

Concerning these which are adiudged to dye, the citizens of Rome doe shewe themselues very charitable & peitiful, for they haue amongest other, a Societie named the companie of mercie, whoe receaue into their custodie, all such as are condemned to dye, towardes whom they vse all humanitie and gentle dealing, neuer leauinge them day nor nighte, vntil the time of executiō be past. If the prisoner haue any children, they promise him to take order for them, and soe they doe, as also for his debtes, if he be trowbled with any: if he haue any enemies, they bring them vnto him to be reconciled: after that, they reade good bookes vnto him and cause vertuous men to preache and make exhortations to like effecte: they watche also with him, and cause praiers to be saied for him, and finallie they accompanie him to the place of executiō, & thẽce receaue his body & burie it, causing certaine Masses to be saied for his soule [sig. G4v–G8].

The graphic and precise nature of such writing, revealing as it does Persons' vivid pictorial imagination, his faculty for arrangement, and his sense of rhythmical expression, is surely in the best tradition of English prose and, to borrow the words of Swift, 'with very few Allowances would not offend any present reader'.*

8. MISCELLANEOUS CONTROVERSIAL AND DOCTRINAL WORKS

JOHN MORWEN'S *An Addicion with an Appologie*

The pamphlet which forms the subject of this notice was written in answer to Bishop Pilkington's sermon of 8 June 1561 on the burning of St. Paul's Church on 4 June 1561.† It was spread abroad in writing and was entitled, according to the printed copy incorporated in Bishop Pilkington's reply:

An Addicion with an Appologie to the causes of brinnynge of Paules Church, the which causes were vttred at Paules Crosse by the reuerend Bysshop of Duresme the. viii. of Iune. 1561.

* *The Tatler*, as before.

† An official pamphlet touching the burning was put out by William Seres 10 June 1561, entitled 'The True Report of the burning of the Steeple and Church of Paul's in London'.

It is of no literary importance, though it may be said to have some historical value as a contemporary document. The theme may be gathered from the following quotation:

> As in Saint Paules Church in London by the decrees of blessed fathers, euery night at midnight they had Mattines, all the fore noone Masses in the Church, with other deuine seruice and contynuall prayer: and in the steple Antimes and prayers: were hadde certayne tymes: but consider how farre nowe contrarye the Churche hais bene vsed, and it is no maruaile yf God haue sende downe fire to brinne parte of the Churche as a signe of his wrath. And where a reuerende Byshop at Paules crosse did exhort the people to take the brinninge of Paules to be a warninge of a greater plage to folowe to the Citye of London if amendment of life be not had in all estates, it was well said: but we muste adde *Accidentem ad deum opportet credere* [sic], the Scripture sais, he that will come to God muste first beleue . . . First searche whether the faith and religion nowe vsed, was taught with the blessed fathers in Chrystes Church in times past: ye shal proue by no recorde of authoritie or Chronicle that this maner of seruice now vsed in the Churche was euer hard tell of afore Luthers time, which is not. xl. yeares old. Therefore it is to be reiected and put awaye as a newe fangled doctrine and scismaticall: therefore come backe againe into the old fathers steppes as well in faith and religion, as godlye conuersation and liuinge or a greater plage is at hande. Also where the said Preacher did recite certain abuses of the said Church as talking, biyng and sellinge, feightinge and brawlinge (although these be verye euill and worthie much rebuke) yet there be worse abuses, as blaspheming God in lyinge Sermons, polluting the Temple with Schismaticall seruice, destroying and pullyng downe holye aulters, that were set vp by good blessed men, & there the sacryfice of the blessed Masse ministred according to the order of Christes catholycke Church. Yea where the alter stode of the holy Ghost, the new Bishops haue made a place to set their tales vpon, and there sit in the iudgement of such as be Catholycke and liue in the feare of God. Some they depriue from liuinges, some they commit to prison, excepte they will forsake the Catholicke faith and embrase a faith and religion that hais no foundacion layde by generall Counsell, nor blessed fathers in times past but inuented by Heretikes that do not agree one with another nor themselfes [sigs. A3–4].

The reply of James Pilkington is contained in:

The burnynge of Paules church in London in the yeare of oure Lord 1561. and the iiii. day of Iune by lyghtnynge, at three of the clocke, at after noone, which continued terrible and helplesse vnto nyght [1563].

JOHN FECKENHAM'S PAMPHLETS

The two pamphlets that we have here to record were both disseminated in manuscript and are extant only in the printed 'Answers' of Feckenham's opponents. The first is an Address entitled

To the right worshipfuls, Sir Frauncis Iobson Knight, Lieuetenaunt of the Toure, Sir Henrie Neuell Knight, and M. Pellam Lieuetenaunt of the Ordinaunce [1570].

Feckenham had been asked by these gentlemen what he thought of a sermon preached by John Gough in the Tower of London on 15 January 1570, and 'vppon your lycence graunted and obteyned', though loth to do it, he set forth his opinion under four heads, ending his pamphlet with a plea to be excused further attendance at the sermons. Two replies were forthcoming to this Address, viz.:

(1) *The aunswer of John Gough to maister Fecknams objections against his sermon lately preached in the Tower* (1570).*

printed by John Awdley; and

(2) *An Answere to certein Assertions of M. Fecknam, somtime Abbot of Westminster which he made of late against a godly Sermon of M. Iohn Goughes, preached in the Tower the xv. of Ianuarie. 1570*,

written by Laurence Tomson and printed by Henry Bynneman. The second pamphlet, which is commonly known as 'An Apology of a Papist' is headed:

Certaine considerations and causes, mouyng me not to bee presente at, nor to receiue, neither vse the seruice of the newe booke, otherwise called the Common boke of praiers. [1571].

William Fulke replied to this in:

A confutation of a Popishe and sclaunderous libelle, in forme of an apologie: geuen out into the courte, and spread abrode in diuerse other places of the Realme (1571).

Judging by these pamphlets one cannot claim any great distinction for Feckenham as a writer of English, but that his prose does not move in the rut of the conventional and common-

* cf. Maitland's catalogue of early books in the Lambeth Palace Library.

place, but has both spirit and humour, will be evident, I think, from the two following short quotations:

> Wherein the aucthors composers and deuisers of this newe religion haue dealed muche like as one maister Molande Vicar of sainct Peters in Oxforde, did with Clare the Butcher, a neare neighbour and parishner of his, vnto whom by the waie of a merie ieste, he made sale of an horse, all by negatiues on this wise, saiyng vnto hym how that his horse had not a greate heade, his horse hadde not a paire of Asse eares, his horse had not one touth in his heade longer then an other, his horse had not a sadle backe, no Splent, Spauen, or Ringbone, hys horse was not pincromped, sicle hought, nor broke winded, and so forth all by negatiues, he soulde his horse to Clare the Butcher, not expressyng what his horse hadde, but what his horse had not. Dealyng therin with muche like faieth and truthe, as our Preachers dooe with the people of this Realme, which goe aboute to plante a new religion amongest theim, which standeth as I haue here expressed wholy by negatiues, in affirmyng nothyng, and deniynge all thinges.*

> Who would desire to liue in that Realme, where such vices are of subiectes openly cõmitted, whiche in all other Christian realmes thei feare to doe in secrete? and where all that thei desire, thei procure, and all that thei procure, thei doe attaine, and all that is euill, thei thinke, and all that thei thinke, thei saie, and all that thei saie, thei maie dooe, and that that thei may dooe, thei dare do, and putte in operation. And therfore, I can haue by no righte reason, any desire of enlargemente of libertie, or yet hope any while to liue.†

A Notable Discourse

The anonymous translation of John de Albine's *Discours Chrestien* (1566)‡ consists of an original Preface to the Reader and text in forty-three chapters. The title runs as follows:

> *A notable Discourse, plainelye and truely discussing, who are the right Ministers of the Catholike Church: written against Caluine and his Disciples, By one Master Iohn de Albine, called de Seres, Archedeacon of Tolosa in Fraunce* . . . (1575).

It was answered by Thomas Spark in

> *An Answere to Master Iohn de Albines, Notable Discourse against heresies (as his frendes call his booke) compiled by Thomas Spark pastor of Blechley in the County of Buck.* (1591).

* *An Apollogie of a Papiste*, cited from Fulke's *Confutation*, sig. i8v.
† ibid., sig. p3v.
‡ See bibl. ent. 2.

The English author of the *Notable Discourse* would appear to be a scholar and one well versed in the art of writing. There is little, however, in his prose to distinguish him from many of his contemporaries. The two passages which follow will, therefore, do little more than serve to illustrate what are the well-known marks of much Elizabethan prose writing. The colloquial ease and vigour of the expression, the familiar images, the proverbial locutions, the trick of redundancy in order to obtain emphasis and melody, all contribute to a style which is unmistakably Elizabethan. Our first extract is taken from the Preface to the Reader:

> Again, he would haue such rulers to call themselues shepherdes and feeders of men, rather then otherwise. So *Homer* calleth a king *pastorem populi*, a shepherde and feeder of the people. And *Plato* in his Dialogue called *Minos*, writeth, that *Minos* and *Radamanthus*, which gaue lawes to ye men of *Crete*, were the true shepherdes of men, whiche was not spoken of so noble a Philosopher without a iust cause: for nothing doth more nourish, mainteine and vpholde a common wealth then lawe, which, as *Tullie in secūdo de natura deorum sayth, est recti praeceptio, prauique depulsio*, a commaunder of that which is good and honest, and an expulser of all that is noughte and vnhonest. Now, as a shepherdes care is to see his sheepe fedde in wholsome pastures, and to be kepte safe from wolues, & al other beastes that would wery and destroy them: and if any in the flocke be infected with any outwarde scabbe, or inward maladie, to remedie it betime: or if the contagion admit no helpe, but is incurable, to haue suche a one away from the flocke, that he hurt none of them that be whole: Euen so must he that will be a shepherde of men, studye for the good ordering and quietnes of the multitude, ouer whom he hath charge, and that all enormities that might disturbe a common wealth, whether it be spirituall or ciuill, be expelled, and that all faultes be redressed with due correction, vsing lenitie and seueritie, after as hope or dispaire of amendment shall appere. Neither hath the name of a shepherde lacked his preheminence at any time. That good Abell, *ad cuius munera deus respexit*, to whose giftes & sacrifice God had respect, was a shepherde: Abraham, in whose seede God promised, that all nations should be blessed, was a shepherde: so was Isaac his sonne, and Iacob his nephewe, and his sonnes also . . . This noble king Dauid was a shepherde. These I suppose almightie God woulde haue to be ensamples to all them that be in authoritie, for as Paule sayth: *Quaecunque scripta sunt, ad nostram eruditionem scripta sunt*, All thinges that are written, are written for our instruction,

that as they fedde that seely innocent cattell, so shoulde all Magistrates that professe his sons name, learne to gouerne the people in the obedience of his doctrine, that they might be *innocentes manibus, & puro corde: nec iurantes in dolo proximo suo,* Innocents of their handes, and of a pure heart, which vse no deceipt towardes their neighbours, but in al their doinges shewe themselues to be *veras oues pascuae Christi,* the true sheepe of the pasture of Iesus Christe, who sayeth: *Bonus pastor animam suam dat pro ouibus suis,* A good shepherd geueth his life for his sheepe. Fewe wordes, but full of pith: And neuer could mo thinges be spoken more compendiouslye.

In our second extract, from the same source, the Ciceronian fulness and balance of the expression will be noted:

I haue hearde, read, and seene manye thinges, yet can I not reade, heare, or see any worlde more contaminate and prone to all kinde of vices then this our age is. And howbeit afore our dayes haue beene in all times and ages men and women verye vitious and monstrous in their liuing, yet then vertue was vertue, and vice was vice: But nowe in our corrupt time, we haue lost the true names and vse of all thinges, and vertue with vs is taken for vice, and contrarily, vice is coumpted for vertue. They that be studious of modestie, obseruers of temperancie, and louers of sobrietie, they be nowe a dayes called Pinche pennyes, and such that hunger droppeth out of their noses.* If any be vertuous, & folowers of the Catholike, which is ỷ true religion, they be called Phariseys & Papists: The discrete mā, he is called an hipocrite, & the small talker a foole and an ignorant person. On the other side, they that leade their liues in all kinde of ryote, they be called hansome men, men of the right making, and such as can tell howe to keepe honest mennes companye. Agayne, the statelyer that one goeth, the higher that he looketh, and the stouter and malapertlier that he speaketh, the more is he praysed among ỷ worldlings for a wise man, who will not suffer himselfe to be ouertroden and made a laughing stocke to euery Rascall. With such vayne glorious prayses be such proude *Thrasoes* extolled and magnifyed of the more parte, and no small number are geuen to flatterie, and enhausing of Clawbacks,† that neuer could that saying of *Terence* be better verifyed then it is nowe: *Obsequium amicos, veritas odium parit,* To holde vp mennes yea and their naye, in holding with the hare, and running with the hounde, getteth a man frendes, but he that will lay flattery aside, and tell the playne truth, shall get nothing but hatred. Thus in these dayes vice is extolled, and vertue contemned: Ill rule is made of, and good rule neglected.

* A proverbial expression for a skinflint. † i.e. praising of sycophants.

LAURENCE VAUX'S *Catechisme*

One of the most popular of the Recusant publications was the Catechism compiled by Laurence Vaux in the year 1567. Originally written, as he tells us, for his pupils at the school which he kept for the exiles in Louvain, it soon came to have a very large circulation for those days and times, there being certainly eight published editions between 1567 and 1605. He refers to his sources in the following terms: 'What I haue set furth in this litle booke, the grounde and substance I haue collected & translated out of the Scripture, & generall Councells, out of the bookes of D. Petrus de Soto, and D. Canisius, addinge here and there some sentences of the auncient Fathers, S. Cypriā, Athanasius, Ambrose, Hierome, Damascene, & S. Bernard.'* The title, as it appears in John Fowler's reprint of 1574, is as follows:

> *A Catechisme, or a Christian Doctrine, necessarie for Children & ignorant people, briefly compiled & set forth by Laurence Vaux Bacheler of Diuinitie. With an Instruction newly added of the laudable Ceremonies vsed in the Catholike Churche* (1574).†

With regard to the character and contents of this little book we may refer to the comments of T. G. Law in his recension of the edition of 1583 for the Chetham Society, published in 1885. Law there describes the work as an 'orthodox, honest, and plain-spoken exposition' of Catholic doctrine. He also calls attention to 'a few relics of antiquated forms and customs, some of which had become out of date at least before 1583', and instances, as an example of Vaux's conservative habits, his question: 'Why is the Aue Maria vsed so oftē to be said for a praier seing ther is no petition in it?', pointing out that the Sarum Breviary, printed at Paris in 1531, had already introduced the longer form‡ and that the Roman Breviary had also adopted it when the revision was made by authority of Pius V in 1568. Yet this is not revised, he comments, in the 1583 edition of the *Catechisme*. He further refers to Vaux's fondness

* ed. 1583. The Author to the Reader.

† For a full account of the various editions of Vaux's *Catechisme*, see Appendix IV.

‡ i.e. with the appended 'Sancta Maria, Mater Dei, ora pro nobis', etc.

for details and mentions as a case in point his enumeration of reserved cases for confession, a thing which 'is not usually found in Catechisms intended for children and ignorant people'.

That the book had its influence in making converts we may gather from the recorded instance of a young Jesuit, John Grosse, who, in 1603, tells us that, when he was a student at Cambridge, he had asked the loan of a Catholic book from Mr. William Alabaster, then a Jesuit and no mean scholar. Alabaster lent him the catechism, 'and having read it', says Grosse, 'I began to imbibe the light of divine grace'.

As for points of style, Vaux himself disclaims any ability for 'finesse of sentence, and eloquence of words',* nor should we expect in a work of this nature to find ingenuity and rhetorical artifice. We may remark, however, 'a pleasant quaintness in the concluding paragraph', cited below, in which he exhorts the reader to put his instruction into practice, and the passage on charity, also cited below, 'almost rises to eloquence'.

> And here nowe let vs make an ende. For after thou knowest once (Gentle Reader, or diligent learner) what thou ought to beleeue, & how thou ought to lyue (which two pointes I haue prosequuted in this short Catechisme) what remayneth but to make an end? For the rest now is to be committed vnto thy practise, that like as thou knowest through my simple and plaine instruction, what is to be done, so thou study and labour to exemplifie & shewe in thy conuersation that which thou knowest.
>
> Especially, whereas I now haue no more to say vnto thee, and God wil beginne to haue a saying vnto thee, except thou kepe his lawes & cōmaundemēts. For whē the Son of mā shal come in his maiesty, & al nations shal be gathered together before him &c. the wicked shall go into euerlasting punishment, & the iust into life euerlastīg. Be faithful therfore in al articles that are to be beleeued, be deuout in thy praiers, be louing & obedient as touching the Commaundements of God & his Churche, be wise in receiuing the Sacraments, & make not light of the remedies of thy synnes and infirmities. Be diligent in the workes of mercy, and take in good part this my smal labour, which I trust, shal bring great profit vnto thee, & God graunt it may be so great, as I haue & shal wish it to be. Amen.†

* Address to the Reader.
† ed. 1568, fol. 110b.

> How must we honour God by Charitie?
>
> We must loue God with al our hartes so firmely, that neither for feare nor flattery, prosperity, nor aduersity we be caried away from God. And that the loue of no creature remaine in our hartes, but for God and godlines. With al our soules we must loue God so faithfully, that we had leuer our soules should be seuered from our bodies, then from God. This loue maketh al thinges light and easy, this loue caused the glorious Martyrs to suffer al kynd of tormentes, both patiently and gladly for the feruēt loue of God. This ardent loue vnto God, caused the blessed fathers in wyldernes to take great paynes and penance vpon them, in fasting, and praying, weping and mourning. For their meate and drincke they vsed dry bread and cold water, herbes, rootes, and barkes of trees, for their clothyng, heare and sacke, the colde earth for a bedde, a hard stone for a pyllowe, and were ready to suffer any cruel death for Christes sake, their hartes were so kindled with a burning Charitie towardes God.*

That a reply to the *Catechisme* was contemplated by the Protestants we learn from Fulke's lists of 'Popish Bookes either aunswered, or to be aunswered', given at Appendix V. It had, however, no directly controversial aim and was clearly compiled with a view to the normal circumstances of Catholic life. In this connexion we may note that although it is, of course, quite unequivocal as to what the Catholic Church is, who are its true pastors, etc. –

> The Church is a visible companye of people, first gathered together of Christ & his disciples, continued vnto this daye in a perpetuall succession, in one Apostolicke fayth, liuinge vnder Christ the head: and in earth, vnder his Vicar, Pastour and cheefe Bishoppe –

or again –

> In this Church is confessed and worshipped one God, one faith is cōfessed and taught, one baptisme and one vniforme order of Sacramētes are ministred without schisme or diuision, hauinge one Head in earth, Gods Vicar ī the Apostolicke See, successor to S. Peter –

yet there is no direct reference to Elizabeth's supremacy nor to the English heresy.

* ibid., fol. 29. Vaux's preliminary Address to the Reader, which exhibits both a sympathetic nature and an attractive modesty, will be found cited at bibl. ent. 146.

TRANSLATIONS TOUCHING JUSTIFICATION
OF
THOMAS COPLEY AND JOHN FOWLER (?)

The *Treatie of Iustification* of Cardinal Pole, with the additional translations which form the subject of this notice, was printed for the first time by John Fowler in 1569. Strype comments on the publication in the following terms: 'We must not omit the mention of a discourse that had laid by many years, but set forth in print this year [i.e. 1569] at Lovain in quarto. It was a treatise of Justification, found among the writings of cardinal Pole, remaining in the custody of Henry Pynning, Chamberlain and general receiver of the said cardinal, late deceased in Lovain. Also certain translations touching the said matter of justification. In the preface the noble author saith, he followeth St. Augustin. And it is so writ, as though he intended to publish it himself; for he makes a preface to the reader.'* In this Preface Pole writes: 'I haue (Christian Reader) with the hope of Gods helpe indeuoured my selfe to laie before thine eies particularly as briefely and plainely as I coulde, the maner of our Iustification in Christ, Grounding my selfe chiefely in al pointes through the Treatie vpon the Scripture and holy Worde of God.' The two additions, it will be seen, are thus supplementary to the original Treatise of Pole, the first, a translation, probably by John Fowler, of the Decree touching Justification from the proceedings of the sixth session of the Council of Trent (13 January 1547), bringing to the question the latest official statement on the subject, the second, the work of Thomas Copley,† buttressing the argument by reference to various treatises or sermons of the Fathers upon the subject. Copley's translations are introduced by means of a second descriptive title, also dated 1569, which begins thus:

> *Certaine Treaties of the Auncient Holy Fathers, touching the Doctrine of good woorkes*, etc.,

the 'Treaties' being drawn, as we learn from the chapter-headings, from SS. Augustine, Chrysostome, Basil, Leo and Cyprian.

Copley sought, in order to edify his readers and to stir their

* *Annals* (1824), Vol. I, pt. 2, pp. 304–5. The exact title will be found at bibl. ent. 118.

† See bibl. ent. 118.

hearts to good works, to transform his originals into the colloquial and familiar speech of his own day. 'I haue made them' (his translations), he writes, 'to speake in English, as faithefully, as truly, and as familiarly, as I coulde possibly doo, not swaruing one iote from their wordes and meaning. Accepte my poore labour in good parte, which I haue taken to edifie many, to offend none. And our Lorde of his mercy geue bothe to thee (gentle Reader) and to me, of his holy Grace, that we may folow and practise in woorkes, that which these holy Fathers do teach vs in woordes. That as sinne hath bene the cause of this horrible schisme and manifolde heresies that nowe raigne, so amendment of life maie be a meane to stay the raging course thereof, and to call vs home to vnite againe, to the honour of God, and peace of his Church. Amen.' To this aim we may add his careful regard for word-order and the rhythmical structure of the sentence, and this, together with a general absence of those verbal conceits, so dear to Elizabethans, gives to his style a vividness and freshness which is in the best tradition of sixteenth century pulpit oratory. The following characteristic passage, with its varied and skilful use of inversion, is taken from his translation of St. Basil's sermon on fasting, and is a model of direct and natural expression:

> Fasting quenched the force of the fier. Fasting stopped the mouthes of the lions.* Fasting sendeth praier vp to heauen: being as it were a winge thereunto, to carry it vpward. Fasting is the wealth of the howse: the mother of health: and the schoolemaster of youth. Fasting is an ornamente to olde menne: a good companion to wayfaring persons: a safe, and trusty conuictour to such as dwell together. The husband suspecteth not to be deceiued by his wife, when he seeth her delight in fasting. The wife fretteth not with ielousie, when she seeth her husband geeuen to fasting. Who euer sawe a house decaie by fasting? Vewe what thinges are at this daie within thy house, and surueie them agayne hereafter, and thou shalt find nothing thereof wanting, through fasting. No beast or other liue thinge lamenteth his death. No bloud is seene in thy house. No heauie sentence of death, geeuen by the vnsatiable belly against the poore beastes. The cookes knife is at rest. The table of the faster is content with such thinges, as voluntarily do rise and growe of the earth. The Sabaoth was geeuen to the Iewes: *That thy beast* (saith God) *and thy seruant may be at rest.* Let thy fasting be a rest of continuall labours, vnto thy seruantes, that serue

* References are to Daniel iii. and vi.

thee all the yeere. Suffer thy cooke to be quiet. Geue rest vnto thy Sewer. Forbeare the hand of thy cupbearer, and butler. Let him haue some repose, who prepareth thy manifold Iouncats and bancketting disshes. Let thy house sometime be quiete from those innumerable tumultes, from smoke, fulsom sauour of rost, and from the running vp and doune of them that do nought but minister vnto the bellie, as to a dame, that can neuer be pleased. Euen exacters of tributes do sometime affoord some libertie to the subiectes. Let the belly likewise geue some truce to the mouthe. Let that which is euer crauing, and neuer ceasseth: which receiueth to day, and forgetteth to morrowe, geue vs truce for fiue daies. When it is full, then it disputeth of abstinence. When the meate is a litle passed, then it forgetteth quite all such doctrine. Fasting knoweth not the nature of death. The table of the faster dooth not sauer of vserie. The fathers vseries doo not strangle the litle child of the faster, in his nonage, winding about him like serpentes. And truly besides all this sometime to faste, is a meane to the increase of pleasure and delight. For as thirst maketh drinke to seeme pleasaunt, and as hunger gone before, doth make the furnished table the more delightsome, right so dooth fasting encrease the gladsome lyking of meates. For that putting it selfe betwene, and thereby interrupting in part the continual glut of delicacies, shall make the receiuing thereof againe, the more pleasaunt, euen as of a friend retourned from far countries. Wherfore if thou wilt make vnto thy selfe thy table pleasaunt, take vnto thee somtime a chaunge by fasting. But thou that art excessiuely possessed with the looue of deliciousnes, doost not perceiue that thou diminishest much of thy delight, by continuall vsage thereof: and for looue of pleasure lesest in dede the chiefest pleasure. For nothing is so pleasaunt, but that by continuall fruition it waxeth fulsome. But of those thinges which are rarely had, the fruition is delightsome.

Euen in this sort, he which hath made vs, hath deuised: that by chaunge and orderly retourne of thinges in this life, the pleasure of those thinges which he hath graunted vs, might still remaine with delight vnto vs. Doest thou not see how after night, the sonne is more bewtiful? And waking more pleasaunt after sleepe? And health the more desired, and esteemed, after feeling of sicknes and aduersitie? Euen so after fasting, is the table also the better welcome both vnto riche menne, and suche as haue it well furnished, and also to poore folke, which haue but from hand to mouth, that which the earth yeldeth.*

The translation of the 'Decree touching Justification', which I have attributed to John Fowler, provides yet another example of that power, so peculiarly Elizabethan, of transferring an

* *A Treatie of Iustification*, sig. NN4v.

original 'literally in body to another language'. The short excerpt from the thirteenth chapter here appended is a fair specimen of the whole, and will be recognized as a piece of intelligible, natural and idiomatic prose writing:

> The like maie be saied of the gifte of pers[eu]erance, wherof it is writen: *Who so perseuereth vntil the ende, he shall be saued:* the whiche thing can not be had from anie other, then from him, which is able to stay him, that standeth, that he maie continually stand, and to set him vp againe that falleth. No man maie promise him selfe any thing of certaintie, with an absolute certaintie, although all men ought to settle and repose a most sure hope in the helpe of God. For God, (excepte they do not their parte according to his grace) *as he hath begon a good woorke, so will he ende it, woorking in them to will, and to make perfecte.* Howbe it *let them, that thinke them selues to stande, take heede, that they fall not*: And let them *with feare and trembling woorke their saluation*, in labours, in watchinges, in almesdeedes, in praiers and offeringes, in fastinges and chastitie. For, knowing that they are regenerated in hope of glorie, and not as yet in glorie, they haue cause to misdoubt of the battaile, whiche remaineth with the flesh, with the worlde, and with the diuel: in the whiche battaile they can not be conquerors vnlesse with the grace of God they obey the Apostle, saying: *We be debtors, not to the flesh, to liue according to the flesh: for if you liue according to the flesh, you shall die: but if you shall mortifie the deedes of the fleshe by the spirite, you shall liue.**

THOMAS BUTLER'S *Treatise of the Holy Sacrifice*
T.I.'s *Catechisme*

We may dismiss very briefly the two translations which remain to be dealt with in this chapter. Thomas Butler's short treatise is a translation from the Italian of Fr. Antonio Possevino, S.J., the Roman jurist, under the following title:

> *A Treatise of the Holy Sacrifice of the Altar, called the Masse. In the which by the word of God, & testimonies of the Apostles, and Primatiue Church, it is prooued, that our Sauiour Iesus Christ did institute the Masse, and the Apostles did celebrate the same* (1570).

The work, which is described in the Prologue to the Reader as 'a short collectiō of such testimonies and reasons, as do confirme the veritie of ẏͤ blessed Sacrifice of the Altar', and which the translator elsewhere commends for its perspicuity and briefness,† is in the main a straightforward exposition of doc-

* ibid., sig. Z3.

† Dedicatory Epistle to Bishop Goldwell.

trine, without controversial bias. The translator follows his text closely, while exhibiting an easy and fluent manner of writing his native tongue.

T.I.'s anonymous translation of the very popular *parvus Catechismus* of Canisius has the following title:

> *Certayne necessarie Principles of Religion, which may be entituled, A Catechisme conteyning all the partes of the Christian and Catholique Fayth. Written in Latin by P. Canitius, one of the holy societie of the Iesuites, and nowe amplified and Englished by T. I.* [1578–9?].*

The main body of the work is divided into five chapters ('all the partes of the whole booke resting on fiue pointes'), 'conteining the doctrine of a Christian man', as follows: (1) 'Fayth, and the Creede'; (2) 'of Hope, and the Lords prayer'; (3) 'of Charitie, and the tenne Cōmaundements'; (4) 'of the Sacramentes'; (5) 'of the offices of Christian iustice'. Its purpose is described in the translator's Address to the Reader as to train up 'little ones and younglings . . . after the playnest and readyest waye' to meet the attacks upon their Faith from 'the common enimie of mankind, who like a roaring Lyon neuer ceasseth to seeke whom he may deuour', though, the writer adds, it will also be found useful for those of 'further yeeres . . . so that suche as are of tender yeeres may both suck holsome milke, and others also may eate heere strong meate'. The translator is, in the main, content to follow his original with its 'absolute and playne order'; in certain places, however, as the title suggests, he amplifies his text, not after the manner of the ornate writers with their 'coloured and painted words', for 'religion and the worde of God', as he says, 'ought not to be set out in plausible termes, that may delight and tickle the eares, but in all simplicitie and truth', but by means of description and example to make it 'so playne that any maye well vnderstande the same'.† Not the least interesting part of the book are the translations from the Scriptures, which compare very favourable with contemporary versions. The work affords yet one more proof that the writing of good, straightforward, rhythmical English prose was no rare accomplishment in the days of Queen Elizabeth.

* The probability of this date is discussed at bibl. ent. 67.

† Citations are from the translator's Address, which will be found quoted at some length at bibl. ent. 67.

CHAPTER IV

DEVOTIONAL WORKS AND THE RHEMES NEW TESTAMENT

WHEN we consider the excellence of the extant devotional writings of our authors we may well regret that there are comparatively few works of this nature in the period covered by this thesis. The long chapter just ended tells its own tale. The age was essentially an age of religious controversy, and the necessity of the time left to the exiled Catholics little opportunity for the composing of works of edification. That this was a matter of concern to the Recusants themselves we may gather from the words of their two most prominent leaders in controversy. Both Harding and Persons deplore the effect of controversial writings which, though necessary, are 'not profitable to devotion'. Good life, says Persons in his Preface to the Christian Reader at the entrance of *The Christian Exercise*, is 'a meane to right faithe', and he exhorts his readers, both Catholic and Protestant, to put aside 'all hatred, malice and wrathfull contention', adding the words, 'let vs ioyne together in amendmēt of our lyues, and praying one for an other'. So, too, Harding, as cited by Richard Hopkins in the following extract:

> It is nowe about foureteene yeares agoe, since the time that Master Doctor Hardinge (a man for his greate vertue, learninge, wisdome, zeale, and sinceritie in writinge againste heresies, of verie godlie and famous memorie) perswaded me earnestlie to translate some of those Spanishe bookes into our Englishe tounge, affirminge, that more spirituall profite wolde vndoutedlie ensewe thereby to the gayninge of Christian sowles in our countrie from Schisme, and Heresie, and from all sinne, and iniquitie, than by bookes that treate of controuersies in Religion: wich (as experience hath nowe plainelie tried) doe nothinge so well dispose the common peoples myndes to the feare, loue, and seruice of almightie God, as bookes treatinge of deuotion and howe to leade a vertuous life doe. The dewe consideration whereof hath so prouoked or rather pricked me in conscience . . .*

In the circumstances it is perhaps not surprising that of the thirteen works with which we have to be content only a small

* *Of Prayer, and Meditation*, as below, sig. a6v.

proportion can claim to be quite original. These thirteen works fall naturally, according to their subject-matter, into four groups or sections, which we may designate: (1) General Spiritual Directories, (2) Penance, (3) Rosary, (4) Psalters and Hours. According to this grouping they will be reviewed in this chapter. A fifth and last section of the chapter will be devoted to that crowning glory of this first period of Recusant literature, the Rhemes *New Testament.*

1. GENERAL SPIRITUAL DIRECTORIES

Six works may be included under this heading, viz. Thomas More's *A Dialogue of Cumfort* (1573), newly set forth by John Fowler; the anonymous *Certayne deuout Meditations* [1576]; Stephen Brinkley's *The Exercise of a Christian Life* [1579]; Thomas Hide's *A Consolatorie Epistle to the afflicted Catholikes* (1580); Robert Persons' *The First Booke of the Christian Exercise, appertayning to resolution* (1582); and Richard Hopkins's *Of Prayer, and Meditation* (1582). Of these only Persons' *Christian Exercise*, Hide's *Consolatorie Epistle*, and the anonymous *Certayne deuout Meditations* are in any sense original works. The treatises of Brinkley and Hopkins are translations, and Fowler's *Dialogue of Cumfort* is a revision of More's well-known tractate.

First in importance among these works is Persons' *Christian Exercise*, described in the title as laying down 'the causes & reasons that should moue a man to resolue hym selfe to the seruice of God' and removing 'all the impedimentes . . . which may lett the same'.* It is a remarkable achievement when we consider the difficulties amidst which it was compiled, and both its excellence as a devotional treatise and its influence upon later devotional works give it an outstanding place in Recusant devotional literature. The early history of the book is worth recording.

When he decided to leave England in the early autumn of 1581, Persons had already begun to write, or at least projected, three books: one, *The Defence of the Censure*; another, a letter in Latin treating of the things he had observed *About the English Persecution*; and a third, entitled *The Resolution*, 'in which were contained the principal motives to encourage Catholics to virtue and specially to patience and firm resolve to bear the

* For further details of title and editions see bibliography.

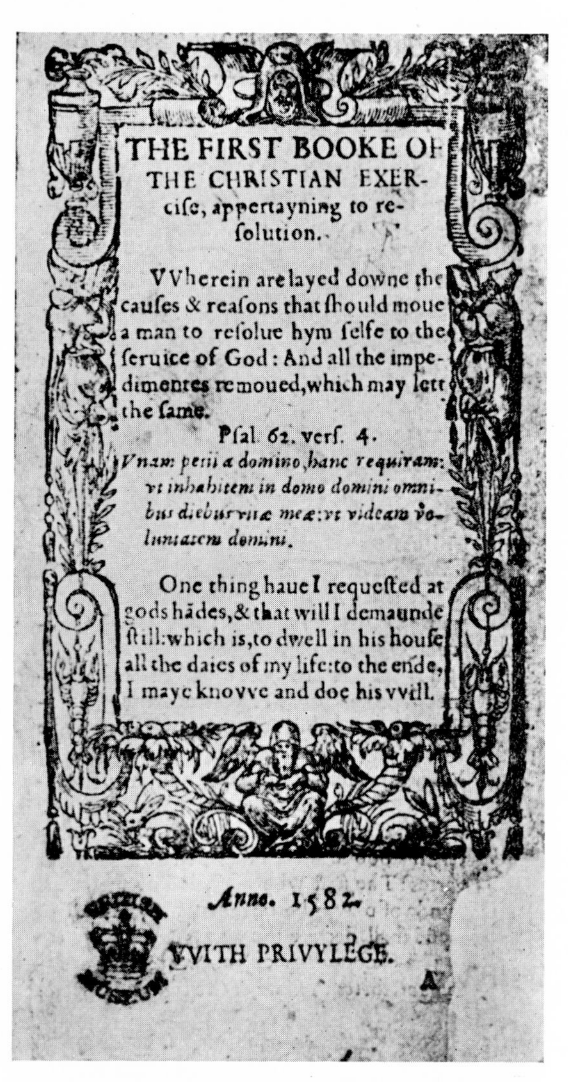
THE FIRST BOOKE OF THE CHRISTIAN EXERCISE, appertayning to resolution.

VVherein are layed downe the causes & reasons that should moue a man to resolue hym selfe to the seruice of God: And all the impedimentes remoued, which may lett the same.

Psal. 62. vers. 4.

Vnam petii a domino, hanc requiram: vt inhabitem in domo domini omnibus diebus vitæ meæ: vt videam voluntatem domini.

One thing haue I requested at gods hãdes, & that will I demaunde still: which is, to dwell in his house all the daies of my life: to the ende, I maye knovve and doe his vvill.

Anno. 1582.

VVITH PRIVYLEGE.

A

TITLE-PAGE OF THE FIRST EDITION OF R. PERSONS' *CHRISTIAN DIRECTORY*

Printed by George L'Oyselet, Rouen

present persecution'. Having no means of getting them printed within the realm of England, he passed over to Rouen in France to finish the books above mentioned that he had in hand and which were also printed and sent to England together with others. So much we may learn from his 'Notes concerning the English Mission'.* The *Book of Resolution*, as it is commonly called, was written therefore during the winter of 1581–2.† A duodecimo volume of some four hundred pages, it owes its inception to the treatise of Gaspar Loarte which Stephen Brinkley had recently translated and published under the title of *The Exercise of a Christian Life*,‡ and, as Persons himself tells us in his Advertisement to the Reader, was, in fact, intended originally to include this translation of Brinkley's together with certain commentaries of his own. However, Persons soon found that he could not combine Loarte and himself, and he was therefore, he goes on, 'inforced, to resolue vpon a further labour . . . which was, to drawe out the whole three bookes himself'. The fact was that he found Loarte's appeal was too limited for his purpose. His work was written for the faithful only, whereas he himself wanted above all things to preach to the unconverted by setting out the reasons which would call forth the sinner's resolution to turn to God. He needed, therefore, to broaden the basis of his book, to widen its appeal, and it is this which mainly distinguishes Loarte's work from his own. In this, too, I imagine, lies the secret of the book's appeal to the Protestants.§ As it turned out he was able to finish only the first of the three books he had promised, owing to his embarrassed circumstances, and this was printed at the press of George L'Oyselet in Rouen early in 1582, whence, as we have already noted, copies were in due course conveyed to England. The book immediately became a popular favourite and before long the first edition was sold out. This is referred

* Cath. Rec. Soc. *Miscellanea IV* (1907); cf. also C.R.S. *Miscellanea II* – 'Father Persons' Autobiography', where he says that one cause of his going to France 'was to printe some books wch I had written in England or was in wryting, as the defence of the Censure, the latin epistle of persecution and the book of resolution in the first edition all which were printed at Roan this winter' (i.e. 1581–2).

† cf. again, Autobiography: 'all this winter [1581–2] Father Persons remained at Rouen in France, where he finished and printed the books before mentioned for the help of Catholics'.

‡ As above.

§ cf. *Reformation und Spanische Andachtsliteratur*, by Dr. Maria Hagedorn (Leipzig, 1934), pp. 110 et seq.

to specifically by Persons in the Preface to his revised edition of 1585.* There he writes: 'I perceaued many monethes before, that al the first copies of the said former booke (though not so wel done as iustely I might haue wished) were wholy dispersed and none remaining to be had.' It is *primarily* for this reason, then, he says, that he has resolved to take the first book again and 'to polish and fil vp some thinges, wherin before for want of leasure and time, I could not geue to my self any reasonable contentation, as also to adioine certaine new chapters'. He further promises a second volume which is to contain the second and third books mentioned above.† He then goes on to give an added reason for his reprint, which we quote in full. The matter was, he says, 'wel forward for the print' when 'I was enformed of two other editions come forth of my forsaid booke without my knowledge, the one by a Catholique (as it seemeth) who perceuing al copies of the former print to be spēt; for satisfying of them that desired the booke, procured the same to be set forth againe, albeit somewhat incorrected, and very disordrely, not hauing the consent or aduise of such, as therin should haue geuen him best direction. The second was published by one Edmund Buny minister at Bolton Percy (as he writeth) in the liberties of Yorke; who with publicke licence vnder my Lord Archbishop of Yorke his protection, set forth the same to the benefite of his brethren; but yet so punished and plumed, (which he termeth purged;) as I could hardly by the face discerne it for mine, when it came vnto my handes, and I tooke no smale compassiō to see how pitifully the poore thing had bene handled. Of this edition then of M. Buny, (letting passe th'other as a matter onely of indiscretion without malice,) I haue to aduertise the reader some few things . . .'‡

The two editions referred to in this paragraph of Persons were a Catholic pirated edition, which was issued from the L'Oyselet press in 1584, and the well-known bowdlerized edition of Edmund Bunny, Calvinist Vicar of Bolton Percy, also of 1584 and printed in London.§ The preface of the latter, in

* *A Christian directorie, guiding men to their saluation, commonly called the Resolution . . . with reproofe of the falsified edition by E. Buny.*

† Save for a further apology for their non-appearance at the end of the volume, this is the last we hear of Books II and III.

‡ Preface to the revised edition, sigs. a4–5.

§ See bibliography.

which Bunny explains his aim and his procedure, must surely rank as a *locus classicus* on literary usurpation. 'I perceived', he writes, 'that the booke insuing was willingly read by divers, for the persuasion that it hath to godlines of life, which notwithstanding in manie points was corruptly set downe: I thought good in the end, to get the same published againe in some better manner than now it is come foorth among them; that so the good, that the reading therof might otherwise do, might carrie no hurt or danger withal, so far as by me might be praevented. For this cause I have taken the pains, both to purge it of certain points that carried either some manifest error, or else some other inconvenience with them: and to join another short Treatise withal, to exhort those that are not yet persuaded, to join with us likewise in the truth of Religion.'* Bunny later replied to Persons' reproof of his edition in his *A Briefe Answer, vnto those idle and friuolous quarrels of R. P. against the late edition of the Resolution* (London, 1589), where, we may note, he accuses Persons of making 'much a doe about nothing', and there, as far as we are concerned, the controversy ends. We shall pass over, therefore, the many references to this book in contemporary and later writers, the various Protestant adaptations and editions (there were nine issues of Bunny's edition between 1584 and 1600), the numerous reprints of the author's original in several languages, the fact that the Protestant version 'was even read aloud, as we learn from a controversialist writer in 1604, by ministers in their churches',† and conclude this history by recording only what is perhaps the most remarkable testimony of all to the influence of this book. It comes from the pen of no less a person than 'the Catholic Puritan', Richard Baxter, Vicar of Kidderminster, who ascribes his own inner conversion to reading it in these words: 'a poor Day-Labourer in the Town (he that I before mentioned that was wont to read in the Church for the old Parson) had an old torn book which he lent my Father, which was called Bunny's Resolution, (being written by Parson's the Jesuit, and corrected by Edm. Bunny . . . And in the reading of this Book (when I was about Fifteen years of Age) it pleased God to awaken my Soul, and shew me the folly of Sinning and the misery of the Wicked, and the

* Preface to the Reader, sig. *2.

† Maria Hagedorn, op. cit., quoting H. Thurston from *The Month*, 1894, p. 468.

unexpressible weight of things Eternal, and the necessity of resolving on a Holy Life, more than I was ever aquainted with before. The same things which I knew before came now in another manner, with Light, and Sense, and Seriousness to my Heart'.*

The *Christian Directorie*, to give the book its revised title of 1585, may best be described as a free adaptation of its Italian original, Gaspar Loarte's *Essercitatio della vita christiana*, published at Barcelona in 1569. In point of fact Persons draws his matter not only from Loarte, but also, in respect of his illustrations, comparisons and quotations, from Luis de Granada's *Guia de Pecadores* (1573), as has been clearly pointed out by Dr. Hagedorn.† And here, too, as the same writer shows, he uses his original with considerable freedom. By avoiding Granada's circumlocutions and many repetitions and by the vigour of his English idiom he produces, like so many contemporary translators, what is in fact essentially an English book. If we turn to the pages of the book we shall be struck by the homeliness of the language, the familiarity of the phrasing, the suggestiveness of the images.

> Consider attentyuely, as a good marchand factour is wonte to doe, when he is arriued in a strãge countrye: or as a captaine sent by his prince to some great exployte is accustomed, when he comethe to the place appointed [sig. C1].

> If a man had to make a iourneye but from Englãde to Cõstãtinople, albeit he had made the same once or twyse before, yet would he not passe it ouer withe oute greate & often consideration, especially whether he were right, and in the waye or no, what pase he held, howe neere he was to his wayes ende, and the lyke [sig. B11].

> If the marchand factour (which I spake of before) after manye yeares spent beyond the seas, returninge home to geeue accountes to his maister, should yeald a reconninge of so much tyme spent in singinge, so much in daunsinge so muche in courtinge, and the lyke: who would not laughe at his accountes? but beinge further asked by his maister, what tyme he bestowed on his marchandise which he sent hym for . . . [sig. C3].

* *Reliquiae Baxterianae* (1696), p. 3, cited by M. Hagedorn, as before.

† op. cit., pp. 115 et seq. Dr. Hagedorn points to a whole series of correspondences between the two works as evidence of this fact and refers to Persons' praise of Granada's devotional works in his preface to the 1585 edition.

> If a poore man, that were out of his waye, wanderinge alone in a durtie lane, in the mydesst of a darke and tempestuous night, farre from companie, destitute of money, beaten with rayne, terrified with thunder, styffe with colde, wearied out with labour, almost famished with hungre and thurst, and neare brought to despare with multitude of miseries, should vpō the suddain, in the twinkling of an eye, be placed in a goodlie large and riche palace, furnished with all kynde of cleare lightes, warme fyre, sweete smelles, dayntie meates, soft beddes, pleasant musike, fine apparell, and honorable cōpanie: all prepared for hym, and attending his cōmyng, to serue hym, to honour hym, and to annoynt and crowne hym a king for euer: what wold this poore man doe? [sig. I4^{v}].

There are three things, says Persons, necessary to a Christian in this life. They are (1) a firm resolution to serve God, (2) knowledge of how to begin to do this, and (3) knowledge of how to persevere to the end. The *Christian Directorie* deals with the first of these only, dividing the theme as between the two parts of the book in the following manner: Part I – (1) of obstinancie, (2) consideration, (3) the finall end, (4) particuler end, (5) of accompte, (6) the nature of sinne, (7) godes benefites, (8) the daye of deathe, (9) of punishement, (10) the rewardes. Part II – (1) of the difficultie, (2) of tribulation, (3) of the world, (4) presumption, (5) of delaye, (6) three impedimentes. The method of presenting the subject is, as in most contemporary works of this kind, part instructional and part edificational, very much after the manner of the sermon, and in some places, as we shall see directly, very much after the manner of the *medieval* sermon. To begin with, here is a short passage which can hardly be distinguished from pulpit eloquence of the best kind. The dramatic effect of the balancing movement of the paragraph will be noted:

> And for the vnderstandinge of this iniurie, we must note that euerie tyme we cōmitt a mortall sinne, there dothe passe thorowgh our hart (though we marcke it not) a certaine practick discourse of our vnderstandinge, (as there doth also in euerie other election) whereby we lay before vs, on the one side, the profit of that sinne which we are to committ, that is, the pleasure that draweth vs to it: and on thother parte, the offēce of God, that is the leesinge of his frindshippe by that sinne yf we doe it: and so hauinge as it were the balances there before vs, and puttinge God in one end, and in the other the aforesayde pleasure: we stāde in the middest deliberatinge and

> examininge the wayght of both partes, & finallie we doe make choise of the pleasure and doe reiect God: that is, we doe chuse rather to leese the frindshipp of God, with his grace, and whatsoeuer he is worth besides, than to lose that pleasure and delectation of sinne [sig. D9v].

Here, as elsewhere in this treatise, the reader will probably be struck by the correctness of the writer's syntax. In the handling of his sentences Persons shows himself indeed to be thoroughly modern. At the same time, as we believe the passages following will show, there is a kinship of temper and style in this work with the great English devotional writings of the fourteenth century and the native medieval sermon. Let us be quite clear about this. We have seen that Persons' work is derivative, and therefore we must admit that his manner to some extent is likely to be tempered by that of his original. Yet we must not make too much of this. We must not see in it a cause for doubting his real affinity with the earlier English tradition in devotional writing. We must not assume, that is to say, that his work bears this particular stamp because he read and translated Loarte. It is equally probable that he found his inspiration in that writer because he was himself the kind of person who was inclined to write in that manner, and as we follow him in the drawing out of his theme of Resolution we become the more certain of this probability. For instance, if we could imagine Richard Rolle writing his *Form of Living*, not for a recluse disciple but for the wider secular public that Persons had in mind, after making allowances, of course, for Rolle's particularities of style, such a passage as the following, in the directness of its manner, would not seem out of place in that work:

> And yet, how easilie men of the worlde doe committ sinne, & how litle scruple they make of the matter, Iob signifieth, vhen [sic], talking of suche a man, he sayeth, *bibit quasi aquam iniquitatem*: He suppeth vp sinne, as it were water: that is, with as great facilitie, custome, and ease, passeth he downe any kynde of sinne, that is offered him, as a man drinketh water, when he is athirst. He that will not beleeue the sayeing of Iob: let hym proue a litle, by his owne experiēce, whether the matter be so or no: let hym walke owt, into the streetes, beholde the doeinges of men, vewe their behauioure, consider what is done in shoppes, in halles, in consistories, in iudgemente seates, in palaces, and in common meetinge places abroade: what lyeinge: what slanderinge: what deceyuinge there is. He shall finde, that of

all thinges wherof men make anye accompt, nothing is so litle accounted of, as to sinne. He shall see iustice solde, veritie wrested, shame lost, and equitie despised. He shall see the Innocent condemned: the guiltie deliuered: the wicked aduanced: the vertuous oppressed. He shall see manye theeues florishe: manye vsurers beare greate swaye, many murderers and extorsioners reuerēced & honoured: many fooles putt in authoritie: and diuers which haue nothing in them but the forme of men, by reason of money, to be placed in greate dignities for the gouernmēt of others. He shall heare at euerie mans mouthe, almoste, vanitie, pride, detraction, enuie, deceyte, dissimulatiō, wantōnesse, dissolution [dissoluteness], lyeing, swearing, periurie, and blaspheming. Finallie, he shall see the most parte of men, to gouerne them selues absolutelie, euen as beastes doe, by the motion of there passions, not by lawe of iustice, reason, religion, or vertue [sig. P12v].

Even more striking, in respect of its realism, its vividness, and its homeliness, is the resemblance of the *Book of the Resolution* to the rather more modern *Scale of Perfection* of Walter Hilton, which Persons must have known quite well. The homeliness of image and language, which, we are told, runs right through the *Scale*, is certainly also one of the principal marks of Persons' own style in the *Resolution*. It is to be observed in our next passage, where the strongly personal touch is yet another link in the chain which binds our author to the medieval tradition in devotional writing. Persons is speaking of the soul's ascent to glory:

Imagine besides all this, what a ioye it shall be vnto thy soule at that daye, to meet with all her godlie freendes in heauen, with father, with mother, with brothers, with sisters: with wyfe, with husband, with maister, with scholares: with neyghboures, with familiares, with kynred, with acquayntance: the welcomes, the myrthe, the sweete embracementes that shall be there, the ioye whereof (as noteth S. Cyprian) shalbe vnspeakable. Add to this, the dalye feasting and inestimable triumphe, whiche shalbe there, at the ariuall of new bretheren and sisters coming thither from time to time with the spoyles of their enemies, conquered and vanquyshed in this world. O what a cōfortable sight will it be to see those seates of Angells fallen, filled vpp agayne with men & wemen from day to day? to see the crownes of glorie sett vpon their heades, and that in varietie, according to the varietie of their cōquestes. One for martyrdome, or confession against the persecutor: an other for virginitie or chastitie against the flesh . . . [sig. I4].

Dr. G. R. Owst in his two important works on medieval preachers and preaching* has drawn attention to the 'realistic' habit of mind which reveals itself constantly in the sermon literature of the Middle Ages. This realistic habit of mind we have already seen in many places in the controversial works of our period. It is equally to be found in the devotional treatises which are now under discussion. The following instance from Persons – and such instances might be multiplied – strongly reminiscent of one type of medieval sermon, points decisively to the continuation of the English sermon tradition in these works:

> Imagine then (my freende) thow I saye which art so freshe and froelicke at this daie, that the ten, twentie, or two yeres, or perhaps two monethes, which thow hast yet to lyue, were now ended, and that thow were euen at this present, stretched out vppon a bed, wearied and worne with dolour and paine, thy carnall frindes aboute the weepinge and howlinge, the phisitions departed with theire fees, as hauinge geeuen the ouer, & thow lyinge there alone mute and dumme in most pitifull agonie, expectinge from moment to moment, the last stroake of death to be geeuen the. Tell me in this instant, what would all the pleasures and commodities of this world doe the good? what comforte would it be to the, to haue bene of honour in this world, to haue bene ryche and purchassed muche, to haue borne office, and bene in the princes fauoure? to haue left thy children or kynred wealthye, to haue trodden downe thyne enimies, to haue sturred much, and borne greate swaye in this lyfe? what ease (I saye) or comfort would it be to the, to haue ben fayre, to haue ben gallant in apparell, goodlie in personage, glytteringe in golde? would not all thes thinges rather afflict than profit the at this instant? for now shouldest thow see the vanitie of thes trifles: now would thy hart begyn to saye within the? "o follye and vnfortunate blindenes of myne, Loe, heere is an end now of all my delytes and prosperities: all my ioyes, all my pleasures, all my myrth, all my pastymes are now finished. Where are my frindes whiche were wont to laugh with me? my seruantes wont to attende me, my children wont to disporte me? where are all my coches & horses, wherwith I was wont to make so goodlie a shew, the cappes and knees of people wont to honour me, the troupes of suters followinge me? where are all my daliances and trickes of loue? all my pleasant musicke, all my gorgeous buyldinges, all my costlie feastes and banquettinges? and aboue all other, where are my deare and sweete frindes, whoe seemed they would neuer haue forsaken me? but

* *Preaching in Medieval England* and *Literature and Pulpit in Medieval England*.

> all are now gone, and hath left me heere alone to aunswere the reckoninge for all, & none of them will doe so muche as to goe with me to iudgemēt, or to speake one worde in my behalfe.
>
> Woe worthe to me, that I had not foreseene this daye rather, & so haue made better prouisiō for the same: it is now to late, and I feare me I haue purchased eternall damnation, for a litle pleasure, and lost vnspeakable glorie, for a flooting vanitie . . . [sig. F9v].

There would seem, then, to be evidence enough in the *Resolution* to show that it is to the writers of the fourteenth century, to Rolle and Hilton and the medieval preacher, that we must look if we would wish to trace the literary descent of Persons and his fellows. Nor is there anything really remarkable in this. Modern research has established that there was no real gap between the fourteenth and sixteenth centuries in the matter of religious prose. During the fifteenth century, we are told, practical works of devotion and collections of sermons were widely disseminated;* amongst these the works of Rolle had probably pride of place. Second only to Rolle was Walter Hilton. In respect of the *Scale*, it has been pointed out that the number of manuscripts extant of this work, 'the fact that it was printed as early as 1494 and that new editions appeared in 1507, 1519, 1525, and 1533, are evidences of Hilton's popularity in his own day and after'.† Further to our point, in an important section of his *Continuity of English Prose*, so often cited in these pages, which he heads 'Evidence for the Continuous Influence of Fourteenth-Century devotional Literature, through the Fifteenth, into the Sixteenth Century', Professor Chambers writes: 'So, when Thomas More determined to be an author, not merely in Latin, but in English also, he had not to make an English prose. He found it ready to hand: not in Chaucer's *Parson's Tale*, not even in Malory, whose book he may perhaps never have opened, but in the living tradition of the English pulpit, and in the large body of devotional vernacular litera-

* cf. H. S. Bennett, *The Author and his Public in the Fourteenth and Fifteenth Centuries* in *Essays and Studies by Members of the English Association, XXIII*, p. 21. See also R. W. Chambers, *Continuity of English Prose*, as before, p. cviii.

† Helen L. Gardner, *Walter Hilton and the Mystical Tradition in England* in *Essays and Studies by Members of the English Association, XXII*, p. 123. Miss Gardner goes on to say that 'in the storm that swept away the religious houses of England, [Hilton] and his fellows were forgotten. But in corners the tradition lingered on'. So far we may follow her. But not her later contention that 'in the main stream of English literature, Hilton and his fellows, as a direct influence, have no place'.

ture dating from the Fourteenth Century and the early Fifteenth'.* Elizabethan England, the writer goes on to say, had little use for this literature; on the other hand, there is evidence enough to show that these books of devotion (Chambers refers particularly to *The Cloud of Unknowing*) continued to be studied during the latter half of the sixteenth century among our Recusant exiles. In view of this evidence, and of such internal evidence as we have been able to adduce in this present notice, we may with some confidence conclude that the roots of these works of Persons and his fellows strike back into the medieval tradition and must thus be regarded as providing an important link in the continuity of our English prose.

It is fitting that we should next consider Stephen Brinkley's translation of Loarte, referred to by Persons above. The title of this book is as follows: *The Exercise of A Christian Life. Written in Italian by the Reuerend Father Gaspar Loarte D. of Diuinitie, of the Societie of Iesus. And newly translated into Englishe. By I. S.* From the subscription to the dedication we learn that it belongs to the year 1579, and that the initials I. S. stand for James Sancer, or Sanker, which, as Persons tells us, was Brinkley's pseudonym. I have been able to trace only a single copy of this original edition of Brinkley's work, viz. that in the Lambeth Palace Library. A revised edition appeared in 1584, and this was reprinted in 1600, 1610 and 1634.† The book, which is a practical handbook of the Christian life, a guide to conduct and a help to prayer and meditation, is dedicated by Brinkley to the members of the Society of Jesus and is marked by the simplicity and straightforwardness of its style. That this was the translator's aim we learn from the following words of the dedication:

> God graũt my skil haue answered to my wil, than shal I without al affectation haue translated that into plaine, and not impure Englishe, which was first written by a woorthy Father of your company, in plaine and right pure Italiã. Accept therfore, Reuerend Fathers, and Brethren, a birde of your owne broode, plucked out of her natural plume, and garnished with forreine fether.

Here, first, is a short quotation, chosen not altogether at random, displaying this plainness of style. It comes from the

* p. cxxiv.

† For further important bibliographical details, see entry 20 in the bibliography.

twenty-third chapter, which deals with Remedies against Pride, and is cited as a parallel passage with that from Persons' *Resolution*, set out above at p. 190. The comparison with Persons is useful, for whereas, on the one hand, little difference will be observed between the two writers in respect of language, on the other, as a result of the comparison, in respect of style, the realism of Persons will perhaps be the plainer, whilst the plainness of Brinkley will perhaps be the better realized:

> And therfore marke wel the wordes that Saint Austine writeth to this purpose. If thou vaunt thee of thy riches (saith he) and of the nobilitie of thine auncestors; if thou glory in thy country thy cōlines of body, & the renowm, which the worlde respecteth thee with; consider with thy selfe, howe thou art mortal, earth, and shalt bee come earth. Beholde where those are now that earst enioyed the same titles and stiles, which thou art presently puft vp with? where be they that so ambitiously desired to rule & gouerne countreys? where be these insuperable and vnuanquished Emperours? where be the Generals, and chiefe captains of armies? where be those that erst ridd so proudly, moūted on their stately palfreys? where be they that tooke plesure in their pompes and ceremonies? now is al turned to earth and ashes? now is the memorial of their liues conteined in fewe lines: Looke nowe into their graues, and see, if thou canst knowe the master from the man; the poore felowe from the penifather?* Discerne now, if thou canst, the bondslaue from the king; the strong man from the weak; the comly personage from the deformed criple? [sig. R1^{v}].

But Brinkley's concern with the style of his work is even more evident from a comparison of the first edition of his translation with the revised edition of 1584. His endeavour to be 'plain' is emphasized by the many alterations and simplifications which he introduced into this latter version. We cannot do better, then, than examine the two versions side by side with a view to establishing this claim to plainness of style. The following passages from the third chapter afford instructive comparison:

1579

> Descending nowe to more particularitie, for that such things as be wel and orderly disposed, be both more durable and profitable too: I haue therefore thought good to aduertise thee, what course and order thou oughtest euery day to keepe. Which let be this: first, to rise in the morning so earlye as thou mayest, hauing before taken conuenient rest and sleepe, which is had

* Skinflint.

betwixt sixe and seuen howres, litle more or lesse, according to the diuersitie of complexions. So soone as thou art awake, it is a good & godlye deuotion, before thou settle thy minde to any other thing, to offer vp to God the first fruits of al thine actions, and powers of thy whole body: as for example, thy heart, thinking of thy Creatour, and sighing after him: thine eyes, casting them vpon some godly picture, or vp to heauen: thy legges, kneeling humbly before his presence: thy handes, lifting them vp to adore and thanke him: thy mouth, saying some short prayers, as the Pater noster, Aue Mary, and the Crede: and then mayest thou afterwards, according as thy deuotion shal teache thee, briefly geue him thankes for hauing preserved thee the night past, desiring him likewise to defend thee that present day from al sinne, and to geue thee grace to spende it better in his diuine seruice.

1584

Descending now to more particularitie, for that things orderly disposed, be both more durable and profitable also, I haue thought good to aduertise thee, what order thou oughtest euery day to keepe. Which let be this: first to rise in the morning so earlye as thou mayest, hauing before refreshed thy self sufficiẽtly with slepe, that is the space of Sixe or seuen howres, litle more or lesse, according to the diuersitie of complexions. So soone as thou art awake, it is a good & godlye deuotion, before thou settle thy minde to any other thing, to offer vp to God the first fruits of al thine actions, and powers of thy whole body: as for example, thy hart, thinking of thy Creator, & sighing after him: thine eyes casting them vpon some godly picture, or vp to heauen: thy legges, kneeling humbly before his presence: thy handes, lifting them vp to adore & thanke him: thy mouth, saying some short prayers, as the Pater noster, Aue Mary, and the Crede: and then mayest thou afterwards, according as thy deuotion shal teache thee, briefly geue him thankes for hauing preserued thee the night past, desiring him likewise to defend thee that present day from al sinne, and to geue the grace to spend it fruitfully in his diuine seruice.

1579

The residue of time from supper til thou goe to bed, thou maiest bestowe in some honest talke, or other good exercise and recreation, taking heede yet of occupying thy selfe in any suche thing as may hinder and disturbe the quietnes of thy minde.

Afterwardes hauing made some smal pause and resting while, see thou prepare thy selfe to bedward, considering that a good christian ought to dispose him selfe in such wise therto, as if he were that night to depart this life.

1584

The residue of time from supper, til thou goe to bed, thou maiest bestowe in some honest talke, or other good exercise and recreation, alwaies taking heede of occupying thy self in any such thing as may hinder and disturbe the quietnes of thy minde.

Afterwardes (hauing thus reposed thy self some time,) see thou prepare thy selfe to bedward, cōsidering that euery good christian ought in such wise to dispose him self thervnto, as if he were that night to depart out of this life.*

There can be little doubt that such alterations as are made in the above passages are all to the good. Chiefly they consist in the removal of redundancies and, in one or two places, in the improvement of the rhythm. Here is a passage where the changes are less happy. In his endeavour to attain more dignified utterance, Brinkley loses in vividness:

1579

And thus his handes and most holy feete being with sharpe nailes fastned to the crosse, they hoiste him vp on high, hanging moste pitifullye thereon. Weigh here diligently, what griping griefes his moste rueful virgin mother suffered, hearing the strokes of the hammer, wherewithal they crucified him, and seeing him afterwardes hoisted so vp vpon that hard crosse with such opprobrious shame, and infinite paines and tormentes [fol. 30b].

1584

And thus his handes and most holy feete being with sharpe nailes fastned to the crosse, they reare him vp on high, hanging most pitifullye thereon. Weigh here diligently, what wonderful griefes his most rueful virgin mother suffered, hearing the strokes of the hammer, wherewithal they crucified him, & seing him afterwardes reared vp vpō that hard crosse with such opprobrious shame, & infinite paines & tormentes [p. 53].

Finally here are a series of phrases and sentences which further exhibit our author's manner of revision:

1579. which thou art to allot and destinate [fol. 21].
1584. which thou art to allot [p. 37].
1579. listning thy wordes [fol. 21b].
1584. listnīg to thy wordes [p. 38].
1579. thou shouldest bye and bye fling out of dores and occupie thy selfe in forraine thoughtes [fol. 90b].

* 1579 – fols. 8 et seq.; 1584 – pp. 14 et seq.

1584. thou shouldest bye and bye ronne out of the dore . . . [p. 157].

1579. that the time & hours thus prefixed, maye admonishe and prouoke thee therto; and a good custome once got take awaye the difficultie [fol. 21].

1584. that the time & hours thus prefixed, maye admonishe & prouoke the thereunto, and a good custome once gotten take awaye the difficultie therof [p. 37].

1579. with other innumerable commodities too many to rehearse [fol. 19b].

1584. with other singuler commodities toe many to rehearse [p. 35].

Altogether we may say that the revision is very thorough, words, punctuation, and occasionally even paragraphing receiving careful attention. Not least among the improvements is the careful distinction, which seems to be generally observed, in the use of the relative pronouns 'that' and 'which'.

Owing to their common origin there are naturally many points of resemblance between this translation of Brinkley's and the work of Persons which we have just examined. It is hardly necessary, therefore, to quote Brinkley at greater length. We may allow ourselves, however, one more passage: from the prayers with which Brinkley closes his book and which do not appear in his original. Since the object here is to stimulate spiritual fervour, the language is naturally more 'coloured' than that which we find in other parts of the book:

> I salute thee, O most beautiful and glittering [1584. glistering] lillie of the gratious and pleasant springtime, moste sacred virgin Mary. I salute thee, O odoriferous floure of diuine suauitie. I salute thee, O louely Rose of celestial delightes, whereon our Sauiour Iesus Christe, the brightnes of his fathers glorie, and figure [1584. the figure] of his substance vouchsafed to be borne and nourished; Obteine me, gratious [1584. for me, O gratious] Ladie, of thy louing sonne, what thou seest most needful [1584. whatsoeuer thou seest to be most needful] for my soul. Help, most [1584. O most] pitiful mother, helpe the weaknes and debilitie of my spirite, in al my tentations and necessities; and vouchsafe to succour me in the hour of death, that through thy gratious fauour and helpe, [1584. fauour and mediation] I may be assured in so perillous and extreme a daunger.
>
> O most happie Angelical spirites, who with one voice doo with pleasaunt and wel-tuned melodie glorifie our common Lorde, and enioye perpetually the taste of his delights, take

pitie vpon me poore miserable wretche, [1584. I humbly beseech you] namely, thou, O holy Angel, the guardian of my soule, to whom [1584. vnto whom] I am especially committed, haue thou continually a diligent and careful eye vpon me. And yee, O Saints of al sortes, which are after the nauigation of these rough and stormie seas, happilye deliuered of this exile, [1584. which after the nauigation . . . are happily deliuered out of this exile] and arriued to the harbour of celestial abode, be, I humblye beseeche you al, mine Aduocates [1584. to be mine Aduocates] and Intercessours, praying to our Lorde [1584. vnto our Lord] for me, that I maye in fauour of your merites and praiers, be not onely fauored [1584. thorough the fauour of your merites and holy intercessions not onely be fauored] of him at this instant, but euen to the very last daie and end [1584. vnto the very last daie and houre] of this my temporal life. Amen [sig. EE5].

One of the most striking successes of the Recusant writers was Richard Hopkins's translation of Luis de Granada's *Libro de la Oracion y Meditacion* (Salamanca, 1554), the title of which is as follows: *Of Prayer, and Meditation. Wherein are conteined fowertien deuoute Meditations for the seuen daies of the weeke, bothe for the morninges, and eueninges. And in them is treyted of the consideration of the principall holie Mysteries of our faithe. Written firste in the Spanishe tongue by the famous Religious father. F. Lewis de Granada, Prouinciall of the holie order of preachers in the Prouince of Portugall* (1582). It is to be observed that this is the first translation of one of the great sixteenth-century Spanish devotional treatises into the mother-tongue, and in thus introducing the works (he also published a translation of Granada's *Memorial de la Vida Christiana* in 1586) of Fray Luis to the Elizabethan public, Hopkins may be said to have had, at least indirectly, an important influence upon the course of later sixteenth-century literature in this country. The popularity of Granada in England is without question. He was a stylist after the Elizabethan heart. 'His reputation rose with that of Lyly, and was based upon the same fundamental grounds.'* 'So widely was he read in our country in the sixteenth and seventeenth centuries† that he may well have inspired men like Vaughan and Crashaw with whom he has much in common.'‡

* J. G. Underhill, *Spanish Literature in the England of the Tudors* (1899), p. 206.

† At least twenty editions, Catholic and Protestant, of his works were published in English before 1640.

‡ E. Allison Peers, *Spanish Mysticism* (1924), p. 20; cf. also M. Hagedorn, op. cit., who would add the names of Donne and Thomas Browne.

There was a measure of audacity in the manner in which Hopkins introduced his translation to the English public. In view of the laws prohibiting Catholic books in the realm and in view of the fact that Spain was the arch-enemy of England, it was certainly a bold move first to name the author (one of the hated Spanish nation) on the title-page, and second to dedicate the book, as he does, to the gentlemen of the Inns of Court, those, that is to say, who were at the very centre of Elizabethan London life.* And, to cap all, Hopkins sent a copy of his book to Francis Walsingham himself. Yet, however provocative we may think the author's action, we may accept his own apology for it, which we must suppose was uttered in all sincerity. Both in the covering letter which accompanied the copy of the book sent to Walsingham,† and in the Dedication, he endeavours to forestall criticism by calling attention to the non-theological character of the writing and to his desire only to do honour to Almighty God and to further the welfare of his fatherland. The words of the Dedication reveal very clearly what was in Hopkins's mind. The signs of the time, he believed, all pointed to the coming of Antichrist, when the devil shall be let loose for a short time before the end of the world:

> in this our vngratious age suche a number of horrible sectes, and heresies, and suche a generall corruption with pride, dysobedience, lyenge, detraction, gluttonie, incontinencie, infidelitie, Atheisme, and all kinde of dissolute wickednes doe abounde and raigne more and more in all partes of Christēdome, woe bee therfore to the Lande, and sea, (as the holye Angell hath forewarned vs) because the Deuill is nowe discended, and let lose towardes the ende of the worlde for a smale time, hauinge a greate rage, for that he Knoweth he hathe but a shorte tyme to continewe his tyrannous kingdome in this worlde . . .

Chief among these signs was the steady decrease in the solemn observances of the Christian faith:

> Nowe emonge all the wylie deceitfull deuises of Satan for ouerthrowinge of the Christian Religion, and so to prepare the waie for Antichristes comminge, there is none (in my simple iudge-

* cf. the late Fr. J. H. Pollen's comment in *The Month* for January 1910 on the words from Fr. Persons' *Life of Campion*: 'Hilary term being ended the most part of gentlemen were retired home into their counties.' Fr. Pollen writes: 'It was the Law Courts, not the Parliament, which kept people in town in those days.'

† S.P.O., Vol. 155, no. 10. The letter, which flatters Walsingham for his moderation in dealing with the Catholics, is dated from Paris 21 August 1582.

> mente) of greater force, and consequence, than his so earnest endeuour to procure all Christians vtterlye to contemne and forgette all the holie misteries of the Christian faithe . . .

This is the explanation of the rise of Puritanism in England:

> And to write here freelie my minde as I thinke, it woulde seeme verie meruailous vnto me . . . howe the deuill coulde preuaile so farfoorthe, as to induce a whole newe late secte of heretikes that be called Puritans (professinge in gaie wordes to be more pure, more sincere, and better professours of Christes gospell than anie other Christians either be or haue bene in anie age since the Apostles time) to write of late so vnchristianlie by common consent euen in an Englishe printed booke againste obseruinge in the Churche the most auncient yearelie solemne holie feastes of *Easter*, and *Pentecoste*, and againste all speciall meditations at anie one solemne time of the yeare more than at others of Christs Resurrection, or of the Comminge of the Holie Ghoste, or of the hower of our death:* because (saie theie) theise meditations shoulde be vsed continewallie euerie daie in the yeare, and owght not to be appoynted by the gouernors of the Churche to be vsed at anie one speciall time more than at others . . .

In this manner the Puritans will in time extinguish all memory of the Church festivals and so prepare the way for the coming of Antichrist. For it is through her festivals and holy days of remembrance that the Church has kept alive the faith in her children. Thus, in order to combat these dangers, he has translated the works of Fray Luis:

> And for this purpose I haue translated out of the Spanishe tongue diuers bookes of a verie holie and famous learned religious father called Lewis de Granada, whose deuoute manner of writinge hath (in my simple iudgemente) a singular rare grace to pearce the harde harte of a dissolute sinner, and to moue and dispose his minde to the abhorringe of sinne, to the contempt of the world, and to the fear, loue and seruice of Almightie God –

and in answer to those who consider his teaching too downright and severe for the ordinary person he appeals to Granada's wide experience in spiritual matters:

> The Author beinge (as I am informed) not onelie a greate

* Marg. 'In the puritans replie againste D. Whitgifte, pag. 120. 121. 122. & 163.' If the reference is to Thomas Cartwright's attack on Whitgift, the reader may be referred to *A Replye to an answere made of M. Doctor Whitegifte. Againste the Admonition to the Parliament* (1573?), pp. 151 et seq., and to *The rest of the second replie of Thomas Cartwright agaynst Master Doctor Whitgifts second answer* (1577), pp. 188 et seq. I have not traced the edition to which Hopkins here refers.

learned and religious deuout olde father, but also of greate wisdome, grauitie, iudgemente, discretion, and of longe experience as well in preachinge, and hearinge of Cōfessions, as in diuers gouernementes in his religious order, and perceyuinge verie euidentlie that farre more Christian sowles be loste in this our corrupte age with ouermuche presumptuous confidence and securetie of their saluation, than with ouermuche feare of leesinge the same –

nor is any nation, he believes, more urgently in need of such teaching than the English and Scottish peoples, who have lost all fear of God and his 'court of punishment' in the conviction that belief alone may save. For his misled compatriots he knows of no better remedy than these Meditations of Granada:

> And if theise and suche like godlie Meditations and considerations of the terrible threateninges and iudgements of almightie God againste the wicked, be not a fitt remedie for their conuersion from their careles dissolute lifes, what other remedie then can possiblie be deuised for them?

Which brings us finally to the point of the dedication itself, viz. his appeal to the high authorities of English justice to play their part in the saving of his countrymen:

> And for so muche as I am verie warie and assured that this boke conteineth not anie thinge whereby I maie iustlie incurre anie penaltie prescribed by anie lawes of our Realme, I am the bolder humblie to recommende it by this my dedicatorie Epistle vnto your Honours and woorshipps: partelie for that I haue spente some parte of my time in the studie of our Common Lawes in the Middle Temple emonge you, and am verie moche bounde vnto diuers of you: But chiefelie for that I knowe right well the greate capacitie and dexteritie of your spirites, the grauitie of your iudgementes, and your wisdomes, experiences, authoritie, and example, to be of suche principall estimation, and worthie respect in our Realme, that in case ye doe zelousely emploie your endeuours to the due reuerente consideration of the holie Mysteries of the Christian Religion, (as I doute not but verie manie emonge you doe) your holie example will generallie allure a greate nomber throughout our whole Realme from all contentious disputinge, and iarringe about theise late newe controuersies in Religion, to embrace firmelie and zealouselie the aunciente Catholike beliefe.*

* That there were many sympathizers amongst the Templars would appear from the returns as to recusancy among members of the four London Inns, demanded by the Government in 1577. The numbers of such Recusants given by H. N. Birt, *The Elizabethan Religious Settlement* (1907), p. 544, citing P.R.O. Dom. Eliz. 118, nos. 68–71, were: Middle Temple 18, Gray's Inn 51, Inner Temple 60, and Lincoln's Inn 40.

A second and most important feature of this introductory matter to the Treatise is Hopkins's Advertisement to the Learned Reader. In it he displays his critical acumen not only by noting the fact that Fray Luis had revised his original version of the *Libro* several times, but also by the added information that he himself had compared the Spanish original with the Italian versions in order to arrive at a sound edition from which to work. Critical method of this kind, as we noted above in the case of Stapleton and Harpsfield,* was exceptional in sixteenth-century editing. Here is the Advertisement in full:

> For so muche as the Author of this booke hath published at diuers times seuerall editions thereof in the Spanishe tongue, and in the later editions hath from time to time verie muche and often corrected, altered, and augmented the same, not onelie in manifolde wordes, and sentences, but also in diuers chapiters, otherwise than in the former editions, that were printed either in *Toledo*, *Salamanca*, *Lisbone*, *Andwarpe*, or in anie other place before the yeare of our Lord. 1567. I thinke it verie conueniente to giue notice of it to the Reader: and withall that in my Translatiō I doe folowe the edition in the Spanishe tongue printed at Andwarpe by *Christopher Plantine*, in the yeare of our Lorde. 1572. For I perceaue that the frenche trāslation differeth in duers [sic] places from this best corrected edition of Plantins: and so doe likewise all the Translations that I haue seene in the Italian tongue printed in diuers yeares at *Rome*, *Naples*, and *Venice*, by *Michaël Tramezzino*, *Horatio Saluiani*, *Iouãni Baptista Guerra*, and *Gabriel Iolito*: vntill that nowe of late all the Authors workes haue bene newlie translated into the Italian tongue, and printed at *Venice* by *Georgio Angelieri*, in the yeare of our Lorde. 1581 [sig. b3].

Hopkins translated only the first of the three parts of Granada's *Libro*. Even so the result is a considerable volume of about 650 pages. Its eleven chapters comprise Meditations for the mornings and evenings of one week, together with much supplementary matter. The various subjects of the Meditations are illustrated with appropriate plates. There are twenty-five of these all told (in very fine condition in the Bodleian copy of the work), the subjects being sometimes dealt with in naive fashion. One might mention, for instance, the 'Christ before Herod' at sig. I8, where the company of Elizabethan courtiers and the poodle in the foreground would have delighted John Ruskin, or 'The Miseries of this Life' at sig. Y1, with its small

* p. 132.

child being beaten on its bare backside by an irate mother. The presence of these illustrations, which are not in the Spanish original, may be explained by the fact that the book was designed chiefly for the use of the laity.

According to M. Hagedorn, to whose work on *Luis de Granada in England* we have so often referred in these pages, Hopkins has given a fairly word-faithful translation of his original. Actually, he amplifies Granada somewhat, and perhaps, as Miss Hagedorn suggests, thus loses something of the beauty of the Spanish original. Certainly the criticism which J. G. Underhill has applied to Granada would naturally apply to Hopkins himself. Granada, Underhill writes, 'attempted to stimulate emotion by a profusion and concord of words rather than by the expression of significant and discriminated ideas. Grandiosity, verbosity, elaboration of the obvious, and utter subordination of thought to phrase, are continually discernible in his pages'.* Such ordering of the expression, with its conscious endeavour after the rhetorical phrase and the superlative word is, of course, permissible in this kind of writing, but (and it must be remembered here that we are solely concerned with literary expression) it must not be overdone. Just to what extent Hopkins (and Granada) is guilty of over-elaboration and insincerity in this work we leave the reader to judge for himself by examination of such a characteristic passage as the following, taken from the meditation on 'How our Sauiour carried the crosse vpon his shoulders':

> Now goeth the sweete innocent Iesus forwardes on his waie, with that so heauie dolorous burthen vpon his weake, and torne shoulders, great multitudes of people folowinge after him, and manie a pittiefull, and sorowfull womā accompanienge him with grieuous teares, and lamentations. What stonie harte had bene able to abstaine from most bitter weepinge, beholdinge the Kinge of angells, to goe thus faintlie, with such a great, and weightie burthen: his knees tremblinge vnder him: his bodie crowchinge vnder the crosse: his modest eies, and face, all blouddye: with that dolorous garlande of thorne vpon his head: and besides all this, annoyed with those most shamefull opprobrious exclamations, and outcries, which they gaue out in the waye against him?

* op. cit., pp. 206–7. Elsewhere he suggests a comparison of Guevara and Granada and concludes that whereas Guevara was Euphuistic, Granada was grandiloquent and more nearly approached the Arcadian style of Sidney.

But now in the meane tyme (o my soule) withdrawe thyne eies a little while from this cruell sight, and hye thee with quicke speede, with heauines of harte, and greate store of teares trickelinge downe by thy cheekes, towardes the howse of the blessed virgine Marie. And when thou art come thither, cast thy selfe downe at her feete, and speake these wordes in most dolefull, and lamentable wise vnto her. O Ladye of angells, and Quene of heauen? O gate of paradice, and aduocate of the worlde? O refuge of sinners, and health of the iust? O ioye of the Sainctes, and Teacher of vertues? O mirrour of cleannes? O patterne of patience, and example of perfection? Woe is me (O blessed ladie) woe is me, why am I preserued aliue, to see this present howre? How can I liue, hauinge now seene with myne eies, that dolefull sight, which I haue seene? What neede more wordes? Alas deere virgine, and most blessed mother: I haue left thy onely begotten sonne, my sweete Lorde and Sauiour in the cruell handes of his malitious ennemies, with a crosse vpon his shoulders, where vpon he shalbe crucified.

* * *

Now the holie virgin walkethe towardes her sweete sonne, and the great desire she hath to see him, restoreth vnto her againe the force, and strengthe, which sorrowe, and greife, had taken awaie. She hearethe a farre of the classhinge of armour, the trowpes of the people, and those most shamefull exclamations, and outcries, which in most dispitefull wise were thundered by his outragious cruell enemies against him. And incontinentlie she seethe the glisteringe speares, and halbardes, which were holden vp a loft. She fyndethe in the waye, the droppes and traces of bloude, whereby she might easelie tracke him, which waie he had gone, and she needeth none other gwide to conduct her vnto him. She approcheth nearer, and nearer, vnto her deerlie beloued sonne, she openeth her eies, which were verie sore dymmed with sorowfull weapinge, to proue whether she might see him, whom her soule so exceadinglie loued. O what a strange combatte was there now of feare, and loue, in the dolorous harte of the most blessed virgin Marie? In one respecte she had a desiere to see him, and in an other, she was vnwillinge to see him thus miserablie and most cruelly disfigured. At the lengthe, when she was come where she might see him indeede: then those two lightes of heauen, doe beholde one an other, and theire hartes embrace sweetly together by meanes of theire eies. Howbeit the sight of one an other in this dolefull wise was a very great corsie to bothe theire afflicted soules. Theire tongues were dōme, so that neither of them both for a while spake one worde, but the naturall affection of that most sweete sonne, spake priuely to the heauie hart of the most blessed virgin, and saied vnto her.

Why commest thou hither my doue, my beloued, and my deere mother? Thy sorowe increaseth myne, and thy tormentes do augment my paines, and be a great torment vnto me: Departe my deere mother, departe I beseach thee, and retourn home againe to thy howse. For it is not seemelie for thy virginall shamefastnes, and puretie, to be here in the companie of murderers, and theeues. And if it woulde please thee so to doe, it woulde certeinly asswage both thy sorrowe and myne. And I will remaine here to be sacrificed for the worlde. For this office apperteineth not to thee, but vnto me, and thy innocencie deserueth not this torment. Retourne therefore my doue to the arcke, vntill such time as the waters of the floude doe cease: forsomuch as here thou shalt finde no place, where thou mayst rest thy feete. There mayst thou attende to thy accustomed diuout praier, and contemplation. And there, by liftinge vp thy soule in godlie meditations aboue thy selfe, thou shalt passe ouer more easely this thy dolefull sorowe and greiffe.

Now this beinge saide, the sorowfull heauie harte of the holie mother made answere to her sonne, and saied vnto him. Why doest thou commaunde me to doe thus my deere sonne? Why wouldest thou haue me to depart awaie from this place? Thou knowest (o my Lord God) that in thy presence each thinge is lawfull vnto me, and that there is non other Oratorie but where thou arte. How can I then departe awaie from thee, vnles I shoulde departe from my selfe? This greife and sorrowe so possesseth my harte, that trewlie I can not thinke vpon anie other thinge. I can goe no whither without thee; neither can I seeke, or receaue comfort of any other, but of thee. Vpon thee, is fixed all my whole harte. Within thee, haue I made my habitation. And my life whollie dependeth of thee. Seinge therefore thou hast vowchesaffed for the space of nine monethes to inhabite within my bowels, and to take my bodie for thy dwellinge place, why maye not I for these three daies, take thy bowels for my habitation? If thou wilt thus receaue me within thee, when thou art crucified, then shall I be crucified with thee: and when thou arte buried, then shall I be buried also together with thee. With thee woulde I drinke of the gaule, and vineger. With thee woulde I suffer vpon the crosse. And with thee woulde I yeelde vp my ghost.

Such wordes as these spake the blessed virgin in her dolefull harte as she went: And after this sort, she passed ouer that painfull and ircksome waie, vntill she came to the place of the Sacrifice [sig. M2^{v}–5].

The reader will probably agree that it would be a mistake to lay too much stress on the stylistic features of such writing as this. The purpose of Granada's work, and of Hopkins's translation was, first and last, to lead souls to Heaven, and it might well be argued that it is beside the point to call attention to the methods employed by the two writers to give force and vividness to their message.

To round off our estimate of Hopkins a word must be said about his translations from the Scriptures. Each of the daily Meditations in Granada's book is based upon a text from one of the Gospels, which immediately precedes the Meditation itself. Hopkins's translation of these texts compares very favourably with contemporary versions, as the reader may judge from the specimen which we here append from the thirteenth chapter of the Gospel of St. John. The translation, it may be remarked, is rather nearer the Genevan version of 1557 than the Rhemes version of 1582:

> When supper was done, he rose vp from the table, and put of his garmentes: and takinge a towell, he girded him selfe with it. After that, he powred water into a basyne, and beganne to washe his disciples feete, and to wype them with the towell, wherewith he was girded. Then he came to Simon Peter. who said to him. Lord, dost thou washe my feete? Iesus answered, and said vnto him: what I doe, thou knowest not now: but thou shalt knowe it hereafter. Peter said vnto him. Thou shalt neuer washe my feete. Iesus answered him. If I washe thee not, thou shalt haue no part with me. Simon Peter said vnto him. Lord, not onely my feete, but my handes, and head also. Iesus said vnto him. He that is wasshed, needeth not to washe, sauinge onely his feete: but he is cleane euerie whit. And ye are cleane, but not all. For he knewe, who should betraie him. And therefore he said: ye are not all cleane. So, after he had wasshed there feete, and had taken his garmentes, and was set downe againe: He said vnto them. Knowe ye, what I haue done to you? ye call me master, and Lord. And ye saie well. For so I am in deede. If I then, being your Lord, and master, haue wasshed your feete: ye owght also to washe one an others feete. For I haue geuen you an example, that ye should do, euen as I haue done to you [sig. E2–3].

The Authorized Version shows little variation from this of Hopkins.

The success of Hopkins's translation of Granada is vouched for by two pieces of evidence. The first comes from his own pen. In dedicating his later translation of Granada's *Memoriall of a Christian Life* (1586) once again to the gentlemen of the Inns of Court, he refers to the excellent reception his *Book of Medita-*

tion had had amongst them: 'Vnderstanding by good intelligence, of the general wel liking, and gratefull acceptation, that your Honours and worshippes haue had, of the *Boke of Meditations*, of the reuerend Religious father *F. Lewis de Granada*, published of late by me in our English tongue, and dedicated vnto you, I haue bene thereby much the rather prouoked to dedicate also vnto you this boke of the same Godlie Awthor.'* The second and more striking piece of evidence is provided by the fact that at least three Protestant editions of the translation appeared before the end of the reign of Elizabeth. All three were published anonymously and no acknowledgement was made of Hopkins's authorship. Indeed, the first of the three, which bears the date 1592, suppressed even Granada's name, if Llanza's statements are correct. According to this author the title-page of the edition runs: *Of Prayer and Meditation. Contayning foure teene Meditations, for the seauen dayes of the weeke: both for Mornings and Euenings. Treating of the principall maters and holy misteries of our fayth. London. Printed for Thomas Gosson and John Perin: and are to be solde at the signe of the Angell in Paules Churchyard, 1592.*† The second Protestant edition, which appeared in 1599, restores Granada's name to the title-page. It was also printed in London, by P. Short for William Wood. The third edition of 1601 follows that of 1599, save that the printer this time is I. Harison. Needless to say, the plagiarist, by elimination or modification, changes the appearance of the book in order to bring it into harmony with Protestant views. For instance, 'Catholic Church' becomes 'Church of Christ', 'priest' becomes 'minister' or 'pastor', 'the blessed Sacrament of the Altar' becomes 'the sacrament of the Lord's Supper', and passages like the one quoted above from the Carrying of the Cross are omitted altogether. The fact that, further, he interchanges the morning and evening meditations and varies their sequence, makes it certain that this anonymous editor intended to conceal as far as possible the connexion between his work and that of Hopkins.

Very different from this work of Hopkins is the book of Meditations printed at Douay in 1576, to which we shall now

* Dedicatory Epistle, init.

† *Bibliografia del V. P. M. Fr. Luis de Granada de la Orden de Predicadores por Fr. Maximinio Llaneza* (Salamanca, 1926), 4 vols., entry 105. The only copy known, I think, of this edition is, or was, in the Harmsworth Library.

refer. It is a handy little 16mo brochure in black-letter, some 120 pages long, consisting of a series of short meditations for each day of the week. The title describes the work as: *Certayne deuout Meditations very necessary for Christian men deuoutly to meditate vpon Morninge and Eueninge, euery day in the weeke: Concerning Christ his lyfe and Passion, and the fruites thereof.* The anonymous author in his Preface enlarges somewhat upon this by describing the Meditations as a consideration, according to five chief points, of the life and passion of our Lord. 'The first', he writes, 'is fetched from Christ his infancy. The second is deduced out of his life, the other three are taken from his passion.' The Meditations, if we may except Friday's Exercise on charity, are intended to inculcate the practice of the 'general' virtues, those virtues which St. Francis de Sales described as not the noblest but 'none so necessary and universally appropriate in practice'. Beginning on Sunday with humility, the well-spring of all such virtues, the writer continues through the course of the week with mildness, patience, obedience, loving kindness, charity, and, on Saturday, bountifulness. The form the Exercises take is not that of the full-dress Meditation, such as we met with in Hopkins, rather the author sets out quite simply the five points of each Meditation solely in order to direct the attention of the meditator. Anything which would be likely to distract that attention is thus eschewed, and it is for this reason, we must suppose, that there is no elaboration of the theme, no use of imagery, and a complete absence of ornament. This, however, will not account for the occasional careless construction of the sentences, which adds to the somewhat undistinguished character of the writing. We do not propose to quote from this author's work. To indicate his method it will be enough to epitomize, shall we say, the Meditation for Friday on 'the merueilous burning charitie of Christ our Lord'. The five points are set out as follows: Our Lord's charity is exemplified –

(1) in the Flight into Egypt –

So, too, 'flee thou into the loving heart of Christ';

(2) in His call to those in misery: 'Come (saith he) all you that live in heaviness and are heavy laden and I will refresh you –

So, 'come thou unto Him';

(3) in the manner that He wasted all His strength during the three hours' agony on the Cross –
  So, 'spend all thy strength in his love';

(4) in the seven words uttered from the Cross –
  So, 'be thou lowly and gentle in words', etc.;

(5) in His most shameful death –
  So, mortify yourself and use yourself as one dead to the world.

The same practicality as is to be found in the Meditations is to be observed also in the Prayers for special occasions which follow towards the end of the volume. These include a series of 'Prayers to be sayed in the schole before lectoures be giuen' for each day of the week. That for Monday, to God the Son, is as follows:

> O Thou who art the wisdom that proceeded out of the mouth of the hyest, who reachest from one quarter of the worlde, to the other most valiantly & settest all things in a most plesaunt order, come & teach vs the way of thy wysdome.
>
> Lord Iesu Chryst who art the eternall worde of the Father, and the verye flowinge springe of all wysdome put into our myndes aptnesse to learning and the lyght of vnderstanding, that these our studies haue good successe, whereby we may haue such furtherāce $\overset{t}{y}$ we therbi may come to the perfect vnderstāding of thee and euerlasting truth, and also to $\overset{e}{y}$ sincere loue of thy goodnesse. Who liuest & raignest god world without ende. Amen [sig. G5^{v}].

The three hymns which are also included in this part of the volume are of so little literary merit that they hardly call for quotation.

It will be evident from those treatises which we have already examined that the devotional works of the Recusants differ considerably the one from the other, both in respect of content and style and in respect of worth. A singular instance exemplifying this varied temper to be found in their writings is furnished by Thomas Hide's *A Consolatorie Epistle to the afflicted catholikes*, printed at Louvain in 1579. If the style of Hopkins may be described as having kinship with the 'Arcadian' style of Sidney,* the style of this Epistle of Hide's may equally be said to have kinship with the 'Euphuistic' style of John Lyly. Alliteration, antithesis, paranomasia, rime, far-fetched simili-

* See above, footnote, p. 202.

tudes from natural history, all the common devices peculiar to this form of writing, are to be found in his Epistle. Nor need we trouble the reader with any particular examples of Hide's ingeniousness, for Euphuism, be it never so witty, is apt to be wearisome. Rather would we call attention to something which much more properly particularizes the character of Hide's work.

Hide's method of dilating his theme is quite unlike anything we have so far met with in the devotional writings of the Recusants,* though it affords one further example, and a most striking one, of the connexion between these writings and medieval sermon literature. The medieval sermon habit 'of developing the several features of some natural object chosen as a symbol' has been clearly pointed out by Dr. Owst.† In English homilies of the medieval period 'familiar objects, whether from Scripture or from every-day life, provide the preacher with a whole series of pegs upon which to hang the chief points of his theme. From Scripture comes Jacob's ladder, or that Galilean boat of the Gospel story in which Christ sat to preach, as figured by Rypon. From current life come the "Castellum Diaboli", or "Castellum Religionis", and the social parable set forth by the chessmen and their moves. As Dr. Brandeis says, the symbol "is set in motion, as it were, by expanding it into a sort of allegorical action" '.‡ Now this exactly describes Hide's method in this Epistle. He begins his introductory note, sermon-wise, with a text from the eighth chapter of the Gospel of St. Matthew:

> Christ and his disciples went into a ship, when sodenly arose a great tēpest in the sea, so that the shippe was couered with waues. Christ slept. His disciples awaked him and said, Master saue vs, we perish. Christ said vnto thē, Why are you fearfull, you of litle faith? Then he arose, rebuked the winds, and there followed a great calme –

and thus continues:

> You haue heard Christes fact, mark the mysterie. This shippe resembled the Church militant, wherin all Christian passengers do sayle, and be tossed with tempestes, whiles they driue toward their countrie, the quiet hauen of heauen, that is, the

* Heskyns's method in *The Parliament of Chryste* (see Chapter III) affords some sort of parallel, but the scale of that work is too vast to invite any real comparison with Hide.

† *Preaching in Medieval England*, as before, p. 325.

‡ ibid.

> Church triumphant. The sea resembleth the course of the world, which is alwayes troublous. And by the tempest is signified all suche pressure, and persecution, as they must expect that follow Christ into this shippe . . . There hath bene no age of men, nor course of time sithence Christ, wherein this shippe, (that is to say the militant Church of Christ) hath not bene tēpested. *The vngodly drew out their sword, bent their bow to cast down the simple, and to slaie such as goe the right way.* These wordes of the prophet were verified after Christs ascension, when there arose greate tempests, to wit, diuers persecutions against the Church, open persecution, and secret persecution, persecution violent, and persecution fraudulent, persecution of tyrannie, and persecution of Heresie, the one openly, the other secretly, the one by sworde, the other by worde . . .

finally drawing from the figure consolation for his afflicted brethren in these words:

> To you therefore (dearely beloued countrie men) to you that be afflicted Catholikes for Religion, in what case and place soeuer you be, I addresse this Consolatorie Epistle, wherein my endeuour is to declare suche comfortes, as the selfe cause of religion seemeth to yeelde. Seeinge now the violent windes blow & bluster not onely against the kingdomes of the world, but against the church that is the kingdome of God, and knowing that they haue shaken out of the shippe many, and too many lost Christians, I offer vnto you that yet remayne & suffer in the shippe, these comforts, euen out of the body and bosome of religion. I make common to you that suffer for religion, such comfortes as I laboured to gayne to my selfe in the great troubles of these countreis, wherein were vsed manye mischieuous meanes to deface religion [sig. A1–4].

In the Epistle proper the 'mysterie' or symbol of the ship is unfolded typically in a series of anagoges. The following example amply illustrates the care which is bestowed upon these spiritual interpretations:

> You, I say, that sayle in the shippe which now is tempested with contrarious winds, feare you not, our Lord is with you, you be safe, *Dominus ibidem.* Asee, who is that Lord by whom you be gouerned in this shippe. Christ the sonne of God is hoysted into the mast of the ship, that is, on the crosse. God the father gouerneth the hinder parte, the holy ghost sitteth in the fore parte. Ther be twelue roers in this ship, to wit, the twelue Apostles, and these driue forwarde the ship, bringing her through the straits of this troublesom sea into the quiet port. Christe our Lorde that prayed for his Church, doth still pray. Though this shippe be tossed, yet can she not be drowned,

because Christe prayeth. Thoughe this shippe be shaken with the violent windes of secular attempts, yet is she safe from wrack, because Christ gouerneth. And the holy ghost our Lorde that sitteth in the foreparte of the shippe, strengthneth all suche as be windshaken [sig. B7v].

At the conclusion of the *Epistle* the gnomic wisdom of the writer finds expression in a series of 'considerations', pregnant yet familiar, from which we select the following:

1. Christians are nowe put together, as it were in a potte ouer the fire to be tried, as golde is tried frō other metals. The fire flameth, the potte seetheth, the waters be thicke, the scomme is cast away.
2. Catholikes are in the forge vnder the workemans hande to be refined. They are in the forge not as coles that burne & turne to ashes, but as gold that is tried. The forge is the world, you are the golde, tribulation is the fire, God is the worke man.
3. Harde thinges maye be mollified, straite thinges maye be loused, and heauie thinges shall litle greeue them that can beare them hansomly.
6. Though God suffer for a time the wicked to rage, and the hypocrite to raigne, yet the same hande that woundeth, healeth, the same hand that presseth, refresheth. Gods pitifull grace will quench the firebrands, asswage the rage, and relieue the innocentes.
7. The wisedome of the worlde maketh worldlye heades deflecte from God. Good mens heartes be create of God, and be restles in the worlde, but when they reste in God [sig. G3–4].

John Fowler's redaction of More's *A Dialogue of Cumfort against Tribulation*,* which he published in 1573, was intended to serve the same purpose as Hide's *Consolatorie Epistle*. The *Dialogue*, as Fowler points out in his Address to the Reader, speaks of man's need of comfort in this vale of woe, and though the author applies his discourse to Hungary 'sore persecuted and oppressed by Turks', yet, as he says, its teaching is applicable to all. 'Al that is sayd of the Turke, is in a parable meant of Heretikes & Shismatikes.'† Herein, too, lies the significance of his dedicating the book to that great friend and benefactress of the exiled Catholics, 'the Ladie Iane, Duchesse of Feria'.

* First published by Tottel in 1553 under the title, *A dialoge of comfort against tribulacion, made by Syr Thomas More Knyght, and set foorth by the name of an Hūgariē, not before this time imprinted*, and reprinted in the Collected Works, edited by Rastell in 1557.

† Marg. A4v.

It is not within the province of this thesis to discuss in detail this work of More's. To one thing, however, I should like to draw attention, and that is the fact that this recension of Fowler's is a sincere attempt on his part to publish a *good* text.

> These six or seuen yeres (he writes) haue I bene desirous, to haue so good a Booke come forth againe in some smaller volume then it was in before, being in deede not so handsome for the priuate vse and cōmoditie of the Reader, as I trust it shalbe now. But it hath not bene my chance through one let or other, to accomplish that desire of mine, til now. And that is in deede the chiefe thing that I haue done therein, which I may accompt as mine: I meane, in that I haue brought it into this smal volume, and withal, by conferring of sundry Copies together, haue restored and corrected many places, and thereby made it muche more plaine and easie to be vnderstood of the Reader.*

Whether Fowler based his text upon Tottel's quarto of 1553 or on that of the collected edition of 1557 I do not know, but a comparison with the latter reveals only small differences – save in the punctuation, which is definitely improved. In order further to assist the reader he adds a running commentary in the margin. The volume includes a woodcut of St. Thomas, with commendatory verses by the editor in Latin together with an English translation.

2. PENANCE

The two short tractates which belong to this section call for only brief consideration. The earlier of the two, John Fowler's *A Brief Fourme of Confession*, is a translation from some Spanish original,† dedicated, like his recension of More's *Dialogue*, to the Duchess of Feria, in the year 1572, but not printed until 1576. This little volume contains, besides Fowler's translation (comprising three chapters and a short conclusion), a number of devotional items, which include a brief treatise on receiving the Blessed Sacrament by St. Thomas More, together with certain of More's prayers and meditations. The title runs as follows:

> *A Brief Fourme of Confession, Instructing all Christian folke how to confesse their sinnes, & so to dispose themselues, that they may enioy the benefite of true Penāce, dooing the woorthy frutes therof,*

* Dedicatory Address.

† I have been unable to trace this original.

according to th' vse of Christes Catholique Church. Newly translated into English and set foorth together with certaine other godly brief Treatises and Praiers, as is to be seene in the side folowing. 1576.

Fowler describes the work as 'a brief fourme or *Doctrine* of Confession',* and that it is not a mere examen, but rather of the nature of a Christian Directory may be gathered from the following passage on the deadly sin of Sloth. The passage may be taken as a fair sample of the translator's style:

> Slouth is a slackenes or lothing in beginning and pursuing the things that belong to walke in the waie of God.
>
> In this sinne doe offend the dul & weake sprited, which euer finde lettes and inconueniences in good things. Also such as are cold, luke warme, negligent, in despaire, and the wretches that wil put themselues to no labour, nor to nothing that good is: the slacke delaiers who walke from day to daie, differring good things: such as haue no regard of the good name of a Christian nor of the duety of their owne vocation in the way and seruice of God, especially in praier. Also they that put away frō them inspirations and good motions, & contemne the good counselles of God and the Gospelles, and the examples of the Saintes, and do not that which God and his Spiritual Officers do commaund, for, and at suche time as they commaund the same. Also they that leese and spend their time ill.
>
> *Of the contrarie vertue vnto Slouth, which is Hope.* This accursed sinne is put away from the soule, by the exercise of the Diuine vertue of Hope, through the which a man doth attempt things that are hard and aboue himself, apperteining to God and his holy wil. This vertue maketh vs to set nought by trauailes, to plucke vp all impedimentes and contradictions, & to passe litle on the difficulties that may come and fal in the waie. S. Paule calleth it the Anker: and very wel. For it worketh that effect in the soule, which the Anker is wont to do in the sea in the time of stormes and tempestes: that is, to hold and keepe the soule fast and vnmoueable in her purpose which is good, although vnto the sense it seme most vnpossible or hard, which we hope for, or though it shalbe long delaied, or be yet farre of, whiche we loke for. The which wheras it is the very fruite of the holy Ghost, it cannot be gotten nor kept without continuing much in holy praier. And therefore it is necessarie, that the same be much vsed in the whole processe and course of this perilous life, if we wil not haue the kingdome of sinne to preuaile and kepe vs away from our beginning, which is God. [sig. f7v.]

The second item which we have to consider here is a small pocket manual of thirty-two pages entitled *A short and an*

* Dedicatory Epistle. Italics are mine.

absolute order of confession most requisite of all persons to be ouer Loked before they confesse them. It is without date or printer* and would appear to be part of some longer work, for it begins 'Hauing treated before of contricion, we will heare likewise shew a way how they should prepare & examine themselues, which often vse to be confessed . . .' Unlike Fowler's *Brief Fourme,* it is principally concerned with examination of conscience, as these words would suggest. The style of the pamphlet is poor and shows the hand of an unpractised writer.

3. ROSARY

The first of the two little books of meditation upon the Rosary which fall within our period is an anonymous publication of the year 1576 entitled *A breefe Directory, and playne way howe to say the Rosary of our blessed Lady: With Meditations for such as are not exercised therein. Whereunto are adioyned the prayers of S. Bryget, with others.* It is a small black-letter volume of some seventy pages and is edited by a certain I. M., who, in a dedicatory epistle from the English Charterhouse at Bruges 'to his deare and weldisposed Sister, A. M.', reports upon its publication as follows:

> The talke which we had together (moste deare and welbeloued Sister) the day before I tooke my iourney to come into these countreis, haue not bin, neither are of me forgotten, and amōng al other your request concerning the Rosary of our Lady. Which request want both of yeres and knowledge woulde not permit me to fulfill: but after I had bene here a whyle, I gat acquaintance of one, who for vertue and good life is accounted among the cheefe, to him vpon a time I declared what I had promised you, and likewise my vnability in performing it, beseching him for Gods cause to take a litle paynes in the matter, whom I founde as ready to satisfie my request, as I was to demaunde him. When it was by him finished, and I somewhat busied in copying the same to be sent vnto you, by chance came into my chamber my cosen and freende I. Noil, who perswaded me to leaue off writing, and promised to procure it to be Printed, for I haue (sayd he) a fit thing to be ioyned thervnto, which was deliuered me by a good Gentlewoman, with earnest request to haue it printed. Wherto I willingly cōsented . . .†

* For the probable date (1576–80) and name of printer see bibl. ent. 6. The title is a text-title.

† The Dedicatory Epistle is cited in full at bibl. ent. 81. See there also the note identifying I.M. with John Mitchell, the Carthusian, together with further bibliographical details.

The additions referred to in this passage are evidently the St. Briget's prayers with those following them. The volume further contains a short treatise upon the Passion from St. Bonaventure, to which is appended the following 'exhortation to penance and pacience':

> Since sinne is not pardoned but through such great smart,
> To purge sinne then much paine take with willing hart:
> For so doth this paterne Chryste teache to obteyne
> Forgiuenes of sinnes by great sorowe and payne,
> And then for paynes past in all ioyes to remayne.

It is difficult to appraise in terms of ordinary criticism a work which was written only for the purpose of stirring up devotion in the average layman. The nature of such writing, with its emotional emphasis, calls for sympathetic understanding rather than cold-blooded analysis. Since the writer's chief aim in such a work is a quickening of sensibility and a hardening of resolve in the reader, we must expect that he will sacrifice, to some extent, truth of actuality to truth of feeling. He is, in this respect, nearer to the poet than to the writer of prose. Apprehending his theme intuitionally, the fruitful expression of his own passionate experience will be his chief concern, and this must be the measure of his work. Its practicality will be decided by the needs of those for whom he writes. In the two illustrations which follow the strength of the feeling will be found to be subserved by the naturalness and simplicity of expression and by a certain grave realism of detail. It is, indeed, in the accumulation of concrete details, simply expressed, that the writer makes vivid his subject-matter and brings it home to the reader:

> Joseph therefore and our Lady, hasting them selues to Bethlehem, when they came there, our Ladies time beeing come for her deliuery, beholde there was no place in the towne for her & her sweete Sonne in anye Inne, the Towne was so full of people, the lodginges were all taken vp. And therefore was the Mother of God enforced to turne into an Oxe stall that stoode by the high way, no better then an houel or cotage, and there brought foorth that blessed babe her deare Sonne, betweene an Oxe & an Asse, lapping him in suche poore cloutes as she had, & layde him in the maunger. Where ye may beholde our Lady borowing a little hay from the sely Asse, to lay her child vppon. And here ye maye consider with your selfe the great goodnes of God, that for his onely sonne prouided nothing that the world accompted needful, not housrome, not chāber, not

chimney, not fyre, not bolster nor pillowe to lye vpon: and yet hath sent vs al these things with many moe, not onely to serue our necessities, but also to satisfie our vanities, As fine chābers right costly hanged, fayre bedstedes curiously carued, soft beds, not onely of fethers, but of downe also: Couerlets and counterpoyntes ful of silke, and testers with curtens richely wroughte and imbrodred, ful of al vanity and superfluitie. And yet scant cōtent our selues therwith: or if we be content, we be neuer the more thankefull vnto God, neither can we easily abyde to beholde or thinke vppon poore Christe lying in the maunger. Who in this poore estate not regarded of men, with great ioy is proclaymed of the angels vnto the Shepheards singing with marueylous melodie, Glory be to God on high, & in earth peace to men of good wyl. Then walk againe with the shepheardes, and beholde poore Christ in the Crib, fal down with the shepheardes and worshippe him that was borne that day thy sauiour Christ our Lorde. And considering how ioyful his mother was of al these, say the thirde *Pater noster* and ten *Aues*.*

O Iesu, very true and plenteous vine, haue mind of the most exceeding & abundant effusion of bloud, that thou sheddest moste plentiouslye, as it had bene crusht out of a ripe cluster of grapes, whē thou vpon ẏ crosse diddest treade that presse alone, and gauest vs drinke both bloud & water out of thy syde, being perced with a knightes speare, so that in al thy body was not lefte a drop of bloud ne of water, thē at the last like a bundle of myre thou wast hanged on the crosse on high, where thy tēder flesh waxed wan, & the licour of thy bowels, & the marowe of thy bones was dried vp: for minde of this thy most bitter passion, sweete Iesu, woūd my hart that the water of penance, and the teare of loue maye be my foode both night and day. And, good Iesu, turne me whole to thee, that my hart maye be euer to thee a dwelling place, & that my liuing maye be euer plesant & acceptable, and that the end of my life may be so cōmendable, that I may perpetuallye deserue to prayse thee with all thy saints in blisse. Amen.†

Our second Rosary book is a translation by John Fen‡ of Gaspar Loarte's *Istrutione e avvertimenti per meditar i misterii del Rosario, della Santissima Vergine Madre* (Rome, 1573). The date and place of origin of the book are nowhere given in the work itself, but we may reasonably conclude that it was printed in London, probably by William Carter, about the year 1580. It

* From the third Joyful Mystery, sig. A4–6.

† The last of the prayers of St. Briget, usually named the fifteen Oes, each prayer beginning with this letter. sig. B5v–6.

‡ According to Dodd. For evidence of this and for further bibliographical details, see bibl. ent. 39.

runs to some 250 pages with the literal title of *Instructions and Aduertisements, How to meditate the Misteries of the Rosarie of the most holy Virgin Mary*. Each of the fifteen Mysteries has its appropriate full-page illustration and is set out under three headings with a 'dilatation' thereon, followed by a prayer. The book concludes with a special Litany of the Blessed Virgin in Latin for each day of the week and some short 'spiritual advices'.

A consideration of Fen's earlier translation from Osorius (above, p. 122) left us in no doubt as to his ability to command the English tongue, and we noted in this connexion the considerable liberty he used in turning his Latin original into good colloquial English and the vigorous effect which this imparted to his style. In the present work, although we may note something of the same natural easy expression as we found in his *Osorius*, yet we cannot get away altogether from the suggestion of translation. Both idiom and vocabulary occasionally show traces of foreign influence, nor does the translator attempt 'to retrench the superfluities of expression' which are characteristic of Loarte's style. Fen would seem, in fact, to have fallen under the spell of his original, and though we may justify the repetitions and the doublings of the expression on the ground that the language of feeling will naturally diverge in this respect from the language of our less exalted moods, yet we must admit that from the point of view of English prose style Stephen Brinkley's more controlled translation of the same author, which we considered earlier in this chapter, is a far more effective piece of work. There is an austerity and strength in Brinkley's prose which is lacking in Fen's more literal translation of his original.

Let us take by way of illustration two examples from the first and third quinaries, which will make the foregoing observations plain. The first is a passage from the third Joyful Mystery, parallel with that we considered from the *Breefe Directory*. The reader may note how the exuberant manner of our author contrasts with the more restrained expression of that work:

> The meditation of the thirde point wil furnish thee of fitt matter to moue compassion, if thou consider, howe this moste mightie monarche, this King of al kinges, he whom neither the heauens nor earth can holde and comprehende, hath in such

> wise debased, humbled, and throwen himselfe downe in a harde manger vpon a litle haye; he, whom the Angels doo adore, and in whose presence the powers of heauen doo quake againe, lieth quaking himselfe for colde betwixt two brute beastes. O diuine darling, what meaneth this geere? what humilitie and basenes is this, O Soueraine King of glorye? what hast thou to doo with the crib, thou that hast thy throne aboue the Cherubins? how art thou made thus dombe, O eternal worde of the Father? whye weepest and wailest in such sort, thou, that art the ioye of al the holy Angels? verily, thou haste masked thy diuine nature with our humane nature, to be the King and Sauiour of Israel, and of the vniuersal world. The desire which thou hast to redeeme vs, moueth thee to doo these strange matters; the loue which made thee weleare [sic] descend frō heuē for our walfare, causeth thee nowe to be borne, and to cloake thy puissance with such penurie and extreme want of al thinges, that we shoulde thereby learne to meeke and humble ourselues, and to detest al pride, al pamperinges and delicacies of the fleshe, louing the lowlines, the penance, and the pouertie, which thou diddest chuse and teach vs, and wouldest for this cause haue thy natiuitie announced to poore Sheppardes, of whom thou wast visited and adored, the which their visitation and adoration we ought attentiuely to ponder, and diligently to imitate [sig. C7–8].

Our second example comes from the fourth Glorious Mystery, 'Of the Assumption':

> Yea, we may not only affirme this to be most true, but beleeue with godly deuotiō, that not onely the Angels, but that which is more, the king of Angels in proper person vouchsafed to come and doo her this honour. Hereupon is it, that some doo contemplate, how the most holy mother being vpō the last hour of her blessed departure, her most sweet sonne descended from heauen, associated with the celestial powers, and entred into that blessed house where she laye; and beholding her with those his amiable eyes, spoke that with a most sweet voice to her, which the husband said to the spouse in the Canticles; *Thou art al faire, my frend, and there is no blemish at al in thee; come from Liban, my Spouse, come from Liban, and crowned shalt thou be.* That is to saye, Come receue the recompence of thy desertes, the treasure which thy most holy workes haue merited, the crown that is due to thy so excellent vertues; Get vp, my Doue, it is nowe high time to issue out of this exile; no toiles, no teares, no sobbes or sorrowes any more. Come to enioye the pleasure of those woundes, which when they were geuen, did occasionate thy so great woes; come nowe and rest thee for the paine which thou hast taken. Come, nowe be merye, for that thou hast wailed and wept, and for that thou humbledst thy

selfe so lowlye, come nowe to reigne perpetually. . . . Doo thou therefore contemplate, what consolation, what ioye, what iubilation this most holy soule receaued with such woordes, with such a sight, and with such a companye; with what confidence and securitie did she depart this life, the most Soueraine King of heauen, taking her in his most sacred armes, kissing & cherishing her most louingly according as S. Bernard meditateth. O glorious Ladye, what tongue can possiblye declare the ioye thou feltest, seing thy selfe thus highly honoured, and thus embraced betwixt those sacred armes of thy dere sonne. . . . Behold now, O moste blessed mother, al thy desires fulfilled, nowe hast thou obteined that which thou requiredst; now hast thou found that which thou soughtest for; now doest thou possesse that which thou desiredst. Sweet were the kisses thou gauest him, and the louing intertainment thou usedst towardes him, when thou borest him being a litle one in thine armes into Egipt; but farre sweeter were those which thou receauedst of him, when nowe being a great one he caried thee to heauen, to enioy the greatest goodes, the greatest riches, the greatest felicitie that was euer graunted to any creature. For if so be no eye hath seene, no eare heard, nor humane vnderstāding can possibly conceaue the goods that God hath prepared for those that loue him. Who can possibly cōceue or imagine those which he hath prepared for thee, which diddest not onely loue him more then al, but diddest engender him of the most pure bloud in thy body? a priuiledge graūted to thee alone, and worthye thee alone [sig. N5–7].

4. PSALTERS AND HOURS

The three works which comprise the subject-matter of this section of our chapter are *Jesus Psalter*, *The Psalter of St. Hierome* and *Jesus Matins*. The first two of these were printed, and to some extent edited, we must suppose, by John Fowler in 1575–6; the third, by an anonymous translator, is of uncertain date. We shall review the three books in this order.

Jesus Psalter

It is impossible to come to any certain conclusion as to how far Fowler himself 'edited' this Psalter, the authorship of which has been ascribed to Richard Whytford, the Brigittine. Its great popularity as a devotional exercise in the sixteenth century undoubtedly gave rise to numerous manuscript copies besides the many printed editions of the work. It is possible, therefore, that, as against his having set about revising one of the extant printed editions of the work, Fowler may simply have been following some manuscript copy, since lost, in his version. His edition of 1575 certainly does not agree exactly with any of those printed by other hands during the century,* nor, it should be noted, does it agree with the earliest manuscript copy, a late-fifteenth-century document, which was edited by H. Godwin in 1885. This is all that we can say with any certainty. However, on the ground of lack of evidence to the contrary, we may be allowed to assume that his work is a revision, a modernized revision, of the old *Psalter*, and that there was good reason for contemporary reference to it as 'Fowler's Psalter'. If we add to this the fact that it occupied a very prominent place in the Catholic devotional literature of our period, and, further, that it gave rise to some controversy, which found expression in 'lame' Thomas Sampson's *A Warning to take heede of Fowlers Psalter* of 1578, we shall find, I think, sufficient reason for including it in a book which is concerned with Catholic Recusant literature in the reign of Elizabeth.

The original title of the *Psalter* seems to have been *An invocacyon gloryous named ye psalter of Iesus*. So it is called in the earliest known printed edition of 1529, and so it continues to be headed in the reprints in the Salisbury Primers. Fowler, in his print of 1575, adopts a new title: *Certaine deuout and Godly petitions, commonly called Iesus Psalter* – and all subsequent editions, at any rate down to 1610, follow him in this.† The two modern critical reprints of H. Godwin (referred to above) and S. H. Sole have thrown much light on the history of the *Psalter*, and the writer is indebted very largely to the prefaces of their two works for the comments which he is now about to make.‡

Let us begin with a word as to Whytford's authorship of the *Psalter*. The general consensus of opinion seems to be that it is the work of Richard Whytford, the younger, 'the wretch of Sion', as he styles himself, and not of Richard Whytford, a Flintshire gentleman, uncle to the younger Richard, as Godwin suggests. The evidence for attributing it to Richard Whytford, the Brigittine, would seem to be principally based upon

* The nearest edition to Fowler's is that printed by L'Oyselet in 1580 (?). But this was probably intended as a reprint of that edition.

† Full bibliographical details will be found at bibl. ent. 44, and at Appendix II.

‡ *The Psalter of Jesus. From a manuscript of the fifteenth century; with variations from some later copies* (1885). Preface is signed H. G. *Jesu's Psalter . . . by the Reverend Samuel Haydon Sole* (1888).

a statement of Anthony à Wood, who enumerates 'The Psaltery of Jesus' among Whytford's works without question. A comparison with his known works affords good internal evidence in corroboration of Wood's statement. The fact that his name never appears with it is, in Sole's judgment, no argument against his having written it. It seems, indeed, says Sole, to have been so well known that 'the simplest inference is that public use had made the form of devotion impersonal'. We may add to this that what we know of Whytford's early life (he was elected fellow of Queens' College, Cambridge, about 1495, and was the close friend of Erasmus and More*) in no way precludes the possibility of his authorship.

The careful structure of the *Psalter* next deserves attention. It derives its name, like the Rosary or Lady Psalter, not from being composed of Psalms, but only from the number of its parts. Just as the Rosary, that is to say, with its 150 Aves, is shaped after the number of the Psalms of David, so Jesu's Psalter consists also of 150 Petitions. These Petitions are divided into fifteen decades for the fifteen principal Petitions, and these again are divided into three series according to the three stages of spiritual life: purgation, illumination, and union. A further analogy with the Rosary may be seen in the secondary Petitions which are added to each of the principal Petitions. These correspond to the Meditations which support the vocal prayer of the Rosary.

Let us turn now to the style of the writing of the *Psalter*. We have already suggested in the previous section that the writer of devotional prose is nearer to the poet than to his more pedestrian brother. This approximation to the poet's art will be yet more apparent in our present work. For not only is the interplay of feeling and will the controlling element of the expression here, but, beyond this, our author is working to a prescribed pattern, so that, like the poet, he must adjust, to some extent, what has to be said to that pattern. We must allow him, therefore, something of the poet's licence and we must not be surprised at his use of poetic devices to accomplish his end. Yet such stylistic expedients as he uses are manifestly intended only

* A letter to him from Erasmus, dated 1 May 1506, ends: 'Both of us [i.e. More and himself] certainly you equally love; to both also equally dear. Farewell, Richard, my delight and most agreeable friend.' Cited by Sole.

to increase devotion, and not to support or emphasize literary values. This should be clear from our examination of his text.

Apart from the vocabulary, which is both free and rich, and which is admirably suited to the meaning or the rhythmical sense, the outstanding feature of the style of the *Psalter* is its beautiful rhythm with its supporting rhymes. The rhythm, says Sole, 'depends primarily upon the rise and fall and rounded period of phrase and sentence; and, secondarily, upon the use of an ever-recurring rhyme which is so unaffected as never to weary'. The rhyme depends chiefly on the use of the forms 'me' and 'Thee' set one against the other in final phrases, serving thus to intensify the contrast between the Creator and the creature. Alternative forms are to be found in such words as 'charity', 'mortality', 'iniquity'. One of rare occurence, but bolder, is the group 'salvation', 'damnation', 'glorification'. Besides these are the rhymes and assonances which occur in such verses as that from the fifteenth Petition –

> O my lord, my lyfe, my might, my sight, lead me,
> feede me, and speede me, in the pylgrimage of this mortalitie –

'where the strength of the cry is enforced by setting in rapid succession words of one sound, or of one principal sound'. All these rhymes, let us repeat, assist the sense rather than restrict it; and this is especially true of the 'me' and 'Thee' rhymes, which are in perfect keeping with the essential form of the prayer: the redemption of the individual and his single growth towards the divine.

The following two *exempla* from the *Psalter* should suffice to illustrate these points.

From the fifth Petition:

> Iesu, make me constant & stable in faith, hope, and charitie, with continuance in vertue, and will not to offend thee.
> Make me oft to remember thy Passion and bitter paines, which thou suffredst for mee.
> Sende me perfect pacience in all tribulation and aduersitie.
> Preserue me fro pryde, Ire, enuie, couetyse, and from all offences to thy lawes contrary.
> The catholike obseruāces of the church make me to keepe truely.
> Make my soule to holy doctrine obedient, & to things pertein-ing to my ghostly weale for the loue of thee.
> Suffer no false delight of his deceiueable life, by fleshly tempta-tion, and fraude of the fende, for to blind mee.

To ye houre of my death, my v.wittes, Iesu, Keepe I beseche thee.
From excesse in speakinge, in feeding, and workinge, preserue my frailtie.
Haue mercy on all sinners, Iesu, I beseech thee: turne their vices into vertues, & make them true obseruers of thy lawe, & louers of thee: bring them to blisse in euerlasting glory.
Haue mercy also on the soules in purgatory for thy bitter Passion, I beseech thee, & for thy glorious name, Iesu.
The holy Trinitie, one very God haue mercy on me [sig. B1–2].

From the twelfth Petition:

Iesu grau̅t me grace & specially in ye time of te̅ptation, to cal for help to thee, & then with faithfull mynd to remember thy passion which thou suffredst for me: tha̅ most merciful lord, keepe my soul fro conse̅t of sinne for very true loue of thee: than let sin appeare stinking & abhominable to me.
Let the remembraunce of the pains of hell, & dampnatio̅ horrible, & terrible, & ful of thine enmitie, with the merytes of thy meke patie̅ce, through charitie & chastitie, mittigate the pronitie [i.e. proneness] to sinne and frailtie in me.
In my temptations, Lord, I beseech thee, help me, for the tender loue, that thou didest shew to thy mother, and she to thee.
Repel thy [the] power of my aduersaries, which entende the dampnation of me.
Inhabite my soule, O Sauiour, which with all humble subiectio̅ desireth ye blessed prese̅ce of thee.
Make me pure in spirite, meeke in speaking, pacient in suffering, hungery of rightuous working, and mercifull to all them that be in misery.
Make me peaceable in conuersation, cleane in heart with holy meditation, and ioyefull to suffer persecution in the cause of thee.
Let all my powers and desires be ruled according to the will of thee: and all my petitions order to thy wisdome, and to the euerlasting profit of me.
Haue mercy on all sinners . . . [*as before*] [sig. C5–6].

The Psalter of St. Hierome

Tradition has it that this abbreviation of the *Psalter* was taught to St. Jerome by an angel. According to the *Primer* of Wynkyn de Worde (*c.* 1494), it was thus abbreviated for the sake of those who, on one count or another, were unable to recite the whole *Psalter*.* A familiar medieval devotional exercise, its earliest recorded appearance is in the *Psalters* of the

* 'Beatus Iheronomus in hoc modo disposuit hoc psalterium ubi angelus Domini docuit eum per Spiritum Sanctum porro propter hoc abbreviatum est, quod hi qui solicitudinem habent, vel qui in infirmitate iacent, aut qui in operibus occupantur,' &c. Cited by Hoskins, *Horae*, p. 115.

fourteenth century.* Later it begins to be incorporated in the *Primers*, which continued to be printed in various forms at least down to the year 1564, the date of *Preces Privatae* (printed by William Seres), where it is described as 'Flores psalmorum, quos Psalterium Hieronymi appellant'.† After that date it seems no longer to occupy a place in Protestant books of devotion and is found, so far as I have been able to ascertain, only in Catholic manuals. Fowler's edition, which is dated 1576, is entitled *The Psalter of Sainct Hierome, with certaine dayly exercises and other deuout and necessary Prayers*. It is again difficult to state how far the translation of the Psalms is his own. He must certainly have known some of the earlier English versions; at the same time his translation differs from these often enough to warrant at least a suspicion that he did not depend primarily on them. Such a conjecture is strengthened by our knowledge of his own scholarly attainments. But, of course, it remains conjecture. The fact that the Address to the Reader affords no evidence one way or the other on the point need not surprise us, as it is hortatory in tone, and states only that this *Psalter* has been added to the *Psalter of Jesus* (with which it is bound up) to lead the devout Christian who may have little time for longer exercises to follow St. Jerome's example in well-doing.‡

Any translation into English of the *Psalter*, or a part thereof, must almost inevitably invite comparison with such well-known versions as those of Coverdale and the Authorized Version, and it may be stated at once that both in style and idiomatic character these versions are everywhere superior to this translation. Cramped by fidelity to the Latin text, Fowler's recension lacks the flexible and musical rhythm and the smoothness of diction which is characteristic of the Protestant versions, and, though his translation on the whole is not without felicity, it suffers as a consequence a certain loss of that emotional force which is a distinguishing quality of our standard English versions of the Psalms. His aim would appear to have been to produce as nearly as possible a rendering which would be an adequate substitute for the Vulgate original for the sake of those who had not sufficient Latin to use St. Jerome's text – an aim very similar to that of Richard Rolle in *his* translation of the

* Hoskins, op. cit., Introd., p. xii. † ibid., p. 261.
‡ The Address is given in full at bibl. ent. 45.

Psalter. The words of the latter in his Prologue to the *English Psalter* might very well be applied to Fowler's work:

> In þis werk I seke no strange Inglis, bot lightest and comunest and swilke þat es mast like vnto þe Latyn, so þat þai þat knawes noght Latyn, be þe Inglis may cum tille many Latyn wordes. In þe translacioun I folow þe letter als mekil als I may, and þare I fynde na propir Inglys I folow þe witte of þe word, so þat þai þat sal rede it, þam thar noght dred errynge.*

The passage here appended represents a collection of verses from Psalms v, vi, xiii, xvii, xix, xxii, xxv, xxvi and xxvii. In many respects it shows a distinct improvement upon the version of the *Primers*; occasionally, too, it improves upon the sense of Coverdale and the A.V.

> O Good Lord, receiue my wordes in thine eares, vnderstand my crying.
> O my king, my God intende to the voyce of my prayer.
> O good Lorde reproue me not in thine ire, and in thy furor doe not destroy me.
> Haue mercy on me good Lord for I am weake, heale me good lord for all my bones are troubled.
> And my soule is greatly vexed, but O thou good Lord how long.
> Turne thee good Lorde, & deliuer my soule, make me safe for thy mercy.
> Looke vpon me and heare me, O Lord my God.
> Illumine mine eyes that I sleepe not in death.
> Performe my goinges in thy pathes, that my steppes may not be remoued.
> I haue cryed out for thou hast hard me God incline thyne eare to me, and heare my words.
> Make the mercy maruailous, thou which sauest them which trust in thee.
> Kee[p]e me good Lorde, like the balle of thyne owne eye, defende me vnder y shadow of thy wings from the face of ye wicked which haue troubled me.
> Clense me good Lord from my secret faultes, and from straunge thinges spare thy seruant.
> But thou good lord let not thy helpe bee from me, loke vnto my defence.
> O God deliuer my soule from the sword, and my darlinge from the hand of the dogge.
> Saue me from the mouthe of the Lion, and my humilitie from the hornes of Vnicornes.†

* *English Writings of Richard Rolle. Edited by Hope Emily Allen* (1931), p. 7.

† Clearer in sense than Coverdale's 'thou hast heard me also from among the horns of the unicorns'. (Similarly A.V. xxii. 21.) The image has reference to the strength and pride of the ungodly.

I shall shewe thy name to my brethren in the middes of the cōgregacion I shall prayse thee.
O Lord make thy waies knowen vnto me & teach me thy paths and direct me in thy truth.
Haue mynde good Lord of thy mercies, and of thy mercifulnes, which hath been from the beginning of the world.
The offences of my youth, and myne ignorances do not remember good Lord.
Accordinge to thy mercy haue remēbraunce of me for thy truth good Lord.
For thy names sake thou shalt take pitie of my sinne, for why it is great.
Beholde my humilitie and my labour, and forgiue all myne offences.
O God do not destroy my soule with ye wicked, nor my lyfe with the bloudy men.
Lord here my voyce with the which I haue cryed to thee, haue mercy on me, and heare me.
Tourne not thy face from me, nor in thy wrath doe not decline from thy seruaunt.
Good Lord be thou my helper, doe not forsake mee, nor doe not despise me, O God my health [sig. A2–4].

Jesus Matins

This small black-letter volume is a translation of the *Little Office of Eternal Wisdom* from the *Horologium Sapientiae* of Blessed Henry Suso, the fourteenth-century Dominican mystic, which he composed some time between the years 1335 and 1338. The *Little Office* is usually found at the end of this work.* A comparison of the translation with such versions as appear in the sixteenth-century *Primers* would suggest that the work is original, this independence of the anonymous translator being further emphasized by the fact that, even in respect of the Versicles and Canticles, where a tradition might have been followed, it is not possible to trace any real connexion between his work and the current versions of the sixteenth century. The copy of the work in the British Museum has no title-page and is without date,† but a text-title runs: *Certayne sweete Prayers of the glorious name of Iesus, commonly called, Iesus Mattens, with the howers therto belonging: written in Latin aboue two hundred yeres agoe, by H. Susonne*. The work includes devotions for each of the seven

* cf. *Oeuvres Mystiques du Bienheureux Henri Suso de L'Ordre des Frères Prêcheurs* (2 vols., 1899), by Fr. G. Thiriot – Preface, Vol. I, pp. xxiv and lii.
† For date see bibl. ent. 7.

'Hours', together with a 'Salutation', which, it may be noted, occurs neither in the original nor in the versions of the Salisbury *Primers*.

The theme of the *Office* is the eternal Wisdom of Almighty God manifest in the Person of Jesus Christ, and this acts, as it were, as a *leitmotiv* to each one of the 'Hours', finding expression in the short versicle, 'Jesus, who is the Wisdom of the Father, give us health both of body and soul', with which each 'Hour' opens. And herein lies the inspiration of the several beautiful prayers and hymns, which the translator, with a fine sense for liturgical writing and hymnody, renders into no less beautiful English, providing yet further evidence of the literary excellence of these Catholic devotional books. The 'Salutation', of which we have spoken, runs as follows:

> My Soule hath desired thee in the night season, and I haue also watched for thee in spirite and mind al the morning (O wisedome most excellent) beseeching thee that thy presence, whiche I so sore haue longed for, expel from vs al such thinges as are agaynst vs, water the secrets of our hartes with thy manyfolde graces, and mightily inflame the same with thy loue. And nowe my moste sweete Lorde Iesu Christ, I rise and come earely to thee in the morning, and pray to thee from the botome of my hart. And a thousande thousande of blessed Saints in my name salute thee, and ten hundred thousand thousande glorifie thee, who are euer in thy sight ready at al times to doo thy will and pleasure. I pray also, that the sweete accorde of all creatures may prayse thee in my behalfe, and that thy triumphant name be our shielde and protection, and blesse vs euermore. Amen [sig. A1].

And here is the Collect for Prime, which may serve as an example of the translator's fine workmanship in his rendering of the prayers:

> Let the brightnes (O Lorde) of thy eternall wisedome illuminate our harts, that they be not dimmed with the darknes of this world, but that we may come to that countrey where is perpetual light: through our sayde Lorde Iesus Christe thy sonne [sig. B7^{v}].

This is certainly an improvement upon its counterpart in the Salisbury *Primer*:

> Lord god with thy eternal lyght of sapyens lyghten vs so that we may auoyd here the darknesse of thys world and agaynst it strongly to preuaylle so that after thys transytory lyff we may se the in thyne eternal glory.

But it is to the hymns of the *Office* that we would especially draw the reader's attention. The translator's genius for this kind of writing is unmistakable. Terseness and simplicity of language, ease and yet, at the same time, elevation of the expression and rhythm, qualities which are most valuable in hymns intended for congregational use, these serve to distinguish his style, and mark an achievement which is the more noteworthy when we remember that he was writing at a time when the development of hymnody had been checked. A particular interest therefore attaches to these short hymns, and in view of this we propose to cite four of them at length, the supplementary references to the versions of the *Primer* of 1536 being given by way of emphasizing those points to which we have called attention. Here, then, is the first of the hymns, from the Office of Matins:

O Iesu meeke, ẏ swetest thought,
That yeldes eche hart true ioy:
More swete it is thē yet was ought
Thy presence to ioioy [sic].

No sweeter tune or note can be
More pleasaunt to the eare,
Nor thoght foūd out so sweete as he
That is Gods sonne and heyre.

Thou Iesu hope to sinners all,
On thee that cry with willing mind
How louing art and naturall,
To them that thee doo finde.

To Father thine al glory be,
All wisdome eke to thee most pure,
The holy ghost in Trinitie,
Be praysed for euer to endure. Amē [sig. A4].

This is rendered in the Salisbury *Primer* as follows:

Most swetest Iesu memoriall
Aboue al other the trew cordiall
Of swetnesse no hony in emynens
So dulcet Iesu is thy presens

There is no Armony so melodious
Nor yet thyng herd so iocundious
Nor yet with hart may be thought
Lyke to thy sone by whome al is wrought

To penytentys thou art the hope
Thou art so meke to them that grop
When we deesyre thou art our helth
Then shal we fynd thou art our welth.

Of sapience thou art eterne
Frome the and thy father who can the werne
The holy ghost and you al in one
Without end to gouerne alone.

The superiority of the later version over that of the *Primer*, not only in the diction but also in the rhythmic structure of the verse, will be at once apparent. Similarly, the hymn for 'Lauds' exhibits a rhythmic smoothness which is in the best tradition of hymnody:

O Iesu wondrous king,
That dost triumph in blisse:
To all men thee desiring,
Thy ioy exceeding is.

No tong hath shewde by speache,
Ne letters euer tolde,
Nor Iesus loue may teache,
But triall can vnfolde.

O pearles Iesus loue,
For which I languishe sore,
My hart with pleasure moue
Of thee my hart and store.

All wisedome be to thee,
And to thy father glory,
The holy ghost prayse wee,
One God in persons three. Amen [sig. B3].

Perhaps there is more 'rustic simplicity' in our author's version of the hymn for 'Nones' than in the foregoing:

What coastes to trace I minde,
I Iesu alwayes would:
Howe glad if I him finde,
But blisse if I him holde.

Then clipping and kissing,
That passeth pleasure all:
In these without staying,
I will to Iesus call.

Nowe what I sought I finde,
And founde I hold at laste:
For Iesus loue I pinde,
And burnt within full faste.

All wisedome be to thee, &c. [sig. C4].

Even so, despite the somewhat 'hobbling' rhythm of the second stanza, it is preferable to the version of the *Primer*:

To what place where so euer I goo
I do desyre Iesu and no moo
How gladde I am hym for to seke
And moch gladder hym for to kepe.

Then clepynge oft I do hym kysse
None erthely thynge that I do wysshe
But in my fayth to cryst conioynt
In maryage thys is the hyghest poynt.

And now I se that I haue sought
With inward eye that me hath wrought
For by fayth I do hym fynde
And there vnto I do me bynde

Of sapience thou art eterne &c.

Finally, here is our author's translation of the hymn for 'Terce':

Thy loue, O Iesu, is
A passing sweete repaste,
Not lothsome ought iwis,
But suger all in taste.

That thee do tast, they hunger stil,
They drinke and yet are dry,
They wold none haue by their good will,
Saue Iesus him on hye.

A thousande times I thee desire,
How glad thou wouldst me make,
If thou wilt come as I require,
And cause my hunger slake.

All wisedome be to thee, &c. [sig. B8].

5. THE RHEMES *New Testament*

The publication of the Rhemes *New Testament* in the year 1582 must surely rank as one of the outstanding events of the earlier part of the reign of Queen Elizabeth. It has been referred to as the 'crowning glory' of our English Recusant literature, and there is substance in this claim. The translation was the work of a single, ailing man, Gregory Martin, who, at the request of Cardinal Allen, had set to work less than four years previously to translate the whole Bible out of the Vulgate into the vulgar English tongue. Owing to lack of funds, however, the publication of the *Old Testament* had to be withheld, and consequently the complete version of Martin's translation, the Douay version of the Scriptures as it is called, did not see the light of day until the year 1609, long after Martin's death. It is indeed remarkable that sufficient money was forthcoming (a modern estimate has put the publishing costs at well over £3,000) to enable even the *New Testament* to be printed in 1582. When we remember the great difficulties with which Allen was faced in finding even the bare minimum of support for the needs of the English College which he had founded at Douay – despite the generosity of the reigning popes and King Philip – owing to the mulcting of the Catholic population by the Queen's Ministers, not to speak of the other obstacles which were created both at home and abroad to hinder the raising of the necessary moneys for English Catholic purposes, when we remember also the numerous calls on his purse for assistance from the many Catholic refugees who had been forced to seek a home on the Continent, and when we further remember the limited possibilities of the sale of English Catholic books, we may well begin to wonder how he ever dared to embark upon such an ambitious and unprofitable undertaking. Bishop Goldwell, we know, contributed to the expense of the printing, and it is likely, too, that George Gilbert, whose purse was always at the disposal of the Church, contributed something. But these two can hardly have accounted for more than a small part of the sum expended. The remainder, we may be fairly certain, came mainly from the pockets of the impoverished Catholic brethren abroad. To their generosity and sure support Allen therefore looked to enable him to put the work in hand, and to John Fogny, Allen's printer at Rhemes, belongs the final honour of producing one of the most beautifully printed English books of the period.

The history of this publication may be briefly told. The project for a new Catholic translation of the Scriptures dates back to the year 1567, when on the 11th of June Thomas Harding and Nicolas Sander wrote to Morone, the Cardinal Protector, to the effect that the evil which resulted from the Protestant Bibles and their heretical interpretations might be remedied by a Catholic translation from the Vulgate into English of parts of the *Old Testament* and the Gospels and Epistles of the *New*.* This idea of countering the various Protestant versions of the Bible was principally in Allen's mind when, ten years later, he set Gregory Martin to work on the Catholic translation. In a letter to his friend and adviser, Dr. Vendeville, dated 16 September 1578, he writes:

> We [i.e. the students of Douay College] preach in English, in order to acquire greater power and grace in the use of the vulgar tongue, a thing on which the heretics plume themselves exceedingly, and by which they do great injury to the simple folk. In this respect the heretics, however ignorant they may be in other points, have the advantage over many of the more learned catholics, who having been educated in the universities and the schools do not commonly have at command the text of Scripture or quote it except in Latin. Hence when they are preaching to the unlearned, and are obliged on the spur of the moment to translate some passage which they have quoted into the vulgar tongue, they often do it inaccurately and with unpleasant hesitation, because either there is no English version of the words or it does not then and there occur to them. Our adversaries on the other hand have at their fingers' ends all those passages of Scripture which seem to make for them, and by a certain deceptive adaptation and alteration of the sacred words produce the effect of appearing to say nothing but what comes from the bible. This evil might be remedied if we too had some catholic version of the bible, for all the English versions are most corrupt. I do not know what kind you have in Belgium. But certainly we on our part, if his Holiness shall think proper, will undertake to produce a faithful, pure and

* See McKee's translation of Meyer's *England and the Catholic Church under Queen Elizabeth* (1916), Appendix XII. Letter cited from Arch. Vat., Arm. LXIV, t. 28, fols. 60, 61. 'Cui malo [i.e. the said evil] videtur quibusdam remedium afferri posse, si saltem historici et morales libri veteris testamenti atque evangelia et epistolae vulgari idiomate a catholicis ederentur. Ita enim demum persuaderi posset populo, ut veteres libros corrupte interpretatos abiiceret, si novi accurate ad vulgatae editionis fidem conversi eis traderentur. Qua in re nos sedis apostolicae iudicio et praescripto subiicimus.'

> genuine version of the bible in accordance with the edition approved by the Church, for we already have men most fitted for the work –*

and thereafter proceeds:

> For although it would perhaps be desirable that the sacred writings should never be translated into the vernacular, nevertheless since in these days, either because of the spread of heretical opinions or for some other reason, even men of good will are apt to be inquisitive, and moreover there may arise the need for reading the Scriptures in order to confute the adversaries, it is more satisfactory to have a faithful catholic translation than that they should endanger their souls by using a corrupt one, especially since it is possible to counteract the dangers consequent upon reading certain more difficult passages by means of suitable annotations.†

It was, indeed, natural and fitting that Allen should have been the prime mover in this matter of translation. His interest in Bible learning was both thorough-going and scholarly. The course of studies which he drew up for his students at Douay included a daily lecture on the *New Testament*, together with a daily exposition of one chapter of the *Old Testament* and one chapter of the *New* at table after dinner and supper. He ordained also weekly disputations in the College on controversial passages of Holy Scripture, which led to bi-weekly sermons by the students upon the controverted themes. In this way the

* *Douay Diaries*, Introducton, pp. xl and xlii.

† The text of the letter is given in *Letters and Memorials* (pp. 64–5) as follows: Id autem anglice facimus ut vernaculae linguae facultatem maiorem et gratiam, qua haeretici mire sibi placent et insigniter aliis simplicioribus nocent, assequamur. In quo genere vel imperiti alioquin haeretici multis doctioribus catholicis saepe praestant, quod hi in academiis et scholis educati non habent fere Scripturae textum nec allegant nisi latinum, quem cum concione indocta coguntur mox in vulgarem linguam vertere, quia statim alicuius versionis vulgaris verba non sunt aut non occurrunt, saepe parum accomodate et non sine ingrata haesitatione transferunt; ubi adversarii ad unguem tenent ex haeretica aliqua versione omnia Scriptura loca quae pro ipsis facere videantur, et quadam composita fraude ac mutatione sacrorum verborum efficiunt tandem ut nihil loqui videantur nisi ex Bibliis. Cui malo utrinque mederi possit, si et nos haberemus aliquam catholicam versionem Bibliorum; omnes enim anglicae versiones sunt corruptissimae. Quales in Belgio vestro habeatis nescio; certe nos si sua Sanctitas faciendum iudicabit, id etiam agemus ut fideliter, pure et genuine secundum approbatum ecclesiae editionem Biblia vertantur; cum ad hanc rem viros iam habeamus aptissimos. Licet enim optandum esset fortasse ut nunquam in barbaras linguas Scripturae verterentur, tamen cum tanta sit hodie vel ex haeresi vel aliunde curiositas hominum etiam non malorum, et saepe etiam propter confutationem adversariorum legendi necessitas, satius est ut fidelem et catholicam habeant translationem, quam ut cum periculo aut ad perditionem utantur corrupta; praesertim cum periculis ex difficiliorum quorumdam locorum lectione commodis quibusdam annotationibus occurri possit.

Old Testament was gone through twelve times in about every three years, 'the time the students usually remain with us in order to obtain sufficient instruction in these matters before they return home',* the *New Testament* being read through sixteen times in the same period. Beyond this we must reckon the fact that he was appointed by Cardinal Carafa, probably in 1579, to be one of his assistants in preparing an emended edition of the Septuagint as an aid to the revision of the Vulgate then in contemplation† – a sure testimony to the care which he would be likely to exercise in the production of an accurate and serviceable version of the Scriptures. In Gregory Martin he had a colleague of outstanding ability to assist him in the performance of this task.

Martin, who was an excellent Graecist and Hebraist, with, moreover, a wide knowledge of the existing versions of the Bible, both English and foreign, began work on the translation about 16 October 1578.‡ His method, we are told, was to translate two chapters daily, which were then carefully looked over by Allen and Dr. Bristow and amended where necessary.§ It is pretty certain that William Rainolds and Henry Holland, *alumni* of the College, were also called upon to give some assistance in the work of revision. But the bulk of this work was certainly done by Allen and Bristow, at any rate up to the latter's departure from the College for England on 23 September 1581, and these two were also mainly responsible for the annotations. Martin must have finished his work not later than January 1582 (probably earlier), as is evident from Allen's letter to Fr. Agazzari under date 7 February of that year, when he writes that the printing was almost done ('Testamenta ista iam pene excusa').|| That the work was finally out of the printers' hands in the following March we learn from an entry in *Douay Diaries* of March 1582, which states that in that month the finishing touches had been put to the English edition of

* Cited *Douay Diaries*, Introduction, p. xli. † ibid., p. lxxxiv.

‡ All the evidence points to this year. For the month, cf. the citation in *Douay Diaries*, p. 145: 'Octobris 16 vel circiter D. licent. Martinus Bibliorum versionem in Anglicum sermonem auspicatus est.'

§ *Douay Diaries*, as before: 'et ut opus istud, ut speratur longe utile, citius prodeat, ipse vertendo quotidie duo capita absolvit; ut autem emendatius, eadem ipsa capita praeses noster D. Alanus et mr n.D. Bristous diligenter perlegunt, atque etiam, si quidquid alicubi dignum videatur, pro sua sapientia fideliter corrigunt'.

|| *Letters and Memorials*, p. 112.

the *New Testament* ('Hoc ipso mense extrema manus Novo Testamento Anglice edito imposita est'). A further letter from Allen, this time to George Gilbert, dated 12 May 1582, indicates that the copies were already being distributed among the faithful by that time.

> You are desirous of two Testaments (he writes) one for your selfe and another for your good son, (i.e. godson) . . . But I think it not good to send them, as you require, by post ether of your pourse or ours; for they will stand in 10 or 12 crownes the cariage by post, and by muliters they will not coom to you this halfe yeare; and therefore I thought better to stay both them and two other bookes, that F. Robert sendeth, of devotion till som of our owne folkes coom by horse.*

Altogether it would seem that some five thousand copies were printed and distributed† – an unusually large edition for those days. That a fair number of these found their way into the hands of the 'adversaries', we may gather from some words of William Whitaker, in his 'reply' to the Rhemists (see below), as cited by the Catholic writer, William Rainolds: '*we . . . are very wel content to see them so common, that as now children may play with them in the streetes*'.‡ Rainolds himself bears further witness to this fact. 'Why', he asks, 'burne they such as fal into their hands?' and then proceeds: 'euery corner of the realme was searched for those bookes . . . the portes were layed for them, Paules crosse is witnes of burning many of them, the Princes proclamation was procured against them, in the Vniuersities by soueraigne authoritie, Colleges, chambers, studies, closets, coffers, and deskes, were ransackt for them . . . auncient men and students of Diuinitie were imprisoned for hauing of them'.§ Even so, a large part of the issue must have remained in the treasured possession of the Catholics, and this probably accounts for the number of surviving copies at this present day.

A second edition of the *Testament* was published in Antwerp by Daniel Vervliet in 1600, which differs from the first merely in the augmentation and rearrangement of some of the Notes. Subsequent issues, based upon this edition, were printed in 1621 and 1633. Further reprints which have been noted are those of

* ibid., p. 135.

† Persons alone wanted not less than 4,000; cf. Allen to Agazzari (Rhemes, 23 June 1581): 'Expetit P. Rubertus tria vel quatuor millia aut etiam plura ex Testamentis Anglicis, cum illa a multis desiderentur.' ibid., p. 96.

‡ *Refutation*, as below, sig. FF6v.

§ ibid.

the years 1738, 1788, 1789 (Liverpool – the first edition to be published in this country) and 1834 (an American publication).*

It was hardly likely that such a publication as the Rhemes *New Testament*, with its cater-cousin, Martin's *Discouerie of the Manifold Corruptions of the Holy Scriptures* (see below), would go unchallenged, and almost before the ink was dry upon its pages William Whitaker had penned his Latin Preface (below), and William Fulke, arch-answerer for the Protestant side, was at work on the first of the 'replies'. Henry Cotton, somewhat unfairly, has described the annotations of the Rhemes Bible as a 'studied series of deliberate insults',† and that this was also the view of Fulke, as it was of his compeers, we may gather from the title of his work, which runs: *A Defense of the sincere and true Translations of the holie Scriptures into the English tong, against the manifolde cauils, friuolous quarels, and impudent slaunders of Gregorie Martin, one of the readers of Popish diuinitie in the trayterous Seminarie of Rhemes.* With the publication of this reply in 1583, following upon Whitaker's *Preface*, the hunt may be said to have been up, and almost immediately, to vary the metaphor, the flood of criticism was in full spate. It would not be in place here to enlarge upon the manner of Fulke's animadversions, nor is it necessary to set out in detail the subsequent attacks on Martin's two works. For this the reader may be referred to the bibliography at the end of this book. It will be sufficient for us to record that the later participants in the Protestant onset included John Rainolds (1584), William Whitaker (1585), Thomas Bilson (1585), Edward Bulkeley (1588), George Wither (1588), William Fulke, in a second attack (1588), and Thomas Cartwright (1602 and again in 1618).‡ On the Catholic side

* See Henry Cotton, *Rhemes and Doway. An attempt to shew what has been done by Roman Catholics for the diffusion of the Holy Scriptures in English* (1855), for a full account of these various editions.

† *Rhemes and Doway*, as before, p. 15.

‡ The slenderest of the 'replies' was Whitaker's Latin preface to his *Ad Nicolai Sanderi Demonstrationes Quadraginta . . . responsio*, of 1583. The most elaborate replies were those of Fulke and Cartwright, the former in his parallel version of the Bishops' and Rhemes *Testaments* of 1588, the latter in the posthumous *Confutation of the Rhemists translation* (1618), where again the Rhemes version is printed in full, with annotations subjoined to each chapter. Cartwright had not quite finished this work before his death in 1603 and so the annotations on the last seven chapters of the *Apocalypse* were added from this second work of Fulke's. Two later volumes bearing upon the Rhemes *New Testament*, as recorded by Henry Cotton, are: Dr. Richard Montagu's *A Gagg for the New Gospel* (1624), a reply to Matthew Kellison's *A Gagg for the Reformed Gospel* (1615 or 16), and Richard Bernard's *Rhemes against Rome* (1626).

William Rainolds, the brother of John, defended the Catholic translation, as against Whitaker, in a work published in Paris in 1583; the latter replying in his volume of 1585. Reference will be made to their controversial works later in this chapter when we come to discuss in detail Martin's *Discouerie*.

We have already referred to Martin's wide knowledge of those versions of the Scriptures, both English and foreign, which were current in his own day, and there can be little doubt that he used the English versions in preparing his translation. This would be the natural inference to draw from a reading of his own Preface to the Reader, which we shall shortly quote at some length, and from the many references to the English translations and the Scottish version by his collaborator, William Rainolds, in his *Refutation* of Whitaker. Yet it would be incorrect to say that the earlier English versions were the 'very groundwork' of the Rhemes *Testament*. Both J. G. Carleton and Brooke Foss Westcott would appear to hold this view.* The latter, in particular, in a footnote to his chapter on *The Rhemes and Doway Bible*, lays special emphasis on this point. The note is worth careful consideration, coming, as it does, from so well-known an authority. 'This will appear', he says, 'at least in the New Testament, by a comparison of any chapter in the Rhemish version with the earlier English translations. The coincidences with the Genevan revision alone (1560) in a single chapter are striking. Rom. i. 6 *the called* of Jesus Christ; 10 *have a prosperous journey*; 12 *be comforted together* in you; 17 *revealed*; 23 *corruptible*; 28 a *reprobate* sense. . . . Some of these words may have come independently from the Vulgate, but a comparison with Wycliffe shews that it is unlikely all did.'† This is not convincing. Martin, we know, on the excellent authority of William Rainolds (see below), in preparing his version carefully collated the Latin with the Greek and Hebrew texts,‡ and not infrequently he rejected the Latin in favour of the Greek reading. This would seem to have been the course he followed in respect of those divergences from the Vulgate which Westcott notes in the examples quoted above. In every

* Carleton in *The Part of Rheims in the Making of the English Bible* (1902), and Westcott in *A General View of the History of the English Bible* (3rd edition, revised by William Aldis Wright, 1905).

† op. cit., p. 245.

‡ As far as concerns the *New Testament* the Hebrew was consulted in cases of quotation from the *Old*.

case except two (viz. 'revealed' and 'reprobate', which are the exact equivalents of the Latin 'revelatur' and 'reprobum') the Greek word supplies the key to his translation of these words. Thus 'the called' finds its counterpart in κλητοί; 'have a prosperous journey' in εὐοδωθήσομαι; 'be comforted together' in συμπαρακληθῆναι; and 'corruptible' in φθαρτοῦ. He may, of course, have consulted the Genevan version (among others) in order to find his English equivalents for the Greek. That would be entirely in accordance with his practice. But it by no means follows from this that he depended upon these earlier English versions for his translation in the sense that Westcott and Carleton would suggest.

A more considered view must lead us to suppose that Martin, as he himself asserts on his title-page* – and I see no reason to doubt his word – based his translation not upon the earlier English versions, but upon the Vulgate. It is surely impossible to believe that a scholar of his standing, with strong prejudices against the English versions, should turn to those versions in order to supply the 'very groundwork' of his translation. William Rainolds, to whom we have so often referred, and who, as we have seen, was a consultant in the process of revising Martin's daily work on the text, insists upon this fact that the Vulgate was the basis of the translation, and as proof that his opponent (Whitaker) seems also to have recognized this, we have the following words cited from Whitaker by Rainolds:

> There is now abrode a certaine english translation of the new testamēt, set forth & laboured by that new colledge at Rhemes to which I am right gladde that our translatiō is nothing like . . . It is altogether framed according to the forme of the old latin edition.†

A little later Rainolds asserts that the translation followed the common and best-corrected points of the Latin, and that this was no idle boast we may gather from the detailed reference to the current texts which were at hand and which he enumerates as –

> the common printes of Andwarp or Louayne &c. of the yeres 1563, 1564, 1565, 1569, 1570, 1574, 1577, 1580 set forth by Brickeman, Tiletane, Grauius, Plantine, & sundrie others.‡

* *The New Testament of Iesus Christ, translated faithfully into English out of the authentical Latin, according to the best corrected copies of the same, diligently conferred with the Greeke and other editions . . .*

† *Refutation*, sig. Ee6v–7.

‡ ibid., sig. Gg4 and Gg5.

In the face of such evidence we may well doubt the relevance of Westcott's stricture (for so we must regard it) cited above, nor will our doubt be lessened when we find that at a later page in his work the author, in a passage which would seem to endorse the contention of the Rhemists, writes: 'As it stands, the Doway Bible' – and I take it that he here includes both *Old* and *New Testaments* – 'is simply the ordinary, and not the pure, Latin text of Jerome in English dress', and supports this statement by reference to Martin's translation of the *Psalter* as a 'signal example' of the latter's failure to distinguish the corrupt from the pure text of his original. 'The Psalter', he says, '(to take one signal example) is translated, not from Jerome's version of the Hebrew, but from his revision of the very faulty translation from the Septuagint which commonly displaced it in Latin Bibles.'* Actually, this point had been met some three hundred years previously, when Rainolds wrote in reference to the purity of the Vulgate text as compared with the Hebrew and Greek:

> The like we say of the old testament, a great part whereof was translated by S. Hierom by order of the same Pope [Damasus], most of al corrected and brought in to ecclesiastical vse: sauing the psalmes, which could not be done so easely because throughout Christēdom, the principal part of the Seruice in al churches consisted of them, and therefore could not wel be altered without much trouble and scandal, as we gather by S. Austin, and which therefore we retaine stil as they were vsed in the primitiue church long before S. Hieroms time according to the version of the 70.†

Doubtless, a closer survey of the works of the period would have led Westcott to clarify his views both as to the origin and the process of Martin's translation.

A more judicial statement of this matter comes from the pen of another Biblical scholar, A. W. Pollard. The latter raises no question as to the prototype of the Rhemes *New Testament*, but doubts the advisability of Martin's translating from the 'ancient vulgar Latin'. 'Here', he writes:

> Here it may be well to remind any reader struck with the superficial absurdity of translating from a translation instead of an original, that if St. Jerome worked from better Greek manuscripts than any which were known in the sixteenth century, his Latin translation might, at least theoretically, represent the original Greek better than any manuscript used by

* op. cit., p. 249.

† *Refutation*, sig. T4v.

> Erasmus. Practically, of course, the question would be one of balance between loss and gain, and in striking this balance Gregory Martin, or whoever wrote the preface, was probably very insufficiently conscious that if the available Greek texts were corrupt the available Latin texts were very corrupt also, and far from representing what St. Jerome really wrote. Thus from the point of view of scholarship the decision to translate from the Vulgate was doubtless wrong, but it was not absurd, and there is ample evidence that Martin and his supervisors were good Graecists, and on any point, such as the use of the article, on which they felt free to interpret the Latin by the Greek, did so with conspicuous success.*

This we may pass without comment; only, in fairness to the Rhemists, recalling that very considerable attention must have been given by them to this difficult matter of a pure text before they decided in favour of the Vulgate over the Hebrew and Greek versions. This must be clear both from the care with which Martin examines the question in his preface to the *Testament* and from such learned evidence as Rainolds marshals in the long twelfth chapter of his *Refutation* of Whitaker. Nor can we imagine that Allen, one of the leading Biblical authorities of his day, would pass over the matter lightly.

The criticisms which have been levelled at Martin's work from the time of Fulke onwards have almost invariably been connected with the number of Latinized words which he employed in his translation and his close adherence to the idiom of the Vulgate. Usually a sinister motive has been attributed to his practice. Thus Fulke wrote in 1583 (and he was generally followed by his contemporaries) that he followed this course 'of purpose to darken the sense' and in order that the Bible might 'be kept from being understood'. Similarly in later days J. G. Gardiner has written: 'His [Martin's] purpose was, though making a translation into English, to reproduce slavishly every word which in the course of the Middle Ages had acquired any ecclesiastical or theological connotation or even a suspicion of such connotation. He and his superiors intended to send the layman continually to the priest for the interpretation of the Scriptures.'† It would, of course, be idle to deny that Martin laid great store by tradition in his interpretation of the sacred text: he himself admits as much in his Preface; but we must

* *Records of the English Bible* (1911), p. 35.
† *The Bible as English Literature* (1906), p. 341.

never forget that he was inspired also by a deep reverence for the Word of God, and it was from this primarily that there flowed, as his Preface again makes clear, that purpose of fidelity to word and sense which caused him, on occasion, to darken the meaning, and led him in places into a style that was literal and stiff. But the instances of such formal defects are not nearly so common as is popularly supposed. Let us again quote A. W. Pollard in this connexion:

> Another point which must be made is that the translation is much simpler than popular accounts of it make out. It is quite true that the translators acted up to their declaration, 'we presume not in hard places to mollifie the speaches or phrases, but religiously keepe them word for word, and point for point, for feare of missing or restraining the sense of the holy Ghost to our phantasie', and it is possible to quote verses, especially from the Epistles, which remain utterly unintelligible until we know the original. In this the translators seem to have forgotten the needs of popular preaching which Cardinal Allen made the main ground for setting Gregory Martin to work. But 'hard places' do not occur on every page of the New Testament, and it is easy to find long passages in the Gospels without a difficult word in them, and which a good reader could make all the more dramatic because of the abruptness of some of the constructions and transitions.*

This view has the support of G. P. Krapp, who writes: 'In justice to the Rhemish translation it should be said, however, that the effect of the whole is not as grotesque as might be inferred from the more extreme examples of learned locutions just cited. Consecutive passages of some length are frequently found which differ but slightly from the earlier English translations based on Tindale, and many readings which differ in the Rhemish translation from the earlier translations are familiar to us now because they were incorporated in the Authorised Version of 1611.'† And even Gardiner allows that where Martin's principle of translation allowed him to be so, he was exquisitely sensitive to the shades of meaning in the English words and the expressiveness of English style'.‡

But it is time to hear Martin in his own defence, and for this we must turn to the Preface already referred to. We may observe first Martin's deep sense of the value of his original and

* op. cit., pp. 35–6.

† *The Rise of English Literary Prose By George Philip Krapp Professor of English in Columbia University* (1915), p. 246.

‡ op. cit., p. 342.

his consciousness of the importance of the task which he had undertaken. This is the burden of the two passages, taken from the earlier part of the Preface, which we here cite:

> They [the Protestants] feele no such depth of Gods science in the scriptures, as S. Augustine did, when he cried out, *Mira profunditas eloquiorum tuorum, mira profunditas* (*Deus meus*) *mira profunditas: horror est intendere in eam, horror honoris, & tremor amoris. that is, O wonderful profoundnes of thy wordes: wonderful profoundnes, my God, wonderful profoundnes: it maketh a man quake to looke on it: to quake for reuerence, and to tremble for the loue thereof.* they regard not that which the same Doctor affirmeth, that the depth and profunditie of wisedom, not only in the wordes of holy Scripture, but also in the matter & sense, is so wonderful, that, liue a man neuer so long, be he of neuer so high a witte, neuer so studious, neuer so feruēt to attaine the knowledge thereof, yet when he endeth, he shall confesse he doth but begin. they feele not with S. Hierom, that the text hath a hard shel to be broken before we come to the kirnel. they will not stay them selues in only reading the sacred Scriptures thirtene yeres together, with S. Basil & S. Gregorie Nazianzene, before they expound them, nor take the care (as they did) neuer otherwise to interpret them, then by the vniforme consent of their fore-fathers and tradition Apostolike [sig. b1].

> We therfore hauing compassion to see our beloued countrie men, with extreme danger of their soules, to vse onely such prophane translations, and erroneous mens mere phantasies, for the pure and blessed word of truth, much also moued there-vnto by the desires of many deuout persons: haue set forth, for you (benigne readers) the new Testament to begin withal, trusting that it may giue occasion to you, after diligent perusing thereof, to lay away at lest such their impure versions as hitherto you haue ben forced to occupie. How well we haue done it, we must not be iudges, but referre all to Gods Church and our superiors in the same. to them we submit our selues, and this, and all other our labours, to be in part or in the whole, re-formed, corrected, altered, or quite abolished: most humbly desiring pardon if through our ignorance, temeritie, or other humane infirmitie, we haue any where mistaken the sense of the Holy Ghost. further promising, that if hereafter we espie any of our owne errors, or if any other, either frende of good wil, or aduersarie for desire of reprehension, shal open vnto vs the same: we wil not (as Protestants doe) for defense of our estimation, or of pride and contention, by wrangling wordes wilfully persist in them, but be most glad to heare of them, and in the next edition or otherwise to correct them: for it is truth that we seeke for, and Gods honour: which being had either by

> good intention, or by occasion, al is wel. This we professe onely, that we haue done our endeuour with praier, much feare and trembling, lest we should dangerously erre in so sacred, high, and diuine a worke: that we haue done it with all faith, diligence, and sinceritie: that we haue vsed no partialitie for the disaduantage of our aduersaries, nor no more licence then is sufferable in translating of holy Scriptures: continually keeping our selues as neere as is possible, to our text & to the very wordes and phrases which by long vse are made venerable, though to some prophane* or delicate eares they may seeme more hard or barbarous, as the whole style of Scripture doth lightly† to such at the begīning: acknowledging with S. Hierom, that in other writings it is ynough to giue in trāslation, sense for sense, but that in Scriptures, lest we misse the sense, we must keepe the very wordes [sig. b2].

Our author's firm belief in the purity of the Latin as opposed to the surviving Greek texts has already been remarked. The reasons for this belief he sets down under ten headings. These, however, need not concern us here, beyond perhaps noting that, in support of his statement that the Latin text has the weight of authority on its side, he cites not only the ancient Fathers, Erasmus, and the Council of Trent, but also Beza and the Calvinists. It is the aim and limitations which the Rhemists set themselves in translating the Holy Scriptures which is most relevant to our purpose, for these gave rise to most of the subsequent controversy over Martin's translation, and they form a necessary background to an intelligent understanding of the manner and style of this great work. They are set down in considerable detail, the intention being, in part at any rate, to forestall criticism while expounding the difficulties. That the writer, in company with every translator of Holy Writ, is fully conscious of the need to strike a balance between conformance to the genius of the language into which he translates and fidelity to the word and sense of his original will become evident as the argument develops.

> In this our translation, (he writes) because we wish it to be most sincere, as becōmeth a Catholike translation, and haue endeuoured to make it: we are very precise & religious in folowing our copie, the old vulgar approued Latin: not onely in sense, which we hope we alwaies doe, but sometime in the very wordes also and phrases, which may seeme to the vulgar Reader & to common English eares not yet acquainted there-

*Lay, unecclesiastical. † Commonly.

with, rudenesse or ignorance: but to the discrete Reader that deepely weigheth and considereth the importance of sacred wordes and speaches, and how easily the voluntarie Translatour may misse the true sense of the Holy Ghost, we doubt not but our consideration and doing therein, shal seeme reasonable and necessarie: yea and that al sortes of Catholike Readers wil in short time thinke that familiar, which at the first may seeme strange, & wil esteeme it more when they shal otherwise be taught to vnderstand it, then if it were the common knowen English.

For example we translate often thus, *Amen, amen, I say vnto you.* Which as yet seemeth strange. but after a while it wil be as familiar, as *Amen* in the end of al praiers and Psalmes. and euen as when we end with, *Amen*, it soundeth far better then, *So be it*: so in the beginning, *Amen Amen* must needes by vse and custom sound far better, then, *Verily verily.* Which in deede doth not expresse the asseueration and assurance signified in this Hebrue word. besides that it is the solemne and vsual word of our Sauiour to expresse a vehement asseueration, and therfore is not changed, neither in the Syriake nor Greeke, nor vulgar Latin Testament, but is preserued and vsed of the Euangelistes and Apostles them selues, euen as Christ spake it, *propter sanctiorem authoritatem*, as S. Augustine saith of this and of *Allelu-ia*, *for the more holy and sacred authoritie thereof, li.2. Doct. Christ. c.11.* And therfore do we keepe the word *Allelu-ia.* Apoc.19. as it is both in Greeke and Latin yea and in al the English translations, though in their bookes of common praier they translate it, *Praise ye the Lord.* Againe, if *Hosanna*, *Raca*, *Belial*, and such like be yet vntranslated in the English Bibles, why may not we say, *Corbana*, and *Parasceue*: specially when they Englishing this later thus, *the preparation of the Sabboth*, put three wordes more into the text, then the Greeke word doth signifie. Mat. 27, 62. And others saying thus, After the day *of preparing*, make a cold translation and short of the sense: as if they should trãslate, Sabboth, *the resting.* for, *Parasceue* is as solemne a word for the Sabboth eue, as Sabboth is for the Iewes seuenth day. and now among Christians much more solemner, taken for Good-friday onely. These wordes then we thought it far better to keepe in the text, and to tel their signification in the margent or in a table for that purpose, then to disgrace bothe the text & them with translating them. Such are also these wordes, *The Pasche. The feast of Azymes. The bread of Proposition.* Which they translate *The Passeouer, The feast of swete bread, The shew bread.* But if Pentecost Act.2 be yet vntrãslated in their bibles, and seemeth not strange: why should not *Pasche* and *Azymes* so remaine also, being solemne feastes, as Pentecost was? or why should they English one rather then the other? specially whereas *Passeouer* at the first was as strange, as *Pasche* may seeme now, and perhaps as many now vnderstand *Pasche*, as *Passeouer*. and as for *Azymes*, when they English it, *the feast of sweete bread*, it is a false interpretatiō of the word, & nothing expresseth that which belongeth to the feast, concerning vnleauened bread. And as for their terme of *shew bread*, it is very strange and ridiculous. Againe, if *Proselyte* be a receiued word in the English bibles *Mat.23. Act.2*: why may not we be bold to say, *Neophyte*. 1 Tim. 3? specially when they translating it into English, do falsely expresse the signification of the word thus, *a yong scholer*. Whereas it is a peculiar word to signifie them that were lately baptized, as *Catechumenus*, signifieth the newely instructed in faith not yet baptized, who is also a yong scholer rather then the other, and many that haue been old scholers, may be *Neophytes* by differring baptisme. And if *Phylacteries* be allowed for English Mat. 23. we hope that *Didragmes* also, Prepuce, Paraclete, and such like, wil easily grow to be currant and familiar. And in good sooth there is in al these such necessitie, that they can not conueniently be translated. as when S. Paul saith, *concisio, non circumcisio*: how can we but folow his very wordes and allusion?* And how is it possible to express *Euangelizo*, but as we do, *Euangelize*? for *Euangelium* being the Gospel, what is, *Euangelizo* or *to Euangelize*, but to shew the glad tydings of the Gospel, of the time of grace, of al Christs benefites? Al which signification is lost, by translating as the English bibles do, *I bring you good tydings*. Luc.2.10. Therfore we say *Depositum*, 1 Tim.6. and, He *exinanited* him self, Phil.2. and, You haue *reflorished*, Philip.4. and, *to exhaust*, Hebr.9,28. because we can not possibly attaine to expresse these wordes fully in English, and we thinke much better, that the reader staying at the difficultie of them, should take an occasion to looke in the table folowing, or otherwise to aske the ful meaning of them, then by putting some vsual English wordes that expresse them not, so to deceiue the reader. Some time also we doe it for an other cause. as when we say, *The aduent of our Lord*, and, *Imposing of handes*. because one is a solemne time, the other a solemne action in the Catholike Church: to signifie to the people, that these and such like names come out of the very Latin text of the Scripture. So did *Penance*, *doing penance*, *Chalice*, *Priest*, *Deacon*, *Traditions*[,] *aultar*, *host*, and the like (which we exactly keepe as Catholike termes) procede euen from the very wordes of Scripture.

Moreouer, we presume not in hard places to mollifie the speaches or phrases, but religiously keepe them word for word, and point for point, for fear of missing, or restraining the sense of the holy Ghost to our phantasie. as Eph.6. *Against the spirituals*

* The reference is to *Philippians* iii. 2. The following note is appended: 'He calleth the carnal Christiā Iews that yet boasted in the circūcision of the flesh, concisiō: & him self & the rest that circūcided their hart and senses spiritually, the true *circumcision*'.

of wickednes in the celestials. and, *What to me and thee woman?* [marg. *Io.2*] whereof see the Annotation vpon this place. and 1 Pet.2. *As infants euen now borne, reasonable, milke without guile desire ye.* We do so place, *reasonable*, of purpose, that it may be indifferēt both to infants going before, as in our Latin text: or to milke that foloweth after, as in other Latin copies and in the Greeke. *Io.3* we translate, *The spirit breatheth where he wil &c.* leauing it indifferent to signifie either the holy Ghost, or winde: which the Protestants translating, *winde*, take away the other sense more common and vsual in the auncient fathers. We translate Luc.8,23. *They were filled*, not adding of our owne, *with water*, to mollifie the sentence, as the Protestants doe. and c.22. *This is the chalice, the new Testament &c.* not, *This chalice is the new Testament.* likewise, Mar.13. *Those daies shal be such tribulation &c.* not as the Aduersaries, *In those daies*, both our text and theirs being otherwise. likewise Iac.4,6. *And giueth greater grace*, leauing it indifferent to the *Scripture*, or to the *holy Ghost*, both going before. Whereas the Aduersaries to to boldly & presumptuously adde, saying, *The Scripture giueth*, taking away the other sense, which is far more probable. likewise *Hebr.*12,21 we translate, *So terrible was it which was seen, Moyses said &c.* neither doth Greeke or Latin permit vs to adde, *that* Moyses said, as the Protestants presume to doe. So we say, *Men brethren, A widow woman, A woman a sister, Iames of Alphaeus*, and the like. Sometime also we folow of purpose the Scriptures phrase. as, *The hel of fire*, according to Greeke and Latin. which we might say perhaps, *the firy hel*, by the Hebrue phrase in such speaches, but not, *hel fire*, as commonly it is translated. Likewise *Luc.*4,36. What *word* is this, that in power and authoritie he cōmaundeth the vncleane spirits? as also, *Luc* 2. Let vs passe ouer, and see the *word* that is done. Where we might say, *thing*, by the Hebrue phrase, but there is a certaine maiestie and more signification in these speaches, and therfore both Greeke & Latin keepe them, although it is no more the Greeke or Latin phrase, then it is the English. And why should we be squamish at new wordes or phrases in the Scripture, which are necessarie: when we do easily admit and folow new wordes coyned in court and in courtly or other secular writings? [sig. c3–4].

The general tenor of this defence will be abundantly clear to the reader. Martin admits the inclusion in his version of a number of unusual terms; unusual, that is to say, to English ears. He also admits that occasionally he has indulged in ambiguous expression and has adopted into his text Latin idioms which, we must acknowledge, in some cases hardly resemble English at all. Yet he justifies his practice. The so-called unusual terms will, he believes, with usage become in time familiar, as in practice many strange terms of the Protestant Bibles already have. His desire to be precise and not to mislead is the sole ground for his adoption of these terms and for sacrificing elsewhere the sense to the expression. Moreover, the annotations should assist in interpreting such difficulties of reading as may be met with. In short, 'we haue endeuoured', he says, 'by al meanes to satisfie the indifferent reader, and to helpe his vnderstanding euery way, both in the text, and by Annotations: and withal to deale most sincerely before God and man, in translating and expounding the most sacred text of the holy Testament'.* Such is his answer to those who, like George Wither,† might charge him with having deliberately obscured the meaning of the text for some sinister purpose. We shall do well to bear it in mind in estimating the value of his work. However, in spite of the fact that Martin, unlike his opponents, was under the stern necessity of not straying one hair's breadth from the traditional interpretation and wording of the Scriptures, the number of passages affected by this Latinization is not large. Much of the *New Testament* is, as has already been pointed out, thoroughly idiomatic, and it abounds in happily turned expressions, many of which, as we shall see directly, have become familiar to us through their adoption into the *Authorized Version* of James I. If the reader will compare, let us say, any of the well-known passages of that version with the parallel passages in Martin's work, he will, I think, be struck more by the resemblances than by the differences of the two. And yet, so eminent a critic as Bishop Westcott remembers only the differences when he writes of the Catholic version: 'The style, so far as it has a style, is unnatural, the phrasing [as a rule] is most unrhythmical.'‡ Undoubtedly it can be held that the *Authorized Version*, in style and rhythm, is in many respects superior to all the earlier English editions. But it is also possible to hold, as

* Preface, as before.

† 'Their Translation (how much soeuer they brag of paines, care, and conscience to deale sincerely) is fraudulently framed to make poore men thinke the Scriptures to be more obscure and darke a great deale, than they are, and so to fray them (as much as in them lieth) from taking paines to read them . . . they haue studied therin for nothing lesse, than perspicuitie, & plainnes. For they haue both hunted for words of purpose, which the people do not vnderstand . . . And also left their sentences vnperfect, halt, maimed, and without sence, and all to strike simple persons in a maze,' &c. *View of the Marginal Notes of the Popish Testament* (1588), Preface.

‡ op. cit., p. 249. The bracketed words are Aldis Wright's.

J. S. Phillimore held, that even in those places where Rhemes departs from the traditional expression of the Protestant Bible its individual style and rhythm have an attraction denied to its sister-versions. It is not our intention here to attempt to decide as between the opinions of Westcott and Phillimore. The dangers of generalizing on such a theme are manifold and to do more would lead to a closer examination of the texts than the scope of this work would allow. One thing, however, we may permit ourselves to say. In judging the style of such writings as the sacred Scriptures we are apt to bring to our judgment, in a degree far greater than in the case of writings of a secular type, emotional associations and intellectual predispositions which it is very difficult for us to shed, and more often than not it is the coincidence of these with those that the writer himself brings to his work which will determine for us the validity of our judgment. To concentrate our attention thus, not upon the essentials but upon the accidents of style, is the main hindrance to a just criticism of Bible literature, and it is well to remind ourselves of this before we attempt any sort of comparison of one version of the Scriptures with another. With this word of caution we must leave the reader to discover for himself the merits of the Catholic version of the *New Testament.* He may do this most satisfactorily by consulting Bagster's *English Hexapla*, where the versions of Wicliffe, Tindale, Cranmer, Whittingham, Rhemes and the *Authorized Version* are arranged side by side.

The significance of the Rhemes *New Testament* in the history of English Literature may be measured by the influence which it exercised upon the Bible of King James. This influence is assuredly much greater than has sometimes been supposed, and it has been stressed by those modern Biblical scholars whose works we have so often referred to in these pages. According to Pollard, for instance, Martin deserves to rank with Tindale, Coverdale, Whittingham and Parker as one of the builders of the *Authorized Version.** 'All that was valuable of [Martin's] labours', writes Gardiner, 'was taken over by the Authorized Version.'† Dr. Carleton, after referring to 'the magnitude of the debt which the translators [of the *A.V.*] owe to the Rhemish New Testament', goes on to say – 'If one were to assess the

* loc. cit. † op. cit., p. 344.

degree of obligation due from the former to the latter, it might, I think, fairly be said, that while the Translation of 1611 in its general framework and language is essentially the daughter of the Bishops' Bible, which in its turn had inherited the nature and lineaments of the noble line of English versions issuing from the parent stock of Tindale's, yet with respect to the distinctive touches which the Authorized New Testament has derived from the earlier translations, her debt to Roman Catholic Rheims is hardly inferior to her debt to puritan Geneva.'* The evidence which Carleton supplies in support of this statement is both important and decisive, and a short summary of it may fitly conclude this notice of the Catholic *Testament*.

The impact of version upon version is described under thirteen separate headings, illustrated by well over a thousand words and phrases, many of which are newcomers to the English *New Testament*:

(1) *Vulgate-Latin influences through Rhemes*. About two hundred examples are given, fifty-three of which are new. These latter include: *usury*, *malefactor*, *more tolerable*, *clemency*, *spectacle*, *contemptible*, *illuminated*, *letters*, *communication*, *sobriety*, *austere*, *Areopagus*, *theatre*, *schism*, *scandal*, *equality*, *humility*, *malice*, *unction*.

(2) *English in place of Latin words* (i.e. where the *A.V.* has accepted the *Rhemes* preference for the home-born as opposed to the Latin word). Twenty-one examples given, two of which are new: *stock* (for 'generation') and *unskilful* (for 'inexpert').

(3) *Modernizations*. Some seventy examples are given, out of which *moisture* (for 'moistness') and *senses* (for 'wits') are new. Other examples include: *it seemeth to me* (for 'me thinketh it'), *adorned* (for 'did . . . tyre'), *immediately* (for 'anon'), *according to* (for 'after'), *themselves* (for 'them' reflexive), *country* (for 'coasts'), *the lame walk* (for 'the halt go'), *know how to give* (for 'know to give' or 'can give'), *who* (for 'which' in reference to personal antecedent), *danger* (for 'jeopardy'), *murderer* (for 'manslayer'), *others* (which almost completely displaces 'other' as a plural form).

(4) *Archaisms*. Seven examples: e.g. *if haply* (for 'to see if'), etc.

(5) *Improvements* (where *Rhemes* plainly emends faulty or defective translations handed down by English traditional interpretation). These include: questions of vocabulary (forty-eight

* op. cit., p. 31.

examples); tenses (twenty-three examples); number (thirteen examples); Greek article enforced (twenty-three places recorded); absence of Greek article enforced (twenty places recorded); due observance of the Greek δέ; together with a number of miscellaneous improvements (sixty separate usages are recorded in all), such as *the whole* for 'all the' (as in ὅλην τὴν πόλιν – the whole city), *I know not* (οὐκ οἶδα) for 'I cannot tell', *by him . . . and without him* (δι' αὐτοῦ . . . καὶ χωρὶς αὐτοῦ) for 'by it . . . and without it' in reference to the Logos of John i. 3, etc.

(6) *Changes for the worse.* Forty-eight examples are given in respect of words, grammar and inferior readings.

(7) *Participial construction introduced* (to replace conjoined finite verbs). Over forty examples given.

(8) *Literal renderings. Rhemes,* as we have seen, is avowedly literal, even sometimes to the point of unintelligibility. Over one hundred examples are given where the *A.V.* would appear to have availed itself of the more literal interpretations of *Rhemes* for the looser or more periphrastic older versions. Among nine locutions which are new we note: *confused* (for 'all out of order'), with great *astonishment* (for 'out of measure'), the times of the *restitution* of all things (for 'the time that all things shall be restored'), to *revenge* (for 'wherewith to take vengeance on'), the *engraffed* word (for 'the word that is graffed in you'), the *foster brother* of Herod (for 'which had been brought up with Herod').

(9) *Concise renderings* (by omitting intruded adjectives, adverbs, etc.). Over eighty examples recorded.

(10) *Change in the order of words* (to produce smoothness, right emphasis, etc.). Over ninety recorded instances.

(11) *Familiar words and phrases.* Carleton here writes: 'It is remarkable how often some familiar phrase, some well-known term in our English New Testament proves on examination to have been suggested by the version of Rheims.' Out of 102 examples listed eighteen are given as new. Among these latter are: 'throng and *press* thee', 'being *privy* to it', 'to *blaze* abroad the matter', *creditor* (for 'lender'), *straitened* (for 'pressed into a narrow room'), *slaves* (for 'bodies' or 'servants'), *transparent* (for 'thorow shining'), *decease* (for 'departing'). Other notable examples, though not new to the Bible, are: *striveth for the mastery* (for 'proveth masteries'), *unto me to live is Christ, and to die is gain*

(for 'Christ is to me life, and death is to me advantage'), *evil communications* (for 'evil words' – 1 Cor. xv. 33), *the one shall be taken and the other shall be left* (for 'the one shall be received and the other left alone'), *ever and ever* (for 'evermore'), *it came to pass* (for 'so it was'), etc.

(12) *Less notable words.* About a hundred examples are given, fourteen of which are new. These latter include: *abode* (for 'dwelling'), *tempestuous* (for 'stormy'), *renounced* (for 'cast from us' – 2 Cor. iv. 2), *stock* (for 'kindred'), *folly* (for 'madness'), *limiteth* (for 'appointeth' – Heb. iv. 7), *silly* (for 'simple'), *overruling* (for 'being lords over').

(13) *Suggestions only taken.* Here *Rhemes* gives the necessary hint for *A.V.*'s rendering. Thus the 'white exceedingly' of *Rhemes* (for 'very white') becomes in *A.V.* 'exceeding white'. Where *Rhemes* reads 'with honour preventing one another' (for the earlier 'in giving honour going one before another'), *A.V.* reads 'in honour preferring one another', and so on. Altogether fifty-seven examples are considered under this head.

It is, of course, possible that in respect of some of these recordings the translators of the *Authorized Version* may have arrived at their final choice of word and expression quite independently of any reference to the Rhemes version of the scriptural text. But the importance of this evidence lies not in the fact that in this case or in that concurrence between these two versions may be observed, but in the extensive and diverse nature of the examples which Dr. Carleton has adduced. In the face of such evidence, therefore, the judgment of those we have cited above must stand, viz. that *Rhemes* played no small part in finally shaping the Book which in the estimation of all competent critics has had more influence than any other single work in setting a seal upon our national style, thinking and speaking.*

Complementary to the translation of the *New Testament* was Martin's *A Discouerie of the Manifold Corruptions of the Holy Scriptures by the Heretikes of our daies, specially the English Sectaries, and of their foule dealing herein, by partial & false translations to the aduantage of their heresies, in their English Bibles vsed and authorised since the time of Schisme.* This work, described by the author as a 'handmaid of the New Testament', was, save for the Preface, actually finished in January 1582, that is to say, some two or

* cf. Sir Arthur Quiller-Couch, *On the Art of Writing* (1921), p. 124.

three months earlier than the publication of the translation of the Scriptures, though it was not printed until towards the end of the following June.* The fact that the printing of both works was in the hands of John Fogny, whose means of production in English was from the very nature of the case strictly limited, together with the fact that the printing of the *New Testament* was of major importance to the Catholic cause, will probably account for this delay in publication. The reason for not incorporating the notes of which the work consists in the *New Testament* may be gathered from the Preface, where Martin states that his book

> wil deale principally with the English translations of our time, which are in euery mans handes within our countrie the corruptions whereof, as they are partly touched here and there in the Annotations vpon the late new English Testament Catholikely translated & printed at Rhemes, so by occasion thereof, I wil by Gods help, to the better cōmoditie of the reader, and euidence of the thing, lay them closer together, and more largely display them . . . esteeming the weight & importance of so many as I thought good to note, specially in the new Testament [sig. a8v].

The corrupt English translations to which this paragraph refers were chiefly, as the Preface goes on to inform us, the editions of the Great Bible and the Genevan Bible of 1562, 1577 and 1579.† Parker's Bible (the Bishops' Bible), which was also reprinted in 1577,‡ was not included in Martin's survey. As Strype points out in his *Life and Acts of Parker*§ most of the 'corruptions' complained of are, in fact, not to be found in that Bible. With the publication of the *Authorized Version*, which adopted many of Martin's readings, much of the critical work embodied in the *Discouerie* ceased, of course, to have significance in respect of the Protestant Bible.

The matters treated in Martin's examination of the 'heretical Translations of the Bible' cover pretty well the whole field of theological controversy which separated the two sides and include such topics as Tradition, Idolatry, Priesthood, Purgatory,

* The evidence for this will be found at bibl. ent. 87.

† sig. b1v. The Great Bible was reprinted by George Harrison in 1562, and the Genevan by Christopher Barker in 1577. Under 1579 I note three reprints of the Genevan version in the British Museum catalogue. One of these was set up in Scotland.

‡ *The Holy Byble . . . Whereunto is joyned the whole service used in the Churche of Englande.* In two parts, and printed by Richard Jugge.

§ Ed. 1821, Vol. I, p. 414.

Limbo, Hell, Justification, Merits, Freewill, Faith, Penance, Satisfaction, Baptism, Confession, Holy Orders, Matrimony, Blessed Sacrament, Sacrifice, Altars, and Invocation of Saints. These are dealt with under their various headings largely in the form of notes. We shall hardly look, therefore, for quotable passages of sustained eloquence in this work, though perhaps we may catch a glimpse of our author's ability to write animatedly in those occasional passages where he is led to exclaim vigorously against his opponents' translations. One such passage is the following, where the disputable points turn upon the interpretation or usage of a word:

> We spake a litle before of the double signification of wordes, the one according to the original propertie, the other according to the vsual taking thereof in all vulgar speache and writing. These wordes (as by the way we shewed before vpon occasion of the Aduersaries graunt) are to be translated in their vulgar and vsual signification, not as they signifie by their original propertie. As for example: *Maior* in the original signification is, *greater*. But when we say, The *Maior* of London, now it is taken and soundeth in euery mans eare for such an officer: and no man will say, The *Greater* of London, according to the original propertie of it. likewise *Episcopus* a Greeke word, in the original sense is euery ouerseer, as Tullie vseth it and other profane writers: but among Christians in Ecclesiastical speache it is a Bishop. and no man wil say, My Lord ouerseer of London, for my L. *Bishop*. Likewise we say, Seuen *Deacons*, S. Steuen a *Deacon*. no man will say, Seuen *Ministers*, S. Steuen a *Minister*. although that be the original signification of the word Deacon. but by Ecclesiastical vse & appropriation being taken for a certaine degree of the Clergie, so it soundeth in euery mans eare, and so it must be translated. As we say, Nero made many Martyrs: not, Nero made many *witnesses*: and yet Martyr by the first originall propertie of the word is nothing els but a witnes. We say *Baptisme* is a Sacrament: not, Washing is a Sacrament. Yet Baptisme and washing by the first originall propertie of the word is all one.
>
> Now then to come to our purpose, such are the absurde translations of the English Bibles, and altogether like vnto these. Namely, when they translate congregation for Church, Elder for Priest, image for idol, dissension for schisme, General for Catholike, secrete for Sacrament, ouer-seer for Bishop, messenger for Angel, embassadour for Apostle, minister for Deacon, and such like. . . . [sig. D5^{v}–6].

The undercurrent of ridicule which may be discerned in this extract is not uncharacteristic of the more 'open' passages of

Martin's treatise. It is sometimes even more strongly evident than here: as in the relation of John Keltridge's preaching before the Jesuits and Seminarists in the Tower, when Keltridge referred to St. Luke's Gospel as though the whole New Testament had been written in Hebrew and that the Seventy had translated it into Greek 'who were dead three hundred yeres before S. Lukes Gospel and the new Testament was written';* or in the following:

> and *so his soule in Hel*, as the holy Scripture speaketh, shal be, *his body in the graue*, as Beza plainely speaketh, and the Bezites couertly insinuate: and white shal be blacke, and chaulke shal be cheese, and euery thing shal be any thing that they wil haue it. And al this their euident false translation, must be to our miserable deceiued poore soules, the holy Scripture and Gods word [sig. G4].

But the particular value for the literary student of such a work as this lies principally in the light it may throw upon current Elizabethan usage. It would seem obvious that these little-known sixteenth-century treatises which are the main subject of this thesis, all written by Englishmen who had distinguished themselves in one branch of learning or another, might very well contain matter pointing the way to a solution of some of those problems which continually engage the attention of students of Tudor and Stuart literature. For this reason, if for no other, it would seem that they are worthy of patient examination. In Martin's *Discouerie* we have what must appear to be on the face of it most unpromising ground for literary research, yet, in addition to its value as a forerunner of the *Authorized Version* (we may note, for instance, its influence on that version of the Bible in the choice of such locutions as 'Tradition', 'Idolater', 'Church', and 'Hell'), we shall find it a useful source of proverbial expression and spoken idiom. The reader may have already noted this in the two passages cited above. We may further instance such expressions as:

> Why do your translations, like cuckoes birdes, sound continually, images, images? [sig. D2].

Or

> turning catte in panne – [sig. B7].

where the meaning is not the generally accepted one of 'to

* sig. S3v. The reference is to Keltridge's *Two Godlie and learned Sermons, appointed and Preached before the Jesuites . . . In May 7 and 21 Anno 1581.*

change sides', but 'to turn the wrong way round', as we may learn from the context.*

Or

> I would once see them precise in following the Greeke and the Hebrue. if not, we must looke to their fingers – [sig. M6].

Or again

> the Hel of the damned, from whēce is no returne – [sig. G8v],

a common gloss which is used to remind us of the distinction between the uttermost Hell (whence is no 'delivery' or 'salvation') and the Hell of purgatory,† and which may possibly throw light upon the well-known crux in *Hamlet* (III, i):

> Who would these Fardles beare
> To grunt and sweat vnder a weary life,
> But that the dread of something after death,
> *The vndiscouered Countrey, from whose Borne*
> *No Traueller returnes*, Puzzels the will,
> And makes vs rather beare those illes we haue,
> Then flye to others that we know not of.

It remains before we conclude this section and chapter to say something of the intervention on the Catholic side of William Rainolds in the controversy which followed the publication of Martin's two works. It will be remembered that one of the earliest replies to Martin had been contained in William Whitaker's Latin Preface to his *Ad Nicolai Sanderi Demonstrationes Quadraginta* of 1583 (see above). Whitaker, it may be pointed out, had for some time been awaiting the opportunity to answer Martin's attack upon the Protestant Bible. He had already replied in a somewhat abusive Latin pamphlet entitled *Responsio ad Rationes Edmundi Campiani* (1581) to the more general charge which Edmund Campion had put forward in the first two of his *Rationes Decem*,‡ that the old heretics had perverted

* See also above, p. 114.

† I note the same gloss in the translation of Psalm xxix. 4 (Vulgate) in the *Manual* (1595), a popular Catholic Elizabethan prayer book:

> Thou haste brought my soule out of hell: thou haste holden me vp from falling into the deepe lake, frō whence no man returneth –

where the words 'whence no man returneth' occur neither in the Latin nor the Greek version, and are used solely to make clear that 'the deepe lake' is the Hell of the damned.

‡ *Rationes Decem: Quibus Fretus, Certamen aduersarijs obtulit in causa Fidei, Edmundus Campianus, e Societate Nominis Iesu Presbyter: Allegatae ad clarissimos viros, nostrates Academicos* (1581). For the history of this celebrated little book the reader may be referred to Richard Simpson's *Edmund Campion* or the more recent biography of the author by Evelyn Waugh.

the meaning of the Scriptures and that Anglicans had done the same with those parts which gave too clear a witness against them. But a detailed reference to scriptural texts was beyond the scope of Campion's little book, and he must perforce bide his time in order to answer the more specific charges of Martin which Campion promised his readers would in due course be forthcoming.

> Here I passe ouer (wrote Campion) such things, as they haue depraued in their false translations, though there be intolerable matters wherewith I may well charge them. I am very loath to take away any part of the matter, either from my old Colledge fellow Master Gregory Martin, a man of excellent great knowledge in the three tongues, which will handle this matter farre more learnedly and copiously than I can . . .*

Very well, replied Whitaker, we will wait for this Martin. 'And I doubt not but we shall be able to maintaine our translations, both Latin and English, against your Martin and all your colleagues.'† Which brings us once again to Whitaker's Latin Preface.

This Preface, which is incorporated in his Reply to the eighth book of Nicolas Sander's important *De Visibili Monarchia Ecclesiae*, bears no relation to the substance of that work, but is entirely occupied with Martin's *Discovery* and the Rhemes *New Testament*. It is not very long and handles no great variety of matter, as Whitaker himself confesses, and it was clearly intended as no more than a preliminary skirmish in the attack which was to develop against the Catholic censure of the Protestant translations. Nevertheless, it provoked a reply (the only reply so far as we know), published in the same year, both 'long and large' from William Rainolds, who was assisted in his task by Robert Anderton, the martyr.‡ The title of this work was – *A Refutation of sundry reprehensions, cauils, and false sleightes, by which M. Whitaker laboureth to deface the late English translation,*

* From Richard Stocke's translation of Whitaker's *Responsio: An Answere to the Ten Reasons of Edmund Campian the Iesuit* (London, 1606), p. 22. Campion's original words, of which these are a translation, are to be found towards the end of the 'First Reason', where the sentence concludes – 'nec aliis, quibus id laboris esse iam prae manibus intellexi'.

† ibid., p. 55.

‡ J. H. Pollen, *Acts of English Martyrs* (1891), p. 67, citing the contemporary relation of Fr. William Warford who wrote: '[Anderton] was very proficient in the sacred language [Hebrew], chiefly on account of his intimacy with Gregory Martin and William Reynold, both well skilled in that tongue. He took great pains in helping the latter while he was writing his books, especially against Whitaker'. Anderton suffered in the Isle of Wight, 25 April 1586.

and Catholike annotations of the new Testament, and the booke of Discouery of heretical corruptions. The printer was the Englishman, Richard Verstegan, who was at this time living in Paris.* The length of the book (it consists of nearly 700 pages), together with the difficulties of printing English works abroad, 'where straungers are the workers, cōpositors, & correctors', makes the achievement of getting it through the press in less than a year a remarkable one, and especially so since it is no mere 'huddled up' answer to Whitaker, but exhibits the painstaking and careful scholarship which one would expect from its learned author. In this connexion it is worthy of note that, like Harpsfield and Stapleton, in order to prevent misunderstandings, Rainolds prints in an Advertisement to the Reader a list of those books referred to in the text according to the editions he has used: an unusual procedure, as we have elsewhere pointed out, in those days. He also shows in the same place a scholarly concern for the right usage of the terms he employs, distinguishing carefully between such closely related sects as Sacramentaries, Zwinglians, Calvinists, Puritans, and what he calls Parliament Protestants. Further indication of his erudite treatment of his subject is to be found in the many references in his text to contemporary Bibles, dictionaries, and Catholic and Protestant writings.

Like his Protestant brother John, Rainolds was a born controversialist, though he asserts plainly in his Preface a hearty dislike for the whole business of controversy.

> I vtterly abhorred (he writes) in the middest of my course of studies and better exercises, to spend any good houres ether in reading or refuting heretical bookes, which neuer edifie to vertue, deuotion and saluation, but distract mens mindes from the meditation of al such religious spiritual and heauenly exercise, and fil their heads only with contentions, disputes, and brawles of wordes, *Pugnis verborum*, as the Apostle calleth them, the end whereof (as Tertullian of old noted) is commonly no other, but to wearie our selues, offend the readers, and exasperate the aduersarie, whose proud spirite of contempt and contradiction is lightly incorrigible [sig. a3v].

However, since he is under obedience to answer Whitaker, he has no alternative but to comply with his superiors' request and forthwith take the matter in hand. As his audience is to be an

* Full bibliographical details will be found at bibl. ent. 120.

English one he naturally writes in English, and not as Whitaker had done in the more learned tongue.

The main purpose of Whitaker's book was, as we have seen, to confute Sander, the Preface alone dealing with Martin's two works. Rainolds's immediate object, on the other hand, was, as the title of his book indicates, not to defend Sander, but to vindicate the Catholic translation of the Scriptures. To this end the general body of his work is directed, and when Whitaker complains later in his *Answer* to Rainolds that the latter had 'answered nothing to the principall question' but had 'written onely against the preface',* he is merely demonstrating what is already evident. As far as he (Rainolds) is concerned it is the Preface which contains the offending matter. He deals summarily, therefore, with the attack on Sander in his own Preface, indicting Whitaker upon the general charge of having followed Jewel's method of irrelevant quotation from his opponent's work in order to divert his readers from the main argument. The charge is supported by citation of a number of instances of Whitaker's practice which the writer brings to an end with the following characteristic comment:

> This maner of answering is not to search out the truth, as becometh Diuines, or to bring men into the right way, as is the dutie of Christians, but only to keepe mens heads in musing & expectation of new bookes, to make them mispend their time, to keepe the printers occupied, and as it were to walke and talke on a stage for no other purpose but to passe away the time. This is truly to be *Carnifex papiri. A murderer of paper*, as Illyricus cōmonly calleth the Zuinglians. this is in deede to be *Miserabilis librifex*, A miserable bookewright, as Luther malapertly nameth king Henry, a learned prince and of famous memory [sig. f1].

The mordant quality of the style which is discernible even in this short passage, and which is certainly the most effective rhetorical weapon that Rainolds has in his armoury, presages the method of attack which he is most consistently to employ in the main body of his work in ridiculing his opponents' attempts at interpreting the text of Holy Scripture in accordance with the Protestant system of belief. In turning, therefore, to our author's text, wherein *his* principal question is handled, we

* *An answere to a certein Booke, written by Maister William Rainolds* . . . (1585), sig. A3v.

may fitly focus our attention upon those passages which will illustrate more cogently this distinctive mark of his style. In the first, which ends with a sly hit at the Regius Professor of Divinity in the University of Cambridge, he would seem openly to testify to this characteristic method of baiting his adversary. The priestly office is in question:

> If he say Christ is a priest for euer: we affirme no lesse. that his priesthod passeth not from him: it is our beleefe. that the force and vertue thereof endureth for euer: we liue and die therein and all the baptismes, recōciliations, sacrifice, sacramentes, al grace, vertue, sanctification, which is in the church Catholike, dependeth of this faith, and floweth from the eternity of this one euerliuinge priest and priesthode. But will he inferre hereof, that therefore there ought to be no other inferior priestes, and that this derogateth from his priesthode? this lo, is so chyldish, that amongest meane learned diuines, it deserueth rather laughter then answeare. *Christe is a priest for euer, therefore there are no priestes:* whie, then let vs argue, Christ is a true man for euer, therefore we are not, or he hath a soule for euer, therefore we haue none, or he is a kinge for euer, therefore let vs depose all princes, and remoue princelie authoritie. Christ is our doctor, maister, and teacher for euer, and so farewel al maisters, and doctors, & so the Eschequer shal saue that, which the Q. Maiestie bestoweth on the Vniuersitie readers . . . [sig. E6v–7].

The element of ridicule, palpably present in this extract, is perhaps even more strongly evident in that which follows. The passage has reference to the Protestant appeal to the literal translation of the Scriptures as opposed to the traditional interpretation of terms according to ecclesiastical usage:

> Let vs suppose in our grandfathers time, some Catholike priest or Byshop in our realme to haue exhorted his people to charitie, deuotion, & reformation of their liues. Suppose he spake vnto them in this sorte.
>
> I that am your *priest* & *bishop*, placed in this *church* by the *holy Ghost* for the feeding of your sowles, do denounce vnto you in the name of *Christ* our *Lord*, that except you with more deuotion come to receaue the *B. Sacrament*, and performe better your promise made to God in *baptisme*, you shal be bodie and sowle condemned to *hell*: your portion shal be with the *deuils*, I say with *Beelzebub* and his *angels*. The meaning of this euery Christian doth know, and no doubt it might and I thinke would moue a Christian audience. Let vs now after your translations, turne the same into the phrase and stile of the new gospel, and see how it wil sound. Let vs suppose some of your

> youthful ministers or superintēdēts to make the same exhortatiō. Thē thus must it rūne.
>
> I that am your *elder* or *surueyer* and *superintendent*, placed in this *synagoge* by the *holy wynd*, for the feeding of your *carcasses*, do denounce vnto you in the name of the *Anointed* our *Baal*, that except yow with more deuotion come to receaue the thankesgeuing, and performe better your promise made to God in *washing*, you shal be condemned bodie and *carcas* to the *graue*, with the *slaunderers*, I say with the *Lord of a flye* and his *messengers*. How deepely this would sinke into the hartes of your Euangelical auditorie, let their owne conscience be iudge [sig. R6v–7].

But perhaps the most downright example in this kind is to be found in a passage where the writer, in answer to Whitaker's stricture upon the 'monstrous noueltie of wordes' in the Rhemes *New Testament*, turns the tables on his opponents by showing how 'vpon most childish affectation to seeme somwhat skilful in the hebrew, [they] reduce al sacred names to the old Iudaical sound'. He quotes in evidence Oecolampadius's translation of the proper names in Esaias I. i.: 'The vision of Iesaaiahu the sonne of Amoz, which he saw vpon Iehudah and vpon Hierusalem in the daies of *Yziiahu, Iotham, Ahhaz, Iehhizkiiahu, Kinges of Iehudah*.' 'Why for Christ vse they not Ieschua,' he goes on to ask, 'for our Lady, Miriā, for S. Peter, Cepha' &c., and concludes, 'If their owne eares abhor this wanton curiositie, and their owne iudgment tel thē it is apish arrogancie, & peevish affectation of popular praise, let them confesse the like in pronouncing Beltshazzar, Nebucadnezzar, Iehuda Iehhizkiiahu, for Baltasar, Nabugodonosor, Iuda, Ezechias. for the case is al one.'*

It must, of course, be admitted that a work which depends for its final effect as much on the proved statement as on the vigour of a keen wit cannot be securely judged only from such *disjecta membra* as have here been offered. In fact these very extracts, to give them their full significance, would require to be quoted in their complete contextual setting, a course which, unfortunately, it is not possible to follow, at least generally, in this present work. We must be content, therefore, with the procedure we have followed, here as elsewhere, of confining our attention to certain prominent features of our author's style, leaving the reader himself to pursue the subject further, should

* sig. Ff4–5 *passim*.

he be so disposed. And in this connexion perhaps we may be allowed one word more before we conclude this notice. We have already referred on a previous page to the fact that many of these Recusant works may justly be regarded as source-books, not only of linguistic usage and idiomatic expression, but also of contemporary life and letters. Rainolds's *Refutation of Whitaker* is no exception to this general rule, and is fairly rich in Elizabethan locutions and proverbial expressions and in references to contemporaneous objects and events. To bring to an end, therefore, this somewhat hurried review, let me append a few scattered examples which may serve as specimens of what our author's work has to yield in this kind. Here, for instance, is a piece of invective which, in its use of a natural and familiar idiom and in the vigour of its phrasing, is essentially Elizabethan in its general complexion:

> Now graunt we al these faults of *tautologia*, an *absurde sentence*, an *idle repetition* &c. where lie these faults? doubtlesse not so much in the Euangelist, who wrote them, as in our Sauiour who spake them. Suppose I say it seeme harde to your delicate and Ciceronian eares. must therefore Christ be sett to schole to learne his lesson of that fierbrande of sedition, that sinke & gulfe of iniquitie Theodore Beza? and what is the absurditie you find in these words? mary that *that which was in the chalice was shedde for our sinnes*, and therefore consequently, it was the real bloud of our Sauiour, which is plaine Papistrye and against our Communion booke. Is it so? Then to hell with your Communion booke, and you to, if that be so opposite to the Gospel of Christ, & you dare mainteyne it by open checking and controling Christ the eternall wisdome of God [sig. P8v].

So, likewise, is this short comment on the 1562 reprint of the Great Bible:

> Only the English translator of the yere 1562. foloweth nether the 70. nor greeke, nor latin, but the brainsicke fansie of his owne head, making a mingle mangle, and thrusting in a patch of his owne [sig. V4v].

Proverbial expressions afford further examples of Elizabethan usage. For *an argument of little or no value* we read:

> [they] are withall as cōmon, as are the Postilions bootes [sig. M2].

To proclaim the obvious is expressed in:

> an obiection, as common & plaine to them that know oughte in diuinitie as Dunstable hye way [sig. E1v].

Wasted labour is:

> to cast water into the Tems, or light a candel at noone daye [sig. R4].

And *stale news* is graphically set forth in:

> to be matched with such blunt aduersaries whose maner of writing is now to cloy vs with *crābe recocta, coleworts twise*, yea tē times *sodden*, & nether thē selues can bring any new stuffe, nor scoure more brightlie or otherwise mend vp their old [sig. S6ᵛ].

As for contemporary references, Henry VIII's jester, Will Summers, receives this mention:

> to babble about the mettal of the chalice, is more meete for William Sommer the Kings iester, then for M. William Whitaker the Quenes reader [sig. P5ᵛ] –

a parallel possibly inspired by the *History of the Life and Death of Will Summers*, if we may conjecture so early a date for that work.*

The Vice of the Elizabethan stage is thus alluded to:

> Such kinde of iesting would better become some merie felow making sport vpon a stage, with a furred hood & a wooddē dagger, thē either a learned bishop, such as M. Iewel tooke him selfe to be, or a profound Reader of diuinitie, as I think M. W. would gladly be accounted [sig. Kk6].

And, finally, here is a reference to the Puritan monster, which was already beginning to raise its formidable head in the mid-years of Elizabeth:

> Reade M. Carliles disputation† which publikely he mainteined in your Vniuersitie . . . Much more hath he against your bibles which you so loue as being perfect and immaculate, and by verie many plaine demonstrations proueth them to be so filthelie corrupted, as they rather resemble Mahomets Alcoran, then the word of the holie Ghost [sig. S1].

* The earliest known edition is, I believe, that of 1676, but this is almost certainly a reprint of a sixteenth-century work.

† *A Discourse concerning two divine Positions* (1582), by Christopher Carlile, fellow of Clare Hall, Cambridge.

CHAPTER V

MISCELLANEOUS WORKS

TOGETHER WITH A NOTE ON THE SCOTTISH WRITERS

THE doctrinal and devotional works which have been the subject of our study in the two preceding chapters are clearly the most important element of our early Recusant literature. But they by no means constitute the whole of it. There still remains a number of works of a more general nature which could not strictly be included in these chapters, but without which no survey of our period could be complete. They embrace the writings of such well-known names as Allen, Campion, John Leslie, Martin and Sander, all of whom, with the exception of Leslie, we have already met. The principal of these writings will, therefore, be our chief concern in this penultimate chapter of our thesis. Before we close the chapter we shall refer very briefly to those Scottish writers who also contributed to the Catholic cause.

We may begin with Allen, who by virtue of his position among the Recusants and by reason of his importance as a writer deserves our first consideration.

WILLIAM ALLEN

The two further works which concern us here are Allen's *An Apologie and true declaration of the institution and endeuours of the two English Colleges, the one in Rome, the other now resident in Rhemes: against certaine sinister informations giuen vp against the same* (1581), and, supplementary to this, his *A Briefe Historie of the Glorious Martyrdom of xii. Reuerend Priests* (1582), both published by John Fogny of Rhemes. Both works contribute to our historical knowledge of the Recusant movement, and the first, the *Apologie*, most certainly establishes Allen's reputation as a writer of English prose.

The nature and scope of this work will be better understood if we briefly recall the circumstances which led to its writing. For these we must go back to the beginning of the year 1580. At that time information reached Elizabeth's Government through Cobham, the English ambassador at Paris, of a Grand

Papal League said to have been arranged between Rome, Spain and Tuscany for the invasion of England.* Cobham's information was later confirmed by a document (counterfeit, as it has since turned out) which came into his hands through the agency of John Leslie, Bishop of Ross, Mary Stuart's former advocate and ambassador, purporting to set out the aims and objects of the League in ten articles.† Leslie's object in acting thus as the devil's advocate seems to have been to curry favour with the English ambassador in the interest of his mistress. It is difficult to believe that he could have foreseen the consequences of his action. Especially is it difficult to understand his motives for compromising Dr. Goldwell, the aged bishop of St. Asaph, and Dr. Morton (and, incidentally, Allen, with whom at this time these two were closely associated), whom he named as agents for carrying out the proposals in the articles. The fact remains that the result of it all was an increase in the persecution at home and a further attempt on the part of the English Government to hamper and, if possible, to bring to an end the activities of the English seminaries abroad. The immediate consequence was the Queen's Proclamation of 15 July 1580 against traitors in foreign parts, appealing for political loyalty from all subjects of the realm, and threatening those who were disaffected. Though there is no explicit reference in this Proclamation to the colleges, it is clearly indicated in the wording that the Government at home believed that the League was being fostered and promoted by Allen and his fellow exiles. The opening sentences will show this:

> The Queenes Maiestie findeth the continuance, or rather increase of the traiterous and malitious purposes, and solicitations of such Rebels and Traitours as doe liue in forraine partes, and ioyning to them others that are fled out of the Realme, as persons refusing to liue here in their natural countrey, both which of long time haue wandred from place to place, & from one Princes Court to another, but specially to the Citie of Rome, and therein haue falsely and traiterously sought and practised by all meanes possible, to irritate all estates against her Maiestie and the Realme, and therewith, as much as in

* The history of this bogus league has been fully treated by Fr. J. H. Pollen in *The English Catholics in the Reign of Queen Elizabeth*, pp. 236 et seq.; cf. also the same, p. 339.

† According to Pollen, Cobham sent in the news to the English Government about 2 July, 1580.

> them might lye, to moue hostilitie, wherein by Gods goodnesse and speciall fauour to this Realme, their desseignes haue bene hitherto frustrate: yet for a further demonstration of the increase of their rancour, they haue caused to be deuised in writings, & the same haue published, that the Pope, the King of Spaine, and some other Princes are accorded to make a great Armie to inuade this Realme of Englande, and other her Maiesties Dominions, and to dispose of the Crowne, and of the possessions of the Subiectes, and of the Realme at their pleasure, thereby intending to moue the people of the Realme to some murmuring as they imagine, whereby some of theirparteners might be made bolder to persist in their unduetifulnesse, some others to be afrayde to continue duetifull. . . .*

Allen understood the imputation. Three months previously (2 April 1580) he had himself returned from Rome to Rhemes, whither he had been on the business of the two colleges, accompanied by Fr. Thomas Darbishire, S.J., Dr. Bavant, Dr. Sanderson, Dr. Humphrey Ely and others, and shortly afterwards Goldwell and Morton, Leslie's two promoters of the League, had joined him there; in the *Apologie* he admits that a mission had been sent during the first half of the year (1580) from the college at Rhemes to the Papal Court for the purpose of enlisting further help from the Pope; nor does he doubt that other members of the English community abroad had probably visited the courts of other princes for a like reason, though he will not speak certainly of this; but he denies stoutly any knowledge whatsoever concerning the articles of confederation between the Pope, the King of Spain and other princes for an invasion of England, and asserts strongly that there was no truth in the rumour that he and his fellow Rhemists were engaged in stirring up arms against the motherland.†

We may understand, then, from the *Apologie* itself that Allen regarded the July Proclamation as aimed principally at the two seminaries which he was now called upon to defend. A letter from the Cardinal of Como, written in November or December in reply to some letter of Allen's concerning the same edict,‡ commending the idea of his writing in their defence and asking

* Dyson's *Proclamations* (B. M. Grenville, 6463). A condensed version of the Proclamation will be found in Pollen, op. cit., p. 340.

† References from *Douay Diaries*, under date 2 April 1580, and *Apologie*, Chapter II.

‡ Allen had previously sent to the Cardinal a copy of the Proclamation; cf. Simpson, *Edmund Campion*, p. 237.

for a copy of the work when it is finished, confirms this view. The Cardinal writes:

> Consilium tuum de conscribenda Apologia placet, ea praesertim ratione ut nihil procaciter nec contumeliose in alios, ut decet Christi athletas atque discipulos; sed cum perfeceris mittes ad nos.*

And if further justification be needed as to what the Proclamation of July intended, we have it in a second Proclamation of 10 January 1581 'for reuocation of Students from beyond the seas, and against the reteining of Iesuites'. This Proclamation is both more explicit and stronger than the former, and its object was pretty obviously to try to kill the seminaries. Amongst other things it enjoins the return within four months of all students from the colleges abroad, and forbids their parents and others to send them money or means of support if they remain away. A clause requiring the Queen's licence for any person or persons departing out of the realm aims at cutting off the supply of recruits to the seminaries. It further seeks to deter Catholic missionaries by denouncing all receivers and favourers of Jesuits, seminary men, or other such persons, and by offering monetary reward to informers or utterers who should cause their apprehension.† How far such an edict was likely to achieve its aim may be judged from the comment upon it which occurs in the following passage of the *Apologie*:

> For, these late terrours (thanks be to God) trouble them [the seminarists] so litle, that diuers straight vpon the arriual here in Rhemes of the late Proclamation of Ianuarie, came to their Superiors, to desire leaue to go in: and being answered that the times were not seasonable, they said, it was no Godamercie for a Priest to enter in at other times, but that they were brought vp and made specially for such daies: and nineteene persons, the same weeke folowing, tooke holy Orders. Such is their desire: but for their going in, they shall be moderated as reason requireth [L5v].

We may take it that this second Proclamation came to Allen's notice when his book was already under way, and possibly it speeded his writing of the defence. Anyhow, the work seems to

* *Letters and Memorials*, p. 92.

† Dyson, as before. A Latin version of the edict will be found in Bridgewater's *Concertatio* (1588), fols. 243–4, where with the later edict of 1 April 1581, in which Jesuits and other traitor priests are denounced, it prefaces a Latin version of Allen's *Apologie*.

have been well advanced by March 1581, when he sent a copy of what he had written to Rome for the making of the Latin version. This we learn from a letter of Bishop Goldwell, dated from Rome, 17 April 1581, in reply it would seem to instructions he had received from Allen in respect of the proposed translation. Goldwell writes:

> Upon the xiv^th^ of thys monthe after evynsonge I recevyd your letters of the xiv^th^ of the last monthe, but not the part of your Apollogy, by cause the father gave hyt to be translate as sone as he had red your letter. Wherfore the next day, as sone as I had sayd masse, I went to the colledge and informed Father Rectore* that owt of Ingland yow have byn prayed to use no words nor termes towards the Qwene but honorable, for feare lest hyt shold torne to the power catholycks more trouble at home. I ordeyned also that in the titull shold be wryttyn *Autore Gulielmo Alano Praesidente Collegii Remensis*, and that the colleges shold be called the Popes colleges, wyth suche other thyngs as yourself ordeyne in your letters.†

A few weeks later, probably some time in May, Allen's difficult and delicate task was completed, and by the middle of June copies of the printed English version of the work were in process of distribution amongst both Catholics and Protestants in the mother country.‡ Allen, we are told, himself sent a copy 'through a merchant in Paris to the English ambassador, Sir Henry Cobham, who forwarded it to Walsingham', 15 June 1581,§ and he believed that Queen Elizabeth herself was presented with a copy which she read.|| The wide approval of the book by both Catholic and Protestant readers is witnessed to in a contemporary letter from some unknown priest to Fr. Agazzari, cited by Simpson, which states:

> The Queen published some outrageous proclamations against all Jesuits, priests, scholars of seminaries, and against the col-

* Fr. Alfonso Agazario (Agazzari), the Italian Jesuit, who had recently succeeded Dr. Maurice Clenock as Rector of the English College.

† *Letters and Memorials*, pp. 92–3.

‡ See Allen's letter of 23 June 1581 to Fr. Alphonsus Agazzari, where he writes: '[Fr. Persons] dicit omnia ibi recte procedere et Apologiam nostram valde probari' (i.e. in England); and the further quotation below. Both quotations from *Letters and Memorials*, pp. 96 and 98.

§ Martin Haile, *An Elizabethan Cardinal, William Allen* (1914), p. 192. The date is Simpson's; op. cit., p. 528.

|| 'Nostra Apologia (ut audio) versatur in manibus tam adversariorum quam amicorum, et illius amplissimae legationis Gallicae princeps, qui vocatur Princeps Delfinus [i.e. the Prince Dauphin of Auvergne] dedit eam legendam ipsi Reginae.' Letter as above.

> leges themselves. But Dr. William Allen, who may most justly be called the father of this vineyard, wrote an apology for them with such prudence, moderation, and weight of argument, that the heretics themselves, ready enough to be offended, praised his book highly, while the Catholics gained no little increase by it.*

A belated reply to the *Apologie* was made by Dr. Thomas Bilson, Warden of Winchester, who devotes the first two parts of his *The true difference betweene christian subiection and vnchristian rebellion*, published in 1585, to this end.

The reader will have already met with two passages from Allen's masterly defence of the seminaries in the second chapter of this book,† and from these he may gather somewhat of Edmund Bolton's meaning when he calls the *Apologie* 'A Princely, graue, and flourishing Peice of natural, and exquisite *English*'.‡ The attractiveness of Allen's writing is indeed undeniable, and even in the two short extracts referred to we may discern the persuasive force which owes little or nothing to self-conscious artistry, but which springs from an open, generous, and withal intensely vivid nature. The sustained eloquence of his appeal never falters throughout the 220 pages of this little octavo volume, and at every point this reader at any rate is conscious of a sincere and impassioned mind. Allen writes because he must; and if, in the illustrations which follow, the careful marshalling of the subordinate elements in the sentence and in the paragraph appear to be purposive in the way they throw more strongly into relief and enforce the essential matter of the discourse, this may be ascribed to the natural clearness, discipline, and orderliness of his mind.

He divides the actual Apology into six short chapters, which are described in the 'Contents' in the following manner:

(1) The reason of our absence and liuing out of our natiue Countrie.

(2) Of our resorting sometimes to the citie and court of Rome.

(3) The meaning and purpose of the institution of the Seminaries.

* op. cit., p. 288. The letter is dated July 1581.

† Above, pp. 15–16 and 18–20.

‡ *Hypercritica* (ed. by Anthony Hall, 1722), p. 233. According to the Calendar of State Papers, as cited by Martin Haile, *Cardinal Allen* (as before), p. 182, Edmund Bolton (1575?–1633) was a Catholic, but allowed to live in peace to that conscience in which he was bred. Fr. J. H. Pollen states that he was a Protestant in his reprint of Allen's *Briefe Historie* (1908).

(4) That we liue not in them against the lawes of God and our Countrie: with a duetiful exhortation to the Queenes Maiestie.

(5) That the Students therof be not trained vp in erroneous doctrine.

(6) Of Priests and Iesuites, and for what cause they are sent into England.

To these is added a seventh chapter, addressed to the persecuted Catholics at home, and entitled 'An admonition and comfort to the afflicted Catholikes'. No writing of Allen's mirrors more faithfully his mind and his temper than does this last chapter, which is a model of that sustained eloquence to which we have referred, and which perhaps surpasses all else that he wrote in English in this kind.

In the following two passages, and many others might easily be selected, the reader will note the simplicity of the language and the rhythmic sweep of sentence and paragraph, which combine to create that almost perfect harmony of utterance which is the peculiar grace of Allen's style in this work. The first is taken from Chapter IV:

> We answer then, that if the lawes of God and the lawes of the Realme did alwaies consent and concurre in deede, as in this clause and other common writings and speaches proceding from authoritie, they be lightly in wordes couched together against vs: hardly could we defend our doctrines and doings from errour and vndutiefulnes towards our Prince. But seing the lawes of Kings and Countries are not euer consonant but may be contrarie to Gods commaundemēts, we may iustly mislike the one without disloyaltie to the other . . . If our Prince or Realme had the promis that their faith should not faile, that Hel gates should not preuaile against thē, that Christ would be with them to the end of the world, that when so euer they meete together in consultations, him self would be in the middes of them: that the holy Spirit should perpetually direct them into al truth, that he would be in their mouth, and the mouth of their childrē, and the mouth of their childrens children euerlastingly: if in doubtes of doctrine we were by the Scriptures referred to them, if the States there assembled might iustly vse this clause of ancient Councels, *It hath pleased the holy Ghost and vs:* then should our Statute-lawes euer cōcurre with Gods lawes, and the breach of one sort should condēne vs of trāsgression of both. Wherof now we neede not feare, knowing that no temporal King, nor Commonwealth, hath such priuileges of

Gods protection, being the special prerogatiues of the Churches tribunals: whose lawes therfore neuer swarue frō Christes commaundements, as our Parliaments haue done (by our Aduersaries iudgement) al these worldes past together, and we are sure that these later haue done, and that al other presuming to determine of matters Ecclesiastical must needes do.

And it were the pitifullest hazard, and vncertainty of our faith and saluation, that could be, so to hang on the Princes will, or the lawes (commonly wholy thereon depending) that there could be imagined no neerer way to religion, then to beleeue what our tēporal Lord and Maister list. And it is the turpitude of our Nation through the whole world, whereat we blush before strāgers that sometimes fall into discourse of such things, that in one mans memorie and since this strange mutation began, we haue had to our Prince, a man, who abolished the Popes authoritie by his lawes, and yet in other pointes kept the faith of his fathers: we haue had a child, who by the like lawes abolished together with the Papacie, the whole ancient religion: we had a woman, who restored both againe, and sharply punished Protestants: and lastly her Ma.[tie] that now is, who by the like lawes hath long since abolished both againe, and now seuerely punisheth Catholikes, as the other did Protestants: and al these strange differences within the compasse of about 30 yeres.

* * *

These strange and vnnatural dealings, these procedings dishonorable to her Ma.[tie] and the Realme, these lawes against Gods expresse comaundements which prescribe obedience and subiection to our Prelates, these decrees that limite Gods constant and permanent truth to the mutabilitie of temporal statutes, to mortal mens willes and fansies: these are the lawes of the Realme (and not the Ciuil ordinances of our Prince) that we refuse to obey: and which not onely in our life and doctrine, but vnto death and yelding our bloud, we trust to withstand: wishing that so at the least God wil haue mercie on our Countrie, and wipe away the ignominie of such violent disorders, which to all our posteritie must needes breede shame and rebuke, and to vs Gods indignation [sigs. E1, 2 and 5].

Our second passage comes from the beautiful *Admonition*:

Our daies can not be many, because we be men: neither can it be either godly or worldly wisdom, for a remnant of three or foure yeres, and perchance not so many moneths, to hazard the losse of all eternity. They can not be good in these euil times, much like to those wherof S. Polycarpe complained thus: *Lord, vnto what times hast thou reserued vs?* And were they neuer so many or good, to him that refuseth his faith and Maister, they shal neuer be ioyful, but deadly and doleful. Corporally die once we must euery one, and but once, and there vpon immediatly iudgemēt, where the Confessor shal be acknowledged, and the Denyer denyed againe.

No Martyrdom of what length or torment so euer, can be more greuous, then a long sicknes and a languishing death: and he that departeth vpon the pillow, hath as litle ease as he that dieth vpon the gallowes, blocke, or bouchers knife. And our Maisters death, both for paines and ignominie, passed both sortes, and all other kinds either of Martyrs or malefactors. Let no tribulation then, no perill, no prison, no persecution, no life, no death separate vs from the charity of God, and the society of our sweete Sauiours passions, by and for whose loue we shal haue the victory in all these conflictes. Neuerthelesse, if by Gods suffering, for causes hidden vnto vs, any shrinke (which Christ forbid) for feare of death, torments, or tribulations, from the felowship of your happy confession and crownes prepared for the same, as in the time of S. Cyprian and alwaies diuers did, and as one of the 40 did, whose glorious fight S. Basil describeth, and the Church celebrateth the 9 of Marche: be not scandalized or troubled thereat, but vse such with all lenitie, taking compassion of their infirmitie, considering that your selues also, or any of vs all, may be tempted and ouerthrowen with Peter, and by Gods grace afterward repent and rise with him againe. Though it be perilous to presume theron, many mo folowing him in his fall and miserie, then attayning to his Martyrdom and mercie [sig. P5v–6].

Allen's aim in this work, we may say, is 'to give forth what he has within him'; he has something to *say* rather than something to *write*; and though we may discover some of those traits of style which we observed when dealing with his *Defense* and his *Treatise* in a former chapter,* yet here, perhaps more than in any other place, he writes, not according to rule, but out of the 'abundant spring' of his own enthusiasm, and in this lies the secret strength of his simple but eloquent appeal.

Whatever bitterness Allen may display in his writings against the Adversary springs without doubt from that persecution, even unto death, which was meted out to so many of his former students and associates. The martyrdom of such men as Edmund Campion, Ralph Sherwin, and Alexander Briant, on 1 December 1581, and the further execution of eight more com-

* Chapter III above.

panions of the Faith in the ensuing months, was truly sufficient to dry up the springs of even his abundant charity. How far this may have influenced his later political decisions it is difficult to say. It would seem that some idea of a policy of appeasement had been present in his mind when he published his *Apologie* in the middle of 1581, a work which is remarkable for the moderation of its expression. It is certain that as the worthlessness of such a policy began to be apparent in the increased persecution of the Catholics by the English Government, so, too, Allen's outlook seems to change, perhaps fundamentally, and we find him adopting in his letters and his other writings a much more openly hostile attitude towards Elizabeth and her Ministers. Before this mid-period of the Queen's reign we can hardly conceive, for instance, that he would have written quite in the vein of the memorandum to the Pope entitled 'A short Note of the standing conditions of affairs in England, to show the easiness and opportuneness of the *sacred expedition*' (*c.* 1584), cited at length by Simpson and roundly denounced by him as puerile;* or in the manner of his reply to Burghley's *Execution of Justice*, in which he sets out to prove, among other things (to quote his own words), 'that it is not only lawful, but even our bounden duty to take up arms at the Pope's bidding, and to fight for the Catholic faith against the Queen and other heretics';† or that he would have penned the libellous *Admonition to the Nobility and People of England* (1588). Be this as it may, there can be no doubt that he felt the persecution of his brethren bitterly, and was herein confirmed in his resolution to compel the attention of Catholic Europe to the state of religion in England by spreading abroad the story of the martyrs which is set out in his *A Briefe Historie*, published in the early autumn of 1582.

The necessity for such action on Allen's part was not lessened by the action of the Adversaries. Very soon after the deaths of Campion, Sherwin and Briant, Anthony Munday and others had been publishing broadsides and pamphlets in defence of the Government‡ and in reply to Thomas Alfield's *True Report*

* *Edmund Campion*, as before, pp. 477 et seq.

† The reply is entitled *A True Sincere and Modest Defence of English Catholiques that suffer for their Faith both at home and abrode*, and was published in 1584, shortly before the Note to the Pope.

‡ A bibliography of these works will be found in Simpson's *Edmund Campion*, Appendix, pp. 495 et seq.

(see below). These were crowned eventually by the official account of the martyrdoms published by the Council some time in June 1582, and this required something like an official answer. Allen was the obvious person to do this job, and we may take it that his *Historie* was ultimately intended to be the Catholic reply to that document.

The Council's action in drawing up this paper seems to have been determined by the spreading influence of the Catholic reports of the martyrdoms. 'England and the Continent', writes Simpson, 'were inundated with accounts of the martyrs. By January 4, 1582, a French account was published;* and on the 14th of that month Cobham wrote to Walsingham that the book was "cried in the streets with outcries, naming them to be cruelties used by the Queen's majesty in England" . . . On the 23rd of March, 1582, Anthony Standen wrote from Florence to Mannering at Paris, "The discourse of the deaths of those good men at home is familiar in these parts to the best sort, and our cases more pitied than heretofore, as by certain letters exhortatory from his Holiness to all princes for the succour and support of the seminary in Rheims is manifest, those being directed to all archbishops and bishops, to make gatherings and collections for that purpose".'† In this diffusion of a Catholic relation of the martyrdoms Allen had a hand almost from the beginning, as we may learn from his letters written to Fr. Agazzari from Rhemes at this time.‡ Thus, in an early letter dated 7 February, he sends, as he states, certain exemplars of a collection of engravings, some printed on pure silk, some on paper, for distribution in Rome.§ One, rather better than the rest, he intends for the Pope. Others were to be given to Cardinal Moroni, the Protector of England; to the Cardinal of Como; to the Fr. General of the Jesuits; and to Goldwell, the Bishop of St. Asaph. Further copies would follow, in order that there might be plenty of them to spread abroad (*ut abundetis*).

* This French translation of Alfield's *True Report* was the earliest published version of that work. The Privilegium is dated 30 December 1581. For further details, see bibl. ent. 9.

† op. cit., pp. 468–9, quoting S.P.O. France, 4 January 1582 and S.P.O. Italian States, 23 March 1582.

‡ The Latin originals of these letters may be found in *Letters and Memorials* under their various dates.

§ These were evidently those prints, representing a martyr's progress, which were included in the Italian version of the *Briefe Historie*, published at Macerata in 1583, and which Fr. Persons appended to his *De Persecutione Anglicana* of 1582.

There is a final expression of hope that a larger history of the Acts of the English Martyrs will in due course be possible (*Nos meditamur prolixiorem de martyrio et actis istorum in Anglia historiam, si Deus vitam et quietem dederit*). Five days later, on 12 February, he fulfils his promise of more copies of the engravings, which he encloses in a note recording details of the constancy of the Confessors just received from a special messenger arrived recently from England and from Fr. Robert Persons. Further letters of March and April witness to his continued activity in disseminating the information which he is patiently collecting for that 'larger history' of which he speaks. In face of this and the like provocation, the English Government were under the necessity of framing some reply in defence of their policy, and as a preliminary measure they published some time in June the tract, said to have been drawn up by Burghley himself, entitled *A particular declaration or testimony, of the vndutifull and traiterous affection borne against her Maiestie by Edmund Campion Iesuite, and other condemned Priestes, witnessed by their owne confessions: in reproofe of those slaunderous bookes & libels deliuered out to the contrary by such as are malitiously affected towards her Maiestie and the state*. The purpose of this tract was to show from documentary evidence that the execution of the martyrs had taken place not on account of 'points that concerned matters of conscience, but for treason', and to this end, besides the inclusion of certain other matter, the confessions of Campion, Sherwin and Briant, and of ten others, viz. Luke Kirbie, Thomas Cottam, Laurence Richardson, Thomas Forde, John Sherte, Robert Johnson, John Hart, William Filbie, James Bosgrave and Henry Orton, were set out for all to see. In order to meet this challenge Allen immediately set about the publication of such evidence as he had been able to collect in support of the martyrs' case.

So much is plain from his letter to Fr. Agazzari of 23 June.

> Even as I write (he says) there has come to me a history written by the heretics concerning the deaths of the aforesaid martyred priests, from which, in spite of its source, one can quite easily discover their unchanging constancy and how greatly the Adversary strove to draw even one of them over to his side. We are publishing here forthwith a true account of the whole affair, which you shall have by the grace of God within one month.

Actually it was rather more than two months before his work was complete. Meantime he kept Agazzari informed of its progress. On 17 July he writes:

> I have already written concerning my sore affliction at the fate of our martyred brethren, ours and yours, and now it falls to my lot to write an account of their deaths and also the deaths of certain others, in English first, because my compatriots strongly desire this and have sent instructions to that effect, afterwards also, maybe, in Latin. Here you will see in all respects the constancy of the martyrs of old; and the effect has been to move and to change the minds of men marvellously, the good or the indifferent to penitence, the bad and the hostile to wonder. Truly the shedding of so much innocent blood has a strong appeal. Many thousands of sermons could not have revealed the splendour of the faith and of the apostolic religion as the savour of these holy sacrifices, sweet-smelling to God and to men, has done. The rest of the confessors become more fervent, our own people here become keener, the harvest becomes more abundant. With God as our leader, by labour and constancy we shall conquer; moreover, our enemies are angrier than ever, for they wholly despair. I am continually being sent fresh material upon which to work. What with this and looking after the college and the rest of our own affairs I am almost worn out, especially since, in respect of the business of writing, I am further handicapped owing to the death and illness of Bristow and Martin, there being hardly anyone here who can help me in this kind of work.

A month later (16 August) he sends Agazzari some advance sheets of the publication:

> I am sending to you, or rather to the Rev. Fr. Confessor and to George Gilbert, in order that they may translate it for you and for others, the martyrology which we have got ready as far as our employment allowed. By this means the martyrology which you yourself purpose will be more complete. To it I have prefixed an epistle to vindicate the innocence of our martyrs – a few pages which I hope will be acceptable to our men. The work is now in the press. I enclose some advance sheets; the rest I shall send by the next messenger. We shall send further and more perfect copies by our scholastics. If the whole History should be translated into Latin and Italian it would please us much and would, I believe, edify all. The work has been written in English in the first place for the use of our countrymen. They specially asked me to do this, because it is a great help to those at home and is a source of inspiration to them in this altogether wonderful struggle. I do not believe the martyrs of the early Church were put to greater trial than these.

Finally, on 3 September, a copy of the complete work is forwarded to Fr. Agazzari with the words:

> I now send a copy of the complete work (*integrum libellum*) about our martyrs, which formerly I transmitted to you in parts as it came from the press. We should like someone either from the College or the Society to translate it into Latin, since we have no one here to spare who is accomplished enough for this kind of work.

According to the excellent custom of the times the title of Allen's book briefly summarizes for us what the book contains. Here it is: *A Briefe Historie of the Glorious Martyrdom of xii. Reuerend Priests, executed within these tweluemonethes for confession and defence of the Catholike Faith. But vnder the false pretence of Treason. With a note of sundrie things that befel them in their life and imprisonment: and a preface declaring their innocencie. Set furth by such as were much conuersant with them in their life, and present at their arraignement and death.* The naming of twelve martyred priests only in the title, '*executed within these twelve months*', was doubtless due to Allen's intention to emphasize the connexion of his book with the current persecution. Actually the records of fifteen martyrs are set out, the additional names being those of Cuthbert Maine, John Nelson, and the layman, Thomas Sherwood, the three forerunners of the Jesuit and Seminarist martyrs. Of the thirteen priests referred to in the Government pamphlet as having been subjected to examination, Allen omits in his recapitulation of their confessions John Hart's 'answer', which he refused to subscribe to, and the answers of John Bosgrave and Henry Orton, which were in the nature of recantations. The twelve priests of our title thus include the names of ten of these thirteen, together with two more which fall within the twelvemonth period, viz.: Edmund Campion, Ralph Sherwin, Alexander Briant (m. 1 December 1581), Thomas Forde, John Sherte, Robert Johnson (m. 28 May 1582), William Filbie, Luke Kirbie, Laurence Richardson, Thomas Cottam (m. 30 May 1582), John Paine (m. 2 April 1582), and Everard Haunse (m. 31 July 1581). The documents which Allen saw fit to publish as witnessing to the constancy of these martyrs are detailed in the bibliography which forms the second part of this volume and need not be repeated here. We would remark only, in this connexion, that Thomas Alfield's *True Report*, which we shall be considering directly, was incorporated almost *in toto* in Allen's book and, indeed, forms the nucleus of his records in much the same way as these later became the core of Bridgewater's *Concertatio*, that invaluable treatise, which in its second and enlarged edition of 1588 contained 'notices of more than a hundred martyrs, and six hundred confessors, exiles and other sufferers for the Faith'.

It would hardly be worth our while to reproduce passages illustrative of Allen's literary manner in this work. Its main interest lies in the information it supplies with regard to the last days of these Confessors, and from the point of view of style bears no sort of comparison with, say, a book like the *Apologie*. There are, as Fr. Pollen has pointed out, no passages of sustained rhetoric or ingenious argument. The writer has one object, and one object only, namely to set before us the death-scene, as viewed by eyewitnesses. He gives their words as far as he can, reproducing even their use of the first person singular.* This, often sudden, introduction of the eyewitnesses' accounts in the first person is sometimes very confusing for the reader. However, some of the documents which Allen cites certainly have some literary value and go to show once more what has been so often said, namely, that the writing of excellent prose was no uncommon gift in Queen Elizabeth's time. We quote here a single letter of Fr. Sherwin's, written from the Tower to his friends, as evidence of this:

> Being wearie of wel doing, and yet desirous not to do nothing (my deare companions) I chose rather by writing vnto you to performe my duetie then otherwise to recreate my head with cogitations lesse necessarie.
>
> Your liberalitie I haue receiued, and disposed thereof to my great contentation, when hereafter at the pleasure of God we shal meet in heauen, I trust you shalbe repaied *Cum foenore.* Delay of our death doth somewhat dull me, it was not without cause that our Maister him selfe said, *Quod facis fac cito.*
>
> Truth it is I hoped ere this, casting of this body of death, to haue kissed the pretious glorified woundes of my sweete Sauiour, sitting in the throne of his fathers owne glorie. Which desire as I trust descending from aboue hath so quieted my minde, that since the Iudicial sentence proceded against vs, neither the sharpnes of the death hath much terrified me, nor the shortnes of life much troubled me.

* Introduction to the reprint of the *Briefe Historie* (published by Burns & Oates, 1908). See note at bibl. ent. 13.

My sinnes are great I confesse, but I flee to Gods mercie: my necligences are without number I graunt, but I appeale to my redeemers clemencie. I haue no bouldnes but in his bloud, his bitter passion is my only consolation. It is comfortable that the Prophet hath recorded, which is, that *he hath written vs in his handes*. Oh that he would vouchsaffe to writ him self in our harts, how ioyful should we then appeare before the tribunal seat of his Fathers glorie: the dignitie whereof when I thinke, my flesh quaketh, not sustaining by reason of mortal infirmitie the presence of my creators Maiestie.

Our Lord perfect vs to that ende whereunto we were created, that leauing this world, we may liue in him, and of him, world without ende. It is thought that vpon Munday or Tewsday next we shal be passible [i.e. liable to suffer] God graunt vs humilitie, that we following his fotesteps may obteine the victorie [sig. f3].

We need not seek to discover the qualities of tone and temper which mark this letter as an example of true eloquence. The brightness of spiritual endeavour, which shines through and sustains the writing, most surely gives it a 'beauty which forces itself upon the mind'.

It would be outside the limits which have been set to this thesis to discuss in detail the further controversy which resulted from the publication of these two works of Cardinal Allen. We must therefore be content here to state barely, that a more elaborate justification of their policy was issued by the Government at the end of 1583, this time certainly from the pen of Lord Burghley,* under the title of *The Execution of Iustice in England for maintenaunce of publique and Christian peace, against certeine stirrers of sedition*; that Allen replied to this in the following year in his *A True Sincere and Modest Defence of English Catholiques that suffer for their Faith both at home and abrode: against a false, seditious and slaunderous Libel intituled; The Execution of Iustice in England*; and that this defence of Allen's called forth two further Protestant publications: Thomas Bilson's *The true difference betweene christian subiection and vnchristian rebellion* (1585) and John Stubbs's *Vindication of the English Iustice* (1587).

* The importance attached by the Government to this work may be gathered from the fact that it was translated into Latin, French, German and Italian.

A true r[illegible] ar-
tyrdome of M. Ca[illegible]pion Iesuite and
preiste, & M. Sherwin, & M. Bryan
preistes, at Tiborne the first of
December 1581.

Obseruid and written by a Catholike
preist, which was present therat

Wheruuto is annexid certayne verses
made by sundrie persons.

Apoca. 7.
These are they that came out of gret
tribulation, and haue washed their
stoles and made them white in the
bloud of the Lambe.

TITLE-PAGE OF T. ALFIELD'S *TRUE REPORT OF THE MARTYRDOM OF M. CAMPION*, ETC.

Printed at a secret press in London by Richard Verstegan in 1582

THOMAS ALFIELD

The printing of the English version of Thomas Alfield's report upon the deaths of Campion, Sherwin and Briant at a secret press in Smithfield within six months of the taking of the secret Greenstreet House press in August 1581 must have caused something of a sensation in Government circles. That it became 'a Star-chamber matter' is a measure of the Government's concern and of its determination to prevent the recurrence of such 'plots and practices'. The full story of these two secret Catholic presses will be told in the next and last chapter of this book. Meanwhile it will be enough to note here that Recorder Fleetwood on behalf of the Government took immediate steps to discover and destroy this press. Fleetwood's search quickly led not only to the seizure of the press and a number of copies of the printed report, but also to the taking of Alfield, Edward Osborne, Edward Cooke, William Dean and some others, who were accused of distributing the copies.* The printer, Richard Verstegan (or Rowlande, as he was then called), managed to flee the country, but Stephen Vallenger, who was associated with him in the production of the book and who was (incorrectly) accused of having written the report, suffered punishment in the pillory with the loss of both his ears and subsequent imprisonment for life.†

* State Papers, Eliz. Dom., Vol. 152, no. 54 [February 1582].

† See bibl. ent. 9 for reasons for attributing the *Report* to Alfield and not to Vallenger. The proceedings of the Star Chamber are thus recorded in Brit. Mus. Harl. MSS. 6265, p. 373: 'In the Star Chamber. 16 May 1582. This man Vallenger present at the Barre being charged by the Queens learned Councell in sorte as you haue hard to be the author and spreader of these Libells denieth all. But that he and none other is the partie culpable, these thinges do trulie argue.

First a booke written all with his owne hand, found in his lodging, shewed in this courte, and confessed by him, wherin amongst other thinges is conteyned all the printed libells before spoken of worde for word without varying in anie thinge, which by his owne confession was written in Januarie last, wheras by good triall it is founde that the same was not printed till february then next. The other libell also that is written in Rythmes confessed by himself to be all of his owne hand.

Secondly his answear both upon his owne examination, and here in Courte, that he receaued the Coppies of them by the hande of his Boye, sent vnto him by a man, whome he neuer knewe nor can name, is a very slender excuse, and doth plainely accuse him, and layeth the matter directly vpon himself as the principall deviser of theise infamous libells, for not being able to produce the partie that made them, he is both by lawe and reason to be taken for the author of them himself.

Thirdly the person is not the least thing to be noted, a vayne man, and so termed in common speech, knowne also to be a master of Rythmes and such vayne thinges, without any likelyhood to mainteyne himself withall. A masterlesse man, making a trade of such lewde devises to liue by, hyring of fellowes to write Copies

It is hardly necessary for us here to marshal the evidence which establishes the identity of the various hands who contributed to the making of this pamphlet. For this the reader may be referred to the bibliography (bibl. ent. 9). We need note only in this place that both title and text refer to a Catholic priest as author of the report proper, and that the State Papers are quite unambiguous as to Alfield's presence at the execution of Campion and about the taking of the notes which were subsequently handed to Verstegan for publication. The printing was undoubtedly prompted by an anonymous black-letter tract which appeared at the end of 1581, possibly that advertisement read by Hearne, the schoolmaster, at the execution,* justifying the Government's action in passing sentence upon the martyrs. The title of this tract was as follows: *An Aduertisement and defence for truth against her backbyters, and specially against the whispering fauorers and colorers of Campions, and the rest of his confederates treasons*. Alfield's pamphlet was entitled: *A true report of the death and martyrdome of M. Campion Iesuite and preiste, & M. Sherwin, & M. Bryan preistes, at Tiborne the first of December 1581. Obseruid and written by a Catholike preist, which was present therat Wheruuto* [sic] *is annexid certayne verses made by sundrie persons*. In addition to the 'annexed' verses, the *Report* includes 'A caueat to the reader touching A,M his discouery', clearly written later than the report itself and probably from the pen of Vallenger.† It was inspired by Munday's *A Discouerie of E. Campion and his Confederates, their most horrible and traiterous practises, against her Maiesties Most Royall Person and the Realme . . . whereto is added, the Execution of E. Campion, R. Sherwin, and A. Brian, executed at Tiborne the 1. of December* (1582) and purposes to discredit the author by reference

of such thinges, and offring them againe for aduantage. All these appearing manifestly to the Courte, there remaineth no doubt but that he is the very principall Author Inventor and spreader of these false and slaunderous libells, though with slender shifte he hath sought to avoyde it. So as for conclusion there resteth now only to consider what punishment he ought to receaue for so greate an offence, and if that he should be, according to the rule of Justice, secundum qualitatem delicti, it would goe neerer him then this Courte doth ordinarily proceed in. For it maye safely be drawen to an abetting of Traytors, and their accounts: But here in this place lesse cannot be layde vpon him, then Imprisonment during the Queens pleasure, fyne to the Queene, 100Li. And to make him a publique example for so publique an offense, to stand vpon the pillorie j daie in the pallace at Westminster, & one other daye in Cheapside, and to loose at eache place one of his eares, to remain as a perpetuall note of his lewd dealing.'

* cf. Simpson, op. cit., p. 452.

† Simpson attributes the *caveat* to Pound, wrongly I think, and cites a portion of it not quite correctly; op. cit., p. 439.

to his past record. Anthony Munday, it will be remembered, was one of the spies of the notorious anti-recusant agent, Richard Topcliffe, and had been an active witness against Campion and the others at the trial in Westminster Hall. Vallenger, if Vallenger it was, takes him up in the following terms:

> Anthony Munday, or as it is [not without some consideration] thought, that some macheuillian in mnndayes [sic] name hath shufled out of late a Discouery of M, Campions & his confederates treasons . . . My self . . . haue thought good in the conclusion of this reporte for the more credit of this his discours to aduertise the reader, of the qualities and conditions of this davus . . . who first was a stage player [no doubt a calling of some creditt] after an aprentise which tyme he wel serned [sic] with deceauing of his master then wandring towardes Italy, by his owne report became a coosener in his iourney. Comming to Rome, in his short abode there, was charitably relieued, but neuer admitted in the seminary as he pleseth to lye in the title of his booke, and being wery of well doing, returned home to his first vomite againe. I omite to declare howe this scholler new come out of Italy did play extempore, those gentlemen and others whiche were present, can best giue witnes of his dexterity, who being wery of his folly, hissed him from his stage. Then being therby discouraged, he set forth a balet against playes, but yet (O constant youth) he now beginnes againe to ruffle vpon the stage. I omit among other places his behauior in Barbican with his good mistres, and mother, from whēce our superintendent might fetch him to his court, were it not for loue (I woulde saye slaunder) to their gospel. Yet I thinke it not amiss to remember thee of this boyes infelicitie two seueral wayes of late notorious. First he writing vpon the death of Euerard Haunse,* was immediatly controled and disproued by one of his owne hatche, and shortely after seting forth the aprehension of M. Campion† was disproued by George (I was about to saye) Iudas Eliot, who writing against him, proued that those thinges he did were for very lucers sake only, and not for the truthe, althogh he himself be a person of the same predicament‡ . . . Therfore good reader examine this mans

* Above, p. 276.

† Simpson records this work as *A breefe Discourse of the taking of Edmund Campion and divers other Papists in Barkshire: gathered by A. M.* (London, 1581, July 29); op. cit., p. 495.

‡ In *A very true report of the apprehension and taking of that Arche Papist Edmond Campion the Pope his right hand, with three other lewd Iesuite priests, and diuers other Laie people, most seditious persons of like sort. Conteining also a controulment of a most vntrue former booke set out by one A. M. aliâs Anthonie Munday, concerning the same, as is to be proued and iustified by George Ellyot one of the ordinary yeomen of her Maiesties Chamber. Authour of this booke, and chiefest cause of the finding of the sayd lewde and seditious people, great enimies to God, their louing Prince and Countrie* (1581).

> honesti so reported, & snspend [sic] thy iugement against these good preists, vntill by gods grace the whol maner, course, and order, araignment, accusation, condemnation, and answeres, shal come forth, which is shortly intēded for thy benefite and satisfaction* [sig. D4v–E1v].

Munday replied to this pamphlet and its French counterpart† in *A breefe Aunswer made vnto two seditious Pamphlets, the one printed in French, and the other in English. Contayning a defence of Edmund Campion and his complices, their moste horrible and vnnatural Treasons, against her Maiestie and the Realme* (1582). His answer to the English version carries the further text-title: *An Aunswer vnto an other seditious Pamphlet printed in Englishe, and named: A true report of the death and Martirdome of Maister Campion, Iesuite and Preest, Maister Sherwin, and Master Brian Preests, at Tiborne the. 1. of Decemb. 1581. Obserued and written by a Catholique Preest, who was present thereat*, and this is followed by a recension, from Munday's own pen, of the verses of the *True Report* in praise of Campion, so changed as to comply with Protestant prejudice. The effect is curious, to say the least. It is only just that we should add that in this reply Munday disposes of the charge in the *Caveat* that he deceived John Allde, the Stationer, to whom he was apprenticed. He quotes Allde's own statement as saying: 'This is to let all men vnderstand, that Anthony Munday, for the tyme he was my Seruant, dyd his duetie in all respectes, as much as I could desire, without fraude, couin or deceyte: if otherwise I should report of him, I should but say vntrueth. By me Iohn Allde.' It would also appear that despite the statement to the contrary he *was* received into the seminary at Rome, but under another name.‡ Following upon this Answer, as a further counter to the *True Report* and in defence of their anti-recusant policy, the Government printed a paper entitled *A particular declaration or testimony, of the vndutifull and traiterous affection borne against her Maiestie by Edmond Campion Iesuite, and other condemned Priestes, witnessed by their owne confessions: in reproofe of those slaunderous bookes & libels deliuered out to the contrary by such as are malitiously affected towards her Maiestie and the state* (1582). This was the work which, as recorded above, prompted the publica-

* The reference is, of course, to Allen's *Briefe Historie*.

† See above, p. 273.

‡ The evidence afforded by Munday's *The English Romayne Lyfe* (1582) is quite satisfactory on this point.

tion of Allen's *Briefe Historie* and which led later to his more elaborate *Modest Defence of English Catholiques*, for distributing copies of which Alfield lost his life.

EDMUND CAMPION

The events in Campion's life which preceded and led up to the writing of his *Historie of Ireland* have been faithfully set forth by Richard Simpson and Evelyn Waugh in their lives of Campion. We need not, then, repeat here what is already sufficiently well known, but may confine ourselves to reporting certain details more immediately connected with the composing of this work, information about which Campion himself furnishes in the two Addresses which serve as an introduction to his discourse.

We gather from these sources that the Irish History was begun early in the year 1571 in the house of Sir James Stanyhurst, the Recorder of Dublin and Speaker in the Irish House of Commons, and that it was hastily completed within about ten weeks. It would appear that the motives which prompted its composition were threefold: (1) antiquarian interest; (2) to excuse the author's presence in Ireland; and (3) to interest Leicester in the state of Ireland and to invite his patronage. As for his difficulties – 'it is well knowne to the learned in this land', so runs the Address to Leicester, 'how late it was ere I could meet with *Gerald* of Wales, the onely Author that ministreth some indifferent furniture to this Chronicle, and with what search I have beene driven to piece out the rest by helpe of forreine Writers (incidently touching this Realme) by a number of briefe extracts of rolles, records and scattered papers'.* Our author has, in fact, had to make the best of a bad job. The second Address, 'to the loving Reader', with its more explicit reference to sources, exhibits the same underlying tone of dissatisfaction with his work. At the point where Giraldus Cambrensis fails him he employs, he says, for the events down to the year 1370 the work of 'a nameless Author'. From that date down to the time of Henry VIII 'because nothing is extant orderly written, and the same is time beyond any mans memory, I scamble forward with such records as could be sought up'. From Henry VIII

* Unless otherwise stated the citations are taken from Sir James Ware's edition of the *Historie*, referred to later above.

down to his own day – 'I tooke instructions by mouth, whatsoever I bring besides these helpes, either mine owne observation hath found it, or some friend hath enformed me, or common opinion hath received it, or I reade it in a pamphlet, or if the Author be worthy the naming I quote him in the margent'. For Scottish Histories he has used John Major and Hector Boethius. For English 'wherein the state of Ireland is often implyed' Fabian, Polidore, Cooper, Hall, Grafton and Stowe. Perhaps somewhat ruefully he adds an expression of hope that later writers will make good the gaps in these sources and 'pollish the stone rough hewed to their hand'. Yet, conscious as he is of the handicap under which he has laboured and of the limitation of his efforts, he is not unconscious of the debt he owes to those who have enabled him to perform his task. Above all, he gratefully acknowledges his obligation to his Irish host, James Stanyhurst, for, he continues, 'notwithstanding as naked and simple as [his *Historie*] is, it could never have growne to any proportion in such post-haste, except I had entred into such familiar societie, and daylie table-talke with the worshipfull Esquire Iames Stanihurst, Recorder of Dublin. Who beside all curtesie of Hospitality, and a thousand loving turnes not heere to be recited, both by word and written monuments, and by the benefit of his owne Library, nourished most effectually mine endeavour'. This second Address is dated 'from Droghedah the 9. of Iune. 1571', and this fixes the date of the completion of the work.

Before we proceed to illustrate Campion's method and style in his *Historie* some comment must be offered by way of textual criticism on this most important of Recusant publications. This does not mean that we are here proposing to resolve the textual problems in which the work abounds, but rather that we wish to draw attention to the fairly extensive variations of reading which occur in those texts which can claim some sort of contemporaneity with Campion's original Chronicle. We may observe, then, that the work is extant in two early manuscript versions (one in the possession of the College of Heralds, one in the Library of the British Museum) and that it also appears in three early printed versions, viz. as part of the two editions of Holinshed's *Chronicles* of 1577 and 1587 and in Sir James Ware's *History of Ireland*, published in Dublin in two separate issues in

1633. It will be convenient to begin with a word or two about each of these versions in turn. And first, the two manuscript versions. That in the Library of the Heralds' College I can only refer to in general terms since I have not had an opportunity of examining it. According to Black's *Catalogue of the Arundel Manuscripts in the Library of the College of Arms* (1829)* it is 'a fair copy in folio, written upon 45 leaves of paper, by five different hands, in the reign of Elizabeth'. It is inscribed 'The Historie of Ireland, Devided into two Bookes; compiled by Master Edmund Campion, fellowe of Saint Jhon Baptist colledge in Oxford, in the yeare of Grace 1571'. It differs from the B.M. copy and from the printed editions in that it 'contains a statistical view of Ireland in a tabular form . . . intitled, "This that followeth was taken out of Mr. Stowe's Coppye, and [was] not written by Mr. Campion, but by [Mr.] Longe. – Anno 1574" ', and further, 'several marginal notes, evidently genuine'. Of the Cottonian MS. in the British Museum I may speak more explicitly. The text of this version differs materially from the three printed editions, and, in the matter of a pure text, as I hope to indicate shortly, must be regarded as an invaluable corrective to all of them. The work of a single late sixteenth-century scribe, it consists of seventy-five quarto leaves of paper (much damaged by fire) and is entitled 'The Two Bookes of the Histories of Ireland Compiled by Edmonde Campion Fellow of St Iohn Baptistes colledge in Oxforde'.† In respect of the three printed versions that of the Irish antiquary and historian, James Ware, must surely hold pride of place. As we have already pointed out, this edition, which incorporates similar works by Edmund Spenser and Meredith Hanmer, was issued in Dublin under two separate titles in the year 1633. These two issues are thus designated: (1) *Two Histories of Ireland. The one written by Edmund Campion, the other by Meredith Hanmer D*[r] *of Divinity*; and (2) *The Historie of Ireland, collected by three learned authors viz. Meredith Hanmer Doctor in Divinitie; Edmund Campion sometime Fellow of St. Johns Colledge in Oxford; and Edmund Spenser Esq.* The text of our author's *Historie* in these two volumes closely resembles that of the Museum MS. and is clearly intended as

* This copy was given by Henry, Duke of Norfolk, in 1678 to the Library of the Heralds' College; cf. Simpson, p. 501.

† Further details as to the form and content of this MS. will be found at bibl. ent. 27.

a version of Campion naked and unadorned. We cannot say as much of the two Holinshed texts, to which we now turn.

The inclusion of Campion's *Historie* in Holinshed's work seems to have been due more to a piece of good luck than to deliberate contriving. Reginald Wolfe, the publisher, under whose auspices the *Chronicles* were planned, had come across, as Holinshed informs us, 'a copie of two bookes of the Irish histories, compiled by one Edmund Campion' – quite possibly the original copy of Campion's manuscript which the officers had seized when Campion embarked for England in June 1571 and which seems to have come into the hands of Lord Burghley towards the end of the following year – and was so taken with them that he persuaded him, Holinshed, to include them in his work. So, says Holinshed, 'I resolued to make shift to frame a speciall historie of Ireland, in like maner as I had done of other regions, following Campions order, and setting downe his owne words, except in places where I had matter to inlarge that (out of other authors) which he had written in breefe'.* Actually, Holinshed's revision of Campion's text ceases at the year 1509. Finding that Campion thereafter became his sole source of information, he turned over the task of completing the Irish history down to the end of Henry VIII to Campion's old pupil and friend, Richard Stanyhurst. The latter thus became responsible for 'The thirde Booke of the Historie of Ireland, comprising the raigne of Henry the eyght', as the text-title has it, to which must be added the short introductory treatise, descriptive of Ireland, and occupying folios A to D, which is also the work of Stanyhurst's hand. Both editors deal pretty freely with their prototype, and though in the result they preserve a general uniformity of character with the other parts of the work, it is clear, as we shall shortly see, that such uniformity has been obtained by sacrificing much of Campion's original method and style. Two things call for immediate brief notice. Campion's last chapter, the tenth of the second book, which deals with the reigns of Edward VI, Mary and Elizabeth, is naturally omitted from Holinshed. This chapter closes with two speeches delivered at the prorogation of the Irish Parliament on 12 December 1570, which Campion professes to report from his own notes, as near as he could, in the same words and

* Introductory Epistle to *The Historie of Irelande*.

sentences in which he heard them.* The first of these is an oration of James Stanyhurst, Speaker of the Parliament, who pleads on behalf of Irish education – for the foundation of a university, for grammar schools in every diocese.† The second is a review of the situation in Ireland by Sir Henry Sidney, the Lord Deputy, in answer to Stanyhurst. The speeches provide a fitting corollary to the work and give significance to what might otherwise be regarded as mere (albeit picturesque) historical relation. The second comment we wish to make is this. In the 1577 edition of Holinshed as it was originally published were passages relating to Gerald FitzGerald's rebellion and to the character of John Alen, Archbishop of Dublin (1528–39). Although the Queen ordered the cancellation of these passages, presumably for political reasons, copies still exist of the *Chronicles* which include the cancelled leaves. It is advisable, therefore, to point out that Campion was not the author of either of the expunged passages. A careful comparison with the rest of Campion's writing points convincingly enough to its being the work of his editor, Richard Stanyhurst. The passages, needless to say, do not occur either in the Cottonian manuscript or in Ware's printed transcript.

Just as Stanyhurst had set out to improve upon Campion in the first edition of Holinshed, so in the second edition of 1587 the editor, John Hooker (uncle of Richard), set out in his turn to improve upon Stanyhurst. The variations in this case are, however, only slight, the most notable departure from the earlier edition being the substitution of Hooker's own translation of Giraldus Cambrensis for the rather shorter version of Campion used by Stanyhurst. Hooker also restored to the text the account of Cardinal Wolsey, from the ninth chapter of Campion's second book, which Holinshed had omitted, no doubt on account of the fact that the cardinal had already received due notice in the English part of the *Chronicles*. If, then, we except these two passages, this edition of 'The Chronicles of Ireland' may rightly be regarded as being at two removes from the original Campion, and, as such, will call for no

* cf. Simpson, op. cit., p. 52.

† Spenser, in his *View of the State of Ireland* (1596), stresses the same point: in every parish 'a pettie Schoole-master', and 'in every Countrey or Baronie, they should keepe another able Schoole-master, which should instruct them in Grammar'; p. 111 of Ware's edition.

particular comment in the detailed analysis of the variants in the early texts which follows hereunder.

Let us begin this analysis by submitting two complete passages, the one from Ware, the other from Holinshed (i.e. Stanyhurst), which may give the reader some idea as to how far Stanyhurst has wandered from his original. The subject is the childhood of St. Brigid, Patroness of Ireland. Here is Ware:

> *Brigide* was base Daughter of Dubtachus a Captaine in Leinster, who perceiving the Mother with child, sold her secretly, fearing the jealousy of his wife, to a Irish Poet, reserving to himself, the fruite of her wombe, she was there delivered of this *Brigide*, whom the Poet trained up in letters, and so conveyed her home to her father. The Damosell was schooled in the faith by S. *Patricke*, preaching then in those parts, she became so religious, and so ripe in judgement, that not onely the multitude, but a whole synode of Bishoppes assembled by Dublin, used her advice in weighty causes, and highly esteemed her. One fact of hers being yet a childe, made her famous. The King of Leinster had given to *Dubtachus* in token of singular affection, for his good service, a rich sword. Now it befell, that the maiden visiting her sicke neighbours, diversly distressed for hunger, (her father being a sterne man, his Lady a shrewe) she saw none other helpe to releive these wretched people, but to part the Iewels of that idle sword among them. This matter was haynously taken, and came to the Kings eares, who (comming shortly after to a Banquet in her fathers house) demaunded the Girle, not yet nine yeares old, how she durst presume to deface the gift of a King, shee answered, that it was bestowed upon a better King, then hee was, whom (quoth she) finding in such extremity, I would have given all my father hath, and all that thou hast, yea your selves and all, were yee in my power to give, rather then Christ should starve [p. 43 – sig. D4].

And here is Stanyhurst:

> Brigide, otherwyse called Bride, was base daughter to one Dubtactius, a Capitayne in Leynister, who perceyuyng the mother wyth chylde, solde hir secretely (fearing the iealousie of his wyfe) to an Irishe Peet,* reseruing to himselfe the fruite of hir wombe.
>
> She was there delyuered of thys Bridget, whome the Peet trayned vp in learning, and vertuous education, and at length broughte hir home to hir father.
>
> The damosell also was instructed in the faith by saynte Patrike, that preached then in those quarters, whervpon she

* The margin here reads: 'Peet, that is, Magus in latin or (as we may say) a Magitiã or soothsayer in English.' I have been altogether unable to confirm Stanyhurst's explanation of this strange word. The Cottonian MS. reads with Ware 'Poet'.

> became so religious and ripe in iudgement, that not only the multitude of people, but also a whole Synode of Bishops assembled neere to Diuelyn to heare hir aduise in weightye causes. Suche estymation they had of hir. One fact of hir beyng yet a childe, made hir famous.
>
> The king of Leynister had giuen to hir father Dubtactius as a tokē of his good liking towardes him for his valiant seruice a riche sworde, the furniture wherof was garnished with many costly iewels. And as it chaunced, the Damosel visiting the sicke neighbours, diuersly distressed for wante of necessarie reliefe (hir father beeing a sterne man and his ladie a cruell shrew) she could deuise no other shift to help to relieue the wante of those poore and needye people, but to imparte the same iewelles of that ydle swoorde among them.
>
> This matter was heynously taken, and being brought to the Kings eares, it chaunced that shortely after he came to a banket in hir fathers house, and calling the maid afore him that was not yet past.ix.yeres of age: He asked hir howe shee durste presume to deface the guyfte of a king in such wise as she had done his. She answered that the same was bestowed vpon a better king than he was, whom (quoth shee) finding in such extremetie, I woulde haue giuen all that my father hath, and all that you haue, yea your selues to and all, were ye in my power to giue, rather than Christ should starue [p. 11, col. 2 – sig. A6].

The reader will not be in doubt concerning this amplification of Campion's plain tale: how much the story has lost in Stanyhurst's retelling may well, therefore, be left to his own judgment. The point we wish to emphasize here, however, is not the superiority of Campion over his editor, but the striking differences exhibited in Holinshed's text from what is clearly the purer text of Ware. Stanyhurst's version is just not Campion, and Campion cannot therefore be judged as a writer of English prose by that version as it stands. To further our argument a little let us set down a few random readings from Holinshed, side by side with similar readings from the Cottonian MS. and from Ware, designating Holinshed as H, the Cottonian manuscript as C, and Ware as W. It will be noted that Stanyhurst's divergence from C and W not only exhibits his habit of amplifying and amending his original, but also shows that at times his readings would seem to be plainly corrupt.

C – 'our infinite necessitie prayeth your fauors' (p. 90^b)
W – 'your infinite necessities pray your favours' (p. 30)
(*this makes nonsense of the context*)
H – 'our urgent necessitie besecheth your fauors' (p. 6)

C – 'resembling the wildernes of that rude world' (p. 123b)
W – 'resembling the wydenesse of the rude world' (p. 100)
H – 'resembling the rudenesse of the rude world' (p. 73)

C – 'resemble a man of straw' (p. 131)
W – 'resemble a man of straw' (p. 113)
H – 'resemble a scarcrowe or a man of straw' (p. 82)

C – 'contente to take egges and bring him in at leisure' (p. 131)
W – 'is glad to take egges for his money and bring him in at leisure' (p. 113)
H – 'content to bring him in at leysure' (p. 82)

C – 'abuse the ignorance of our state and contrie' (p. 131b) (*this makes the best sense*)
W – 'abuse the ignorance of their state and Countrey' (p. 114)
H – 'abuse the ignorance of your state and contrie' (p. 83)

C – 'strength to saue his owne' (p. 132)
W – 'strength to save his owne' (p. 114)
H – 'strength to saue his crowne' (p. 83)

C – 'As touching my Kingdome (my Lord) I would you and I had exchanged' (p. 132)
W – *the same* (p. 114)
H – 'Touching my Kingdome I know not what your Lordship shoulde meane thereby' (p. 83)

C – 'such an odious storme' (p. 132)
W – *the same* (p. 114)
H – 'such an odious terme' (p. 83)

Having thus demonstrated something of the manner in which the Holinshed text diverges from the two versions of Ware and the Cottonian manuscript, we propose now to call attention to the way in which these two versions themselves differ, a thing which must already be evident to the reader. As before, let us begin with a short continuous passage, this time, however, as a preliminary to indicate that despite differences there is a close resemblance between the two versions. Short though the extract is, it will suffice. It is taken from the narration of the early life of St. Patrick. The text is that of C, the readings of W being placed within square brackets.

> Now were the Irishe throughe ye helpe of the Scottes and Pictes arche pirates of the narrow seas and used to sake litle weak villages scatered alonge the shore [and] for wante of other pray to bringe the inhabitantes home captiues, with other was also [others also was] taken this Patricius [a ladde] of xvj yeres old

> being then a student of seculer lerning, and [became] the villeyn of an Irishe Lord [called] Macbuaim from whome after sixe yeres he redemed him self with a pece of gold, which he founde in a clodd of earthe newlie-torned vpp by the swyne he kept. the tyme of his banishement (as afliction commonlie maketh men relligious) [This]* with the regard of his former education printed in hym suche remorse and humilitie, that being [from] thensforth vtterlie weaned from the world he betoke hym sellf to contemplacon euer lamenting the lack of grace and truthe in that lande [p. 94].

It will be noted that the additions of W in this extract might all have been due to the work of a careful editor writing up the rather bare text of C and might suggest, therefore, no more than a redaction of C. A more detailed examination, however, of the two texts reveals differences striking enough to warrant our belief that Ware must have had a second manuscript in his hands, upon which he probably based his text, and sometimes his readings are so obviously corrupt that we may well doubt whether he knew C at all. Let the reader himself be judge of this by examining the textual differences between the two versions exhibited below. All save three are taken from two consecutive pages in the earliest part of the work.

C	W
voyage	poore voyage
farre countries	forraine countryes
I am beholden	I have beene beholding
iudgement seated	judgement setled
[*blank*] on	gazeth on
to be deemed praiseable [when] they lodge	to be denied, praiseable when they lodge
are placed in your bres[t]	are planted in –
benefitt resort of daylie suters	benefit an infinite resort –
your tree	your noble tree
to doe you seruice	to your service
the same time is	the same is time
all be reported . . . yet	although they be reported . . . yet
to spare vpon this buysines	to spare about –
lighted into familiar socyetie	entred into such familiar –
to lende their good liking to my good will	to bend their good liking –
not reaching forthe to sea nookes and elbowes of land as Brytan doth	not reaching forth to Sea, in nookes and elbowes of Land –
you are in fault	well, we are in fault: why? because you are
his vnciuill neighbors	his vincible neighbors
him he tho[ught]eth to be kindled	him he thought eith to be kindled

* Probably a piece of bad editing by Ware, whose version here runs 'newly turned up by the swyne hee kept the time of his Banishment (as affliction commonly maketh men religious.) This with the regard of', &c. The passage so punctuated makes nonsense.

It is, of course, no part of our aim here to attempt to decide which of these two texts provides the better version of Campion's *Historie*. Our object in presenting these parallel readings has been solely to draw attention to certain differences existing in the best texts we know. However, from a fairly thorough examination of the two texts we have been unable to avoid arriving at certain plain conclusions, which may be stated as follows: (1) In some cases where the meaning of C is quite clear the readings of W make nonsense, as in the phrase of W 'to be denied, praiseable' for C's 'deemed praiseable' or in W's 'thought eith' for 'thoughteth'; (2) sometimes C provides the better sense simply, as in the description of the Irish coast as 'not reaching forthe to sea nookes [i.e. sea-nooks] and elbowes of land as Brytan doth', or in the phrase 'vnciuill neighbors' as against W's 'vincible neighbors'; but (3) more often than not the W version is plainly superior to that of C. This being so, it would seem natural to conclude that, although in certain respects we must allow the superiority of C over the printed version, the MS. upon which the latter was based (it being highly improbable that it was based upon C itself) was probably superior to C, but that neither C nor W is satisfactory as it stands. We would suggest, therefore, that since it would appear that no proper printed edition of this important work as yet exists, an edition, collated from the MS. sources, is now called for, and we would venture to commend this suggestion to the officers of the *E.E.T.S.* That the work deserves the distinction of an authentic text we hope to show in the paragraphs which follow.

We cannot claim for Campion's *Historie* that it is written according to the principles of the modern scientific historian, whose aim is to unfold the 'logic of events', 'to trace', as Lingard says, 'the silent progress of nations from barbarism to refinement, and to mark their successive improvement in the arts of legislation and government'.* Nor can we claim for it as a piece of early historical writing the importance that, say, R. W. Chambers attaches to More's *Richard III*, that 'first great piece of modern English history',† or that we ourselves would attach to the Harpsfield-Stapleton *Counterblast*.‡ It does not, in fact, pretend to be much more than a plain record

* Advertisement to Vol. I of the *History of England*.
† *Continuity of English Prose*, as before, p. xlviii.
‡ See above, p. 126.

of those documents and evidences which its author had been able rather hurriedly to put together during his stay in Ireland. Yet Campion is no mere annalist. He had a clear conception of the main principles of historical criticism and he understood the importance of first-hand sources. He also understood the value of legend in the writing of history as a means of reflecting the manners, the moral philosophy, and the theology of the race which makes it. It is, indeed, in his use of legend that he shows most clearly his powers of bold discrimination and reveals the broad purpose underlying his work, which may be described as a closer understanding of the Irish nation and its people, their character and their needs. This is the common-sense of his book, which fitly concludes with a striking appeal for the education of the Irish, an appeal which Edmund Spenser was to revive a quarter of a century later in his *View of the State of Ireland*, and it was this which led Simpson to declare that the work 'is almost as much a pamphlet to prove that education is the only means of taming the Irish as a serious history'.* However, whether we regard it as a simple chronicle of the Irish people or as a tractate on Irish claims to education matters little for our present purpose. For us the important thing is that both as chronicle and tractate it has its place in the history of English prose, and it is this aspect of the work which is here our special concern.

The most striking tribute which has been paid to Campion as a writer comes from the discerning pen of Evelyn Waugh, who summarizes our author's manner in the *Historie* in the following terms: '*The History of Ireland* is a superb piece of literature, comparable in vigour and rhythm to anything written in his day. With all its imperfections of structure and material, it is enough to show that, had Campion continued in the life he was then planning for himself, he would, almost certainly, have come down in history as one of the great masters of English prose. From the lovely cadence of the opening sentences, describing the physical character of the country which "*lieth aloof in the West Ocean, in proportion like an egg, blunt and plain at the sides, not reaching forth to the sea in nooks* [sic] *and elbows of land as Britain doth*", to the balanced, Ciceronian speeches at the end it is manifestly the work of a stylist for whom form and matter

* op. cit., p. 42.

were never in conflict; there is no shadow of the effort and ostentation which clouds all but the brightest genius of the period.'* To this estimate of Campion's worth as a writer of English prose we may wholeheartedly subscribe. We may note in the first place the almost complete absence in the *Historie* of those embellishments so dear to most Elizabethan writers of secular prose. Campion writes (if one must give it a name) in what has been called the Direct Style, a style which by reason of its economy, directness and speed is eminently suitable for certain types of historical narration. The primary aim of the writer in this style is to convey a sense of actuality to the reader, and this is done for the most part by the careful selection of objects or events and by their simple objective presentation. Hence the absence of artifice in this kind of writing. Where emphasis is called for it must be sought in the order and movement of the writing, and to this end Campion resorts most frequently to the use of inversion and the manipulation of the balance of the sentence and phrase, which thus become the chief contributory elements in the rhythmical structure of his prose. In the hands of a lesser artist these devices will often lead to a dull or mechanical mode of expression. There is nothing dull or mechanical, however, about Campion. His fine sensibility to form, which everywhere controls the material he handles, together with the boldness of his phrasing, offsets any such possibility and induces an animation of rhythm and a vigour of expression which, if one may venture a comparison, at times strangely recalls the prose style of C. M. Doughty.

In illustration of Campion's practice, the reader will, we think, be best served if, in conclusion, we cite a complete chapter of the *Historie*. The chapter chosen is the thirteenth of the first book, on account of its more general interest. It is entitled 'Of Saint Patrickes Purgatory'. The version followed is the 1809 reprint of Ware.† Variations in the Cotton MS. are printed in square brackets.

> Every History of Ireland that I have seene, maketh one severall title *De mirabilibus Hiberniae*, and therein with [a] long processe treateth of severall Ilands, some full of Angels, some full of devils, some for male only, some for female, some where poore

* *Edmund Campion* (1935), pp. 37–8.

† *A Historie of Irelande, Written in the Yeare 1571. By Edmund Campion . . . Reprinted at the Hibernia Press* [Dublin] . . . *1801*.

[none] may live, some where none can dye: finally such effects of waters, stones, trees, and trinkets, that a man would weene them to be but heedlesse and uncertaine tales by their complexion.

Verily, being inquisitive of these matters, I could finde no one of them soothed* by such persons upon whose relation I am disposed to venture. Onely the place behinde [beyond] Ardmagh called S. *Patricks* Purgatory, because it is knowne and confessed, and because I would be discharged of my Readers expectation, who perhaps with the name of S. *Patricke* looketh to bee informed thereof, I can bee content to put so much in writing, as Bookes and reports affirme with most likelyhood.

Two things I muse at [must – *followed by blank*], that neither the time nor the author of so strange erection was preserved. Concerning the time one Record putteth it in Anno Domini 302. which is 128. yeares before S. *Patricke* converted Ireland, and sixty sixe yeares before his birth. Againe *Cambrensis* who [who *omitted*] maketh curious recitall of wonders in the land, never uttereth word of this Purgatory; & though a negative authority be not invincible, yet considering the propertie [purpose] of that man, and what sort of trifles he taketh paine to justifie, it may serve for a vehement suspition, that the place was then either not found [founded], or not miraculous. Concerning the Author, very few there are that referre it to this *Patricke* their Apostle, but rather to an Abbot of the same name, whom I marvaile I finde not in the mighty bigge volume of their Saints: Notwithstanding these Originalls might bee either lost or altered, but the thing it selfe being extant, must needes have had a beginning, whereof possibly there are monuments in that Church, or in the Irish tongue to me unwitting.

Therefore I hold him unwise that will utterly mistrust the principall, because the circumstances vary: or condemne the whole, because he could not reach to the undoubted truth of some part. If any man bee so delicate, that not a jote thereof [no iott hereof] will sinke into his head, who shall controule him? neither hee nor wee are bound to believe any story besides that which is delivered us from the Scriptures, and the consent of Gods Church. Let the discreet Reader judge of it.

This [thus] I learne, that the holy Abbot *Patricius secundus*, not the Bishop their Apostle, laboured the conversion of the people of Vlster, which being now Christians, could yet at no hand be wonne to renounce their olde sensuality, cruelty, murthers, extortion. And when he much inforced the life to come, they replyed unto him with contempt, that unlesse they saw proofes of these loyes† and paines hee preached, they would never leese possession of the pleasures in hand, for hope or dread of things

* Corroborated.

† A misprint for the 'Ioyes' of Ware's original edition. It occurs again later in the passage.

to come they wist not when. At their importunacie [importunytie] hee besought God, were it his good [when it is good] pleasure to give out some evident token of the maters they required: finally by the special direction of God he found in the north edge of Vlster a desolate angle hemmed in round, & in the mids [the mids *omitted*] thereof a pit, where he reared a Church, closed the same with a wall, bestowed therein Canons regular, at the East end of this Church yarde, a doore leadeth into a closet of stone, which they call the Purgatory, because devout people have resorted thither for penance, and reported at their returne, strange visions of paine and blisse appearing to them. They used to continue therein [theare] foure & twenty [24] houres, which [with] doing one while with [with *omitted*] ghostly [godlie] meditations, and another [other] while a dreadfull [adradd for] conscience of their deserts, they saw as they say [They say they see], a plaine resembling [resemblance] of their owne faults and vertues, with the horror and comfort thereto belonging, that one so terrible, the [that] other so joyous, that they verily deeme themselves for the time to have sight of heaven and hell [hell and heauen]. The revelations [relacons] of men that went in (Saint *Patricke* yet living) are kept written within the saide Abbey. When any person is disposed to enter (for the doore is ever sparred) he repaireth first for advice to the Archbishop, who casteth all perils, and disswadeth him, because they say diverse never [men] came backe againe, but if the party be resolute, he recommendeth him to the Pryor, who in like manner favourably exhorteth him not to hazard such a danger, if notwithstanding he finde [fyndeth] the party fully bent, he conducteth him to this [the] Church, enjoyned [enioyneth] him to begin with prayer, fast and vigill of 15. [fiftene] dayes, so long together as in discretion can be endured. This time expired, if he yet persevere in his former purpose, the whole Convent accompanieth him with solemne procession and benediction to the mouth of the cave, where they let him in, & so barre up the doore till the [the *omitted*] morrow, & then with like ceremonies they awaite his returne, & reduce him to the Church. If he be seene no more, they fast & pray 15. dayes after. Touching the credit of those [theis] matters, I see no cause but a Christian man assuring himself that there is both hel & heaven, may without vanity upon sufficient information, be persuaded that it might please God at somtime for considerations to his infinit wisdome known to reveale by miracles [miracle] the vision of Ioyes & paines eternal, but that altogether in such sort, & so ordinarily, & to such persons, and by such meanes as the common fame & some records therof doe utter, I neither believe, nor wish [them *supplied*] to be regarded. It appeares [appereth] by *Trevisa* in his additions [audit-] to *Polichronicon*, that a superstitious opinion of this Purgatory was then conceived, which he disproveth. And a man of [an *supplied*] indifferent judgement may soone suspect that in the drift and strength of Imagination [ymaginacons], a contemplative person would happely suppose the sight of many strange things which he never saw. Since writing hereof I met with a Priest, who told mee that he had gone the same pilgrimage, and affirmed the order of the premisses: But that he for his owne part saw no sight in the world, save onely fearefull dreames when he [when he *omitted*] chanced to nod, and those he saith were exceeding horrible: further he added, that the faste is rated more or lesse, according to the quality of the penitent, and that the place seemed to him scarcely [well *supplied*] able to receive sixe persons.

GREGORY MARTIN

Shortly after Martin's death in 1582 Richard Verstegan published in Paris (*anno* 1583) *A Treatyse of Christian Peregrination, written by M. Gregory Martin Licentiate, and late reader of diuinitie in the Englishe Coleadge at Remes. Whereunto is adioined certen Epistles written by him to sundrye his frendes: the copies whereof were since his decease founde amonge his wrytinges.* The volume comprises: (1) 'A treatise of Pilgrimage and Relicks'; (2) 'A letter sente to M. N. a maried priest'; (3) 'A letter sent to his Sisters, maried to protestants, and them selues trained vpp in heresie, where he sheweth and proueth the Catholicke Church to be the true Church'; and (4) 'A letter sent to M. D. Whyte then warden of newe colleadge in Oxford, touching his folowing the worlde and dissembling in religiō agaynst his conscience and knowledge'. Of the treatise, which runs to some sixty-six octavo pages, there is nothing in particular to record, beyond noting once again our author's use of common and familiar expression in treating a learned subject. He describes his opponents' terminology, for instance, in one place as 'deuysed by heretikes as buggishe baubles to feare babyes', and refers in another place to their having made 'sore bugges-wordes' of the names of Pilgrim and Pilgrimage. Such common doublings of the expression as 'dolts and dysards' (blockheads), 'culled and kissed', are also not infrequent in his text. And there is, too, the usual plentiful supply of examples of Elizabethan construction and phrasing scattered about his pages. But it is the three letters in this volume which afford its principal interest, and we shall therefore proceed to deal briefly with these in turn.

One of Allen's rules for his collegians at Douay was that they should write letters to their friends and relatives at home in order to move them to attend to the salvation of their souls and to draw them, if possible, into the fold of the Church. The letters of Martin which had influenced Campion in his decision to leave Oxford and a little later to seek his vocation among the exiles at Douay are specimens of the practical utility of this rule. We have Campion's own attestation to this fact when he writes to Martin: 'I remember too how earnestly you called me from Ireland to Douai, how you admonished me, and how effective were your words. Before that, I remember how from the Duke of Norfolk's house you dealt with me to keep me from the ecclesiastical dignity, which, as a friend, you feared might betray me into serving these wretched times. In these words, as I consider, you were even prompted by the Holy Ghost, – "If we two can live together, we can live for nothing; if this is too little, I have money; but if this also fails, one thing remains, – they that sow in tears shall reap in joy." What you foretold is fulfilled.'* Only a sprinkling of these letters has survived, chiefly in manuscript form, and we owe a debt of gratitude to Verstegan for having studied to preserve for us these examples of Martin's penmanship, revealing as they do a side of Martin which we have not met with in those works of his which we have considered hitherto. Here we may mark the modesty and moderation of our author, as also that burning desire for souls which, we maintain, was ever the root and the spring of our Recusant literature and which saves it, even when most controversial in tone, from degenerating into the scurrilities and mere abuse of a writer like Lewis Evans† or the authors of the Marprelate tracts.

First in order of date (15 October 1575) is the third letter in our volume, to Dr. Whyte.‡ Dr. Whyte's was a not uncommon case in the reign of Elizabeth. He appears to have been a Catholic at heart and seems to have had a wide influence in the university. Martin, who had known him in his Oxford days, recalls in his letter how he had received some benefit at his hands at that time, and it is largely on the strength of this connexion – 'many thinges moued me', he writes, 'especially my

* The letter is dated from Prague, 3 July 1577, and is thus cited by Simpson (op. cit., p. 126) from *Opuscula* (Antwerp, 1631, p. 389), where the date appears to be given as 10 July.

† Above, p. 116.

‡ See bibl. ent. 88.

charitie towardes you to whom I am beholding for causes which you may remember' – that he now presumes to address himself to the elder man and to plead with him to give up temporizing and to declare himself. It is a modest appeal, couched altogether in the simple and unpretentious language of the following lines:

> For a Catholicke you are esteemed, and learned and wyse: Many good meaning men that gladly would doe well depende vpon you, harken what you say, looke what you doe, and because they are determined to folow you, by your doing ill and saying worse, you doe pitifully infecte many hartes, either with error or dissimulation, and wounde their soules to euerlasting death: and that because they compte you a Catholicke, and therefore are perswaded, that you will not teach them amisse.

The second letter in the *Treatyse* was written about the time of Martin's return from Rome to Rhemes in 1578. That is the date of its original printing, when it appeared under the simple title *The Loue of the Soule Made by G. M. Printed at Roane 1578.** Whether Martin himself undertook the publishing of this little 16mo volume we cannot say, though it could hardly have been printed without his knowledge. It evidently enjoyed some popularity as it was thrice reprinted before 1640: about 1600, in 1619, and again in 1633. And here let us digress for a moment. To each of these later editions of the letter was annexed a set of verses entitled 'Catholike Questions to the Protestants'. The late Miss Guiney, in her anthology *Recusant Poets,*† attributes these verses to Martin himself, apparently, since they are unsigned, on the sole ground that they are printed in a volume bearing his name. Martin's authorship may be doubted. The title of the volume in which the verses first appear, and which later editions follow, is certainly not conclusive on the point. It runs: *The Loue of the Soule. Made by G. Mar. Whereunto are annexed certain Catholike questions to the Protestants,*‡ where the word 'annexed' may quite fairly be taken to indicate the hand of a second author; and this especially in view of the fact that it was not unusual in the sixteenth and early seventeenth centuries for an editor or publisher to enlarge a volume with additional matter, which, when occasion served, might come from

* Details with regard to both the date of the letter and the printing of this volume will be found at bibl. ent. 85.

† Sheed & Ward, 1938.

‡ This is the volume which I date about 1600. It was answered by John Rhodes in *An answere to a romish rime* (1602) where the 'Catholike questions' are printed along with his reply.

the pen of another writer.* Moreover, we have no good evidence beyond these verses that Martin ever put his hand to the writing of English verse. Furthermore, it is difficult to believe that Martin could have been guilty of such doggerel as:

> Where haue you bene so long a time?
> to whom did your light shine?
> Where did your principall Pastor sit?
> who kept your keies, who fed your sheep?
> Shew some Churches you haue bilt,
> I can shew many you haue spilt.†

These considerations, we suggest, serve to emphasize the need for sound positive evidence of Martin's authorship of these verses, and until this is forthcoming it will be wise at least to postpone our judgment on the question.

To return to Martin's letter. The simple eloquence, springing as it were from the double fount of a deep sincerity and an ardent zeal, will, we think, explain its popularity. The familiar address, the direct and open expression, the absence of artifice, the moving appeal, all combining to disarm criticism and to captivate the mind, are the means by which that eloquence is sustained. The reader will have already met with a short extract from the letter, in substance autobiographical, in an earlier part of this book,‡ which affords an excellent example of these characteristics of Martin's style. The short excerpts which follow have, therefore, been chosen rather to serve as an epitome of the letter than to provide further examples of Martin's powers of eloquence, a thing which would have been done better by citing one or two longer pieces. Even so, the passages are not without their value in this respect. The letter begins:

> Deere Sisters, my care, my loue, & of al worldly things (next to my good mother) my greatest comforte and ioye. Vnlesse you did thinke, that I doe most hartely loue you, you coulde not alwaies heretofore haue declared your exceeding loue so plentifully towards me, for the which almightie God rewarde you. This my loue because it is not a naturall affection onely, but sincere and true charitie, forceth me to wish vnto you, my louing Sisters, not onelie manie worldlie commodities, which

* Numerous instances of this practice could be cited. Most pertinent to our present argument is the fact that the 1619 edition of Martin's letter had added to it a catalogue of the popes, which we should hardly ascribe to our author's pen.

† Ed. 1600 (?); sig. A6v.

‡ Above, p. 52.

(God be thanked) you lacke not: but much more, all spirituall treasure and heauenlie riches, wherof you can not haue great store, because you dwell not where it groweth.

The state of the Catholics in England is described:

And now also in all these countries, how many are there thinke you of secret catholickes that wish for the olde religion againe with all their hart, and folow the new onely for feare? Nay how many are there especially in *England* that doe yet openly professe the Catholike Faith?

Aske good Sisters aske, and you shall learne that all the prisons not only of *London*, but of *England* are full of them, because they will not yeeld to these new proceedings, nor contaminate their soules with this newe seruice, and leaue the olde true and Catholicke fayth: besides a number of sundrye degrees, which are deade in prison: namely twentie three Bishops all depryued of their liuing these twētie three yeres, & now but two of them alyue: I omit *Doctors*, *Deanes*, *Archdeacons*, *Knights*, *Squires*, partlie in prison, partly departed the Realme and forsaking all, rather then they will forsake God, and his moste true and vndoubted religion.

He recalls Henry VIII's deathbed repentance:

. . . as for King *Henry*, he wente nothing so farre as they are now come: but whereas for his pleasure he had put awaye the Popes authority, and for his profit had plucked downe Abbaies, he let all other poyntes in maner remayne as before: and of this also repented before he died, as it is knowen.*

He makes a final appeal:

I pray you when the three wise men came from the East to worship Christ, what did they see in him? Forsooth a yong infant, not able to helpe himselfe suckinge his mother a poore carpenters wyfe, and that in an oxe stawle: yet they fell downe and worshipped him as a God: Is it not as easie to beleeue the body of Christ is vnder the forme of bread, as that almightie God himselfe was then vnder the shape of a seely weake infante? O good Sisters, vnlesse you beleeue, you shall neuer vnderstande: beleeue once Christ his wordes, and that he is Almightie,

* This repentance of Henry VIII seems to have been persistently rumoured during the Queen's reign. Allen refers to it as a fact in his *Apologie of the English Seminaries*, when he addresses the Queen in these words: 'Your Highnes noble father (as of worthy and wise mē we haue heard) was fully determined to giue ouer the title of Supremacie, and vnite him self and his Realme to the See and Church Apostolike againe: but being preuented by death, could not accomplish his most necessarie and honorable designement, and therfore may be both an example and a warning to your Ma.tie the last of al his deerest Children, to accomplish that thing, which to his great wisdom, at the very going out of this life, was thought so necessarie for his soul, his people and posterity' [sig. G2]. It is referred to also by John Leslie in his *Treatise of Treasons* at sig. L6. So far as the writer knows the rumour was never contradicted.

> and that he is able to doe whatsoeuer he sayeth, and you will thinke that all is easye: returne to the Catholike Church, and be content to learne that which you know not, of them that wil not for all the world deceaue you, and you shal fynde exceeding comfort.

and ends with the following valediction:

> Commend me to your selues, your louing husbands, and your litle ones: and when you haue learned to beleeue ryght your selues, bringe them vp accordingly, & teach them to feare God. Make much of this berer I praye you: and saue him harmelesse by your wyse and discreate dealings. Almighty God preserue you, and by his holy spirite leade you into all truth. Amen.

Our third letter, the first of our volume, is dated from Paris, 15 February 1580, and is addressed to an apostate priest, an old friend of Martin's. It affords a further example of the simple eloquence of our author, and may be taken as expressing something of that affliction of spirit which must have been endured by many Elizabethan Catholics on account of the defection of their friends. The following extracts will form a fitting conclusion to this notice:

> O M. N. you should rather be ther where those handes should handle the blessed body of Christ, for which they were anointed and cōsecrated: where those lippes should say ordinarie *Mattins*, *Masse*, and *Euensong*, as you are boūd also by precepte, then to employ your whole bodie vpon the dailie doing of such thinges, which good preests dare not thinke once vpō (but against their wil) for feare of sinne. Or if you can not be in place to doe as you shoulde, yet you may alwaies be in place to refraine from that which you shoulde not doe.
>
> Good M. N. consider at length the case deepely as it deserueth. As it is odious before God and man that you haue thus fallen, so it shal be alwaies honorable for you to rise againe: we haue knowen maried priestes, afterwarde holie men, and by their repentance no lesse esteemed then if it had neuer bene. The Church of God (as also God him selfe) is alwaies glad of a penitent sinner, and the Angels in heauen reioise therat: let it suffice you that you haue taken your pleasure all this time, and geue God thankes that he hath spared you and reserued you al this time to repentance, wheras you might haue died in your sinnes and so haue bene damned euerlastingly: despise not his calling of you vnto him selfe and to his Catholike Church.
>
> * * *
>
> You see vvhat might be said if a man vvere disposed to set your selfe before your ovvne eies as in a glasse: but I hope you are vvise ynough to gather much of this litle: & I vvould to

God I had novv as good oportunitye to talke vvith you face to face as I haue had heretofore: I doubte not, by the grace of God, but I should reclayme you: for I persvvade my selfe that you vvould doe vvell, but the vvorld and the flesh ouercometh you: and yet (alas) flesh and bloud shall not possesse the kingdome of heauen. Thinke then of the losse of heauen, nay thincke on the paines of hell, vvhich shal beginne perhaps to morovv, perhaps one yere hence, and shal continevv for euer, for euer, for euer, (this is a long day,) and in more terrible torment then can be imagined in this life. And yet the verie goodnes and loue and benefites of God & of our Sauiour Christ, should make vs to doe vvel and to please him, more then the feare of hel paines. Slaues and seruantes vvill not vvorke vvithout stripes: but children ought to doe vvell of verie loue and conscience.

* * *

For a farewel, remember the later ende of man, the accompte to be made, the consequent thereof, hel or heauen, and before all other respectes doe well for his sake that made you, redeemed you, sanctified you, and hath hitherto preserued and enriched you, and will hereafter in heauen fully rewarde you, if you wil come euen now at the ninth and eleuenth howre. Our Lord keepe you.

Your louing frend vndoubtedly G. M.

NICOLAS SANDER

The fact that Sander, one of the leaders of the Louvainists, should have rounded off the English works which he put out from Louvain with a treatise on usury, a subject which can hardly be described as coming within the orbit of the attack which the Recusant scholars, established in that city, were directing against the Anglican schism, provides one more indication of the importance with which this subject was regarded in the sixteenth century. It is quite clear that his treatise is not directed against anything the Anglicans had written on the subject, for it is one of the interesting facts of the English Reformation that upon this one burning question of the time Anglicans and Catholics were in full agreement. Latimer in his sermons, Ponet in his *An Exhortation, or rather a Warning, to the Lords and Commons*, Crowley in his *The Way to Wealth* and *Epigrams*, Lever in his sermons, Becon in his *The Jewel of Joy*, Sandys in his sermons, Wilson in his *A Discourse upon Usury*, and Jewel – to mention but the best-known names – had all appealed on the question to the traditional teaching of the Church as it was to be found in the Bible, the Fathers and the Schoolmen, the decretals, church councils, and commentators on the canon law, and all had, therefore, held the orthodox and Catholic view that by the laws of the Church usury is simply and generally prohibited.* Furthermore, even the Act of 1571 had subscribed to the same orthodox view in one of its sections in declaring that 'all usurie being forbydden by the lawe of God is synne and detestable'.† If Sander, then, had intended aiming a shaft at the Anglicans by his treatise, he could hardly have undertaken a barrener task. In face, therefore, of this coincidence of view, as between Anglicans and Catholics, we may very well ask what was Sander's purpose in publishing a further English work on the subject of usury. The answer to this question would seem to be twofold and to have a particular and general reference. We may suppose that first (and this is to interpret Sander's action in the narrower and more parochial sense) the growing practice of usury throughout the realm called for some authoritative statement in English from a Catholic source to set side by side with the Protestant literature on the subject; and second (and here we are basing his action on wider and more general grounds) the spreading influence of Calvinistic teaching on all social questions in the reformed Churches threatened the whole system of Catholic and medieval thought. 'The theory of usury', writes Tawney, 'which the divines of the sixteenth century inherited was not an isolated freak of casuistical ingenuity, but one subordinate element in a comprehensive system of social philosophy, which gave its poignancy to the controversy of which it became the centre. The passion which fed on its dusty dialectics was fanned by the conviction that the issue at stake was not merely a legal technicality. It was the fate of the whole scheme of medieval thought, which had attempted to treat economic affairs as part of a hierarchy of values, embracing all interests and activities, of which the apex was religion.'‡

* I am indebted to R. H. Tawney's important work, *Religion and the Rise of Capitalism* (1929), for the detailed references and for some of the wording in this statement; cf. especially pp. 82, 158 and 306.

† Tawney, op. cit., pp. 180–1. The Act was that of 13 Eliz., c.8, and was introduced to repeal the more stringent regulations against usury of the Act of 1552.

‡ op. cit., pp. 153–4.

To interpret exactly and fully the position which confronted Catholic and Anglican divines alike in respect of the theory and practice of usury in the reign of Elizabeth would require a much more detailed discussion of the subject than this short notice permits. The reader will be well advised himself to consult the work of Tawney, upon which are based these few preliminary remarks, for such discussion, and also the same writer's compendious introduction to Thomas Wilson's *Discourse.** Here we must confine our attention to one or two leading details which may serve to define more sharply the opposition on the part of the orthodox to the new movement in social ethics and which may help to elucidate the motives which prompted Sander to intervene on behalf of the Catholics. And first a word as to the interpretation placed on the term usury itself by those who were opposed to its practice. 'The truth is', writes Tawney, 'that any bargain, in which one party obviously gained more advantage than the other, and used his power to the full, was regarded as usurious.' Thus 'not only the taking of interest for a loan, but the raising of prices by a monopolist, the beating down of prices by a keen bargainer, the rack-renting of land by a landlord, the sub-letting of land by a tenant at a rent higher than he himself paid, the cutting of wages and the paying of wages in truck, the refusal of discount to a tardy debtor, the insistence on unreasonably good security for a loan, the excessive profits of a middleman – all these had been denounced as usury in the very practical thirteenth-century manual of St. Raymond; all these were among the "unlawful chaffer", the "subtlety and sleight", which was what the plain man who sat on juries and listened to sermons in parish churches meant by usury three centuries later'.† There is plenty of evidence that the traditional view which is expressed in these words had to some extent been modified in practice throughout the later Middle Ages. And it would seem that ethical theory also had not been wanting in order to justify a restricted form of capitalism. Tawney quotes St. Antonino (fifteenth century), for instance, as having attempted 'to maintain the principle of the just price, while

* *A Discourse upon Usury* (Bell & Sons, 1925). The Introduction, which covers some 200 pages, examines the medieval background which lies behind Wilson's writing.

† As before, p. 153. For Raymund of Pennafort's manual the reader is referred to *Raimundi de Penna-forti Summa Pastoralis* (Ravaisson, *Catalogue Général des MSS. des Bibliothèques publiques des Departements*, 1849, Vol. I, pp. 592 et seq.).

making allowance for practical necessities' and as having concluded that 'the fairness of a price could at best be a matter only of "probability and conjecture", since it would vary with places, periods and persons'.* But it is the open pronouncements of the extreme Protestant School of Calvin, Bucer and Bullinger which represent the real break with the tradition which 'stigmatized the middleman as a parasite and the usurer as a thief',† and there can be little doubt that Sander had these writers in mind when he wrote his brief treatise in defence of the orthodox view.

Modern opinion will not, of course, find anything obnoxious in the doctrine of usury as it was propounded by these Reformers; but to the medievally-minded Catholic it appeared as a subversion of the moral law of which the Church was the guardian and the exponent. The doctrine may be roughly summarized in the declaration which another Catholic writer, to whom it was equally distasteful, put into the mouth of a sympathetic exponent of Calvinism. The statement, which is in the nature of an *obiter dictum*, is undoubtedly a bald one, but it will suffice. It runs: 'Divine law does not teach us that all forms of usury are to be condemned, but only that kind which is extravagant in its demands, which "exhausts" the borrower, and ruins him by excessive exactions. So Bullinger writes: "If a man should give money to another, whereby he may purchase a property, or a farm, or fields, and so may trade and at length make a profit on his purchase, I do not see why the lender of the money should not be allowed to receive an equal profit (over and above his capital) for the money hired out as it were from his own estate", and having gone on learnedly to support this view from Holy Scripture he finally concludes: "Therefore usury is prohibited by divine law only so far as it injures one's neighbour (as I read the Scriptures) and brings about his ruin; and in respect of this it is the duty of the accredited Magistrates to restrain usurers by just laws, and to fix, according to the conditions of times and places, persons and things, what should be equitable, just, and allowed, in order that in the business of borrowing and lending usurers may not oppress the unfortunate" – which is the opinion also of Bucer and Molinaeus'.‡

* As before, pp. 40 and 296. The references given are *Summa Theologica*, pars. ii, tit. i, cap. viii, §1, and cap. xvi, §iii.

† ibid., p. 104.

‡ William Rainolds, *Caluino-Turcismus* (1597), p. 306.

The principles which this statement embodies, it will be observed, are not unlike those expressed by St. Antonino, referred to above, and, on the face of it, would seem to be no more than a natural development of the teaching of some at least of the medieval jurists on the subject of money-lending. In fact, the crucial point of divergence from the traditional doctrines was that the Reformers were ready to treat as *normal* what had hitherto been regarded as *exceptional*; they were prepared, to use Bacon's expression, 'in a sort [to] authorize usury, which before was in some places but permissive', and it was in this respect that their teaching ran counter to the whole conception of the theory of usury inherited from the Middle Ages. As for the wider implications of the new teaching as it affected moral values and social conduct, though these are not irrelevant to our theme, to speak of them here would carry us far beyond the scope of this short notice and our immediate purpose. This much only need we add: that in their vigorous reassertion of the traditional doctrines our sixteenth-century English writers were undoubtedly influenced by the unhappy state of affairs which had resulted from usurious practice in their own country. Dr. Thomas Wilson, who, as Master of Requests, spoke from first-hand knowledge, is insistent upon this point, and he foresees, as indeed did Jewel and Sander, the most grievous danger to the commonwealth in the continuance of the practice.*

It is in the light of these facts, therefore, that we may understand the greater stringency of both Anglican and Catholic opinion concerning the practice of taking interest, and herein lies the explanation of the reaffirmation of the medieval doctrine by both Sander and the sixteenth-century Anglican divines.

Sander's work carries the following title: *A Briefe Treatise of Vsurie, made by Nicolas Sander D. of Diuinitie. Luc. 6. Mutuum date, nihil inde sperantes. Geue to lone, hoping for nothĩg therof*,† and we may discern in its reference to *St. Luke* (vi. 35 to be precise) one of the principal differences between the orthodox attitude on the subject of usury, with its appeal to Scriptural authority, and that of the Reformers, who rejected the commonly quoted

* cf., for instance, the Address to Leicester which prefaces his *A Discourse vppon vsurye*, where he sums up: 'For as I thinke, and must saye stil, vsurie onely, is the cheefest cause of the greatest miserie in thys lande, aswell to geeue occasion of great waste, as also to make much wante, and wil be in the ende, the vndoynge of all, yf it bee not loked to in tyme.'

† See bibl. ent. 132.

passages from the Scriptures and the Fathers as irrelevant, 'because designed for conditions which no longer exist'.* This appeal to divine law, as it is revealed in the word of Scripture, together with the argument from natural law, as it is set forth in the *Politics* of Aristotle, provides the basis upon which Sander seeks to build his main thesis that payment of interest for capital is unjustified and unjustifiable. The high light of his exposition is, of course, the all-important Latin text from *St. Luke*, quoted in the title, which is given, medieval fashion, the following ingenious, if somewhat disconcerting, turn:

> The Latin name [*mutuum*] is compounded of two wordes, *meum* and *tuum*, myne, and thine, as if we might say in english Mynethine: whereby is mēt, that the thing which before was mine, is by lending made thine, to the end thou maist vse it, being thine owne, and the value thereof must again of thine be made myne when it is restored back vnto me [sig. B7].

In respect of the main substance of his argument, following as it does the traditional lines, a simple reference to the headings of the ten short chapters should be enough to acquaint the reader with its general tenor and its uncompromising nature. Here they are:

1. The occasion of this Treatise, and the argumentes which are commonly made for the defense of vsurie, and what is vsurie.
2. That vsurie is forbidden by Gods Lawe, vnder the paine of euerlasting damnation.
3. Whence bargaines proceede, and why Almosdedes are so acceptable to God.
4. Of geuing to lone or lending, which are naturally free contractes.
5. How much it importeth, that the boundes and limites of euerie contract belonging to the law of nations, should be inuiolably kept and maintayned.
6. That the vsurer in setting out his mony for gayne, doth, and can not but geue his monie to lone.
7. How heynouse, and how much against the nature of geuing to lone, and against the law of al Nations the vice of vsurie is.
8. That the Heathens condemned vsurie.
9. That the Ciuil lawe doth not acknowledge vsurie to spring or arise of the nature of suche thinges as are geuen to lone, but rather to be contrarie therevnto.
10. Certaine examples of vsurie, whereby yt may the better be knowen, what is vsurie, and what is not: and of the restitution which the vsurer is bound to make.

* Tawney, as before, p. 107.

The heart of the argument is to be found in Chapter 4, where, following the interpretation of the text of *St. Luke* given above, the Christian ethics of lending is developed according to the juristic principles of canon law. The chapter concludes with the following admirable summary:

> Hytherto we haue learned, first, that geuing to lone is a contract in nature next vnto almose deedes, or to a free gift, not differing at al from it, for the time that it dureth.
>
> Secondly, that yt ought allwaies to be free: otherwise it is no lone at al, but a selling or setting to hyer.
>
> Thirdly, that yt differeth from simple lending, because the proprietie of the thing geuen to lone, becometh his owne who boroweth yt, which is not so in simple lending.
>
> Fourthly, it insueth herevpon, that in geuing to lone, the danger and losse is his only who boroweth, and not at al his who geueth to lone: because the lord of euerie thing alwaies beareth the losse, and not he who had nothing to do withal.
>
> Fifthly, thinges geuen to lone be such as consist of weight, number and measure: as wine, oyle, corne or graine.
>
> Last of all, monie is of those thinges which are geuen to lone, and cōsequently he is not lord of yt who lent yt, but he only who boroweth it. And therefore if the mony lent, be stolen, or doe perish by what soeuer mischance, without any default in the world of him who doth borowe yt: yet he that gaue it to lone, may with safe conscience aske so much again as he lent, and the borower (if he be able) is bound to repaie yt [sig. C6–7].

As for the style of the treatise, there is little we can add to what has already been said of Sander's writing elsewhere in this book. There is the same plain and unequivocal statement as characterized his earlier *Treatise of Images*, the same precision in the handling of his material, the same lucid expression. It may be that at times the presentation of the theme reminds us that a Regius Professor of Canon Law is speaking, as in the summary just quoted, and that the English retains in some measure the scholastic method of exposition; but the terminology as a rule is not scholastic, but derives from the native idiom, and there are passages where markedly the 'vigorous sap of native English phrase' (to borrow an expression from Saintsbury) gives to the argument a cogency which is at several removes from the cold dry tones of the Schoolmen.

JOHN LESLIE

The name of John Leslie, Bishop of Ross, will be familiar to historians of the Elizabethan period as the ambassador of Mary Stuart to the English Court and later as her agent abroad. As a person of note he thus occupies an important place among our Catholic refugees, and though one would hesitate to class him as of outstanding ability as a writer, yet his skill as a dialectician and his legal and historical learning, in which he has been compared to his learned fellow-Scot of the reformed party, George Buchanan,* give to his writings a documentary interest which no student of English and Scottish relations in the reign of Elizabeth can neglect.

In the bibliography to this work (s.v. *Leslie*) reference will be found to some fourteen of Leslie's compositions.† These include certain foreign translations and retranslations of his own works – which, of course, are not our present concern, though, on account of their variations from their originals, both by amendments and additions, they are each and all important for any complete estimate of our author's views on the general current of contemporary English and Scottish affairs. They include also the *History of Scotland*, which equally does not concern us here, since it is written in the Scottish vernacular and not in 'Southron'. Three works only of the fourteen actually fall within the scope of our present inquiry and these are, in chronological order: the *Defence of the honour of the right highe, mightye and noble Princesse Marie Quene of Scotlande and dowager of France* (1569) – with its second edition of 1571, entitled *A Treatise concerning the Defence*, etc.; the *Treatise of Treasons against Q. Elizabeth* (1572); and *The Copie of a Letter writen out of Scotland* (1572?). Since the occasion of the writing and the history of these three works is fully dealt with in the bibliography at the end of this book, we may turn at once to an examination of their matter and their style.

The *Defence of the honour*, which is described in the half-humorous allegorical colophon of the earlier edition as printed 'at London in Flete strete at the signe of Iustice Royal, againste the Blacke bell, by Eusebius Dicaeophile', and to be sold 'in

* T. F. Henderson in the *D.N.B.*, s.v. *Leslie*.

† Probably an additional six more writings of varying sorts may be ascribed to his pen, according to the *D.N.B.*

Paules churche yearde, at the signes of Tyme & Truthe, by the Brasen Serpēt, in the shoppes of Ptolomé and Nicephore Lycosthenes brethren Germanes,' was in truth printed abroad by Allen's printer, John Fogny of Rhemes. It is a small octavo volume of some three hundred pages and comprises three books or parts, dealing in turn with Mary's innocence with regard to certain calumnies which were being spread abroad respecting her private and public life, with her right to 'the Succession of the crowne of Englande', and with the more general question of the Rule of Women. Leslie's own version of his reason for writing this defence of his mistress is given in the Address to the Reader, where the following general statement occurs. We quote from the rather more elaborate form of the second edition of 1571:

> How be it, considering the world so farre corrupted, as at this day it is, and fearing, least the infamie of their slanders haue seduced certaine of to light persuasion, to geue ouermuch credite therevnto: I haue thought it expedient, to declare her innocencie to the whole world, and to iustifie the same in such plaine and true wise, by answering to al their slanderous and spiteful accusations (so far foorth as the time present may yet permit to be published and disclosed) and in such forme I trust, as the discrete Reader shal plainly see, how iniuriously the noble and innocent Queene hath bene slandered by her malitious Aduersaries . . .

A more particular statement in respect of Part I singles out the Queen's marriage with Darnley, the casket letters, and the Norfolk match as the principal points of issue raised by Mary's calumniators which are to be resolved. It runs:

> The effect and drifte of the whole tendeth to this, that first they would we should beleeue: that after her mariage her minde was as it were alienated from her husband.
>
> Secondly they pretende certain letters, that they surmise and would haue, to haue bene written by her Grace: wherby they seeke to inferre against her many a presumption, as their wily braines imagine. But the most weighty of them al seemeth to them to be her pretensed Mariage, whereof we wil lastly entreate [sig. A4].

With Part II we pass on to matters less directly personal. Here our author is concerned mainly with the legal aspect of the Queen's succession. For much of the matter of his argument he was indebted, as he freely acknowledges in his *Discourse*, to

Anthony Brown, Lord Chief Justice of Common Pleas, and to Mr. Carell, another learned and judicious lawyer.* As we might expect, the style of this part of the *Defence* is less free, the expression rather more technical, than in Part I. Part III, which declares 'that the Regiment of Women is conformable to the lawe of God and Nature', returns again to the more vehement fashion of Part I. It may be regarded in some degree as a sop to Cerberus, since the question involved the prestige of Elizabeth as well as that of Mary Stuart. It also afforded Leslie a parting shot at his old antagonist, John Knox, who had oppugned the right of women to rule in his *First Blast of the Trumpet against the Monstruous Regiment of Women*, a tract that was originally aimed at Mary of Lorraine, the Scottish Regent, and Mary I of England. It is worthy of notice that in this third part our author writes as though he were an Englishman and not as a Scotsman, a trick he was to repeat in the later *Treatise of Treasons*. One thing further with regard to the subject-matter of the *Defence* must be here recorded. It is that in the second (revised) edition of 1571 the attitude of the writer towards Elizabeth has completely changed. Whereas in the earlier edition Mary's claims to the throne were regarded as secondary to those of Elizabeth, now they are no longer so regarded, and she is treated as the only true heir to the English crown. No wonder that it gave greater offence to the English Court than the prior edition, and that Charles Bailley, one of Queen Mary's servants, was apprehended for introducing copies of the book into the country.†

The *Treatise of Treasons*, as the title indicates, is divided into two parts, 'whereof, The firste Parte answereth certaine Treasons pretended, that neuer were intended: And the second, discouereth greater Treasons committed, that are by few perceiued'. The first part, in other words, is a reply, paragraph by paragraph, to the tract *Salutem in Christo*, published by Richard Grafton, to defend the Duke of Norfolk's execution in 1571; the second, a strong attack upon Cecil and Bacon (the former of whom is designated as Synon), who Leslie believed were behind this pamphlet.‡ Incidentally, the author is at pains to defend himself against the charge that he was '$\overset{e}{y}$ chiefest cause

* See bibl. ent. 75. † See bibliography, as already cited.
‡ For further details, see bibliography as before.

of the Dukes calamitie, whome before and aboue al other, next vnto his Souueraigne and Mistresse, he hath euer honoured and serued, as his publike dedes do sufficiētly testifie',* and to justify his conduct as Mary Stuart's ambassador to the English Court. J. B. Code has described the *Treatise* as one of the most important of the political pamphlets of the whole Elizabethan period,† and, by way of summary, we cannot do better than quote his own words in support of this statement. The chief value of the pamphlet, he writes, 'consists in that it gives the feelings of the English Catholics before the persecution had reached its heighth, when already many believed that Cecil was the power in England, sharing his position, however, with Sir Nicholas Bacon. Fines, imprisonments, and even executions, so it states, had already created a state of suffering for the Catholics simply because of their refusal to subscribe to the change of religion. Already Elizabeth was regarded as being in the hands of her ministers. The author of this pamphlet gives a story of intrigue, deception, disregard for law, poverty, heavy taxation, piracy, help to rebels, and a widespread moral decadence. Graphic as are the details with which the narrative is given, more striking is its insistence that England has broken with a tradition of long standing, a break that is not only political, but economic and religious. It is to be noted that the characteristic common to the earlier [Recusant] writings, namely the clemency of Elizabeth, is dwelt upon here at length'.‡

A brief compendium of this *Treatise*, published under the initials 'G. T.', probably in the year following the publication of the original, and summarizing its contents, will be discussed along with another of G. T.'s works in our next notice (below, p. 317).

The *Copie of a Letter*, published anonymously by John Fowler from Louvain, probably in 1572,§ a very rare black-letter pamphlet of 130 pages, is an account by a contemporary, evidently in the closest touch with the Queen's affairs, of the connexion of Mary with the murder of Darnley. It is, in fact,

* sig. G4v. † *Queen Elizabeth and the English Catholic Historians* (1935), p. 72.

‡ ibid. A footnote in connexion with this last point cites: 'Behold how her mildness and clemency in government for many years together, by speech and print was justly commended and remaineth, no doubt, in her good nature still: and the renown thereof redounding to her great honour' (fol. 162).

§ It is without name of author, place or date. See bibl. ent. 79.

a reply to the charge that, in order to marry Bothwell, Mary connived at, even if she did not prompt, the murder of her husband. It is the work of a skilled advocate, the line followed being very much that which we find in the *Treatise concerning the Defence*; in fact, a comparison with that work affords substantial evidence for the single authorship of the two books. On account of the extreme rarity of the little volume, and since its subject is of considerable historical interest, we propose to offer a short summary of the principal points which the writer puts forward in support of his case. The Regent, James Stewart, Earl of Moray, Mary's half-brother and her chief enemy, is pointed to incisively as the villain of the piece, the argument running somewhat as follows:

(1) That it was contrary to Mary's character to connive at murder.

(2) If she had wished to rid herself of Darnley she might have employed the ordinary course of the law against him in respect of his dagger found sticking in her secretary David's body when he was murdered. She would appear, therefore, to have gone out of her way in order to seek unlawful means for his destruction.

(3) She would not countenance divorce from her husband. She believed Darnley would in time grow into a more responsible person. She was further not insensible of her duty to him as her husband. Moreover, she had been completely reconciled to him before his death.

(4) The absence of motive on her part. *Cui bono?* She could gain nothing by Darnley's murder, the Earl of Moray everything.

(5) To the charge that she was already intriguing with Bothwell during Darnley's lifetime, a charge grounded upon the finding of a letter from the Queen to Bothwell in a box taken upon Dugglish, the Earl of Bothwell's man, who was sent to the Earl from Sir James Balfore, Captain of Edinburgh Castle, it is replied that it is most improbable that Bothwell's enemy, Balfore, would so help him.* Further, there is not a scrap of evidence to show that Mary had written the letter. Nor would it be like the Queen to write such a letter.

* Sir James Balfour (d. 1583) was, however, a great time-server, and changed sides more than once.

(6) As against the contention that Mary's marriage with Bothwell, one of Darnley's murderers, three months after the death of Darnley provided supporting proof of her guilt, it is replied that the Earl of Moray himself (in letters extant) persuaded the Queen to this course for, as he intimated, the good of the realm.

The writer concludes that even if these arguments are not decisive in exonerating the Queen, Moray's complicity in the murder can be established beyond doubt from other sources.

> If suche vehement presumptions as are before remembred, (he writes) could be slightly past ouer, as things that rather make likely, then cleerly proue true yͭ which is gathered therof: yet is it not to be mistrusted, but so many witnesses directly accusinge Murrey & his complices, at the houre of their death, Murreys foretelling the night when the Lord Darley shoulde be killed, the flatte and weightie testimonie of the Noble Lord Harris yet liuing, and lastly the Indenture of that traiterous conspiracie, signed and sealed with the knowen hand and seale of the Lord Murray and his Confederates,* will fully satisfie all men yͭ haue their commō sense, and geue them matter inough cleerely to see, who were the procurers of that horrible murder, wherof the guiltie malefactours haue so vnnaturally slandered their good and guiltlesse Queene.†

Leslie's use of English rather than Scottish in these three tracts or treatises is to be explained by the fact that he was writing for an English audience. This, together with his sense of style, accounts for the care he took in submitting the first of them (we have no information on this point with regard to the other two) for revision to his friend and physician, Dr. Good, in order to ensure the purity of the expression. Dr. Good seems to have done his work well, for we can find no obvious trace

* cf. *Treatise concerning the Defence* (sig. F6): 'We can tel you, that there were interchangeable Indentures made and subscribed by you, that he which had the best opportunitie offered to make him away, should furthwith take it in hande and dispatche him.'

† sig. D2^{v}–3. The complicity of Moray in the murder is substantially echoed in *The Sakeless Queen: A Ryme in defence of the Q. of Scotts against the Earle of Murray* (1568), cited by Miss Guiney in *Recusant Poets* (1938), p. 250. The indictment of the Earl is briefly set forth in the following lines:

> A scholler sure of pregnant wit and apt for such a place
> who trayned up was in the schole of lyeinge *Sathans* grace.
> where he hath learned a finer feate then *Richard* earst did see
> to doe the deede and laye the blame on them that blameless be
> for he and his companions eake agreeing all in one
> did kill the kinge and laye the blame the sakelesse Queene upon.

of Scotticisms in the *Defence*. Only rarely, too, in the *Treatise of Treasons* does the writer reveal himself as not being completely *au fait* with the English tongue. There are occasional difficult expressions and twisted idioms, and perhaps an even more occasional Scotticism, but that is all. The writing is not unattractive in the vigour and the homeliness of the expression. But there is, to set off against this, especially in the *Treatise*, a strong tendency to orotundity, not to say volubility, and in some passages, where the Elizabethan predilection for rhetoric is most marked, the whole bag of rhetorical tricks is exhibited to our gaze.

There is little, therefore, in the general style of Leslie's writing to distinguish him from his fellow-rhetoricians, and we do not propose here to offer the reader further examples of a style with which he must be thoroughly familiar. Leslie's books, as we have already suggested, are principally interesting for their subject-matter and for the light that they throw upon contemporary events, and though we must not overlook their usefulness in providing, in phrase and idiom, just that kind of colloquial evidence the absence of which is so often baffling to the student of our earlier literature,* yet it is on these considerations that their worth must ultimately be judged.

One further thing we would add before we bring this review of Leslie to an end. More than one modern writer has suggested that the origin of certain elements in our English prose tradition is to be found in the ancient English alliterative verse. The trick of balanced sentences and alliteration so common in sixteenth-century writing would certainly seem to demand some such explanation. G. P. Krapp avers that with the Middle-English revival of alliterative verse – and he refers especially to Langland – the verse of this tradition passed over into popular alliterative prose which 'in its looseness of form and its picturesqueness and homely vigor . . . resembles the degraded survival of the older alliterative long line known as "tumbling verse" '.† There seems no reason to dispute this statement. That this alliterative tradition, fostered in part by pulpit oratory, was very much alive at the beginning of the sixteenth

* Numerous examples of words and expressions, either earlier or later than the recorded usages in the *N.E.D.*, are to be found in Leslie's works.

† *The Rise of English Literary Prose*, as before, p. 18.

century, R. W. Chambers has pointed out in his *Continuity of English Prose*.* That it was still alive and working towards the end of the century, Leslie will bear witness. It would, we think, be difficult to find more striking evidence of this fact than is supplied by the following alliterative lines, taken at random from the *Treatise of Treasons*:

> From fasting fishdaies to flesh on Fridaies.
> A Russianlike russhing into al vice.
> Lulled and culled in Catilines armes.
> It bended and tended to a farre other marke.
> These painted pretenses of plausible things.
> What must this purposed & prepended defamation
> Of these Princes in prison promise and portend?

'G. T.'

Before turning to an examination of the two works of the anonymous writer who signs himself 'G. T.', let us say a word about their author. There is no evidence, so far as I have been able to ascertain, pointing to his identity at all, nor is there any very certain evidence for attributing both the works, grouped here under a single designation, to the same person. Each is signed with the same initials, 'G. T.'; both writers, when occasion serves, write with the same gusto, and they are alike in their use of certain rhetorical tricks, such as that of repetition; both also were pretty certainly abroad at the time of writing. There our evidence of a common identity ends, and although it is sufficient perhaps to justify our present arrangement of grouping the two works together it can hardly be regarded as conclusive.

The earlier of the works, which purposes to be a short summary of Leslie's *Treatise of Treasons*, was published abroad by John Fowler probably in the year 1573. The only exemplar in existence, as far as the writer knows, is that in the Lambeth Palace Library where it is bound up with a copy of the *Treatise*, but is without title-page and lacks the end leaves of the second and third (last) of the octavo gatherings. It thus comprises forty-four pages instead of the full complement of forty-eight. These are divided between a dedicatory epistle to Elizabeth (five pages), the *Table* (twenty pages), a letter addressed to Sir Christopher Hatton and delivered to him at Spa on 5 July

* See especially, p. cxxiv.

1573, subscribed 'From Antwerp. the 26. of Iune 1573. By yours to his power. G. T.'* (three pages), and some additional points, incorporated after the *Table* had been handed to Hatton, 'implying vehement demonstrations of the present peril' of the Queen's life and person (fourteen pages). The main text-title to the pamphlet runs: *A Table gathered owt of a Booke named A Treatise of treasons against Q. Elizabeth, and the Croune of England. Latelie compiled by a stranger and sent owt of France, Printed in the yeare of our Lord 1572.*

The reason for the drawing up of the *Table* is stated in the epistle to Elizabeth as being due to the belief that Burghley and Bacon, the two chief conspirators named in the *Treatise*, had prevented the Queen's seeing the original. It was being sent to Sir Christopher Hatton in the hope that he would be able to circumvent the two councillors and bring it to Elizabeth's notice.† Hatton was singled out for this mission partly on account of his accessibility at Spa, whither he had gone to recuperate after a serious illness, partly because he was believed to be sympathetic towards the Catholic cause, and notably because of his known good favour at Court. These points are indicated in the covering letter to the Queen's Vice-Chamberlain which concludes with the words:

> '[The Table] is addressed vnto yow, that you should thereof make speedie conveye, in sort that the same may not faile to passe directlie to her heighnes handes. in the dutie whereof it is hoped yow wil not faile, for that it is firder intended that the said Table shal also be consigned to others of your qualitie, and shortlie come to print, and be published so, as both her highnes and the world may be wittnes that some one that loueth her'‡ &c.

In summarizing the *Treatise* 'G. T.' does not follow the order of the original, but plans to bring together the various points under the following headings:

> Treasons in general.
> Treasons in particular against the Queenes person, the realme and right succession.
> Particular Treasons of the Conspirators against the Queene of Scotl. the Realme and the Prince.

* i.e. 'to the utmost of his ability', a variant of 'yours at all power'.

† See bibl. ent. 143 for the text of the Epistle.

‡ sig. $**6^v$–7. One of the others to receive the *Table* was undoubtedly Burghley himself. See the latter's letter to Parker, cited at bibl. ent. 78.

> Treason to both the Crowns of England and Scotl. fol. 118. 125. &c. Where yow shal finde. xi. politicque and abondant prouisions made for the establishment of the third line, the howse of Suff. where unto the Capitaine conspiratours haue vnited them selues, and incorporated their children.
> Sicilian trickes and policies tending to the conspiratours final pourposes and treasons.
> What detrimentes and preiudices haue ensued to the Q. and to the Realme . . .
> Violation of common Iustice: and priuat Iniustice vsed to the furtherance of their final pourpose.
> A description of the English Sinon [Burghley].

From the last we cite the following summary:

> Of base parentage, ambitious minde, of subtil witte, of smooth tongue, of shamelesse face, of little honestie, of no cōscience: ennemie to the old blood Royal: Intollerablie insolent in authoritie: vile and abiect in aduersitie . . . Sinons sophistrie . . . Sinons falsehood in felowshippe . . . Sinons Credo. vnder King H. catholique, vnder King E. protestāt vnder Q.M. a creper to the crosse. vnder Q.E. first a Lutheran, then a Caluenist, then a puritane, nowe a Macheuelian if not an Anabaptist &c. fol. 97.

There follow two further sections, viz.:

> Dispersed Notes in the booke worth the consideration.
> A frindlie Alarme.

Among the twelve additional points in the fourth part of the pamphlet we observe that the abridger intimates to the Queen that Sinon 'tournithe over a new leafe', and that a new policy was afoot to make James the successor to the English throne in order that the conspirators might thereby conserve their power for their own ends. 'What lack they', he concludes, 'but that they looke when tyme will so tempre, as to set forward their terrible tragedies wich muste ende with the Dispatche of 3. Princes, the Q. of Scotl. her Soon, and your selfe, to the vttre confusion and ruine of a florishing Realme.'

The later work of our anonymous author is an English translation of de Launoy's French version of Fr. Persons' well-known *De Persecutione Anglicana Epistola* (Bologna? 1581)* with an accompanying address by the translator to the Lords of the Council. It is entitled *An Epistle of the Persecution of Catholickes in Englande. Translated owt of frenche into Englishe and conferred*

* The place of origin was really Rouen. See Chapter VI below and bibl. ent. 144.

withe the Latyne copie. by G.T. To whiche there is added an epistle by the translator to the right honorable Lordes of her maiesties preeuie councell towchynge the same matter. Like that of its prototype, the title-page is misleading as to its place of origin. It states that it was printed at Douay, whereas the printer was pretty certainly George L'Oyselet of Rouen, who was working under the superintendence of George Flinton at this time for the Refugees.* Appended to the translation is a letter from the Catholic martyr, Alexander Briant, to the Fathers of the Society of Jesus asking that he may be received into the Society *in absentia*, and a short Address to the Reader.

G. T.'s letter to the Lords of the Council, which is, of course, of minor importance compared with the translation, may be briefly epitomised. The writer begins by contrasting the Marian persecution with that of Elizabeth and then goes on to point out the great advantages enjoyed by a State where Catholic conditions prevail. These advantages are derived from the principles of conduct inherent in Catholic doctrine and governing the life of a Catholic people. The principles may be summarized as follows: the necessity of restitution (=prevention of theft); observation of vows; abstinence from flesh (=economy); fasting (=economy); celibacy of clergy and religious (problems of overpopulation and poverty solved); prohibition of the raising of rents, save moderately and upon great cause; divorce forbidden; obedience to magistrates; the wise distinction of venial and mortal sin; the effect of reward and punishment hereafter; encouragement to good works; and confession, 'which thinge is the verie hedge and wall of all vertuous life, and the cheefest brydle of Lycentiousnes in a common wealthe'. The letter ends with a plea for toleration.

It is not at first sight easy to see why our translator should have chosen to employ the French version of Persons' work for his translation instead of Persons' original, since, as he himself intimates on his title-page, he had the latter beside him for the purpose of checking de Launoy. It is possible that we have here yet one more example of that allegiance or respect which was paid to French models by English writers in the sixteenth century. It is again possible that our author, finding ready to his hand in de Launoy's version one which had already to some

* Chapter VI below.

extent adapted the more severe style of the Latin to suit contemporary taste, decided to avail himself of his contemporary's labour in order to lighten his own task of substitution. In any case, whatever may have been his reason, the effect upon his work is manifest. The natural ease and flow of the French style is carried over into the English version, and it is from the French that the English borrows much of the vivacity and freedom of expression which is its distinguishing trait. Two examples must suffice to illustrate these marks of the translator's style. Both have reference to the treatment meted out to notable Recusants by the authorities. The first, as the margin indicates, concerns 'M. Tirwit sonne to Sir Robert Tirwit':

> A certein yong gentleman, of an auncient and right woorshipfull familie, was accused for hearing of a masse celebrated (as it was reported) at the mariage of his sister. Where vppon he fled from his fathers house, and kept hym selfe secret in London the yere last past. And there, by reason of his trauaile in flyeing awaye, and (as I think) through the intemperature of the sōmer, he fell in to a greuouse feuer. The aduersaries hearing hereof, doe runne vnto him by and by, and in all haste will nedes pull hym oute of the house, and throwe hym in to prison, euen as he then was, feble, faynt, and greuouslye sicke. This semed to the beholders thereof to be a maner of dealing bothe churlishe & detestable. They pray, they intreate, they make intercession, they vse all the means they can, to moue the aduersarie to haue consideration of the sick, not to heape sorow vpon sorow, nor affliction vppon an extremely afflicted man, not to take away the lyfe of so comelie a yong gentleman: they proffer as sufficient assurance for his forth coming, as his aduersaries wolde demaund, and to vndertake for his appearance before the iustices immediatlie vpon the recouerie of his health: but it will not be accepted. The phisitions come, they affirm for certein, that he is vtterlie vndone and castē away, yf he shoulde be remoued forthe of that place in to the inconueniēces of a prison. All this is nothing regarded: they layd hands on the sickeman, haled hym away, shut hym vp in prisō, & with in two days next after he dyed: they burie hym, and make no bones of the matter, nor scruple, or anie regarde at all [sig. G1^{v}].

The second recounts the inhuman treatment accorded to Mr. Dimmock, a son-in-law of the Earl of Lincoln. In spite of the fact that he was suffering from some form of paralysis he was carried off to prison.

> What folowed? by these inconueniences in verie short space after, he dieth. And yet they leaue hym not when he is dyeing: yea then they vexe and afflict hym more. For they come when he is extreme sick, they come whiles he is wrestling with the pangs of deathe, they come as he is passing oute of this lyfe, they come whiles he is yeelding vp the Ghoost: then they trouble hym: thē they doe not suffer hym to rest, nor permit hym to die in suche sorte as he desired to die: (for his desire was to die according to the custome of the vniuersall christian churche:) but then the ministers flocke aboute hym: thē they intrude them selues vpon hym: then they vrge him to praye such sorie prayers of their owne making, as in healthe he cōtemned, in sicknesse with open voice he reiected, and (nowe dum & halfe deade,) by his countenaunce, by signes & tokens, & by gesture of his bodie he dyd vtterlie detest and abhorre. What greater vncourtesie, or crueltie rather, can be imagined than this? [sig. G3].

These extracts, let us add, are a fair sample not only of the translator's style, but also of the contents of Persons' volume, which is full of such references to persons and events connected with the Catholic persecution. These naturally fall outside the scope of our present study; nor are they properly the concern of the literary historian. On the other hand, as documentary evidence of a contemporary they have their value for the historian of the period, and, we would suggest, in this respect the testimony which in most cases they afford should not be overlooked.

ROGER BAYNES

The two dialogues which we are now to consider were both written during the reign of Elizabeth, though the second and later one was not actually published until the year 1617. Strictly speaking this latter falls outside the period we are discussing in this present volume, since, as we learn from the internal evidence of the text itself, it was composed some time after the death of Mary, Queen of Scots, probably about 1590. However, as it is the only other surviving work of our author and thus completes what evidence we have of his method and style of writing, we believe we shall best be serving the interests of the reader by including it here with the earlier volume of 1577.

Both dialogues are social in character and are intended to be popular in their appeal; which will account for our author's resort to this particular literary form, common enough in the sixteenth century as a device for sugaring the didactic pill. In the 'General Proeme' of *The Baynes of Aquisgrane*, the second of the dialogues, he defends his practice. Here are his words which, it may be observed, are meant to forestall the criticism of the learned as well as to explain and justify the method of the dialogue as an instrument for serious argument:

> In Dialogues it is not to be expected, that all which is written, is to be continuate doctrine, but that some Interlocutions are to enter betwixt; the which being passed ouer, then the matter of doctrine returneth againe.
>
> This trace hath *Count Baltazar Castiglio* in his *Courtier*, and *Boetius* in his *Consolation* directly followed; and *Plato* in his Compositions more then any other. The which Interlocutions though perhaps they may not fall out still to be so pleasing as the doctrine it-selfe; yet so long as they be not unproportionable to the matter which they concerne, they may be permitted to passe: because when all is done, he who will haue good store of corne, must be content withall to take some chaffe. Yet I cannot well deny, but that some motions I haue had, to diminish heere and there some discourses of the Interlocutors, had I not considered withall, that one thing it is to publish a Booke, and another thing to publish but a Pamphlet; and also a Booke or Bookes of such particuler titles, as without some amplification made, some of them doe render of themselues but small discourse of matter.

The reader will hardly fail to be struck by the *naïveté* of this statement, and if it were the complete measure of Baynes's practice his two dialogues might well be dismissed as unworthy of further notice. Happily there is more to it than this. The 'Interlocutions' of which he speaks are not mere digressions, but lend some weight and vivacity to the argument itself, and, moreover, the general handling of the dialogue, at any rate in respect of the *Baynes of Aquisgrane*, to which the words are especially intended to apply, with its easy, informal movement and its real figures, lifts it out of the region of mere debate and imparts to it that semi-dramatic quality which we are given to understand was the peculiar literary attraction of the great sixteenth-century masters of polemical dialogue.* But this is to anticipate.

* I have especially in mind the remarks of C. H. Herford on such masters of dialogue as Erasmus and Hutten in his *Studies in the Literary Relations of England and Germany in the Sixteenth Century* (1886).

The earlier dialogue, which carries the London imprint of Francis Coldocke and Henry Bynneman, was published in 1577 and bears the following title: *The Praise of Solitarinesse, Set down in the forme of a Dialogue, Wherein is conteyned, a Discourse Philosophical, of the lyfe Actiue, and Contemplatiue.* It is a black-letter quarto of some ninety-four pages and is dedicated to the Elizabethan poet and courtier, Sir Edward Dyer, whom the author calls 'my approued frende'. As dialogue it is definitely inferior in quality to the *Baynes*, since it lacks the interplay of character and speech which marks that work, following rather the more formal and pedantic lines of the medieval school debates. On this account it is hardly worth while troubling the reader with direct quotation from the book. On the other hand, owing to the great rarity of both this volume and its companion, that the reader may not be left entirely in the dark as to its contents, we shall presume to set forth very shortly the substance of its argument, and add a brief comment on the manner of its execution.

The theme of the discussion is simple enough and progresses by easy, leisurely stages through the two parts into which the discussion is divided. The occasion is a chance meeting in Venice of three friends, *Lysippus*, *Eudoxus* and *Tales*, who agree to pass the time pleasantly together in talk in a gondola, rather after the manner of the four friends in Dryden's *Essay of Dramatic Poesy*, who, it will be remembered, carry out their discussion in a barge on the river Thames. One of the three, *Eudoxus*, has just returned from the Isle of St. George whither he had escaped, as he says, for the sake of quietude. This at once raises the question upon which the theme of the dialogue is based. How far can Virtue be practised and preserved in a Society which is predominantly vicious? Does not solitariness (or the life of contemplation) provide a better field for the cultivation of Virtue than society (or the active life)? The answer will depend, says *Tales*, upon what we mean by Virtue, which it is agreed is nothing less than goodness itself. Pursuing this theme, *Tales* next draws a distinction between good and what he calls 'selfe-good'. Virtue is a good, but not a self-good. He means by this, if we may interpolate, that it is not a good in its own right, but only good in so far as it finds expression in the right activity of the soul under such conditions as make for its right exercise, following the well-known Aristotelian dictum that moral states have no existence apart from the activities corresponding to the moral states themselves. Later he follows this up with the further statement that 'Vertue is alwaies one and the selfesame thing, notwithstanding, that according to the diuersitie of matters wherein it is handled, it taketh diuerse names'. The point goes home and finds an echo in the rejoinder of *Lysippus*, who exclaims in a half-bantering tone: 'Verily Tales, then haue we in my opinion bene greatly fortunate, in this our brief disputation, for where we sought but for one onely *Vertue*, we haue now found out a whole worlde of *Vertues* to be resiaunt among men.' The discussion on Virtue is finally rounded off by *Tales*, who pronounces Virtue to be 'nothing else, than a good constitution of the soule and minde', and by *Lysippus*, who is allowed to add the all-important words – 'gotten by vse and exercise'. A short discourse upon the mind (which governs all our dispositions) and upon study (emphasizing above all the importance of the study of divine letters) follows this final pronouncement, and this brings the first part of the dialogue to a close.

The ground having thus been cleared, largely, as it will be observed through the instrumentality of *Tales*, *Eudoxus* and *Lysippus* now carry on the argument alone. *Eudoxus*, of course, favours Solitariness as against Society as the best means of embracing the virtuous life; *Lysippus*, as we should expect, takes the opposite view. Neither disputant is convincing. The fact is that with the absence of *Tales* as a principal in the debate the reader's interest inevitably slackens. He has come to depend so much upon *Tales* as the exponent of the author's views, and *Eudoxus* and *Lysippus* are so clearly made to play second fiddle in the first part, that the result is they are handicapped at the outset when they take over the discussion and have little or no chance of establishing themselves or of gaining the reader's confidence. It may be the author himself had little confidence in them, for the dialogue in the second part proves itself to be little more than a contest of debate (at one point the dispute degenerates into a mere verbal quibble) with each side playing for a win, and when finally *Lysippus* takes possession of the field and is about to overwhelm his opponent with the numerous *exempla* he adduces in support of his case, *Tales* is again called in to settle the question, which he does by effecting a compromise between the two contesting views. And so the dialogue ends.

As for the author's workmanship (and this is of more immediate interest to us) it must be already clear even from this rough sketch of the dialogue that the first part, with its carefully elaborated theme, is superior to the second, with its more limited range of matter. We may note further that, whereas in Part I the dialogue may definitely be said to give some support to the unfolding of the argument, thus contributing to the liveliness of its presentation, in Part II the debate is scarcely relieved by one dramatic touch or by one hint of play of emotion and character, with the result that it lacks verisimilitude and, as we have already suggested, suffers the consequent loss of the reader's interest. In respect of the dialogue as a whole let us repeat that it fails to reach the excellence of the later *Baynes*. This is partly to be accounted for by the purely allegorical nature of the characters employed, but even more than this by the fact that it savours strongly of the intellectual figment, common to early dialogue, of the first speaker maintaining, the second objecting, and the third deciding.

In turning to the second of the two dialogues, *The Baynes of Aquisgrane*, the first thing that must strike the reader is the ambitious nature of the projected work. Let us recall the circumstances out of which the dialogue takes its rise. Three men of one nation have come to the ancient city of Aquisgrane (Aix la Chapelle), presumably to take the waters for which it is famed. They are *Aquilonius*, 'a dexterous Northern-man, who being the conducter of a certaine Gentlemans sonne of those quarters, and a Politician by profession, was come thither only for stipend and remuneration of his seruice'; *Favonius*, 'a far borne Western-man, & by profession a Protestant, but of the ciuiller sort'; and *Subsolanus*, 'a middle dwelling Estern-man . . . a Catholike exiled'. The three meet in *Subsolanus*'s lodgings, and since they have twenty-seven days before them they agree to pass the time in argument upon the Variety of the World, the Subordination thereof, and the Folly of the same. Nine days are to be allotted to each of these three subjects. At the suggestion of *Subsolanus*, who proves himself to be a thorough schoolman in his methods of dichotomizing, the discussion on the Variety of the World is to be divided into three parts, viz. (1)

'Humane Nature', (2) the 'Mynd of man', and (3) the 'Body of man', three days being allowed for each of these subjects. In order to space out the time as neatly as possible a further sub-division is also proposed, one day being set apart for each of the subordinate themes. Thus *Human Nature* will be discussed from the point of view of (*a*) Profit, (*b*) Pleasure and (*c*) Honour; the *Mind of Man* from that of (*a*) Ignorance, (*b*) Opinion and (*c*) Science; and the *Body of Man* from that of (*a*) Education, (*b*) Travail and (*c*) Repose. It would seem, though it is not very clear, that the author intended to print two volumes to cover the discussion on Variety. This we learn from 'the general proeme' to his book, which adds that other volumes were to follow 'touching', as it says, 'Policy and many other curious matters'. In view of this statement and of the evidence furnished by the treatment of the first part of the subject it is not unduly fanciful to suppose that the same elaborate method was to be used for the remaining two parts, from which it would appear that the author must have anticipated publishing not less than six volumes in order to cover the whole of his work. A pretty ambitious undertaking in the circumstances. As it is, only that part of the first volume which embraces the subject of Profit seems to have seen the light of day, although the printer himself expected to publish the complete work. 'This present volume', he writes, 'and the rest that are to follow, though they haue not come to the Presse till now, yet haue they byn written some yeares ago, in the tyme of the late Queene Elizabeth.'* Why the printing should have abruptly ceased (if that is what happened) we shall probably never know. Of this, however, according to this statement, we can be certain, viz. that the author's extensive manuscript was in the printer's hands in the year 1617, and we may, I think, rightly regret, since Baynes has some claim to distinction as a writer of English prose, that no more of it has survived than that comprised by the curtailed volume under our present consideration.

The title of the volume, with its punning reference to the author, is as follows: *The Baynes of Aquisgrane, The 1. Part, & 1. Volume, intituled Variety. Contayning Three Bookes, in the forme of Dialogues, vnder the Titles following, Viz. Profit, Pleasure, Honour. Furnished with diuers things, no lesse delightfull, then beneficiall to be*

* The Printer to the Reader.

knowne, and obserued. Related by Rog. Baynes Gent. a long Exile out of England, not for any temporall respects. Qui nihil sperat, nihil desperat. Printed at Augusta in Germany. M.DC.XVII. Like *The Praise of Solitarinesse* it is a small quarto, but in roman letter, and is about twenty pages longer than that work. As a dialogue it is undoubtedly superior to its predecessor. In place of the purely allegorical figures of the earlier colloquy we have three characters, distinctly marked, whose very names suggest something of their nature. *Aquilonius* is a good hard-headed Northerner in his worldly-wise attitude towards the subject of wealth, in his stubbornness in persisting in his views about riches and honesty, and in his defence of Mary Queen of Scots against the English. *Favonius*, a Westerner, adopts a mildly tolerant Protestant attitude in defending the execution of Mary against the Northern man, but agrees with him in sticking to concrete facts and in his dislike of abstractions. *Subsolanus*, whose name suggests the cold and penetrating East wind, proves himself the thorough-going schoolman, both in his love of dividing and classifying and in his fondness for abstract conceptions. He is, of course, the more redoubtable opponent and provides an admirable foil to *Aquilonius*, who being a plain man dislikes intensely his hair-splitting and his method of *reductio ad absurdum*. 'Sophistication', he calls it, and occasionally when he gets very rattled he shows temper and waxes sarcastic at *Subsolanus*'s expense. But he never gives way, though he appears to be routed again and again, at least not until he is finally driven into silence by the final discourse of *Subsolanus*, who, as we might expect, is given the last word. On the whole the dialogue moves swiftly to and fro and it is rendered the more vivid not only through the quite considerable play of emotion which both *Aquilonius* and *Favonius* in turn manifest, but also from a number of humorous allusions. There is, of course, in places some clogging of the movement, due to the customary rhetorical trick of piling up words or phrases or *exempla*, and *Subsolanus* is especially an offender in this whenever he really gets into his sermonic stride. On the other hand, the use of the vernacular and the racy Elizabethan idiom are a compensating medium in interruptions of this kind to the flow of the argument, so that even in such passages the writing is not necessarily dull.

We propose to illustrate the style of the dialogue with two

extracts. The first, a very short one, we offer as exemplifying excellently the diverse manner of the three characters. Here it is:

> *Subsolanus.* In these mysticall reckonings of yours, me thinks you pay one another like as a souldier of Ægipt did, who only with the sound of his money paid a brawling Cook, for the smel of his rost-meate; since what with variety, and what with obscurity you determine of nothing.
>
> *Aquilonius.* Indeed, as you say, we Northern borderers be very obscure fellowes, for that we call a Hare a Hare, and a Dogge a Dogge, when we talke togeather in our owne domesticall language.
>
> *Favonius.* So that you leaue, I perceaue, vnto me (said *Favonius*) to answer vnto the imputed variety of our talke, as also to the not determining of our things somewhat better. And therefore to follow our proposition a little more strictly then before, I say now: That whereas worldlines transgresseth most of all in excesse, if it be on your part amended, & temperately moderated, the reckoning will be easily made vp betwixt vs.
>
> *Aquilonius.* As though in such a man (sayd *Aquilonius*) as followeth the world attentiuely, there might not be tolerated, sometimes, an once of excesse in his actions, to get thereby a pound of credit.
>
> *Favonius.* This kind of merchandize I do not well vnderstand . . . [sig. A4^{v}].

and so on. Our second, and longer extract, will serve to illustrate the nature and the manner of the interlocutions which our author defends in his proeme. *Subsolanus* is here pleading the cause of Poverty and commending its excellence:

> *Subsolanus.* Where, I pray you, was that couetous Wisdome, you speake of, at the very first beginning of things, when there was not yet in the world any kind of money, or riches to be found at all, but that ech where [i.e. everywhere] one commodity was changed for another? Belike the men of those dayes, if wisedome, as you say, had chiefly consisted in riches, were all fooles, and yet some Wise men haue said, That happy, and most happy were they, who liued in that so simple and honest an age, while no vanityes were as yet discouered amongst men, nor any disordinate appetites obscured the light of the vnderstanding, with the temptations of the fraile and deceiuable senses; and while there were as yet no weapons, nor warres, nor locks, nor doores, no robbing, nor stealing, nor any violent temptations vnto any kind of wickednes. For though women and men did conuerse togeather no lesse then they do now, yet

the women were modest and shamefast, and the men myld, and both of them continent, being accustomed to mortify and suppresse the disobedience of the flesh, partly with abstinence, and partly with assiduous labour, so as they felt no great motiues vnto sinne: I meane that innocent and pacificall age, when no Mettall was as yet digged out of the earth, nor no oxe, nor horse emploied to till the ground, but that euery one liued of that which the earth it selfe of it owne accord brought forth, without the help of any industry or art; for so God of his bounty had ordayned, that all those things, whereof man had need, as flesh, fruites, and the like, should be prouided for him, & produced for his vse aboue the gound [sic], hyding and burying all those other things which were superfluous (as gold, siluer, and the rest) within the bowells of the earth it selfe, to the end he should neither loue them nor desire them, nor be tempted to vse them, in respect of the great harme he might receiue by them. Besides that, no timbred Oake, nor Firre, nor Pyne had then byn framed into ships, to furrow the windy seas, either for curiosity to passe from one Country to another, or els to fetch home the variety of forrayne vnknowne delicacyes . . . (ô gentle Pouerty!) thou, I say, who when thou obseruest the Lawes of Nature, doest subdue all paynfull industry, doest ouercome all mortall honour and doest contemne the vayne discourses of men, not caring for the heat of the summer, nor much esteeming the cold of the winter, but contented to repaire the one with the shaddow of the leaued trees, and to withstand the other with the help of the cheap vntawed skins of beasts, whereby in that homely weed thou shunnest the temptations of all idle loue, of all vaine lasciuiousnes, & of all shamefull lust, as also all the enuy of men, all the daunger of theeues, and all the disturbance of broken sleeps: wherefore to thee be the eternall praise of all ingeniosity, of all inuentions, and of all arts, as vnto the egregious Mother of all study, of all speculation, and of all operation: whose vertues (to conclude) be many, whose refuges more, and whose benefits be infinite.

Aquilonius. These be Sophisticall fictions, rather then reasons, all of them found out by the art and malignity of such, as vnder a certaine kind of Philosophicall authority, do attend to inuent those abstracted arguments, thereby to giue credit and reputation to the beggarly and bare state of their owne base fortune, because they are not able to attayne vnto more . . . [sig. K2^{v}–4^{v}].

In this last rejoinder of *Aquilonius* the reader may trace the aggressive conceit of the one-time typical Northerner defending his partiality for his beloved brass.

RICHARD VERSTEGAN

Verstegan's *Post of the World* is the only one of his many printed works which was written during the period which this volume comprises. It is a small guide-book or itinerary for the European traveller, translated from the German as the writer tells us in his dedicatory address to Sir Thomas Gresham, and was published in London by Thomas East in 1576. It has no particular literary value, and is chiefly interesting as an early indication of the translator's interest in antiquarian studies. The main title affords an excellent description of the contents of the book, as follows: *The Post of the World. Wherein is contayned the antiquities and originall of the most famous Cities in Europe. With their trade and traficke. With their wayes and distance of myles, from country to country. With the true and perfect knowledge of their Coynes, the places of their Mynts: with al their Martes and Fayres. And the Raignes of all the Kinges of England* . . . while a second title informs us that it was published by the translator under the assumed family name of Rowlands. For fuller details as to the origin and contents of the work the reader is referred to the bibliography at the end of this volume.

THREE ANONYMOUS PAMPHLETS

The inclusion of the two earlier of these three extremely rare pamphlets in a work upon Catholic Recusant Prose demands a word of explanation, since there is no sure evidence to support the view that they were Recusant publications. There can be little doubt that they are the work of one hand, but there is no indication at all in the pamphlets (nor elsewhere) as to whose that hand was. Nor does the subject-matter of the two pamphlets provide any certain clue as to their origin, whether Catholic or Protestant. And yet we think it would be rather more difficult to establish a Protestant origin for them than a Catholic. The very fact that they were printed abroad anonymously at the time when they were (in 1565), in a city which was one of the harbourages of the early Catholic refugees, would naturally lead us to suppose that they were the work of some English Catholic, and if we add to this the further point that, speaking generally, the contents are of such a kind as to suggest that the writer was not without Catholic sympathies, it would seem, at any rate in the absence of proof to the opposite effect, that there is a *prima facie* case for including them in this present volume.

Each of the pamphlets of which we speak came from the same press at Ghent, each carries the same date, 27 August 1565, and each relates to an important current event. Of historical rather than of literary interest, they are among the earliest examples of English news pamphlets now extant and, as such, may be said to contribute rather to the curiosities of our literature than to afford further examples of serious prose writing. On these grounds the following detailed account is accordingly set down. And here, to begin with, are their titles: (1) *A brief rehersal & discription, of the Coronatiō of the hye and myghti Prince Maximilian Kyng of Romans, Boheme Hungeri &c. Don at the famus citie of Francford yn the year of owr lord. 1562. the month of Nouember, wyth the cōming yn of the great Turcks Embassater, & of the presents by hym gyven, & other thyngs worthy to be known*, and (2) *Certayn and tru good nues, frō the syege of the Isle Malta, wyth the goodly vyctorie, wyche the Christenmen, by the fauour of God, have ther latlye obtayned, agaynst the Turks, before the forteres of saint Elmo. Translat owt of Frenche yn to Englysh.* Let us take them in the order of the events to which they relate.

The first may be described as an eyewitness's account of the ceremonies connected with the crowning of Maximilian II as King of the Romans (or German King) at Frankfort in November 1562.* It consists of four leaves only and is stated to have been written in order that the gentle reader might 'refresh hys mynd a lyttel wyth the noveltie of the matter, and content hymself wythal'. While we must, of course, accept the author's statement that his pamphlet was intended primarily to satisfy the curiosity of his English readers for the strange and unusual, the question yet presents itself as to why he should have set about recording events which were nearly three years old when the pamphlet found its way into print. Doubtless the interest aroused by the recent death of Ferdinand and the succession of

* It may be remembered that in the Middle Ages the title King of the Romans was usually bestowed upon the successor to the Head of the Empire if elected during the latter's lifetime. Maximilian was so elected in October 1562, about a month prior to the events described in the pamphlet, succeeding to the Empire and the Kingdoms of Hungary and Bohemia on the death of his father, Ferdinand, in July 1564.

Maximilian to the Empire provided reason good enough for publishing it in the year 1565. But one cannot help wondering, especially in view of the simultaneous publication of the *News from Malta* (the second of our pamphlets), whether something in the nature of a reproach was not intended in thus directing the attention of his English readers to Continental affairs and, above all, to the menace of the Turk at a time when England had deserted the common cause of Christendom. It is true that the events to which we refer were not entirely without official recognition in this country. Bishop Grindal, for instance, had preached a funeral sermon to commemorate the death of Ferdinand, which was printed by John Day, 8 November 1564; but his object had been mainly to laud Ferdinand's liberal tendencies in religion and to attack the Catholic doctrine of Purgatory. Again, Queen Elizabeth had ordered prayers to be said in all the churches for the Knights of the Order of St. John of Jerusalem in their heroic defence of the Island of Malta; but this, we must suppose, was rather from reasons of sentiment than from any desire to give a direction to national policy. The fact remains that Malta was saved and the Battle of Lepanto was won without any assistance from England, and it was to the Emperor Maximilian and his Catholic allies and not to Elizabeth that England owed her immunity from the inroads of 'the watchful and unwearying Turk'. It is, therefore, in the light of such considerations that we would suggest that these two news pamphlets may be properly understood.

Our second news pamphlet is concerned with the great siege of Malta, which, the reader may remember, began 18 May 1565 and continued without intermission for some four months. It consists of a brief account of the Turkish attack upon the fort of St. Elmo, as recorded in a letter from Jehan Parisot de la Valette, the Grand Master of the Knights Hospitallers, to Don Garcia de Toledo, the Viceroy of Sicily (under date 18 June 1565), and in a relation made at Messina nine days later (27 June) by Orlando Magro, 'pilot to the chyff galley of the great master'. La Valette's letter, while announcing the news of the defeat of the Turks before St. Elmo, at the same time appeals for Don Garcia's help to keep off the Turk. Orlando Magro's short account of the assault and the operations records the final repulse of the Turks in the somewhat laconic statement:

> One valiant knyght hauing a two handed swerd yn hys hand, saying that he wold dye for the Cristian fayth, gave to all the rest suche currage, that they obtayned at last the victori. Item that the great master was veari sorrowful for the death of Capitayne mirande [sig. A4v].

La Valette's appeal seems to have been heard, for, although the gallant little body of 1,200 Knights of St. Elmo was in the end overcome, but not before they had disposed of 7,000 Turks, with the forts of St. Angelo and St. Michel still holding out, the island was finally relieved and the siege raised on 8 September by the reinforcements of Don Garcia, sent at the express order of King Philip.

The general political and religious interest of both Protestant and Catholic Englishmen in the Wars of Religion in France finds expression in a series of pamphlets, published both at home and abroad, which more or less cover and jump with the various stages of the Catholic-Huguenot struggle. They are in the main translations of Huguenot and Catholic Declarations and Decrees and were presumably intended to be informative as well as directive of public opinion. To this series the third and latest of our three anonymous pamphlets may be said to belong. It is a translation of the two Edicts promulgated by Charles IX of France in September 1568 at the beginning of the third phase of the struggle between the Catholics and Huguenots. Published at Louvain towards the end of October 1568 by John Fowler, who may possibly also have been the translator, it carries the following title: *An Edict or Ordonance of the French King, conteining a Prohibition and Interdiction of al preaching and assembling, and exercise of any other Religion, then of the Catholique, the Apostolique, and the Romaine Religion. Item an other Edict oe* [sic] *the same King, remouing al Protestants from bearing any Office vnder the King, in the Realme of France. Newly translated out of Frenche into English.* It is a small octavo volume of forty pages and, save for the imprimatur (dated 29 October 1568), contains nothing beyond the bare text of the two Decrees.

The *Edict of the French King*, to give the pamphlet its running title, follows up an earlier Edict of the same year issued at the conclusion of the Peace of Longjumeau (23 March 1568), which ended the second phase of the Huguenot War. This Edict had been published in London under the title: *The Kinges Edict or* *decree, vpon the pacification of the troubles of his Realme, made the xxiij. of March. 1568 . . . And also certayn requestes, made by the Protestants, with the Kings answeres therevnto* (1568). By it very favourable terms had been offered the Huguenots, giving them nearly all they had asked. The peace was, however, short-lived, and with the renewal of hostilities in the following September the earlier concessions were largely revoked. The new Edict, according to our translated text, recalls the toleration which had been shown to the Huguenots in the past years, and their repeated refusal to live quietly and orderly; it also stresses the fact that there should be no conscience test – 'we meane not, ne wil not, that those of the saied Religion pretended refourmed, be by any meanes examined vpon their consciences, so that they refraine from the exercise of all other Religion, then of the said Catholique and Romaine'. There is thus to be no enforced attendance at Mass, though, on the other hand, there is to be no *open* practice of Protestant worship. 'We leaue it to the Bishops and Pastors of the Church', the Edict goes on to say, 'to do their duty in reclaiming the lost sheep.' As for the 'Ministers of the saied Religion pretended refourmed', they 'bee bounde within xv. dayes after the publication of these presentes, to auoide and departe our saied Realme . . . vppon payne of confiscation of bodie and goodes'. This penalty was attached also to any Minister exercising any other religion 'then onely the Catholique, and Romaine'. The contrasting parallel to the position of the two religious parties at home afforded by this declaration lends, perhaps, some extra significance to this Catholic translation of the two decrees.*

THE SCOTTISH WRITERS

The six Scottish writers who are included in this last section of our chapter are, in chronological order of their works, Quintin Kennedy, Ninian Winzet, James Tyrie, John Hay, John Hamilton and Nicol Burne. The various items of composition, which the reader will find listed under their names in the

* An extremely rare and little-known item which also belongs to this group of Catholic-Huguenot translations is Thomas Jenye's *A discours of the present troobles in Fraunce, and miseries of this tyme, compyled by Peter Ronsard, gentilman of Vandome, and dedicated vnto the quene mother*. The original, written in Alexandrines, is entitled *Discours des Miseres de ce Temps. A la Royne mere du Roy. Par P. de Ronsard Vandomois. A Paris* (1563). According to Sidney Lee (*The French Renaissance in England*, p. 213), Jenye's translation is in English verse. See my further note at bibl. ent. 69.

bibliography to this work, comprise five by Winzet,* four by Kennedy, two each by Hamilton and Burne,† and one each by Tyrie and Hay. They include books, pamphlets, letters and orations, all of which are controversial and are directed against the Protestant Reformation in Scotland and its leader, John Knox. Their most interesting feature is the strong national note which they all strike. The writers appear to have been keenly aware that the alliance with England, largely engineered by Knox, was mainly responsible for the success of the Reformation in Scotland. Here was the principal cause of their country's ruin, and hence their detestation of all things English. They stood, therefore, as the champions not only of the old religion, but also of Scottish life and tradition, and for this reason they regarded it as a point of honour to write in what they believed to be the purest Scots. We have already referred to this matter in an earlier page of this thesis,‡ where we cited statements of both Winzet and Hamilton to this effect. How far the 'auld brade Scottis' (to use Winzet's expression) in which they claim to write preserves the dialectic integrity of Middle Scots, or how far it rather exhibits the rapid changes which were taking place in the literary language of Scotland at that time, it is for the student of such things to decide. One certainly notes in passing the presence of a number of early Southern forms together with a fair sprinkling of Gallicisms and Latinisms especially in Winzet's writing; and Tyrie would seem to acknowledge his imperfect command of the dialect in which he writes when, in reply to John Knox's strictures as to his language and orthography, he says 'for quhow impropir that euer my language be I am verray excusabill, be resson of my lang absence from my awin cuntray and hanting of the latine toung and vther languagis mair nor my awin'.§

The literary value of these writings is perhaps not very great, despite the fact that all the writers were men of considerable eminence and first-class controversialists. On the other hand, as specimens of early Scottish prose, by reason of the great rarity of such exemplars, they certainly warrant the special attention which has been bestowed on them by such important

* Pronounced Win-yet or Win-gate.

† Hamilton's second work belongs to the year 1600 and is not, of course, our present concern.

‡ Above, p. 57.

§ *Refutation*, sig. †5v.

bodies as *The Scottish Text Society*, *The Wodrow Society*, *The Maitland Club*, and *The Bannatyne Club*. As for their historical value, Bishop Keith pointed out long ago that Winzet's *Tractates* are among 'the most valuable Monuments of the Ecclesiastical Affairs in Scotland in the XVI. Age; so far as they contain and discover the Causes and Manner of the Eversion of the ancient Form of Religion in this Kingdom',* and this is true also, though possibly to a lesser extent, of the works of Kennedy, Hamilton and Burne.

* *History of the affairs of Church and State in Scotland* . . . (1734), pp. 203–4.

CHAPTER VI

PUBLISHERS AND PRESSES

THE earliest books of the Catholic exiles were nearly all printed in the well-known printing houses of Antwerp and Louvain. Aegidius Diesthemius or Diest (Gilles Coppens), John Latius (van Laet), William Sylvius, all of Antwerp, and John Bogard, of Louvain, between them printed some twenty of these English books in the eighteen months prior to the year 1565, when the Englishman, John Fowler, established himself as publisher in Louvain.* Considering the difficulties under which these printers worked this is a remarkable achievement, for they were printing in a tongue which they did not understand and were without a competent English supervisor of the print. It is the more remarkable when we consider the size of the books they produced. Allen's *Defense of Purgatory* (John Latius. 1565), for example, is an octavo of about 300 folios or leaves; Dorman's *Disproufe of M. Nowelles Reproufe* (John Latius. 1565) is a quarto of over 200 folios; and Harding's *Confutation of the Apologie of the Church of England* (John Latius. 1565) is a quarto not far short of 400 folios. Small wonder, then, that under 'faultes escaped' we are continually meeting with such expressions as: 'Good Reader beare with these small faultes, or other, which in this difficulty of printing, there where oure tonge is not vnderstāded, must needes be committed';† or 'If yow finde any other faultes I trust yow will frendely amende them youre selues, and considre that we printe not withe suche ease as doe oure aduersaries, whose bookes yeat lacke not their faultes'.‡ Even so, save for certain eccentricities of spelling (not uncommon in Elizabethan books), the reader is little hampered in his reading. The faults are surprisingly few.§

Yet, if there were to be English books, the need of an English printer was obvious. John Martiall, the 'corrector' of Harding's *Answere to Maister Iuelles Chalenge* (1565), addresses the Reader to this effect in the following passage:

* The contribution of Sylvius and Bogard to this total was, however, only one book apiece.

† Allen, *Defense of Purgatory*, sig. A7v.

‡ Dorman, *Disproufe*, sig. *6.

§ In proof whereof the reader is invited to examine the quoted passages in this book.

> I wishe oure louing countrie men to consider how harde it is for aliantes to print English truly, who nieither [sic] vnderstand, nor can pronounce the tonge rightly. As for the correctour, where the faultes of the printers be infinite for the vnskill of the language, were he as full of eyes as Argus, or as sharpsighted as Lynx, yet shoudle [sic] he passe ouer no small number vnespied. Were there here an Englishmā who had skill in settīg a print, and knew the right Orthographie of ouer speach, then mightest thou reader looke for bookes more correctly set forth: for lacke whereof we do as we maye.*

John Fowler, Wykehamist and late Fellow of New College, Oxford, has the distinction of first supplying this need. As we shall see below (p. 342), he was admitted stationer in Louvain on 5 May 1565, only four months after Martiall's Address was written.

1. EVIDENCE OF THE TYPE

It is desirable, before we proceed to a detailed account of the subject of this chapter, to refer to those typographical features of a sixteenth-century book which may assist us in tracing it to its source.† This is a matter of great importance in regard to these Recusant works. We shall see, for instance, how, in the case of the aforesaid John Fowler, a knowledge of the print leads us to correct certain mistakes which have been made about his life. But it is especially important because, owing to the danger involved in publishing, both at home and abroad,‡ many of the books were printed without any indication of publisher or place of origin or date, and some are purposely misleading in their titles.§ In order, therefore, to get at the source of the imprints we are often compelled to rely entirely upon the typography, which makes the work of investigation both arduous and difficult. The task is not made easier by the fact

* sig. A3v. See bibl. ent. 49.

† The summary which follows below is based solely upon an examination of the works included in the bibliography of this book and kindred works. It does not attempt to deal with the printing of the period in any wider aspect.

‡ Richard Verstegan provides the classic example of the danger abroad. For printing certain Catholic books he was, at the representation of Sir Edward Stafford, the English ambassador, thrown into prison by order of the French king, and was also in danger of being extradited (January 1584). See *Cath. Encycl.*, s.v. *Verstegan.*

§ The reader is referred to the bibliography for examples. They become more numerous after 1582.

that most of the books are extremely rare and are widely scattered.*

We may summarize the typographical features most useful in tracing a print to its source as follows:

(1) *Ornamental Initials*

These are extremely useful for distinguishing printers. They appear invariably to have been *hand cut* and not *cast* in the period under consideration.† This means, of course, that no two are precisely alike. Since, furthermore, it is unlikely that borrowing of such small pieces by another printer would take place, we may state with some degree of certainty that the appearance of a particular initial or set of initials indicates a particular printer. When the initial is defective in any way – and this applies not only to initials but to all kinds of ornaments – the indications are likely to be even more certain. A word of caution is necessary with regard to factotum initials. When these are composed of small printers' ornaments, as they often are in these Recusant works, they are generally quite useless for the purpose of identifying a particular printer.‡

(2) *Large Printers' Ornaments*

Such are head-pieces, tail-pieces, large conventional ornaments, etc. These are also very useful for distinguishing printers,

* I have purposely omitted all reference to devices of printers and publishers in the summary which follows. Where these occur they offer no problem to the bibliographer. The single exception, the so-called Jesuit device (the Greek IHS with heart and nails – to be found, incidentally, on the title-pages of many books not of Jesuit origin), is more properly an ornament than a device.

† The safest evidence for this is usage. When a printer never uses the same initial on the same side of a sheet but invariably substitutes another when the letter is called for, it points pretty certainly to his having only one of the kind, which, in its turn, points to a cut letter and not a cast one. Again, the number of initials one meets with at this period which are copies, differing from each other only in small details, points the same way. R. B. McKerrow suggests that 'a very large percentage of the initials after about 1570 and a good many earlier ones' were cast (*An Introduction to Bibliography*, 1928, p. 117). My experience, which, however, must be much more limited than his, would lead me, of course, to put the date later. Elsewhere McKerrow has pointed out that probably by 1583 large ornaments were beginning to be cast (see note below). There seems to be no reason, therefore, why ornamental initials should not have been cast at least as early as that date. But the question is an exceedingly difficult one and must await a final answer.

‡ C. Sayle seems to have been the first to draw attention to the use for purposes of identification of 'the initials used in English books printed abroad at the cryptic presses, and generally supposed to have emanated from such places as St. Omer, and Douai, and Paris'. See his monograph, 'Initial Letters in Early English Printed Books', in *Transactions of the Bibliographical Society* (1904), Vol. VII.

since, like initials, they appear to have been hand cut. It has been suggested that these large ornaments may have been lent about from printer to printer.* This, of course, would lessen their value as detectors considerably. The books that I have examined, however, do not suggest this.† The casting of large ornaments appears to date from about 1583. Their evidence, therefore, after that date must be accepted with caution.‡

(3) *Small Printers' Ornaments*

These are almost useless for purposes of detection. They were always of metal cast from matrices, and were evidently supplied wholesale to all kinds of printers by the founders. The rather larger kind that were cast for making up into lacework ornaments are equally useless.

(4) *Type*

Apart from measurement of type and type face, which are, of course, always to be regarded, certain peculiarities in the print (mainly to be found in roman and italic founts) may help in distinguishing printers. Such are the absence of the letter W (together with the particular substitute employed by the printer – VV, VU, UU and V are all found) and of the ligature sh; the presence of an imported W or K in the fount;§ lack of Greek or Hebrew type for learned works; or insufficient variety of type for the purpose in hand, and so on.

(5) *Composition*

The value of composition as evidence of a particular printer is small. However, when a compositor is working under such difficulties as are suggested under (4) above we may probably glean something from his method of meeting those difficulties:

* McKerrow, op. cit., p. 115.

† The more elaborate ornaments, such as borders and compartments, are another matter. The title-pages of two of John Leslie's foreign translations, for instance, dated 1587, carry borders which seem to have been passed from John Fogny of Rhemes to George L'Oyselet of Rouen.

‡ 'The earliest certain evidence of the casting of anything large and elaborate that I have come across dates from 1583, when on the title-page of Day's quarto edition of Sternhold and Hopkins's *Psalms* we find two blocks of the well-known ornament of archers with dogs &c., at the head and at the foot of the page. The blocks are so exactly similar that I think there can be no doubt that they were cast, and hardly touched up at all by the graver afterwards.' R. B. McKerrow, *Printers' and Publishers' Devices in England and Scotland, 1485–1640* (London, *Bibl. Soc.*, 1913), p. xxxix.

§ The absence of the letters W and K and of the ligature sh usually clearly distinguishes Continental from English printing at the end of the sixteenth century.

the composing of his title pages and text-titles, for example, will be worth observing if he is short of type. When we are dealing with books from small presses, where possibly a single compositor was at work, even made-up ornaments may give us a hint as to the printer.* The distinction between u and v (the former as vowel, the latter as consonant), which is beginning to be observed after 1580, may also provide a clue.

2. JOHN FOWLER

We may now return to the main subject of this chapter and to John Fowler, who is far the most important person connected with the printing of the early Recusant works. We have already seen that he started on his career as publisher in Louvain in 1565. Between that date and 1579, the date of his death, in addition to a number of works in Latin, he saw through the press thirty-one English books – nearly a third of the total number published during our period. For four of these he was personally responsible. The most careful statement we have of his activities in the Low Countries is that of van Havre:

> Jean Foulerus, originaire de Bristol, vint habiter Louvain, où il fut admis comme libraire, le 5 mai 1565. Le 20 juillet 1570, Christophe Plantin lui accorda le certificat exigé par l'ordonnance du roi Philippe II, du 19 mai 1570. Les lettres d'examen portent: *scait le latin, françois, italian, espagnol, avec son maternel anglais et aucunement le grec et le flameng.* Il était en relation d'affaires avec Plantin qui lui ouvrit un premier compte, le 21 janvier 1568. Il résulte des comptes qui suivent que Jean Foulerus vint s'établir à Anvers, en 1576, et y resta jusqu'en l'année 1578. A cette époque il quitta cette ville pour aller habiter Douai . . . De cette date [le 24 août 1582] au 13 juillet 1601, les comptes de livraisons faites par l'imprimerie plantinienne portent le nom d'Alice Foulers, veuve de Jean, à Douai &c.†

* There is no doubt that the made-up ornaments in the books printed by George L'Oyselet tend to repeat themselves from book to book. The same thing may even be said of some of the productions of John Fogny's press.

† *Marques Typographiques des Imprimeurs et Libraires Anversois recueillies par le Chev. G. van Havre* (1883), s.v. *Fowler.* The reader in Flemish will find the ordinance of 19 May 1570, which concerned Printers, Booksellers and Schoolmasters, in the splendid collection of the Ordinances of Philip II in the Netherlands in the George III Library of the British Museum. It is entitled *Ordinancie, statuyt ende gebot prouisionnael onss Herren des Coninx, Aengaende de Printers, Boeckvercoopers ende Schoelmeesters,* and was printed at Brussels in 1570. Fowler's business relations with Plantin, and later those of his widow, were doubtless connected with his bookselling, not his publishing, activities. On Alice Fowler's death Balthazar Beelaert, printer at Douay, undertook to discharge the larger part of her debts due to the house of Plantin. (van Havre, loc. cit.)

Two important facts emerge from this statement: (1) that Fowler was a 'stationer' (*libraire*), a fact already alluded to above, and (2) that he resided at Louvain until the year 1576. Neither of these facts has been generally understood in the past. The short biographical notices of Fowler which have appeared from time to time have, with the single exception of that of van Havre, described him as a printer,* and have either suggested that he had two presses, one at Antwerp and the other at Louvain, or imagined him restlessly passing from one place to the other and back again. The mistake has arisen from relying upon the title-pages of his publications as evidence of their place of origin,† that and the supposition that he was printer.

Van Havre's statement, which I think we may take as authoritative, points then to Fowler's having been engaged in publishing at Louvain continuously up to the year 1576. Now, if we examine the print of the books which bear Fowler's name, we find they are linked up by initials, ornaments and type in such a way as to suggest one certain conclusion, namely that they are the work of a single printer. The printer was Velpen of Louvain.‡ Comparison with books known to have been printed by the Velpen family puts this beyond doubt.§ This

* Thus Pits refers to him as 'arte Typographus', and again as 'partim Antuerpiae, partim Louanij typographiam exercens' (*De illustribus Angliae Scriptoribus*, 1619, p. 771). He is followed by Wood (*Ath. Oxon.*) and subsequent writers. Cardinal Allen, in a letter to Fr. Agazzari, S.J., dated 18 November 1583, had described him as 'catholicissimus et doctissimus librorum impressor' (Knox, *Letters and Memorials*, p. 216). The word 'impressor' is, however, capable of a wider interpretation than Pits's 'typographus'.

† The title-pages alone would lead us to conclude that Fowler was publishing in Louvain, 1565–6; in Antwerp, 1566; in Louvain, 1567–72; and in Antwerp again, 1573–7.

‡ The Velpen family were printing at Louvain from about 1545 to 1580, first in partnership with Jacob Bathen and afterwards, from about 1553, on their own account. The names of both Reynier and Rutger Velpen (they were probably brothers) appear in the books printed after this latter date. Rutger Velpen, after a short association with John Maes in 1579, migrated to Mons in 1580, where he printed until 1585, when he finally moved to Brussels; cf. H. Rousselle, *Annales de l'Imprimerie à Mons* (1858).

§ One may refer, for purposes of comparison, to such works as: *Elegiarum de Rebus Cestis Archiducum Austriae, Lib. duo, Ioanne Ramo Goesano Autore &*c., which has the following colophon – 'Louanii Typis Reyneri Velpij Diestensis Typo. Iurat. Anno 1553'; or *Proditionis ab Aliquot Sectiae Perduellibus aduersus serenissimam suam Reginam non ita pridem perpetratae brevis & simplex narratio . . . Louanii, Apud Rutgerum Velpiu Bibliop. Iurat. Sub Castro Angelico. An. 1566*; or Nicolas Sander's *De Visibili Monarchia Ecclesiae*, which was printed by Reynier Velpius 'Ioannis Fouleri cura & impensa' in 1571; or John Leslie's *Congratulatio Serenissimo Principi et Illustrissimo Cardinali Alberto Archiduci Austriae*, printed at Brussels by Rutger Velpius in 1596. All these books carry hand-cut initials which are repeated in several of Fowler's English publications.

would seem, then, to confirm van Havre's statement, since it is highly improbable that Fowler would have printed in Louvain, but published in Antwerp. There were plenty of printers in Antwerp to accommodate him if he had been living in that city and, in fact, we find that when he moved to Antwerp in 1576 he employed an Antwerp printer, Gerard Smits, to print for him.* It would follow, since we know of no other publisher of English books for whom Velpen was printing, that those English books which are without name of publisher or place, but which are Velpen's printing, were also published *apud Ioannem Foulerum* in Louvain.

The question remains, why did Fowler substitute Antwerp for Louvain on the title-pages of so many of his English publications. The answer to this can only be that he wished to mislead the English authorities. It is, perhaps, not without significance that *all* the English works published by him after the year 1571 either bear no name of place at all or are assigned to Antwerp; for it was on the eleventh of October in that year that a certain Henry Simpson gave evidence under examination at York that

> Mr. Fowler, an Englishman, prints all the English books at Louvaine written by Mr. Harding or others, and the Duke of Alva's printer, who lives in Brussels, all the Latin that are against the doings in England. Wm. Smith, a Welshman, servant to Dr. Harding, commonly brings the books to the printing.†

Fowler published no more English books after his removal to Antwerp in 1576. He died at Namur early in the year 1579.

3. JOHN LION

Since his name appears on the title-pages of five Recusant works, some consideration must here be given to John Lion. Very little is known about this English bookseller. He had been active in the Catholic cause in England and, it appears, in order to escape imprisonment had fled the country. He arrived at the college at Douay on 15 February 1578. Under that date in the *Douay Diaries* is the following entry:

* Gerard Smits was admitted to the St-Lucasgild in Antwerp as *libraire* in 1571. (See van Havre, op. cit., s.v. *Smits*.) He printed Fowler's *M. Maruli Spalatensis Dictorum Factorumque Memorabilium Libri Sex* in 1577, 'apud eundem Iohan. Foulerum'.

† *Calendar of State Papers*, *Eliz. Dom.*, *Addenda, 1566–1579*. Ed. M. A. E. Green, Vol. XIX, no. 78, p. 365.

> Die 15 venit ad nos ex Anglia librarius quidam dictus Lions. Erat ille multum ab haereticis ad carceres quaesitus, quippe qui eo nomine exosus eis fuit quod eius opera plurimi divulgarentur in Anglia libri catholici.

How long he stayed at the college we do not know, but it is unlikely that he accompanied Allen and the rest to Rhemes when the college moved there in the following month. A further reference to him is contained in a letter written by Cardinal Allen from Rhemes to Richard Hopkins at Louvain under date 5 April 1579. Hopkins had clearly written to Allen on Lion's behalf for help. Allen replies:

> For John Lyon because he is no student, though I most heartily would and he well deserveth, I cannot tell what to say. Our profession and good will is to help every body: many the students and priests be in special recommendation. Yet if Mr Lyon can find no means, somewhat for service about our house he shall be allowed, as long as we are able; which is the condition we must add to every matter.*

How we are to interpret these words I do not know. What help did Lion need? Was he, like so many of his Recusant brethren, simply destitute? Or was he merely seeking assistance in order to set up in his own trade, that of bookseller, hoping, perhaps, to succeed Fowler as publisher of English books in Louvain? Whatever view we take, there can be no doubt that he did actually start on a career of publishing, for, before the year was out, the first book to bear his imprint came from the press of John Maes of Louvain. As I hope to show, this was the only book he himself actually published.

The five books which bear the imprint of John Lion are:

(1) T. Hide's *A Consolatorie Epistle*. 1579. 'Imprinted at Louaine by Iohn Maes, for Iohn Lion.'

(2) T. Hide's *A Consolatorie Epistle*. 1580. (A reprint of no. (1)) 'Imprinted at Louaine by Iohn Lyon.'

(3) R. Bristow's *Reply to Fulke*. 1580. 'Imprinted at Louaine by Iohn Lion.'

(4) R. Persons' *A Briefe Discours*. 1580. 'Imprinted at Doway by Iohn Lyon.'

(5) R. Persons' *A Brief Censure*. 1581. 'Imprinted at Doway by Iohn Lyon.'

* T. F. Knox, *Letters and Memorials of Cardinal Allen*, p. 77.

As we have already hinted, there seems no reason to doubt the witness of the title-page to Lion's part in the production of the *Consolatorie Epistle* of 1579. Allen's letter (quoted above) is evidence that Lion was living at Louvain at this time, and the book was undoubtedly printed by John Maes, the well-known Louvain printer. We cannot say as much of the reprint of 1580 (no. (2) above), however. As far as possible it reproduces the original edition, but it differs from it materially in the following respects:

(1) The cuts (there are three of them: a resurrection lamb on the title-page; Christ bearing the cross; and a Calvary) are careful reproductions of those of the 1579 edition; they are not from the same blocks.

(2) A different black-letter fount is used from that employed by Maes.

(3) The roman fount of the 1579 edition has no w and no ligature sh, whereas that of 1580 has both.

The fact that the later edition definitely attempts to reproduce the earlier, but yet differs from it in such material particulars as the above, points almost certainly not only to another printer, but to *one who was not printing in Louvain.* The mere fact that the three cuts have been carefully copied, when the printer, if he had been printing in Louvain, might quite easily have borrowed them, is most significant. The reader will find that below this edition is referred to the Greenstreet House Press. The two books of Robert Persons (nos. (4) and (5) in the list above) also came from the Greenstreet House Press (see below). Bristow's *Reply to Fulke* (no. (3) above) is rather more of a problem. The fact that it bears the same imprint as Hide's *Consolatorie Epistle* (1580) of course looks suspicious, and the printing certainly points to an English rather than to a foreign source. Yet it is a considerable work to have come (as I am going to suggest) from a secret press, and I have been unable to discover any external evidence to support this view. The evidence of the print is set out below. Meanwhile, it may be remarked that the putting of John Lion's name on the title-pages of these books secretly printed in England was not without its point. The man the pursuivants had hoped to lay by the heels for publishing abroad Catholic books in England, was now, apparently, printing them on the Continent.

4. DOUAY, RHEMES AND PARIS

After the two great publishing centres of Antwerp and Louvain, the four most important continental towns where Recusant works were produced during the period 1559–82 were Douay, Rhemes, Rouen and Paris.* We will deal first with the printing of Douay, Rhemes and Paris, reserving that of Rouen for a separate and final section of this chapter.

Five English books appear to have been published at Douay during our period – four by John Bogard and one by John Beelaert. Beelaert's connexion with Douay, however, is very shadowy. He was admitted to the St-Lucasgild in Antwerp as 'libraire' in 1559,† and as far as is known carried on his business as 'stationer' in Antwerp until his death in 1595.‡ There is no evidence that he ever published books elsewhere, except the title-page of this one book, John de Albine's *Notable Discourse* (bibl. ent. 2), which bears the imprint 'Duaci. Per Iohannem Bellerum. 1575'. It is surely strange to find that Beelaert, who was publishing in Antwerp in 1574§ and again in 1576,|| in 1575 was producing a book in Douay. It is perhaps stranger still to find him employing a Bruges printer, Hubert Holost,¶ to print this book for him. We might well ask what can be made of a book which is printed in one place and published in a second place by a publisher who has his business in yet a third place. And perhaps we had best leave the matter at that.

John Bogard, who has already been referred to as a printer of English works in Louvain, established himself as publisher

* Ghent and Bruges complete the list. Two anonymous pamphlets were published at Ghent in 1565 (see bibl. ent. 5 and 8) and Hubert Holost printed and published John Mitchell's (?) *Brief Directory how to say the Rosary* at Bruges in 1576 (see bibl. ent. 81).

† van Havre, *Marques Typographiques*, p. 23; cf. also McKerrow (following Olthoff), in *Dictionary of Printers and Booksellers*, p. 30.

‡ Whether he was printer as well as publishing bookseller is a debatable point. Duthilloeul (*Bibliographie Douaisienne*, 1842, p. 405), following Adrien Baillet (*Jugemens des Savans*, 1722, Vol. I, p. 390), describes him as a printer in his day second only to Plantin himself. I have no knowledge of any book, however, which can definitely be said to be his printing. On the other hand, the two editions of Simon Verrepé's *Precationum Piarum Enchiridion*, which he published at Antwerp in 1576 and 1580 (?), were both printed by Gillis van den Rade, master printer in the St-Lucasgild.

§ J. N. Paquot refers to 'Compendium Precum Liturgicarum in vii. dies digestarum. Antv. Joan. Bellerus, 1574'. *Memoires* (1765), Vol. I, pp. 124–6.

|| See note above.

¶ See bibliography (entry 81) for the reason for attributing the printing to Holost.

in Douay in the year 1574.* The four English books published (and probably printed) by him at Douay between 1576 and 1580 are dealt with in detail in the bibliography and therefore require no further notice here.†

There is also little to add to what the reader will find in the bibliography with regard to John Fogny or Jean de Foigny of Rhemes. He seems to have become official printer to the English college after its removal from Douay to Rhemes in 1578, printing and publishing between 1581 and 1583 five English books in all. Previous to this he had published in 1569 John Leslie's *Defence of the Honour of Marie Quene of Scotlande*, with its strikingly satiric imprint and colophon. He is probably the best known of the foreign printers of English books on account of that noble production of his art, the Rhemes *New Testament*.‡

Eight books written in the vernacular by English and Scottish authors were printed in Paris between 1573 and 1583. Three of these (Hay, *Certaine Demandes* (1580); Hopkins, *Of Prayer and Meditation* (1582); and Tyrie, *Refutation of ane Ansuer be Schir Iohne Knox* (1573)) were published by Thomas Brumen, two (Martin, *Treatyse of Christian Peregrination* (1583); and Rainolds, *A Refutation* (1583)) were supervised in the printing by Richard Verstegan, and three (Burne, *Disputation* (1581), *Admonition* (1581); and Hamilton, *Catholic and Facile Treatise* (1581)) afford no sufficient clue as to publisher or printer. The Scottish books must have offered a pretty problem to the printers. The Scottish use of z (for y), y (for th), qu (for w), not to speak of w itself, must have looked remarkably strange to a French

* Duthilloeul, op. cit., p. 403. McKerrow gives Bogard's dates at Louvain as 1564–7 (op. cit., p. 40). We have evidence, however, that he was printing in Louvain as early as 1562 and as late as 1573. Four pamphlets of Dr. Richard Smith's, bound up together in a volume in the British Museum Library (699.c.2.), carry the imprint 'Louanii Apud Ioannem Bogardum, Sub Bibliis Aureis. Anno 1562' together with Bogard's device; and Duthilloeul, referring to Peter Peck's *Ad regulas Iuris Canonici Commentaria* (1574), states that the second part of this book was printed at Louvain in 1573 and has the imprint 'Lovanii, ex officina Joannis Bogard', &c. (op. cit., p. 16).

† Entries 4, 6, 7, and 67.

‡ Probably the last work to be printed for the English College by Fogny was Edward Rishton's edition of Nicolas Sander's *De Origine ac Progressu Schismatis Anglicani* (1585). This book has the imprint 'Coloniae Agrippinae', but a comparison with Fogny's printing, in respect of initials, ornaments and type, puts the matter beyond doubt. Edward Rishton, after his expulsion from England early in 1585, spent a short time in the English College at Rhemes before proceeding to the University of Pont-à-Mousson, and I would suggest that it was while he was there that he edited Sander's work for the press. It will be remembered that he died on 29 June in the same year (*Douay Diaries*).

compositor. The reader may judge this for himself from the following short passage from Hay's *Demandes*:

> Quhou expone ze ane infinite nomber of scriptures in ye quhilk vve reid that it is gevin to man to his chose, gyf he vil do gude or evvill or quhat auailes ye commandements gevin be God, and zour daily preachings ād exhortatiōs, gyf ane man have na frie vvill bot be constrained be necessitie to do quhat somever he dois, and quhat difference make ze betuene ye action of ane man, and of ane beast, gyf ye vvill of man be subiect to necessitie as is ye appetite and inclinatiō of beastes.*

The difficulties in printing this 'strange tongue' would certainly lead us to suppose that the printer who had printed the two earlier works of Tyrie and Hay would have also been entrusted with the later works of Burne and Hamilton. This does not appear to have been the case. Brumen's printer was the well-known Paris printer, Jean Le Blanc.† I have searched through some twenty exemplars of Le Blanc's printing, of various formats, but have been unable to establish any certain connexion with these books.

I have also failed to trace to their printer the two English books which Richard Verstegan saw through the press in Paris. Both books contain initials of a distinctive character. It is possible that these are cuts of Verstegan himself.‡

5. SECRET CATHOLIC PRESSES IN ENGLAND

Those who remember the Marprelate controversy will not be surprised to learn of the existence of secret Catholic presses in England during Elizabeth's reign. The difficulty of importing Catholic books into England, witnessed by the repeated Proclamations against Recusant works, was undoubtedly a primary cause of their existence, though the need of meeting their adversaries with the least possible delay also influenced both Verstegan and Fr. Persons in printing at home rather than abroad. Of necessity the printing was secret. 'The rigorous enforcement of the policy of regulating printing in the interests

* sig. D1. T. G. Law gives an interesting list of specimens from these Scottish texts in *Catholic Tractates of the Sixteenth Century, 1573–1600* (1901). Amongst others I note vyer (vther), vyfues (pl. of wyf), vvse (vse), vvoue (voue), selfvvs (pl. of self), varld (warld).

† Described by Jean de Lacaille as 'un des habiles Imprimeurs de son temps, & qui a le plus travaillé pour les Libraires'. *Histoire de l'Imprimerie et de la Librairie* (Paris, 1689), p. 149.

‡ Further reference to Verstegan will be found in the next section.

of church and state naturally drove the opponents of the establishment, the papists on the one side and the puritans on the other, to resort to secret printing.'* Three of these presses were at work between the years 1578 and 1582 in London: William Carter's press on Tower Hill, Stephen Brinkley's at Greenstreet House and elsewhere, and Richard Verstegan's in Smithfield. The three presses probably printed ten books between them. They were all eventually discovered and dismantled.

The first of the three presses to be set up was that of William Carter, who had served his apprenticeship to the printing trade with John Cawood, Queen's printer.† Carter afterwards acted as amanuensis to Nicholas Harpsfield until Harpsfield's death in 1575. Bishop Aylmer says that during this period he actually published some of Harpsfield's works:

> Then he attached himself to Doctor Harpsfield, a man well-known to me, and an evil fellow and very pig-headed (I had a mighty public disputation with him in 1553). This Carter was Harpsfield's amanuensis and not only wrote his books which he published [*edidit in lucem*] for him while he was alive, but also took the greatest pains to scatter them broadcast after his master's death.‡

This, I think, must be taken as an *ex parte* statement, at any rate if the word 'published' is to be understood here in its ordinary sense. The only work of Harpsfield's printed during his lifetime was the *Dialogi sex*, published at Antwerp in 1566.§ It was only after Harpsfield's death that Carter turned to the printing and publishing of Catholic books. Aylmer states that he had two presses for this purpose.||

> Moreover, he secretly printed Papistical books, (for he kept two presses [*duo praela*] for the purpose, which after a careful search

* *Camb. Hist. of Eng. Lit.* (1919), Vol. IV, p. 411.

† 'Wylliam Carter the sonne of Roberte Carter of London Draper hath put hym selfe apprentice vnto John Cawood Cytizen and Stacioner of London from the feaste of the puryfication of the blessed lady saynte mary [2 February] *Anno* 1562 [i.e. 1563] tenne yeres.' Arber, *Transcript of Stationers' Register* (1875), Vol. I, p. 196.

‡ From the account of the evidence of Aylmer at Carter's trial, as set forth in Bridgewater's *Concertatio* (1588), sig. Kk3v.

§ See R. W. Chambers, *Life and Works of Nicholas Harpsfield*, in *Harpsfield's Life of More* (*E.E.T.S.*, 1932), p. cxcvi et seq.

|| It is probable that he obtained his printing materials from Gabriel Cawood, who had succeeded on his father's death in 1572 to the printing business. Cawood was certainly sympathetic towards the Catholic cause. Persons says that he was actually imprisoned about 1581 *ob quiddam ad religionem pertinens* (*De Persecutione Anglicana Epistola*. Admonition to the Reader).

> were seized) with which books he incited the public to sedition; nor, I am sure, can this bad man in any way show that he ever printed a good book.*

Whether Carter printed more than the three books I have attributed to him in the bibliography I have been unable to discover. Aylmer's letter to Lord Burghley, which follows, seems to suggest that he did. If this is so, we can only suppose that they suffered the fate of many other 'lewd pamphlets' of the time, for all trace of them has disappeared. I give the letter in full:

> Right honorable and my singuler good L. I have founde out a presse of pryntynge wth one Carter, a verye lewed fellowe who hath byne dyvers tymes before in prison for printinge of lewde pampheletes. But nowe in searche of his Howse amongest other nawghtye papystycall Bookes, wee have founde one wrytten in Frenche intyled the inosencey [mg. in anr. hand, Innocency] of the Scotyshe Quene, a very dangerous Book. Wherin he calleth her the heire apparant of this Crowne. he enveyth agaynst the Execūcon of the Duck of Norfolke, defendeth the rebellion in the north, and dyscourseth agaynst yo^{w}, and the Late L. keper.† I doubt not but that yor L.shipp hath seene yt, neverthelesse I thought good to signyfye thus muche vnto yor L. shipp that yo^{w} maye deale wth the fellowe (who ys nowe neare yo^{w} in the Gate-howse) as to yor wysdom shall seme good. I can get nothinge of him, for he dyd denye to answere vppon his othe. When yor L.shipp shalbe at any leasure to deale in the matter: I will sende to yo^{w} the wardens [sc. of the Stationers' Company], wch will enforme yo^{w} further of an other Booke, wch ys abrode wherin her ma^{tie} ys towched‡/and of certayne other newe formes of Lr̃es [sc. type: probably initials] wch he hath made and will not confese them. Thus wth my humble dewtye vnto yor Lordshipp I take my leave from my Howse at London by Pawles this xxxth of December 1579
>
> Yo^{r} L.shipps humble to comaund
> John London.§

* Bridgewater, *Concertatio*, loc. cit.

† The book is, of course, Bishop Leslie's *L'Innocence de Marie Royne d'Escosse* (1572). Strype understood Aylmer to mean that Carter had printed this book: 'He [Carter] had printed several books against the queen and the state of the church established; and against the queen's statesmen, particularly the lord treasurer Burghley and the late lord keeper Bacon' (*Annals of the Reformation*, 1824, Vol. II, pt. 2, p. 271). The typography of the book, however, points certainly to John Fogny of Rhemes as the printer.

‡ *A Treatise of Schisme* (1578), by Gregory Martin. The book which Carter had printed and which was to cost him his life.

§ Brit. Mus. Lansdowne MS. 28, no. 81. Cited by Strype, op. cit., pp. 271–2; Arber, op. cit., II, 749; cf. also Strype, *Life and Acts of Aylmer*, p. 30; *D.N.B.*, s.v. *Carter*, &c.

The story of Carter's taking (by Topcliffe), as recorded in the letter above, his later transference from the Gatehouse to the Tower in June 1582,* and his subsequent trial, and death on 11 January 1583–4, have been duly recorded by all the authorities.† It remains only to say something about the charge of treason on which Carter was condemned. The charge was a bogus one, and was based upon a passage in Gregory Martin's book, *The Treatise of Schisme* (Carter's printing), which refers to the slaying of Holofernes by Judith. It was maintained that the passage was intended as an incitement to 'Catholike gentlewomen' (*Reginae famulas* – 'the Queen's Maids of honour', according to Camden) to emulate the example of Judith and to seek means to destroy the Queen. This has been generally accepted as a correct interpretation of Martin's words,‡ and even the *Dictionary of National Biography* has lent its support to this view. But anyone who will take the trouble to examine the passage as a whole will see at once the absurdity of the charge:

> Iudith foloweth, whose godlye and constant wisedome if our Catholike gentlewomen woulde folowe, they might destroye Holofernes, the master heretike, and amase al his retinew, and neuer defile their religion by communicating with them in anye smal poynt. She came to please Holofernes, but yet in her religion she woulde not yeelde so muche as to eate of his meates, but brought of her owne with her, and tolde him plainelye, that being in his house, yet she must serue her Lorde and God stil, desiring for that purpose libertie once a day to goe in & out ye gate. *Non potero manducare ex his quae praecipis mihi, ne veniat super me offensio.* I maye not eate of that which thou commaundest me, least I incurre Gods displesure. Which her constancie (a wonderful thing to tel) was the very means afterward, wherby she caried away his head safely, the porters presupposing that she went forth (as before) to pray to her God. He hoped wel to haue had the company of her body, and so to possesse her altogether: but God did so direct her religious mind, that she confounded him and al his, not once touching

* According to the prison lists published in C.R.S., *Miscellanea II*, p. 228, he appears to have been committed to the Tower early in June 1582.

† cf. Stowe, *Annals*; Holinshed, *Chronicles* (1587); Camden, *Annals*; Wood, *Athen. Oxon.*, &c.

‡ For example, by the authorities already quoted. The Rev. W. K. Clay, in his edition of *Liturgies and Occasional Forms of Prayer set forth in the Reign of Queen Elizabeth* (Parker Society, 1847), further opines that an allusion in the preface to a prayer 'for the preservation of her Majesty and the Realm, from the traitorous and bloody practises of the Pope, and his adherents' to Holofernes may have been suggested by Carter's reprint [sic] of *A Treatise of Schisme;* p. 596.

A
BRIEF CENSVRE
vppon two bookes
WRITTEN IN AN-
swere to M. Edmonde
Campions offer of
disputation.

Deuter. capit. 5. ver. 5.
Yow feared the fyre, and therfore you
ascended not vp the mountayne.

Imprinted at Doway by Iohn Lyon.
1581.
WITH PRIVILEGE.

TITLE-PAGE OF R. PERSONS' *A BRIEF CENSURE*
Printed at the Greenstreet House Press, London

> of his meats: Her good maid waited vpon her al this time. And surely one constant Iudith shal easily make many like seruants, a thing much to be wished, for the Catholike bringing vp of yonge gentlewomen, who otherwise are in daunger of Holofernes, and his vngratious ministers.*

Quite clearly Judith is being held up to the 'Catholike gentlewomen' for her steadfastness in religion, and of course she provides an excellent example for those whom the writer is exhorting 'to abstaine altogether from heretical Conuenticles'.

The press, which for convenience' sake we have named the Greenstreet House Press, was originally set up by Fr. Robert Persons at Greenstreet House in East Ham some time in October 1580.† The idea of printing Catholic books in England had been in mind before he left Rome (he arrived in England in June 1580), for among the faculties granted to Frs. Robert Persons and Edmund Campion for the mission, under date 14 April 1580, was one which was to enable them to publish such books anonymously:‡ 'Ut liceat libros catholicos imprimere et edere tacito nomine auctoris, loci et typographi, non obstante concilio Tridentino. Ut liceat etiam his facultatibus in aliis vicinis regionibus, nominatim in Scotia, Hibernia et Mona et aliis adiacentibus locis, uti, et etiam in eis, qui ex aliis regionibus in haec loca venerint.'§ Quite naturally, therefore, the subject of the press was mooted at the conference between Persons and Campion held at Uxbridge in October 1580. Immediately afterwards, we are told, Persons retired to London, where ('with characteristic energy and ingenuity' says T. G. Law)|| he busied himself about putting the project into effect.¶ The difficulties which he encountered and the subsequent history of the press are now common knowledge. We may content

* *Treatise of Schisme*, sig. D2. T. Cooper, the writer in the *D.N.B.* (surely with some *naïveté*), stops short in his quotation of the passage at the words 'in anye smal poynt' and so gives an entirely wrong emphasis to Martin's words (s.v. *William Carter*).

† Persons' *Brief Discourse* was printed at the press before 6 November 1580, and it was not the first book to be printed.

‡ The faculty was necessary on account of the Tridentine decree *de editione et usu sacrorum librorum* (Session IV of the Council), which forbade *imprimere vel imprimi facere quosvis libros de rebus sacris sine nomine auctoris, &c.*

§ S.P.O., Dom. Eliz., Vol. 137, no. 26, §8. Cited by A. O. Meyer, *England and the Catholic Church under Queen Elizabeth* (translated by the Rev. J. R. McKee), London, 1916, at Appendix XVII, p. 487.

|| s.v. *Persons* in the *D.N.B.*

¶ Simpson, *Edmund Campion* (1896), pp. 251, 257 and 260.

ourselves, therefore, with a very short *résumé* of the principal facts.*

The 'large and fair house' situated 'near a place they call Greenstreet', which Persons rented for his press, was chosen on account of its seclusion – *recessum opificio aptissimum.* It was five or seven miles from London, and thither, with the help of Stephen Brinkley, Persons conveyed the necessary materials for the print. Brinkley engaged the workmen – *nec defuere (fauente coeptis Deo) fidelissimae operarum Catholicarum manus* – and took charge of the printing. To evade suspicion the workmen paraded the neighbourhood disguised as gentlemen:

> Eos vbi Brinclaeus, auertandae suspicionis gratia, in modum nobilis familiae, eodem instructos corporis cultu, a pedibus, equitans parumper publice circumduxerat, domum reductos, fallaci exutos pompa, vrgendo prelo volentes fatigabat.†

Cardinal Allen, in a letter to Fr. Alphonsus Agazzari from Rhemes, dated 23 June 1581, states, on the authority of George Gilbert, who was Persons' constant companion at this time, that there were seven workmen employed under Brinkley and that Gilbert provided the necessary funds for the venture:

> Habet ipse [sc. Persons] septem homines continuo laborantes in praelo quod habet constitutum extra Londinum, ne rumor illius machinae obaudiatur in urbe . . . Ita mihi narrat iste D. Gilbertus, individuus ejus per totum hunc annum comes, quique in discessu P. Ruberto [Persono] reliquit septem equos ad necessaria sacerdotum et patrum itinera et negotia obeunda; summamque vim pecuniae ad necessarium rerum apparatum, nempe, chartae, praeli, caracterum, atramenti et similium impendit.‡

After printing at least one book Brinkley took the press away. When, however, Persons decided to print again the press was set up anew, this time, however, at a house provided by Francis Browne, the brother of Lord Montague, who also supplied books, food and servants. Here the printing continued until

* The principal original authorities for the history of the press are Bombinus, *Vita et Martyrium Edmundi Campiani* (1620), Persons' *De Vita Campiani*, and his later *Memoirs*. These originals (and it is to be remembered that Bombinus's informant was Fr. Persons himself; cf. the words at p. 147 of his book 'narrabat mihi, cum haec scriberem, Personius') present difficulties – the result, it would seem, of Persons' uncertain memory.

† This and the preceding Latin quotations from Bombinus, op. cit., pp. 137–8.

‡ Knox, *Letters and Memorials of Cardinal Allen*, p. 98. An English translation of this letter is given in full by Simpson, op. cit., p. 293 et seq.; cf. also Persons in a letter to the Pope, dated 24 June 1581, quoted by Simpson at p. 291 et seq.

some time in March 1581, when, owing to the increasing vigilance of the authorities, it was removed to the house of Dame Cecilia Stonor near Henley. Fr. Persons' records of these latter moves are to be found both in his *Domesticall Difficulties* and his *De Vita Campiani* (c. 18). I submit the relevant passages, observing only that in respect of the move to Francis Browne's house mentioned in the *De Vita Campiani*, but not in the *Domesticall Difficulties*, the former work must carry more weight, since it appears to be the first of Persons' writings about Campion and himself, having been begun in December 1593.* Here, then, is Persons' account in the *De Vita Campiani*:

> obtulit se Brinklaeus ut eo proelum reveheret, si ego responderem [to the attack by Charke and Hanmer against Campion's *Challenge*]: sed deerat locus, deerant libri: solicitum tenebat suspicio famuli [Alfield] qui petebat ad patrem suum Gloucestriani proficisci: tandem Franciscus Brunus obtulit domum, libros escam, servitium, et praestitit . . .

The passage from the *Domesticall Difficulties* is as follows:

> Soone after this, againe having procured a print and printers in a village called Greensted 7 mile out of London whereof Mr Steven Brinkley above said was the corrector and overseer, the said Father also lyving there in secrett and wryting against Charke, Nicols, & others, the said Brinkleys man that went in and out betwene London and that place was taken by treason and carried to the Tower and tortured out of hande, wherupon they were constrayned to fly with print, presse, paper & all, and to place the same in another countrey which was nere to Henley upon Thames in the house of the Lady Stoner, whether came also F. Campion out of Lancashire to print his boke, in Latine called 'Decem rationes ad Academicos'.†

The *Rationes Decem* was the last work to be printed by Brinkley's press. At the beginning of August 1581 Sir Henry Neville and another were instructed by the Council 'to repair unto the Lady Stonor's house, and to search for certain Latin books dispersed

* I am indebted to Fr. Leo Hicks, S.J. for this information, as also for the quoted extract from the *De Vita Campiani*. The whole incident connected with this move is dealt with by Fr. Hicks in his *Letters and Memorials of Father Robert Persons* already cited.

† *Memoirs II. Domesticall Difficulties*. C.R.S. *Miscellanea II* (1906), p. 182. The details which follow the above extract both in the *Memoirs* and in Bombinus, who appears to have been using the *Memoirs*, are confused. For a more exact account of what happened later, see Fr. J. H. Pollen's edition of Campion's *Ten Reasons* (1914). Fr. Pollen there quotes (from C.R.S., IV, 14–17) a rather different version by Persons of the same events. Evelyn Waugh, in his account of Brinkley's press in his recent *Edmund Campion* (1935), largely repeats what Pollen says.

already in Oxford at the last commencement, which Campion hath confessed to have been there printed in a wood. And also for such English books as of late have been published for the maintenance of Popery, printed also there, as is thought, by one Parsons – a Jesuit, and others. And further for the press and other instruments of printing, thought also to be there remaining'.*

On 8 August the press was seized† and Brinkley and his four associates John Harris, John Hervey, John Tuker and John Compton, were taken into custody.‡ Brinkley was committed to the Tower where he remained for nearly two years, being discharged on 24 June 1583 'by the intercession of friends and on bail'.§ He forthwith crossed the Channel and, after a short visit with Fr. Persons to Rome, towards the end of the year settled in Rouen, in order to assist George Flinton, who was engaged in publishing Catholic books under Persons' direction.

We would suggest that Brinkley printed altogether six books at his secret press, as follows:

T. Hide: *A Consolatorie Epistle*, 1580.

R. Bristow: *Reply to Fulke*, 1580.

R. Persons: *A Briefe Discours*, 1580; *A Brief Censure*, 1581; *A Discouerie of I. Nicols*, 1581.

E. Campion: *Rationes Decem*, 1581.

The last four of these (the three books of Persons and Campion's *Rationes Decem*) offer no problem. It will be clear from what has already been written above that they were all printed by Brinkley.|| The two books of Hide and Bristow, however, have never been referred to Brinkley's press. It will be necessary, therefore, to examine their claims to inclusion in the above list in some detail.

* Cited by Simpson, op. cit., p. 344.

† J. H. Pollen, *Cath. Encycl.*, s.v. *Persons.*

‡ J. H. Pollen, quoting from Rishton's *Diary of the Tower*, in his edition of Campion's *Ten Reasons* (Manresa Press, 1914). On the 30th of the month the Privy Council wrote to Neville to thank him for apprehending the printers. (See Fr. John Morris's article in *The Month* for July 1889.)

§ Fr. John Morris, quoting Rishton's *Diary*, in *The Month*, as before. The incident of Brinkley's taking is referred to in the *Douay Diaries*, under date 27 August 1581, thus: 'Audivimus etiam sub finem, ni fallor, Julii D. Brinkleum, J. civilis bacm, a D. Henrico Nevell, equite aurato, captum fuisse et arce Londinensi inclusum. Hujus autem fidelissima industria, antequam caperetur, in libellis typo mandandis usus est pater Robertus' [Persons].

|| But see also the notes to Persons' books in the bibliography.

Both books came from the same press. The printing puts this beyond doubt. The three founts employed, viz. a black letter, a twelve-point roman, and a six-point italic, are the same in both, and both use the same single initial I.* Both were printed in England. We have already given reasons for supposing that Hide's book was not printed in Louvain, as the title page indicates (p. 346): we need not look further than the printer's Address to the Reader in Bristow's book for evidence of its English origin. The Address is as follows:

> In two thinges I am to desire thee (curteous and friendly Reader) to extend thy accustomed gentlenes in perusing and reading of this godly worke: One is, that thou wilt friendly correct with thy penne these faults, and what others els thou shalt therin espie committed in the Printing: for although I haue had great care and bene very diligent in the correcting thereof, yet because my Compositor was a straunger and ignorant in our Englishe tongue and Orthographie, some faultes are passed vnamended of me. The other, that thou wilte not like the worse of this learned worke, because it hath not the varietie of letters which is requisite in such a booke, and as the Printers in England do customably vse, my abilitie was not otherwise to do it, and hauing these Characters out of England, I could not ioyne them together with any others, and so was forst to vse one Character both for the words of Fulke, and for all Allegations. Remember that when man can not do as he would, he must do as he may. John Lyon.†

The 'curteous and friendly Reader' will probably agree that the printer doth protest too much. For it may reasonably be asked why John Lyon should import his 'Characters out of England' into Louvain, when John Maes and others had already shown that English printing could be done quite reasonably well with foreign founts; and why, after printing Bristow's and Hide's books, no other works were forthcoming from his press, since he had gone to this expense and trouble; and whether his unwillingness to mix his type accounts also for the absence of Greek and Hebrew type from the text; or whether we are to understand that these were not available in Louvain.‡ It will

* Both at sig. A1. The I is slightly defective, which makes it certain that it is the same letter.

† sig. Eee4v.

‡ Twelve Greek words or phrases occur in the text at different places, all printed in roman character, and there is one Hebrew sentence also in roman. Bristow was both a Greek and Hebrew scholar and would himself certainly have used the alphabets of the originals.

also be remarked that, in spite of the compositor being 'a straunger and ignorant in our Englishe tongue and Orthographie', he has produced one of the most correctly printed of all the Catholic Recusant works.*

If, then, the book was printed in England (and I think we may conclude from what has been said that it was) it follows (and this applies equally to Hide's *Consolatorie Epistle*) that it must have been printed at some secret press, for it is beyond possibility that any licensed printer would have put his hand to such a work. We are thus left with no alternative but to assign it and its companion volume to Brinkley's press, and, in confirmation thereof, we may add that the type employed in both works is similar to that used in the other Greenstreet books and that the subject of Hide's book exactly answers the description of Brinkley's first printing as understood by Simpson, namely that 'the first book that issued from this [Brinkley's] press was probably some book of devotions or *of encouragement to persecuted Catholics*'.†

After the Greenstreet House press had been seized it is probable that Richard Rowlande, or Verstegan as he later called himself, intended to carry on the work of printing Catholic books in this country. His attempt to do so, however, was short-lived, for, after printing secretly in London Thomas Alfield's compilation, *A true report of the death and martyrdome of M. Campion* [1582], his press, too, was seized and he himself was compelled to flee the country. The facts are quite clear. We learn from the State Papers for May (?) 1582 that notes of Campion's words and his manner of execution were delivered to 'Rowlande the prynter in Smythefild'.‡ Again, in a letter to Lord Burghley, dated 14 April 1582, Recorder Fleetwood describes his taking of Rowlande's press:

> it fell owt y^t in the first wike of lent that there was a booke cast a brood in com̃endinge of *Cmpian* and of his fellowes, and of

* Whether any significance can be attached to the compositor's use of the English letter W in his signatures I do not know. It is certainly unusual in English printing of the period, nor does it occur in the signatures of any other of the Recusant books.

† op. cit., p. 261. Italics mine. Fr. J. H. Pollen (*Ten Reasons*, 1914) has shown very clearly that the press Brinkley used at Stonor Park had a very limited amount of type. Since no such shortage is apparent in the books actually printed at Greenstreet (and we refer especially here to Bristow's work), we must conclude that the difficulties of transporting the press to Stonor were responsible for this.

‡ Passage cited in full at p. 377 below.

theire deathe. I pursued the matter so nere that I found the presse, the lr̄es, the figures, and a nosmber of the bookes.*

And again in a State Paper of February (?) 1582, in reference to the same work, we read: 'One Norwoode of Symons Ine publisher of these books knowethe the prynter And was the cause of his flyenge and escaype'.† With the taking of this press the printing of Catholic books in England ceased altogether for a few years. The snake was scotched, however, not killed, and in a later volume we hope to return to this part of our subject with an account of the secret presses of Robert Southwell, Henry Garnet and James Duckett. Meanwhile, Recusant works continued to be printed on the Continent,‡ and it is to a foreign press, with which for a short time Fr. Robert Persons was closely associated, that, lastly, we must turn our attention.

6. GEORGE L'OYSELET'S PRESS AT ROUEN

When Persons left England in the autumn of 1581 he first proceeded to Rouen, where he intended to continue the work of publishing Catholic books which had been interrupted by the seizure of the press at Stonor Park. He found there, in Rouen, a comparatively unknown printer named George L'Oyselet, who had already been engaged in printing English books during the two years previous to his arrival. Whether he was aware, before he left England, of the existence of L'Oyselet's press and had been prompted by this to set up again at Rouen, or whether it was simply a happy coincidence which led his steps thither, must be matter of conjecture. This is certain – that forthwith L'Oyselet became Persons' printer. As supervisor of the printing Persons employed an English merchant named George Flinton, who continued to act in that capacity until his death in 1585.§

* Brit. Mus. Lansdowne MS. 35, no. 26. There follow the words 'my lo. I have sent vnto yor honor a box of suche stuffe as these Libellers vse for theire Printe'. The MS. is endorsed '14. April. 1582 Mr Recorder to my L. wth a boxe of popish stampes'. The letter is cited in full in C.R.S., Vol. V, pp. 27–9; cf. also Strype, *Annals* (1824), Vol. III, pt. 1, pp. 124 and 197.

† Cited by C.R.S., as before, p. 27, from S.P.O., Dom. Eliz., Vol. 152, no. 54. The document has no date, but this may be determined by its reference to the arrest of William Deane on 21 February and from the date of Fleetwood's letter recorded above.

‡ Verstegan himself plays no small part in their production, first in Paris and later on in Antwerp. The Paris prints have already been referred to above (p. 348). Verstegan's later Antwerp publications fall outside the scope of this present volume.

§ The view, hitherto accepted, that Flinton himself did the printing at some private press set up by Persons, does not fit the facts.

Thus we read in Persons' *Notes on the Mission of England* for the year 1581: 'F. Persons procured that a merchant, very pious and zealous, called George Flinton, would undertake wholly to that exercise of printing: which he did afterwards during some years up to the time of his death'.*

L'Oyselet was by far the most important printer of Recusant works on the Continent during the decade 1580–90.† He printed altogether some twenty of these books between the years 1580 and 1587, most of them anonymously, without place or printer. Fortunately, three books have survived which bear his imprint and, starting with these as a nucleus, we can gather together, with tolerable certainty, the remainder of the group of books for the printing of which he was responsible. This group includes the five books which, without any doubt, were 'supervised' in the printing by George Flinton, as we shall proceed to show. The three books are:

(1) Richard Hopkins's translation: *Of Prayer and Meditation.* 'Imprinted at Rouen by George L'oiselet.' 1584.

(2) Richard Hopkins's translation: *A Memorial of a Christian Life.* 'Imprinted at Rouen, by George L'oyselet.' 1586.

(3) John Leslie's *Du Droict et Tiltre de la . . . Marie Royne d'Escosse.* 'G. l'Oyselet: Rouen' [1587].

Now a connexion can be clearly established between these three books and the two which L'Oyselet printed before the arrival of Persons in Rouen, viz. the *Jesus Psalter* of 1580–1 (?) and Vaux's *Catechism* of 1581 (?).‡ The evidence for this connexion is, of course, purely typographical and is based largely

* The reference is, of course, to the printing at Rouen. The original passage, as cited by T. F. Knox in *Letters and Memorials of Cardinal Allen* (footnote, p. 198), reads: '[F. Persons] procurò che un mercante molto pio e zeloso chiamato Giorgio Flintono s'aplicasse totalmente a quell' essercitio della stampa: il che fece da poi per alcuni anni sino alla morte.'

† L'Oyselet is given by L.-C. Silvestre as printer at Rouen, 1584–1602 (*Marques Typographiques*, Vol. I, p. 330). The earlier date 1580 may, I think, now be taken as correct. As for the later date, I have at present no knowledge of any book printed by L'Oyselet after 1587. R. B. McKerrow (*Dictionary of Printers and Booksellers, 1557–1640*) gives the dates as 1584–99, basing the later date on a reprint of R. Hopkins's translation, *A Memoriall of a Christian Life*. This book certainly bears the imprint 'G. L'Oyselet, Rouen', but it was actually printed by James Duckett in London, and so is not evidence.

‡ Both these books are without place, printer and date. Evidence for their early date is set out at pp. 524 and 533. Let me add that it is by no means certain that L'Oyselet printed two books only at this date. It is quite possible, for instance, that he printed *The Scale of Perfection* about the same time, though no copy of such an edition has yet come to light. See Appendix II.

upon the ornamental initials used in these works; but, as we have already pointed out (p. 340), these provide the strongest possible evidence for the print of these Recusant books. So, too, in respect of the four books (referred to below) which were printed at the press before the end of 1582, the evidence of the print is equally conclusive. They can all be shown to be directly related to these three and to the other books of the L'Oyselet group in respect of both initials and type. And, if we chose to pursue the matter still further, we should find the same thing true of the remaining books of the group.* The result is, we have a very clearly defined group of books with marked characteristics in these issues from this Rouen press, and it is with some degree of certainty, therefore, that we are able to assign the books published by George Flinton to L'Oyselet's printing.†

The four books which were printed by L'Oyselet for George Flinton, or under Flinton's supervision, before the end of 1582 were:

(1) Persons' *De Persecutione Anglicana, Epistola.* 'Bononiae apud Io. Baptistam Algazarium.' 1581.

(2) *An Epistle of the Persecution of Catholickes in Englande.* (A translation of (1) by G. T.) 'Doway in Artois.' [1582].

* To set out the evidence in full for this interconnexion of the books would mean a very lengthy statement indeed. I offer, therefore, the following very partial statement only, as witness to the facts: Hopkins's *Memorial* (numbered (2) above) has an initial T at sig. N4 which we find also used in Vaux's *Catechism* of 1581 (?) at sig. G1. It also has a number of initials which are to be found in John Leslie's *A Treatise Touching the Right, Title and Interest of . . . Marie, Queene of Scotland* (1584). Again, the *Catechism* of 1581 (?), already referred to, carries an initial I which appears again in George Cotton's *The Contempte of the World* of 1584. *The Contempte of the World* again has numerous points of resemblance (initials, &c.) with Persons' *First Booke of the Christian Exercise* (1582), which was one of the books printed under Persons' own supervision at Rouen. We can establish in the same manner a connexion between John Leslie's *Du Droict et Tiltre* (numbered (3) above) and Persons' *First Booke of the Christian Exercise* by way of Leslie's *Declaration del Titulo y derecho que la Serenissima Princesa Donă Maria* (1587 – the Spanish version of *Du Droict et Tiltre*) and *The Contempte of the World*, and so on.

† If further proof is needed that Persons did not print his Rouen books at some private press of his own, we may refer to the Catholic pirated edition of Persons' *Book of Resolution* of 1584, *which was printed at the same Rouen press as the other books of Persons, but without Persons' knowledge.* He writes in the preface to the revised edition of that work of 1585: 'I was enformed of two other editions come forth of my forsaid booke without my knowledge, the one by a Catholique (as it seemeth) who perceuing al copies of the former print to be spēt; for satisfying of them that desired the booke, procured the same to be set forth againe, albeit somewhat incorrected, and very disordrely, not hauing the consent or aduise of such, as therin should haue geuen him best direction.'

(3) Persons' *The First Booke of the Christian Exercise.* (No place or printer.) 1582.

(4) Persons' *A Defence of the Censure.* (No place or printer.) 1582.*

It remains only to say a word about the order of their printing. The date of number (1) is fixed by the imprint on the title, and it must, of course, precede number (2), G. T.'s translation of it 'out of Frenche into Englishe and conferred withe the Latyne copie'. The grounds for putting the English *Epistle of Persecution*, *The First Booke of the Christian Exercise* and the *Defence of the Censure* in that order are typographical. The *Epistle* has no roman w, whereas the *Christian Exercise* begins with a small but inadequate supply of oversized w's. About half-way through this latter book a new roman w appears and thenceforth there is no lack of this letter.† The *Defence of the Censure* has a plentiful supply of lower case w throughout.

Persons' connexion with L'Oyselet's press seems to have come to an end in 1585 with the printing of his second edition of *The Book of Resolution.* A brief narration of the events connected with that publication will bring this chapter to a fitting close. In the autumn of the previous year (1584) Persons returned to Rouen in order to prepare the matter for the press. With him were Stephen Brinkley, the Greenstreet House printer (released from the Tower in 1583), and George Flinton.

> Wherupon (he writes) I buying myself dyverse sortes of good books returned to live for the next winter in Roan in a voyde house given to the Society in a garden, where were with me Mr Stephen Brinkly, a vertuous gentleman that translated Loartes book under the name of James Sanker, and Mr Flinton, an honest marchant, who both of them did help me to set forth my 2d edition of the book of Resolution much augmented.‡

He left Rouen for Flanders 'about mid-Lent, 1585',§ leaving Brinkley and Flinton to carry on with the preparing of the copy

* The imprints of the first two are, of course, bogus, and point to the endeavour to keep the place of printing secret.

† The change is observed at sig. Q2. The first line of Q2 has one of the oversized w's. Thereafter vv is used until the last line but one of the page, when the right-sized w appears.

‡ Autobiographical Notes by F. Persons. Stonyhurst MSS., pp. 231, 232. Cited by T. F. Knox, *Letters and Memorials of Cardinal Allen*, p. 222 (footnote).

§ T. F. Knox, ibid. The passage goes on to state that he remained in Flanders until the autumn, when he went with Dr. Allen to Rome.

for the print. Towards the end of March or at the beginning of April of the same year Flinton died,* and Brinkley was left to complete the task alone. He appears finally to have seen the book through the press some time in the following autumn.† With its publication he passes from our sight. It is possible that he continued to assist with the English books which issued from L'Oyselet's press, but we have no information on the point. The date of his death is not known.

* From the information supplied by Nicholas Berden (*alias* Roger), spy to Walsingham, as a result of conference with Richard, servant to Dr. Allen: 'He allso toulde me that Flynton is dead at Roane within these xiiii dayes, as Hartely reportethe [margin – 'This Hartely was prysoner in the Marshallsea'], and his bookes delivered to Mr Shelton.' Cited C.R.S., Vol. XXI, p. 75, from S.P.O. Dom. Eliz. 178, no. 19. Under date 13 April 1585.

† We learn from the Preface to the book, which is dated 29 July 1585, that the matter was 'wel forward for the print'.

PART II

BIBLIOGRAPHY

Note to the Bibliography

FROM the point of view of the bibliographer the bibliographical details which follow in this section of the book will probably appear to be lacking in certain necessary features; from that of the student of literature they may appear to be unduly elaborate. Let me state, therefore, before descending to particulars, that the descriptions have been designed primarily as a help to the literary student, that is to say, as far as possible to show *what is in the books* recorded rather than *of what the books are made.* At the same time, since these Recusant works are very scattered and are often difficult to get at, and since they are so largely anonymous in one way or another, it has been felt necessary to give sufficient bibliographical detail as will enable the student who may come to deal with the books themselves to recognize with some certainty the book he is handling. Even so, in drawing up the bibliography the bibliographer has never been entirely out of my mind, and I trust the details given of the various books may be of some use also to him.

To turn, then, to particulars:

I. *Works included in the bibliography:*

(1) All works in English by Catholic Recusant writers printed between 1559 and 1582, the latter date being interpreted somewhat liberally.

(2) All such works known to have been written between these dates, but only subsequently printed.*

(3) Under reference titles, all such works printed after 1582, the authors, etc. of which are already included in the full title-list.

(4) Two manuscripts – A. Langdale's tract (entry 74), because of its particular relation to a work of Persons, and E. Campion's *Historie*, for the reason given in the note below.

* In one case, viz. E. Campion's *Historie of Ireland* (entry 27), a record of the original MS. has been substituted for the printed work on account of the wide divergence between the written and the printed word.

II. *Description of title-page:*

In each case the title of the earliest extant edition is set out as closely as possible to its original within the convention adopted. The following points should be noted:

(1) No attempt has been made to reproduce the great variety of founts (upper and lower case) as they appear in the originals.

(2) Capital letters of the original titles are used when a capital letter is clearly indicated, otherwise modern procedure has been followed.

(3) The printing difficulty of the letter W (upper and lower case) has been carefully preserved in the titles, though not elsewhere.

(4) The word [ornament] in the titles refers to all kinds of ornaments, including signs, but not to cuts and devices. When the word is followed by a period it means 'ornamental'.

(5) The abbreviation [mg] in the titles indicates a marginal reference, the reference being placed at the end of the passage referred to, though it may not actually so occur in the original. This placing has been necessary owing to such references often being out of alignment.

(6) Where printer's or publisher's name, place of origin, or date is not given in the original title these are supplied as far as possible, the information being given within square brackets. The bibliographical notes supply the necessary information where these details occur on the title-page incorrectly.

III. *Library references:*

The library reference at the end of the titles usually refers to that copy of the book which is most complete and is at the same time most easily available. Pollard and Redgrave's *Short Title Catalogue* will generally supply further information on this point. Absence of such reference means the best available copy of the book is in the library of the British Museum. The following abbreviations have been used: Bod. (Bodleian Library, Oxford),

Camb. (Cambridge University Library), Sir R.L.H. (Library of the late Sir Leicester Harmsworth), Lamb. (Lambeth Palace Library), Lincoln (Lincoln Cathedral Library).

IV. *Bibliographical descriptions:*

In the descriptions which accompany the titles the following special abbreviations have been used: Fol. (foliation), Not fol. (not foliated), Pag. (pagination),* Cw. (catchwords), Mg. (marginalia), Rt. (running title). Following McKerrow, the convention π has been used for leaves without signature.

* The numbering of leaves and pages is so seldom perfect that no special reference has been made to this unless it occurs at the last numbered leaf or page of a book.

TO THE READER

THE judicial reader will easily understand that the faults here set down which occur in the titles following (and others which he may espy) are not to be imputed to the present printers, viz.:

'oe' for 'of' (entry 3); 'wheruuto' for 'wherunto' (entry 9); 'latly' for 'lately' (entry 14); 'Bristo' for 'Bristow' (entry 23); 'nowe' for 'newe' (entry 34); 'seth-furth' for 'sett-furth' (entry 57); 'questōis' for 'questiōs' (entry 83); 'puplished' for 'published' (entry 88); *κρατεῖτο* for *κρατεῖτω* (entry 122); 'tanslation' for 'translation' (entry 137).

ANONYMOUS

1. An Apologie / of priuate Masse, spred a / broade in writing without name / of the authour: as it seemeth, a- / gainst the offer and protestacion / made in certayne Sermons by / the reuerent father Bisshop of / Salsburie: with an answer to / the same Apologie, set foorth / for the maintenance and / defence of the / trueth. / Perused and allowed, by the reuerent / father in God Edmonde Bisshop / of London, accordynge to the / order appoincted in the / Queenes maiestes / Iniunctions. / Londini. / Mens. Nouemb. / 1562.

[colophon on V7v] ¶Imprynted at London in / Fleetestreete, by Thomas / Powell.

8°. B.L. A–T in eights+V7. Fol. 1[A1]–31[D7]; 1[E5]–123 (wrongly numbered 121) [V7]. Cw. Mg. Rts – (1) An Apologie / of priuate Masse; (2) The defence / of the trueth. (1) Title [A1]. (2) Blank [A1v]. (3) Text of the *Apologie* [A2–D7v]. (4) New Title as follows:
[within a compartment] An Answere in / defence of the truth. / Againste the / Apologie / of / priuate / Masse. / Londini / Mens. Nouēb. / 1562 [D8]. (5) 'The cheefe poinctes touched in this defence of the trueth' [D8v]. (6) 'The preface to the Reader' [E1–4]. (7) Blank [E4v]. (8) Text of the *Answere* [E5–V7v]. (9) Colophon [V7v].

Owing to the curious history which is attached to this book I have thought it proper to set out title and bibliographical details in full, although, as it stands, it can hardly be described as a Recusant publication. Actually there were three separate issues of the book in the month of November 1562, each with a different title-page. The two later titles are as follows:

2. [ornament] A Levvde Apo- / logie of pryuate Masse, sedyci- / ously spred abroade in wrytynge / without name of the authour: / as it seemeth, against the offer / and protestacion made in cer- / taine Sermons by the re- / uerende father Bishop / of Salesburie: / [ornament] With a learned and godly answere to the same Apo- / logie, set foorth for the / maintenance and / defence of the / trueth. / Londoni. / Mens. Nouemb. / 1562.

3. An Apologie / of priuate Masse sedici- / ously spredde abroade in wri- / tyng without name of the au- / thour: as it semeth, against / the offer and protestacion / made in certain sermons / by the reuerende fa- / ther Byshop of / Salesburie. / With an answere and confu- / tacion of the same, set forth / for the defence and / maintenance of / the trueth. / Londoni. / Mense Nouemb. / 1562.*

The third of these issues differs from the two previous ones in its Address to the Reader on the verso of the title-page [A1v]. In this Address the author of the *Answere* thus accounts for the later issues:†

* I give the three issues in the order in which they were published. See A. Esdaile in *Transactions of the Bibliographical Society* (*The Library*. Fourth Series. Vol. I, p. 161) for 1920.

† The reader will note the insertion of the word 'lewd' in the second title. The author evidently hoped thus to scotch the 'shameless shifts' of his opponents. The device was apparently ineffective, hence the third issue. See A. Esdaile, loc. cit.

'If it had not ben knowen before, that nothing coulde be so sincerely done, but that malice woulde peruerte it to an euill purpose: It might haue ben sufficiently learned by the late publishyng of this little boke. For of honest meanyng I placed this Apologie by it selfe, to this ende, that it might be seene in the whole discourse as it was written, & that the patrone of priuate Masse might not iustly pretend, that his doyng was mangled by setting it in partes, as other men commōly haue vsed. But there hath not lacked lewdly disposed mindes, which, to animate their fauourers to thexpectacion of their longe loked day, haue quite seperated the confutaciō from the Apologie, and sendyng it abroade vnto their frindes, haue said, that it was now published in defence of their masse, by the alowance of the reuerend father in god bishop of London. wherfore, seing plaine and honest dealinge can not be saulfe from their shameles shiftes, I am cōstreigned (gentle reader) by this note openly to let the vnderstād, as wel the maner of their vnhonest dealyng, as also that this Apologie was not set foorth & allowed for the doctrine therin conteined. but that it might be compared with the answere, and confutacion of the same.'

The author of the *Apologie* is unknown.*

The *Answere* is from the pen of Bishop T. Cooper.† Bishop Cooper was answered by John Rastell in *A Replie against an answer (falslie intitled) in Defence of the truth* (1565) [entry 124].

The *Apologie* has been reprinted by the Parker Society in *An Answer in Defence of the Truth against the Apology of Private Mass . . . Edited . . . by the Rev. William Goode, M.A., F.S.A.* Cambridge, 1850.

2. [ornament] A notable / Discourse, plainelye and / truely discussing, who are the right / Ministers of the Catholike Church: / written against Caluine and / his Disciples, By one Master Iohn / de Albine, called De Seres, Arche- / deacon of Tolosa in / Fraunce. / With an Offer made by a Catholike / to a learned Protestant, wherin shall / appere the difference betwixte the open / knowen Church of the Catho- / likes, from the hid and vn- / knowen Congregati- / on of the Prote- / stantes. / Duaci. / Per Iohannem Bellerum. / 1575.

Bod.

* It was thought to be the work of Thomas Harding at the time of its spreading abroad, owing, no doubt, to some autobiographical details in the text, which might well have been applied to him (at sig. A2). Harding, however, expressly denies authorship. He can only be referring to this book when, in *An Answere to Maister Iuelles chalenge* (1565), he writes of 'a certaine exercise of a learned mā of fiue or six sheetes of paper spredde abroade in the Realme in defence of some of these Articles by M. Iuell denyed' and adds it 'was fathered vpō me, which in dede I neuer made sentēce of' (sig. C4).

† On the testimony of Dr. E. Cradocke in a work published in 1572. See introductory note to the *Parker Society* reprint, p. *v*.

8°. B.L. ¶–¶¶+A–M in eights+N²+A–C in eights. Fol. 1[A1]–98[N2]. The repeated signatures, A–C, are not foliated. Cw. Mg. Rts–(1) A notable discourse / Against heresies. (2) An Offer to the / Learned Protestant. (1) Title [¶1]. (2) Blank [¶1ᵛ]. (3) 'The Preface to the Reader' [¶2–¶¶7ᵛ]. (4) Blank [¶¶8]. (5) Text of the Discourse in 43 chapters [A1–N2ᵛ]. (6) Text of the Offer: 22 Articles, followed by 6 'Signes' [A1–C7]. (7) Blank [C7ᵛ–8].

The first part of this work is a translation of *Discours Chrestien et Aduertissemens salutaires au simple & treschretien peuple de Frãce . . . Par Iehan d'Abin de Valzerg, dit de Seres, Archediacre de Tolose.* 1566. The translator omits the *Epistre au peuple de France* and certain other portions of the French version, substituting his own 'Preface to the Reader'. The author of the original is known variously as de Albynne, de Seres, Albin de Valsergues, etc.

The 'Offer to the Learned Protestant' is a version of Card. Allen's Articles with an additional six 'signes'. Edward Rishton, editor of Sander's *De Origine ac Progressu Schismatis Anglicani* (1585), has been named as the editor of these Articles, but on insufficient evidence.* Nor is it possible to say whether the two parts of the book are the work of one hand. Probably they are not, since the writer of the preface to the translation and the writer of the six signs (the two original sections of the book) use different versions of the Vulgate.

The 'Offer' was replied to by R. Crowley in *A Deliberat answere made to a rash offer, which a popish Antichristian Catholique, made to a learned protestant (as he saieth) and caused to be publyshed in printe: Anno.Do.1575.* London, 1588. The six 'signes' are dealt with separately under the heading 'A new offer, touching the sixe seuerall signes'.

The 'Notable Discourse' was replied to by T. Spark in *An Answere to Master Iohn de Albines, Notable Discourse against heresies (as his frendes call his booke) compiled by Thomas Spark pastor of Blechley in the County of Buck.* Oxford, 1591. He answers the whole book, excepting, however, the twenty-two demands, since 'Doctor Fulke long ago hath answered those demaundes, and that also nowe of late Master Crowley hath at large aunswered, both them and that which is added concerning those signes'. He continues 'Doctor Fulkes answere thereunto maie be had vnder the title of an aunswere of a Christian protestant, to the proude Chalenge of a popish Catholicke, and it is prefixed commonly before his booke written in confutation of Allens of Purgatorie. Indeed concerning the six signes hee saieth nothing, not because of any greater matter in them than in the rest, but because at the first they were not published with the other' [sig. A4]. Hereby he unwittingly distinguishes two of the versions of Allen's Articles referred to in Appendix I. Finally, he doubts

* See Appendix I, where this question is discussed.

whether the Notable Discourse is a translation at all (you never can tell what these Catholics may not be up to!) and whether there is such a person as the Archdeacon of Tolosa, for the writer in the preface does not once hint in what language the author wrote it.

The printer of this volume was probably Hubert Holost, the 'Duaci' of the title-page representing the place of publication or sale of the book. John Bellaert, the publisher and printer, appears to have lived uninterruptedly at Antwerp from 1553 to 1595.* I have no information of any other work of his emanating from Douay.

3. An Edict or Ordonance / of the French / King, conteining a Prohibi- / tion and Interdiction of al preaching / and assembling, and exercise of any / other Religion, then of the Catho- / lique, the Apostolique, and / the Romaine Re- / ligion. / [ornament] / Item an other Edict / oe the same King, remo- / uing al Protestants from bea- / ring any Office vnder the / King, in the Realme / of France. / Nevvly translated out of Frenche / into English. / Louanii, / Apud Ioannem Foulerum, / Anno 1568.

BOD.

8°. Second edict in italic. A–E in fours. Not fol. Cw. No Mg. Rt–An Edict of the French King. (1) Title [A1]. (2) Blank [A1v]. (3) First Edict [A2–D2v]. (4) Blank [D3]. (5) Second Edict [D4–E4]. (6) Imprimatur: 29 October 1568 [E4]. (7) Device [E4v].

A translation of the two Edicts given by Charles IX at St. Maur de Fossez in September 1568. Their publication by Fowler in English was probably to draw attention to the toleration which had been extended to the Protestants by the Catholic party in France, which they (the Protestants) had lost only on account of their perversity in refusing to live quietly and orderly. It is likely that Fowler himself was the translator.

4. Certayne deuout Me- / ditations very / necessary for Christian men / deuoutly to meditate vpon / Morninge and Euen- inge, / euery day in the / weeke: / Concerning Christ his lyfe and / Passion, and the fruites / thereof. / Vigilate & orate, vt non intretis in / tentationem. Math. 26. / Watch and pray, least you fall / into temptation. Math. 26.

[colophon on H8v] Duaci apud Iohannem Bogardi [sic]. 1576.

16°. B.L. A–H in eights. Not fol. Cw. No Mg. Rt. varies. (1) Title [A1]. (2) Blank [A1v]. (3) 'The preface of the Author to certaine Meditaciōs

* See R. B. McKerrow, *Dictionary of Printers and Booksellers* (*Bibl. Soc.*), 1910, and H.-R. Duthilloeul, *Bibliographie Douaisienne*, 1842; cp. also the note in reference to this work at p. 450.

which must be dayly saide according to the nombre of the seauen daies in the weeke' [A2–4v]. (4) Meditations for each day of the week [A5–D8v]. (5) Prayers, Hymns, and Meditations for special occasions [E1–H8]. (6) Colophon [H8v].

Author not traced.

5. [C]ertayn and / tru good nues, / frō the syege / of the Isle Malta, wyth the goodly / vyctorie, wyche the Christenmen, by the / fauour of God, have ther latlye obtayned, / agaynst the Turks, before the forteres / of saint Elmo. / Translat owt of Frenche yn to Englysh. / [ornament] / And nuli prented yn Gaunt, / the 27. of August. / [rule] / M.CCCCC.LXV.

LAMB.

8°. A4. Not fol. Cw. on verso only. No Mg. No Rt. (1) Title [A1]. (2) 'The copie of a letter writen, by the ryght noble & worthke [sic] Capitayn, don Garcia of Toledo Capitayn general to the kyng of spayn. Contayning the late nues last com from Malta, wyth the horrible & pytiful assautes made by the Turks apon the sayd fortressis, and the fayer victori, wych the Christians had before saynt Elmo, the xv. & xvj. day of Iune last past': ends, 'From Malta the xviij day of Iune 1565. Subscribed By me I. Vallet' [A1v–3]. (3) 'Relation made by Orlando Magro pilot to the chyff galley of the great master comāder of the Rhodes, now Malta the wyche aryued at Messina the xxvij. day of Iune 1565' [A3–4v].

Translator unknown, but probably by the same hand as *A brief rehersal* [entry 8]. The printer is certainly the same as printed that pamphlet.

6. [*Text-title.*] A short and an absolute order of confession most requisite of all persons to be ouer loked before they confesse them. [John Bogard. Douay? 1576–80?]

16°. B.L. A–B in eights. Not fol. Cw. No Mg. Rt – An absolute order, / of confession. Text [A1–B8v].

Author unknown.

This short pamphlet appears to be a part of some larger work. It begins: 'Hauing treated before of contricion, we will heare likewise shew a way how they shuld prepare & examine themselues, which often vse to be confessed . . .'

The printer is undoubtedly the printer of *Iesus Mattens* [entry 7, q.v.] with which the British Museum copy is bound up; and it seems likely that it was printed about the same time as that book.

7. [*Text-title.*] Certayne sweete Prayers of the glorious name of Iesus, commonly called, Iesus Mattens, with the howers therto belonging: written in Latin aboue two hundred yeres agoe, by H. Susonne. [John Bogard. Douay? 1576–80?]

16°. B.L. A–C in eights+D4. Not fol. Cw. No Mg. Rt – Iesus Mattens. (1) Text [A1–D4]. (2) Blank [D4v].

A translation of the *Officium aeternae sapientiae* of the fourteenth-century mystic, Blessed Henry Suso. Translator unknown. The Office is usually to be found appended to the *Horologium Sapientiae* of the same author.* It was later incorporated into some of the Salisbury Prymers, both in Latin and in English.† The latest printing, previous to that of the above, seems to have been in 1558.‡

A comparison of this book with two similar books known to have been printed by John Bogard, viz. *Certayne necessarie Principles of Religion* [entry 67], and *Certayne deuout Meditations* [entry 4], points almost certainly to the same printer. The type employed (both black-letter and roman) and the style of printing are the same for all three. The fact that the same series of block capital letters is used in this work and in *Certayne necessarie Principles of Religion* (a series not found elsewhere) puts the matter pretty well beyond doubt. We may date the book tentatively, then, with the other two as 1576–80.

8. A brief / rehersal & discription, of / the Coronatiō of the hye and myghtī / Prince Maximilian Kyng of Romans, Bohe / me Hungeri &ç. Don at the famus citie of Franc- / ford yn the year of owr lord. 1562. the month of / Nouember, wyth the cōming yn of the great / Turcks Embāssater, & of the presents by / hym gyven, & other thyngs wor- / thy to be known. / [ornament] / Newli prented yn Gaunte, the 27. of August / M.CCCCC.LXV.

8°. 4 folios. No signatures or catchwords. Not fol. No Mg. No Rt.

Author unknown.

Maximilian was elected Roman king 27 October 1562, though he was not officially recognized by Pius IV till February 1564. Possibly this pamphlet found its way into print in 1565 in order to commemorate his succession as Emperor of Germany on the death of Ferdinand in July 1564.

The pamphlet is badly printed and curiously spelt. The unusual medial v's are to be noted.

* e.g. in the edition printed at Venice in 1482 (Brit. Mus. IA.24149) it follows immediately upon the *Horologium* with the introductory words: 'Incipit cursus seu officium de eterna sapientia compositum a beato Henricho syso ordinis predicatorum.'

† e.g. in the *Hore beate Marie virginis secundum usum Insignis ecclesie Sarum* (1503), in Latin (Hoskins. 26); and in the English *Prymer of Salysbery vse* printed in 1536 (Hoskins. 122).

‡ See the note under *Jesus Psalter* at p. 413.

ALFIELD, THOMAS
d. 1585

9. A true report of the death and mar- / tyrdome of M. Campion Iesuite and / preiste, & M. Sherwin, & M. Bryan / preistes, at Tiborne the first of / December 1581. / Observid and written by a Catholike / preist, which was present therat / Wheruuto is annexid certayne verses / made by sundrie persons. / [device] / Apoca. 7. / These are they that came out of gret / tribulation, and haue washed their / stoles and made them white in the / bloud of the Lambe. [Richard Verstegan. London. 1582.]

8°. B.L. A–F in fours+G². Not fol. Cw. Mg. No Rt. (1) Title [A1]. (2) Blank [A1ᵛ]. (3) 'To the Reader' [A2–3ᵛ]. (4) Text of the 'True Report': ends, 'God saue the Queene' [A4–D4]. (5) 'A caueat to the reader touching A, M his discouery' [D4ᵛ–E1ᵛ]. (6) The Verses: (i) 'Vpon the death of M Edmund Campion, one of the societie of the holy name of Iesus'. (ii) 'An other vpon the same.' (iii) 'A Dialogue betwene a Catholike, and Consolation.' (iv) 'The complaynt of a Catholike for the death of M. Edmund Campion.' [E2–G2]. (7) 'Good reader pardon all faultes escaped in the printing and beare with the woorkmanship of a straingre.' [G2]. (8) Blank [G2ᵛ].

Campion, Sherwin and Bryan had been put to death on 1 December 1581. This little volume is a monument to these martyrs, and is intended to set at nought the 'divers and many slaunders raised since by some maliciously blinded' and 'to satisfie & content all such as do desire to vnderstand the manner of the same' [sig. A2]. We read that it was also written 'in part to diminishe those sinister rumors which are raysed against these good men by a notable and most infamous libel, entituled, *An Aduertisement and defence for truth against her backbyters, and specially against the whispering fauorers and colorers of Campions, and the rest of his confederates treasons:* published there, and openly read, printed abrode without authoritie of seen and alowed, a pamphlet, false, impudent, and farssed with lyes and vntruthes'* [sig. A4ᵛ]. Cardinal Allen used the narrative portion of the *Report* for his *Briefe Historie of the Glorious Martyrdom of XII Reuerend Priests* [entry 13]. The official reply to Alfield was a pamphlet entitled, *A particular declaration or testimony, of the vndutifull and traiterous affection borne against her Maiestie by Edmond Campion Iesuite, and other condemned Priestes, witnessed by their owne confessions: in reproofe of those slaunderous bookes & libels deliuered out to the contrary by such as are malitiously affected towards her*

* This anonymous B.L. pamphlet of four leaves was put forth at the end of 1581 in justification of the sentence passed on Campion and his fellows at Westminster, 20 November 1581. As usual, the coming of the Jesuits into England is associated with Sander's expedition to Ireland.

Maiestie and the state. London, 1582.* A reply came also from the pen of Anthony Munday, viz., *A breefe Aunswer made vnto two seditious Pamphlets, the one printed in French, and the other in English. Contayning a defence of Edmund Campion and his complices, their moste horrible and vnnatural Treasons, against her Maiestie and the Realme. By A. M.* London, 1582.†

The book, it will be observed, is made up of a preface, an account of the martyrdoms, a warning about Munday, and certain verses. It has been variously ascribed to Vallenger, Thomas Pounde, Alfield, and even Robert Southwell. It is, however, necessary to distinguish. With regard to the account of the martyrdoms, the evidence is in favour of Alfield. We note the statement in the title, 'Observid and written by a Catholike preist, which was present therat'. A personal reference in the text of the *Report* by the writer provides the evidence for this statement: 'many good catholike gentlemen . . . presented them selues at the place of execution, and my selfe a Catholike preist pressed to that bloodie spectacle' [A4]. The writer of the address to the reader refers to this last statement in the following words: 'Amongst the diuers reportes of the behavior of M. Campian, M. Sherwin, & M. Bryā at their death (passing among freindes from hand to hand) I hapned vpon one geven out as it seemeth by a Catholike priest, who as it apereth pressed to obserue & marke those dealings: which report I have here published, cōsidering the divers & many slaunders raised since by some maliciously blinded to satisfie & content all such as do desire to vnderstand the manner of the same: I hope that consideration which hath movid me hereto, wil also perswade that preist to the wel liking of this my doing.' That the priest was Alfield seems fairly certain from the evidence of a State Paper of May (?) 1582. The Paper is concerned with the two young Dolmans, who were at this time students of Gray's Inn. It reports of them as follows: 'For beinge of Graisine They lodged Thom^{as} Aulfild, a not^{ed} Seameanarye

* This anonymous pamphlet was incorporated almost *in toto* by Allen in his *A Briefe Historie of the Glorious Martyrdom of XII Reuerend Priests*, referred to above.

† The French work referred to must be the earliest of the printed books in defence of Campion's martyrdom (the Privilegium is dated 30 December 1581). It is entitled *L'Histoire de la mort que le R. P. Edmond Campion prestre de la compagnie du nom de Iesus, & autres ont souffert en Angleterre pour la foy Catholique & Romaine le premier iour de Decembre, 1581. Traduict d'Anglois en François.* Paris, 1582. The text-title of the answer to the English work is *An Aunswer vnto an other seditious Pamphlet printed in English, and named: A true report of the death and Martirdom of Maister Campion* . . . This answer is followed by 'Verses in the Libell, made in prayse of the death of Maister Campion . . . here chaunged to the reproofe of him, and the other Traitours'. The verses are given as follows: (1) 'Why doo I vse my paper, inke and pen . . .'; (2) 'What iron hart, that would not melt in woe . . .'; (3) 'A Dialogue betweene a Christian, and Consolation'; (4) 'The Complaint of a Christian remembring the vnnaturall treasons of Edmund Campion, and his Confederates'. They are signed Anthony Munday. The effect may be imagined.

now prisoner in the tower who haunted the Northe. And heard him saye a nomber of masses in there chamber and in another mans chamber. And one of those Dolmans did accumpany. Aulfild to Campyans execucōn, took noates of his wordes and maner of Execucyōn And delyuerid the same to Rowlande the prynter in Smythefild and Aulfild did delyuer iij of the bookes prynted vnto one of theis too Dolmans And dyuers other Seameanaryes did haunt to theis too Dolmans.'* The presence of Alfield at the execution, the taking of the notes, the delivery of the same to the printer – the record of these events, together with the evidence of the book itself, emphasizing the fact that it was the work of some Catholic priest, can leave little doubt as to Alfield's authorship of the *Report*.

It will be obvious from a perusal of the extract from the 'address' printed above (and, we may add, the warning about Munday, which is pretty certainly by the same hand as the address) that this part of the work was not written by Alfield. Of the three remaining possibilities, Vallenger, Pound and Southwell, Pound had been removed to the Tower from Stortford Castle at the end of August 1581, and was subject to the strictest surveillance. It is most unlikely, therefore, that he was in any way connected with the book.† Southwell was not in England, nor did he arrive here until some four years later.‡ We are left, then, with Vallenger, unless Verstegan, the printer, edited as well as printed the book. Quite a possibility. For Vallenger's claim we have the evidence of the proceedings before the court of Star Chamber, 16 May 1582, when Vallenger was condemned 'to stand upon the pillorie j daie in the pallace at Westminster, & one other daye in Cheapside, and to loose at each place one of his eares' for being 'author and spreader of these Libells'.§ This evidence, however, does not seem conclusive, for Vallenger, although he admitted that the written copy of this work found in his possession was 'written all with his owne hande', yet denied that he was the author of it, and the argument that 'for not being able to produce the partie that made them [the libels], he is both by lawe and reason to be taken for the author of them himself' || is not very impressive. However, we must assume that Vallenger was the author of this part of the book, in the absence of more certain information.

The question as to the authorship of the poems has been thoroughly investigated by the Rev. J. H. Pollen, S.J., in the introduction to his reprint of *A Briefe Historie of the Glorious*

* State Papers, Eliz. Dom., No. 78 – 1582, May (?) (Vol. 153). Cited in *The Gentleman's Magazine* for November 1865, and quoted, in part, by Gillow, *Bibl. Dict.* II, p. 91.

† See his personal narrative of his sufferings recorded by Br. Foley, *Records S.J.*, III, p. 650.

‡ See *D.N.B.* art. 'Southwell'.

§ Brit. Mus. Harleian MS. 6265, p. 373.

|| ibid.

Martyrdom of Twelve Reverend Priests (1908). He inclines to the view that the first two poems are the work of Fr. Henry Walpole, S.J., the remaining two being the work of some unknown author or authors.*

Evidence for the printer of this book is furnished by the passage already quoted from the State Papers: 'And one of those Dolmans did accumpany Aufild to Campyans execucōn, took noates of his wordes and maner of Execucyōn, And delyuerid the same to Rowlande the prynter in Smythefild.' This Rowlande or Rowlands was the well-known Catholic printer, Richard Verstegan, who eventually settled in Antwerp. Corroborative evidence is to be found in the unusual medial 'v's', which are a mark of Verstegan's printing.†

The date, 1582, is settled by the proceedings in the Star Chamber, under date 16 May 1582, when Vallenger was convicted. One of the points which was said to argue for his authorship of the book was that, whereas the book 'written all with his owne hand . . . was written in Januarie last', it was found 'by good triall' that it 'was not printed till february then next'.‡

ALLEN, WILLIAM, CARDINAL
1532–1594

10. A Defense / and Declaration / of the Catholike / Churchies Doctrine, / touching Purgatory, and pra- / yers for the soules departed. / by William Allen / Master of Arte and student / in Diuinitye. / Mortuo ne prohibeas gratiam. Eccles.7. / Hinder not the departed of grace and fauoure. / [device] / Imprinted at Antwerp by Iohn / Latius, with Priuilege. / Anno. 1565.

8°. A–Z+Aa–Oo in eights. Fol. 1[A1]–289 [Oo1]. Cw. Mg. Rts – (1) A Defense / of Purgatory &c. (2) Of Prayer for the / Soules Departed. (1) Title [A1]. (2) Privilegium: Brussels. 14 March 1564. *Stilo Brabantiae* [A1v]. (3) Address to the Reader: Antwerp. 2 May 1565 [A2–7]. (4) Errata: introduced by 'Good Reader beare with these small faultes, or other, which in this difficulty of printing, there where oure tonge is not vnderstāded, must needes be committed' [A7v]. (5) Ornament [A8]. (6) Blank [A8v]. (7) Preface [B1–C5]. (8) Text of Book I in 13 chapters [C5v–Q2v]. (9) Text of Book II: preface and 17 chapters [Q3–Oo1]. (10) Imprimatur: 8 March 1564. *Stilo Brabantiae* [Oo1v]. (11) Arguments of the chapters [Oo2–7]. (12) Blank [Oo7v–8].§

* Dr. Augustus Jessopp suggests that Vallenger, like Walpole, came from Norfolk, and that they were old friends. (*One Generation of a Norfolk House* (1878), p. 102.) This may help to explain their association in this publication.

† See Cap. VI: section *Private Presses*.

‡ Brit. Mus. Harleian MS. 6265, p. 373. Recorder Fleetwood writing to Lord Burghley, 14 April 1582, says that the book was published 'in the first wike of Lent' of that year. Brit. Mus. Lansdowne MS. 35, n.26. Cited in *C.R.S. Publications*, Vol. V. Fleetwood also records in this letter the seizure of a number of copies of the book; cp. Strype, *Annals* (1824), Vol. III, pt. 1, p. 124.

§ The dates are interesting, since they show that the Brabantians did not follow the Spanish reckoning but kept to the Old Style.

This book, which was written principally in answer to Jewel's *Challenge*, is Allen's earliest work. It was composed while he was studying theology at Louvain, three years previous to publication. Fitzherbert, Allen's secretary, writes of it as follows:

> Dum illic [i.e. at Louvain] haeret, partim sua sponte partim provocatus aliorum exemplo qui per id tempus multa scripsere praeclare de rebus controversis et maxime contra Juellium Anglorum haereticorum antesignanum, librum confecit de Purgatorio, lingua (ut alii) patria, sed ea doctrinae et eloquentiae laude conscriptum ut permagnam inde nominis famam et apud omnes aestimationem sibi collegerit.*

Gillow says the book 'attracted so much notice that in a writ issued by the Queen, 21 February 1567, to the High Sheriff of Lancashire, for the apprehension of "certain persons who, having been late ministers in the Church, were justly deprived of their offices of ministry for their contempt and obstinacy", Allen heads the list under the designation of "Alen, who wrote the late booke of Purgatory" '.†

W. Fulke replied to Allen in his *Two Treatises written against the Papistes, the one being an answere of the Christian Protestant to the proud challenge of a Popish Catholicke: the other a confutation of the Popish Churches doctrine touching Purgatory & prayers for the dead.* London, 1577.

Allen's book has been reprinted under the title of *Souls Departed: Being a Defence and Declaration of the Catholic Church's Doctrine touching Purgatory*, etc., by T. E. Bridgett, C.SS.R., 1886. The spelling has been modernized in this edition, and there are a few notes.

11. A Treatise / made in defence / of the lauful power and au- / thoritie of Priesthod to / remitte sinnes: Of / the peoples duetie for confession of their / sinnes to Gods ministers: And of / the Churches meaning concer- / ning Indulgences, com- /monlie called the / Popes Pardōs. / By William Allen M. of Arte, and / Student in Diuinitie. / Iudae.1. / Vae illis qui perierunt in contradictione Core. / Wo be vnto them that perished in the / disobedience and contradictiō of Cores. / [ornament] / Lou- anii, / Apud Ioannem Foulerum, / Anno D. 1567.

8°. B.L. $\star^8 + \star^4$ + A–Z + Aa–Bb in eights + Cc^{10}. Pag.1[A1]–412[Cc6]. Cw. Mg. Rts – (1) Power of Priesthode / to remitte sinnes. (2) Confession of

* *Nicolai Fitzherberti . . . De Alani Cardinalis vita, libellus*, Rome, 1608. Cited by Knox: *Letters and Memorials of Cardinal Allen*, p. 5.

† *Bibl. Dict.* under Allen. A copy of the Queen's writ is given in Knox: *Letters and Memorials of Cardinal Allen*, p. 21, from P.R.O. Dom. Eliz., vol. 46, no. 32. The names are on the back of the paper. They are Alen, Vause, Murray, Marshall, Hargrave and Norreys.

sinnes / to a Priest. (3) Of the Popes Pardons / and their meaning. (1) Title [*1]. (2) Blank [*1v]. (3) 'To the Christian Reader' [*2]. (4) 'Faultes in the printing' [*3]. (5) Privilegium: Brussels. 26 April 1567. (The book is here referred to as 'A necessary Doctrine of the office of a Priest &c.') [*3v]. (6) Preface [*4–**4v]. (7) Text of Part I: 11 chapters and conclusion [A1–Q5v]. (3) Text of Part II: 12 chapters [Q6–Cc6v]. (9) Imprimatur: Louvain. 20 April 1567 [Cc6v]. (10) Table of Contents [Cc7–10v].

According to Nicholas Fitzherbert this work of Allen's was composed during his sojourn in England (1562–5):

> Interim vero in hac quiete ac secessu [near Oxford] libros duos de Sacerdotio et de Indulgentiis ad scrupulos omnes ex quorundam animis evellendos anglice composuit.*

It called forth from W. Fulke *A Confutation of a Treatise made by William Allen in defence of the vsurped power of Popish Priesthood to remit sinnes, of the necessity of Shrift, and of the Popes Pardons. By William Fulke.* Cambridge, 1586.†

12. An Apologie / and true decla- / ration of the insti- / tution and endeuours of the tvvo / English Colleges, the one in Rome, / the other novv resident in Rhemes: / against certaine sinister informa- / tions giuen vp against the same. / 1.Pet.3. / Sanctifie our Lord Christ in your hartes, ready alwaies / to satisfie euery one that asketh you an accoumpt of / that hope which is in you, but with modestie and / feare, hauing a good conscience, that in that which / they speake il of you, they may be confounded which / calumniate your Good conuersation in Christ. For it / is better to suffer as doing wel (if the wil of God / will haue it so) then doing il. / [ornament] / Printed at Mounts in Henault. / 1581.

8°. A–P in eights+Q^3. Fol. 1[A1]–122[Q2]. Cw. Mg. Rt – An Apologie of the / English Seminaries. (1) Title [A1]. (2) Table of Contents [A1v]. (3) Text: introductory matter and 7 chapters. Ends, 'Your louing felow and seruant in Christ Iesus. William Allen' [A2–Q2v]. (4) Ornament [Q3]. (5) 'The faultes in some copies escaped' [Q3v].

There are numerous references in the *Douay Diaries* to Allen's *Apologia.* All we need note here is that it was contemplated to-

* *Nicolai Fitzherberti . . . De Alani Cardinalis vita, libellus,* Rome, 1608. Cited by Knox, *Letters and Memorials of Cardinal Allen,* p. 6; cp. also Wood, *Ath. Oxon.,* ed. Bliss (1813), I, 616: 'So that going to a certain place near Oxon he . . . wrote two books in English, one *Of the Authority of the Priesthood,* and the other *Of Indulgences.*'

† Full title at entry 96. C. H. Hartshorne, in his introduction to *A Defence of the Sincere and True Translations of the Holy Scriptures into the English Tongue* (Parker Soc. reprint, 1843), says this work of Fulke's was published separately and was also appended to *A Treatise against the Defense of the Censure.* I have not met with this separate publication. Gillow (under Allen, *Bibl. Dict.*) gives *Two Treatises written against the Papistes . . .* 1577, as a reply of Fulke's to this book of Allen's. This is incorrect.

wards the end of 1580,* and that it was published, at the latest, in the following June.† The occasion of its writing may best be seen in a letter from an unknown English priest to Fr. Agazzari, S.J., Rector of the English College at Rome, dated July 1581. He writes: 'The Queen published some outrageous proclamations against all Jesuits, priests, scholars of seminaries, and against the colleges themselves. But Dr. William Allen, who may justly be called the father of this vineyard, wrote an apology for them with such prudence, moderation, and weight of argument, that the heretics themselves, ready enough to be offended, praised his book highly, while the Catholics gained no little increase by it.'‡

The proclamations alluded to in the letter were those of 15 July 1580 and 10 January 1581.§ There is express reference to these in the text of the *Apologie*. Thus: 'wheras we be closely charged in the Edict of the 15 of Iulie 1580, that we be fled into forraine partes and refuse to liue in our natural Countrie;' || and again, 'For, these late terrours (thankes be to God) trouble them so litle, that diuers straight vpon the arriual here in Rhemes of the late Proclamation of Ianuarie, came to their Superiors, to desire leaue to go in' (i.e. into England).¶ Nicholas Fitzherbert states that Allen's *Apologie* was also a reply to some book. He writes:

> non solum [magistratus] nova ac severa edicta in Jesuitas ac seminaristas promulgat, sed eosdem etiam libello edito passimque sparso multis calumniis et criminibus falsis onerat . . . Huic libello alio suo, cui Apologiae seminariorum titulum praefixit, Alanus ita respondit.**

* The Cardinal of Como writes to Allen in November or December 1580: 'Consilium tuum de conscribenda Apologia placet.' *Letters and Memorials*, p. 92.

† Allen writes to Fr. Alphonsus Agazzari on 23 June 1581: '[Fr. Persons] dicit omnia ibi recte procedere et Apologiam nostram valde probari' (i.e. in England), ibid., p. 96.

‡ Quoted by Simpson, *Edmund Campion* (1896), p. 288.

§ The earlier proclamation, that of 15 July 1580, is discussed very fully by Fr. J. H. Pollen, S.J., in his *English Catholics in the Reign of Queen Elizabeth* (1920), pp. 339 ff. Surprisingly he states that although 'all contemporary writers declare [the proclamation of July 15] to have had great influence in aggravating the persecution, yet none of them quote it or had it before them when writing' (p. 339). This is contradicted by the evidence given above. Allen also refers to it explicitly in his letter to the Cardinal of Como, dated 12 September 1580 (cited by Knox, *Letters and Memorials of Cardinal Allen*, p. 90). The later proclamation may be found in Strype, *Annals* (1824), Vol. III, pt. 1, pp. 57–61. Both proclamations appear in Humfrey Dyson's Collection of Proclamations in the Brit. Mus. (Grenville 6463).

|| Note how these words echo the Proclamation's 'such Rebels and Traitours as doe liue in forraine partes, and ioyning to them others that are fled out of the Realme, as persons refusing to liue here in their natural countrey'.

¶ The two references are from *Apologie*, sigs. A5 and L5^{v} respectively.

** *Nicolai Fitzherberti . . . De Alani Cardinalis vita libellus*, Rome, 1608. Cited by Knox, *Letters and Memorials of Cardinal Allen*, p. 13.

There is no express reference to a book in the *Apologie*, but there are statements which certainly hint at an answer to William Charke's *An answere to a seditious pamphlet* (1580).*

Allen's *Apologie* had a wide circulation. A copy was put into the hands of Walsingham,† and it is probable that Queen Elizabeth herself read it.‡ It was translated into Latin and incorporated in Bridgewater's *Concertatio* with the Proclamations of 10 January 1581 and 1 April 1582 prefixed. Thomas Bilson devotes the first two parts of *The true difference between christian subiection and vnchristian rebellion* (Oxford, 1585) to answering it.§

The *Apologie* was printed by Allen's printer at Rhemes, John Fogny. Mounts in Henault is a blind. The ornamental capital letters employed in the text and the printer's ornaments, together with the bold roman type, put this beyond doubt.|| It is interesting to note that Allen paid a visit to Mons (Mounts in Henault) on 4 July 1581, returning to Rhemes on 3 August following.¶ Possibly the idea of this visit suggested the place on the title.

13. A / Briefe Historie / of the Glorious / Martyrdom of XII. Reue- / rend Priests, executed vvithin these tvveluemo- / nethes

* This book was entered on the Stationers' Register, 20 December 1580. The alternative to Charke's book would be Meredith Hanmer's *The Great bragge and challenge of M. Champion a Iesuite*, entered on the Stationers' Register, 3 January [1581]. But I can find nothing in Allen's *Apologie* which could be described as specifically answering Hanmer. There are, on the other hand, four references in Charke to Ireland, suggesting a connexion between Sander's expedition thither and the coming of the Jesuits to England. (This, be it noted, is also broadly hinted at in the Proclamation of January 1581.) Allen, in his chapter 'Of Priestes and Iesuites', is at some pains to show the impossibility of this connexion. Again, although his main theme is treason, Charke refers in section 3 of his book to poperie as being 'in gold and siluer & pearle, and crucifixes, and Agnus deis, all for the eye'; and again, in the same section, to Masses, pardons, 'holie graines', and copper pieces of Agnus dei. Allen asks, 'What hath Masse, Matins, Confession, Absolution, beades, Agnus deies . . . in nature with treason?' [K2]. There is nothing in the two Proclamations to which these words could refer.

† 'Allen sent a copy [of the *Apology*] through a merchant in Paris to the English ambassador, Sir Henry Cobham, who forwarded it to Walsingham.' Martin Haile, *An Elizabethan Cardinal, William Allen* (1914), p. 192.

‡ 'Nostra Apologia (ut audio) versatur in manibus tam adversariorum quam amicorum, et illius amplissimae legationis Gallicae princeps, qui vocatur Princeps Delfinus [i.e. the Prince Dauphin of Auvergne] dedit eam legendam ipsi Reginae.' Allen to Fr. Alphonsus Agazzari, S.J., in his letter of 23 June 1581. Cited in Knox, *Letters and Memorials of Cardinal Allen*, p. 98.

§ Full title at entry 86. Cp. Strype, *Annals* (1824), Vol. I, pt. 2, p. 337, and Vol. III, pt. 1, p. 448.

|| H. Rousselle suggests Rutger Velpius as the printer. The suggestion seems to be based solely on the reference to Mounts in Henault on the title-page, coupled with the fact that Velpius had removed his press to Mons in 1580, where he was, at this time, the only printer. *Annales de L'Imprimerie à Mons* (1858), p. 140.

¶ Cp. *D.D.* Under date 4 July 1581 we read that on that day Allen had set out 'versus montes in Henalte'. Under date 3 August 1581 we read, 'a montibus in Henalt rediit dignissimus D. Praeses cum servo suo H. Browne'.

for confession and defence of the Ca- / tholike Faith. But vnder the false pre- / tence of Treason. / VVith a note of sundrie things that befel them in their life / and imprisonment: and a preface declaring their / innocencie. / Set furth by such as were much conuersant vvith / them in their life, and present at their / arraignement and death. / Occidistis, sed non possedistis. / that is / You haue slaine them, but / you haue not gotten / possession. / 1582. / [rule] [John Fogny, Rhemes.]

8°. a–f+A–D in eights. Not fol. Cw. Mg. No Rt. (1) Title [a1]. (2) 'The names of these glorious martyres with the day and yere of their suffering' [a1v]. (3) Preface to the Reader [a2–c8]. (4) 'A True Report of the death and Martyrdom of F. Campion Iesuite and Priest, M. Sherwin, and M. Bryan Priestes': includes letters from Frs. Campion, Sherwin and Bryan, followed by elegiac verses in Latin describing Campion's life by 'an old fellow of F. Campions' [c8v–f8]. (5) 'The Articles ministred to the 7 priestes, and others condemned with them, with the answeres of these 7 to the same. 13. Maij. 1582' [A1–A4]. (6) 'The Martyrdomes oe the Reuerend Priestes M. Thomas Forde, M. Iohn Sherte & M. Robert Iohnson, the XXVIII. of Maye, 1582' [A4v–B1]. (7) 'The Martyrdomes of the Reuerend Priests, M. William Filbe, M. Lucas Kirbie, M. Laurence Richardson whose right name was Iohnson, and M. Thomas Cottam the 30 of May 1582': includes a letter of Kirby's [B1–C3]. (8) Martyrdoms of the Priests, John Paine (2 April 1582), Everard Haunse (31 July 1581), Cuthbert Maine (29 Nov. 1577), John Nelson (13 Feb. 1578), and of Thomas Sherwood (7 Feb. 1578): includes a letter of Everard Haunse [C3–D8v]. (9) Ends: 'Gentil Reader, consider our difficulties in printing, and beare with the faults escaped vs.' [D8v].

The many references in Allen's letters printed in Knox, *Letters and Memorials of Cardinal Allen*, leave no doubt as to Allen's editorship of this work.* This has already been pointed out by the Rev. J. H. Pollen in his reprint, and the reader may be referred to the evidence collected by Fr. Pollen in his introduction to that volume.† The work, as Fr. Pollen points out, represents, as far as possible, a faithful eyewitness's account of the various martyrdoms. Information was thus derived from a number of sources, including the pen of Fr. Robert Persons.‡ Thomas Alfield's *A true report* (referred to in the note below) is

* For example, the letters to Fr. Agazzari under dates 7 Feb., 12 Feb., 23 June, 17 July, 16 Aug., 3 Sept. 1582.

† *A Briefe Historie of the Glorious Martyrdom of Twelve Reverend Priests Father Edmund Campion & his Companions By William Cardinal Allen With Contemporary Verses by the Venerable Henry Walpole, & the Earliest Engravings of the Martyrdom Reprinted from the (probably unique) Copy in the British Museum, and edited by the Rev. J. H. Pollen, S. J.* (London, 1908). The verses are taken from Thomas Alfield's *A true report of the death and martyrdome of M. Campion* [entry 9]. The engravings, which depict a martyr's progress, are reproduced from the first Italian translation of the *Briefe Historie* (Macerata, 1583).

‡ Thus, Allen writes to Agazzari, 12 February 1582: 'haec nunc adicio . . . partim ut significem id quod mihi peculiaris nunc ex Anglia nuntius narrat, et quod etiam aliunde R. P. Rob. [i.e. Fr. Robert Persons] scribit'. Cited in Knox, *Letters and Memorials of Cardinal Allen*, p. 113.

the basis of the narrative in that section which deals with Campion, Sherwin and Bryan. Publication took place in August or early September 1582,* and in the following year translations appeared in Latin and Italian. Later there was a Spanish version.†

A comparison of the printing of the *Briefe Historie* (lettering, ornaments, etc.) with that of works known to have been printed by John Fogny of Rhemes points conclusively to its being the work of the same printer.

14. [within a border] A / true report / of the late ap- / prehension and im- / prisonnement of Iohn / Nicols Minister, at Roan, and his / confession and ansvvers made in the / time of his durance there. / Vvherevnto is added the satisfaction of cer- / taine, that of feare or frailtie haue / latly fallen in England. / [ornament] / Printed at Rhemes, / By Iohn Fogny. / [rule] / 1583.

8°. A–E in eights+F². Fol. 1[A7]–34[E8]. Cw. (verso only) No Mg. No Rt. (1) Title [A1]. (2) Blank [A1ᵛ]. (3) Preface [A2–6ᵛ]. (4) Text: letters etc. concerning John Nicols, Laurence Caddey, Richard Baines, Edward Osberne, James Bosgrave [A7–E8ᵛ]. (5) 'An Admonition to the Reader': 1 June 1583 [F1–2ᵛ].

The earlier career of John Nicols is referred to at entry 94. This collection of documents continues his story and adds that of other lapsed Catholics.

Dr. George Oliver supposed that Persons was the editor of this book.‡ This is unlikely. Persons was in Spain, and was, moreover, a sick man during the early part of 1583, when the book was in preparation.§ He only returned to Paris at the end

* Allen to Agazzari, 3 September 1582: 'Mitto nunc integrum libellum de martyribus nostris.' Cited in Knox, ibid.

† The Latin version appears to have been made by Fr. John Gibbons, S.J. It is printed in Bridgewater's *Concertatio* (1583, 1588, etc.).

‡ 'I believe he was the Author of "a true Report of the late apprehension and imprisonment of John Nicols, Minister, at Roan".' *Collectanea* (1845), p. 162. No reasons are given.

§ He had gone to Spain in connexion with the plans of the Duke of Guise concerning Scottish affairs. There are several references in letters of Allen at this time to his illness. The fullest account is to be found in his own *Notes Concerning the English Mission*: 'Persons was going to return to France, but falling seriously ill at the port of Bilbao in Biscay he was in great danger of his life. It was reported he was dead, as Dr. Allen wrote to Father Agazario on December 29 [should be '30'] of this year: "As to our good Father, about whom you make inquiry, in truth I fear that he has died on his journey, for we have been expecting him these two months, and even ere this with tears, and yet he appears not." Thus wrote Allen. But, having recovered a little, he went to the College of the Society in the University of Oñate, where he remained until the spring of the following year.' [1583]. *Publications of Catholic Record Society*, Vol. IV, p. 63; cf. also p. 103, where further details are given.

of May, when it was already in the press. Since, as we learn from the 'Admonition to the Reader', despatch in publication 'was compted necessary', the editing must have been done by someone on the spot. There are reasonable grounds for attributing it to Allen. Allen was at Rhemes during the period when the events recorded in the book took place. The apostatas naturally addressed themselves to him, as the head of the English Catholics in the Low Countries. His own printer, John Fogny, was employed to print the book. In addition to this, his letters at this time to Fr. Agazzari in Rome give a complete account of the preparation and the printing of the work, implying thereby his own connexion with it. So, after reference in three letters during March 1583 to the submission of the apostatas, he writes on 14 April, 'We are now having printed the confessions of Caddey and Nicols and probably of Osborne as well'.* He follows this on 20 May with the news 'By the next messenger we shall send the confessions of Nicols and other lapsed [Catholics]; they are already in the press'.† And finally writes on 30 May: 'I send now the little book in English containing the various accounts of the apologies and repentance of the Catholics who have lapsed in this persecution . . . You will see, you will see the admirable confession of our priest-prisoner' (i.e. Richard Baines).‡

It follows that there is, at least, a strong presumption in favour of Allen's having edited this *Report*. When we turn to the style of editing the presumption becomes pretty well a certainty. The *Report* closely resembles, in this respect, a similar work of Allen's, viz. *A Briefe Historie of the Glorious Martyrdom of XII. Reuerend Priests* [entry 13].

15. A True Sincere and Modest Defence of English Catholiques that suffer for their Faith both at home and abrode: against a false, seditious and slaunderous Libel intituled; The Execution of Iustice in England. Wherin is declared, how vniustlie the

* *Damus nunc praelo confessiones Caddei et Nicolai atque fortassis etiam Osburni.* Knox, *Letters and Memorials of Cardinal Allen*, p. 188. Fr. Richard Barret, who was with Allen at Rhemes at this time, and may also have had a hand in the editing of the work, is even more explicit. In a letter of the same date to Fr. Agazzari he writes, 'the whole history of Nicols and his confession is going to be printed in a week's time'. (*Iam statim post unam septimanam esset imprimenda*) *D.D.*, pp. 323 and 324.

† *Per proximum nuntium mittemus confessiones Nicolai et aliorum lapsorum; sunt enim jamdudum sub praelo. Letters and Memorials*, p. 192.

‡ *Mitto hoc tempore libellum anglicum continentem varias diversorum hominum in hac persecutione lapsorum satisfactiones et poenitentias . . . Videbitis, videbitis mirabilem confessionem nostri incarcerati sacerdotis.* Ibid, p. 194. This copy which Allen sent to Agazzari was evidently an advance copy. The reader will note that the 'Admonition' was dated 1 June, and was evidently added subsequently. The March letters referred to above will be found in Knox, at pp. 177, 182 and 186.

Protestants doe charge Catholiques with treason; how vntrulie they deny their persecution for Religion; and how deceitfullie they seeke to abuse strangers about the cause, greatnes, and maner of their sufferinges, with diuers other matters perteining to this purpose. Psal. 62. Vt obstruatur os loquentium iniqua. That the mouth may be stopped of such as speake vniustlie. Psal. 49. Os tuum abundauit malitia, & lingua tua concinnabat dolos. Thy mouth hath abounded in malice, and thy tongue hath coninglie framed lies. [Rouen. 1584.]

16. The Copie of a Letter written by M. Doctor Allen: concerning the yeelding vp, of the citie of Dauentrie, vnto his Catholike Maiestie, by Sir William Stanley Knight. Wherin is shewed both howe lawful, honorable, and necessarie that action was: and also that al others, especiallie those of the English Nation, that detayne anie townes, or other places, in the lowe countries, from the King Catholike, are bound, vpon paine of damnation, to do the like. Before Which is also prefixed à gentlemans letter, that gaue occasion, of this discourse. Matth. 22. Reddite ergo quae sunt Caesaris, Caesari: Render therfore the things that are Caesars, to Caesar: Imprinted at Antuarpe, by Ioachim Trognaesius, Anno 1587.

17. An Admonition to the Nobility and People of England and Ireland concerninge the present warres made for the execution of His Holines Sentence, by the highe and mightie Kinge Catholike of Spaine. By the Cardinal of Englande [i.e. Card. Allen]. A°. 1588 [Antwerp].

BAINES, RICHARD
fl. 1583
(see entry 14)

BAYNES, ROGER
1546–1623

18. [within a compartment] The Praise / of Solitarinesse, / Set down in the forme / of a Dialogue, / Wherein is conteyned, a Dis- / course Philosophical, of the / lyfe Actiue, and Con- / templatiue. / Imprinted at Lon- / don by Francis Coldocke and / Henry Bynneman. / 1577. / [rule] / Qui nihil sperat, / Nihil desperat.

4°. B.L. A–L in fours + M³. Pag. 1 [B1]–86 [M3ᵛ]. Cw. Mg. Rt – The prayse / of Solitarinesse. (1) Title [A1]. (2) Blank [A1ᵛ]. (3) 'To the Right Worshipfull my approued frende, Mʳ. Edwarde Dyer, increase of estimation according to his vertue': Roger Baynes [A2–4]. (4) 'To the Reader': 'Vale. Qui nihil sperat, Nihil desperat' [A4ᵛ]. (5) 'The prayse of Solitarinesse, sette downe in the forme of a Dialoge, wherein is contayned a discourse Philosophical, of the lyfe Actiue, and Contemplatiue. The Speakers. Lysippus. Eudoxus. Tales' [B1–M3ᵛ].

19. The / Baynes of / Aquisgrane, / The 1. Part, & 1. Volume, / intituled / Variety. / Contayning Three Bookes, in the forme of Dialogues, / vnder the Titles following, Viz. / [rule] / Profit, Pleasure, Honour. / [rule] / Furnished with diuers things, no lesse delightfull, then be- / neficiall to be knowne, and obserued. / Related by Rog. Baynes Gent. a long Exile / out of England, not for any temporall respects. / [ornament] / Qui nihil sperat, nihil desperat. / Printed at Augusta in Germany. M.DC.XVII.

4°. ⋆ + A–O in fours. Pag. 1 [A1]–112 [O4ᵛ]. Cw. No Mg. Rt – The Baynes of Aquisgrane. / Part 1. Lib. 1. (Of Profit.) (1) Title [⋆1]. (2) 'The Printer to the Reader. This present Volume, and the rest that are to follow, though they haue not come to the Presse till now, yet haue they byn written some yeares ago, in the tyme of the late Queene Elizabeth.' Beneath these words is an heraldic shield within a wreath, with the words 'Nihil Sperat, Nihil Desperat' [⋆1ᵛ]. (3) 'The general proeme made by the relator of this Worke, Vnto the first Part therof, intituled Variety, Dedicated in the Names of the Authors themselues, vnto the future Posterity of England' [⋆2–4ᵛ]. (4) Text-title: 'The Baynes of Aquisgrane. The I. Part, and I. Booke, Intituled Profit.' Followed by 'The Dedication of the Relator, to the Professors in England of Thrift' [A1–1ᵛ]. (5) Text of Dialogue: three characters – Aquilonius, Favonius, and Subsolanus [A2–O4ᵛ].

The printer's statement in respect of further volumes of this work (bibl. details (2) above) can have been no more than a pious hope, for no trace of any subsequent volume has been found. Nor does the manuscript, which was evidently in his hands, seem to have survived. We are informed in the text of the dialogue that the subject of Variety was to be treated under the further headings of Ignorance, Opinion, Science, Education, Travaile and Repose, making nine in all. The work was to be completed with a discussion on (1) the Subordination of the World, and (2) the Folly of the Same.*

BOSGRAVE, JAMES, S.J.

1547?–1623

(see entry 14)

* In addition to the above two works there is a short poem by Roger Baynes 'in the due commendation of the Author' in George Turbervile's *Tragical Tales* (1587).

BRINKLEY, STEPHEN
fl. 1584

20. [within a compartment]. [upper panel] The / Exercise / [middle panel] of / A Christian / Life. / Written in Italian by the / Reuerend Father Gaspar / Loarte D. of Diuinitie, / of the Societie of / Iesus. / And newly translated / into Englishe. / by I.S. / [medallion enclosing the IHS device] / [lower panel] Dilexi decorem domus tuae, Domine. [William Carter? 1579.]

LAMB.

8°. **+A–Z+AA–EE in eights. Fol. 1[A1]–224[EE8]. Cw. Mg. Rt – The Exercise of / a Christian Life. (1) Title [**1]. (2) Blank [**1v]. (3) 'To al those of the Reuerend Societie of the name of Iesus, perpetual increase of al vertues, from him that geueth them': 'At Paris, the.20. of Iune. 1579, Your most bounden beadsman, and dutiful frende for euer. Iames Sancer.' [**2]. (4) 'The Authour to the deuout Reader' [**3]. (5) Table of Chapters [**4–6]. (6) 'A Sonnet to the Christian Reader' [**6v]. (7) 'Militi Christiano Tetrastichon' [**7]. (8) 'Carmen in Natiuitatem Christi' [**7v]. (9) Two cuts, with verses in Lat. and Eng. [**8 and 8v]. (10) Text in 33 chapters, followed by two prayers. Cuts occur at D5v and H3v [A1–CC4]. (11) Translator's Prayer [CC4v]. (12) Cut, with verses in Lat. and Eng. [CC5]. (13) 'To the Reader' [CC5v]. (14) Prayers and 'A Protestation to be made in time of sicknes' [CC6–EE6]. (15) 'A most straunge and excellent monument, prouing apparantly the Reuerend antiquitie of our Catholike Religion; found at Rome, in Iuly last past, in the yere of our Lorde. 1578. and is of al wise men beleeued to be the blessed virgin S. Priscilla her Churchyarde' [EE6–8]. (16) 'The faultes escaped in printing . . .': ends, 'Pardon al faultes, good Reader, and beare with the Printers of a vulgare tongue in a forreine countrey' [EE8v].

The work is a translation of Loarte's *Essercitatio della vita christiana. Composto per il R.P.D. Gaspar Loarte*, first published at Barcelona in Spain in 1569.* Fr. Persons refers to the translator in his *Memoirs* as 'mr Stephen Brinkly, a vertuous gentleman that translated Loartes book under the name of James Sanker'.†

The initials N. R. are appended to the 'Sonnet to the Christian Reader' in the revised edition of the work referred to below. They are probably those of Nicholas Roscarrock, who was closely associated with Brinkley in the Catholic cause.‡

Evidence for date is to be found in bibl. details (3) and (15) above. The printing corresponds in every respect (cuts, ornamental caps., type, etc.) with that of Fen's *Instructions and Aduertisements*. The reasons for attributing it to William Carter are therefore set out at that entry [no. 39]. Brinkley's reference to

* cf. Alegambe, *Bibliotheca Scriptorum Societatis Iesu* (1676), p. 278.

† *Memoir I. Publications of the Catholic Record Society*, Vol. II, p. 33. Further notes on Brinkley will be found at p. 354.

‡ cf. Gillow, *Bibl. Dict.*, s.v. *Roscarrock*. Roscarrock also contributed verses to John Bossewell's *Workes of Armorie* (1572), and (possibly) to George Gascoigne's *The Steele Glas* (1576).

Paris in the subscription to the Address (bibl. details (3) above) can only be meant to mislead. There is no evidence that he was in Paris before 1583.

A revised edition of his translation, 'with certaine very deuout exercises and prayers added therunto, more then were in the first edition', was published by Brinkley at Rouen, where he was assisting Fr. Persons in the publication of books, in 1584. This edition was reprinted about 1600. There were further reprints in 1610 and 1634.

BRISTOW, RICHARD, D.D.
1538–1581

21. A Briefe / Treatise of di- / uerse plaine and sure wayes / to finde out the truthe in this doubtful / and dangerous time of Heresie: contey- / ning sundry worthy Motiues vnto the / Catho-like faith, or Considerations to / moue a man to beleue the Ca- / tholikes, and not the / Heretikes. / Sette out by Richard Bristow Priest, / Licentiat in Diuinitie. / [ornament] / Antuer-piae, / Apud Iohannem Foulerum, Anglum. / M.D.LXXIIII. / [rule] / Cum Priuilegio.

Bod.

8°. B.L. ★^{8}+★★^{4}+A–Y+a in eights. Fol. 1[A1]–176[Y8]. Cw. Mg. Rt – Motiues to the / Catholike Faith. (1) Title [★1]. (2) Blank [★1^{v}]. (3) Two quots. in Lat. and Eng. [★2]. (4) 'To the Reader' [★3–★★4]. (5) 'The approbation of this Boke, according to the order of the Councel of Trent. Sess.4.'. Signed by William Allen [★★4^{v}].* (6) Text: 48 Motives in all, headed, and each numbered in margin [A–Y8]. (7) 'Bristow to the Reader' [Y8^{v}]. (8) Table of Motives [a1]. (9) Table of principal matters [a2–8]. (10) 'Faultes escaped in the printing' [a8^{v}].

An interesting history attaches to this rare book. We learn from Bristow's *Reply to Fulke* [entry 23] that it was based on certain rules of truth,† which had been drawn up by Cardinal Allen some years previously, and was compiled at Allen's express wish. Copies were scarce 'partly because there were but few

* The 'Approbation' appears in both Latin and English. The English version is as follows:

'This Treatise written in the English tongue by my louing frind Richard Bristow Licētiat in Diuinitie: conteining with great perspicuitie, order, & art, diuers most excellent marks, whereby to discerne in Religion the true iudgement of the Catho-like Church from the false vanitie of the Heretikes: is in al pointes Catholike, learned, and worthy to be read and printed. which alone if my Countrey most sweete vnto me, wil earnestly & diligently reade, it wil meruaile, that from the grounded Faith of al times, Nations, and Doctors, it can be remoued by so few, so new-risen, so busie, so euil, so vnlearned felowes, and so at variance amongst themselues. So do I geue my censure, William Allen, the Kings Professor of Diuinitie at Douay. 30. Apr. 1574.' sig. ★★4^{v}.

† *Certain Brief Reasons concerning the Catholic Faith.* By Cardinal Allen. See Appen-dix I, where the question of this work and its relation to Bristow's book is discussed.

printed, partly because a great parte of those few fell into Heretickes handes'.*

This suppression of the copies led to the revised *Demaundes* [next entry]. W. Fulke replied to this work of Bristow's in *A Retentiue, to stay good christians, in true faith and religion, against the motiues of Richard Bristow.* London, 1580. Oliver Carter's reply† is referred to at next entry.

The *Motives* was heartily disliked by the Protestants, and indeed Card. Allen in his *Answere to the Libel of English Justice* says of Bristow's reference in this book to 'the controuersie betwixt our two superiors' (i.e. the Pope and Queen Elizabeth): 'Manie Catholiques were sorie therefore, and wished the matter so offensiue had neuer bene touched, but committed onelie to higher powers, and especiallie to Gods iudgement . . . Wherupō afterwardes not onely D. Bristow omitted in his second edition or abridgement of his booke that odious point, not fit at that time to be handled . . .'‡ The section referred to by Allen is entitled 'Obedient Subiects' (Motive 40). Passages from this section and from Motives 6 and 15 were submitted to Edmund Campion and his fellows when on trial for their lives.§ It is to be observed that the 1599 Antwerp reprint does not omit this section.

22. Demaundes to bee / proponed of Ca- / tholickes to the / Heretickes. / By Richard Bri- / stow Priest and Doctor / of Diuinitie. / Taken partely out of his late En- / glishe Booke of Motiues to / the Catholicke faith, partely / out of his intended Latin / booke of the same / matter. / [cut]. [J. Duckett. 1599?].

Bod.

12°. B.L. A–F in twelves. Pag.1 [A2]–123[F3]. Cw. Mg. Rt – Demaundes vnto / All Heretickes. (1) Title [A1]. (2) Q.iots. in Lat. and Eng. Imprimatur by William Allen [A1v]. (3) Text [A2–F3]. (4) 'The Titles of the Demaundes' (51 in all): ends 'In M. Edward Rishtons *Table of the Church*, may

* Actually 367. See MS. Lansdowne, Vol. 42, No. 78 (B.M.), which reads: 'Trayterous and popish bookes intercepted. 1584. [a mistake for 1574] . . . 367. Motiues to the catholicke faith, by Richard Bristowe proeste Licentiate in Diuinitie. Imprinted at Antwerpe 1574'; cp. Strype, *The Life and Acts of Matthew Parker* (1821), Book IV, p. 392, entry 477, where the correct date is given.

† Referred to by Strype, *Annals* (1824), Vol. II, pt. 1, p. 498.

‡ *A True Sincere and Modest Defence of English Catholiques*. By Card. Allen. sig. D8v [entry 15].

§ The importance that was attached to the *Motives* may be seen in Richard Simpson's account of the trial of Edmund Campion (*Edmund Campion. A Biography* (1896), pp. 406 and 407). The passages submitted are referred to in the same work at p. 385. The six articles (the fifth of which specially refers to Bristow's *Motives*), ministered to the seven priests who suffered subsequently, are to be found in English in Allen's *A Briefe Historie of the Glorious Martyrdom of XII Reuerend Priests* (see entry 13) and in Latin in John Bridgewater's *Concertatio Ecclesiae Catholicae in Anglia . . .* (1588), sig. X4v. See also M. A. Tierney, *Dodd's Church History* (1839), Vol. III, Appendix iii.

be sene with the very eie, all wel neare that hath bene saide in this Booke' [F3v–4v]. (5) 'The Continual Succession of the Popes of Rome' (from Peter to Gregory XIII), with an appended note [F5–11]. (6) Blank [F12].

See previous entry for the occasion of writing. In his introductory matter Bristow states that he was 'not minded to repaire the Printe' of the *Motives*, but 'thought good . . . for further propagatiō of the truth, to the saluation of my deare deceaued Countreimē, to set out this litle Pāflet. which albeit to some may for the quantity seme but a trifle, yet whosoeuer will voutsafe to peruse it, shal finde it (I trust) full of most iust & weightie considerations to beleeue the Catholikes, of this time also, & not the Heretickes . . . But if any man desire a larger declaration of them, he shall in my late booke of Motiues for most of thē find enough; and for all of them much more in my Latine booke which I minde with Gods help to make, as sone as I can cōueniently, of the same matter, and that somewhat of an other sort, & in another order thē I did before in English, which by these Demaundes may partly be coniectured'* [A2–A3 *passim*].

Oliver Carter replied to the *Demaundes* in *An Answere made by Oliuer Carter, Bacheler of Diuinitie: Unto certaine Popish Questions and Demaundes*. London, 1579.† Dodd suggests that there was a London edition of the *Demands* in 1592, and he gives as a reply, 'To the seminary Priests late come over, &c. Answer to Dr. Bristow's 51 Demands, 4to, 1592'.‡ Dr. J. Rainolds also replied to Bristow.§

The *Demaundes* was first published early in 1576. We have as authority for this date Bristow's words in his *Reply to Fulke*, where, in the Address to the Reader, he writes 'this was the occasion . . . of my *Demaundes* in the beginning of the year 1576'.|| The following passage from the *Douay Diaries*, under date March 1576, also refers to the publication of the *Demaundes* (described as an epitome of the *Motives*):

> Denique hoc mense ornatiss. vir Do.Ric.Bristous, S.Theologiae doctor, cum libros illos quos, Motivorum nomine nuncupatos, ad Anglos suos ad unitatem fidei catholicae revocandos non multo ante miserat, magna ex parte in haereticorum manus incidisse certo cognoverat, audito etiam plurimorum jam in Anglia studio vehementi et illorum librorum avidissimo desiderio, novis impensis alios plurimos

* The Latin Version was edited and published in 1608 by Dr. Thomas Worthington. The printing difficulty seems to have precluded publication in Bristow's lifetime. See *D.D.*, p. 319. Letter of Gregory Martin.

† See the article by J. E. Bailey on Carter in the *D.N.B.* Also the note on Carter at Appendix V.

‡ C. Dodd, *The Church History of England* (1737), Vol. II, p. 60. See also entry in *Pollard and Redgrave*.

§ See the reference at entry 87.

|| The passage is given in full at Appendix I.

(quasi priorum illorum brevem quandam epitomen ad modum quaesitionum eruditiss[e] et ad omnium captum lucidissime propositarum explicatum) curavit imprimi, et per Anglum quendam mercatorem non longe antea suo opere ad fidem catholicam revocatum Angliam remisit; quos libros, ut de prioribus jam certo cognovimus et quotidie experimur, plurimum apud omnes profuturos speramus.*

No copy of this edition seems to be extant. The Bodleian copy, from which the bibliographical details above are taken, is a reprint, and came from the secret press of James Duckett, who was printing about 1599–1600. He reprinted Bristow's *Motives* in 1599, and it would seem reasonable to assign this edition to the same date. Lambeth Palace Library possesses a copy of this same edition.

23. [ornament] A Reply to Fulke, / In defense of M. D. Allens scroll of Articles, / and booke of Purgatorie. / By Richard Bristo Doctor of Diuinitie. / Tit.3. / Haereticum hominem post vnam & secundam cor- / reptionem deuita: sciens quia subuersus est, qui / eiusmodi est, & deliquit cum sit pro- / prio iudicio condemnatus. / Auoyde the Heretike man after the first and second / correption: knowing that he which is suche, / is subuerted and sinneth, syth that he / is condemned by his owne / Iudgement. / Perused and allowed by me / Th. Stapleton. / [ornament] / Imprinted at Louaine by Iohn Lion. / Anno Dom. 1580.

4°. B.L. π^1+A–W–Z+Aa–Ww–Zz+Aaa–Fff in fours. Pag. 1[B1]–415[Eee4]. Cw. Mg. Rt – A Reply to Fulke. (1) Title [π]. (2) Blank [π^v]. (3) To the Reader [A1–4]. (4) Blank [A4^v]. (5) Text [B1–Eee4]. (6) 'The Printer to the Reader': John Lyon. 'The Errata' (Eee4^v]. (7) 'The contentes of this Booke at large' [Fff1–3]. (8) Blank [Fff4].

Fulke's book was entitled *Two Treatises written against the Papistes, the one being an answere of the Christian Protestant to the proud challenge of a Popish Catholicke: the other a confutation of the Popish Churches doctrine touching Purgatory & prayers for the dead: by William Fulke . . .* 1577.† Bristow's view of this work is contained in his address *To the Reader* as follows: 'And now after all this, the last yeare 1577. commeth foorth from one *W. Fulke* an heretike, a pretended answere to the first copie aboue mentioned, or to some extract thereof, ioyned with another like answere of the same Authors to D. Allens *booke of Purgatorie*, and to my handes it came a fewe weekes agoe, euen this late Christmas

* *D.D.*, p. 102.

† The first of these treatises was republished in the same year under the title of *An Answer of a true christian to the proude challenge of a counterfet Catholike.*

[margin reads 'an.1578 stylo R.']. Sith which time reading it twise ouer, I finde, that he neuer so much as once mentioneth either my Motiues, or my Demaundes, and much lesse doth he euer goe about to infringe any of my probations therein conteined. And yet notwithstanding this depe silence, in one place he bewrayeth him selfe to haue knowen of them, where he glaunceth at the diuine worke of a certayne healing which I reported in my Motiues' [A1]. He goes on to describe Fulke's work as 'only for shew of an answere to my Motiues and Demaundes, specially seeing that, where as D. Allens writing was called onely by the name of *Articles*, this man at euery Article hath also printed the worde *Demaundes*, because euery Article consisteth of certayne Demaundes: by meane whereof I knowe already my selfe, some that are deceyued, and thinke it to be an answere vnto me, yet in trueth it toucheth not me at all, neither maketh any iuste answere to D. Allen, but all so simply and so feebly, that he is fayne to set it out without priuiledge, as also his other booke against Purgatorie, though that booke *was authorized* (he saith) *almost two yeares ago*' [A2].* Fulke replied to Bristow in *A Reioynder to Bristows Replie in defence of Allens scroll of Articles and Booke of Purgatorie.* 1581. [Full title at entry 128.]

The *Reply to Fulke* was probably printed at the Greenstreet House Press by Stephen Brinkley, not as the title indicates 'at Louaine by Iohn Lion'.

BRYAN, ALEXANDER, S.J.

1553–1581

(see entry 13)

BURNE, NICOL

fl. 1581

24. The / Disputation / concerning the / controversit headdis / of Religion, haldin in the Realme of / Scotland, the zeir of God ane thou- / sand, fyue hundreth fourscoir / zeiris. Betuix. / The praetendit Ministeris of the deformed Kirk / in Scotland. / And, / Nicol Burne Professor of philosophie in S. / Leonardis college, in the Citie of Sanctan- / drois, brocht vp from his tender eage in the / peruersit sect of the Caluinistis, and nou be / ane special grace of God, ane membre of / the halie and Catholik kirk. / Dedicat / To his Souerane the kingis M. of Scotland, / King Iames the Saxt. / Nisi conuersi fueritis, gladium

* Further reference to this Address will be found at p. 519, where Allen's 'scroll of Articles' is discussed. For Allen's 'booke of Purgatorie' see entry 10.

suum vibrabit: arcum / suum tetendit, & parauit illum. 1. / Vnles ze be conuerted, God vil drau his suord: he hes / bendit his bovv, and preparit it / Psalm.7. / Imprented at Parise the first day of / October. / 1581.

[colophon on Z7^{v}] Imprentit at Pareis, the first day of / October, The zeir of / God, 1581.

8°. ā+A–Z in eights. Fol. 1 [A1]–190[Z4]. Cw. on fol. 8^{v} of each gathering only. Mg. Rt. varies. (1) Title [ā1]. (2) Quots. in Latin and Scots [ā1^{v}]. (3) 'To the maist nobil, potent, and gratious King of Scotland King Iames the saxt': 'At Parise the 24. day of Iulij. 1581. Zour M. Maist humil, faythful subiect, and daylie Oratour. Nicol Burne' [ā2–5^{v}]. (4) 'To the Christiane Reidar': Paris. 24 July 1581 [ā6–8]. (5) Quots. in Scots, with explanation [ā8^{v}]. (6) Text of the *Disputation* in 41 chapters (numbered incorrectly as 37). At sig. M5 is the translation from Beza's book of Epigrams of his verses 'Theodorus Beza de sua in Candidam & Audebertum beneuolentia'. At sig. X2 are two woodcuts [A1–Z4^{v}]. (7) 'The materis of controuersie quhilk ar intreated in this conference ar thir' [Z5–6^{v}]. (8) Quots. in Latin and Scots [Z7]. (9) Colophon [Z7^{v}]. (10) Ornament [Z8]. (11) Blank [Z8^{v}].

The disputation, which Burne admits 'I haue sumpairt amplifeit ād inlargeit [but only so far as his own answers were concerned] findand greitar commoditie of buikes heir [i.e. in Paris] nor in Scotland', seems to have taken place during his imprisonment in the Tolbooth at Edinburgh (14 October–30 January 1580), and to have been concluded at Paisley. Those who took part in the discussion were Andrew Melville, a Mr. Blackwood (who intervenes at chapter 12), Walter Balcanquhal and John Durie (who take up the discussion at chapter 21), John Brand (at chapter 22), and a Protestant, unnamed (who appears in chapters 23 and 24). Then 'Smeton tuik on him the disputation in Paislay, in audiēce of the maist honorabil the Maister of Ross, the lairdis of Caldual, blackhal, Ihonestone, Quhytfurd, and sindrie vtheris' [sig. N2] (chapters 25–8). Finally, an unnamed Minister and a Protestant conclude the disputation.*

The printing is the same as that of Hamilton's *Ane Catholik and Facile Traictise*. Possibly the publisher was Thomas Brumen, from whose house issued most of the Scottish tracts. There is not sufficient evidence, however, to fix this certainly.

* I give the numbers of the chapters as they appear in the book. The names of the disputants are again referred to in *An Admonition* (next entry). Short biographical notes will be found in *Catholic Tractates of the Sixteenth Century 1573–1600*, edited for the Scottish Text Society by T. G. Law (Edinburgh and London, 1901). This excellent work reprints excerpts from the following books: Tyrie's *Refutation* (1573); Hay's *Demandes* (1580); Hamilton's *Catholik Traictise* (1581); Burne's *Disputation* (1581); Canisius's *Catechism* (tr. 1588); Hamilton's *Facile Traictise* (1600); and *Ane Schort Catholik Confession* (printed from a manuscript, without date). In addition there are facsimile title-pages, an appendix (which includes two later works), and a glossarial index.

25. [headpiece] / Ane Admonition / to the Antichri- / stian Ministers In the De- / formit Kirk of / Scotland. / [ornament] / Exurgat Deus et dis- / sipentur inimici eius. / 1581. [Paris. T. Brumen?].

SIR R.L.H.

8°. Italic. A^4+B^3. Not fol. No Cw. One marginal ref. ('S.P.' (St. Peter) against the words 'thy Rock' in the last stanza). No Rt. (1) Title [A1]. (2) 'To the Louing Reider', (two introductory quatrains) [A1ᵛ]. (3) Text (45 eight-line stanzas, with a last stanza of ten lines) [A2–B3ᵛ].

This poem is, of course, an attack upon the Scottish reformers, the author inviting them at frequent intervals (with variations) to

Kilt vp zour Conneis, to Geneue haist with speid.*

It was issued both as an addendum to the *Disputation* (previous entry) and as a separate publication. J. Cranstoun attributes it, rightly, to Burne on these grounds: (1) the tenor of the piece; (2) the date of publication; and (3) the circumstance of its being appended to a few copies of the *Disputation.*† The printing is the same as that of the *Disputation.*

BUTLER, THOMAS, LL.D.

fl. 1570

26. A Treatise / of the Holy / Sacrifice of the / Altar, called the / Masse. / In the which by the word of / God, & testimonies of the Apo- / stles, and Primatiue Church, it / is prooued, that our Sauiour / Iesus Christ did institute the / Masse, and the Apostles did ce- / lebrate the same. / Translated out of Italian into / English, by Thomas But- / ler, Doctor of the Ca- / non and Ciuil / Lawes. / Louanii, / Apud Ioannem Foulerum. / Cum priuilegio. / 1570.

STONYHURST.

12°. B.L. A–G in twelves+H^6. Fol. 1[B1]–78[H6]. Cw. Mg. Rt – A Treatise of the / Most holy Masse. (1) Title [A1]. (2) Imprimatur: Louvain. 14 March 1570 [A1ᵛ]. (3) 'To the right Reuerend Father in God, and m[y] singuler good Lord, the Lord Byschop of S. Assaph, helth and perpetual felicitie': 'At Rome the first of Ianuarie. 1570. Your Lordships most bounden oratour, Thomas Butler' [A2–7ᵛ]. (4) 'The Prologue to the Reader' [A8–B1]. (5) Table of Chapters [B1ᵛ–2ᵛ]. (6) Text in 30 chapters [B3–H6]. (7) Printer's device [H6ᵛ].

* 'Pack up your traps', etc. Melville, Blackwood, Balcanquall, Durie, Brand and Smeaton are all pilloried.

† *Satirical Poems of the time of the Reformation. Edited by James Cranstoun, LL.D. Two Volumes* (Scottish Text Society, 1891), p. liv. These poems cover a period of about twenty years (1565–84). Catholic interest is represented by *A Lewd Ballet; Ane Exclamatioun maid in England vpone the Delyuerance of the Erle of Northumberland furth of Loch-leuin*; and *Ane Admonition . . .* (as above). The *Admonition* is also reprinted in J. Sibbald's *Chronicle of Scottish Poetry; from the thirteenth century, to the union of the crowns* (4 vols., 1802), Vol. III, pp. 450–63.

The author of the original of this treatise was Fr. Antonio Possevino, S.J., the well-known Roman jurist. His work is entitled 'Trattato del Santiss. Sacrificio dell' Altare detto Messa. Nel quale per la sancta parola di Dio, e per i testimonij de gli Apostoli, et della chiesa primitiva si mostra che il Signor Giesu Christo institui la Messa, et gli Apostoli la celebrarano. In Lione, appresso Michele Gioue. All' insegna del Giesu, 1563'.*

Strype, in referring to the interception of Catholic books which were being clandestinely imported in January 1574, mentions nine copies of this translation of Butler's as having been seized. He gives the work as having been printed at Antwerp in 1570.†

CADDEY, LAURENCE

fl. 1583

(see entry 14)

CAMPION, EDMUND, S.J.

1540–1581

27. The Two Bookes of the Histories of Irelande Compiled by Edmonde Campion Fellow of St Iohn Baptistes colledge in Oxforde [1571].‡

Brit. Mus. MS. Cotton. Vitellius F.ix.

Paper. Late 16th. century. 4°. Ff. 75, having 31 to 37 lines to a page. The manuscript has been much damaged by fire.

(1) Title (as above) [f.71]. (2) Blank [f.71b]. (3) ['To the right honourable Robert Dudley, Baron of Denbigh, Earle of Leicester, Knight of the noble Order of the garter, and S. Michaels, Master of the Queenes Majesties horse, and] one of her priuie Councell highe [Chauncellour of the] Vnyuersity of Oxforde my singuler good Lorde': ends, 'from Dyuelyn 27 maij 1571 your L. humble to comaunde Edmond Campion' [f.72]. (4) ['To the loving Reader']: ends 'Farewell from Dorghedaghe the. 9. of Iune. 1571' [f.73]. (5) Book I (15 chapters) [ff.74–101b]. (6) Book II (10 chapters; closing with 'The oration of Iames Stanihurst Speaker of the parliament', Sir Henry Sidney's answer, and a few words in praise of Sidney) [ff.102–146]. (7) Blank (146b]. (Blanks occur also at ff.76a, 85a, 112b, and 130a.)

* de Backer, *Bibliothèque des Écrivains de la Compagnie de Jésus* (1872), Vol. II, col. 2106. de Backer goes on to say: 'Ce traité fut traduit en anglais et imprimé en Belgique l'an 1584.' This seems to be an incorrect transcript of the entry in Alegambe 'qui liber Anglice versus prodijt in Belgio 1564' (*Bibliotheca Scriptorum Societatis Iesu* (1676), p. 81). There is, however, no evidence for a translation by Butler of that date.

† *Life and Acts of Parker* (1821), Vol. II, p. 392. Strype must be in error with regard to the place of printing. No Antwerp edition of this book is known. He is followed by Cooper, *Athen. Cantab.*, s.v. *Butler*, and Gillow, *Bibl. Dict.*

‡ A slightly fuller title is provided by Arundel MS. 37 in the Library of the College of Arms: *The Historie of Ireland, Devided into two Bookes; compiled by Master Edmund Campion, fellowe of Saint Jhon Baptist colledge in Oxford, in the yeare of Grace 1571* (Black, *Catalogue of the Arundel Manuscripts*). The manuscript is described as 'a fair copy in folio, written upon 45 leaves of paper, by five different hands, in the reign of Elizabeth'.

On account of religious difficulties Campion had left Oxford for Ireland 'with the approbation of the Earl of Leicester' in 1570.* The *Historie* was 'huddled up' during the last ten weeks of his stay in that country, in 1571. This fact we learn from the Dedicatory Address to the Earl, where the following two causes are given for the dedication: 'First that by the patronage of this boke, you maie be induced to waighe the state and become A patron to this noble realme, wch claymeth kindred of yo^{ur} eldest auncestors, and loveth entierlie yo$^{ur.}$ noble vertues the fame wherof is now caryed by those straungers that have felt them, into many farre countries that never sawe yo^{ur} person. Secondly because theare is none that knoweth me familiarly but he knoweth w^{t}hall how many waies I am beholden to yo^{ur} Lordship', etc. In the Address to the Reader Campion makes careful reference to his authorities, which include Giraldus Cambrensis, a 'nameless author', Hector Boethius, Hall, Grafton, Stowe, etc. He concludes this Address with a graceful tribute to James Stanyhurst, in whose house he was domiciled during the greater part of his stay in Ireland, as follows: 'Notwithstanding as naked and simple as it [sc. the *Historie*] is, it could never have growne to any proportion in such post-haste, except I had entred into such familiar societie and daylie table-talke with the worshipfull Esquire Iames Stanihurst, Recorder of Dublin. Who beside all curtesie of Hospitality, and a thousand loving turnes not heere to be recited, both by word and written monuments, and by the benefit of his owne Library, nourished most effectually mine endeavour.'†

The *Historie of Ireland* was first printed, in a much edited and embellished form, in Holinshed's *Chronicles* (1577).‡ In his introductory Epistle Holinshed describes how he came to use it. He states that Wolfe, the publisher of the *Chronicles*, had met with 'a copie of two bookes of the Irish histories, compiled by one Edmund Campion, fellow sometime of S. Iohn Baptists college in Oxford, verie well penned certeinlie, but so breefe, as it were to be wished, that occasion had serued him to haue vsed more leasure, and thereby to haue deliuered to vs a larger discourse of the same histories . . . § But how breefe so euer I found him,'

* Simpson, *Edmund Campion* (1896), p. 34. Campion's *Historie* is dealt with by Simpson at pp. 42–59.

† I follow Ware's edition here.

‡ Not 1587 as the *D.N.B.* (s.v. *Campion*) states. Simpson (op. cit.) says 1586.

§ The *Historie* had been seized by the officers after Campion had escaped from Ireland and had been sent, in November 1572, by Archbishop Parker to the Lord Treasurer, who was desired to communicate it to the Earl of Leicester. This, no doubt, accounts for Wolfe's copy. See Simpson, op. cit., p. 59. Also cp. Strype, *Life and Acts of Parker* (1821), Vol. II, p. 164. Campion was to write later to Gregory Martin concerning 'those writings of mine about Irish history which you have, to find some way of sending them to Prague in perfect safety'. He is either referring to a second copy, or, more probably, to a rough draft of the original. The letter is cited by Simpson at p. 131.

he continues, 'at the persuasion of maister Wolfe, vpon the hauing of that copie, I resolued to make shift to frame a speciall historie of Ireland, in like maner as I had doone of other regions, following Campions order, and setting downe his owne words, except in places where I had matter to inlarge that (out of other authors) which he had written in breefe. And this I haue thought good to signifie, the rather for that I esteeme it good dealing in no wise to defraud him of his due deserued praise'. He adds that he took the history down to the year 1509, and then, finding that Campion thereafter became his sole source of information, he entrusted the remainder of the work to Richard Stanyhurst, who completed it down to the end of the reign of Henry VIII.*

In the second edition of the *Chronicles*, published under the editorship of John Hooker in 1587, Campion's work has suffered a still greater change. In addition to further 'editing', Hooker has substituted his own translation of Giraldus Cambrensis for the Campion-Holinshed version in the earlier edition.†

In 1633 Sir James Ware, the Irish antiquary and historian, published Campion's *Historie* in its original form. It appears in a small folio volume entitled *Two Histories of Ireland. The one written by Edmund Campion, the other by Meredith Hanmer Dr of Divinity. Dublin. Printed by the Society of Stationers. M.DC.XXXIII.*‡ The text of this edition differs materially from that of the Cottonian MS.

28. Letter to the Lords of the Council. 1580.

This letter was not printed by Campion, but circulated in manuscript.§ It was printed for the first time in *The Great bragge and challenge of M. Champion a Iesuite, cōmonlye called Edmunde Campion, latelye arriued in Englande, contayninge nyne articles here seuerallye laide downe, directed by him to the Lordes of the Counsail, cōfuted & aunswered by Meredith Hanmer, M. of Art, and*

* Campion's tenth (and last) chapter thus finds no place in Holinshed. It is to be noted that the expurgated passages of the *Chronicles*, relating to Gerald FitzGerald's rebellion and the character of John Alen, Archbishop of Dublin, cancelled by order of the Queen, are not from Campion.

† The *Cambridge History of English Literature* (1918), Vol. III, p. 319, wrongly attributes this translation of Giraldus to Richard Hooker and transfers it to the first edition of the *Chronicles*.

‡ The sheets which make up this volume are also bound up with Ware's publication of Spenser's *View of the State of Ireland*, in a volume entitled *The Historie of Ireland, collected by three learned authors viz. Meredith Hanmer Doctor in Divinitie; Edmund Campion sometime Fellow of St Johns Colledge in Oxford: and Edmund Spenser Esq.* Dublin, 1633. Ware's edition of Campion was reprinted in 1809 under the title, *A Historie of Ireland written in 1571.*

§ The circumstances of the composing of its nine articles are told fully in Simpson's biography of Campion and in J. H. Pollen's *The English Catholics in the Reign of Queen Elizabeth* (1920). Both these writers set out the articles in full; cp. also Strype, *Annals* (1824), Vol. III, pt. 2, App. VI.

Student in Diuinitie. London, 1581. Charke also replied to Campion in *An answere to a seditious pamphlet lately cast abroade by a Iesuite, with a discouerie of that blasphemous sect. By William Charke.* London, 1580.

COLE, HENRY, LL.D., D.D.
d. 1580

29. Letters to Bishop Jewel.

These letters are printed in *The True Copies of the Letters betwene the reuerend father in God Iohn Bishop of Sarum and D. Cole, vpon occasion of a Sermon that the said Bishop preached before the Quenes Maiestie, and hyr most honorable Cōusayle. 1560. Set forthe and allowed, according to the order apointed in the Quenes Maiesties Iniunctions. Cū gratia & priuilegio Regiae Maiestatis ad septemniū* [September 1560].*

This book is made up as follows:

(1) 'The Copie of a letter sent from D. Cole to the Bishop of Sarum, vpon occasion of a Sermon that the saide Bisshop had preached in the Courte before the Quenes Maiestie': '18.Martij. Henricus Cole' [A2–4]. (2) 'The Bishop of Salisburies answere vnto the letter afore written': '20.Martij. Io. Sarum' [A4v–B1]. (3) 'D. Coles seconde Letter to the Bishop of Sarum': '24.Martij. Henricus Cole' [B1v–6]. (4) 'The answere of Io. Bishop of Sarum vnto D. Coles seconde Letter': '29.Martij. Io. Sarum' [B6v–D4v]. (5) 'Doctour Coles answere to certaine parcelles of the Seconde Letters of the Bishop of Sarum, set forthe in such sorte as it came from the Authour. 8. Aprilis. An.1560': '8.Aprilis. Henricus Cole' [D5–E3v]. (6) 'A Letter sent from the Bishoppe of Sarum to Doctour Cole, wherin he requireth of him a true and a ful Copie of the former answere': 'From Shirebourne ye xxij. of Iuly. An. 1560. Io. Sarum' [E4–5]. (7) 'Vnto this Letter D. Cole, beyng bisides by messenger earnestlie required, would make no answere one waye or other. Therefore vpon his refusall, it was thought good to answere his Letters as they were' [E5v].† (8) 'The Replie of the Bishoppe of Sarum to the Letter

* Entered on *Stationers' Register* 26 September 1560. Colophon on sig. R3: *Imprinted at London by Iohn daye dwellyng ouer aldersgate. Cum gratia & priuilegio Regiae Magestatis* [sic]. The book is sometimes found bound up with *The copie of a Sermon pronounced by the Byshop of Salisburie at Paules Crosse the second Sondaye before Ester in the yere of our Lord. 1560. wherupon D. Cole first sought occasion to encounter, shortly set forthe as nere as the authour could call it to remembraunce, without any alteration or addition . . .* This latter carries a colophon on sig. H6v: *Imprinted at London, by Iohn Day, dwelling ouer Aldersgate, beneath Saint Martins. Cum gratia & priuilegio Regiae Maiestatis per Septennium. These bokes are to be solde at his shop vnder the Gate.*

† Jewel's account, in the letter referred to, is that Cole had recently been before the Queen's visitors at Lambeth when he was accused of having spread abroad a letter in answer to Jewel. This Cole acknowledged, saying, however, that 'it was mutch abridged, and that the originall was twise asmutche'. For this reason he demanded Cole's 'owne copie full and large' so that he might answer not only a part but the whole. 'I praye you', he concludes, 'lette me here from you with expedition, for I meane plainly, and therefore haue caused the print to staie vpō your answere.' As Cole did not reply he had to be content with the answer he had originally written (bibl. details (7) and (8) above); cp. Strype, *Annals* (1824), Vol. I, pt. 1, p. 301.

aboue written, whiche D. Cole contrarie to euen dealing had geuen out and sent abroade, not to the said Bishop to whome he wrote it, but priuely and secretly vnto certaine of his owne Frendes': '18.Maye. 1560. Iohn. Sarum' [E6–R3].*

COPLEY, SIR THOMAS
1514–1584
(see entry 118)

DORMAN, THOMAS, D.D.
1532?–1577†

30. A Proufe of Cer- / teyne Articles in Reli- / gion, denied by M. Iuell, / sett furth in defence of the Catholyke be- / leef therein, by Thomas Dorman, / Bachiler of Diuinite / VVhere-unto is added in the end, a conclusion, conteinyng. xij. / Causes, vvhereby the Author acknovvlegeth hym self to haue / byn stayd in hys olde Catholyke fayth that he vvas / baptized in, vvysshyng the same to be made / common to many for the lyke stay / in these perilouse tymes. / Augustinus contra literas Petiliani. lib 2. cap.16. / Si quaeras, quibus fructibus vos esse potius lupos rapaces cognoscamus, obijcio schismatis / crimen, quod tu negabis, ego autem statim probabo. Neque enim com-municas omnibus / gentibus, & illis ecclesijs Apostolico labore fundatis. that is to say. / If thou demaundest (he speaketh to Petilian the Heretick) by vvhat fruictes I / knovv you to be rather the rauening vvolues, I obiect to you the fault of / scisme, vvhich thou vvilt deny, but I vvil out of hand proue. for / thou doest not communicat vvith all Nacions, not vvith / those churches founded by th' apostles labour. / [device] / Im-printed at Antwerp by Iohn Latius, at the / signe of the Rape, with Priuilege. / Anno. 1564.

* For the controversy which has its beginning in Jewel's sermon, see p. 60. Reprints of the above work will be found in the two collected editions of Jewel's works, edited by R. W. Jelf (1848) and J. Ayre (for the Parker Society, 1850) respectively.

† The date of Dorman's birth, in the absence of external evidence, can be computed from the following statements made by himself: 'It prycketh now fast (if my memory fayle me not) ryght worshipfull sir, towardes the poyncte of seuenteen yeares, when I, beyng a yong nouyce of Caluyns relygyon, was fyrst by my frendes brought, to that famouse schole at Wynchester, of bishop Wyckham hys founda-tion . . . I was the same yeare . . . brought home agayn to Chrystes churche from whence I was strayed.' (Dedication to Harding in *A Proufe of Certeyne Articles in Religion.*) 'I left youre pestilent and perniciouse opiniōs being of age betwene fiftene and sixtene.' (Words addressed to Nowel in *A Disproufe of M. Nowelles Reproufe* – sig. Tt1.) The date, then, is 1564 less 32 (17+15), i.e. 1532 roughly.

4°. A–Z+Aa–Nn in fours+Oo^3. Fol.1[B1]–143 (for 142)[Oo2]. Cw. Mg. Rt – A Proufe of Certeyne Articles / in Religion, denyed by M. Iuell. (1) Title [A1]. (2) Privilegium: Brussels. 14 July 1564 [$A1^v$]. (3) Dedication to Harding [A2]. (4) 'To the Readers': Antwerp. 26 July 1564. Thom. Dorman [A3]. (5) Table of the four Articles proved [A4]. (6) Blank [$A4^v$]. (7) Text, with preface and conclusion [B1–Oo2]. (8) Imprimatur: Louvain. 9 July 1564 [$Oo2^v$]. (9) 'Faultes committed in the Printing' [Oo3]. (10) Ornament [$Oo3^v$].

The writer deals with four of Jewel's twenty-seven Articles, one concerning the headship of the Church and three concerning the Sacrament.* In the dedication he refers to his conversion from Calvinism seventeen years previously at Winchester as being due to Harding. He writes from Aquicinctum 'the seat of my banyshment'.† Alexander Nowell replied to Dorman in two books, both dealing with the single question of the headship of the Church (Dorman's Article I), viz.: (1) *A Reproufe, written by Alexander Nowell, of a booke entituled, A Proufe of certayn articles in religion denied by M. Iuell, set furth by Thomas Dorman, Bachiler in Diuinitie.* London, 1565 (May);‡ and (2) *The Reproufe of M. Dorman his proufe of certaine Articles in Religion &c. continued by Alexander Nowell. With a defense of the chief authoritie and gouernment of Christian Princes as well in causes Ecclesiasticall, as ciuill, within their owne dominions, by M. Dorman malitiouslie oppugned.* London, 1566.§

31. A Disproufe of / M. Novvelles / Reproufe. / By Thomas Dorman Bachi- / ler of Diuinitie. / Dignare ergo rescribere nobis, vt sciamus quomodo fieri possit, vt ecclesiam suam / Christus de toto orbe perdiderit, & in vobis solis habere coeperit. August. ad Honorat. / epist.161. / Vouchesaufe to write againe to vs, that we maye knowe howe it can be, / that Christe shoulde leese his churche ouer all the worlde, and beginne to / haue it emongest yow onlye. / [device] / Imprinted at Antwerp by Iohn Laet, / Anno Domini 1565. 3 Decembris, / with speciall priuileage.

4°. B.L. preface. ✠^{4}+★^{6}+A–Z+Aa–Zz+Aaa–Ggg in fours. Fol.1[A1]–211[Ggg3]. Cw. Mg. Rt – A Disproufe of M. / Nowelles Reproufe. (1) Title [✠1]. (2) Privilegium: Brussels. 17 Oct. 1565 [✠1^v]. (3) The Preface to the Readers (B.L.) [✠2–★5^v]. (4) 'Faultes escaped in printing' [★6]. (5) Royal

* Referred to by Strype, *Annals* (1824), Vol. I, pt. 2, p. 113.

† It would seem, then, that Dorman was at this time staying in the Benedictine Abbey at Anchin (Aquicinctum) in Hainault, which later (17 January 1569) established and endowed Anchin College in the University of Douai. See *D.D.* Historical Introd. init.

‡ There was a second issue of this work in July of the same year.

§ There is no reference to Dorman's second work, *A Disproufe of M. Nowelles Reproufe* (see next entry) in this book of Nowell's. Gillow is wrong in suggesting it is a reply to the *Disproufe* (*Bibl. Dict.* under Dorman).

Arms (subscribed 'God saue the Quene') [*6v]. (6) Text in 33 chapters [A1–Ggg3v]. (7) Imprimatur: Louvain. 16 Oct. 1561 [Ggg3v].* (8) Blank [Ggg4].

Answered by Alex. Nowell's *A confutation as wel of M. Dormans last boke entituled 'A disproufe &c.' as also of D. Sander his causes of transubstantiation.* London, 1567.†

32. A Request / To M. Iewell. / That he kepe his promise, made by so- / lemne protestation in his late ser- / mon at Pauls Crosse the. 15. of Iune. / Anno.1567. / By Thomas Dorman, Bacheler of / Diuinitie. / [device] / Louanii, / Apud Ioannem Foulerum. / Anno D. 1567.

LINCOLN.

8°. Italic. A–B in eights. Fol.1[A1]–16[B8]. Cw. Mg. Rt – A Request / to M. Iewel. (1) Title [A1]. (2) Privilegium: Brussels. 1 Sept. 1567 [A1v]. (3) Text: ends 'Amen. Tho. Dorman' [A2–B8]. (4) Imprimatur: Louvain. 30 August [B8v].

The protestation made by Jewel is quoted in the text as follows: 'Nowe here I protest before God: my consciēce is free and clene frō al falshod that euer I vttred: yet I am a mā, ād may be deceiued, ād if there be any such (error) this mouth shal cōfesse it, ād this hand shal retract it: they would be loth to cōfesse their errours: they seeke to glory in theyr fleashe.'

The Lincoln copy of this pamphlet appears to be unique.‡

EVANS, LEWYS
fl. 1574§

33. [ornament] Certaine Tables / sett furth by the right Reuerend father / in God, William Bushopp of Rurimun- / de, in Ghelderland: wherein is detected / and made manifeste the doting dange- / rous doctrine, and haynous heresyes, of / the rashe rablement of heretikes: trans- / lated into Englishe by Lewys Euans, / And by hym intituled, / The betraing of the beastlines / of heretykes. / Reade, and iudge, let selfe will walke: / Peruse the booke, before thowe talke. / [ornament] / Imprinted at Antwerpe by Aegidius Diest, / with Priuiledge. 1565.

* An obvious misprint for 1565.

† See Strype, *Annals* (1824), Vol. I, pt. 2, p. 247, where the Dorman-Nowell controversy is discussed. Also *Life and Acts of Parker* (1821), Vol. I, pp. 359–60, 403.

‡ Dorman's part in the Challenge controversy is set out at pp. 62, 64 and 65.

§ I include here only those works which are definitely associated with Lewys Evans's recusancy. I have, therefore, omitted *The Abridgement of Logique*, which was probably published before Elizabeth's accession. Other works noted by *Pollard and Redgrave*, and not included here, are: *A new balet entituled how to wyve well.* London, 1561; and *A short treatise of the mysterie of the euchariste.* London, 1569.

Bod.

8°. Tables in B.L. A–E in eights. Not fol. Cw. Mg. Rt – The Betrayng / of Heresye. (1) Title [A1]. (2) English Verses [A1v]. (3) 'To Maister Grindal Lewys Euans wisheth perfeicte healthe': 'From Antwerpe the 29. of Iune.' [A2–2v]. (4) 'L. Euans to the Reader' [A3–8]. (5) Text: 4 Tables, each followed by a short disquisition, with some final quotations from Fridericus Staphylus [A8–E8]. (6) Short Apology for his book, followed by small cut with couplet in English [E8v].

Lewys Evans translates from *In hoc libello contenta: Tabulae Grassantium passim Haereseôn anasceuasticae, atque analyticae authore D. Wilhelmo Lindano Dordraceno, Doct. Theologo atque Palatij Haghen. Decano. Quibus subtexitur Sectae Lutheranae Trimembris Epitome, per Fridericum Staphylum Regis Rom. consiliarium.* Antwerp, 1562. He uses four only of the original seven Tables. 'It was,' he says, in his address to Grindal, 'it was my chaunce to meete with certayne Tables, sett furthe by the right Reuerend Father in God Willm̄ Bushop of Rurimunde in Ghelderlande: in fowre of the which tables, I thē perceaued the peruerse purpose of heretikes so painted, as more then a wonder vnto me yt was, howe anie man, beholding the same, colde longer lye in suche lothesome sinckes of heresie & synne,' etc.

34. [within a border, within a rule] A brieue Admonition / vnto the nowe made / Ministers of Englande: / Wherein is shewed some of the / fruicte of this theyr late framed / fayth: Made by Lewys Euans stu- / dent in Louain. 24.Aug. 1565. / [rule] / Ioan.8. / Vos ex patre Diabolo estis, / & desideriis patris vestri / vultis obsequi. / Ye are of your father the deuyll, / and the lustes of youre father / yowe wyll doe. / [ornament] / [rule] / Antuerpiae / Typis Ae. Diest. / M.D.LXV.

8°. A–B in eights. Not fol. Cw. Mg. (in B.L.). Rt – An Admonicion vnto the nowe / made Ministers of Englande. (Rule between Rt. and Text.) (1) Title [A1]. (2) Cut, with verses in English subscribed L.E. [A1v]. (3) Text [A2–B8v]. (4) Errata [B8v].

Some time after the publication of this work the author apostatized and proceeded to an answer thereof. Anthony à Wood writes: 'Afterwards the said Evans being reconcil'd to the ch. of England by some of his friends; did, to shew his zeal for the love he had to it, write and publish a book as full of ill language against the Roman catholics, as the other was full of good to them.'*

The book is: *The Castle of Christianitie, detecting the long erring estate, aswell of the Romaine Church, as of the Byshop of Rome: together with the defence of the Catholique Faith: Set forth, by Lewys Euans*. London, 1568.

* *Athen. Oxon.* (ed. Bliss, 1813), Vol. I, p. 411. More succinctly, in his Catalogue of 'Popish Bookes either aunswered or to be aunswered', William Fulke writes, 'Maister Euans answered by himselfe'. (See Appendix V.)

One other controversial work came from Evans's pen, viz. *The Hatefull Hypocrisie and rebellion of the Romishe prelacie. By Lewys Euans.* 1570.*

FECKENHAM, JOHN, ABBOT, O.S.B.
1518?–1584†

35. A Declaration of such scruples and stays of conscience, touching the oath of Supremacy, as Mr. John Feckenham by writing did deliver unto the lord bishop of Winchester, with his resolution made thereto. London. 1564.‡

The original treatise was called *The Answere made by M. Iohn Fekenham, Priest and Prisoner in the Tower, to the Queenes highnes Commissioners, touching the othe of the Supremacie.* Feckenham devised this before his first release from the Tower, intending to deliver it 'to the Commissioners (if any came) as the staie of his conscience, concerning the refusall of the foresaid othe' (i.e. the oath of the Queen's Supremacy). § The Commissioners, however, did not put in an appearance, and when Feckenham passed into the custody of Robert Horne, at Waltham in Hants (October 1563), Horne pressed him for his views in writing, promising that no harm should come thereby. He then handed Horne this treatise. The treatise was afterwards increased by Horne's answers and Feckenham's replies. After his return to the Tower in 1564 Feckenham sent one copy to Leicester and one to Sir William Cecil – 'with the same title that the printed book conteineth' – both of them being delivered by the Lieutenant of the Tower.

No copy of the work as printed in 1564 seems to be extant, but it is printed in full, according to custom, in Horne's Answer, which runs: *An Answeare Made by Rob. Bishoppe of Wynchester, to*

* The reasons which seem to have prompted this work are set out in the Address to the Reader. Evans there writes: 'Beinge of late in the vniuersite of Oxforde, I herd ther, not by any mean mã but by the learnest, how myne aduersaries, na, how the truethes aduersaries had bruited, that I had reuolted from, the Gospell, & that I was agayne gonne beyonde the seas, I hearde also nowe at my cominge to the Citie of Londen, howe yt was in the mouthes of manye, that I was deade. two tales, & yet neuer a one true . . . in despight of satan, saye mine enemies what they will, thinke men as they liste, it is the law of God that I professe, & it is traiterouse Papacy that I detest. & this is it which moued me at this time (Gentle reader) to set furthe these few leafes.'

† Earlier works of Abbot Feckenham, not included here, are: *A certayne communication, betwene the Lady Iane, & Master Feckenham, iiii dayes before her death* (printed in *An Epistle of the Ladye Iane*, 1554); *A notable sermon.* London, 1555; *Two homilies upon the creed.* London [1555?]. The two latter I get from *Pollard and Redgrave.*

‡ I cite this title from Strype, *Annals* (1824), Vol. I, pt. 2, p. 178. In his list of 'Old printed Books' used in the *Annals*, Strype refers to it as 'Abbot Fecknam's Decla. of Scruples and Stays of Conscience, 1564'. (*Annals*, Vol. II, pt. 2, p. 714.)

§ See Stapleton's 'Answere to the Preface' in *A Counterblast to M. Hornes Vayne Blaste* (entry 142). The substance of what follows here comes from that work.

a Booke entituled, The Declaration of suche Scruples, and staies of Conscience, touchinge the Othe of the Supremacy, as M. Iohn Fekenham, by wrytinge did deliuer vnto the L. Bishop of Winchester, with his Resolutions made thereunto. London, 1566.*

Horne was answered in his turn by Thomas Stapleton in *A Counterblast to M. Hornes vayne blaste against M. Fekenham.* Louvain, 1567† (entry 142).

36. [*Text-title*]. To the right worshipfuls, Sir Frauncis Iobson Knight, Lieuetenaunt of the Toure, Sir Henrie Neuell Knight, and M. Pellam Lieuetenaunt of the Ordinaunce. [1570]

Printed in full in *An Answere to certein Assertions of M. Fecknam, somtime Abbot of Westminster which he made of late against a godly Sermon of M. Iohn Goughes, preached in the Tower the xv. of Ianuarie. 1570.* By Laurence Tomson. London. Feckenham states that he had been asked by the three gentlemen what he thought of Gough's sermon, and 'vppon your lycence graunted and obteyned', though loth to do it, he has set forth his opinion under four heads. The document occupies sigs. A2–C1 of Tomson's volume.

Another answer came from Gough himself, viz. *The aunswer of Iohn Gough to maister Fecknams obiections against his sermon lately preached in the Tower.* London, 1570.‡

37. [*Text-title*]. Certaine considerations and causes, mouyng me not to bee presente at, nor to receiue, neither vse the seruice of the new booke, otherwise called the Common boke of praiers. [1571?]

This is undoubtedly the Apology referred to by Fulke in his catalogue of 'Popish Bookes' as 'Fecknams Apologie, aunswered

* Horne's Preface affords further evidence of the date and publication of Feckenham's book. He writes: 'It is nowe an whole yeere paste, since I herde of a booke secretely scattered abroade by M. Fekenham emonge his freendes: And in April laste [he is writing under date 25 February 1565, O.S.] I came by a copie therof . . . I woulde haue paste it ouer with silence . . . But seeing the chiefe ende and principall purpose intended, as may be iustly gathered in publishyng the booke, was, to ingrafte in the mindes of the subiectes a mislikyng of the Queenes Maiestie', etc.

† There is a full account of the Feckenham-Horne controversy in Strype, *Annals* (1824), Vol. I, pt. 2, pp. 178–87. See also Vol. II, pt. 2, pp. 714–15, and *Life and Acts of Grindal* (1821), p. 117.

‡ Miss E. T. Bradley, in her article on Feckenham in the *D.N.B.*, states, in referring to the above work of Feckenham's, that it was 'printed by John Hoodly, London, 1570'. This is an error, which can be traced to a misreading of a note in *Lansdowne MS.* No. 982, f. 63 (Brit. Mus.). The reference there to Gough's *Aunswer* has a marginal note, 'Printed by John Awdley. 1570'. The script is such that a casual reader might easily read Awdley as Hoodley. It may be supposed that Miss Bradley knew that Awdley (Awdeley) was the printer of Gough's *Aunswer*, and therefore referred Feckenham's document to this 'ghost'.

by W. Fulke'.* It is printed in *A confutation of a Popishe and sclaunderous libelle, in forme of an apologie: geuen out into the courte, and spread abrode in diuerse other places of the Realme. Written by William Fulke.*† London, 1571. (Running Title – 'An Aunswere to a Popishe apologie'.) Fulke gives the following account of his Answer: 'There was found in the court, either cast of purpose, or lost of negligence, a certain small pamphlette, conteinyng an Apollogie, or aunswere of a Papiste, to some frendes of his, that perswaded hym to conforme hymself, to the Religion now receiued in the realme, by publike aucthoritie: which when it came to my handes, supposyng it might do some hurte emonge them that are ignoraunte, I thought good, briefly to confute it. But because the copie whiche was founde, was vnskilfully written, I had some diff[ic]ultie to reade it in certaine places, and sometymes I mighte plainely perceiue, that the aucthours meanyng was chaunged by vntrue writyng: So that the aucthour, or his frendes, maie haue some occasion to cauill at my publishing of the copie, whiche was so muche corrupted: In cōsideratiō wherof, I would haue been verie glad, to haue had the principall copie of the aucthours owne hande, if I could haue knowen how to come by it. But seyng I was out of hope of that, I perused, and restored the copie that I had, as faithfully as I could,‡ desiryng the aucthour, or his frendes, that haue the originall, if I haue erred in any woorde of any momente, to lette me haue knowledge thereof, and I will thereby reforme the apologie, and alter myne answere thereto accordyngly' [aj]. The Apology occupies altogether about twenty pages out of the 116 of Fulke's Answer.

FEN, JOHN
d. 1615

38. A Learned and / very Eloquent / Treatie, writen in Latin by / the famouse man Hieronymus Osorius / Bishop of Sylua in Portugal, wherein / he confuteth a certayne Aunswere / made by M. Walter Haddon against / the Epistle of the said Bishoppe / vnto the Queenes / Maiestie. / [ornament] / Translated into English by Iohn Fen stu- / dent of Diuinitie in the Vniuer- / sitie of Louen. / [ornament] / Louanii, / Apud Ioannem Foulerum, / Anno 1568. / Cum Gratia & Priuilegio.

* See Appendix V for this catalogue.

† Gillow (*Bibl. Dict.*, art. 'Feckenham') gives this title with the words 'by M. J. Fecknam' interpolated. None of the extant editions carries these words on the title.

‡ Fulke appears to have used two copies for his Answer. He writes at page 70b: 'The seuenteenth negation was altogether lefte out in the copie which came first to my handes, I suppose by negligence of the writer, but in another copie I finde it thus'.

8°. *[4]+A–Z+AA–MM in eights+NN[4]. Fol.1[A1]–283[NN3]. Cw. Mg. No Rt. (1) Title [*1]. (2) Blank [*1v]. (3) 'To the Catholic Reader': Louvain. 1 Nov. 1568. John Fen [*2–*4v]. (4) Text in 3 books [A1–NN3v]. (5) Imprimatur: Louvain. 3 Sept. 1568 [NN4]. (6) Device [NN4v].

Osorius's Treatise was entitled *Amplissimi atque Doctissimi Viri. D. Hieronymi Osorii, Episcopi Syluensis, in Gualterum Haddonum Magistrum Libellorum Supplicum . . . libri tres.* Olissipone, 1567. Fen gives as his chief reason for translating Osorius's reply* that 'it conteineth a briefe confutation of manie erroneous opinions of much heretical and pestilēt doctrine, comprised in a litle booke, set out these late yeares in the name of M. Haddon: wherin was pretended an answere to the Epistle of Osorius . . . but in effecte was nothing els, but a numbre of stout assertions faintly prooued, be sprinkled here and there with bitter tauntes, vnsauerie gyrdes, and other the like scomme or froth of vndigested affections' [*3].

39. Instructions and / Aduertisements, / How to meditate the / Misteries of the Rosarie of the most / holy Virgin Mary. / Written in Italian by the Reuerend Father / Gaspar Loarte D. of Diuinitie of the So- / cietie of Iesus. And newly trans- / lated into English. / [cut] / Non nobis Domine, non nobis, sed Nomi- / ni tuo da gloriam. [William Carter? 1579?]

8°. **[4]+A–P in eights+Q[4]. Fol.1[A1]–125[Q3]. Cw. Mg. Rt. varies. (1) Blank (?) [**1]. (2) Title [**2]. (3) Blank [**2v]. (4) 'The Authour to the deuout Reader' [**3–4]. (5) Cut [**4v]. (6) Author's Preface [A1–B2]. (7) Totius Libri Summa (in 4 Latin verses) [B2v]. (8) Text: each quinary is preceded by a full-page title, and there is a full-page cut for each mystery [B3–O7v]. (9) Cut and Latin verses [O8]. (10) Cut [O8v]. (11) Litanies of the Blessed Virgin in Latin [P1–Q3]. (12) Spiritual advices [Q3v–Q4]. (13) Faults escaped [Q4v].

De Backer gives Loarte's original work as *Istrutione e avvertimenti per meditar i misterii del Rosario, della Santissima Vergine Madre. Raccolti per il Reverendo P. Gasparo Loarte Dott. Theologo della Compagnia di Giesu. In Roma, M.D.LXXIII.*† C. Dodd attributes the translation to Fen in his list of Fen's works, as follows: 'Mysteries of the Rosary: Tr. from Gaspar Loartes.'‡

* This was the second reply to Haddon, a year previous to this, Emanuel Dalmada, Bishop of Angra, having replied on behalf of Osorius in his *Epistola Reuerendi Patris Domini Emanuelis Dalmada Episcopi Angrensis . . . Aduersus Epistolam Gualteri Haddoni*. Antwerp, 1566. The British Museum copy of Dalmada's work contains the well-known satire in verse on the Osorius-Haddon controversy, 'Chorus alternatim canentium', with the accompanying caricature of Haddon, Bucer and Vermigli (Peter Martyr) as dogs drawing a car on which Osorius is seated in triumph. For a further note on the Osorius-Haddon controversy, see entry 133.

† *Bibliothèque des Écrivains de la Compagnie de Jésus*. Vol. II, col. 770, s.v. *Loarte*.

‡ *Church History* (1737). Vol. I, p. 510. I have been unable to trace Dodd's authority for this.

The printing of this book may be attributed to William Carter on the grounds of its resemblance to that of Gregory Martin's *Treatise of Schisme* (1578), which Carter acknowledged to be his printing. We note:

(1) The style of the printing is similar, and

(2) The three principal founts employed by the printer (10pt. roman, 8pt. roman and a small italic) are in every respect similar to the three founts used to supplement the black-letter fount of the *Treatise.**

It is not surprising, then, to find what seems to be a specific reference to Brinkley's *Exercise of a Christian Life* (entry 20) and to Fen's *Instructions and Aduertisements, How to meditate the Misteries of the Rosarie* in Cardinal Allen's words concerning Carter: 'The said yong man Cartar, of whos martyrdome we last treated, was examined vpon the racke, vpon what Gentlemen or catholique Ladies he had bestowed or intended to bestowe certaine bookes of prayers and *spiritual exercises* and *meditations* which he had in his custodie.'†

It follows, if Carter was the printer, that Fen's work cannot be later than 1579, for it was towards the end of that year that Carter's press was seized and he himself imprisoned. Aylmer writes on 30 December 1579 to Lord Burghley: 'I have founde out a press of pryntynge wth one Carter, a verye lewed fellowe who hath byne dyvers tymes before in prison for printinge of lewde pampheletes . . . I thought good to signyfye thus muche vnto yor L. shipp that yo^{w} maye deale wth the fellowe (who ys nowe neare yo^{w} in the Gatehouse) as to yor wysdom shall seme good.'‡

40. The Life of the Blessed Virgin, Sainct Catharine of Siena. Drawne out of all them that had written it from the beginning. And written in Italian by the reuerend Father, Doctor Caterinus Senensis. And now translated into Englishe out of the same Doctor, by Iohn Fen Priest & Confessar to the Englishe Nunnes at Louaine. With permission of Superiors. Anno 1609.

* On the other hand the factotum capitals of the *Treatise of Schisme* are nowhere repeated either in Fen's work or in Brinkley's *Exercise of a Christian Life* (same printer). This, however, is to be expected, since the printer was trying to escape detection.

† *A True Sincere and Modest Defence* [1584]. By Cardinal Allen. The italics are mine.

‡ Lansdowne MS. 28. No. 81. Brit. Mus.

FOWLER, JOHN

1537–1579

41. An Oration / Against the Vnlawfull In- / surrections of the Protestantes of / our time, vnder pretence to / Refourme Religion. / [ornament] Made and pronounced in Latin, in the / Schole of Artes at Louaine, / the. xiiij. of December. / Anno. 1565. / [ornament] By Peter Frarin of Andwerp, M. of / Arte, and Bacheler of both lawes. / And now translated into English, / with the aduise of the Author. / [device] / Antuerpiae, / Ex officina Ioannis Fouleri. / M.D.LXVI.

8°. B.L. A–L in eights. Not fol. Cw. Mg. Rt – Against the Vnlawful / Insurrections of the Protestantes. (1) Title [A1]. (2) Blank [A1v]. (3) Scriptural texts (Lat. and Eng.) [A2]. (4) Privilegium: Brussels. '14.Martij. Anno. 1565. stilo Brabantiae' [A2v]. (5) 'The Translatour to the Gentle Reader': Antwerp. 9 May 1566. Ihon Fouler [A3–7v]. (6) Text [A8–K3]. (7) Imprimatur [K3]. (8) Blank [K3v]. (9) 'The Table of this Booke set out not by order of Alphabete or nūbre, but by expresse figure, to the eye & sight of the Christian Reader, and of him also ṫ cannot reade' (36 woodcuts with explanatory verses) [K4–L8]. (10) Blank [L8v].

In his Epistle to the Reader Fowler calls attention to the origin of this book by observing that at Louvain University in December each year lessons cease and a whole week is given over to disputation. 'Amonge diuerse other,' he continues, 'this laste December there, a learned man toward the Law called M. Peter Frarin borne in Andwerp made an oration against the Insurrections of the Protestantes and Sectes of our time . . . which, at the earnest requeste of his frindes, he suffered to be afterwarde printed. And because I thought it no lesse profitable and fruteful, that, as that Oration is in Latine, and like to be shortly in Doutch and Frenche, so it should be in Englishe also to warne my deere Contremen of those mens malice and cruelty: I conferred with him, and by his aduise traslated [sic] it into our Mother tong, with suche notes and farther additiōs as for lack of tyme, whē he pronounced it, were omitted and leafte out in the Latine.'

The cuts, which take the place of a Table of Contents, depict the various activities of the Reformers as they are recorded in the book, with folio reference. Sometimes they are unpleasantly realistic. The verses describe the cuts, usually in exact detail.

Frarin's 'rayling declamation' was answered by Dr. Fulke in *An Apologie of the Professors of the Gospel in Fraunce against the railing declamation of Peter Frarine a Louanian turned into English by Iohn Fowler. Written by William Fulke.* Cambridge, 1586.*

* This answer occurs, with separate title-page, in *A Treatise against the Defense of the Censure* (see entry 96). The Rev. C. H. Hartshorne, in the Parker Society edition of *A Defence of the Sincere and True Translations of the Holy Scriptures into the English Tongue. By William Fulke* (1843), says, in his introductory life of Fulke to that volume (p. x), that it was also published separately.

42. A Dialogue / of Cumfort / against Tribulation, made by / the right Vertuous, Wise and Learned / man, Sir Thomas More, sometime / L.Chanceller of England, which / he wrote in the Tower of / London, An.1534. / and entituled / thus: / A Dialogue of Cumfort against Tribula- / tion, made by an Hungarian in Latin, and / translated out of Latin into French, & / out of French into English. / Now newly set foorth, with many places restored / and corrected by conference of sundrie Copies. / [ornament] / Non desis plorantibus in consolatione. / [mg] Eccli.7. / [ornament] / Antuerpiae, / Apud Iohannem Foulerum, Anglum. / M.D.LXXIII. / [rule]

8°. B.L. *+A–Z+a–d in eights+**4. Fol. 1[A1]–216[d8]. Cw. Mg. Rt – Cumfort against Tribulation. (1) Title [*1]. (2) Device [*1v]. (3) 'To the Right Honourable and Excellent Ladie, the Ladie Iane, Duchesse of Feria': 'From Antwarp, the last of September. An.1573. Your Graces most humble Seruitour Iohn Fouler' [*2–3]. (4) Ornament [*3v]. (5) 'To the Reader' [*4–7]. (6) 'Iohan. Fouleri Bristoliensis in D.Th. Mori effigiem, Hexastichon' (with English verse translation) [*7v]. (7) Cut of Sir Thomas More, with the words 'Thomas Morus Anglus Anno Aetatis 50' [*8]. (8) Blank [*8v]. (9) The Dialogue in three books [A1–d8v]. (10) Table of Chapters [**1–4v].

Fowler thus refers to his recension in his dedicatory epistle: 'These six or seuen yeres haue I bene desirous, to haue so good a Booke come forth againe in some smaller volume then it was in before, being in deede not so handsome for the priuate vse and cōmoditie of the Reader, as I trust it shalbe now. But it hath not bene my chance through one let or other, to accomplish that desire of mine, til now. And that is in deede the chiefe thing that I haue done therein, which I may accompt as mine: I meane, in that I haue brought it into this smal volume, and withal, by conferring of sundry Copies together, haue restored and corrected many places, and thereby made it muche more plaine and easie to be vnderstood of the Reader.'

The *Dialogue* was written primarily for the use of his own family by Sir Thomas More. The first printing was by Tottel in 1553. This was followed by its inclusion in the magnificent collected edition of More, published by John Cawood, John Waly and Richard Tottel in 1557, the edition referred to above by Fowler.* In his own edition, besides corrections and an improved punctuation, Fowler adds a running commentary in the margin.

* I must not miss the opportunity here offered of recording my admiration for the new edition of 1557 in facsimile, now in process of publication, and edited with a modern version of the same by W. E. Campbell.

43. A Brief / Fourme of / Confession, In- / structing all Christian folke / how to confesse their sinnes, & so / to dispose themselues, that they / may enioy the benefite of true / Penãce, dooing the woorthy / frutes therof, according / to th' vse of Christes / Catholique / Church. / Newly translated into English, and set / foorth together with certaine other / godly brief Treatises and Pra- / iers, as is to be seene in / the side folo- / wing. / [ornament] / Antuerpiae, / Apud Iohannem Foulerum. / M.D.LXXVI. / Cum Priuilegio.

BOD. LAMB.

12°. B.L. a–k in twelves. Fol. 1[a2]–114[k12] (fol. 1, 2 and 3 each embraces two leaves, thence it is straightforward). Cw. (irreg.) Mg. Rt – A Brief Fourme / of Confession. (1) Title [a1]. (2) Contents [a1v]. (3) 'To the Right Honourable and Excellent Lady the Duchesse of Feria her Grace': 'From Louen the second of April. Anno D.1572. Your Graces most ready Seruitour, Iohn Fouler' [a2–5]. (4) 'To the Reader' [a5v–6v]. (5) 'A Brief Fourme of Shrift or Confession, according to the vse of Christes Catholike Church' [a7–e9]. (6) Approbation: Louvain. 27 December 1571 [e9]. (7) Cut, with scriptural texts [e9v]. (8) 'A Brief Treatise to receiue the Blessed Bodie of our Lord Sacramentally, & virtually both: made by the excellent learned, wise, vertuous, & godly man, Sir Thomas Moore Knight (sometime Lord Chancelour of Englãd) while he was prisoner in the Tower of London, Anno 1534. & 1535': Rt – 'A brief Treatise / Of the B.Sacrament' [e10–f12v]. (9) 'Certaine Deuout Praiers and Ghostly Meditations made and collected also by the said Sir Thomas Moore, whiles he was prisoner in the Tower of London.' Followed by an Instruction, an Exhortation (in Latin and English), and further Prayers, which include devotions from Ludovico Vives and Sir Thomas More. Cut at 110 [g1–k2]. (10) 'The Goldẽ Litani in English' [k2v–12v].

Owing to its having been 'adjoined' to one of the editions of *A Catechisme or Christian Doctrine* (see below) this book has sometimes been ascribed to Laurence Vaux. T. G. Law points out, however, that 'there are sufficient indications in its preface, its style, and its matter, to make it certain' that it is not Vaux's.* Reference to the dedicatory epistle makes it equally certain that it is Fowler's. He there writes, 'whereas I had also translated out of Spanish a short Treatise cõteining a briefe fourme or Doctrine of Confession . . . I should doe right wel, to dedicate the same smal labour of mine vnto your Honour' [a4v].†

The reprint, referred to above, is as follows: *A Catechisme or Christian Doctrine necessarie for Children and ignorante people, briefly compiled by Laurence Vaux . . . Whereunto is adioyned a brief forme of Confession (necessary for all good Christians) according to the vse of the Catholicke Churche. S. Athanasius. Who so euer wil be saued, before all thinges it is necessarie, that he holde the Catholicke faith. Cum Priuilegio. 1583.*

Subsequent reprints in 1590, 1599 and 1605.

* In the Chetham Society reprint of Vaux's *Catechism*. 1885. (See Appendix IV.)
† I have been unable to trace this Spanish original. The statement of Pits that

44. Certaine deuout and / Godly petitions, com- / monly called / Iesus Psalter. / [cut: with the words 'Non est aliud Nomen / datum hominibus. Act.4.' to left and right] / There is none other name vnder heauen / giuen vnto men, in which we / must be saued. Act.4. / Antuerpiae. / Apud Iohan. Foulerum. Anno. 1575.

16°. B.L. A–D in eights. Not fol. Cw. (irregular). No Mg. Rt – Iesus Psalter. (1) Title [A1]. (2) Blank [A1v]. (3) Text of Psalter [A2–D4v]. (4) 'An admonition' [D5]. (5) 'Here foloweth a wholesome doctrine how to resist and ouercome the ghostly temptations of the fende' [D5v–7v]. (6) 'A Narration' [D7v–8v].

This Psalter, which has for generations been ascribed to Richard Whytford, 'the wretch of Syon', dates back to a MS. of the late fifteenth century,* and has never ceased to be, from that time to this, a favourite Catholic book of devotion. The earliest known printed edition is dated 1529 and is entitled *An invocacyon gloryous named ye psalter of Iesus.*† Subsequently it was printed, under the same title, in the Salisbury Primers of 1532, 1533, etc. According to an entry in the *Stationers' Register* there appears to have been one edition printed in Queen Mary's reign about the year 1558.‡ Fowler's edition, detailed above, is substantially the same as that of the Primers, as far as the actual Psalter is concerned; § he enlarges his introductory matter, however, with a note of procedure, which is not found in the Primer of 1532, and the 'wholesome doctrine' and 'Narration' (bibl. details (5) and (6) above) are substituted for the 'prayers to the trynyte' and the prayer of St. Bernard of that edition.

Fowler seems to have printed two further editions in this same year 1575, || and it is not surprising, therefore, that the work came to be known to the Protestant side as 'Fowler's Psalter', and is referred to as such by Thomas Sampson in *A Warning to take heede of Fowlers Psalter, giuen by Th. Sampson.*

Fowler wrote in English 'ad Ducissam Feriae confessionis formam' (*De illustribus Angliae Scriptoribus* (1619), p. 772) is probably based upon this passage.

* The MS. has been printed by H. Godwin in, *The Psalter of Jesus. From a manuscript of the fifteenth century; with variations from some late copies. London. Pickering and Co. 1885.* Godwin gives a history of the Psalter by way of preface. The 'late copies' are the printings of 1532 and 1624.

† Copy at Blairs College, Aberdeen.

‡ The entry runs (under date 1558) 'John Judson ys lycensed to prynte the boke Called the Spirituall Counsaile / Jesus mattens / Jesus psalter and xv oes all in one boke' (Arber's *Transcript*, Vol. I, p. 32). No copy of this edition seems to be extant. Godwin, who quotes the entry somewhat inaccurately, suggests that the book was never printed (op. cit.). S. H. Sole thinks that the Manresa MS., dated 17 August 1571, is a transcript of this edition, but on insufficient evidence. (*Jesu's Psalter . . . by the Rev. Samuel Heydon Sole.* London, 1888.)

§ The minor differences include change in vocabulary, change in the order of words, and occasional insertions. All these changes seem to point to an endeavour to modernize the Psalter.

|| A note on these and on some subsequent editions will be found at Appendix II.

London, 1578. Gillow's description of the *Psalter*, however, as 'a controversial work' is hardly apt.* It is, of course, purely a book of devotion.

I include the *Psalter* among the works of John Fowler on the grounds of editorial privilege and received usage.

45. [ornament] The Psalter of / Sainct Hierome, with certaine / dayly exercises and other deuout / and necessary Prayers. / [cut: with the words 'Non est aliud Nomen / datum hominibus. Act. 4.' to right and left] / There is none other name vnder heauen / giuen vnto men, in which we / must be saued. Act.4. / Antuerpiae. / Apud Iohan. Foulerum. Anno. 1576.

16°. B.L. A–D in eights. Not fol. Cw. No Mg. Rt – Sainct Hieromes / Psalter. (1) Title [A1]. (2) 'To the Reader' [A1v]. (3) Text of Psalter [A2–C4v]. (4) Prayers [C5–D8v].

An account of St. Jerome's *Psalter*, together with the early printings, will be found in Hoskins (*Horae*). Fowler's recension differs from previous versions only in minor points. Although it is a separate bibliographical unit, and is treated here as such, it is clear from the foreword that it was not a separate publication, but was added to the *Jesus Psalter* for the reasons stated. Fowler writes: 'I haue thought good gentle Reader, for the profit & commodity of eche deuoute Christian, to ad vnto the Psalter of Iesus, this godly and briefe collection of the Psalmes, called by the name of Sainct Hierome his Psalter, & also a dayly exercise taken out of *Officium beata Maria*, with other necessary Prayers, priuatly of the godly to be vsed: the one for that the exāple of that holy Father which collected it & dayly vsed it, may giue thee ensample to folowe his weldoinge. The other that if thy worldly businesse suffer thee not to spende much tyme in Prayer, thou mayst notwithstandinge haue wherewithall to occupy thy selfe aptly that lyttle tyme thou haste permitted thee: which I beeseche thee to take in no worse part then I bestow it. And so I leaue thee to the tuitiō of the almightie. Farewell' [A1v].

HAMILTON, JOHN
d. 1611?

46. Ane Catholik and / Facile Traictise, dra- / uin out of the halie scriptures, treulie ex- / ponit be the anciēt doctores, to confirme / the real and corporell praesence of chry- / stis pretious bodie and blude in the sa- / crament of the alter / Dedicat. / To his souuerane Marie the quenes maiestie / of scotland. / Be /

* *Bibl. Dict.* s.v. *Fowler*. He follows C. Dodd, *Church History*. Vol. I, p. 532.

Iohne Hamilton student in theologie, and re- / gent in philosophie to the maist excellent / and catholik prince Charles of / Bourbon in the royal college of Na- / uarre. / Imprentit at Paris the first of / April. / 1581.

16°. A–V in eights + π (between P4 and P5). Fol. 1[A1]–116[P4]. Cw. on fol. 8ᵛ of each gathering only, except sig. H. Mg. Rt – Of ye Lordis / Supper. (1) Title [A1]. (2) Three quots. in Scots [A1ᵛ]. (3) Dedicatory Epistle to Queen Mary: Iohne hamilton [A2–B2ᵛ]. (4) Text in ten chapters, each preceded by a short Argument [B3–P4ᵛ]. (5) New Title: [ornament] / Certane Ortho- / dox and Catholik / conclusions vith yair proba- / tiōs, quhilkis Iohne Hamil- / ton proponis in name of ye / Catholikis, to the Caluino- / latre ministeris. / Dedicat, / To ye Kingis maiestie of Scotland. / My sone keip ye preceptis of yj father & / put not auay ye lau of yj mother, bind yame / contenuallie in yj hairt, & knit yame about / yj craig. Quhen you gais, let yame pas vith / ye, quhen you sleipis let yame preserue ye, / and valkand speik vith yame. / Prouerb.7. / Imprentit at Paris ye 20. of Aprile. / [rule] / 1581. [π]. (6) Dedicatory Epistle to King James VI: 'Vrittin at Pareis in the Royall college of Nauarre the 20. of Aprile 1581 . . . I. Hamilton' [P5–8ᵛ]. (7) 'Certain Orthodox and Catholik cōclusiones, vith thair probationes, quhilk Iohne Hamilton regēt in ye Royall college of Nauarre, in name of ye Catholikis proponis to ye ministeris in ye deformit Kirk in Scotlād. To be disputit before the Kingis Maiestie ād his honorable coūsall.' 24 'conclusions' in all (without Rt.) [Q1–V2ᵛ]. (8) 'Testimoneis for Antiquitie of religion and succession of Pastoris in the Catholik Kirk, quhilk heretikis as the Caluinolatre antichristian ministers can not schau, quha not entering at ye dur, hes violentlie dispossessit lauchfullie callit pastoris' [V3–6ᵛ]. (9) 'Certane Quaestionis to the quhilkis ve desyre the ministeris mak resolute ansuer at yair Nixt generall assemblie . . .' [V7–8ᵛ].*

In the year previous to this publication Hamilton had written a letter challenging a public conference on religion, to which he had added fifteen theological propositions.† These are the first fifteen of the twenty-four 'Orthodox and Catholik Conclusiones' referred to at (7) above.

The printing of this work is clearly that of Burne's *Disputation* [entry 24].

47. A Facile Traictise, Contenand, first: ane infallible reul to discerne trevv from fals religion: Nixt, a declaration of the Nature, Numbre, Vertevv & effects of the sacraments; togider

* The second title given at (5) above is absent from the British Museum copy of this book and from the copy at St. John's Seminary, Wonersh. As the signatures are complete without it, its absence would not generally be detected. T. G. Law reproduces it in facsimile in his edition of *Catholic Tractates of the Sixteenth Century* (Scottish Text Society, 1901) from a copy in the Drummond collection of the Edinburgh University Library, and the above details are taken from his reproduction. Presumably, then, we have here a cancel. The word 'gais' in the title is a misprint for 'gangis'.

† Answered by William Fowler, a young Presbyterian, in his *An Answer to the calumnious letter and erroneous propositiouns of an apostat named M. Io. Hammiltoun.* Edinburgh, 1581. Hamilton's letter is not extant. He alludes to it in his Epistle to King James in these words: 'I craue the spirituall cōbat quhilk I offerit the last zeir to the ministers in zour hienes realme.' See T. G. Law's biographical notice of Hamilton (op. cit.) for further details.

vvith certaine Prayeres of deuotion. Dedicat to His Soverain Prince, the Kings Maiestie of Scotland. King Iames the Saxt. Be Maister Ihone Hamilton Doctor in Theologie. The Kirk of God, is the piller and sure ground of the veritie. 1.Timoth.3. VVha heiris nocht the Kirk, lat him be to the as a Pagan and Publican. Math.18. At Louan. Imprinted be Laurence Kellam. Anno Dom. M.D.C.

HARDING, THOMAS, D.D.
1516–1572

48. An Ansvvere / to Maister Iuelles / Chalenge, By Doctor / Harding. / 1.Cor.14. / An à vobis verbum Dei processit? aut in vos solos peruenit? / Hath the word of God proceded from you? Or / hath it come among you only? / [device] / Imprinted in Louaine by Iohn Bogard at the / Golden Bible, with priuilege. / Anno 1564.

Bod.

4°. ✶+A–Z+Aa–Zz+Aaa–Ddd in fours. Fol. 1[B1]–193[Ccc3]. Cw. Mg. Rt – An Ansvvere to / M. Iuelles Chalenge. (1) Title [✶1]. (2) Privilegium: Brussels. 15 Sept. 1563. Followed by reference to the Table at the end of the book [✶1v]. (3) 'To the Reader': Louvain. 14 June 1563. Thom. Harding [✶2–3v]. (4) 'A Collection of Certaine Places out of Maister Iuelles Booke . . .' [✶4–A2]. (5) Jewel's challenge, etc. 'in other places of his booke' [A2v–A4v]. (6) Preface to Jewel: Thomas Harding [B1–C3v]. (7) Authorities ('Councelles and fathers') alleged [C3v–4]. (8) Ornament [C4v]. (9) Text in 26 Articles and Conclusion [D1–Ccc3]. (10) 'A Table of the Articles' [Ccc3v–4]. (11) 'A Table of the Chiefe pointes' [Ccc4–Ddd4]. (12) Imprimatur [Ddd4]. (13) Ornament [Ddd4v].

The controversy, which arose from Jewel's challenge delivered at Paul's Cross on 31 March 1560 and to which this book belongs, is discussed fully at p. 60.

It would appear from the address 'To the Reader' that the original version of this treatise was written by Harding while he was still in England, and that it was not intended for publication. He writes: 'Where as Horace sayeth, they that runne ouer the sea, chaunge the ayer, not the mynde: it is so reader, that I passing ouer the sea out of England in to Brabant, haue in some part chaunged also my mynde. For where as being there, I mynded to send this treatise but to one frend, who required it for his priuate instruction, and neuer to set any thing abroade: now being arriued here in Louaine, I haue thought good, by putting it in printe, to make it common to many'[*2].

49. An Ansvvere / to Maister Iuelles / chalenge, by Doctor / Harding. / augmented vvith certaine quotations and additions. / 1.Cor.14. / An à vobis verbum Dei processit? aut in vos solos /

peruenit? / Hath the word of God proceded from you? / Or hath it come among you only? / [device] / Imprinted in Antwerpe, / At the golden Angel by William Syl- / vius the Kinges Maiesties printer. / [rule] / M.D.LXV. / VVith priuilege.

8°. A–Z+Aa–Gg in eights. Fol. 1[A1]–236[Gg4]. Cw. Mg. Rt – An Ansvvere to / M. Iuelles Chalenge. The details of this book follow closely those already set out in the previous entry save for (a) 'The Correctour to the Reader': Antwerp. 12 Jan. 1565. John Martiall; and (b) Privilegium: 15 Jan. 1563.*

The reason for this reprint of Harding's work is given by John Martiall† in 'The Correctour to the Reader': 'If thou wilt knowe gentill Reader for what Causes and by whom this booke is now set forth in print againe, here mayst thou see both the same declared, and his name subscribed. First the booke being good, and conteyning true, holsome, and Catholike doctrine, the more it is made common, the more good thereby is done. Againe whereas many be desyrous of the same, as well in Scotland, Ireland, as in England: in so easy and so profitable a thing not to answer their desires, it were byside all humanitie. Thirdly for asmuch as it is often and constantly reported, that an answere to this booke hath this long time ben and is yet in hande,‡ that, when the same shall come forth men may the better see by conferēce of bookes, where true dealing is, and where falsehed is vsed: it may to any man appeare reasonable, that for so honest and so good a purpose the copies by meane of a newe print be multiplied.' He then goes on to explain how the work came to be augmented: 'That thou findest here sundry quotations, and also certaine briefe additions, which the copies of the first print had not: to the intent I make thee priuey to all, thus it hath ben done. About halfe a yere past coming into M. D. Hardinges chambre, (which to his frēdes is neuer shutte) and there finding a booke newly quoted, and with some annotations augmēted with his owne hande: vppon affiance of his frendship, I was so bolde in his absence, as for a time to take it with me, and according to the same to note myne owne booke, not mynding as then euer to set it in print, but to vse it to my priuate instruction. And the same now hath serued the printer for his copie. Whereas I haue aduentered thus to do without the authors knowledge, whereto himselfe by sundry persons moued could neuer yet be induced: as I knowe not why I should be blamed of any other, so I trust the greatnes of the profit that hereof is like to folowe, shall procure me easy pardon of him, whose slacknes I haue supplied' [A2–3].

* A misprint. Read – 15 Jan. 1565.

† For John Martiall, see entries 82 and 83.

‡ The answer duly arrived and was entitled *A Replie vnto M. Hardinges Answeare.* By John Jewel. 1565. There is no reference to Martiall's recension in this *Replie.*

50. A Confutation / of a Booke intituled / An Apologie of the / Church of England, by / Thomas Harding Doctor / of Diuinitie. / 2.Timoth.3. / Quemadmodum Iannes et Mambres restiterunt Moysi, ita & hi resistunt veritati, ho- / mines corrupti mente, reprobi circà fidem. sed vltrà non proficient: insipientia enim eorum / manifesta erit omnibus, sicut & illorum fuit. / As Iannes and Mambres withstode Moyses, euen so do these felowes also / withstand the truth, men of a corrupt mynde, and castawayes as concerning the / faith. but they shall not preuaile any further: for their folishnes shall be open vn- / to all men, as theirs was. / [device] / Imprinted at Antwerpe, by Ihon Laet, / with Priuilege. 1565.

4°. ★6+!^{6}+A–Z+AA–ZZ+AAA–ZZZ+a–x in fours. Fol. 1[A1]–351[t3]. Cw. Mg. Rt – A Confutation of the / Apologie, &c. (1) Title [★1]. (2) Royal Arms (left and right: E.R. – subscribed 'God saue the Quene.') [★1^{v}]. (3) Address to Queen Elizabeth: 'Your Maiesties most faithfull subiect and bounden oratour Thomas Harding' [★2–6^{v}]. (4) 'To the Reader' [!1–6]. (5) Privilegium: Brussels. 12 April 1565 [!6^{v}]. (6) Text in six parts [A–t3]. (7) Table [t3^{v}–x2^{v}]. (8) 'Faultes escaped in printing. In the Margent' [x3]. (9) Imprimatur: Louvain. 10 April 1565 [x3^{v}]. (10) Blank [x4].

This answer to John Jewel's *Apologia* (1562) is the earliest of the answers in English that that notable work called forth.* 'Two onely,' says Harding, 'I heare of that haue written against it, the one in latin, a learned Spaniard, bishop in the kingdom of Naples, the other an Italian, in the Italian tonge.' He then proceeds, 'myselfe thought it more conuenient to write this Confutation in english, then in latin, that so both falsehed might be refelled, and truth defended, and also that our domesticall faultes might be considered to amendment within the bankes of England, and not by the common tonge blowen abroade through all Christendom, to the contempt and shame of our countrie' [!3^{v}–!4]. Harding uses Lady Bacon's translation of the *Apology*, giving first 'the wordes of the Apologie as I found them translated, sometimes by whole paragraphs, sometimes by mo, sometimes by fewer and briefe sentences'. His confutation follows 'longer or shorter, according to the thing confuted'. 'Here,' he adds, 'shalt thou finde the Apologie whole, sentence for sentence, word for word. That I might seme to deale vprightly, I would leaue out nothing' [!2^{v}]. He wrote the book, he says, in less than three-quarters of a year.

51. To Maister John Jeuell.

This is a large broadsheet,† printed on one side only, and dated Antwerp, 12 Junii 1565. It is printed in full by Strype,‡ who

* The Apology controversy is discussed fully at p. 61.

† Strype, *Annals* (1824), Vol. I, pt. 2, pp. 176–7. ‡ ibid., pp. 524–7.

heads it, 'Harding's letter to bishop Jewel, printed. Dated from Antwerp: requiring a copy of his sermon preached at St. Paul's Cross'.

The facts we elicit from the letter are that Jewel had referred slightingly to Harding's answer to his challenge (see entry 48), impugning the authorities he had quoted in a sermon preached on 27 May previous, and that Harding required 'the true copie of that you said in your sermon to see whether it be as good in substance to the lerned, as for the tyme it semed gay to the people'. The letter is peremptory in tone and Jewel did not comply with the request.

52. [ornament] / A Briefe Answere / of Thomas Harding Doctor of Diuini- / tie, touching certaine vntruthes, with / which Maister Iohn Iuell charged / him in his late Sermon at Paules / Crosse the viii. of Iuly. / Anno. 1565. / [ornament] / Antuerpiae / typis Aegid. Diest. / 26.Iulij. / [ornament]

LAMB.

8°. A1–12. Not fol. Cw. Mg. No Rt. (1) Title [A1]. (2) Blank [A1v]. (3) 'To the Reader' [A2]. (4) Text: Antwerp. 1565. 24 July. Tho. Harding [A2v–12]. (5) Blank [A12v].

In his published letter of 12 June (see previous entry) Harding had asked for a copy of Jewel's sermon of the previous 27 May. Jewel had not obliged him. Instead, he preached a further sermon on 8 July strongly attacking him on the doctrine of the Real Presence, prayers in Latin, etc. This affords the reason for this new pamphlet. Thus he addresses the reader: 'For so muche (Gentill Reader) as Maister Iuell hitherto hath refused my reasonable request, touching his sermon at Paules Crosse of the. 27. of Maie last, to be imparted vnto me, so as he will stand vnto it, and hath since that time eftsones doubled his euill demeanour towardes me, and his iniurie towardes the truth, by his other late sermon of the. 8. of Iuly last: I trust I shall seme to do neither besydes the dutie of an honest man, if I cleare my selfe of slaũder obiected, neither besydes that apperteineth to my calling, if I defend the truth impugned. I confesse in very dede, it shold better become my person to bestowe a iust treatise vpõ these pointes, thẽ such short pamflets, which I wold willingly do after the measure of my simple lerning, if I had the said sermons either printed, or by M. Iuell hymselfe subscribed. But the case standing as it doth, and the same being yet denyed: I thinke it better thus to write briefly, then by silence to seme to acknowledge a gylt, to suffer thee to remaine deceiued, and the truth iniured' [A2]. We learn also from this Address that he has had his information of Jewel's sermon from 'sundry persons aparte' and he is persuaded of its truth since they 'without diuersitie agree in one'. There is again reference in the text to Jewel's coming book – a 'huge booke', this time – and he suggests that these sermons are but the preliminary puffs to rouse expectation, 'which expectation the greater it is, the more it shall cause men to contemne it, and laugh at it, if they shall see so great a hill after so long trauaile, brought a bed of a foolish mouse' [A11].

53. A Reioindre / to M. Iewels / Replie. / [ornament] By perusing wherof the discrete and diligent Reader may / easily see, the Answer to parte of his insolent Chalenge iustified, / and his Obiections against the Masse, whereat the Priest some- / time receiueth the holy Mysteries without present com- / panie to receiue with him, for that cause by Lu- / thers Schoole called Priuate Masse, / clearely confuted. / By Thomas Harding Doctor of Diuinitie. / Prouerb.25. / Nubes, & ventus, & pluuiae non sequentes, vir gloriosus, & promissa / non complens. / Like as is a cloude, and winde, and no raine folowing: so is a man, that cra- / keth much, and performeth not his promises. / [device] / Antuerpiae. / Ex officina Ioannis Fouleri. / Anno. M.D.LXVI.

4°.B.L.★–★★★+ π+ ¶–¶¶¶¶+A–Z+a–z+AA–ZZ+AAa–MMm in fours +NNn^{2}. Fol. 1[B1]–315[LLl3]. Cw. Mg. Rt – A Reioindre to / M. Iewels Replie. (1) Title [★1]. (2) Privilegium: Brussels. 20 May 1566 [★1v]. (3) 'To the Reader' [★2–π2]. (4) 'To M. Iewel': Antwerp. Aug. 1566 [π3–A3].* (5) 'Faultes escaped in printing' [A4]. (6) Text [B1–LLl3]. (7) Table [LLl4–NNn2]. (8) Imprimatur: Louvain. 7 May 1566 [NNn2]. (9) Ornament [NNn2v].

This Rejoinder answers Jewel's *A Replie vnto M. Hardinges Answeare* (1565) and belongs to the Challenge controversy (see pp. 60, et seq.). Harding answers only the first of Jewel's twenty-seven Articles, viz. that dealing with what 'M. Iewel and his companions cal priuate Masse'. Edward Dering replied to the Rejoinder in *A Sparing Restraint, of many lauishe Vntruthes, which M. Doctor Harding dothe chalenge, in the first Article of my Lorde of Sarisburies Replie* (1568). Harding's *Detection of sundrie foule errours* (1568)† (entry 55) was published about a month after this book of Dering's. This will account for there being no reference to it in that work of Harding's.

* Immediately after the date, this address to Jewel continues: 'In which time your brethren of this low Countrie professours of that ye cal the Gospel, haue geuen euident testimonie to ÿ worlde, with what Spirite they be lead by their spoiling and robbing of Churches and religious houses, by destroying of Libraries, by threatning to fyer the places where they be resisted, & with other wicked outrages: through occasion whereof this Treatise could not be printed neither so spedily, nor so exactly, as in quiet times it might haue ben. Thomas Harding.'

† Referred to by Strype, *Annals* (1824), Vol. I, pt. 2, p. 272.

54. A Reioindre to M. / Iewels Replie against / the Sacrifice of the / Masse. / In which the doctrine of the Answere to the. xvij. Ar- / ticle of his Chalenge is defended, and further pro- / ued, and al that his Replie conteineth against / the Sacrifice, is clearely confuted, / and disproued. / By Thomas Harding Doctor of Diuinitie. / Luke.22. / Doo ye this in my Remembrance. / Irenaeus lib.4. cap.32. / Christe (at his last Supper) taught the new Oblation of the / new Testament, which the Churche, receiuing it of the Apo- / stles, offereth vp vnto God through the whole worlde. / [device] / Louanii, / Apud Ioannem Foulerum, Anno.1567. / Cum Priuilegio.

4°. a–n+A–Z+AA–ZZ+AAA–XXX in fours. Fol. 1[c3]–50[n4] and 1 [A1]–262[VVV2]. Cw. Mg. Rt – A Reioindre to M. Iewels Replie / against the Sacrifice of the Masse. (1) Title [a1]. (2) Privilegium: Brussels. Callend. Septemb. 1567 [a1^{v}]. (3) 'To M. Iewel': Thomas Harding (followed by quotation) [a2–c2^{v}]. (4) 'The Preface to the Catholike Reader touching the Sacrifice of the Masse' [c3–n2^{v}]. (5) 'The chiefe, and most common Argument, that the Protestantes make against the Sacrifice of the Masse' [n3–4]. (6) 'Faultes escaped in printing' [n4^{v}]. (7) Text [A1–VVV2]. (8). 'The Table' [VVV2^{v}–XXX4^{v}]. (9) Imprimatur: Louvain. 23 Aug. 1567 [XXX4^{v}].

This book is a continuation of the Rejoinder of the previous year and answered three further Articles.

55. A Detection of sun- / drie foule errours, lies, / sclaunders, corruptions, and other / false dealinges, touching Doctrine, and other matters, vt- / tered and practized by M. Iewel, in a Booke late- / ly by him set foorth entituled, A Defence / of the Apologie. &c. / [ornament] / By Thomas Harding Doctor of / Diuinitie. / Psalm.4. / Filij hominum vsquequo graui corde? vt quid diligitis vanitatem, & / quaeritis Mendacium? / O ye sonnes of menne, how long wil ye be dul harted? what / meane ye thus to be in loue with Vanitie, and to seeke after / Lying? / [device] / Louanii, / Apud Ioannem Foulerum, Anno 1568. / Cum Priuilegio.

BOD.

4°. ★–★★★★★★+A–Z+AA–ZZ+a–z+aa–zz+Aa–Oo in fours. Fol. 1[A1]–417[Nn1]. Cw. Mg. Rt. varies. (1) Title [★1]. (2) Privilegium: Brussels. 24 May 1568 [★1^{v}]. (3) 'The Preface to the Reader': Thomas Harding [★2–★★★★★★4^{v}]. (4) Text in five Books [A1–Nn1^{v}]. (5) Table [Nn2–Oo3]. (6) 'Faultes escaped in the printing' [Oo3^{v}]. (7) Imprimatur: Louvain. 21 May 1568 [Oo3^{v}]. (8) Blank [Oo4]. (9) Fowler's device [Oo4^{v}].

This work is an answer to *A Defence of the Apologie of the Churche of Englande*, by John Jewel (1567). It belongs to the Apology controversy (see pp. 60 et seq.). In the Preface to the Reader

Harding refers to the 'hugenesse' of Jewel's volume (it is some 750 folio pages long), and apologizes for the smallness of this reply (about 900 pages of quarto!). 'The booke of the Defence being alreadie so great, as it is, by that time a iuste answer should be added vnto it, euery man that hath any iudgement in these thinges, maie soone conceiue, of what an huge quantitie my new printed Volume would be. In deed were euery idle point answered, and treated of at ful, it would seeme to matche, yea farre to ouermatche Foxes Huge Booke of his false Martyrs' [*4v].

Jewel finally replied with an enlarged edition of the *Defence* (see p. 66).

HARPSFIELD, NICHOLAS, D.C.L.

1519–1575

(see Appendix III)

HAUNSE, EVERARD

d. 1581

(see entry 13)

HAY, JOHN, S.J.

1546–1607

56. Certaine / Demandes con- / cerning the chri- / stian religion and discipline, pro- / poned to the Ministers of the / nevv pretended kirk of Scotlād, / be Iohne Hay ane Clerk of the / Societie of Iesus. / Stand in the vvaies, and beholde, and aske / for the old vvaie, quhilk is the gvid / vvaye, and vvalke therin, and ze sall / find rest for zour soules. Ier.6. / [cut] / Imprinted at Paris by Thomas Brumen, in clauso / Brunello, at the signe of the Olivve trie. / Anno CIϽIϽLXXX.

16°. A–F in eights+G4. Pag. 1[A1]–104[G4v]. Cw. on verso pages only. Mg. Rt – Demandes vnto / the Ministers of Scotland. (1) Title [A1]. (2) Quots. in Scots, and printer's ornament [A1v]. (3) 'To the Nobilitie of Scotland Iohne Hay vvisheth grace and peace': 'At Pariss, the 25. day of Februar. anno CIϽIϽLXXX. Zours most humble and obedient Seruiteure. Iohne Hay' [A2–4]. (4) Text of the Demands (166 in number) [A4v–F6v]. (5) Conclusion: ends, 'Imprinted vvith licence of the Superiours. Praised be God. Amen.' [F6v–G4v]. (Brumen's monogram appears at sig. A4v.)

In his Address to the 'Nobilitie of Scotland' Fr. Hay gives an account of the occasion of his *Demandes*. He had gone to Scotland for his health and, having apparently engaged in religious controversy, was summoned to appear at Stirling to give an account of himself before the Privy Council. He was examined by the ministers of the reformed religion and offered to dispute before the king and the nobles. Needless to say, his offer was refused.* 'Therefore', he writes, 'nocht heffād the moyen be there refvvse to givve reason in zovvr presence of sik thinges as concernes the controvversie of religion in thir dayes, I am constranead, for the discharge of my conscience, to propone ane certaine nommer of qvvestiones or demādes vnto thame, to the ende yat efer [efter] ze heavve read and considred the said demandes, and cavvsit the Ministers ansovvr directlie therto ze may easelie persavve that the doctreine quhilk is professed in Scotland is na other thing bot other the inuention of Iohne Calvin, or ane rapsodie of avvld condamned heresies manie hvvndrethe zeares afoir, quhilk I hoip in God ze sell do, and prayes him to illvvminet zovvr hartes to acknavvlege the trevvthe, and to assist zovv vvithe his holie Sprit, that ze fvvlfilland his holie commandementes may be participāt of the lyiff eternell.'†

No answer was forthcoming, however, and after waiting four years, as he says in the Dedicatory Epistle to the French edition (see below), Hay translated his work into French in the hope that the Protestants of Nîmes and others would be readier than their Scots *confrères* to answer him. This translation was entitled *Demandes faictes aux Ministres d'Escosse: Touchant la religion Chrestienne, Par M. Iean Hay Escossois, de la compagnie de Iesus, Professeur en Theologie, en l'Vniuersité de Tournon. Reueuës, & de l'Escossois mises en nostre langue Françoise . . . A Lyon, Par Iean Pillehotte. M.D.LXXXIII. Auec priuilege du Roy.*‡ This time Hay

* He arrived in Scotland on 20 January 1579. The result of his examination was that he was ordered to leave the country before 1 October. T. G. Law, Introd. to *Catholic Tractates of the Sixteenth Century*, s.v. *Hay* (Scottish Text Society, 1901).

† The curious interchange of 'u', 'v' and 'w' in this passage is characteristic also of Nicol Burne's *Disputation* and Hamilton's *Traictise*. It points evidently to the same printer having been at work in all three books.

‡ This translation has been persistently referred to Fr. Michel Coyssard, S.J., as a result of the entry under John Hay in the *Bibliotheca Scriptorum Societatis Iesu* (Alegambe, 1676): 'Interrogationes ad Sectarios Praedicantes, quas Michael Coyssardus Gallicas fecit Virduni apud Ioannem Wapii 1583.' Both J. N. Paquot in his *Mémoires pour servir à l'Histoire littéraire des dix-sept Provinces des Pays-Bas* (1765–70), s.v. *Hay*, and de Backer in his *Bibliothèque des Écrivains de la Compagnie de Jésus* (1869), s.v. *Michel Coyssard*, have read the words of the *Bibliotheca Scriptorum* as referring to this Lyons translation. They are followed by T. G. Law and others. An examination of the book itself shows that this cannot be correct. The Address to the Contesse de Rosillion is signed 'Vostre treshumble & tresaffectioné serviteur Iean Hay'. In this Address Hay speaks himself as the translator, warning his hearers also that this work is, as it were, a foretaste of a bigger treatise he is preparing in Latin. The Advertisement to the French Catholic Reader begins: 'Si par aduāture quelques vnes de ces miēnes Demandes', etc. All of which points definitely to Hay as translator. The only conclusion which can be legitimately drawn from the entry in the *Bibliotheca Scriptorum*, which, be it noted, refers to a translation published at Verdun, by Jean Wapius, not at Lyons, is that Michel Coyssard also translated the work, or that he was in some way connected with a second publication of it in the same year, 1583. The Verdun edition does not appear to be extant. A German version, translated from the French, was published at Freiburg in 1885.

was not disappointed. De Chambrun replied in *L'Esprit et Conscience Iesuitique* (Nismes, 1584), and Jean de Serres in *Defence de la vérité catholique* (Nismes, 1586), 'in which he refutes the calumnies of Hay, and sets against his 206 Demands, 412 addressed to the Jesuits'.* There was also an anonymous answer entitled *Réponse aux cinq premières et principaux Demandes de F. Iean Hay, moine Iesuite* (Geneva, 1586).† Hay defended himself in his *Apologie des Demandes proposées aux Ministres Escossois* (Lyon, 1586).‡ Reference to further pamphlets in connexion with the controversy will be found in de Backer.§

HESKYNS, THOMAS, O.P.

fl. 1565

57. The / Parliament / of Chryste auou- / ching and declaring the enac- / ted and receaued trueth of the presence of his bodie and bloode in the / blessed Sacrament, and of other articles concerning the same, im- / pugned in a wicked sermon by M. Iuell, Collected and seth- / furth by Thomas Heskyns Doctour / of dyuinitie. / Wherein the reader shall fynde all the scripturs cōmonlie alleaged oute of the newe Testament, / touching the B. Sacrament, and some of the olde Testament, plainlie and truely expownded / by a nombre of holie learned Fathers and Doctours. / Ecclesiast.viii. / Non te pretereat narratio seniorum, ipsi enim didicerunt a patribus suis. Quoniam / ab ipsis disces intellectum, & in tempore necessitatis dare responsum. / Go not from the doctryne of the elders, for they haue learned of their fathers. For of them thowe / shalt learn vnderstanding, so that thowe maist make answer in tyme of nede. / August. lib.I. de moribus Eccle. cap.xxv. / Audite doctos catholicae Ecclesię viros tanta pace animi, & eo voto, quo ego vos / audiui. / Heare ye the learned men of the catholique Churche with as

* T. G. Law, *Catholic Tractates*, p. xli.

† Paquot suggests that Beza was possibly the author of this; op. cit. Vol. III, p. 616.

‡ 'En français selon le père Alegambe: mais c'est une erreur; car Jean Hay assure, dans sa préface, qu'il l'avait écrite en latin, et qu'elle fut traduite en français par quelques-uns de leurs écoliers. Cette Apologie fut faite contre *le libelle de Jacques Pineton de Chambrun, prédicant à Nîmes*, et imprimęe à Lyon l'an 1586. L'épître dédicatoire, datée du 2 de juillet 1585, témoigne que depuis cinq ans l'auteur lisait publiquement la théologie à Tournon.' P. Bayle, *Dictionnaire Historique et Critique* (1820), Vol. VII, p. 459. Both de Backer (op. cit., Vol. II, col. 66) and the *D.N.B.* (s.v. *Hay*) seem to have referred the date of Hay's book to that of de Chambrun.

§ loc. cit.; cp. also T. G. Law, loc. cit.

quiet a mynde, and with soche / desyre as I haue heard yowe. / [device] / Imprinted at Antvverpe, / At the golden Angell, by VVilliam Silvius prynter to the Kynges / Maiestie. M.D.LXVI. / VVith Priuilege.*

2°. ¶^{6}+A^{4}+B–Z+Aa–Zz+Aaa–Yyy in sixes+(.:.)^{8}. Fol. 1[B3]–400[Yyy6] each fol. being divided alphabetically into eight sections, except gathering A, where the division is into fourteen. Cw. Mg. No Rt. (1) Title [¶1]. (2) 'The names of soche authours as be alleaged in this Booke of the Parliament of Chryste, placed as yt were in two houses, that ys to witte soche as were before a thousand years or verie neer, in the higher house, soche as were since in the lower house' [¶1^{v}]. (3) Full-page plate of 'The Parliament of Christe vpon the matter of the B.Sacrament' [¶2]. (4) Privilegium: Brussels. 7 July 1565 [¶2^{v}]. (5) Address to Jewel [¶3–6]. (6) Prologue to the Reader [A1–B2^{v}]. (7) Text in three books [B3–Yyy6]. (8) Imprimatur: Louvain. 4 July 1565 [Yyy6]. (9) 'The Cheif and moste matters conteined in this booke' [(.:.) 1–7^{v}]. (10) 'Faultes in printing' [(.:.) 7^{v}].† (11) Blank [(.:.) 8].‡

This is part of the concerted answer to Jewel's challenge, delivered at Paul's Cross (see p. 60). Heskins quotes largely from the sermon. The purport of the book is set forth in the Address to Jewel as follows: 'I haue doen to yowe in this booke three things. First, I haue shewed yowe the beginning of the doctrine of the bless. Sacramēt, the progresse and cōtinuance of yt, and the defence of yt. Secōdlie, of the Masse which ys the solēne sacrifice of Chrysts Church, I haue shewed yowe good presidents, certē and assured practises, and these right auncient. Thirdlie, for the Sacramētaries doctrine, I haue shewed whē yt began, by whō yt was inuēted, whē and wher yt was condēned, and so ceassed, and by whom yt was raised again in these our daies, in the whiche yt ys also laufullie again condēned' [¶5^{v}]. In the Prologue to the Reader we are told Book I deals with the Old Testament prophecies etc. with regard to the Sacrament, Book II with the Gospels (S. John vi, S. Matt. xxvi and S. Luke xxiv), and Book III with the Epistles (notably 1 Cor. ii). 'By Christes Parliament house', he says, 'I meen the catholique Churche.'

W. Fulke replied in 'Heskins Parleament Repealed', which is the first part of *D. Heskins, D. Sanders, and M. Rastel, accounted* (*among their faction*) *three pillers and Archpatriarches of the Popish Synagogue,* (*vtter enemies to the truth of Christes Gospell, and all that syncerely professe the same*) *ouerthrowne, and detected of their seuerall blasphemous heresies. By D. Fulke, Maister of Pembroke Hall in Cambridge* . . . London, 1579.

* Gillow [*Bibl. Dict.* under *Heskyns*) refers to a Brussels folio (1565) of this work and he is followed in this by the *D.N.B.* I have not traced a copy of this edition, nor can I find reference to it elsewhere.

† This instruction follows: 'And let the binder looke to the order of the Ternions, for the signatorie letters be some wanting: some mysplaced.'

‡ Some of the above particulars from the Bodleian copy. The last page of the Brit. Mus. copy [Yyy6] is a skilful reproduction of the original of that page.

HEYWOOD, JASPER, S.J.
1535–1598*

58. [ornament] The Sixt Trage / die of the most graue and prudent / author Lucius, Anneus, Seneca, / entituled Troas, with diuers and / sundrye addicions to the same. / Newly set forth in Englishe by / Iasper Heywood stu- / dient in Oxen- / forde. / Anno domini. / 1559. / [ornament] Cum priuilegio ad impri- / mendum solum.

[colophon on F3v] [ornament] Imprinted at London in Fletestrete / within Temple barre, at the signe of the / hand and starre, by Ri- / chard Tottyll. / Cum priuilegio ad impri- / mendum solum.

8°. B.L. A–E in eights+F3. Not fol. Cw. No mg. Rt – Troas / of Seneca. (1) Title [A1]. (2) Blank [A1v]. (3) 'To the most high and verteouse princesse, Elyzabeth by the grace of god Queene of England, Fraunce, and Ireland defender of the faith her highnes most humble and obedient subiecte Iasper Heywood studient in the vniuersite of Oxford wissheth helth welth, honour, & felicitie' [A2–3]. (4) 'To the readers' [A3v–4v]. (5) 'The preface to the tragedye' [A5–6v]. (6) 'The speakers in this tragedie' [A6v]. (7) Text (This includes certain additions. To quote the translator's Preface to the Readers: 'I haue . . . supplied the want of some things, as the fyrst Chorus, after the fyrst act beginning thus. O ye to whom &c. Also in the second acte. I haue added the speche of Achilles spright . . . Againe the three last staues of the Chorus after the same acte, and as for the third Chorus which in Seneca begynneth thus, *Que vocat sedes*: For as much, as nothing is therin but a heaped noumbre of farre & strange countreies . . . I haue in the place therof, made a nother beginning in thys maner. O Ioue that leadst &c.') [A7–F3v]. (8) Colophon [F3v].

59. [within a compartment, the base of which carries the date 1534] The Seconde / Tragedie of / Seneca entituled Thy- / estes faithfully Engli- / shed by Iasper Hey- / wood fellowe of / Alsolne Col- / lege / in Oxforde. / Imprinted at / London in Fletestrete / in the hous late / Thomas Ber- / thelettes. / Anno. 1560. / 26. die Martij.

* In addition to the titles set out above there are three signed poems by Jasper Heywood in *The Paradyse of daynty deuises* (1576). For some conjectures as to further poetical work of his, see *D.N.B.* (s.v. *Heywood*). It is unlikely, as there recorded from J. Ritson's *Bibliographia Poetica* (1802), p. 230, that the initials H.J. prefixed to a couple of stanzas, at the head of M. Kyffin's *Blessednes of Brytain* (1588), may be Heywood's. Ritson also suggests that Heywood may have been the editor of Greene's *Groatsworth of Wit*. The edition he had in mind was probably that of 1617, edited by J.H. This, of course, is much too late for Heywood. The Brit. Mus. Catalogue suggests John Hind as the owner of the initials. A note on Heywood's three tragedies will be found in A. W. Reed's *Early Tudor Drama* (1926), pp. 66 and 67.

[colophon on E6^{v}] Imprinted at / London in Fletestrete, in / the house late Thomas / Berthelettes. / Cum priuilegio ad im- pri- / mendum solum. / Anno M.D.LX.

8°. B.L. *^{8} + ❧^{8} + A–D in eights + E^{7}. Not fol. Cw. No mg. Rt – Thyestes / of Seneca. (1) Title [*1]. (2) Blank [*1^{v}]. (3) 'To the right honorable syr Iohn Mason knight one of the Queenes maiesties priuie counsaile, his daily orator Iasper Heywood wysheth health with encrease of honour and vertue' (in verse) [*2–2^{v}]. (4) 'The translatour to the booke' (in verse) [*3–4]. (5) 'The preface' (in verse) [*4^{v}– ❧8^{v}]. (6) 'The speakers' [❧8^{v}]. (7) Text [A1–E6]. (8) Colophon [E6^{v}]. (9) Blank [E7].

60. Lucii Annei Se- / necae Tragedia prima quae inscri- / bitur Hercules furens nuper recognita, & ab / omnibus mendis, quibus antea scatebat sedu- / lo purgata, & in studiosae iuuentutis vtilitatē, / in Anglicum metrum tanta fide conuersa, vt carmen / pro carmine quoad Anglica lingua patiatur / pene redditum videas. / Per Iasperum Heyvvodum Oxoniensem. / The first Tra- / gedie of Lucius Anneus Seneca, / intituled Hercules furens, newly pervsed and / of all faultes whereof it did before abound di- / ligently corrected, and for the profit of young / schollers so faithfully translated into En- / glish metre, that ye may se verse for verse / tourned as farre as the phrase of the en / glish permitteth / By Iasper Heywood studient / in Oxford.

[colophon on M8^{v}] Imprinted at / London by Henrye Sutton / dvvelling in pater noster / rovve at the signe of the / blacke Boy. / Anno Domini. M.D.LXI. / [cut]

8°. Latin in roman, English in black letter. A^{4} + B–M in eights. Not fol. Cw. No mg. Rt – Hercul. fur Senecae (Sen.) / Hercu. fur. of Sen. (1) Title [A1]. (2) Dedication to William Herbert, Earl of Pembroke [A1^{v}–4^{v}]. (3) 'The Argument of this Tragedy' followed by 'The speakers' [B1]. (4) Text in Latin and English [B1^{v}–M8]. (5) Colophon [M8^{v}].

HEYWOOD, JOHN
1497–1578 (?)*

61. Iohn Heywoodes / woorkes. / [ornament] A dialogue conteynyng the / number of the effectuall prouerbes in / the Englishe tounge, compact in / a matter concernynge / two maner of ma- / ryages. / With one hundred of Epigrammes: and / three hundred of Epigrammes / vpon three hundred pro- /

* Heywood's works, with the exception of that recorded here, all belong to a period earlier than Elizabeth. Recent studies of the Heywood canon which should be noted are R. W. Bolwell's *Life and Works of John Heywood* (New York), Read's *Early Tudor Drama*, and R. de la Bère's *John Heywood: Entertainer*.

uerbes: and a fifth / hundred of E- / pigrams. / Wherunto are now newly added / a syxt hundred of Epigrams / by the sayde Iohn / Heywood. / [ornament] / Londini. / Anno christi. / [rule] / 1562.

[colophon on Ee1v] Imprinted at / London in Fleetestrete / by Thomas / Powell. / Cum priuilegio.

4°. B.L. A–Z+Aa–Dd in fours+Ee². Not fol. Cw. Rt varies. (1) Title [A1]. (2) Preface in verse [A1v]. (3) 'The fyrst parte' in 13 chapters [A2–F1]. (4) 'The seconde parte' in 11 chapters [F1v–L3]. (5) New title as follows: The firste hundred of / Epigrammes. / Inuented and / made / by / Iohn Hey- / wood. / Londini. / 1562 [L3]. (6) 'To the reader' in verse [L3v]. (7) 'The table to this booke' [L4]. (8) Text [M1–Q1]. (9) Cut of John Heywood [Q1v]. (10) New title as follows: [ornament] Three hundred Epi- / grammes, vpon / three hundred / prouerbes. / Inuented and made by / Iohn Heywood. / Londini. / 1562. [Q2]. (11) 'The Table of this booke' [Q2v–4v]. (12) Text [R1–Y2]. (13) Blank [Y2v]. (14) New title as follows: [ornament] The fifth hundred / of Epygrams. / Inuented and / made by / Iohn Heywood. / Londini. / Anno Christi. / 1562. [Y3]. (15) 'To the reader' [Y3v]. (16) 'The table' [Y4]. (17) Text [Z1–Bb2v]. (18) New title as follows: A sixt hundred of / Epi- / grammes. / Newly inuented and made / by / Iohn Heywood. / [ornament] / Londini. / Anno christi. / 1562. / [Bb3]. (19) 'To the reader' [Bb3v]. (20) 'The table' [Bb4]. (21) Text [Cc1–Ee1v]. (22) Colophon [Ee1v]. (23) Blank [Ee2].

HIDE, THOMAS

d. 1597

62. A Conso- / latorie Epistle / to the afflicted / catholikes, set foorth by / Thomas Hide / Priest. / Be strong, and take a Good hart / vnto you, al you that put your / trust in our lord. Psalm. 30. / [cut] / Imprinted at Louaine by Iohn / Maes, for Iohn Lion. / 1579. / VVith Priuilege. / Subsig. Strick.

SIR R.L.H.

12°. B.L. A⁸–K⁴ in alternate eights and fours. Not fol. Cw. Mg. Rt – A consolatorie / Epistle. (1) Title [A1]. (2) Three quots. [A1v]. (3) Text: ends, 'Fare you wel. At Louaine, the last of September. 1579' [A2–K1]. (4) 'A Prayer' [K1–1v]. (5) Cut, with quots. above and below [K2]. (6) Imprimatur [K2v]. (7) Cut, with quot. below [K3]. (8) Blank [K3v–4].

This edition of the *Consolatorie Epistle* is very rare. I know of only one other copy – at Emmanuel College, Cambridge.

The name of John Maes, licensed printer at Louvain, does not occur in McKerrow's *Dictionary of Printers and Booksellers*. A note on John Lion will be found at p. 344. The *Epistle* was reprinted, probably by Stephen Brinkley at the Greenstreet House Press, in 1580.*

* See p. 353.

HOPKINS, RICHARD

d. 1594 (?)

63. Of / Prayer, and / Meditation. / Wherein are con- / teined fovvertien deuoute / Meditations for the seuen daies of the weeke, / bothe for the morninges, and eueninges. And in / them is treyted of the consideration of the prin- / cipall holie Mysteries of our faithe. / Written firste in the Spanishe / tongue by the famous Religious father. F. Lewis / de Granada, Prouinciall of the holie / order of preachers in the Pro- / uince of Portugall. / [cut] / Imprinted at Paris by Thomas Brumeau, at the signe of the / Olyue. Anno Domini. M.D.LXXXII.

8°. a–b+A–Z+Aa–Ss in eights+Tt⁴. Fol. 1[A1]–331 (pr. 231) [Tt3]. Cw. (on verso pages only). Mg. Rt. varies. (1) Title [a1]. (2) Blank [a1ᵛ]. (3) Dedicatory Epistle: 'To the Righte Honorable, and Worshipfull, of the fower principall howses of Cowerte in London, professinge the studie of the Common Lawes of our Realme, Richarde Hopkins wishethe dewe cōsideration of the holye mysteries of the Christian Religion': ends, 'From Paris, vpon the holie festiuall daie of Pentecoste. In the yeare of our Lorde. 1582' [a2–b2ᵛ]. (4) 'An Aduertismente by the translatour to the Learned Reader' [b3]. (5) Exhortation to the Reader: 'Bernard de Fresneda Bishoppe of Cuenca' [b3ᵛ–8]. (6) Blank [b8ᵛ]. (7) Author's Dedicatory Epistle and Prologue [A1–7]. (8) Text in 10 chapters and a 'last chapiter' (chapter 3 is not indicated) [A7ᵛ–Ss6ᵛ]. (9) 'Faultes escaped' [Ss7]. (10) Table of Contents [Ss7ᵛ–Tt3ᵛ]. (11) Blank [Tt4].

Lewis de Granada's work was originally published at Salamanca in 1554. In the 'Aduertismente by the translatour to the Learned Reader' Hopkins writes, 'in my Translatiō I doe folowe the edition in the Spanishe tongue printed at Andwarpe by Christopher Plantine, in the yeare of our Lorde. 1572'. This edition is as follows: *Libro De La Oracion Y Meditacion: En el qual se tracta de la Consideracion de los principales mysterios de nuestra Fe . . . Compuesto por Fray Luys de Granada, de la orden de Sancto Domingo . . . En Anvers, En casa de Christophoro Plantino.* 1572.*

This original has three parts (referred to in the prologue [bibl. details (7) above]). Hopkins translates the first part only. He had been prompted to this work of translation, he says, by Dr. Harding some fourteen years before. 'It is nowe about foureteene yeares agoe, since the time that Master Doctor Hardinge (a man for his greate vertue, learninge, wisdome, zeale, and sinceritie in writinge againste heresies, of verie godlie and famous memorie) perswaded me earnestlie to translate some of those Spanishe bookes into our Englishe tounge, affirminge, that more spirituall profite wolde vndoutedlie ensewe thereby to the gayninge of Christian sowles in our countrie from

* *Bibliographia del V.P.M. Fr. Luis de Granada* (4 vols.). By Fr. Maximino Llaneza. Salamanca, 1927.

Schisme, and Heresie, and from all sinne, and iniquitie, than by bookes that treate of controuersies in Religion: wich (as experience hath nowe plainelie tried) doe nothinge so well dispose the common peoples myndes to the feare, loue, and seruice of almightie God, as bookes treatinge of deuotion and howe to leade a vertuous life doe.' Therefore he has translated 'diuers bookes of a verie holie and famous learned religious father called Lewis de Granada, whose deuoute manner of writinge hath . . . a singular rare grace to pearce the harde harte of a dissolute sinner'. He adds, 'I haue resolued to publishe (godwillinge) in printe all my translations' [a6v–a7, *passim*].*

Hopkins explains his Dedication to the members of the Temple in these words: 'And for so muche as I am verie warie and assured that this boke conteineth not anie thinge whereby I maie iustlie incurre anie penaltie prescribed by anie lawes of our Realme, I am the bolder humblie to recommende it by this my dedicatorie Epistle vnto your Honours and woorshipps: partelie for that I haue spente some parte of my time in the studie of our Common Lawes in the Middle Temple emonge you, and am verie moche bounde vnto diuers of you: But chieflie for that I knowe right well the greate capacitie and dexteritie of your spirites' [b1].†

The plates in this work deserve special mention. There are twenty-five of them in all, representing the various subjects for meditation. Those in the Bodleian copy (a more perfect specimen than the one in the Museum library) are very fine indeed.

It is odd that the printer's name, Thomas Brumen, should appear incorrectly on the title-page (of all places) as Thomas Brumeau. His full printing title is 'Thomas Brumen, au cloz Bruneau à l'enseigne de l'Oliuier'. I can only suggest that the two names Brumen and Bruneau ran together in the compositor's mind, and he produced a 'portmanteau' which was subsequently overlooked.

George L'Oyselet reprinted this translation at Rouen in 1584. Amongst subsequent reprints is to be noted a Protestant version of 1592 under the title: *Of Prayer and Meditation. Contayning foure teene Meditations, for the seauen dayes of the weeke: both for Mornings and Euenings. Treating of the principall maters and holy misteries of our fayth. London, Printed for Thomas Gosson and John Perin: and are to be solde at the signe of the Angell in Paules Churchyard.* The

* 'Diuers bookes' and '*all* my translations' suggest more works from the Spanish than the two recorded here.

† There can be little doubt that it was a copy of this translation which was sent by Hopkins to Francis Walsingham. In a covering letter to Walsingham Hopkins writes: 'takinge occasion to sende your Honour as a token of my readie humble service one of my bookes translated and published nowe by me into our Englishe tounge, contayninge nothinge whereby I maie incurre anie penaltye prescribed by anye manner of Lawes of our Realme'. The letter is dated from Paris, 21 August 1582. (S.P.O. *Dom. Eliz.*, Vol. 155, No. 10.)

absence of Granada's name from the title-page will be noted. It is also to be remarked that the morning and evening Meditations have been transposed in this version and, of course, they have been carefully purged. Later reprints of the Protestant edition are those of 1599 (*At London, Printed by P. Short, for William Wood, and are to be solde at his shop at the West end of Paules, at the signe of Tyme.*), which restores the author's name to the title-page, and of 1601 (printed by I. Harison). These carry a second title: *An Excellent Treatise of Consideration and Prayer. Written by the same Authour, F. Lewes de Granada, in Portugall: and annexed to his Booke of Meditations.*

64. A Manual of Prayers nevvly gathered out of many and diuers famous authours aswell auncient as of the tyme present. Reduced into. 13. chap. very commodious and profitable for a deuout Christian. [cut] 1.Pet. cap.4. Be wise therefore & watch in prayers. But before all things, hauing mutual charitie cō-tinual among your selues. Cum Priuilegio. 1583. [George L'Oyselet. Rouen.]*

65. A Memoriall of a Christian Life. Wherein are treated all such thinges, as apperteyne vnto a Christian to doe, from the beginninge of his conuersion, vntil the ende of his perfection. Deuided into Seauen Treatises: the particulars whereof are noted in the page followinge. Written first in the Spanishe tongue, by the famous Religious Father, F. Lewis de Granada, Prouinciall of the holie order of Preachers, in the Prouince of Portugal. Imprinted at Rouen, by George L'oyselet. Anno Domini. M.D.LXXXVI.

66. The Spiritual Pilgrimage of Hierusalem, contayninge three hundred sixtie fiue dayes Iorney, wherin the deuoute Person may Meditate on sondrie pointes of his Redemption. VVith. Particular Declaration of diuers Saints bodies and holy places which are to be seene in the said voyage: As also sundrie deuout praiers and meditations verie healpful to the Pilgrimes: With Licence. [Boscard. Douay. 1592?]†

I., T.

67. [ornament] Certayne / necessarie Princi- / ples of Religion, which / may be entituled, / A Catechisme conteyning / all the

* There seem to be reasonable grounds for supposing this manual to be the work of Hopkins.

† There are reasonable grounds for supposing that this is Hopkins's work.

partes of the Chri- / stian and Catholique / Fayth. / Written in Latin by P. Cani- / tius, one of the holy societie / of the Iesuites, and nowe / amplified and Engli- / shed by T.I. / Duaci, / Per Ioannem Bogardum. [1579?]

16°. B.L. ¶+A–H in eights. Not fol. Cw. Mg. Rt – A Catechisme / for Catholiques. (1) Title [¶1]. (2) Blank [¶1v]. (3) Missing [¶2]. (4) 'The Translatour to the Reader': 'from Duaci the 17, of February' [¶3–8v]. (5) Text of the Catechism in 5 chapters [A1–G7]. (6) 'Certayne Testimonies taken out of holy Scripture . . .' [G7v–H6v]. (7) 'Three notable sayinges taken out of S. Augustine, moste worthy of remembraunce' [H7–8]. (8) Blank [H8v].*

Translated from the *Parvus Catechismus Catholicorum* of St. Peter Canisius. I have been unable to trace the anonymous translator, T. I.

The circumstances which led to the translating and publishing of the *Catechisme* are recorded at length in the Address to the Reader as follows: 'At suche time as I trauayled betweene *Artois* and *Paris* (beeing occasioned so to doo, bicause of those outragious conspiracies which were raysed all *Flaunders* ouer)† somewhat to appease the sorowes which then pinched my harte full sore (when I sawe the desperate attemptes of such as what in them lay, procured destruction to that whole countrey) I happily chaunced in my iourney, to reade the little Catechisme, compiled in Latin by that learned and godly Father *Canitius*: In perusing wherof I conceyued such pleasure, partlye for the absolute and playne order, and partly for the notable and holsome lessons therein conteined, that in translating it into our Englishe tongue, both the tediousnes whiche chaunced to me in trauayling, and my greefes which troubled me otherwise, were very well mitigated. After I was setled in *Paris*, and had accesse to my accustomed studies, a certayne freende of mine coming to visite me, sawe in my Chamber this said little booke, and reading somewhat of my translation, dealte with me about the imprinting thereof. Agaynst whom I replied, saying, That al pointes of Religion were alredy so excellently well handled by diuers of our countrey men, and that in the Englishe tongue, that this my labour shoulde seeme not onely superfluous, but also ridiculous, for that I shoulde, as the olde Prouerbe goeth, *Post Homerum Iliadas scribere*, that is, to take in hād a needeles work. Besides that, mens eares were so delicate nowe a days, & their stomachs so curious, that they woulde geue eare to nothing, except it were set out goodly in coloured termes, and should pleasantly and smothly passe by the eare, nor their

* Bibliographical details supplemented from a copy in the Gillow Library.

† The reference is pretty certainly to the risings which resulted in Parma's victory on 31 January 1578. The consequence was the departure of the English seminary from Douay to Rhemes on 23 March following. The date is important, as it helps to fix the date of the publication of the *Catechisme*.

quaisie stomacks disgest any thing which were not *Ingenio perfectum, & elaboratū industria*: as a certayne noble Oratour writeth of the Oratours of his time. With that my freende answered, that inasmuche as *Canitius* hath touched all matters concerning our saluation so aptly, and in so good an order, that nothing is superfluous, and yet sufficiently and to the full: for that euery sentence is either taken out of holy scripture, or els selected out of the holy and auncient Fathers: In so much also, that the passing good order and methode therof is so liked of diuers, that the French mē, Italians, Spaniards, & Dutch men, haue translated this sayd Booke: it would be a shame for Englishe men, not to wishe as muche good to their Countrey as any of these doo to theirs. And where as you say further (sayde he) that onely coloured and painted words please now a dayes: the trueth is (as you are not ignoraunt) that Religion and the worde of God ought not to be set out in plausible termes, that may delight and tickle the eares, but in all simplicitie and truth. These and the lyke reasons of my freende, tooke suche force with me, as freendly talke ought to be accounted of him who wyshed wel to his freende, & hurte to none. After this I considered better hereupon with my selfe, and when I saw we had good plentie of Latin bookes, that handled al poyntes of Religion very wel: and yet there was suche scarsitie of Englishe bookes, that we had none except M. Vauces Catechisme, that breefly comprised the principal partes of our Christian and Catholike fayth. Because M. Vauces booke was somewhat rare, and of some weldisposed persons not thought so fitte for the capacitie of little ones and younglings, who are to be trained vp after the playnest and readyest waye: I thought this Pamphlet would not be vnfit for them both, for that the author thereof vseth such perspicuitie, that his preceptes may wel be vnderstanded of any, and for that all the partes of the whole booke resting on fiue pointes, may wel be comprehended of a meane memorie, & also for that things be so handled therein, that whosoeuer is perfect in this little Treatise, he shal be sufficiently instructed in all matters of Christianity: I was also much animated to this my translation, because it may be a good stay to tender & young witts, who are (more is the pitie) caried a wrong and daungerous way, by diuers wicked and pestiferous books, which in these lamentable times flowe al the world ouer.'

The probable date of the *Catechisme* may be fixed by reference to the following:

(1) Presumably the writer left Flanders during the general exodus of the English, referred to above, i.e. in or about January 1578 (N.S.).

(2) The Address to the Reader is dated 17 February, a date

which, of course, cannot be earlier than 17 February 1578, if the presumption of (1) is correct.
(3) The book is listed in Fulke's catalogue of 'Popish Bookes', which occurs in his *D. Heskins, D. Sanders, and M. Rastel, accounted (among their faction) three pillers and Archpatriarches of the Popish Synagogue* (ent. *Sta. Reg.* 2 April 1579).*
The date of publication, then, is sometime after 17 February 1578, and certainly not later than 2 April 1579.

JENEY, THOMAS
fl. 1565–1583

68. Maister Randolphes Phantasey. 1565.

Edited by Dr. James Cranstoun in *Satirical Poems of the Time of the Reformation* (Edinburgh, 1891) for the Scottish Text Society, from a manuscript in the State Paper Office dated 31 December 1565 (Scottish Series, Vol. XI, No. 108).† From this edition I get the following particulars: (1) 'The Epistle dedicatorie To the right wurshipfull Mr Thomas Randolphe, esquyre Resident for the Quenes Maties affaires in Scotlande': ends, 'Thus I take my leave at my Chambre in Edenbrughe the last of Decembre 1565. – Yo^r w.bounden servante Thomas Jenye'. (2) 'To the reader' (seven lines of English verse). (3) 'Maister Randolphe Phantasey: a breffe calgulacion of the procedinges in Scotlande from the first of Julie to the Last of Decembre' (in three parts: (a) ll.1–320: alternate twelves and fourteens rimed; (b) 'The Quenes Matie complante of a mysordered comon weale' – ll.321–733: stanzas of somewhat irregular five foot iambics, with rime scheme ababbc; (c) 'Finis' – ll.734–811: riming couplets as in (a). The poem is signed 'Jenye'.

69. A discours of the present troobles in Fraunce, and miseries of this tyme, compyled by Peter Ronsard, gentilman of Vandome, and dedicated vnto the quene mother, translated in to english by Thomas Ieney, gentilman. Printed at Anduerpe, 1568.

BRITWELL.

4°. A²+B–D in fours+A⁴.

This was one of the books found in John Stow's study when it was searched in 1568.‡ It is a translation of *Discours des Misères de ce Temps. À la Royne mère du Roy. Par P. de Ronsard Vandômois* (Paris, 1563), and according to Dr. James Cranstoun § is 'dedicated to Sir Henry Norries, Knight, L. Ambassadour resident

* See Appendix V.
† MS. is endorsed '1565. Mr Randolphes phantasy of the procedings in Scotland.'
‡ Strype, *Life and Acts of Grindal* (1821), pp. 516–17. § op. cit., Introd.

in Fraunce'. The entry in the *Sales Catalogue of books from Britwell Court* (No. 578), from which the bibliographical details are taken, states that the first part of the book is in English and the second in Latin verse, and refers to the *Elegia Danielis Albimontii Angli, de perturbata Christiani Orbis Republica, Anno 1568* at the end. The Britwell copy, which was probably unique, was bought by Dr. Rosenbach, and is now in the Carl H. Pforzheimer Library.

KENNEDY, QUINTIN, ABBOT
1520–1564*

70. Letter from the Abbot of Crossraguell to James Archbishop of Glasgow; together with the correspondence of the Abbot and John Willock. M.D.LIX.†

These letters occupy pp. 265–77 of the *Miscellany of the Wodrow Society* and relate to a proposed disputation between the Abbot and John Willock. The disputation never came off. Laing states that they serve 'not only to illustrate the manner in which literary disputes were then conducted, but to throw some light on the personal character of the intended disputants'.‡

71. An Oration by Mr. Quintine Kennedy, Commendator of Crossraguell. 1561.

Printed in the Bannatyne Club edition of the *Works of John Knox* (pp. 157–65).§ The *Oration* consists of:

(1) 'Ane Epistol to the Nobilite and Principalis of the Congregatione'; and

(2) 'Ane Oratioune in favouris of all thais of the Congregatione, exhortand thaim to aspy how wonderfullie thai ar abusit be thair dissaitfull prechouris; set furth be Master Quintine Kennedy, Commendatour of Corsraguell, the yeir of Gode 1561'.

* The Abbot of Crossraguell's works, together with a Life, have been printed in (a) *The Miscellany of the Wodrow Society: containing tracts and original letters . . . Selected and edited by David Laing, Esq. Volume first. Edinburgh* (1844); and (b) *The Works of John Knox: collected and edited by David Laing. Volume Sixth. Edinburgh: Printed for the Bannatyne Club* (1864). Previous to the first work described above the Abbot had published *Ane compendius Tractiue conforme to the Scripturis of almychtie God, ressoun, and authoritie, declaring the nerrest, and onlie way, to establische the conscience of ane christiane man, in all materis* (*quhilks ar in debate*) *concernyng faith and religioun* (1558). [Edinburgh. John Scot.]

† First printed by Bishop Robert Keith in his *History of the Affairs of Church and State in Scotland* (1734). Appendix, pp. 193–8. It is followed at p. 199 by a long reference to Kennedy's *Ane compendius Tractiue.*

‡ op. cit.

§ First printed by Sir A. Boswell in his edition of *Heir followeth the coppie of the ressoning which was betuix the Abbote of Crosraguell and Iohn Knox . . . concerning the masse* (Edinburgh, 1812).

It is chiefly intended to controvert John Knox's syllogism 'in his Sermon aganis the Mess':* 'All worschipping, honoring, or service inventit be the brayne of manne in the religion of God, without his owne expres commandement, is ydolatrie: the Mess is inventit be the brayne of manne, without ony commandement of God: tharfor it is ydolatrie.'

Thus did the controversy between the Abbot and Knox originate.

72. Ane compendious Ressonyng be the quhilk is maid manifest, treulie and propirlie, conforme to the Scripturis of Almychtie God (bayth New Testament and Auld) the Mess to be institute be Jesu Christ oure Salveour in the Latter Supper, incontrar the ralling ressonyng of all sic, as dois affirme the Mess to be inventit be the brayne of man. Set furt by Maister Quintyne Kennedy, Commendator of the Abbay of Corsraguell, in the yeir of God ane thousand fyve hundreth threscoir ane yeiris.

Printed (a small part only) in the Bannatyne Club edition of the *Works of John Knox* (pp. 166–8). It consists of:

(1) 'To the Redar in generale, and in speciall to Knox, Willock, Wynrame, Gudeman, Dowglas, Hereot, Spottiswod, Athenis, and all the laif of the famous Precheouris to the Congregatioun'; and

(2) 'Ane familiare Ressonying of the Misterie of the Sacrifice off the Mess, betuix tua brethir, Maister Quintyne Kennedy, Commendatour of Corsraguell, and James Kennedy of Uchtwallure.'

A note states that the MS. fills '46 pages exclusive of the title, dedication and table of contents'. It seems to have been this unpublished work which drew forth George Hay's *The Confutation of the Abbote of Crosraguels Masse*. Edinburgh, 1563.†

73. Heir followeth the coppie of the ressoning which was betuix the Abbote of Crosraguell and Iohn Knox, in Mayboill concerning the masse, in the yeare of God, a thousand fiue hun-

* Delivered before Cuthbert Tunstall, Bishop of Durham, in April 1550. See *Works*, as above, p. 155.

† The printer of this book, Robert Lekpreuik, appears to have had no Greek type. Spaces were therefore left and the Greek was written in by hand. He apologizes to the reader for this and says, 'I haue vsed the help of a moste excellẽt young mã, wel exercised in the tongue, yit the trauel being wearisome . . . I was driuen, and content to borrow the laboure of some Scollers, whome I iudged to be moste expert. Whom vnto it muste be imputed, if ether faut shalbe in lacking of a letter, or otherwayes in accent, and other such accidents'. – 'The Prenter to the Reader'.

dreth thre scoir and two yeares . . . Imprinted at Edinburgh by Robert Lekpreuik, and are to be solde at his hous, at the nether bow. Cum priuilegio. 1563.

Occupies pp. 169–220 of the Bannatyne Club edition of Knox's *Works* referred to above.* Laing states that the dispute lasted three days, and, to counteract the false reports that were circulated, Knox prepared and published this work. It consists of:

(1) Knox's Prologue;

(2) Preliminary correspondence concerning the disputation;

(3) Agreement as to procedure;

(4) Text – the arguments of both sides being set out in full.

KIRBIE, LUKE

1548–1582

(see entry 13)

LANGDALE, ALBAN, D.D.

fl. 1580

Begin:

74. 'And for so muche as yt semethe that this question [sc. of attendance at the Protestant Service] was neuer thus moved, nor the case in experience in any age before this tyme, therfore this is nowe made a question, argumentes are sett dowen for Iudgment, And these be the reasons to prove that in the case sett dowene ys nether. P. nor mortale synn.'

[endorsed] 'a perswasiō d̄d̄ [delivered?] to Mr Sheldō 1580'.

MS. S.P.O. Dom. Eliz. Vol. 144, No. 69.

Paper. Late 16th century. Folio. Pp. 11, having 43 to 50 lines to a page.

For the reasons for attributing this pamphlet to Dr. Alban Langdale, see the notes on Persons' *Briefe Discours* (entry 92). There can be little doubt that it was intended as a reply to Persons, as indeed Persons himself supposed.

* See a previous note in reference to Sir Alexander Boswell's reprint of this work.

LESLIE, JOHN, BISHOP OF ROSS
1527–1596*

75. [ornament] A defence of the / honour of the right highe, / mightye and noble Princesse Marie Quene / of Scotlande and dowager of France, / with a declaration aswell of her right, / title & intereste to the sŭccession / of the crowne of Englande, as / that the regimente of wo- / men ys conformable / to the lawe of God / and na- / ture. / [ornaments] / Imprinted at London in Flete strete, at the / signe of Iustice Royall against the / Blacke bell, by Eusebius Dicaeo- / phile. Anno Dom. / 1569.

[colophon on t2^{v}] Imprinted at London in Flete strete at the / signe of Iustice Royal, againste the Blacke / bell, by Eusebius Dicaeophile, anno D.1569. / and are to be solde in Paules churche / yearde, at the signes of Tyme & Truthe, / by the Brasen Serpēt, in the shoppes / of Ptolomé and Nicephore Ly- / costhenes brethren / Germanes. / [ornament]

Sir R.L.H.

8°. $\dagger^{6}$+a–s in eights+t^{2}. Fol. 1[a1]–148 (rather 146, the numbers 73 and 74 being omitted) [t2]. Cw. Mg. No Rt. (1) Title [†1]. (2) Blank [†1^{v}]. (3) 'The Authour to the Gentle Reader' [†2–6]. (4) 'The printer to the reader' [†6^{v}]. (5) 'A Defence of the Honeur of the ryght hyghe, ryght myghtye and noble Princesse Marie Quene of Scotlande, and Dowagere of France. The fyrst Booke' [a1–g2]. (6) 'The Seconde Booke towchinge the right title and interest of the foresaide Ladie Marie Quene of Scotlande, to the Succession of the crowne of England' [g2^{v}–p5]. (7) 'The Thyrde Booke, where in ys declared that the regimente of whomen ys conformable to the lawe of God and nature' [p5^{v}–t2]. (8) Colophon [t2^{v}]. (No privilegium or imprimatur.)

Although Bishop Leslie's name appears neither in this nor in the second edition (entry 77) of this very rare book, there is abundant evidence to prove his authorship. Queen Elizabeth herself seems to have countenanced the publication, the rigorous suppression of copies being due to 'some factious persons, enemies to the said title'. James Anderson, in his editorial preface to his reprint of the second edition, gives a careful history

* The earliest bibliography of Leslie's works is that of James Maitland in his *Apologie for Maitland of Lethington*, written about 1610 and edited by Andrew Lang for the Scottish History Society, Vol. XLIV. Edinburgh, 1904. The bibliography is to be found in the second of the two volumes which comprise Vol. XLIV, at pp. 158 et seq. Maitland is a credible witness in respect of Leslie's writings. It has not been thought necessary to refer to him in the following account of Leslie's works, except where special occasion demanded.

of the origin of the Defence.* In respect of Leslie's complaint to Queen Elizabeth of books and pamphlets written against Mary he refers especially to three: 'one in 1560, by *John Hales* Clerk of the Hanaper or Hamper, commonly called Club-foot, assisted as it was said by Chancellor *Bacon*, and imprisoned for publishing of it. But whether ever in print till lately in 1713, in the Appendix to the Book intitled, *The Hereditary Right of the Crown of* England *asserted*, I can't be positive . . . also a small Book very scarce, printed in 1565, immediately after her Marriage with *Darnley*: entitled *Allegations against the surmised Title of* Mary *Queen of* Scotts, *and the Favourers of the same*. Wherein are also exceptions against the Title of *Darnley's* Mother . . . and particularly of an Invective by one *Sampson* a Preacher, the supposed Author of the *Discourse touching the pretended Match betweene the Duke of* Norfolke *and the Quene of* Scottis'. 'The Bishop', Anderson goes on to say, 'also particularly complained of the foresaid Allegations against his Mistress's Title to the Crown of *England*, asking leave of Q. *Elizabeth* to have Answers made thereto, which Queen *Elizabeth* was content with, providing the same should not be published in print, until the first Copy should be presented unto her.' Let us proceed with Leslie's own account of what followed.† He writes: 'This libertie beinge graunted me by the Q. I travelled with some that was best learned and moste expert, as well in the civil lawe as in the common lawe of the Realme of *England*, to whome I delivered all treaties or pamphletts, which had bin sett forth againste the Q. my Mistres title in anie times paste, which I had recovered divers waies by diligent meanes, soe that they were all come to my hands, togither with some other breife treaties and collectiouns drawne for defence of the Q. my Sovereignes title, specially by one of the best learned judgs that was in *England*, called Justice *Browne*, and by another as well learned and experimented, called Mr. Carrell, which altogither theise learned men did well consider, and after good advisement and deliberatioun sett forth a treatie for defence of the

* *Collections Relating to the History of Mary Queen of Scotland. In four Volumes.* By James Anderson. Edinburgh, 1727. The preface occurs in Vol. I, and is followed by the reprint. John Scott in his *A Bibliography of Works relating to Mary Queen of Scots. 1544–1700* (Edinburgh Bibliographical Society (1896), Vol. II) – an invaluable work for the student of these books – follows Anderson in respect of the details given above. So, too, T. F. Henderson in *D.N.B.* Scott reproduces the title-page of Leslie's book in his appendix of Facsimiles.

† *A Discourse, conteyninge A perfect Accompt given to the moste vertuous and excellent Princesse, Marie Queene of Scots, And her Nobility, By John Lesley Bishop of Rosse, Ambassador for Her Highnes toward the Queene of England: Of his whole Charge and Proceedings during the Time of his Ambassage, from his Entres in England in September 1568. to the 26th of March 1572.* Printed in Anderson, *Collections*, Vol. III. The Author's Epistle tells us it was 'written in the prison called the Bloudy-towre, within the towre of London, the 26 of March 1572'. The above excerpt is from Anderson, pp. 66–8.

Q. my Mistres title, provinge it to be the first and onely title that should succeed to the crowne of *England*, and that she is just and right heire apparant to the Realme of *England*, failinge of Q. *Elizabeth* nowe presentlie regnant, and the heires of her bodye lawfullie to be begotten . . .

'This treatie was afterward printed and came to the Q and Councells hands; although I had presented a perfect copie therof longe before to the Q. at which time the Councell said unto me it was very learnedly collected and sett forth, soe that all the lawyers in *England* could say noe further in that matter, nor better to that effect, then was contayned in that treatie . . .

'And yet notwithstandinge of the Q. licence given to me to that effect, I sustayned divers wayes trouble and injuries, by imprisonment of my selfe, my servants and others, upon the occasioun of the publyshinge therof, albeit some other causes alsoe was surmised.'*

It is probable that Dr. Good, Leslie's physician and intimate acquaintance, assisted him in the Englishing of his work. Anderson writes: 'It appears that the Bishop left a Copy of the Defence of her Honour with Dr. Good, that he might turn into English any Scottish Words in it, which was returned to the Bishop corrected with some Notes by the Queen to be added thereto'.†

The printer of this first edition of the *Defence* was John Fogny of Rhemes: comparison with the known works of that printer puts this beyond doubt. Since it was probably Fogny's first attempt at printing an English book, the following words of 'the printer to the reader' have a particular interest: 'I require ād hartelie praye the (good and louinge reader) that yf in this praesent Boke thou finde any alligation not dewly coted, or a poinct out of place, a lettre lackīg, or other wise altered: as, n, for, u, and suche littill light faultes against orthographiae, thov wilt neither impute the same to the authour of this worthie worke, nor yet captiouslye controule the errour: but rather of thy humanitie and gentilnes, amende that which is amisse with thy penne. For if thou diddist knowe with what difficulté the imprinting herof was atchiued, thou woldest rather curtouslye of frendlye faueur pardon many greate faultes, than curiouslye withe rigorouse censure to condemne one litl.'

* Camden's account of the matter – and he seems to have drawn upon Leslie's *Discourse* for his facts – is that Elizabeth determined to prohibit the publishing of books against Mary because they were written 'with such boldnesse of spirit', and that therefore she 'suffered by way of connivence the Bishop of Rosse to answer them'. He refers to the second edition by 'Morgan Philips' (*Annals*, third edition (1635), p. 113).

† op. cit., Vol. I. 'Editor's Preface to the Defence of Q. Mary's Honour.' He cites Cotton MS. Cal. 7. C.4, Fol. 249, etc., and C.5, Fol. 6, etc.

76. The Historie of Scotland fra the death of King James the First in the yeir of God M.CCCC.XXXVI. to the yeir M.D.LXI. and sae of the four late Kingis called James Steuartis, and of Quene Marie now Quene of Scotland; Newly collected be Johne Leslye Bischop of Rosse, during the time of his remaning as Ambassadour for the Quene his soverane in Ingland, M.D.LXX.

This History of Scotland was written in the Scottish language during the years 1568–70, when Leslie was resident in England, for Queen Mary and was presented to her in 1571. It remained unpublished until 1830, when it was edited for the Bannatyne Club by T. Thomson.* The title above is quoted from that edition. In the 'Authours Epistle to the Quene' Leslie refers to how he came to write the History: how in 1568 he was in restraint at Burton-upon-Trent and occupied his leisure in reading history and in compiling that part of Scottish history with which this work deals; and again how, when he was in 1569 sequestrate in the Bishop of London's house in London, he revised what he had collected at Burton. The History, which begins with James II and ends with Queen Mary, is divided into five parts corresponding to the lives of the five Scottish sovereigns with which it deals. Leslie, later, incorporated this work in his larger Latin History which was printed in Rome in 1578 under the following title: *De Origine, Moribus, et Rebus Gestis Scotorum libri decem: e quibus septem veterum Scotorum res in primis memorabiles contractius, reliqui vero tres posteriorum Regum ad nostra tempora historiam, quae hucusque desiderabatur, fusius explicant. Accessit noua et accurata Regionum et Insularum Scotiae, cum vera eiusdem tabula topographica, Descriptio. Authore Ioanne Leslaeo, Scoto, Episcopo Rossensi. Romae, in aedibus populi Romani, 1578.*†

With regard to this Latin version, the preliminary notice in

* Under the title *The History of Scotland, from the death of King James I in the year M.CCCC.XXXVI, to the year M.D.LXI. By John Lesley, Bishop of Ross. Printed at Edinburgh: M.DCCC.XXX.* A preliminary notice in this publication deals with the manuscript history of Leslie's work.

† Maitland's account of this publication is as follows: 'He [Leslie] leving at Rome thrie zeirs togither did publiss & set furthe in print in the Latin toong anno 1578 . . . his historie or Chronicle of Scotland fra the beginning to his auin tyme or rather did withe help of vthers put in forme & set togither that historie pairtlie made or collectit be Mr Ninian Winzet Abot of the Scots Abay in Regensburg, pairtlie be Mr Alexander Andersone Principal of the Colledge in Aberdein & pairtlie be Mr James Scheme Chanon & [omission] of the Cathedral Kirk of Tournay, eiking at the end thairof onlie some of his auin informations' (op. cit., p. 164). Leslie, however, was likely to suffer detraction at Maitland's hands, and his indebtedness to these others may be somewhat exaggerated.

T. F. Henderson, in his article on Leslie in the *D.N.B.*, refers to a Latin manuscript in the archives of the Vatican continuing Leslie's History down to 1571. There is an English translation of this in W. Forbes-Leith's *Narrative of Scottish Catholics* (1885), at pp. 84–126.

the Bannatyne Club edition of the History states that it shows that the alterations made by Leslie on his own original sketch do not consist merely in correction and enlargement, 'but that in numerous instances he has been induced to suppress or generalize those more minute details and domestic occurrences which he may have found less susceptible of that classic attire in which he was naturally ambitious of exhibiting his historical work' (p. vi). These words are important as throwing light upon Leslie's methods of revision both here and elsewhere.

A Scottish translation of the Latin version was made by Fr. James Dalrymple, a religious of the Scottish cloister of Regensburg, in 1596. His manuscript has been edited by Fr. E. G. Cody, O.S.B., for the Scottish Text Society (Edinburgh, 1888. 2 vols.).

77. A Treatise / concerning / the Defence of the / Honour of the Right / High, Mightie and Noble Prin- / cesse, Marie Queene of Scotland, and Douager of / France, with a Declaration, as wel of her / Right, Title and Interest to the Suc- / cession of the Croune of Eng- / land: as that the Re- / giment of / women is conformable to the / lawe of God and / Nature. / Made by Morgan Philippes, Bachelar / of Diuinitie, An. 1570. / [ornament] / Leodii. / Apud Gualterum Morberium. / 1571.

8°. π^1+❧2–8+❧❧^{8}+A2–8+B–F in eights+G^3+π^1+a2–8+b–h in eights+i^4+Aa2–8+Bb–Dd in eights. Fol. 1[A2]–50[G3]; 2[a2]–67 (correctly 68: error at fol. 40)[i4]; 1[Aa2]–30[Dd7]. Cw. Mg. Rts – (1) The first Booke / A Defense of her Honour; (2) The second Booke / touching the succession; (3) The third Booke / For the Regiment of women. (1) Title [π]. (2) Blank [π^v]. (3) 'To the Reader' [❧2–❧❧8^v]. (4) Text of Book I [A2–G3^v].* (5) New title as follows: A Treatise / touching the Right, / Title, and Interest of / the mightie and noble Prin- / cesse Marie, Queene of / Scotland, to the succession / of the Croune of / England. / Made by Morgan Philippes, Bachelar of Di- / uinitie, assisted vvith the aduise of Anto- / nie Broune Knight, one of the Iu- / stices of the Common Place. / An. 1567. / [ornament] / Leodii. / Apud Gualterum Morberium. / 1571. [π] (6) Blank [π^v]. (7) Text of Book II [a2–i4]. (8) Imprimatur: Louvain. 6 March 1571 [i4^v]. (9) Text of Book III [Aa2–Dd7^v]. (10) Imprimatur: Louvain. 6 March 1571 [Dd7^v]. (11) 'Errata Libri secundi.' 'Errata Libri tertij' [Dd8]. (12) Ornament [Dd8^v].†

This Defence of Mary Stuart differs from the previous edition of 1569 (entry 75) in that – to quote the words of John Scott – 'the address to the reader has been rewritten and much extended. Passages have been suppressed which, in the first edition, mentioned Queen Elizabeth with respect, and placed

* The text-titles of the three books differ in no important detail from those of the first edition.

† The second imprimatur refers to all three books of the treatise. 'Hos tres libros . . . iudicaui merito edendos esse.'

Queen Mary's rights to the English throne as secondary to those of Queen Elizabeth, or any issue which might spring from her. The second edition artfully reverses the position, and treats Queen Mary as the only true heir to the throne of England. It consequently gave greater offence to the English Court than the prior edition, and was strenuously suppressed'.* 'Some copies', the writer goes on to say, 'immediately on their arrival, were seized at Dover, to which place they had been brought by Charles Bailley, one of Queen Mary's servants.'†

Leslie translated the second and third books of his treatise into Latin, with various additions and amendments (thus following his usual practice), under the following titles:

De Titulo et Iure Serenissimae Principis Mariae Scotorum Reginae, quo Regni Angliae successionem sibi iuste vendicat, Libellus: Simul & Regum Angliae a Gulielmo Duce Normandiae, qui Conquestor dictus est, genealogiam & successionis seriem in tabula descriptam: Competitorum quoque a Lancastrensi & Eboracensi familijs descendentium historiam summatim complectens. Opera Io. Leslaei Episcopi Rossensis Scoti, dum pro eadem Serenissima Principe iampridem in Anglia Oratorem ageret, patrio primum, nunc vero Latino sermone in lucem editus. Accessit ad Anglos & Scotos, vt qui temporis bellorumque iniuria iamdiu distracti fuerunt, tandem aliquando animis consentiant, & perpetua amicitia in vnum coalescant, Paraenesis. Post varias caedes, vnita Britannia tandem Florebit, pace & relligione pia. Rhemis, Excudebat Ioannes Fognaeus, sub Leone. 1580. Cum Priuilegio.

(It is to be noted that Leslie's name appears here on the title, and so in all subsequent editions. Also the genealogical table appears in all editions from this date.)

De Illustrium Foeminarum in Repub. administranda, ac ferendis legibus authoritate, Libellus, Opera Io. Leslaei Episcopi Rossensis Scoti, dum pro Serenissima Principe Maria Scotorum Regina iam pridem in Anglia Legatum ageret, patrio primum, nunc vero Latino sermone in lucem editus. Rhemis, Excudebat Ioannes Fognaeus, sub Leone. 1580. Cum Priuilegio.‡

* op. cit., p. 24. Scott's words are a free quotation from Anderson's 'Preface to the Defence of Q. Mary's Honour'. (*Collections*, Vol. I.) It is, of course, significant that the Bull against Elizabeth had been promulgated in the interval between the two publications. There are a number of smaller changes besides, corrected errors, etc., and the punctuation of the later edition is distinctly better than that of 1569.

† loc. cit. Leslie himself refers to the incident in his *Treatise of Treasons* (entry 78), where he writes: 'Neede they to be named . . . that betraied and diuers waies afflicted Charles Baily a straunger, without colour of cause, other then for seking to publish a Pamphlet in the Defense of their Mistresses honour & title, that impeached not your Q. in any iote?' [E4v]. For an account of Bailley or Baillie, see article in *D.N.B.*

‡ These two Latin editions have been reprinted in Jebb's 'Collections', Vol. I, pp. 37–116 and 117–47.

Strype, *Annals* (1824), Vol. II. pt. 1, p. 78, refers to the former of these two Latin volumes as having been answered by Glover, Somerset herald, about 1580. Glover's book, however, was never published.

It is characteristic of the man that in 1584 he retranslated the Latin version, *De Titulo et Iure*, into English (see entry 80). Here the name of James is first included in the title.* A French translation followed in 1587 under the title *Du Droict et Tiltre de la Serenissime Princesse Marie Royne d'Escosse, & de tres-illustre prince Iaques VI. Roy d'Escosse son fils, à la succession du Royaume d'Angleterre . . . par R. P. en Dieu M. Iean de Lesselie Euesque de Rosse, Escossois . . . nouuellement mis en Francois par le mesme Autheur. A Rouen, De l'Imprimerie de George l'Oyselet.* There was also a Spanish translation of this same date – *Declaration del Titulo y derecho que la Serenissima Princese Doña Maria Reyna de Escoçia, tiene a la Succession del Ingalaterra . . . Compuesto por el Reuerendissimo Señor Don Iohan Lesleo Obispo de Rossa Escoçes . . . traduzido de yngles en latin y de latin en Español por el mismo author . . .*

The second book of the original second edition seems to have been issued also as a separate publication.

The *Treatise* was published at Louvain by John Fowler. The initials and an unusual tailpiece (at sig. G3v) found only in books printed by Velpen, Fowler's printer at Louvain, point conclusively to this. The two title-pages by Morberius are cancels.†

78. A Treatise / of Treasons / against Q.Elizabeth, / and the Croune of England, / diuided into two Partes: / whereof, / The first Parte answereth certaine / Treasons pretended, that neuer were / intended: / And the second, discouereth greater / Treasons committed, that are by few / perceiued: as more largely appeareth in / the Page folowing. / [ornament] / Imprinted in the Moneth / of Ianuarie, and in the Yeare / of our Lord. / [rule] / M.D.LXXII. [Louvain. John Fowler.]

8°. B.L. ā+ē+ī+A–X in eights+Y6. Fol. 1[A1]–174[Y6]. Cw. Mg. Rt – Treasons against Q.E. and / the Crowne of England. (1) Title [ā1]. (2) 'The Argument of this Treatise diuided into two Partes' [ā1v]. (3) 'The Preface to the English Reader' [ā2–ī6v]. (4) 'Allusio ad presentem Angliae conditionem, ex Aeneid. Lib.2' [ī7]. (5) Blank [ī7v–ī8]. (6) Ornament [ī8v]. (7) Text in two parts [A1–Y6]. (8) 'Faultes escaped in the Printing' [Y6v]. (No privilegium or imprimatur.)

The first part of this treatise is a reply to the tract *Salutem in Christo* (by R. G.),‡ which deals with the proposed marriage

* James's name had been already coupled with that of the Queen in this Latin version; not in the title, however, but in the Address to the Queen.

† We need have no doubt that they *are* by Walter Morbers. The second one carries an ornament which occurs in *Canones et Decreta Sacrosancti Oecumenici, et Generalis Concilii Tridentini* . . . printed by Morbers at Liége in 1570.

‡ Leslie understood these initials to refer to Richard Grafton, the printer and publisher. He believed, however, that Cecil and/or Bacon had inspired the tract, which partly accounts for the *quid pro quo* he delivers in Part II. See the *Treatise* at sigs. A4 and L4.

of Queen Mary to the Duke of Norfolk and with the Duke's committal to the Tower. The second part strongly attacks Cecil and Bacon, the former of whom is designated as Synon. They are accused of abusing Queen Elizabeth and her people, by not only desiring to destroy Queen Mary and her son, but Queen Elizabeth herself, so as to settle the Suffolk family on the throne.*

Strype, in referring to this treatise, writes under the year 1573: 'While the Court was here at Canterbury, the Lord Treasurer, in the midst of his feasting, met with sour sauce with it. It was a most venomous book, wrote by some Papist against him and the Lord Keeper: which, yet, was not the first of many that he had felt the malice of. But it grieved much this good man, and made him almost weary of his life, after his painful service and honest heart to the realm and to the Queen, to be so continually slandered and back-bitten. This book he sends to the Archbishop from one of the Prebends' lodgings to peruse, with a letter which ran to this tenor:

"*May it please your Grace*,

You shall see how dangerously I serve in this state, and how my Lord Keeper also, in my respect, is with me beaten with a viperous generation of traitorous Papists: and I fear of some domestic hidden scorpion. If God and our consciences were not our defence and consolation against these pestilential darts, we might well be weary of our lives. I pray your Grace read the book, or so much as you list, as soon as you may; and then return it surely to me; so as also I may know your opinion thereof. When your Grace hath done with this, I have also a second smaller, appointed to follow this;† as though we were not killed with the first; and therefore a new assault is given. But I will rest myself upon the Psalmist's verse, *Expecto* [sic] *Dominum, viriliter age, et confortetur cor tuum, et sustine Dominum.* From my lodgings at Mr. Person's, 11. Sept. 1573.

Your Grace's at commandment,

W. Burghley" '.‡

The book made such a stir that it called forth, in defence of Burghley and Bacon, the Proclamation of 28 September 1573 prohibiting all Catholic 'bookes and libelles'. The point is made in the following extract: 'they [the Catholics] are fallen into another crooked course of malitious persecutyng the happy estate of this countrey and gouernment, by choosyng out of

* cp. Scott, *Bibliography of Works relating to Mary Queen of Scots*, p. 28. See also entry 143.

† Given at entry 143.

‡ *Life and Acts of Parker* (1821), Vol. II, pp. 297–9; cp. also *Annals* (1824), Vol. II, pt. 1, pp. 264–5. For Archbishop Grindal's letter to Lord Burghley (5 October 1573) *apropos*, see *Calendar of State Papers*, Dom. Eliz. (S.P.O.), Vol. 92, No. 33.

certayne shamelesse, spiteful, and furious braynes, hauing a trade in pennyng of infamous libelles, not only in the Englishe, but also in Latine, and other strange languages.

'And by these meanes they haue lately caused certayne seditious bookes and libelles to be compiled . . . and yet to abuse such as are strangers to the state, they haue glosed some of theyr late libelled bookes with argumentes of discoueries of treasons, intended, as they do craftily alleage, by some special persons beyng counsaylers, against her Maiestie . . . bendyng theyr mallice moste specially agaynst two, who be certaynely knowen to haue alwayes ben moste studiously and faythfully careful of her Maiesties prosperous estate.'*

The *Treatise of Treasons* is described in the British Museum Catalogue as an English version of *L'Innocence de la Tresillustre, tres-chaste, et debonnaire Princesse, Madame Marie Royne d'Escosse* (1572), by F. de Belleforest. This is to put the cart before the horse. From a consideration of the dates it will be evident that the *Treatise* came first. It was printed, according to the title, in January 1572. The *L'Innocence* must have been later than this, since the first part is a reply to the French translation of George Buchanan's *Detectio*, viz. *Histoire de Marie Royne d'Escosse*, which itself bears the date 'le 13. de Feurier, 1572', and which is referred to in the text of the *L'Innocence* as 'imprimé du 17. Feburier 1572. enuoyé secrettement, & à cachette exposé par la France'.†

The connexion between the two works, the *Treatise* and the *L'Innocence*, is carefully set out by Scott. He points out that the Introduction of the latter is a reproduction of the second part of the *Treatise of Treasons* and that the third part is the reply to the tract *Salutem in Christo*, translated from the same work. He also points out that the first part (the reply to Buchanan's *Detectio*) could not have been produced by a Frenchman, 'at least not without instruction from some person having an intimate knowledge of the details of recent events in Scotland'. If, then, Belleforest 'had any part in its production, it was only as editor and translator'.‡

* Grenville Proclamations (Brit. Mus.), p. 151. Strype gives the Proclamation in his *Life and Acts of Parker* (1821), Vol. II, at pp. 316–20. Also reprinted by Arber, *Transcript of the Registers of the Company of Stationers of London* (1875), p. 215.

† 'Aduertissement au Lecteur', sig. a3v.

‡ op. cit., p. 29. Scott suggests that Belleforest's name has been connected with this work probably on the authority of Le Long (*Bibliotheque Historique de la France*. Paris, 1769, Vol. II, p. 651), who says: 'François de Belleforest est l'Auteur de cette Apologie', without giving any authority for his statement. It would seem more likely that Leslie himself was the translator. James Maitland (op. cit., pp. 158 and 163) gives the work to Leslie, and it is in keeping with what we know of Leslie that he should have undertaken the translation himself. All the known editions of the book, be it remarked, came from the press of John Fogny, whence issued the first edition of Leslie's *Defence of the Honour of Marie Queene of Scotland*. It was supposed by Strype, on the authority of Bishop Aylmer (Letter from Aylmer to

There are good grounds for attributing the *Treatise of Treasons* to John Leslie. We have already seen that Maitland assigns the French translation to him and that this in itself would point to his authorship of the English version. Internal evidence points to the same conclusion. Perhaps it will be enough to summarize very shortly what this evidence is:

(1) Leslie was a historian and the *Treatise* shows a considerable knowledge of history.

(2) There is a striking similarity in the progress of ideas at one point in the Prefaces of the *Treatise* and the *Defence of the Honour*.*

(3) The intimate knowledge of contemporary Scottish history and Scottish affairs, together with the allusions to the writer's part in 'intreating' the affairs of Queen Mary, points to the Queen's ambassador, Leslie.

(4) The several allusions to the Bishop of Ross by name in the text smack strongly of *self*-defence.†

(5) The tricks of style, notably the fondness for parenthesis and for repetition, are characteristic of Leslie.‡

The ornamental capitals, together with the general style of printing, point conclusively to Fowler as the publisher of this work.

79. [*Text-title.*] The Copie / of a Letter writen out / of Scotland, by an English Gen / tlemā of credit and worship ser / uing ther, vnto a frind and kins- / man of his, that desired to be in- / formed of the truth and circum / stances of the slaunderous and / infamous reportes made of the / Quene of Scotland, at

Lord Burghley, 30 December 1579 – Brit. Mus. Lansdowne MS. 28, f. 177, cited by T. Cooper, s.v. *Carter* in the *D.N.B.*), who had found a copy of the *L'Innocence* in the house of William Carter, the printer, in 1579, that Carter himself printed this book. (*Annals* (1824), Vol. II, pt. 2, p. 271; cf. also *Life and Acts of Aylmer* (1821), p. 30.) A bad guess.

* I am referring here to the *Treatise concerning the Defence of the Honour of Marie Queene of Scotland*, i.e. to the second edition of the *Defence*.

† And, if I may be allowed one quotation, surely Leslie is speaking in this passage: 'Finally, I speake without name vnto you now, bycause with name you may not now be spoken vnto: and I forbeare my name at this time, to the end I may by name speake againe an other time (*as if cause so require, I meane to do historically*) knowing by experience long syns lately and often proued: that if by name I shoulde encounter with this namelesse man, neither should I be permitted to speake, nor you suffered to heare me' [A7]. The italics are mine. Leslie's History was to be published in Rome in 1578.

‡ I note, for instance, that there are forty examples of parenthesis in the first thirty pages of the *Defence*, and that there are over sixty in the first thirty pages of the *Treatise*.

that time / restreined in maner as prisoner / in England, vpon pretense / to be culpable of / the same. [Louvain. John Fowler. 1572?]

CAMB.

12°. B.L. π¹+A–E in twelves+F⁵. Fol. 1[A1]–65 [F5]. Cw. Mg. No Rt. (1) Title [π]. (2) Text of Letter, consisting of introductory matter and 4 chapters [A–E5ᵛ]. (3) Text-title: 'An Exhor- / tation to / those Noblemen of / Scotland, that remaine yet main / teiners and defenders of the vn- / natural and dishonorable / practises against the / Queene' [E6–F5ᵛ].*

Maitland refers to this pamphlet as Leslie's though 'witheout, anie name of Author, printer, date or suprascript';† and again as having been 'writtin be him during his Residens in Ingland'.‡ We may take his word that Leslie was the author. The internal evidence supports this view strongly. That is to say, the argument against Mary's implication in the murder of Darnley, etc. (with which the *Letter* is concerned) is set forth in much the same way as it appears in the *Treatise concerning the Defence of the Honour of Marie Queene of Scotland* (1571).§

With regard to the date, if the *Letter* was written during Leslie's residence in England, as Maitland states, then we can fix it approximately between 1570, the date of Murray's death, mentioned in the *Letter*, and January 1574, when Leslie landed in France from England. ||

Type, initials, and general style of printing all point certainly to Fowler as the publisher of this *Letter*.

80. A Treatise tovvching the Right, Title, and Interest of the most excellent Princesse Marie, Queene of Scotland, And of the most noble king Iames, her Graces sonne, to the succession of the Croune of England. VVherein is conteined asvvell a Genealogie of the Competitors pretending title to the same Croune:

* This Exhortation is referred to in the Letter at sig. E5 as the author's.

† op. cit., p. 158. ‡ ibid., p. 163.

§ A single example will perhaps make clear what is intended by this. Writing of the murder of Darnley, the writer of the *Letter* suggests that Mary might have employed the ordinary course of law against him in respect of his dagger found sticking in the Secretary David's body after the murder (Cap. I). We read in the *Treatise concerning the Defence*: 'Who can nowe reasonably thinke, that where she by lawe and iustice might haue fully satisfied this her falsely surmised will and desire: that she would not take the opportunities in this sort offered . . . By the due and ordinary processe and course whereof he might iustly haue bene conuicted, condemned and executed, aswel for the murther committed vpon Dauid her Secretarie, in whose body his dagger was found stabbed', etc. [A6].

|| There is a reference in the *Letter* to the death of the young Earl of Arran. 'He fel byside him selfe, or rather starke mad, and so lyuing certaine yeares, at the last he died in plaine Lunacie, and in very miserable case' [E2]. And so he did. But this hardly affects our computation, as it happened nearly forty years later in 1609. Leslie seems to have been curiously misinformed.

as a resolution of their obiections. Compiled and published before in latin, and after in Englishe, by the right reuerend father in God, Iohn Lesley, Byshop of Rosse. VVith an exhortation to the English and Scottish nations, for vniting of them selues in a true league of Amitie. An 1584. All Britaine Yle (dissentions ouer past) In peace & faith, will growe to one at last.

M., I.

81. [within a border] A breefe Di- / rectory, and playne way / howe to say the Rosary / of our blessed Lady: / VVith Meditations for / such as are not exer- / cised therein. / Whereunto are adioy- / ned the prayers of S. / Bryget, with / others. / Bruges Flandrorum. / Excudebat Hu. Holost. / 1576.

16°. B.L. ¶^{4}+A–D in eights+E^4+A–B in eights+C^4. Not fol. Cw. No mg. Rt. varies. (1) Title [¶1]. (2) Blank [¶1^v]. (3) 'To his deare and weldisposed Sister, A.M. encrease of grace, with perseuerance in the fayth of Christe': ends, 'From the English Charter house in Bridges, the vigil of the Assumption of our Lady. 1576. Your brother I.M.' [¶2–4^v]. (4) Text of Directory in 3 parts: ends, 'Of your charitie pray for him that wrote this' [A1–D7^v]. (5) 'A breefe Treatise of the most greeuous paynes that our sauiour Iesus Christ suffred for vs wretched sinners: Taken out of Bonauenture vpon the Passion' [D8–E4^v]. (6) 'An exhortation to penance and pacience' (five lines of rimed verse) [E4^v]. (7) 'Fifteene Prayers righte good and vertuous, vsually called the. xv. Oos, and of diuers called S. Brigets prayers, because the holye and blessed Virgin vsed dayly to say them before the Image of the Crucifix, in S. Paules Church in Rome' [A1–B6^v]. (8) Prayers for various occasions [B7–C4^v].

The history of this publication is given in the Address (bibl. details (3) above) as follows: 'The talke which we had together (moste deare and welbeloued Sister) the day before I tooke my iourney to come into these countries, haue not bin, neither are of me forgotten, and amōg al other your request concerning the Rosary of our Lady. Which request want both of yeres and knowledge woulde not permit me to fulfill: but after I had bene here a whyle, I gat acquaintance of one, who for vertue and good life is accounted among the cheefe, to him vpon a time I declared what I had promised you, and likewise my vnability in performing it, beseching him for Gods cause to take a litle paynes in the matter, whom I founde as ready to satisfie my request, as I was to demaunde him. When it was by him finished, and I somewhat busied in copying the same to be sent vnto you, by chance came into my chamber my cosen and freende I. Noil, who perswaded me to leaue off writing, and promised to procure it to be Printed, for I haue (sayd he) a fit thing to be ioyned thervnto, which was deliuered me by a good Gentlewoman, with earnest request to haue it printed. Wherto I willingly cōsented, for in my selfe I perceiue the great discommoditie of ignorance, which causeth me to labour all that I may, to pleasure suche as are like vnto my selfe (I mean in ignorance) And seeing my Cosen hath caused it to be printed although it be not so exactly done, I confesse, as you would desire, yet accept it, I pray you, for the Auctor within three or foure dayes after he had deliuered mee the copie thereof, tooke his iourney into Italie, not thinking that I would publish it'.

The author of the *Directory* remains unknown. Father J. H. Pollen has suggested that the I. M. of the Address may be John Mitchell, a Carthusian of Bruges.*

The printer of this book is the same as that of *A Notable Discourse* (entry 2). Both works are printed in the same bold black letter, and both carry an unusual, rather poor, ornamental capital F. Since the words of the title of the *Directory*, 'excudebat Hu. Holost', can mean *only* that Holost was the printer, we must assume that the *Notable Discourse* was also printed by him. That is to say, John Bellaert was the publisher but not the printer of that work.

MARTIALL, JOHN

1534–1597

82. A Treatyse / of the Crosse ga- / thred out of the / Scriptures, Councelles, and / auncient Fathers of the pri- / mitiue church, by Iohn Martiall / Bachiler of Lavve and / Studient in Di- / uinitie. / Multi enim ambulant quos saepe dicebam vobis (nunc au- / tem flens dico) inimicos crucis Christi quorum finis interitus. / &c. Philip.3. / For many vvalke of vvhome I haue often told youe, / (and novve tell yovve vveping) that they are enemies / of the crosse of Christ, vvhose end is damnation. / [device] / Imprinted at Antwerp by Iohn Latius, / at the signe of the Rape, with Pri- / uilege. Anno. 1564.

8°. A–Z in eights+Aa^{7}. Fol. 1[A2]–169[Z2]. Cw. Mg. Rt – A Treatyse / of the Crosse. (1) Title [A1]. (2) Privilegium: Brussels. 6 Oct. 1564 [A1^{v}]. (3) Address to Queen Elizabeth: Antwerp. 12 Oct. 1564. 'Youer louing subiect and trewe beedes man Iohn Martial' [A2–4]. (4) Preface to the Readers [A4^{v}–B3]. (5) 'The names of the Authours Alleaged' [B3–5]. (6) Text [B5–Z2]. (7) Imprimatur: Louvain. 'quarto calendas octobris' [Z2]. (8) Table [Z2^{v}–Aa5]. (9) 'Faultes escaped in printing' [Aa5–6]. (10) Cut within a border. Latin verses [Aa6^{v}]. (11) Latin hymn, followed by small cut subscribed *Typis Ioannis Latii* [Aa7–7^{v}].†

Although this work contains references to Jewel it does not belong properly speaking to either the Apology or the Challenge controversy. It is rather a general assault on the Protestant economy. The writer addresses the Queen because she is 'so

* *Acts of English Martyrs* (1891), footnote, p. 242.

† Some of these details have been supplied from the Stonyhurst Copy.

wel affectioned to the crosse (which is the matter that I haue taken in hand to treat)' that she has 'alwayes kept it reuerently' in her chapel, 'notwithstanding many meanes haue bene made to the contrary'.*

The answer came from the pen of that staunch Calvinist, James Calfhill, and is an excellent example of Elizabethan 'Limehouse' speech (see next entry).

83. A Replie to / M. Calfhills / blasphemous Answer / made against the Trea- / tise of the Crosse, by / Iohn Martiall, Bachiler / of Lawe, and studient in Di- / uinitie. / Reade and Regarde. / Yf any man teache otherwise, and doth not encline to the hol- / some woordes of our Lord Iesus Christ, and to the doctrine / which is according to godlynes, he is proude, and one that / knoweth nothing, but beating his braynes aboute questõis, / and strife of woordes. 1 Timoth. 6. / [cut within a border] / Imprinted at Louaine by Iohn Bogard at the Golden Bible / with the Kinges Maiesties priuilege. 1566.

4°. ⋆–⋆⋆⋆⋆⋆⋆+A–Z+Aa–Zz+AAa–LLl in fours. Fol. 1[A1]–227[LLl4]. Cw. Mg. Rt – A Replie to the Blasphemous Answer / against the Treatise of the Crosse. (1) Title [⋆1]. (2) Privilegium: Brussels 12 June; followed by two mementoes in Lat. and Eng., headed 'To M. Calfhill' and 'To the Christian Reader' [⋆1v]. (3) 'A Request to Maister Grindal and other Superintendents of the newe Churche of England'; followed by memento (Lat. and Eng.), headed 'To the newe clergie' [⋆2–⋆⋆2]. (4) 'The Preface to the Reader' [⋆⋆2–⋆⋆⋆⋆⋆⋆3]. (5) 'Faultes escaped in printing' [⋆⋆⋆⋆⋆⋆3v–4]. (6) Cut [⋆⋆⋆⋆⋆⋆4v]. (7) Text. Concludes with Latin memento to Calfhill [A1–LLl4].†

Dr. James Calfhill's work was published under the title of *An Aunswere to the Treatise of the Crosse*. London, 1565.‡ William Fulke replied to Martiall (Calfhill had died in 1570) in *T. Stapleton and Martiall (two popish Heretikes) confuted, and of their particular heresies detected. By D. Fulke*. London, 1580.§

* Alex. Nowel, dean of St. Paul's, was publicly reproved by the Queen while preaching in her presence on 7 March 1564 (1565) against Martiall's *Treatise*. He was so 'utterly dismayed' at this reproof that Archbishop Parker had to take him home to dinner to comfort him. Professor J. E. Neale, in his recent book on Queen Elizabeth, refers to this incident (p. 216). See Strype, *Life and Acts of Matthew Parker* (1821), Vol. I, p. 318; also Vol. III, Appendix 29.

† Some bibliographical details supplied from Stonyhurst Copy.

‡ Reprinted by the Parker Society, 1846. See Strype, *Annals* (1824), Vol. I, pt. 2, p. 200; cf. also Vol. I, pt. 1, p. 262. A further reference is to be found in Strype's *Life and Acts of Grindal* (1821), p. 165.

§ Reprinted by the Parker Society, 1848. The part allotted to Martiall is headed, 'A Reioynder to Iohn Martials reply against the answere of Maister Calfhill, to the blasphemous treatise of the Crosse'. The volume contains a useful catalogue of 'Popish Bookes either answered, or to be aunswered, which haue bene written in the Englishe tongue from beyond the Seas, or secretly dispersed here in England haue come to our handes, since the beginning of the Queenes Maiesties reigne'. See Appendix V. The list is revised from that in Fulke's earlier volume on Heskins, Sanders and Rastel (1579). See entry 57.

MARTIN, GREGORY

d. 1582

84. A Treatise of / Schisme. / Shewing, that al Catholikes ought in / any wise to abstaine altogether from / heretical Conuenticles, to witt, / their prayers, sermons. &c, / deuided into foure / Chapters / where- / of / 1. Conteineth sundry reasons to that pur- / pose, grounded for the most part vp- / pon Scriptures and Fathers. / 2. Examples out of holy Scripture. / 3. Examples out of ecclesiastical histories. / 4. Answeres to the chiefe obiections. / By Gregorie Martin Li- / centiate in Diui- / nitie. / Duaci. / Apud Iohannem Foulerum. / 1578.

8°. B.L. **+A–K in eights+L^2. Not fol. Cw. Mg. Rt – A Treatise / of Schisme. (1) Title [**1]. (2) Imprimatur by William Allen [**1v]. (3) Preface to the Reader: 'From Remes within the Octaues of Al Saintes. 1578. By your countriman G.M.' [**2–8v]. (4) Text [A1–L2v].

According to Strype this pamphlet was answered by Lord Burghley's *A Declaration of the fauorable dealing of her Maiesties Commissioners appointed for the Examination of certaine Traitours, and of tortures vniustly reported to be done vpon them for matters of religion*. 1583.* This is a mistake. The *Declaration* was a Government reply to the many reports, books, letters and libels which followed W. Carter's execution (see below). It is entirely concerned in defending the authorities against charges of rigour in administering torture.†

Although John Fowler's name appears on the title-page of the *Treatise*, it was in reality the work of W. Carter, who suffered death for printing it. This, Carter acknowledged at his trial in 1583. The trial is fully recorded in Bridgewater's *Concertatio*, where the following words occur:

> Est is liber eo animo a me [Carter] scriptus, excusus et in lucem prolatus, quo ii schismatici, qui communionem habent cum iis, qui a sua veraque religione sunt alieni, ab hoc errore suo ad vnius Ecclesiae Catholicae cultum obedientiamque reuocarem.‡

More interesting and important is the evidence of Carter's

* Strype, *Annals* (1824), Vol. III, pt. 1, p. 407. This rare document (a quarto of four leaves only) is reprinted in Holinshed's *Chronicles* (1587), Vol. III, p. 1357.

† Campion and Briant are specially referred to as not having been rigorously treated.

‡ Which, the reader will observe, is not very good Latin. The meaning is, however, clear. That Carter is reported as having *written* the book (scriptus) need not disturb us. The evidence of the work itself (see the Preface to the Reader) is proof enough to the contrary. The reference to Bridgewater is *Concertatio Ecclesiae Catholicae in Anglia* (1588), sig. Kk2v. This reference is one of several.

printing afforded by one of the Bodleian copies of the *Treatise*, which has bound up with it a slip of paper on which is written in an early hand:

> Wm. Carter hathe cōfessed he hath printed of theis bookes 1250.
>
> This was founde at Wm Carters: in his house at the Tower hill with the Origenall Coppy sent from Rhemes allowed vnder Doctor Allens owne hand & name subscribed thus: Hic Tractatus est plane Catholicus, & nostris imprimis hominibus hoc schismatis tempore pernecessarius. Ita testor Gulielmus Alanus S. Theologiae Doctor & Professor.*

This copy is without the title-page.† In the complete copies the imprimatur appears on the reverse of the title exactly as it is written here. In view of this evidence it is hardly necessary to point out that the printing of the *Treatise* is quite unlike that of Fowler. The type is poor; the factotum capitals are such as Fowler never employs; moreover, the printer has no Greek type.‡

We may take it that the exact date of printing was December 1578 (two months, incidentally, before Fowler's death), for we read in the *Douay Diaries* under that date (recorded as a marginal reading):

> Hoc mense a quodam alumno seminarii nostri perscriptus et typis mandatus est liber quidam de non communicando cum haereticis.§

85. The / Loue of / the Soule / Made by G.M. / [cut] / Printed at Roane 1578.

16°. A–C in eights+D². Not fol. Cw. No Mg. Rt – The loue of the soule. (1) Title [A1]. (2) Blank [A1v]. (3) Text [A2–D2v].

A letter from the author to his Protestant sisters pleading for their conversion. The date of writing appears in the text as 'the yeare of Christ a thousand fiue hundred, eightie and three'

* The handwriting was noted in the Bodleian exhibition of Catholic books (1935) as being that of Richard Topcliffe, the pursuivant.

† It was evidently this copy which Anthony à Wood saw and which he mistakenly refers to as '*A Treatise of Schisme* published under the name of Jo. Howlet (being one of the copies which was seized before the title-page was printed).' *Ath. Oxon.* (ed. Bliss), Vol. II, 68–9.

Gillow doesn't mend matters when he states that Wood was wrong, and that the book which Carter printed 'was entitled "A Brief Discourse contayning certayne Reasons why Catholiques refuse to goe to Church" . . . by J(ohn) H(owlet, i.e. Robt. Persons), and bearing the running title of "A Treatise of Schisme" '. (*Bibl. Dict.*, under *Gregory Martin*.) This work of Persons comes from the Greenstreet Press, as Gillow himself points out in his bibliographical record of Persons' works.

‡ Further reference to Carter will be found at p. 350.

§ *D.D.*, p. 147.

[B6v]. This hardly agrees with the date of the title. Possibly Martin was reckoning from the true date of our Lord's birth (i.e. from B.C. 5 (?)), and not from the conventional date.

The printing of this book bears no relation to any Rouen printing that I know. It is rather crude and an English fount was employed. It is possible that it may have come from William Carter's press. There is, however, no certain evidence for this.

The Bodleian Library has an augmented edition of this work: 'Made by G. Mar.'; 'Printed at Roan'; without date. The probable date of this copy is after 1600.

86. [within a border, within a rule] The / Nevv Testament / of Iesus Christ, trans- / lated faithfully into English, / out of the authentical Latin, according to the best cor- / rected copies of the same, diligently conferred vvith / the Greeke and other editions in diuers languages: Vvith / Arguments of bookes and chapters, Annota- / tions, and other necessarie helpes, for the better vnder- / standing of the text, and specially for the discouerie of the / Corruptions of diuers late translations, and for / cleering the Controuersies in religion, of these daies: / In the English College of Rhemes. / Psal.118. / Da mihi intellectum, & scrutabor legem tuam, & custodiam / illam in toto corde meo. / That is, / Giue me vnderstanding, and I vvil searche thy lavv, and / vvil keepe it vvith my vvhole hart. / S. Aug. tract.2. in Epist.Ioan. / Omnia quae leguntur in Scripturis sanctis, ad instructionem & salutem nostram intentè oportet / audire: maximè tamen memoriae commendanda sunt, quae aduersus Haereticos valent plu- / rimùm: quorum insidiae, infirmiores quosque & negligentiores circumuenire non cessant. / That is, / Al things that are readde in holy Scriptures, vve must heare vvith great attention, to our / instruction and saluation: but those things specially must be commended to me- / morie, vvhich make most against Heretikes: vvhose deceites cease not to cir- / cumuent and beguile al the vveaker sort and the more negligent persons. / Printed at Rhemes, / by Iohn Fogny. / 1582. / Cum Priuilegio.

4°. a–c in fours + d² + A–Z + Aa–Zz + Aaa–Zzz + Aaaa–Zzzz + Aaaaa–Ddddd in fours + Eeeee². Pag. 1[A1]–745[Bbbbb1]. Cw. Mg. Rt. varies. (1) Title [a1]. (2) 'The Censure and Approbation' [a1v]. (3) 'The Preface to the Reader treating of these three points: of the translation of Holy Scriptures into the vulgar tongues, and namely into English: of the causes why this new Testament is translated according to the auncient vulgar Latin text: & of the maner of translating the same' [a2–c4v]. (4) 'The signification or meaning of the Numbers and Markes vsed in this New Testament' [d1]. (5) 'The

Bookes of the New Testament, according to the counte of the Catholike Churche' (followed by a note on 'the infallible authoritie and excellencie of them aboue al other Writings', with quotations from the Fathers on various points) [d1v–d2v]. (6) 'The Summe of the New Testament' [A1–A1v]. (7) Text: Each book is preceded by an 'argument', except the three Epistles of S. John, which have a single 'argument' for the three. Each chapter has a summary heading and a tail of 'annotations'. The verses of each chapter are numbered, but the chapter is divided into paragraphs. There are margins on each side of the text – one of reference, one of commentary. At the end of the Gospels is 'The Summe, and the Order of the Euangelical Historie: gathered breifly out of al foure, euen vnto Christs Ascension'. This is accompanied by a 'harmony' of the chapters of the four gospels in the margin. At the end of the Acts of the Apostles are two tables summarizing the Acts of Peter and the Acts of Paul. (These go beyond the text of Scripture to the witness of the early ecclesiastical writers. They are accompanied in the margin by a 'harmony' of dates). There follows a short reference to the Acts of the rest of the twelve Apostles, and the Apostles' Creed is cited in its twelve articles. The Epistles are introduced with 'The Argument of the Epistles in General'. Throughout, the Church's use of the various parts of Scripture is referred to, so that the book is a book of instruction for the faithful in regard to Church practice and the Scriptures, as well as an attack upon the 'heretics'. We note the omission of 'S' before Matthew, Paul, etc., at the beginning of each book, thus following, as the Preface to the Reader states, the Greek and the Latin. The 'S' is retained, however, in the running titles [A2–Bbbbb1]. (8) 'A Table of the Epistles and Gospels, after the Romane vse, vpon Sundaies, Holidaies, and other principal daies of the yere, for such as are desirous to know and reade them according to this translation. And therefore the Epistles taken out of the old Testament are omitted, till the edition thereof' [Bbbbb1v–3]. (9) 'An ample and particular table directing the reader to al catholike truthes, deduced out of the holy Scriptures, and impugned by the Aduersaries' [Bbbbb3–Eeeee2]. (10) 'The explication of certaine wordes in this translation, not familiar to the vulgar reader, which might not conueniently be vttered otherwise' (56 entries) [Eeeee2–2v]. (11) 'The faultes correcte thus' [Eeeee2v].

The translation of the New Testament rightly belongs to Martin. William Allen, Richard Bristow and William Rainolds acted as his assistants and supplied the principal commentaries. It appears that the work was published in March or early April 1582,* that is about three months before the publication of Martin's *Discouery of the Manifold Corruptions of the Holy Scriptures* (next entry). It was immediately attacked by W. Fulke who, in his *A Defense of the sincere and true Translations of the holie Scriptures into the English tong*. London, 1583 (full title at next entry), gives a short section to 'Popish annotations vpon the new Testament printed at Rhemes'. Subsequent 'answers' are to be found in:

The true difference betweene christian subiection and vnchristian rebellion: Wherein the princes lawfull power to commaund for trueth, and indepriuable right to beare the sword are defended against the Popes censures and the Iesuits sophismes vttered in their Apologie and Defence of English Catholikes: With a demonstration that the thinges refourmed in the Church of England by the Lawes of this Realme are truely

* See the section on the Rhemes *New Testament* at pp. 231 et seq. above.

Catholike, notwithstanding the vaine shew made to the contrary in their late Rhemish Testament: by Thomas Bilson Warden of Winchester. Oxford, 1585.*

An answere to ten friuolous and foolish reasons, set downe by the Rhemish Iesuits and Papists in their Preface before the new Testament by them lately translated into English, which haue mooued them to forsake the originall fountaine of the Greeke, wherein the Spirit of God did indite the Gospell, and the holie Apostles did write it, to follow the streame of the Latin translation, translated we know not when nor by whom. With a discouerie of many great Corruptions and faults in the said English Translation set out at Rhemes. By E[dward]. *B*[ulkeley]. London, 1588.†

A View of the marginal notes of the Popish Testament, translated into English by the English fugitiue Papists resiant at Rhemes in France. By George Wither. London, 1588.

The Text of the New Testament of Iesus Christ, translated out of the vulgar Latine by the Papists of the traiterous Seminarie at Rhemes. With Arguments of Bookes, Chapters, and Annotations, pretending to discouer the corruptions of diuers translations, and to cleare the controuersies of these dayes. Whereunto is added the Translation out of the Original Greeke, commonly vsed in the Church of England, with a Confutation of all such arguments . . . By William Fulke. London, 1589.‡

Σύν θέῳ ἐν Χριστῷ. *The Answere to the Preface of the Rhemish Testament. By T. Cartwright.* Edinburgh, 1602.§

A Confutation of the Rhemists translation, glosses and annotations on the New Testament, so farre as they containe manifest Impieties, Heresies, Idolatries, Superstitions, Prophanesse, Treasons, Slanders, Absurdities, Falsehoods and other evills . . . Written long since by order from the chiefe instruments of the late Queene and State, and at the speciall request and encouragement of many godly-learned Preachers of England, as the ensuing Epistles shew. By that Reverend, Learned, and Iudicious Divine, Thomas Cartwright. 1618.||

W. Whitaker also took part in this attack. He was answered by W. Rainolds (entry 120).

A second edition of the Rhemes Testament, with certain augmentations, was printed at Antwerp by Daniel Vervliet in 1600.

* The fourth part of this work deals especially with the Rhemes *Testament.*

† cp. Strype, *Annals* (1824), Vol. III, pt. 2, pp. 156–8.

‡ This is the most elaborate 'answer' to the Rhemes N.T. The two versions, the 'Rhemes' and the 'Bishops' ', are set out in parallel columns, marginal references being given in both margins according to the originals. Invaluable for purposes of comparison.

§ Cartwright's *Confutation*, from which this was taken, follows above.

|| The reasons for the delay in the publication of this answer of Cartwright's are given fully in Strype, *Life and Acts of Whitgift* (1822), Vol. I, pp. 481–5; cp. also Strype, *Annals* (1824), Vol. III, pt. 1, pp. 287, 289, 290 and 291.

87. A Discouerie / of the Manifold / Corruptions of the / Holy Scriptures by the / Heretikes of our daies, specially the / English Sectaries, and of their foule / dealing herein, by partial & false trans- / lations to the aduantage of their here- / sies, in their English Bibles vsed and / authorised since the time of Schisme. / By Gregory Martin one of the readers / of Diuinitie in the English College / of Rhemes. / 2 Cor.2. / Non sumus sicut plurimi, adulterantes verbum Dei, sed / ex sinceritate sed sicut ex Deo, coram Deo, in Christo / loquimur. / That is, / VVe are not as very many, adulterating the word / of God, but of sinceritie, & as of God, before / God, in Christ vve speake. / Printed at Rhemes. / By Iohn Fogny. / [rule] / 1582.

8°. a^8+b^6+A–V in eights$+X^4$. Pag. 1[A1]–322[X1v]. Cw. Mg. Rt – A Discouerie of the Haeret. / Translations of the Bible. (1) Title [a1]. (2) Blank [a1v]. (3) Preface [a2–b6]. (4) 'The Arguments of euery chapter' [b6v]. (5) Text in 22 chapters [A1–X1v]. (6) 'The faultes correcte thus' [X2]. (7) Table [X2v–X4]. (8) Blank [X4v].

Although Martin's *Discouerie* had been finished in the preceding January,* it was not printed until the end of June 1582, that is, *after* the publication of the *New Testament.*† Further, Martin in his Preface, in describing the author's intentions, writes that he 'wil deale principally with the English translations of our time, which are in euery mans handes within our countrie the corruptions whereof, as they are partly touched here and there in the Annotations vpon the late new English Testament Catholikely translated & printed at Rhemes, so by occasion thereof, I wil by Gods help, to the better cōmoditie of the reader, and euidence of the thing, lay them closer together, and more largely display them', thus pointing to the same fact.

Replies to Martin came from W. Fulke and J. Rainolds as follows: *A Defense of the sincere and true Translations of the holie Scriptures into the English tong, against the manifold cauils, friuolous quarels, and impudent slaunders of Gregorie Martin, one of the readers of Popish diuinitie in the trayterous Seminarie of Rhemes. By William Fulke D. in Diuinitie, and M. of Pembroke haule in Cambridge. Where vnto is added a briefe confutation of all such quarrels & cauils, as haue bene of late vttered by diuerse Papistes in their English Pamphlets, against the writings of the saide William Fulke.* London, 1583.‡

* Allen mentions it in a letter, written in Italian, to George Gilbert, dated 15 January 1582. He says, 'Of necessity we ought to have it printed'. Knox, *Letters and Memorials of Cardinal Allen*, p. 109.

† *D.D.*, p. 188. See also my note at the previous entry.

‡ Reprinted by the Parker Society, 1843; cp. Strype, *Life and Acts of Matthew Parker* (1821), Vol. I, pp. 413, 414 and 417. Strype complains of Martin's use of the Coverdale version of the Scriptures instead of the later, more orthodox Bishops' Bible. But there was no good reason for his using the latter. It had not a very wide vogue. See also Strype, *Annals* (1824), Vol. III, pt. 1, p. 288.

The Summe of the Conference betwene Iohn Rainolds and Iohn Hart: touching the head and the faith of the Church . . . Penned by Iohn Rainoldes, according to the notes set downe in writing by them both: perused by Iohn Hart, and (after things supplied, & altered, as he thought good) allowed for the faithfull report of that which past in conference betwene them. Whereto is annexed a Treatise intitled, Six Conclusions Touching The Holie Scripture And the Church, writen by Iohn Rainoldes. With a defense of such thinges as Thomas Stapleton and Gregorie Martin haue carped at therein. London, 1584.*

88. A / Treatyse of Christi- / an Peregrination, writ- / ten by M. Gregory Martin Licentiate, / and late reader of diuinitie in / the Englishe Coleadge at / Remes. / VVhereunto is adioined certen Epistles vvrit- / ten by him to sundrye his frendes: the copies / vvhereof vvere since his decease founde a- / monge his vvrytinges./ Novv especially puplished for the benifite / of those, that either erre in religion of simplicitie, / or folovv the vvorlde of frayltie. / [ornament] / Anno Domini / 1583. [Paris. Richard Verstegan.]

8°. π^2+A–D in eights+E^2+1π–5π in eights+6π^2. Not pag. Cw. Mg. Rt – Christian / Peregrination. (No Rt. to addenda.) (1) Title [π1]. (2) 'The contentes of this booke' [$\pi 1^v$]. (3) Printer's Preface: signed, R. V. [π2]. (4) Text [A1–E1^v]. (5) Blank [E2]. (6) 'A Letter sente by M. Licentiate Martin to a maried priest his frende': ends, 'Paris. 15. Fe. 1580 Your louing frend vndoubtedly G. M.' [1π1–7^v]. (7) 'To my louing and bestbeloued sisters': unsigned and undated [1π8–3π6]. (8) 'The copy of a letter written to M. Doctour Whyte Warden of the new Colledge in Oxforde': dated 15 October 1575 [3$\pi 6^v$–6π2]. (9) Blank [6$\pi 2^v$].

This posthumous work of Martin's was printed in Paris by Richard Verstegan (R. V. above), who writes in the Printer's Preface: 'this Treatise came vnto my handes, the which by lycense of my Superiours, I haue here published, and annexed there-unto certayne Episttles of the same Authors, a man of rare vertue and excellent learning'. Verstegan was in Paris in 1583, and a comparison of this work with *A Refutation of Sundry Reprehensions* by William Rainolds (entry 120), also printed at Paris in 1583, makes it quite certain that the two books came from the same press. It is to be observed that Verstegan's printer was without Greek type, and had to resort to Roman spelling of Greek words in the letter to Dr. Whyte.

The letter to his sisters is reproduced from Martin's *Loue of the Soule* (entry 85).

Dr. Thomas Whyte, an old friend of Martin's, became Warden of New College in 1553. He was succeeded by Martyn Colepeper in 1573. Martin thus appears to be two years late with his letter.†

* Two pages only are given to Martin's *Discouery*. On the other hand, Bristow's *Motives* and *Demands* are answered at some length.

† *Historical Register of the University of Oxford* (1900), p. 539.

89. The Holie Bible faithfully translated into English out of the Authentical Latin. Diligently conferred with the Hebrew, Greeke, and other Editions in diuers languages. With Arguments of the Bookes, and Chapters: Annotations: Tables: and other helpes, for better vnderstanding of the text: for discouerie of Corruptions in some late translations: and for clearing Controuersies in Religion. By the English College of Doway. Haurietis aquas in gaudio de fontibus Saluatoris. Isaiae.12. You shal draw waters in ioy out of the Sauiours fountaines. Printed at Doway by Laurence Kellam, at the signe of the holie Lambe. M.DC.IX.

90. The second tome of the Holie Bible faithfully translated into English, out of the authentical Latin. Diligently conferred with the Hebrew, Greeke, and other Editions in diuers languages. With Arguments of the Bookes, and Chapters: Annotations: Tables: and other helpes, for better vnderstanding of the text: for discouerie of Corruptions in some late translations: and for clearing Controuersies in Religion. By the English College of Doway. Spiritu Sancto, locuti sunt sancti Dei homines. 2.Pet.1. The holie men of God spake, inspired with the Holie Ghost. Printed at Doway by Laurence Kellam, at the signe of the holie Lambe. M.DC.X.

MORWEN, JOHN

1518?–1568?

91. [*Text-title.*] An Addicion with an Appologie to the causes of brinnynge of Paules Church, the which causes were vttred at Paules Crosse by the reuerend Bysshop of Duresme the. viii. of Iune. 1561.

This pamphlet was first printed in Bishop Pilkington's *The burnynge of Paules church in London in the yeare of oure Lord 1561. and the iiii. day of Iune by lyghtnynge, at three of the clocke, at after noone, which continued terrible and helplesse vnto nyght.* London, 10 March 1563. It occupies sigs. A2–6. The Bishop's confutation of the pamphlet is printed under the text-title: 'A Confutacion of an Addicion, wyth an Appologye written and cast in the stretes of West Chester, agaynst the causes of burnyng Paules Church in London: whych causes, the reuerend Byshop of Duresme declared at Paules Crosse 8. Iunij. 1561.' After the Confutation thirteen questions, which Morwen had added to his pamphlet, are answered by the Bishop. This section of the book is headed: 'Here folowe also certaine questions propounded by him, whiche are fullye althoughe shortly aunswered' [P4–S2].*

NICOLS, JOHN

1555–1584?

(see entry 14)

OSBERNE, EDWARD

fl. 1583

(see entry 14)

PERSONS, ROBERT, S.J.

1546–1610

92. A / Brief Discours / contayning certayne / reasons why Ca- / tholiques refuse to goe / to Church. / Written by a learned and / vertuous man, to a frend / of his in England. / And / Dedicated by I.H. to the Queenes / most excellent Maiestie / [device] / Imprinted at Doway by Iohn Lyon. / 1580. / With Priuelege.

8°. B.L. ‡–‡‡+A–I in eights. Fol. 1[A1]–70[I6]. Cw. Mg. Rt – The 1. Part Contayning. / Reasons of Refusal. (1) Title [‡1]. (2) Blank [‡1v]. (3) Address to Queen Elizabeth: 'Your Maiesties most humble and obedient subiect. I. Howlet' [‡2–‡‡8v]. (4) Text: nine reasons are given [A1–I4]. (5) 'To the Reader towchinge the omission of the Seconde and Third Parte promised at the beginning' [I4–6v]. (6) Blank [I7–8].

By far the best account of the occasion of this publication, commonly known as *Reasons of Refusall*, is to be found in Fr. Persons' *Memoirs II*. Since there has been some confusion in the matter,† I propose to give this account at length.‡

'And now', he writes, 'was the question [sc. of attendance at the Protestant Service] much more revived upon the coming in of the foresaid Fathers [Persons and Campion], who were

* Bishop Pilkington's book has been reprinted by the Parker Society in *The Works of James Pilkington, B.D., Lord Bishop of Durham*, edited by Rev. James Scholefield, 1842. Morwen's pamphlet is referred to by Strype, *Annals*, Vol. I, pt. 1, pp. 390 and 416.

† By Gillow, for example, in *Bibl. Dict.* (art. *Persons*); and C. Dodd, *Church History*, II, 41.

‡ The *Memoirs* are printed in *Publications of Catholic Record Society*, Vols. II and IV. The passages quoted here are from Vol. II, pp. 179–81. Parallel accounts are to be found at Vol. II, p. 28, and Vol. IV, pp. 3–5.

knowne to hould the negative parte, and for that cause, the Councell hath put in prison presently upon there arivall in England divers men of accompt, as the Lord Pagett, Sir John Arundell, Thomas Tressam, Mr William Catesby, Sir Thomas Frogmorton, Mr Sheldon and the like, threatning them that soone after in the Parlament, which for that purpose they had called, most sharpe lawes should be made against them . . . For answering of which objection and for preventing somewhat the minds of men before the Parlament begane, F. Parsons wrote the boke intituled *Reasons of Refusall*, and gott it printed; in which booke he showed by divers reasons, that conscience and not obstinacy or other evill meaning was the true cause of Catholikes refusing to goe to protestant Churches.

'And when matter stood in these tearmes, and greate expectations were on all sides, whether Catholikes would be constant or noe, behould a new difficulty, for upon the soddaine a little before the parlament begane two principall men yelded to go to the Church, to witt the Lord Pagett and Mr Sheldon, which they pretended to have done upon the persuasion of a new booke secretly spread abroad in wrytten hand, which did teach that in such a case Catholikes might goe to churche,* and for that this booke was thought to have byn gathered by some principall man or men in England (thoughe given out by one William Clytherowe a man little studied thoughe afterward made priest in Flaunders) it was like to make greate motion coming togeather with the storme of persecution, as may appeare in the letter of a grave priest and gentleman named Mr Edward Chambers . . . which letter he wrote to F. Persons going then under the name of Mr Roberts in manner as followethe.'

The letter, which is dated 6 November 1580, refers to 'a certaine peevishe booke cast forth amonge them [sc. 'gentlemen restrayned for not going to Churche'] of late by I knowe not whome, alleadging divers reasons whie yelding to go to Churche in this case is no greate sin, if it be any at all, and in effect it doth contradict the cheefest purpose of the *Reasons of Refusall* of late printed'. The memoir then goes on to state that Persons and Mr. George Blackwell saw the book, 'which was not greate, but peevishly wrytten and very dangerous in such a tyme, for that it made profession to prove all it said out of ancient Fathers: whereby it appeared, that albeit the opinion was the foresaid William Clytherowe, who had byn a Lawiers Clarke had wrytten it out, and given it abroad, yet that he was

* 'A treatise to prove that attendance at the Protestant church was in itself no sin, and therefore might be lawfully submitted to for the purpose of avoiding a persecution so intolerable at present, and threatening to grow so much more so.' Gillow, *Bibl. Dict.*, under *Langdale, Alban.* Mr. Sheldon's copy of this tract is in the S.P.O. Dom. Eliz., vol. cxliv, No. 69 (see entry 74).

not the author therof, but rather Mr D. Langdale that lived with the Lord Monteacute, and permitted him as was said to have English service in his house for his servants, though himselfe went to Masse'.

There follows Fr. Persons' account of how he, together with Mr. George Blackwell, 'went over the River to Southwarke and procured to have a sight of Mr Doctor Langdales Library, who was absent in the country with the Lord Montacute, and there they found not only sufficient bookes, but also the same places coated and marked which were alleadged in the pamphlet newly sett forthe; whereby they gathered, eyther Doctor Langdale had made that booke, or at least gathered the notes for it, for that they were wrytten with his owne hand'. He adds the rider: 'it seemeth that God punished him [Dr. Langdale] in that very kind shortly after, for that a nephew of his a grave man called F. Langdale, who had lived many yeares in the Society of Jesus, leasing upon the soddaine, as it were, his witt and judgment rane out of Italy into England without licence of his Superiours to teach this doctrine, that it was lawful for men to go to Church'; and concludes, the book 'was answered presently by F. Persons, the notes being gathered by Mr Blackwell, and it so repressed the matter for the present, as noe more men of marke fell'.*

From this somewhat lengthy account these facts emerge:

(1) Persons wrote his *Reasons of Refusall* to confirm the faithful and to combat the lax views held by certain of the clergy and laity;

(2) He wrote it prior to Langdale's written pamphlet, which may have been a sort of reply to the views he had expressed;

(3) He believed Alban Langdale (certainly not Thomas Langdale, who, as he points out elsewhere, arrived in England only at the beginning of 1583) was the originator of this written pamphlet;

(4) His answer to the latter was disseminated in writing.

For obvious reasons Fr. Persons is purposely misleading as to the origin of his book in his address 'To the Reader towchinge the omission of the Seconde and Thirde Parte promised at the beginning'. He there writes: 'The wryter of this Treatise, hauing ended this first part and being wel entred into the second, was partlye by euil disposition of bodye, and partlye by other sodaine busines falling vpon him, enforced to leaue the place, wherein he wrote this. Whereupon the messager hastinge awaye

* cf. 'mr Blackwel also and I together made an answer in wryting to Clithero's book: wherupon the cath^s took hart and courage to stand to it, and this was our exercise that wynter [1580] in London.' *Publications*, Cath. Rec. Soc., Vol. II, p. 28.

into Englande, and the other not able, as he desired, so spedely to dispatche him with the whole: was content to impart to him, for his frend, this which he had ended, promising hereafter, (if his health and leasure should permit him) to finish also the other two parts.'*

The following were the replies to Persons' book:

A briefe Confutation, of a Popish Discourse: Lately set forth, and presumptuously dedicated to the Queenes most excellent Maiestie: by Iohn Howlet, or some other Birde of the night, vnder that name. Contayning certain Reasons, why Papistes refuse to come to Church, which Reasons are here inserted and set downe at large, with their seuerall answeres. By D. Fulke. London, 1581.

A Caueat for Parsons Howlet, concerning his vntimely flighte, and scriching in the cleare day lighte of the Gospell, necessarie for him and all the rest of that dark broode, and vncleane cage of papistes, who with their vntimely bookes, seeke the discredite of the trueth, and the disquiet of this Church of England. Written by Iohn Fielde. London [1581].

A Checke or reproofe of M. Howlets vntimely shreeching in her Maiesties eares, with an answeare to the reasons alleadged in a discourse therunto annexed, why Catholikes (as they are called) refuse to goe to Church: Wherein (among other things) the Papists traiterous and treacherous doctrine and demeanour towardes our Soueraigne and the State, is somewhat at large vpon occasion vnfolded: their diuelish pretended conscience also examined, and the foundation thereof vndermined. And lastly shewed that it is the duety of all true Christians and subiectes to haunt publike Church assemblies. London, 1581 [Perceval Wiburn].

Despite the title, the *Brief Discours* was printed at the Greenstreet House Press by Stephen Brinkley.† A second edition was printed by James Duckett (title says Doway) in 1599. There was a further edition printed at Doway in 1601.

* A Welsh carol, composed before 1584 by Richard White, verses Persons' nine reasons 'Against going to Protestant Service' in 'brief poetic way'. See *Publications of the Catholic Record Society*, Vol. V, pp. 91–9, for Mr. Richard White's Welsh carols, where an English translation is added.

The second part of the treatise, which Persons says he was 'wel entred into', does not appear to have been published. He says, in the address quoted above, that its main object was 'to exhorte Catholicks in Englande and to make humble supplication to ther soueraine Ladye and Princesse, for some more fauorable tolleration with them for their cõsciences. For the better obtayninge wherof, he meaneth to lay doune certayne reasons, or motiues, wherby her Maiestie may be the sooner induced, both in respect of God, her selfe, and her whole Realme, to graunte the same'. The Proclamation of 10 January 1581 followed hard upon the publishing of the *Discours*, and no doubt he realized then how useless such an appeal would be.

It is interesting to note that the anonymous author of *A Consolatory Letter to all the afflicted Catholikes in England* [1588?] drew freely upon the *Briefe Discours* for the first half of his work.

† See p. 356.

93. A / Brief Censure / vppon two bookes / written in an- / swere to M. Edmonde / Campions offer of / disputation. / Deuter. capit.5. ver.5. / Yow feared the fyre, and therfore you / ascended not vp the mountayne. / [device] / Imprinted at Doway by Iohn Lyon. / 1581. / With Priuilege.

8°. B.L. A–E in eights+F³. Not fol. Cw. Mg. Rt – A Brief / Censure. (1) Title [A1]. (2) Blank [A1v]. (3) Text in four parts [A2–F3v].

The two books are *An answere to a seditious pamphlet lately cast abroade by a Iesuite, with a discouerie of that blasphemous sect. By William Charke.* London, 1580; and *The Great bragge and challenge of M. Champion a Iesuit, cõmonlye called Edmunde Campion, latelye arriued in Englande, contayninge nyne articles here seuerallye laide downe, directed by him to the Lordes of the Counsail, cõfuted & aunswered by Meredith Hanmer, M. of Art, and Student in Diuinitie.* London, 1581.*

The *Douay Diaries* (under 20 March 1581), after stating that Persons was thought to be the author of this work and that he had 'printed at Louvain' put on the title-page, adds that the book was ready in ten days and that Recorder Fleetwood, on finding a copy outside his door, was amazed at the size of the book, seeing that it had been produced in so short a time and had come all the way from Louvain.†

Charke and Hanmer replied in the following:

A Replie to a Censure written against the two answers to a Iesuites seditious Pamphlet. By William Charke. London, 1581.

The Iesuites Banner. Displaying their original and successe: their vow and othe: their hypocrisie and superstition: their doctrine and positions: with A Confutation of a late Pamphlet secretly imprinted and entituled: A Briefe Censure vpon two bookes written in answeare to M. Campions offer of disputation. &c. Compiled by Meredith Hanmer. London, 1581.‡

* Campion's nine articles are set out at length by Hanmer. They are thus *printed* for the first time.

† 'In fronte cujusque libri positum erat Lovanii excusus &c. Quorum cum unum ante fores suas jacentem Fleetwoddus, rotulorum Londinensium custos et senescallus, invenisset, obstupuisse dicitur, libri magnitudine, temporis angustiis, et Lovanio transmissione diligenter inter se collatis et comparatis. *D.D.*, p. 177. Louvain is, of course, a mistake.

‡ R. Simpson states that Persons thought 'that the proclamation of 10 January 1581, ordering all young men to return from the seminaries, and denouncing all receivers and favourers of priests and Jesuits, was a kind of reply to his Censure'. (*Edmund Campion. A Biography*, p. 262. No reference is given. See my suggestion about this Proclamation at previous entry.) This is hardly possible. We are told that Persons produced his reply some ten days after Hanmer's book was published (see above). The latter was entered on the *Stationers' Register* on 3 January 1581, and since books were usually entered *before* publication (there is no evidence to show the contrary), Persons' work could not have been published earlier than 13

Persons' authorship of this and the two following works (*A Discouerie of I. Nicols* and *A Defence of the Censure*) is put beyond doubt by his plain avowal in his Autobiography. 'I amongst others', he writes, 'wrott and printed the Reasons of Refusall and the Discovery of John Nichols. There hapned also other things this winter, as the coming forth of the books of Hanmer and Chark, whereto I answered by the Censure, and the defence therof made afterwards.'*

Like the *Brief Discours*, this book was printed at the Greenstreet House Press (now lodged in the house of Francis Browne) by Stephen Brinkley.†

94. A Discouerie of I. Nicols / minister, misreported a Iesuite, latelye / recanted in the Tower / of London. / Wherin besides the declaration of the man, is con- / tayned a ful answere to his recantation, with a confuta- / tion of his slaunders, and proofe of the con- / traries, in the Pope, Cardinals, Clergie, Stu- / dentes, and priuate men of Rome. / There is also added a reproofe of an oration and sermon, / falsely pretended by the sayd Nicols to be made in Rome, / and presented to the Pope in his Consistorye. / Wherto is annexed a late information from Rome / touching the autētical copie of Nicols recantation. / [device: to left 'God hathe exalted him, and geuen him a name whiche is aboue all names. Philippens. 2. ver. 9.'; to right 'There is no other name vnder heauen geuen vnto men, wherin we must be saued. Act. 4. ver.12.'] / A lyeing witnes shall haue an yuel ende. Pro.21. / An non ex hac odiosa impudentia, pullulabit mox impoe- / nitentia, mater desperationis? Bern. Ser.42. in Can. [Greenstreet House Press. By Stephen Brinkley. 1581.]

Bod.

8°. B.L. A–M in eights + π^2. Not fol. Cw. Mg. Rt – A Discouerie / Of Iohn Nicols. (1) Title [A1]. (2) 'The Contentes' [A1v]. (3) 'To the indifferente Reader' [A2–4v]. (4) Text in 3 parts [A4v–L6]. (5) 'Touching his oration and sermon' [L6–M6]. (6) 'A new information from Rome of I. Nicols' [M6–7v]. (7) 'An example of Iohn Nicols talent in raylinge at bothe sides' [M7v–π1v]. (8) Blank [π2].

January; that is, three days, at least, *after* the Proclamation. We must assume, therefore, that Simpson has confused the *Censure* with Persons' *Discourse* (1580). He appears not to have known of the latter work, since he states in the same context that the first book issued from Brinkley's Press was 'probably some book of devotions or of encouragement to persecuted Catholics', and suggests that this was next followed by the *Censure*.

* *Publications of the Catholic Record Society*, Vol. II, p. 28. *Pollard and Redgrave* gives the *Censure* under both Persons and Campion.

Persons makes similar acknowledgment of these and other works in his *Warn-word to Sir Francis Hastings Wast-word* (1602).

† See pp. 354 and 356.

John Nichols, the informer, had published, on his recantation, two books, to which this work of Persons is a reply.* They were:

(1) *A declaration of the recantation of Iohn Nichols (for the space almost of two yeeres the Popes Scholer in the English Seminarie or Colledge at Rome) which desireth to be reconciled, and receiued as a member into the true Church of Christ in England.* London, 1581. 14 February.†

(2) *The Oration and Sermon made at Rome by commaundement of the foure Cardinalles, and the Dominican Inquisitour, vpon paine of death. By Iohn Nichols, latelie the Popes Scholler. Which Sermon and Oration was presented before the Pope and his Cardinalles in his Consistorie, the xxvij day of Maie. 1578. and remaineth there registred. Now by him brought into the English tongue, for the great comfort and commoditie of all faithfull Christians. Heerin also is aunswered an infamous Libell, maliciouslie written and cast abroad, against the saide Iohn Nichols, with a sufficient discharge of himselfe from all the Papists lying reports, and his owne life both largelie and amplie discouered.* London, 1581.‡

The 'late information from Rome', referred to in the title, was sent to Persons by Allen, who had received it from Fr. Agazzari.§

Towards the end of his book Persons attacks Thomas Lupton. 'Of late', he says, 'in the middest of our persecutiōs, there came foorth a weightie worke of 40, sheets of paper, made by one Thomas Luptō, intituled *A perswasiō from Papistry*, (he would haue saied, a *disswasion*, but that Papistrie & perswasion began both with a letter).' He then proceeds to examine Lupton's arguments. This brought Lupton into the field against him in *The Christian against the Iesuite. Wherein the secrete or namelesse writer of a pernitious booke, intituled A Discouerie of I. Nicols Minister &c. priuily printed, couertly cast abrod, and secretely solde, is not only iustly reprooued: But also a booke, dedicated to the Queenes*

* Gillow suggests a third, viz. *Iohn Niccols Pilgrimage*. London, 1581. But this book was not entered on the *Stationers' Register* until 4 September 1581, whereas the *Discouerie*, as indicated above, had been printed at least a month earlier.

† Nichols confessed later that this book was an inspired document. He writes: 'M. Stubs gaue me the matter of my booke in the Tower, intituled: *The recantion of Iohn Nicols*, &c. *M. Wilkinson* did write in the margent the notes: and also added to that which I wrote, and corrected the faults by me escaped.' *A True Report of the late Apprehension . . . of Iohn Nicols*. Rhemes, 1583, sig. C6v. Articles on Stubbs and Wilkinson will be found in the *D.N.B.* For an account of Nichols's recanting, see Strype, *Annals* (1824), Vol. III, pt. 1, p. 61. Also *Life and Acts of Grindal* (1821), pp. 390–2.

‡ Nichols suggests that he was invited to marshal arguments *against* the Holy See in this Sermon and Oration for some cause or other. A highly improbable proceeding.

§ See the letter of Allen to Agazzari, dated from Rhemes, 23 June 1581, in Knox, *Letters and Memorials of Cardinal Allen*, p. 96.

Maiestie, called A persuasion from papistrie, therein derided and falsified, is defended by Thomas Lupton the authour thereof. London, 1582. A further reply came from the pen of Dudley Fenner in *An Answere vnto the Confutation of Iohn Nichols his Recantation, in all pointes of any weight conteyned in the same: Especially in the matters of Doctrine, of Purgatorie, Images, the Popes honor, and the question of the Church. By Dudley Fenner, Minister of Gods word.* London, 1583.*

For proof of Persons' authorship of the *Discouerie*, see previous entry. The printing is clearly that of the two previous entries.† The date, 1581, is settled by the fact that Persons' press (the Greenstreet House Press) was seized at the beginning of August 1581. The book must, therefore, have been printed before that date, and not earlier than 2 April 1581, which is the date when Nichols's *Oration* appears on the *Stationers' Register*.

95. [within a compartment] The First Booke of / the Christian Exer- / cise, appertayning to re- / solution. / VVherein are layed downe the / causes & reasons that should moue / a man to resolue hym selfe to the / seruice of God: And all the impe- / dimentes remoued, which may lett / the same. / Psal.62. vers. 4. / Vnam petii a domino, hanc requiram: / vt inhabitem in domo domini omni- / bus diebus vitae meae: vt videam vo- / luntatem domini. / One thing haue I requested at / gods hādes, & that will I demaunde / still: which is, to dwell in his house / all the daies of my life: to the ende, / I maye knovve and doe his vvill. / [beneath compartment] Anno.1582. / VVith Priuylege. [George L'Oyselet. Rouen.]

12°. A[6]+B–T in twelves. Pag. 1[B1]–431[T12]. Cw. (irregular). Mg. Rt – The Christian Exercise / [book, part, chapter with chapter heading in brackets.] (1) Title [A1]. (2) 'The Summarie of the Christian exercise, as it is intended' [A1v]. (3) 'An Aduertisement to the Reader' [A2]. (4) Table of Contents [A3–6v]. (5) 'To the Cristian Reader towchinge two editions of this booke': ends, 'Thy hartie welwiller and seruant in Christ. R. P.' [B1–3]. (6) 'An Induction to the three bookes followinge' [B3v–5]. (7) Blank [B5v]. (8) Text of the first book in two parts [B6–T12v].

The Christian Directory, as this work came to be called later, was originally planned as three books by Persons: the first to be of resolution, in two parts; the second on how to begin well, in two parts; the third, the means of perseverance, also in two

* The *D.N.B.* (s.v. *John Nicholls*) suggests that there were *two* books confuting the *Recantation of Iohn Nichols*, viz. 'A Confutation of John Nicolls his Recantation', answered by Dudley Fenner, and 'A Discoverie of J. Niccols, Minister, misreported a Jesuite', answered by Thomas Lupton. The mistake has arisen from the differences in the reference to Persons' book in the two titles of these answers. Both answers refer explicitly to Persons' *Discouerie* in the text.

† See p. 355; also note on the *Brief Discours* at p. 465.

parts. The first book only was published. Persons writes apropos, in the Advertisement to the Reader, 'I am constrayned to breake of, for the present, & to send thee onelie this first booke of resolutiō'. In this same place he acknowledges his indebtedness to Gaspar Loarte's *Exercise of a Christian Life*. In the address 'to the Cristian Reader' he refers to Stephen Brinkley's translation of this latter work (entry 20), translated 'abowt three yeres past'. He intended, he says, to have it printed again, more fully 'hauing added vnto it, two partes of three, which were not in the former booke'. However, he found he could not combine Loarte and himself and so was 'inforced, to resolue vpon a further labour . . . which was, to drawe out the whole three bookes' himself [A2].

The printing is that of the Rouen Press employed by Persons, from which a number of Recusant works emanated at this time. The book is prior to the *Defence of the Censure* (next entry), also published from Rouen in 1582.*

Within the three years following publication of this work three further editions were published:

(1) A Catholic pirated edition, which was issued from the same press as the original edition in 1584;†

(2) Edmund Bunny's bowdlerized edition, also of 1584:
A Booke of Christian exercise, appertaining to Resolution, that is, shewing how that we should resolve our selves to become Christians in deed: by R. P. Perused, and accompanied now with a Treatise tending to Pacification: by Edm. Bunny. London, 1584;

and (3) Persons' own revised edition of 1585:
A Christian directorie, guiding men to their saluation, commonly called the Resolution . . . with reproofe of the falsified edition by E. Buny [Rouen].

In his Preface to this last edition Persons writes: 'I perceaued many monethes before, that al the first copies of the said former booke (though not so wel done as iustely I might haue wished) were wholy dispersed and none remaining to be had.' Therefore he has resolved to take the first book again and 'to polish and fil vp some thinges, wherin before for want of leasure and time, I could not geue to my self any reasonable contentation, as also to adioine certaine new chapters'. He is still contemplating the second and third books of the *Resolution*, but they must be left for a later volume. He then goes on to refer to the two pirated editions. 'I was enformed', he says, 'of two other editions come forth of my forsaid booke without my knowledge, the one by a Catholique (as it seemeth) who perceuing al copies of the former print to be spēt; for satisfying

* For details about this press and the works which issued from it, see pp. 359–363.
† This edition has an important bearing on the question of the Rouen Press. See p. 361, footnote.

of them that desired the booke, procured the same to be set forth againe, albeit somewhat incorrected, and very disordrely, not hauing the consent or aduise of such, as therin should haue geuen him best direction. The second was published by one Edmund Buny minister at Bolton Percy (as he writeth) in the liberties of Yorke; who with publicke licence vnder my Lord Archbishop of Yorke his protection, set forth the same to the benefite of his brethren; but yet so punished and plumed, (which he termeth purged;) as I could hardly by the face discerne it for mine, when it came vnto my handes, and I tooke no smale compassiō to see how pitifully the poore thing had bene handled. Of this edition then of M. Buny, (letting passe th' other as a matter onely of indiscretion without malice,) I haue to aduertise the reader some few things.' Which he proceeds to do.

Bunny replied to Persons in *A Briefe Answer, vnto those idle and friuolous quarrels of R. P. against the late edition of the Resolution: By Edmund Bunny*. London, 1589.

The Christian Directory was frequently reprinted both in Catholic and Protestant versions in the succeeding centuries. It was also translated into French, Italian, German and Welsh.*

96. [within a border] A Defence / of the Censure, / gyuen vpon tvvo bookes / of william Charke and Meredith Han- / mer, mynysters, whiche they wrote a- / gainst M. Edmond Campian preest, of / the Societie of Iesus, and against his / offer of disputation. / Taken in hand since the deathe of the sayd / M. Campian, and broken of agayne be- / fore it could be ended, vpon the / causes sett downe in an epi- / stle to M. Charke in the / begyninge. / Sap 3. / The sovvles of the iust are in the hande / of God, and the torment of deathe shall not / touche them: they seemed to the eyes of foo- / lishe men to dye, but neuerthelesse they rest / in peace. / An. 1582. / [rule] / Cum Priuilegio. [George L'Oyselet. Rouen.]

8°. A+Aa in eights+Aaa⁴+B–M in eights. Pag. 1[A2]–37[Aaa4]; 1[B1]–173[M7]. Cw. (regular on verso pages; on recto irregular, save on fols. 6, 7 and 8 of each gathering) Mg. Rt – A Defence of the / Censure [followed by the subject of the page on recto pages within brackets]. (1) Title [A1]. (2) 'The corrector of the prynt vnto the gentle reader' [A1v]. (3) 'The Setter forth of this booke vnto William Charke Minister' [A2–7]. (4) 'The Answere to the Preface touchinge Discerninge of Spirites' [A7v–Aaa4]. (5) 'The contents of the former epistle and answere' [Aaa4v]. (6) Text [B–M7]. (7) 'Heere the Authour was interrupted by a Writte *de remouendo*, so as he could not for this present passe on any further: as more at large is shewed at the beginning, in an epistle to M. Charke' [M7]. (8) Table of principal matters [M7v–8]. (9) 'The faultes correcte thus' [M8v].

The two books referred to in the title are given at entry 93.

* Gillow, *Bibl. Dict.*, s.v. *Persons*.

Persons had written most of the *Defence* while he was still in England. On the seizure of his press at Stonor Park, however, on 8 August 1581, he was forced to discontinue writing. He writes in the Epistle to Charke: 'In generall, euery one can imagine by hym selfe, how difficult a thing yt is in England at this daye, for a Catholique man to write any book: where nether libertie, nor rest, nor librarie, nor conference, nor beinge is permitted hym. And in particular, thus muche I must adde, whiche you alredie in part doe knowe: that soone after the publishinge of your reply to the Censure, the Author therof addressed hym selfe to a defence, and had in greate part dispatched the same, redie for the printe, in suche sort as the rigorous tyme of your persecution permitted hym. But God sufferinge at that verie instāt, that the sayd print so long sought, and muche feared by you, should be taken: there was taken, lost, and dispersed therwithall, not onelie all furniture there redy for this booke, but also for sundry other thinges, partlie printed, and partlie in printing, concerning our defence of trueth and equitie, against your falsehood and violent oppressions.

'This disturbance, and losse beinge fallen owt by gods most holy and fatherlie permission: and the Author of the Censure hauing nether tyme, nor place, nor bookes, nor leysure to begynne agayne, nor any hope of print when he should haue done the same: being also necessarilie called awaye at that verye tyme, to a place somewhat farof, vppon vrgent businesse: he resolued vtterlie to gyue ouer the sayd attempt of defence' [A2]. He concludes by saying that, owing to Campion's unfair treatment when on his defence, he has resolved 'to take in hand agayne the Answer of your booke'.

The 'corrector of the prynt', who, in the first Answer to the *Defence*, is dubbed 'some Vsher', in his words to the reader begins somewhat naïvely: 'To the ende this page shoulde not goe emptye, I haue presusemed [sic] (without the Authours knowlege) to put downe for yonge scholers the true declynynge of a Nowne Heretike: whereof we haue more experience in these dayes than olde Grammarians hadde'. He then proceeds to decline the noun 'Heretic' according to its (or his) meaning, in Latin and English.*

* For the curious I give here the English version of his declension.

The singuler number,

An Heretike {
In the Nominatiue or first case (to begin withall) he is *Prowde*.
In the Genetiue case he growethe *Malapert*.
In the Datyue case he becometh a *Lyar*.
In the Accusatiue case he waxethe *Obstinate*.
In the Vocatiue or preaching case he is *Seditious*.
In the Ablatiue or endinge case hee proueeth *an Atheist*, or els *a Lybertine*.
}

The plurall number,

In bothe genders, *Impudent*, throughowte all cases.

Short lives of the first gospellers – Luther, Calvin, Beza, Bucer, etc. – are included in this work, and these are referred to in the preliminary Answer, the title-page of which runs: *An Answeare for the time, vnto that foule, and wicked Defence of the Censure, that was giuen vpon M. Charkes Booke, and Meredith Hanmers. Contayning a maintenance of the credite and persons, of all those woorthie men: namely, of M. Luther, Caluin, Bucer, Beza, and the rest of those Godlie ministers of Gods worde, whom he, with a shamelesse penne most slanderously hath sought to deface: finished sometime sithence: And now published for the stay of the Christian Reader till Maister Charkes Booke come foorth.* London, 1583.* A second Answer, presumably by Charke himself, came forth in 1586, under the title *A Treatise against the Defense of the Censure, giuen vpon the Bookes of W. Charke, and Meredith Hanmer, by an vnknowne Popish Traytor, in maintenance of the seditious challenge of Edmond Campion, lately condemned & executed for high Treason . . . Hereunto are adioyned two treatises, written by D. Fulke: the one against Allens booke of the authoritie of Priesthode to remitte sinnes, of confession of sinnes to a Priest, and of the Popes Pardons: The other against the Railing declamation of P. Frarine.* Cambridge, 1586.†

Evidence for Persons' authorship of the *Defence* will be found at entry 93. The printing (ornamental capitals, etc.) points conclusively to the press used by Fr. Persons at Rouen.

A section of the *Defence*, viz. 'The Answere to the Preface touchinge Discerninge of Spirites' (see bibl. details (4) above), was reprinted with an addition by the Birchley Press in 1620 as follows: *A Little Treatise concerning Trial of Spirits: taken for the most part out of the Works of the R.F. Robert Persons, of the Societie of Iesus. Whereunto is added a Comparison of a true Roman Catholike with a Protestant, wherby may bee discouered the difference of their Spirits. With an Appendix taken out of a later Writer.*

97. Newes from Spayne and Holland conteyning. An information of Inglish affayres in Spayne with a conferrence made theruppon in Amsterdame of Holland. Written by a Gentleman trauelour borne in the low countryes, and brought vp from a child in Ingland, vnto a Gentleman his frend and Oste in London. Anno, M.D.XCIII.

98. A Temperate Ward-word, to the Turbulent and Seditious Wach-word of Sir Francis Hastinges knight, who indeuoreth to slaunder the whole Catholique cause, & all professors therof, both at home and abrode. Reduced into eight seueral en-

* *Pollard and Redgrave* gives Charke as the author. There is no evidence for this in the book itself.

† For Fulke's two treatises, see entries 11 and 41.

counters, with a particuler speeche directed to the Lordes of her Maiesties most honorable Councel. To whome the arbitriment of the whole is remitted. By N.D. Psalm. 71. vers.4. Iudicabit Dominus pauperes populi, & humiliabit calumniatorem. God wil iudge his poore and afflicted people, and will make the slanderer to stoop. Imprinted with Licence. Anno M.D.XCIX.

99. [*Text-title.*] The Copie of a Letter written by F. Rob. Parsons the Iesuite, 9. Octob. 1599. to M. D. Bish: and M. Ch. two banished and consigned Priests, the one in Fraunce, the other in Lorraine, by the suggestions of F. Parsons, for presuming to goe to Rome in the affaires of the Catholicke Church. [Occupies sigs. Gg1 to Ii2 of *The Copies of certaine discourses.* Roane. 1601.]

100. A Briefe Apologie, or Defence of the Catholike Ecclesiastical Hierarchie, and subordination in England, erected these later yeeres by our holy Father Pope Clement the eight; and impugned by certaine libels printed and published of late both in Latine and English; by some vnquiet persons vnder the name of Priests of the Seminaries. Written and set forth for the true information and stay of all good Catholikes, by Priestes vnited in due subordination, to the right Reuerend Archpriest, and other their Superiors. Hebr.13. vers.17. Obedite praepositis vestris, & subiacete eis, &c. Obey your Superiors, and submit your selues vnto them. I.Thess.5. Rogamus vos fratres, corripite inquietos. We beseech you brethren, represse those that are vnquiet amongst you. Permissu Superiorum. [1601]

101. An Appendix to the Apologie, lately set forth, for defence of the Hierarchie, and subordination of the English Catholike Church, impugned by certaine discontented Priestes. Wherin two other bookes or libels of the impugners, the one in English the other in Latin, no lesse intemperate then the former, are examined, and considered, By the Priestes that remaine in due obedience to their lawful Superior. August. lib.17. contra Faustum Manichaeum. Cap.4. Iam puto sufficere, quae dicta sunt ad studiosos commouendos, & ad calumniosos conuincendos. We think that sufficient hath byn sayd now, both to warne good and vertuous men, as also to confute those that delight in slaunders and calumniations. Imprinted with Licence. [1601]

102. A Manifestation of the great folly and bad spirit of certayne in England calling themselues secular priestes. Who set forth dayly most infamous and contumelious libels against worthy men of their owne religion, and diuers of them their lawful Superiors, of which libels sundry are heer examined and refuted. By priestes lyuing in obedience. 2.Tim.3. Their folly, shalbe manifest to all men. Luc 11. The vncleane spirit went foorth and took seauen other spirits, more wicked then himself, and all entring dwelt there, and the ending of those men was worse then the beginning. Superiorum Permissu. 1602.

103. The Warn-word to Sir Francis Hastinges Wast-word: Conteyning the issue of three former Treateses, the Watch-word, the Ward-word and the Wast-word (intituled by Sir Francis, an Apologie or Defence of his Watch-word) togeather with certaine admonitions & warnings to the said knight and his followers. Wherunto is adioyned a breif reiection of an insolent, and vaunting minister masked with the letters O.E. who hath taken vpon him to wryte of the same argument in supply of the knight. There go also foure seueral Tables, one of the chapters, another of the controuersies, the third of the cheif shiftes, and deceits, the fourth of the parricular [sic] matters conteyned in the whole book. By N.D. author of the Ward-word. Tit.3. vers.10. Fly an herttical [sic] man, after one or two warnings, knowing that such a one is subuerted, and sinneth damnably against his owne iudgment. Permissu Superiorum. Anno 1602.

104. A brief, and cleere Confutation, of a new, vaine, and vaunting Chalenge, made by O.E. Minister, vnto N.D. Author of the Ward-word. Wherin Yssue is ioyned vpon the fiue seueral pointes, proposed by the Chalenger: and his egregious ignorance, falshood, and folly, discouered in them all. By W.R. The particular pointes and h[ea]des of euery Chalenge, follow in the second page. Esay.5. vers.20. Wo be vnto yow, who cal euil good, and good euil, darknes light, and light darknes; bitter sweet, and sweet bitter. Concil.Cirtense ad Donatist.

apud.Aug ep.152. No excuse now remayneth, too too hard and diabolical are their hartes, who stil do resist vnto cleere manifestation of the truthe. Imprinted with licence. Anno Domini 1603.

105. A Treatise of Three Conuersions of England from Paganisme to Christian Religion. The first vnder the Apostles, in the first age after Christ: The second vnder Pope Eleutherius and K. Lucius, in the second age. The third, vnder Pope Gregory the Great, and K. Ethelbert in the sixth age; with diuers other matters thereunto apperteyning. Diuided Into three partes, as appeareth in the next page. The former two whereof are handled in this booke, and dedicated to the Catholikes of England. With a new addition to the said Catholikes, vpon the news of the late Q. death. and succession of his Maiestie of Scotland, to the crowne of England. By N.D. author of the Ward-word. Deut.4. & 32. Inquire of auncient tymes before yow; remember th' old dayes of your forefathers; consider of euery age, as they haue passed: aske your father and he will tell yow: demaund of your ancestors, and they wil declare vnto yow. Imprinted with licence, anno. 1603.

106. The Third Part of a Treatise, Intituled: of three Conuersions of England: conteyninge. An examen of the Calendar or Catalogue of Protestant Saints, Martyrs and Confessors, diuised by Iohn Fox, and prefixed before his volume of Acts and Monuments. With a Pararell [sic] or Comparison therof to the Catholike Roman Calendar, and Saints therin conteyned. The first six monethes. Whervnto in the end is annexed a defence of a certaine Triall, made before the King of France vpon the yeare 1600. betweene Monsieur Peron Bishop of Eureux, and Monsieur Plessis Mornay Gouernour of Saumur, about sundry points of Religion. By N.D. S.Aug. lib.3. contra Parmen. cap. 6. Sacrilegious schismatikes and impious heretikes, dare presume when they are punished, to accoumpt the punishment of their fury, for true martyrdomes. Math.25. Vers.32. God shall separate them a sunder (at the day of iudgment) as the shepheard doth separate the sheep from goates. Imprinted with licence, Anno Dñi. 1604.

107. The Third Part of a Treatise Intituled of three Conuersions of England. Conteyninge an examen of the Calendar or Catalogue of Protestant Saintes, Martyrs and Confessors, deuised by Fox, and prefixed before his huge Volume of Actes and Monuments: With a Paralel or Comparison therof to the Catholike Roman Calendar, and Saintes therin conteyned. The last six monethes. Whervnto is annexed in the end, another seuerall Treatise, called: A re-view of ten publike Disputations, or Conferences, held in England about matters of Religion, especially about the Sacrament and Sacrifice of the Altar, vnder King Edward and Queene Mary. By N.D. S.Aug. lib.3. contra Parmen. cap.6. Sacrilegious schismatiks and impious heretiks, dare presume when they are punished, to accompt the punishment of their fury for true martryrdomes. Matt.25. Vers.32. God shall separate them a sunder (at the day of iudgement) as the shepheard doth separate the sheep from goates. Imprinted with licence, Anno Domini. 1604.

108. A Relation of the Triall Made before the King of France, vpon the yeare 1600 betweene the Bishop of Eureux, and the L. Plessis Mornay. About Certayne pointes of corrupting and falsifying authors, wherof the said Plessis was openly conuicted. Newly reuewed, and sett forth againe, with a defence therof, against the impugnations both of the L. Plessis in France, & of O.E. in England. By N.D. Tertullian. lib. de praescript. aduers. haereses. Vinci possunt, persuaderi non possunt. Heretikes may be vanquished, & yet not persuaded. Imprinted with licence. Anno M.DC.IIII.

109. A Reuiew of ten publike Disputations Or Conferences held within the compasse of foure yeares, vnder K. Edward & Qu. Mary, concerning some principall points in Religion, especially of the Sacrament & sacrifice of the Altar. Wherby, May appeare vpon how weake groundes both Catholike Religion was changed in England; as also the fore-recounted Foxian Martyrs did build their new opinions, and offer themselues to the fire for the same, which was chiefly vpon the creditt of the said Disputations. By N.D. Aug. lib.2. against Petilian the Donatist. We are constrayned to heare, discusse, and refute these trifles of yours: least the simpler and weaker sort should fall into your snares. Imprinted with licence Anno M.DC.IIII.

110. An Answere to the fifth part of Reportes Lately set forth by Syr Edward Cooke Knight, the Kinges Attorney generall. Concerning The ancient & moderne Municipall lawes of England, which do apperteyne to Spirituall Power & Iurisdiction. By occasion wherof, & of the principall Question set downe in the sequent page, there is laid forth an euident, plaine, & perspicuous Demonstration of the continuance of Catholicke Religion in England, from our first Kinges christened, vnto these dayes. By a Catholicke Deuyne. Matt.22.v.21, Reddite quae sunt Caesaris Caesari; & quae sunt Dei Deo. Giue vnto Cesar the things that belonge vnto Cesar; and vnto God, those that apperteyne to God. Imprinted with licence, Anno Domini 1606.

111. A Treatise tending to Mitigation towardes Catholicke-Subiectes in England. Wherin is declared, That it is not impossible for Subiects of different Religion, (especially Catholickes and Protestantes) to liue togeather in dutifull obedience and subiection, vnder the gouernment of his Maiesty of Great Britany. Against The seditious wrytings of Thomas Morton Minister, & some others to the contrary. Whose two false and slaunderous groundes, pretended to be drawne from Catholicke doctrine & practice, concerning Rebellion and Equiuocation, are ouerthrowne, and cast vpon himselfe. Dedicated to the learned Schoole-Deuines, Cyuill and Canon Lawyers of the two Vniuersities of England. By P.R. Prou.26. Vers.20. Susurrone subtracto, iurgia conquiescunt. The make-bate being remoued, brawles do cease. Permissu Superiorum. 1607.

112. The Iudgment of a Catholicke English-man, liuing in banishment for his religion: Written to his priuate friend in England. Concerninge A late Booke set forth, and entituled; Triplici nodo, triplex cuneus, Or, An Apologie for the Oath of Allegiance. Against two Breues of Pope Paulus V. to the Catholickes of England; & a Letter of Cardinall Bellarmine to M. George Blackwell Arch-priest. Wherin, the said Oath is shewed to be vnlawfull vnto a Catholicke Conscience; for so much, as it conteyneth sundry clauses repugnant to his Religion. S. Hieron. Comment. in Cap.4. Hierem. Let an Oath haue these companions, Truth, Iudgment, and Iustice; for if these be wanting, it shall not be an Oath, but Periury. Permissu Superiorum. Anno 1608.

113. Dutifull and Respectiue Considerations vpon Foure Seuerall Heads of Proofe and Triall in Matters of Religion. Proposed By the High and Mighty Prince, Iames King of Great Britayne, France, and Ireland &c. in his late Booke of Premonition to all Christian Princes, for clearing his Royall Person from the imputation of Heresy. By a late Minister and Preacher in England. August. lib. contra Iudaeos, Pagan. & Arian. cap.20. You must know (deare brethren) that true faith, sincere peace, & perpetuall saluation is only by the Catholicke faith: for it is not in a corner, but euery where all. If any man depart from it, and deliuer himselfe vp to the errors of Heretickes, he shall be iudged and condemned as a fugitiue bond-man. Permissu Superiorum, M.DC.IX.

114. A Quiet and Sober Reckoning with M. Thomas Morton somewhat set in choler by his Aduersary P.R. concerning Certaine imputations of wilfull falsities obiected to the said T.M. in a Treatise of P.R. intituled Of Mitigation, some part wherof he hath lately attempted to answere in a large Preamble to a more ample Reioynder promised by him. But heere in the meane space the said imputations are iustified, and confirmed, & with much increase of new vntruthes on his part returned vpon him againe: So as finally the Reckoning being made, the Verdict of the Angell, interpreted by Daniel, is verified of him. Daniel 5. vers.27. Appensus es in statera, & inuentus es minus habens. You haue byn weighed in the ballance, & are found to want weight. There is also adioyned a peece of a Reckoning with Syr Edward Cooke, now L. Chief Iustice of the Cōmon Pleas, about a Nihil dicit, & some other points vttered by him in two late Preambles, to his sixt and seauenth Partes of Reports. Permissu Superiorum. M.DC.IX.

115. A Discussion of the Answere of M. William Barlow, D. of Diuinity, to the Booke intituled: The Iudgment of a Catholike Englishman liuing in banishment for his Religion &c. concerning The Apology of the new Oath of Allegiance. Written By the R. Father, F. Robert Persons of the Society of Iesus. Wherunto since the said Fathers death, is annexed a generall Preface, laying open the Insufficiency, Rayling, Lying, and other

Misdemeanour of M. Barlow in his writing. Ex fructibus eorum cognoscetis eos. Matt.7. You shall know them by their fruites. Permissu Superiorum. M.DC.XII.

116. A Memorial of the Reformation of England: containing Certain Notes, and Advertisements, which seem [sic] might be proposed in the First Parliament, and National Council of our Country, after God, of his mercy, shall restore it to the Catholick Faith, for the better Establishment and Preservation of the said Religion. Gathered and set down by R.P. 1596.
[Printed in: *The Jesuit's Memorial, For the Intended Reformation of England, Under their First Popish Prince. Published From the Copy that was presented to the Late King James II. With an Introduction, and some Animadversions, By Edward Gee.* London, 1690.]

POINTZ, ROBERT

1535–

117. Testimonies / for the Real Presence / of Christes body and blood in the blessed / Sacramēt of the aultar set foorth at large, / & faithfully translated, out of six auncient / fathers which lyued far within the first six / hundred yeres, together with certain / notes, declaring the force of those testimo- / nies, and detecting sometimes the Sa- / cramentaries false dealing, as / more plainly appeareth in / the other syde of this / leaf. / By Robert Pointz student in / Diuinitie. / [ornament] / Athan. ad Epict. contra Haeret. / Si vultis filij patrum esse, non debetis sen- / tire diuersa ab ijs, quae patres ipsi cōscri- / pserunt. / If ye will be children of the Fathers, you must / not dissent from those thinges which the Fa- / thers them selues haue written. / Louanii, / Apud Ioannem Foulerum. / M.D.LXVI.

8°. B.L. A–Z+Aa–Cc in eights. Fol. 1[B1]–200[Cc8]. Cw. Mg. Rt – Testimonies for / the reall presence. (1) Title [A1]. (2) 'The summes of the Chapters' [A1v]. (3) 'To the Reader': Robert Pointz [A2–6v]. (4) 'Faultes escaped in printing' [A7]. (5) Quots. from Fathers [A7v–8]. (6) Privilegium: Brussels. 20 Aug. 1565 [A8v]. (7) Text [B1–Cc8]. (8) Imprimatur: Louvain. 7 Aug. 1565 [Cc8v].

This work is part of the concerted reply which Jewel's challenge called forth (see pp. 60 et seq.). The six 'auncient fathers' are SS. Chrysostom, Cyril, Cyprian, Hilary, Augustine and Ambrose.

POLE, REGINALD, CARDINAL
1500–1558

118. A Treatie / of Iustification. / Founde emong the writinges of Cardinal Pole of blessed / memorie, remaining in the custodie of M. Henrie / Pyning, Chamberlaine and General Receiuer / to the said Cardinal, late deceased / in Louaine. / Item, certaine Translations touching the said matter of / Iustification, the Titles whereof, see in the / page folowing. / Prouerb. 4. / Ne declines neque ad dexteram, neque ad sinistram. / Turne not aside to the right hande, nor to the lefte. / [device] / Louanii, / Apud Ioannem Foulerum. Anno. 1569. / Cum Priuilegio.

CAMB.

4°. *+A–Z+a in fours+b²+AA⁶+BB–TT in fours+VV². Fol. 1[A1]–98[b2]; Fol. 1[AA3]–77[VV1]. Cw. Mg. Rt–'Of Mans Iustification' &c. (1) Title [*1]. (2) Table of Translations [*1ᵛ]. (3) 'The Preface to the Reader' [*2–4ᵛ]. (4) Text in two books [A1–X4]. (5) 'The Praier of the Churche' (Lat. and Eng.) [X4]. (6) 'To the Reader' [X4ᵛ]. (7) 'The Sixth Session of the General Councel of Trent holden in the thirtenth daie of Ianuarie, in the yeare of our Lorde 1547' (preface, 16 chapters, and 33 canons) [Y1–b2ᵛ]. (8) Table of chapters of Treatise of Justification [AA1]. (9) New title as follows: Certaine Treaties / of the Auncient Holy / Fathers, touching / the Doctrine of / good woorkes. / Namely, / A Treatie of S. Augustine, whiche he Intituled: Of Faith / and VVorkes. / Item, a Sermon of S. Chrysostome, of Praying vnto God. / Item, a Sermon of S. Basil, of Fasting. / Item, certaine Sermons of S. Leo the Great, of the same matter. / Last of al, a notable Sermon of S. Cyprian, of Almes dedes. / Al newly translated into English. / Tobie. 12. / Bona est Oratio cum Ieiunio, & Eleemosyna, magis quàm The- / sauros auri recondere. Quoniam Eleemosyna à morte liberat, & / ipsa est quae purgat peccata, & facit inuenire vitam aeternam. / Prayer is good with Fasting, and Almes, better then to / hide vppe treasures of golde. For Almes deliuereth / from death, and shee it is which purgeth sinnes, and / maketh to finde life euerlasting./ Louanii, / Apud Ioannem Foulerum. Anno. 1569. / Cum Priuilegio [AA2]. (10) Blank [AA2ᵛ]. (11) 'The Translatour to the Reader' [AA3–6ᵛ]. (12) Text of Translations [BB1–VV1]. (13) Imprimatur: Louvain. 15 Jan. 1569 [VV1ᵛ]. (14) 'Faultes escaped in the printing, of the Translations' [VV2]. (15) Ornament [VV2ᵛ].

In the Cambridge copy of this book, from which the above bibliographical details are taken, on the reverse of the title-page, at the end of the Table of Translations, written in an early Italian hand, occur the words 'by Thomas Lorde Coppley'. Again on the second title-page, at the words 'Al newly translated into English', the same sixteenth-century hand adds 'by Thomas Coppley esquier'.* I see no reason to doubt this

* Thomas Copley was a well-known Elizabethan recusant. He appears to have left England about the time of the publication of this work and spent the remainder of his life in France, Spain, and the Low Countries. 'He died in Flanders in 1584, and in the last codicil of his will styles himself "Sir Thomas Copley, knight, Lord Copley of Gatton in the county of Surrey" '. *D.N.B.*

contemporary evidence. Copley was well equipped for such work. Witness Fr. Persons' account – how 'when Maister Iewells booke [*Apologia Ecclesiae Anglicanae*] was newly come forth, he being also learned himselfe in the Latyn tongue, tooke paines to examine certayne leaues therof', and how, later, at the Earl of Leicester's house after dinner, Jewel was put down by him.* I think, however, it is clear that the words are intended to refer *only* to the translations from the Fathers and *not* to the translation of the decrees of the Sixth Session of the Council of Trent. The repetition of the words *at the second title-page*, and the non-inclusion of the translation of the decrees in this part of the book, both point to this. The translation of the decrees is thus left unaccounted for, for from internal evidence it is clearly not the work of Pole. Quite possibly the printer or publisher, John Fowler, was responsible for it.

POUNDE, THOMAS (approved scholastic, S.J.)†
1539–1616

119. [*Text-title.*] Sixe Reasons set downe to shew, that it is no orderly way in cõtrouersies of faith, to appeale to be tryed only by Scriptures (as the absurde opinion of all the Sectaries is) but the sentence & definition of the Catholike Church, by whome, as by the Spowse of Christ, alwayes inspired with the holy ghost, the holy Scripture is to be iudged.

Printed in *An Aunswer to sixe Reasons, that Thomas Pownde, Gentleman, and Prisoner in the Marshalsey. at the commaundement of her Maiesties Commissioners, for causes Ecclesiasticall: required to be aunswered. Because these Reasons doo moue him to think, that controuersies and doubts in Religion, may not be Iudged by the Scriptures, but that the Scriptures must be Iudged by the Catholique Church. 1. The first is, for that the Scriptures are mute and dum. 2. The second, for that they be full of harde and deepe mysteries. 3. The thirde, for that S. Peter sayth: No Scripture is to be taken after any priuate interpretation. 4. The fourth, for that to appeale to the Scriptures, dooth seeme to denie all vnwritten verities. 5. The fyft is, for that it were a great absurditie, not to haue a certaine Iudge of absolute Authoritie, in the interpreting of Scriptures. &c. 6. The sixt is, for that in refusing the Authoritie of the Churches absolute Iudgement herein: we seeme to denie the holie ghost, to be the spirite of trueth. Written by Robert Crowley.* London, 1581.

* *A Relation of the Triall Made before the King of France, vpon the yeare 1600 betweene the Bishop of Eureux, and the L. Plessis Mornay. . . By N. D.* 1604. Sig. D4.

† See J. H. Pollen, *The English Catholics in the Reign of Queen Elizabeth* (1920), pp. 347 and 366.

Pounde's pamphlet occupies sigs. A4–B3v and ends 'This is my faith, because it is the Catholique faith. Thomas Pownde'.*

In his address 'To all the Pope his Catholiques, in England or else where', Crowley states that in the previous September (1580) he had been appointed to confer with Catholics who were in the Marshalsey and the White Lion, together with Henry Trippe. Pounde, who was in the Marshalsey, refused conference but presented six reasons in a written pamphlet and asked for an answer in writing (7 September 1580). On 9 September Crowley started an Answer. Meanwhile, Pounde was removed to another prison, and when the Answer was ready it could not be delivered. Since Pounde went on distributing copies of his pamphlet, Crowley approached the Bishop of London for leave to print his Answer, which was allowed 4 January 1581.† Crowley's Answer is followed by 'A breefe Aunswer to Maister Pownds six Reasons. Written by Maister Henrie Trippe' (two leaves).

RAINOLDS, WILLIAM
1544?–1594

120. A Refutation of / sundry reprehen- / sions, cauils, and false / sleightes, by which M. Whitaker la- / boureth to deface the late English / translation, and Catholike annota- / tions of the new Testament, / and the booke of Dis- / couery of hereti- / cal corrup- / tions. / By William Rainolds, Student of Diui- / nitie in the English Colledge at Rhemes. / 2.Timoth. 3.v.8,9. / As Iannes and Mambres resisted Moyses, so / these also resist the truth, men corrupted / in minde, reprobate concerning the fayth. / But they shal prosper no further. For their / folly shal be manifest to al, as theirs also / vvas. / Veni & vide. Come and see. Iohn.1.v.46. / Printed at Paris, / the yere 1583. [Richard Verstegan.]

8°. a–f+A–Z+Aa–Nn in eights+Oo⁴+Pp². Pag. 1[a1]–92[f6]; 1[A1]–561 [Nn1]. Cw. Mg. Rt – A Refutation of / M.W. Reprehension. (1) Title [a1]. (2) Blank [a1v]. (3) 'The Preface to the Reader' [a2–f2]. (4) 'An Aduertisment to the Reader' [f2v–6v]. (5) Table of Chapters [f7–8]. (6) Blank [f8v]. (7) Text in 17 chapters and Conclusion [A1–Nn1]. (8) General Table [Nn1v–Pp1v]. (9) 'The faultes correct thus' [Pp2]. (10) Blank [Pp2v].

A reply to William Whitaker's attack on Gregory Martin's *Discouery* (entry 87) and the Rhemes *New Testament* (entry 86) in the Preface to the Christian Reader of his *Ad Nicolai Sanderi Demonstrationes Quadraginta, in octauo libro visibilis Monarchiae positas, quibus Romanum Pontificem non esse Antichristum docere instituit,*

* The Six Articles are printed in Foley, *Records S.J.*, Vol. III, pp. 632–44.
† cp. Strype, *Life and Acts of John Aylmer* (1821), p. 30.

responsio Gulielmi Whitakeri. London, 1583. Rainolds was answered by Whitaker in *An answere to a certeine Booke, written by Maister William Rainolds Student of Diuinitie in the English Colledge at Rhemes, and entituled, A Refutation of sundrie reprehensions, Cauils, &c. By William Whitaker, professor of Diuinitie in the Vniuersitie of Cambridge*. London, 1585.

A comparison with the printing of Martin's *Treatyse of Christian Peregrination* (entry 88), printed in the same year, leaves no room for doubt that Rainolds's book was also published by Verstegan. Since printing the former, the printer had evidently acquired both Greek and Hebrew type. These are both used in the latter book. The following words, which occur in the table of faults, are significant: 'Some other faultes there are . . . al which, considering the ordinarie difficulties of printing, where straungers are the workers, cōpositors, & correctors, (besides other extraordinarie mishaps) I trust the Reader of his curtesie wil easely pardon.' The 'other extraordinarie mishaps', doubtless, are connected with the close watch which was kept on Verstegan in Paris at this time. He was arrested later, at the instance of Stafford, the English ambassador, for printing 'certain catholic books'.

121. A Treatise conteyning the true Catholike and Apostolike Faith of the Holy Sacrifice and Sacrament ordeyned by Christ at his last Supper: With a declaration of the Berengarian heresie renewed in our age: and an Answere to certain Sermons made by M. Robert Bruce Minister of Edinburgh concerning this matter. By William Reynolde Priest. Ioan.6. 51. The bread which I wil give, is my flesh, (the same) which I wil give for the life of the world. At Antwerpe, Imprinted by Ioachim Trognesius. M.D.XCIII.

RASTELL, JOHN, S.J.

1527–1577

122. [ornament] A confutation / of a sermon, pronoūced by M. Iuell, / at Paules crosse, the second Sondaie / before Easter (which Catholikes / doe call Passion Sondaie) An- / no Dñi. M.D.LX. By Iohn / Rastell M. of Art, and stu- / dient in diuinitie. / [ornament. rule] / Miror quòd tam citò transferimini, ab eo / qui vos vocauit in gratiam Christi, / in aliud Euangelium. &c / [mg.] Galat. 1. / I maruell that yow be so sone caried awaie / from hym which called yow vnto the grace / of Christ, in to an other Gospel. / [ornament. rule] / ἔθη ἀρχαῖα κρατεῖτο. / Mores antiqui obtineant. / Lett old customes preuaile. / [ornament] / Imprinted at Antwerp by Aegidius Diest. / 21. Nouemb. Anno. 1564. / Cum Priuilegio.

8°. A–Y in eights+Z^7. Fol. 1[A6]–176[Z5]. Cw. Mg. Rt – A Confutation of / M. Iuelles Sermon. (1) Title [A1]. (2) Privilegium: Brussels. 17 Nov. 1564 [A1^v]. (3) Preface to the Reader: Louvain. Nov. 20 [A2–5]. (4) Text [A6–X4]. (5) 'A Conclusion to the Reader, with a challenge annexed' [X5–Z5^v]. (6) Imprimatur: 11 Nov. 1561 [Z5^v]. (7) Table [Z6–7]. (8) 'Faultes escaped in the printing' [Z7^v].

Jewel's sermon was preached at Paul's Cross, 31 March 1560. Dated correctly in the title, it is misdated in the text (fol. 141.) *The Confutation* was not originally intended for the press, as we learn from the preface, having been composed four years before, in 1560, and addressed to a single friend, M. N. Jewel's posy in Greek, Latin and English (see title) was prefixed to the sermon.

William Fulke's reply to this book appeared in 1579. It was called *A Refutation of Maister Iohn Rastels Confutation as he calleth it of maister Iewels sermon*, and was part of a larger work entitled *D. Heskins, D. Sanders, and M. Rastel, accounted* (*among their faction*) *three pillers* . . . (full title at entry 57).*

123. [ornament] A Copie of a / challenge, taken owt of the / confutation of M. Iuells / sermon made by / Iohn Rastell. / [ornament] / Imprinted at Antwerp by Aegidius Diest, / xx. Ianuarij. Anno M.D.LXV. / Cum Priuilegio.

BOD.

8°. Italic and roman. A–B in eights+C^4. Fol. 1[A1]–18[C2]. Cw. Mg. Rt – A Challenge agaynst / the Protestantes. (1) Title [A1]. (2) Blank [A1^v]. (3) Text [A2–C2^v]. (4) Imprimatur: 11 Nov. 1561 [C2^v]. (5) Blank [C3–4].

This pamphlet is a page by page reprint of fol. 160–76 (sigs. X4–Z5) of *A confutation of a sermon* (see entry 122). The following differences are to be noted: Title is new; fol. 2^a [A2] has been reset and has a different ornamental capital; fol. 2^b [A2^v] has a marg. reference altered; fol. 18^b [C2^v] has been reset. The watermark is the same in both books.

124. A Replie / against an answer / (falslie intitled) in Defence / of the truth, made by Iohn / Rastell: M. of Art, and / studient in diuinitie. / Forte est vinum, fortior est Rex, fortio- / res sunt mulieres, super omnia vincit / Veritas. / [mg.] 3.Esd.3. / Wyne ys strong, A King ys stronger, / Women be stronger, but, aboue

* The Challenge controversy to which Rastell's *Confutation* belongs is set out at pp. 60 et seq.

all / thinges, truth ouercummeth. / [ornament] / Imprinted at Antwerp by Aegidius Diest, / x Martij. Anno M.D.LXV. / Cum Priuilegio.

8°. ¶+†+A–Z+Aa–Bb in eights+Cc^4. Fol. 1[A1]–205[Cc3]. Cw. Mg. Rt – A Replie against the false- / named Defence of the truth. (1) Title [¶1]. (2) Privilegium: Brussels. 10 March 1565 [¶1^v]. (3) 'To the Reader': Louvain. 2 March [¶2–†6]. (4) Two blanks [†7–8]. (5) Text [A–Cc3^v]. (6) Imprimatur [Cc3^v]. (7) Table [Cc4]. (8) 'Faultes escaped' [Cc4^v].

This work is a reply to Bishop T. Cooper's *An Answere in defence of the truth*, which, in its turn, was a reply to *An Apologie of priuate Masse* (see entry 1); not, as Gillow supposed,* a rejoinder to Jewel's answer to Dr. Thos. Harding. This is quite clear, as the thirteen chapters correspond precisely to the thirteen chapters of Cooper's *Defence* and quote chapter and verse from that book.

125. A Treatise / intitled, Beware of / M. Iewel. By Iohn Rastel / Master of Arte and / Student of Di- / uinitie. / Math.7. / Beware of false Prophets, which come vnto / you in the cotes of sheepe, but inwardlye are Ra- / uening wolues. &c. / [device] / Antuerpiae / Ex officina Ioannis Fouleri. / M.D.LXVI.

8°. B.L. A^8+★^{4}+B–Z in eights+℟^{4}. Fol. 1[B1]–180[℟4]. Cw. Mg. Rt – Beware of M. Iewel. (1) Title [A1]. (2) Blank (A1^v]. (3) 'To the Indifferent Reader': Antwerp. 10 May [A2–8; ★1–4]. (4) Privilegium: Brussels. 8 March 1565; and Imprimatur: Louvain. 7 March 1565 [★4^v]. (5) Text in two books[B1–℟4]. (6) 'Faultes escaped in the Printing'. 'Faultes in the Margent' [℟4].

This is Rastell's reply to Jewel's *A Replie vnto M. Hardinges Answeare* (see entry 49). In the preface to the Reader Rastell describes the first book as an answer to 'the foure first Articles' of Jewel's book, and says: 'In the second boke, I come to more particular poyntes.' He then goes on, 'By all which Euidences, if it be not sufficiently proued, that he is a man of little Modesty, Truthe and Conscience, I will shortly set furth a thirde boke against him' (see next entry).†

126. The Third / Booke, Declaring by / Examples out of Auncient Coun- / cels, Fathers, and Later wri- / ters, that it is time to / Beware of / M. Iewel. / By Iohn Rastel Master of Art and /

* *Bibl. Dict.* under *Rastell.*

† Rastell refers at sig. Z2^v to Jewel's contention that the word *Missa* was used in early writings for 'any assemblie of the people . . . For which cause al manner of common praiers many times are called, Missa, as may be seen in Cassianus', &c. (Jewel – *A Replie vnto M. Hardinges Answeare* (1565), at sig. G3). He answers that 'the Masse at Rome is [not] such a kynde of Praier only'. Possibly this is the justification for Shakespeare's use of the term 'evening mass' in *Romeo and Juliet*, Act IV, Scene 1.

Student of Diuinitie. / Math.7. / Beware of false Prophets, which come vnto / you in the cotes of sheepe, but inwardly are Ra- / uening wolues, &c. / [device] / Antuerpiae, / Ex officina Ioannis Fouleri. / M.D.LXVI.

8°. B.L. A^8+*^4+B–Z+AA–GG in eights+HH^7. Fol. 1[B1]–239[HH7]. Cw. Mg. Rt – The third Booke. / Beware of M. Iewel. (1) Title [A1]. (2) Blank [A1^v]. (3) 'To the Indifferent Reader': Louvain [A2–8; *1–2]. (4) Imprimatur: Louvain. 3 Nov. 1566 [*3]. (5) 'Faultes escaped in the Printing' [*3^v]. (6) Text [*4–HH7]. (7) A leaf appears to be missing.

See previous entry.

127. A Briefe Shevv / Of the false VVares packt / together in the named, Apo- / logy of the Churche / of England. / By Iohn Rastell M. of Art and student of / Diuinitie. / Qui nititur Mendacijs, hic pascit ventos, Idem / autem ipse sequitur aues volantes. / [mg.] Prob. 10. / He that leaneth to lies, feedeth yͤ winds: / & the selfe same foloweth yͤ fleyng birdes. / [device] / Louanii, / Apud Ioannem Foulerum. / Anno D. 1567.

Bod.

8°. Italic (quotations from *Apology* in B.L.). $*^4+$A–R in eights+S^4. Fol. 1 [A1]–140[S4]. Cw. Mg. Rt – The False VVares / Of the Apol. of Engl. (1) Title [*1]. (2) Privilegium: Antwerp. 9 July 1567 [*1^v]. (3) 'To the Reader': Louvain. Aug. 21 [*2–3^v]. (4) Imprimatur: 7 July 1567 [*4]. (5) Ornament [*4^v]. (6) Text [A–S4^v].

This book belongs to that group of controversial works which had their origin in John Jewel's *Apologia Ecclesiae Anglicanae* (1562).* Thomas Harding had replied to Jewel's *Apology* in 1565 (see entry 50), and a further reply from Jewel was expected. Rastell refers to this in his address 'To the Reader', and suggests that the extracts which he has gathered together in this book from Harding's *Confutation of the Apologie* should be read before the 'Grosse Booke' which is to follow from Jewel's pen. The text is composed of extracts from the *Apology* followed by Harding's confutation, as set out in Harding's book. Occasionally Rastell will introduce a statement or comment of his own, in one case at least arising out of information which had been conveyed to him by someone who was 'present at M. Iewels sermō at Poules Crosse the fiftenth of Iuly last', when Jewel apparently accused Harding of misquoting him.

ROSCARROCK, NICOLAS
1549?–1634?
(see entry 20)

* See p. 60 for a full discussion of this controversy.

SANDER, NICOLAS, D.D.
1530?–1581

128. The supper of our / Lord set foorth / in six Bookes, according to the truth of the / gospell, and the faith of the Catho- / like Churche. / By Nicolas Saunder Doctor / of Diuinitie. / The contents of euery Booke are to be seen / in the syde following. / [ornament] / Manhu? / [ornament] / What is this? / The figure. Exo.16. / This is the bread which our Lord hath geuen you to eate. / The Prophecie. Prouerb.9. / Come, eate my bread, & drink yͤ wine which I haue mixed for you. / The promise. Ioan. 6. / The bread which I wil geue, is my flesh for the life of the world. / The perfoormance. Mat.26. Luce.22. / Take, eate, this is my body which is geuen for you. / The belefe of the Churche. Hilar. de Trin.8. / Both our Lord hath professed, and we beleue it to be flesh in dede. / The custome of heretikes. Tertul. de Resur. car. / The contrarie part reyseth vp trouble by pretense of figures. / Louanii. / Anno Domini. 1565. [John Fowler.]*

4°. B.L. A–Z+Aa–Zz+Aaa–Zzz+AAaa–ZZzz+Aaaaa–Qqqqq in fours. Fol. 1[A4]–425[Qqqqq4]. Cw. Mg. Rt – The supper / of our Lord [with var.]. (1) Title [A1]. (2) 'The contents of euery Booke' [A1ᵛ]. (3) 'To the Body and Blood of our Sauiour' &c. [A2–3]. (4) 'The Contentes of the first Booke' [A3ᵛ]. (5) 'The preface to the Christian Reader' [A4–C2]. (6) 'Notes concerning the translation' [C2ᵛ–D2]. (7) Text of Book I [D2ᵛ–M2ᵛ]. (8) Text of Books II, III, IV, V and VI with preface and table of chapters in each case [M3–PPpp3]. (9) 'Here vnto is added the seuenth booke, conteining a confutation of the fifth article of M. Iuels Reply against D. Harding, concerning the reall presence of Christes body in the supper of our Lorde': preface, table of chapters and text [PPpp3–Qqqqq4ᵛ]. (10) 'Approbatio septimi libri': Louvain. 20. Dec. 1565 [Qqqqq4ᵛ].

This work by the best-hated English Catholic of the time is, we are told in the Preface, an answer to Jewel's 'Apologie of the Churche of England'. It was answered in part by Alexander Nowell in *A confutation as wel of M. Dormans last boke entituled "A disproufe &c." as also of D. Sander his causes of transubstantiation* (London, 1567), and more fully (the whole seven books coming under review) later by W. Fulke in *A Reioynder to Bristows Replie in defence of Allens scroll of Articles and Booke of Purgatorie. Also the cauils of Nicholas Sander D. in Diuinitie about the Supper of our Lord, and the Apologie of the Church of England, touching the doctrine thereof, Confuted by William Fulke* (London, 1581).†

* See next entry.

† Sander is faithfully dealt with by Strype in *Life and Acts of Parker* (1821), Vol. II, pp. 168–74; 177–80; and Vol. III, Appendices 75, 76 and 77.

129. The supper of our Lord / set foorth accor- / ding to the truth of the Gospell and Catholike faith. / By Nicolas Saunder, Doctor of Diuinitie. / [ornament] With a confutation of such false doctrine as the Apologie of / the Churche of England, M. Nowels chalenge, or M. Iuels / Replie haue vttered, touching the reall presence / of Christe in the Sacrament. / [ornament] / Manhu? / [ornament] / What is this? / The figure. Exod.16. / This is the bread which our Lord hath geuen you to eate. / The prophecie. Prouerb.9. / Come eate my bread, & drink ẏ wine which I haue mixed for you. / The promise. Ioan.6. / The bread which I wil geue, is my flesh for the life of the world. / The performance. Matt.26. Luc.22. / He gaue, sayīg: take, eate, this is my body which is geuē for you. / The doctrine of the Apostles. I.Cor.10. / The bread which we break, is ẏ cōmunicatīg of our Lords body. / The belefe of the Church. Hilar. lib.8. de Trinit. / Both our Lord hath professed, & we beleue it to be flesh in dede. / The custome of Heretiks. Tertul. de Resur.car. / The contrarie part reiseth vp trouble by pretense of figures. / Louanii. / Anno domini 1566. [John Fowler.]

[colophon on Rrrrr2] Louanii. / Apud Ioannem Foulerum / Anno Domini 1566. / Mense Ianuar.

4°. B.L. A–Z+Aa–Zz+Aaa–Zzz+AAaa–ZZzz+Aaaaa–Qqqqq in fours+ Rrrrr². Fol. as 1565. Cw. Mg. Rt. as 1565. (1) Title [A1]. (2) Privilegium: refers to original privilegium as 20 Aug. 1565 (i.e. for the original six books) and to the additional (i.e. the seventh) book, and renews the privilege for the whole seven. Brussels. 22 Dec. 1565 [A1ᵛ]. (3) Imprimatur (for the first six books): Louvain. 7 Aug. 1565. A second Imprimatur (for book 7): Louvain. 20 Dec. 1565 [A1ᵛ]. (4) Text follows 1565 issue (see bibl. notes 2–9 of previous entry). (5) Additional to 1565 issue: (a) 'A briefe table of the whole worke' [Rrrrr1]. (b) 'Faultes and corrections' [Rrrrr1ᵛ–2]. (c) Colophon [Rrrrr2]. (d) Blank [Rrrrr2ᵛ].

A careful examination of the two copies (1565 and 1566) in the British Museum and a comparison with the Stonyhurst copy (1566) shows them to be two issues of the same printing; Fowler being the printer, therefore, of the earlier as well as of the later issue. The following further points should be noted: (a) The 1565 issue, being probably Fowler's first attempt at publication,* omitted such necessary items as the privilegium and the imprimatur for the first six books (we note the *approbatio* of book 7), and there was no table of faults. (b) The title-page of the 1565 issue with its 'in six Bookes' had already been printed before the seventh book was added. The latter was admittedly an after-thought, for the author says in the preface to it that it was written 'after seeing Iuel's reply against Harding, and after

* See p. 342.

the completion of the six books'. (c) In order to repair these omissions, etc., Fowler reprinted the title-page, leaving out the words 'in six Bookes' and making a necessary emendation in the texts, resetting at the same time its companion leaf, sig. A4; introduced the omitted privilegium and the imprimaturs on the reverse of the title-page; and shifted the contents table to the end of the book, adding a table of faults. (d) It may have been necessary to introduce the colophon in order to meet the Spanish printing laws.*

130. The Rocke of / the Churche / Wherein the Primacy of S. Peter and / of his Successours the Bishops / of Rome is proued out of / Gods Worde. / By Nicolas Sander D. of diuinity. / [ornament] / The eternal Rock of the vniuersal Church. / Christ was the rock, an other foundatiō / no man is hable is put. I Cor. 3. & 10. / The temporal Rock of the militant Church. / Thou art Peter, and vppon this Rocke I / wil build my Church. Matth.16. / The continuance of this temporal Rocke. / In the Church of Rome the primacy of / the Apostolike chaier hath alwaies flori- / shed. August. in Epist. 162. / Recken euen from the very seate of Pe- / ter: and in that rew of Fathers, consyder, / who succeded the other. That is the rock / which the proud gates of hel doe not o- / uercome. In Psal. cōt. part. Don. Tom. 7. / Louanii, / Apud Ioannem Foulerum. / Anno D. 1567.

8°. Italic. ‡–‡‡‡‡+A–Z+Aa–Mm in eights+Nn[6]. Pag. 1[A1]–566 [Nn3]. Cw. Mg. Rt – The Rocke / of the Churche. (1) Title [‡1]. (2) Privilegium: Brussels. 27 Febr. 1566 [‡1v]. (3) Address to Parker and others [‡2–‡‡‡‡7]. (4) 'The Chapiters of the Treatise following' [‡‡‡‡7v–8]. (5) Text in eighteen chapters [A–Nn3v]. (6) Imprimatur: Louvain. 25 Febr. 1566 [Nn3v]. (7) Summary of chief points [Nn4–5]. (8) 'Faultes escaped in the printing' [Nn6]. (9) Device [Nn6v].

This work is a further instalment of the attack upon Jewel. It was answered by W. Fulke in *A Retentiue, to stay good christians, in true faith and religion, against the motiues of Richard Bristow. Also A Discouerie of the Daungerous Rocke of the Popish Church, commended by Nicholas Sander D. of Diuinitie. Done by William Fulke Doctor of diuinitie, and Maister of Pembroke hall in Cambridge . . .* London, 1580.†

* A law regulating printing and publishing in Spain, and presumably in the Spanish Netherlands, of 1558 demands the name of author, printer and place of printing to be placed in a book, and there were heavy penalties for its contravention. It would seem that this law was observed at first by the recusant printers, but it must have been waived later on when things became more difficult for them. See paper by G. F. Barwick in *Bibliog. Soc. Trans.*, Vol. 4.

† The *Discouery* has been reprinted by the Parker Society (1848). The original volume contains a catalogue of 'Popish Bookes'. See Appendix V.

I am inclined to put this work earlier than Sander's *Treatise of Images*, which is also dated 1567, on account of the very early date of the privilegium (27 February 1566). The imprimatur of the *Treatise* is undated. Fulke refers to the two works in this order in his *Catalogue of Popish Bookes* (see Appendix V), but this may have no significance.

131. A Treatise / Of the Images of Christ, and / of his Saints: and that it is vnlaufull / to breake them, and lauful to honour them. / With a Confutation of such false doctrine / as M. Iewel hath vttered in his Replie, / concerning that matter. / Made by Nicolas Sander, Doctour / of Diuinitie. / [ornament] / Ecclesiastici. 45. / τὸ μνημόσυνον (τοῦ ἀγαπημένου ὑπὸ θεοῦ) ἐν εὐλογίαις. Memoria dilecti Deo, in benedictionibus est. / [ornament] The Remembraunce or the Memorial of the / beloued of God, is blessed. That is to say, any / thing which maketh vs remember him that is / beloued of God, is worthy of praise and of honor. / Louanii, / Apud Ioannem Foulerum. / 1567.

Bod.

8°. B.L. (preface in roman) *–******+A–Z+AA–BB in eights+CC⁴. Fol. 1[B1]–192[BB8]. Cw. Mg. Rt. varies. (1) Title [*1]. (2) Blank [*1ᵛ]. (3) The Preface [*2–A7]. (4) 'Faultes escaped in the Printing' [A7ᵛ]. (5) 'The Chapiters of the Treatise following' [A8]. (6) Text in seventeen chapters [B1–CC1]. (7) Imprimatur, followed by the words 'cum gratia & Priuilegio Regiae Maiestatis' [CC1]. (8) 'The contents of the principal points of this Treatise' [CC1ᵛ–CC4ᵛ].

By his exposition of the doctrine of Images the writer answers Jewel on this subject. W. Fulke replied in 'A Confutation of an idolatrous Treatise of Nicolas Sander Doctor in Diuinitie, which mainteyneth the making and honouring of Images, by W. F. Doctour in Diuinitie'. This occurs in the volume *D. Heskins, D. Sanders, and M. Rastel, accounted* (*among their faction*) *three pillers* . . . London, 1579 (full title at entry 57).

132. A Briefe / Treatise of / Vsurie, made by / Nicolas Sander D. of / Diuinitie. / Luc.6. / Mutuum date, nihil inde sperantes. / Geue to lone, hoping for nothĩg therof. / [device] / Louanii, / Apud Ioannem Foulerum, An.1568. / Cum Priuilegio. Subsig. / De La Torre.

8°. A–I in eights. Fol. 1[A2]–67[I4]. Cw. Mg. Rt – Of Vsurie. (1) Title [A1]. (2) Blank [A1ᵛ]. (3) Text in ten chapters [A2–I4ᵛ]. (4) Imprimatur: Louvain. 8 Apr. 1568, *stylo communi seu Romano* [I5]. (5) Table of Contents [I5ᵛ–6]. (6) 'Faultes escaped in printing' [I6ᵛ–7]. (7) Device [I7ᵛ]. (8) Blank [I8] *

* Bibl. details in part from Bodleian copy. Sigs. H and I lacking in B.M. copy.

This treatise of Sander's, strangely enough, seems to have been the inspiration of Jewel's discourse on 1 Thess. iv, where the subject of usury is treated. This discourse was one of a series apparently delivered in the cathedral of Salisbury in 1569, the year following the publication of Sander's work.*

SHACKLOCK, RICHARD

fl. 1575

133. An Epistle / of the Reuerend / Father in God Hiero- / nimus Osorius Bishop of / Arcoburge in Portugale, to the most excellent Princesse Elizabeth / by the grace of God Que- / ne of England, Fraunce, / and Ireland. &c. / Translated oute of Latten in to Englishe by / Richard Shacklock M. of Arte and stu- / dent of the Ciuill Lavves in Louaine. / [device] / Imprinted at Antwerp by Iohn / Latius Anno 1565.

8°. A–K in eights. Fol. 1[A1]–78[K6]. Cw. Mg. Rt – A Pearle for / a Prynce. (1) Title [A1].(2)Verses headed 'The Translatour' [A1v].(3) 'To the Reader': Antwerp. 13 March. R.S. [A2–5]. (4) Ornament [A5v]. (5) Text [A6–K6]. (6) Imprimatur [K6]. (7) 'To M. Doctor Haddon': Antwerp. 27 March [K6v–K7v]. (8) 'Faultes escaped in some copyes' [K8]. (9) Blank [K8v].†

The Bishop's book was *Epistola ad Elizabetham Angliae Reginam de Religione* (Paris, 1563). It deals with a number of subjects, including kings and princes, justice, wise men and fools, religion, and it is highly flattering to Elizabeth.

Walter Haddon, Master of the Requests, at the instance of the Government, having replied to Osorius in Latin (1563),‡ this translation of Shacklock's was in some sort an answer to that reply. Shacklock's translation was countered by a translation of Haddon's work by Abraham Hartwell entitled *A sight of the Portugall Pearle, that is the Aunswere of D. Haddon Maister of the requests . . . against the epistle of Hieronimus Osorius, a Portugall, entitled a Pearle for a Prince. Translated out of lattyn into englishe by Abraham Hartwell, Student in the kynges colledge in Cambridge.* 1565.§ Osorius eventually replied to Haddon in a work pub-

* Reprinted in the *Works of John Jewel* by R. W. Jelf (1848), Vol. 7. See also the paper *De Usura*, found in Jewel's study after his death and reprinted in the same volume.

† 'Arcoburge in Portugale' appears to be a mistake. Paquot says, 'Osorio n'étoit pas Evêque d'Arcoburge (nom inconnu) mais de Silves'. *Mémoires* III, p. 231.

‡ *Gualtheri Haddoni pro Reformatione Anglicana Epistola Apologetica ad Hier. Osorium, Lusitanum.* Paris, 1563. Corrections and additions were made by Sir Thomas Smith, Queen Elizabeth's Ambassador in Paris, who was responsible for getting this answer through the press. The licence to print was obtained with considerable difficulty. See Strype, *Life of Sir Thomas Smith* (1820), pp. 75–80 and 90. For a full account of the Osorius controversy, see Strype, *Annals* (1824), Vol. I, pt. 1, pp. 124 ff., pp. 541–2; Vol. I, pt. 2, pp. 69 ff.; and Vol. III, pt. 1, pp. 96–9.

§ *Pollard and Redgrave* gives also *An answer in action to a Portingale Pearle, called a Pearle for a Prince* [*by D. Emilie?*]. 1570.

lished in 1567 and translated by John Fen under the title of *A Learned and very Eloquent Treatie* (1568): see entry 38 above. Haddon started a rejoinder but died before finishing it.* The *Pearle for a Prynce* was reprinted at Antwerp by Aegidius Diest, the reprint carrying the same date as the original edition, 1565. It is a line-by-line copy and bears evident marks of being the later edition.

134. [ornament. rule] / A most excel- / lent treatise of the / be-gynnyng of heresyes in oure tyme, com- / pyled by the Reuerend Father in God / Stanislaus Hosius Byshop / of Wormes in Prussia. / To the moste renomed Prynce Lorde Sigismund / myghtie Kyng of Poole, greate Duke of / Luten and Russia, Lorde and Heyre of / all Prussia, Masouia, Samogitia &c. / Translated out of Laten in to Englyshe by / Richard Shacklock M. of Arte, and student / of the Ciuil lawes, and intituled by hym: / The hatchet of heresies. / [ornament. rule] / Haereses ad suam originem reuocasse, est refutasse. / Of heresies to shewe the spryng, / Is them vnto an end to bryng. / [ornament. rule] / [ornament] Imprinted at Antwerp by Aeg. Diest. / Anno. 1565. the 10. of August. / Cum Priuilegio. / [ornament. rule]

8°. B.L. a–b+A–M in eights+N[7]. Fol. 1[A1]–95[M7]. Cw. Mg. Rt – The Hachet / of Heresyes. (1) Title [a1]. (2) Verses headed 'The Translatoure vpon the figure following' [a1v]. (3) Cut of Satan, Tree of heresy, Hosius with axe &c. [a2]. (4) Verses headed 'The Translatoure vpon the figure before-going' [a2v]. (5) Address to the Queen: Richard Shacklock [a3–8]. (6) Verses headed 'The Translatoure vpon the holy wryter Hosius' [a8v]. (7) Epistle dedicatory to Sigismund: 'Ides of Octobre 1557' [b1–8]. (8) Latin verses of Michael Serinius to the reader; followed by Translator's English paraphrase. Signed R.S. [b8v]. (9) Text [A1–M7]. (10) Latin verses of Shacklock *pro Regina, Regno, et toto Christianismo* [M8]. (11) Table [N1–7].

A translation of Hosius's *De origine haeresium nostri temporis* (Louvain, 1559). In the address to the Queen the translator explains that he has named this book 'the hatchet of heresies. for so muche as to shewe the begynnyng of heresies, is to bryng heresye vnto an end, and to cut it downe none other wyse then an hatchet in man his hand layde to the roote of a plant, sone supplāteth and ouerthroweth it. Euen so truly', he continues, 'thys boke is the hatchet which supplanteth that euel plant which Sathā hath sowed in God his groūde, whose roote is ray-lyng, whose body is rebellion, whose braunches be bloodshedde,

* The rejoinder was eventually published as *Contra Hieron. Osorium, eiusque odiosas insectationes pro Euangelicae veritatis necessaria Defensione, Responsio Apologetica. Per clariss. virum Gualt. Haddonum inchoata: Deinde suscepta et continuata per Ioan. Foxum.* London, 1577. Haddon was responsible for Book I and part of Book II of the three books which this work comprises. It was afterwards translated into English by James Bell under the title *Against Ierome Osorius Byshopp of Siluane in Portingall and against his slaunderous Inuectiues* . . . London, 1581.

whose leaues be lyes, whose frute be the aples of Atheisme, that is to be of no Religion, or to thynck that there is no God at all' [a6v].* He has every confidence in dedicating his translation to Her Majesty, knowing her love of truth and learning, and he offers it in English rather than in 'any fyner forren language' because it tells of matters of great importance and as such would be 'better welcome to youre grace in oure own contrye speche'.

John Barthlet gave the answer direct to Shacklock's book in his *The Pedegrewe of Heretiques*. 1566. To quote the *D.N.B.*: 'Barthlet, scandalised by Shacklock's contempt for the doctrines of the Reformation, tried to show that all Roman catholic doctrines were tainted by heresies traceable to either Judas Iscariot or Simon Magus. His table of heretics is of appalling length, and includes such obscure sects as "Visiblers", "Quantitiners", "Metamorphistes", and "Mice-feeders" '.† To these may be added: Matrimonie Tatians, Diuorcing Montanists, Collyridianes or Marymen, Bysleepers, Lady Dawers, Fayth Flyghters, Gospellfacers, Patrines, Bread Spoylers, and Accident rotters.

SHERWIN, RALPH

1550–1581

(see entry 13)

STANYHURST, RICHARD

1547–1618

135. [within a compartment] 1577. [in upper panel] / The / Historie of Irelande / from the first inhabitation / thereof, vnto the yeare 1509. / Collected by Raphaell Holinshed, / and continued till the yeare 1547. / by Richarde Stanyhurst. / At London, / ¶Imprinted for Iohn / Harison. / God saue the Queene. [in lower panel].

2°. B.L. ☙²+A–C in eights+D⁴+A–D in eights+E⁵+F–G in eights+H⁶+I². Fol. 1[A1]–28[D4]; Pag. 1[A1]–115[H5] (in double columns). Cw. Mg. Rts – (1) The description of Irelande. (2) The Historie of Irelande.‡

* This describes the symbolic tree of the cut at sig. a2.

† *D.N.B.*, s.v. *John Barthlet*.

‡ A copy of this work in the Grenville Library of the British Museum differs from the above in the following particulars: The title-page has 'Imprinted for George Bishop', and the second register runs: A–G in eights+H⁶+I², the additional signatures, E6–8, comprising three cancelled leaves. A fourth cancelled leaf has been inserted after sig. F5. The subject-matter of these cancellands is referred to at entry 27.

The *Historie of Irelande* forms the third part of *The Firste volume of the Chronicles of England, Scotlande, and Irelande* (London, 1577). Stanyhurst's contribution is as follows:

(1) 'A Treatise contayning a playne and perfect Description of Irelande, with an Introduction, to the better vnderstanding of the Hystories, appartayning to that Islande: compyled by Richard Stanyhurst, and written to the Ryght Honorable, Syr Henry Sydney Knight', etc. [A1–D4^{v} (1st register)].

It would seem that this part was added after the original design of the *Historie*, as expressed on the title-page above, had been completed, since there is no reference to this preliminary work of Stanyhurst's there. It is to be observed that it is printed in a different black-letter type from the rest of the *Chronicles*, and it will be noted that it has a separate register. The text is based upon Campion's *Historie of Ireland* (entry 27), which Stanyhurst re-arranges and enlarges.

(2) 'The thirde Booke of the Historie of Ireland, comprising the raigne of Henry the eyght: continued by Richard Stanihurst, and written to the right honorable Sir Henrie Sidney Knight', etc. [F1^{v}–H5 (2nd register)].

Illustrated by numerous woodcuts. Full use is again made of Campion.

136. Thee first fo[u-] / re bookes of Vir- / gil his Aeneis transla- / ted intoo English heroical verse by Ri- / chard Stanyhurst, wyth oother / Poëtical diuises there- / too annexed. / [device] / Imprinted at Leiden in Holland by Iohn Pates. / [rule] / Anno M.D.LXXXII.

4°. Italic and roman. A–P in fours+Q^{1}. Pag. 1[B3]–110[Q1^{v}]. Cw. Mg. (at A4 and N2–3 only). Rt. varies. (1) Title [A1]. (2) Blank [A1^{v}]. (3) 'Too thee Right Honourable my verie loouing broother thee Lord Baron of Dunsanye': 'From Leiden in Holland thee last of Iune. 1582. Youre Lordship his loouing broother Richard Stanyhurst' [A2–4^{v}]. (4) 'To thee Learned Reader' [B1–2^{v}]. (5) Text of the Translation (at the end of Book 4 are the words 'Opus decem dierum') [B3–N1]. (6) Translations of certain Psalms of David into English in various metres, with metrical notes [N1^{v}–4]. (7) 'A Prayer too thee Trinitye' (in English sapphics) [N4^{v}]. (8) Conceits (translations from Latin into English verse) [N4^{v}–P1^{v}]. (9) Epitaphs in Latin and English, with notes [P2–Q1^{v}]. (10) 'Iohn Pates printer too thee curteous reader', followed by errata [Q1^{v}].

The printer's Address is as follows: 'I am too craue thy paciēce and paynes (good reader) in bearing wyth such faultes as haue escapte in printing; and in correcting as wel such as are layd downe heere too thy view, as al oother whereat thow shalt hap too stumble in perusing this treatise. Thee noouelty e of imprinting English in theese partes, and thee absence of thee author from perusing soom proofes could not choose but breede errours. But for thee abridging of thy trauayle I wyl lay downe such faultes as are at this present found to bee of greatest importaũce. And as for thee wrõg placing of an V for an N, or an N for an V, and in printing two EE for one E, or one for two, and for thee mispoyncting of periods; thee correction of theese I must bee forced for this tyme too refer too thye friendlye paynes'.

A second edition was printed by Henry Bynneman in 1583.

STAPLETON, THOMAS, D.D.
1535–1598

137. The Apologie / of Fridericus Staphy- / lus Counseller to / the late Emperour / Ferdinandus, &c. / Intreating / Of the true and right vnderstanding of holy Scripture. / Of the tanslation of the Bible in to the vulgar tongue. / Of disagrement in doctrine amonge the protestants. / Translated out of Latin in to English by Thomas / Stapleton, Student in Diuinite. / Also a discourse of the Translatour vppon the doctrine of the / protestants vvhich he trieth by the three first founders / and fathers thereof, Martin Luther, Philip / Melanchthon, and especially / Iohn Caluin. / Matth.24. Videte ne quis vos seducat. / Take hede that no man deceaue you / Matth.7. Ex fructibus eorum cognoscetis eos. / Ye shal knovve them by their frutes. / [device] / Imprinted at Antwerp by Iohn Latius, / at the signe of the Rape, with Pri- / uilege. Anno. 1565.

4°. A–Z+Aa–Zz+Aaa–Ttt in fours. Fol. 1[A1]–254[Sss4]. Cw. Mg. Rt. varies. (1) Title [A1]. (2) Privilegium: Brussels. 17 Nov. 1564 [A1v]. (3) 'The Preface of the Translatour': Louvain. 12 Nov. 1564. 'Thomas Stapleton' [A2–C4]. (4) Two quots. with comment [C4v]. (5) The Preface of Staphylus to the Bishop of Eystat [D1–H1]. (6) Staphylus to the Reader [H1v–H4]. (7) Text of translation, with the Petigrew at sig. Gg[H4v–Oo2v].* (8) Stapleton's Discourse [Oo3–Sss4]. (9) Imprimatur: Louvain. 16 Nov. 1564 [Sss4v]. (10) Table [Sss4v–Ttt4]. (11) 'Faultes escaped in Printing' [Ttt4]. (12) Blank [Ttt4v].

* This extraordinary woodcut, occupying a whole sheet [Gg], follows on a detailed account of the heresies which have had their beginning in Lutheranism. It is entitled 'A Showe of the Protestants Petigrew, as ye haue it before at large deducted' and represents a tree with a shield at its root displaying 'an ougly Monster brought forth of a cowe, in the yeare 1523. in Waltersdorff . . . much resembling the cowle of a Fryer. Whereby Luthers Monstrous life and doctrine was boded'. Toads appear among the roots of the tree. The trunk shows Luther himself with Katerin Bore – 'A Nonne . . . then coupled her selfe in pretensed wedlock with Martin Luther, a Nonne with a Fryer, Apostatesse with Apostata' – at his right side. From Luther spring three branches: Bernard Rotman, the founder of the Anabaptists, Philip Melanchthon, and Zwinglius. From each of these branches grow the leaves of the heresies. From Melanchthon, most fruitful, grow, however, three further branches: 'Zealous Lutherans' – 'Disordrely and vnruly Lutherans' – 'Ciuil Lutherans'. In addition to the notes the following verses appear at the bottom of the sheet:

The Latin version, of which this is a translation, is *Apologia D. Friderici Staphyli, recens aucta & recognita. De Vero germanoque scripturae sacrae intellectu, De Sacrorum Bibliorum in idioma vulgare tralatione* [sic], *De Luteranorum concionatorum consensione. Latinitate donata, opera F. Laurentij Surij Carthusiani* (Cologne, 1562). The learned translator does not refer directly either to the 'Challenge' or the 'Apology' of Bishop Jewel, although his running marginal commentary afforded opportunity for such references. Nor does he in the *Discourse* which follows. The latter work deals especially with the *Institutions* of Calvin and his sacramental teaching, and is a polemic against the Protestant position in general. Bishop Grindal's sermon at the death of the Emperor Ferdinand (July 1564), in which he enlarged upon Ferdinand's liberal tendencies in religion and attacked the doctrine of purgatory is, however, briefly replied to (fol. 162–75). It seems to have been assumed in previous accounts of Stapleton's works that the *History* (next entry) was the first English publication.* A scrutiny of the dates, however, points to the above work as earlier. It will be noted that both the privilegium and the imprimatur are dated November 1564, whereas the privilegium of the *History* is dated June 1565. Actually, the publication of the latter must have been later than October 1565, since it was published as a single volume with the *A Fortresse of the Faith* (see next entry), and in that work Stapleton's 'Address to the Protestants' is so dated.

An interesting corroboration of the earliness of the date of the *Apologie* is to be found in an autograph on the title-page of the British Museum copy, which reads 'Liber Roberti Hare ex dono authoris. 1564'.† This would put the date of the book not later than March 1565 (N.S.). The presumption following on this is that the printer, John Latius, calculated the new year from 1 January, according to the Spanish reckoning.

138. The History of / the Church of / Englande. / Compiled by Venerable Bede, / Englishman. / Translated out of Latin in to English by Thomas / Stapleton Student in Diuinite. / You being sometimes straungers and enemies in vnderstanding &c.

Bicause no coulours might expresse Luther the friers grace,
As also that such Champions might be knowen by their race,
Nature therefore in his chefe time of wedding and of preaching
Did blase his armes in this Monster to geue the a warning.

Such faire figures, such like truthes, such foule rootes, such ofspring,
Such holy fathers, such good sonnes, such ghospell, such blessing.
Yet thou which maiest read, vpon this Monster do not muse
But to haue more deformites, his broode in this booke peruse.

---

* So, the *Catholic Encyclopedia*; *Bibl. Dict.*, etc.

† Robert Hare, a great benefactor of Cambridge University and a papist, was Clerk of the Pells in 1564. See article in *D.N.B.*

He hath / now reconciled in the body of his fleshe through death &c. If yet ye conti- / new grounded and stedfast in the Faith, and be not moued away from the hope / of the ghospell, which ye haue heard, which hath ben preached amonge all crea- / tures vnder heauen. / [mg.] Coloss.1. / [device] / Imprinted at Antwerp by Iohn Laet, / at the signe of the Rape: with / Priuilege, Anno, 1565.

4°. $\star^{6}$+ $\triangleright^{4}$+ $\|^{4}$+A–Z+AA–ZZ+AAA–CCC in fours. Fol. 1[A1]–192 [BBB4]. Cw. Mg. Rt – The Historie(y) of the / Church of England. (1) Title [★1]. (2) Royal Arms (left and right, E.R.; subscribed 'God saue the Quene') within a border [★1^{v}]. (3) Address to Queen Elizabeth: 'Your highnes most lowly subiect, and bounden oratour, Thomas Stapleton' [★2–▷3]. (4) Forty-five differences between Catholicism and Protestantism gathered out of Bede's History [▷3^{v}–||2^{v}]. (5) Privilegium (*History* only): Brussels. 20 and 23 June 1565 [||2^{v}]. (6) 'The Preface to the Reader': Louvain. 12 June 1565. 'Thomas Stapleton' [||3–C1^{v}]. (7) 'The Life of S. Bede: writen by Trithemius' (with list of Bede's works) [C2–3]. (8) 'Bede to the Reader' [C3]. (9) Bede's address to Ceolwulf (C3^{v}–4^{v}]. (10) The *History* in five books [D–BBB3]. (11) Note by Bede [BBB3^{v}]. (12) Table [BBB4–CCC4]. (13) 'Faultes escaped in Printing' [CCC4^{v}]. (14) Cuts occur on sigs. H3, N4 and V1.

W. Fulke's reply to this publication is referred to at next entry.

There can be no doubt that *The History of the Church of Englande* and *A Fortresse of the Faith* (next entry), which is bound up with it, should be considered as separate bibliographical units. They have, therefore, been given separate entries.* On the other hand, the two works are and were intended to be a single publication. This is evident from the setting out of the 'Differences' (noted above, bibl. n.4) in the front of the *History*, and the appended note, 'All these differences touching doctrine and ecclesiasticall gouernement, are proued to concurre with the belefe and practise of the first vj.C. yeares, in the second part of the Fortresse of our first faith set forthe presently with the History' [||2^{v}].

A reprint of Bede's original version was put forth at Louvain in 1566 as follows: *Venerabilis Bedae Presbyteri Ecclesiasticae historiae gentis Anglorum, Libri V. Cum indice, qui materias insigniores ordine literarum per libros & capita demōstrat. Louanii. Apud Hieronymum Wellaeum, ad Intersigne Diamantis. Anno 1566. Cum Gratia & Priuilegio.*

139. A Fortresse of / the Faith / First planted amonge vs englishmen, and continued / hitherto in the vniuersall Church of Christ. / The faith of which time Protestants call, / Papistry. / By Thomas Stapleton / Student in Diuinite. / Melius erat illis non cognoscere viam iustitiae, quám post agnitionem retrorsum

* An examination of the bibliographical details of the two works will make this clear.

conuerti / ab eo quod illis traditum est sancto mandato. / [mg.] 2.Petr.2. / It were better for them neuer to knowe the waie of righteousnesse, then after / the acknowleadging thereof to re-uolte backe from the holy commaundement / deliuered vnto them. / [device] / Imprinted at Antwerpe, by Ihon Laet, / with Priuilege. 1565.

4°. A^4+b–z+Aa–Ss in fours. Fol. 1[A1]–162[Ss2]. Cw. Mg. Rt – A Fortresse of the Faith first / planted among vs Englishmen. &c. (1) Title [A1]. (2) Privilegium (*Fortresse* only): Brussels. 20 and 23 June 1565 [A1ᵛ]. (3) Address to the Protestants of England: 'Thomas Stapleton'. Antwerp. 17 Octob. 1565 [A2–4]. (4) Text in two parts (forty-five differences between Catholics and Protestants included, as in the Table in the *History*) [b1–Ss2]. (5) Imprimatur: Louvain. 8 June 1565 [Ss2]. (6) Table of Chapters [Ss2ᵛ–4]. (7) 'Faultes escaped in Printing' [Ss4]. (8) Blank [Ss4ᵛ].

Stapleton thus sets out the 'effect' of the *Fortresse*:

'*Papistry is the only true Christianitie* . . . This proposition or rather paradoxe, as it may seeme to many, I will folowe and prosequute in this treatise by two principall partes. In the firste part, I will proue by euident testimonies of holy scripture, of the psalmes, of the Prophetes, and of the newe Testament, by remouing the obiections of the aduersaries made out of the Scriptures, that the church can not possibly erre . . . In the seconde parte after a fewe reasonable and necessary demaundes made vnto protestans, putting the case that the knowen church of these ix. hundred yeares is a kynde off papistry . . . I wil shewe that the faith now of protestāts preached and maintained, is founde different from the faithe first planted amonge vs englishmen, and so many hundred yeares continued, in more then fourty pointes (as farre as the history of venerable Bede reporteth) concerning doctrine, ecclesiasticall gouernement', etc. [b3].

The *Fortresse* thus enlarges the forty-five 'Differences' summarized in the front of the *History*, and, together with that work, is part of the concerted attack upon Jewel's challenge delivered at Paul's Cross.* Both these books came under Fulke's purview in his reply. He notes in his Catalogue of Popish Books† 'Stapletons Differences, & Fortresse of the faith, answered by D. Fulke'. The title of this rejoinder is *An Ouerthrow By W. Fulke Doctor of Diuinitie, and Master of Pembroke hall in Cambridge: to the feeble Fortresse of Popish faith receiued from Rome, and lately aduaunced by Thomas Stapleton Student in Diuinitie.* It is contained in the volume, *T. Stapleton and Martiall* (*two Popish Heretikes*) *confuted, and of their particular heresies detected. By D. Fulke, Master of Pembroke hall in Cambridge.* London, 1580.‡

* The Challenge controversy is discussed at p. 60. We note references to Jewel's *Reply to Cole* at sig. EE1ᵛ, to Jewel's 'last Replie to D. Cole' at sig. Dd1ᵛ, to the *Apology of England* at sig. Cc2ᵛ, etc.

† See Appendix V.

‡ Reprinted by Parker Society, 1848.

140. A Returne of Vn- / truthes vpon M. Ievvel- / les Replie. / Partly of such, as he hath Slaunderously charged D. / Harding withal: Partly of such other, as he hath / committed about the triall thereof, in / the Text of the foure first Ar- / ticles of his Replie. / VVith a Reioyndre vpon the Principall Matters / of the Replie, treated in the Thirde / and Fourthe Articles. / By Thomas Stapleton student in Diuinite. / Magna est Veritas, & praeualet. / Greate is the Truthe, and it preuayleth. / [mg.] 3. Esdr.4. / [device] / Printed in Antwerpe, by Iohn Latius, At the / signe of the Sower. 1566. / With Speciall Grace / and Priuilege.

USHAW.

4°.★–★★★★+||+A–Z+AA–KK in fours+LL^2+a–z+aa–zz+aaa–ddd in fours. Fol. 1[A1]–134[LL2]; 1[a1]–196[ccc4]. Cw. Mg. Rt – A Returne of Vntruthes vpon M. Iewel, &c. (1) Title [★1]. (2) Privilegium: Brussels. 26 April 1566 [★1^v]. (3) 'To M. Iohn Iewel Thomas Stapleton wissheth the loue of Truthe': ends, 'Farre you well in Christ Iesus. Thomas Stapleton' [★2–★★★★2]. (4) Preface to the Reader: Antwerp, 24 July 1566. 'Thomas Stapleton' [★★★★2^v–||4]. (5) 'Faultes escaped in printing of this booke' [||4^v]. (6) Text, in four Articles with conclusion [A1–ccc4^v]. (7) Imprimatur: Louvain. 17 April 1566 [ccc4^v]. (8) 'A Table of the Principall Matters, by the Order of the Alphabet' [ddd1–3^v]. (9) Blank [ddd4].

This is a rejoinder to Jewel's *A Replie vnto M. Hardinges Answeare* (1565) (see bibl. ent. 49). The Preface to the Reader explains the order and manner of setting forth the book: 'I do first laye forthe the wordes of D. Harding printed in a seueral letter [i.e. type], vpon and aboute the which, the Replier hath noted the Vntruthe. Then foloweth īmediatly the Vntruthe and the nūber thereof noted by the Replyer, worde for worde, as it standeth in the Margin of his Replie vpon the text of D.H. After in an other distinct letter, foloweth the Iustifying and discharging of the Vntruth, whereby the Replyer is Recharged, the Vntruthe vpō him Returned, and he proued a Slaunderer.' Stapleton adds that where occasion has required Jewel has been quoted in full and a fuller answer has been given.

Although we are told by W. Fulke in his Catalogue of 'Popish Bookes either answered or to be answered' (1580) [Appendix V] that this work of Stapleton was in process of being answered, I have been unable to trace any direct answer to the book.

141. Of the / Expresse / VVorde of God. / A shorte, but a most / excellent treatyse and / very necessary for this tyme. / VVritten in Latin, by the right Reuerend, / Lerned, and vertuous Father Stanislaus Ho- / sius, Bisshop of VVarmia, Cardinal of the Ho- / ly Apostolyke See of Rome, and one of / the Presidents in the late Gene- / ral Councel holden / at Trent. / Newly translated in to English. / Behold I come to these Prophetes (sayth our Lor- / de) vvhich take their ovvne sayinges, and saye. The / Lorde sayeth it. Ierem.23. / Hilarius lib.2.de Trinitate. / Of vnderstanding not of Scripture ryseth haeresy: / And the meaning, not the vvorde is blamed. / [ornament] / Imprinted in Louayne, by Iohn Bogard at / the signe of the golden Bible: with / Priuilege. An.1567.

8°. Italic. ★4+A–O in eights+P4. Fol. 1[A1]–113[P1]. Cw. Mg. Rt – Of the Expresse / VVorde of God. (1) Title [★1]. (2) Privilegium: Brussels. 4 November, 1566 [★1v]. (3) 'The Translatour to the Reader': Louvain. 3 January [★2–4v]. (4) Quarter-page dedication to Prince Sigismond, followed by Text [A1–P1]. (5) 'A Table of the Principall Matters' [P1v–P4v]. (6) Imprimatur [P4v].

Translated from the *De Expresso Dei Verbo* (Dilinge, 1558) of Bishop Hosius, and attributed to Stapleton by C. Dodd in his list of Stapleton's works in his *Church History*.*

W. Fulke replied to Hosius in his *Gulielmi Fulconis Angli, ad epistolam Stanislai Hosii Varmiensis episcopi de expresso Dei verbo Responsio* (London, 1578). There is no reference to Stapleton's translation in this reply. The author informs us in his short preliminary statement that he had come across this work of Hosius some time previously and had written a reply, which had lain amongst his papers and now for the first time was to see the light of day. The translation was evidently the exciting cause of publication, however, for, in his list of 'Popish Bookes' answered (see Appendix V), we find the entry: 'Hosius of Gods expresse worde translated into English, answered by W. Fulke.'

142. A Counterblast to / M. Hornes vayne / blaste against M. / Fekenham. Wherein is set / forthe: / A ful Reply to M. Hornes Answer, and to euery part ther- / of made, against the Declaration of my L. Abbat of / Westminster, M. Fekenham, touching, The / Othe of the Supremacy. / By perusing vvhereof shall appeare, besides the holy Scriptures, as it vvere a / Chronicle of the Continual Practise of Christes Churche in al ages and / Countries, frō the time of Constantin the Great, vntil our daies: / Prouing the Popes and Bisshops Supremacy in Ecclesiasti- / cal causes: and Disprouing the Princes Supremacy / in the same Causes. / By Thomas Stapleton Student in Diuinitie. / Athanas. in Epist. ad solita. vitā agentes. pag.459. / When was it heard

* C. Dodd, *The Church History of England* (1737, etc.), Vol. II, p. 86. I have been unable to trace Dodd's authority for this. He, however, does not regard Stapleton's authorship as doubtful, and the source of his information may well have been what he describes as 'MS. in my hands'.

from the creation of the worlde, that the / Iudgement of the Churche should take his authoritie from the / Emperour? Or when was that taken for any iudgement? / Ambr. lib.5. epist. 32. / In good sooth, if we call to minde either the whole course of / Holy Scripture, or the practise of the auncient times passed, who / is it that can deny, but that in matter of faith, in matter, I saie, of / faith, Bisshops are wont to iudge ouer Christian Emperours, not / Emperours ouer Bisshops? / [ornament] / Louanii, / Apud Ioannem Foulerum. / An.1567. Cum Priuil.

BOD.

4°. *–*****+A–Z+AA–ZZ+a–z+aa–zz+aaa–zzz+aaaa–yyyy in fours. Fol. 1[A1]–542[xxxx2]. Cw. Mg. Rt – 'The First Booke of the Counterblast' &c. (with descriptive titles in top margins). (1) Title [*1]. (2) Privilegium: Brussels. 27 May 1567 [*1^{v}]. (3) 'To M. Robert Horne, Thomas Stapleton wisheth Grace from God, and true repentance of al Heresies': ends, 'Vale & Resipisce. Thomas Stapleton. τὸ ἀληθὲς ὡς ἀληθῶς ἀληθὲν [*2–****1]. (4) 'The Preface to the Reader': ends, 'In Louaine, the last of September. An. 1567. Thomas Stapleton' [****1^{v}–*****3]. (5) 'An Aduertisement to the Lerned Reader' [*****3^{v}]. (6) Blank [*****4]. (7) Ornament [*****4^{v}]. (8) 'An Answer to the Preface' [A1–B1^{v}]. (9) 'The first booke, conteining many priuat doinges of M. Fekenham, the State of the Questiō, answer to M. Hornes oppositions out of holy scriptures both olde and newe, with a declaration, who are the right Donatists, Protestants or Papistes' (20 chapters) [B2–X4^{v}]. (10) 'The second Booke, disprouing the pretensed practise of Ecclesiastical gouernement in Emperours and Princes of the first. 600. yeares after Christ' (20 chapters) [Y1–b4^{v}]. (11) 'The Thirde Booke: disprouing the pretensed practise of Ecclesiastical gouernmēt in Emperors and Kings as wel of our own Countre of Englande, as of Fraunce and Spayne, in these later. 900. yeres from the tyme of Phocas to Maximilian next predecessour to Charles the. V. of famous memory' (40 chapters with a 'conclusion of the three bookes going before') [c1–fff3]. (12) 'The Fourth Booke: conteyning a ful confutation of M. Hornes answeres, made to M. Fekenhams Reasons, for not taking the Othe of the Supremacye' (14 chapters) [fff3^{v}–xxxx2]. (13) Table [xxxx2^{v}–yyyy3]. (14) 'Faultes escaped in the Printing.' (A mistake in the Greek type at p. 206 is specially noted, and there is added: 'The whole sentence in some Copies is quite leaft vnprinted, which is this . . .' The sentence is omitted in the Bodleian copy. In the copy at Oscott College the sentence is in place) [yyyy3^{v}]. (15) Imprimatur: by F. Ioannes Hentenius, S.T.P., on the approval of Thomas Harding and Nicolas Sander [yyyy4]. (16) Blank [yyyy4^{v}].*

Robert Horne's book was entitled *An Answeare Made by Rob. Bishoppe of Wynchester, to a Booke entituled The Declaration of suche Scruples, and staies of Conscience, touchinge the Othe of the Supremacy, as M. Iohn Fekenham, by wrytinge did deliuer vnto the L. Bishop of Winchester, with his Resolutions made thereunto.* London, 1566.†

We learn from the Preface to the Reader of Stapleton's reply that he had (somewhat unwillingly) undertaken the task because Feckenham himself was not in a position to do so. He

* Bibliographical details in part supplied from the copy at Oscott College.
† Details of the Feckenham-Horne controversy will be found at p. 125.

had been unwilling for two chief reasons: 'First, for that many things in this booke pertaine to certaine priuat doinges betwixt M. Feckenham and M. Horne, of the which I had no skil. Secōdely, for that a number of such priuate matters touching the state of the Realme occurred, as to them without farder aduise, I could not throughly shape any answer. Howbeit', he continues, 'afterward it so happened, that by suche as I haue good cause to credit, there came to my knowledge such Instructions, as well for the one as for the other, that I was the better willing to employ some study and paines in this behalfe . . . I haue therefore by such helpes, as is aboue saied, added my poore labour thereto, and with some diligence in the reste, shaped to the whole booke, a whole and a full Reply.'*

The *Counterblast* was answered by John Bridges in *The Supremacie of Christian Princes, ouer all persons throughout their dominions, in all causes so wel Ecclesiastical as temporall, both against the Counterblast of Thomas Stapleton, replying on the Reuerend father in Christe, Robert Bishop of Winchester: and also Against Nicolas Sanders his Visible Monarchie of the Romaine Church, touching this controuersie of the Princes Supremacie. Answered by Iohn Bridges.* London, 1573.

The first book only is dealt with in this reply.

T., G.

143. [*Text-title.*] A Table gathered ovvt of a Booke named A Treatise of treasons against Q. Elizabeth, and the Croune of England. Latelie compiled by a stranger and sent owt of France, Printed in the yeare of our Lord 1572. [John Fowler. Louvain. 1573?]†

LAMB.

8°.*⁸+**⁷+A⁷. Not fol. Cw. Mg. Rt – A Table. (1) Text-title [*1]. (2) 'The didicatorie epistle to her heighnesse': 'Your heighnes dailie Orator. G.T.' [*1–3]. (3) Text of the Table: ends 'G.T.' (with marg. refs. to fols. of *Treatise of Treasons*) [*3ᵛ–**5]. (4) Blank [**5ᵛ]. (5) 'A Copie of a Lettre addressed from Antwerp the xxvi. of Iune to Mʳ Hatton and deliuered vnto him at Spaw the 5. of Iulie. 1573': 'From Antwerp. the 26. of Iune 1573. By yours to his power. G.T.' [**6–7]. (6) Blank [**7ᵛ]. (7) 'Certain important points added by the Abridger of the Treatise, after the deliuery of the Table to Mʳ. Hattons handes, implying vehement demonstrations of the present peril of your Heighnes life and person' (12 points in all) [A1–7ᵛ]. (No privilegium or imprimatur?)

The *Table of Treasons* was, before publication, sent to Sir Christopher Hatton with a covering letter (see bibl. details (5) and (7) above).‡ It seems to have been published not very long

* The question of the author of the 'Instructions' is discussed fully at Appendix III.

† For *Treatise of Treasons against Q. Elizabeth*, see entry 78.

‡ Hatton was believed to be 'popishly affected'; cp. Fuller, *Worthies* (1840), II, p. 507.

after: that is, if we may take Burghley's letter to Archbishop Parker, dated 11 September 1573, as referring to the *printed* book.* The Argument of the *Treatise of Treasons*, together with the purpose of the *Table*, is set forth in the Dedicatory Epistle as follows:

'Madam this table of treasons doth your heighnes to witt of a booke called, *A treatise of treasons against you and the Croune of England*. That treatise is addressed of gratefull affection borne to yow, and discovereth hidden treasons, which reach to the danger of your person, of your state and life. That treatise discovereth the transposing of the crowne, the extincting of your line, and the hazarding of the Realme. It openeth vnto yow the contrivers of those treasons [sc. Lord Burghley and Sir Nicholas Bacon] to be a couple of companions of base parentes borne: first callid to Courte, thone from booke, thother from butterie: which two be now more then Barons by office and dignitie, more then Earles by possessions and wealth, more then Dukes in authoritie: which two be now your cosoning Counsaillors, though sett vppe by your good fauour in the cheifest places of the Realme, whereby they haue made them selues mightie in money, mariages and allies, and be the two captaine cōspiratours, that haue in their owne power and in the handes of their confederates, all the offices, all the portes, all the fortresses, your treasour, your armour, yea your selfe, your succession and the whole realme to dispose at their will . . .

'Thus that treatise discouereth those two traiterous Counsaillours: who to worke more subtilly their mischeuous intentions and to kepe yow from espying their terrible treasons, haue misleaden yow by a false show of other treasons, wich were neuer intended, and abused yow vndre title of dutie, pretence of seruice, and colour of securitie to hold them vnsuspected.

'In that treatise also your heighnes shal see the vnbuckling and lifting vpp of their visardes and veiles, that wold walke vnseene, and still couertlie circumuent yow by their fine fetches whiles they freelie finish their determined treasons against your person and state.

'That treatise of treasons is abridged into this table, which showeth forth but in breife maner, vvhat in the same is at full enlarged.

'It is therefore passing necessarie, that hauing good regarde of your owne person, the preseruation of the realme, and the rightfull succession of the same, yow call for that treatise, yow reade that treatise, as well for the more full and better vnderstanding of the conspiratours practises finallie ment: as for their mischeuous meanes vsed to bring their practises to passe . . .

'The author of the treatise, and the abridger of the same

* This letter is quoted at p. 445.

beare good affectiō to yow and to the realme: and therefore doe discouer vnto you the present perills that now hang over both: which when yow shal by survew perceave and vnderstand, God giue yow grace, to consider and preuent.

'And Madam for that it cannot be doubted but that those two Conspiratours doe watchfullie care and politickly provide, how to kepe frō yow alletters, bookes and treatesies, which they feare may let or discouer their final purpose: It hath ben thought neccessarie to invent and find owt all good meanes whereby the said treatise or at least the Table of the same, might by some more faithful seruant of yours, be addressed to your owne handes: for the which respect it hath bene by meanes conveighed to the sight of your trustie servant Mr Hatton (and others) who of dewtie and alleageance hath bene thought the most fitt instrument to present yow the same. wherein he shal showe your heighnes, more love dutie and faithful obediēce, then those of your Counsaillors, that so many monethes sithence, haue had the treatise it selfe in their handes and concealed the same, either of doubt their practises might be vntimelie discouered and preuēted, or in deede for lack of love towardes your heighnes person: which standeth in greater perill then yow can beleeve. God geve yow grace to forsee and avoide the same' [*1–3].

I have been unable to trace the anonymous G. T. The printing is undoubtedly that of the books published by John Fowler (evidence from block caps., etc.).* The copy of the pamphlet in the Lambeth Palace Library is probably unique.

144. An Epistle of / the Persecution of / Catholickes in En- / glande. / Translated ovvt of frenche into Englishe and / conferred vvithe the Latyne copie. by G.T. / To whiche there is added an epistle by / the translator to the right honorable / Lordes of her maiesties preeuie coun- / cell towchynge the same matter. / Psal. 105. Ver.38. / They shed innocent blood, euen the blood / of theyr ovvne sonnes and of theyr / ovvne daughters. / Psal.78. Ver.2. / They lay the deade bodyes of thy seruantes (ô Lorde) / for meate to the fovvles of the ayer, and the fleshe / of thy saintes to the beastes of the fielde. / Imprynted at Douay in Artois. / [rule?] [1582?]

8°. A–L in eights+M4. Pag. 1[A1]–167[L4]. Cw. on sig. 8v only of ea. gathering. Mg. Rt – Of the Persecution / in Englande. (1) Title [A1]. (2) Blank [A1v]. (3) 'To the Honorable Lordes of her Maiesties Preeuie Councell': 'Your honours humble oratour and vnfavned [sic] hartie Beadesman. G.T.' [A2–C5v]. (4) Text of the Epistle, addressed 'To his verie louinge frinde. M. Gerarde at Bononie in Italie' [C6–L4]. (5) 'An Admonition sent

* Fowler was also the publisher of the *Treatise of Treasons* (q.v.).

by Gerard to the Reader touching the former epistle' [L4v–5v]. (6) 'The Copie of a Letter sent frome a priest [i.e. Alexander Bryan or Briant] being prisoner in the Tower of London, to the fathers of the Societie of Iesus in England' (short address to the Reader followed by the Letter) [L6–M2].* (7) 'The Translator to the gentle reader' [M2v–4v].†

The French edition referred to in the title is *Epistre de la Persecution meue en Angleterre contre l'Eglise Chrestienne Catholique & Apostolique, & fideles mēbres d'icelle* (Paris, 1582). The French translator was Matthieu de Launoy. The original of this translation is Fr. Robert Persons' *De Persecutione Anglicana, Epistola. Qua explicantur afflictiones, aerumnae, & calamitates grauissimae, cruciatus etiam & tormenta, & acerbissima martyria, quae Catholici nunc Angli, ob fidem patiuntur* (Bologna, 1581).‡ (Actually printed by George L'Oyselet, Rouen.) Apart from the additions noted on the title-page and the final Translator to the Reader, the translator follows his original closely. One exception, however, must be recorded. The incident of Gabriel Cawood's imprisonment in the Clink for having spoken 'three little words in support of Campion against Fulke', which appears in the original at pp. 76 and 77, is referred to only generally (without names) in the translation.§

Walter Travers, the Puritan divine, replied to the Epistle in *An Answere to a Supplicatorie Epistle, of G. T. for the pretended Catholiques: written to the right Honorable Lords of her Maiesties priuy Councell. By Water* [sic] *Trauers, Minister of the worde of God.* London (n.d.).

The printer of the *Epistle* was George L'Oyselet, Rouen. Comparison with books known to have been issued from his press puts this beyond doubt. The words on the title 'Imprynted at Douay in Artois' are, of course, intended to mislead.

TYRIE, JAMES, S.J.
1543–1597

145. The / Refutation / of Ane Ansuer ma- / de be Schir Iohne Knox / to ane letter, send by Iames Tyrie, / to his vmquhyle / brother. / Sett furth by Iames / Tyrie. / Currebant, & ego non

* See also entry 13 (bibl. det. (4)).

† Bibliographical details supplemented from the copy at Foxcote Hall.

‡ Reprinted in *Concertatio Ecclesiae Catholicae* (edited by John Gibbons and John Fen, 1583), and again in the more generally known enlarged edition of 1588 (J. Bridgewater's *Concertatio*). Another Latin edition, containing six woodcuts of a martyr's progress, was printed in Rome in 1582. An Italian edition was also printed in that year, entitled *Della Persecutione de Catolici nel Regno D'Inghilterra. Per ordine di Monsig. Illustriss. Card. Paleotti, Vescouo di Bologna. In Bologna.* It contains a single woodcut of a martyr being dragged on a hurdle to execution. The British Museum copy of the Latin version referred to in the text above is inscribed 'Ex libris. R. P. Jo Leslaei Epi Rossensis' in Lesley's hand.

§ Possibly in accordance with Persons' own desire. See the Admonition to the Reader in Bridgewater (op. cit.).

mittebam eos Hier. 14. / Quomodo predicabunt nisi mittantur? Rom. 10. / [device] / Parisiis / Apud Thomam brumenium in clauso / brunello sub signo Oliuae. / 1573. / Cum Priuilegio.

8°. Italic and roman. †[6]+A–G in eights+H[2]. Fol. 1[A1]–57[H1]. Cw. on fol. 8v of each gathering only (omitted at sig. G). Mg. No Rt. (1) Title [†1]. (2) Blank [†1v]. (3) 'To the Beneuolent Reader': 'Daitit at Paris the 8. of Merche. 1573. Iames Tyrie' (followed by ornament) [†2–6v]. (4) Text (the original letter, Knox's answer, and Tyrie's refutation are given in rotation) [A1–H1v]. (5) 'The Errours' [H2]. (6) Blank [H2v].

There is a full account of the origin of this work in T. G. Law's *Catholic Tractates of the Sixteenth Century.** Tyrie's elder brother, David, we are told, had joined the reformers, and James, anxious to win him back to the faith, corresponded with him from Paris.† One letter, written presumably at the end of 1565,‡ dealing with the visibility of the Church, was shown to Knox in order that he might write a reply to it. Knox's account of this in his *Answer* is that the letter had been presented to him seven years earlier, when he scribbled a reply in a few days, but decided to suppress it. However, he says, since the Jesuits have returned to the attack with the 'same argumentis which Tyrie vsis: amplifyed and set furth', he now publishes his reply. The reply is entitled *An Answer to a Letter of a Iesuit named Tyrie, be Iohne Knox . . . Imprentit at Sanctandrois be Robert Lekpreuik. Anno. Do. 1572.*

Knox died 24 November 1572 and so did not live to see Tyrie's 'Refutation' of his *Answer*. The General Assembly in 1574 appointed a committee to consider an answer to it prepared by John Duncanson, and another, drawn up by George Hay three years later, was also submitted to the Assembly. But neither was published.§ John Hamilton comments caustically: 'nether knox nor ony of his factione sen his dead dorst tak in hand to vrit ane ansuer to maister Iames Tyreis beuk concerning the visibilitie of the kirk: zea quhen sum of thaime scheu thair ansuer to thair general assemblie, it become inuisibil as thair kirk vas before thame selfis . . . christisone of dondie || causit burne the same at the market croce and sa schauit his auin ignorance in place to tak the pen to mak ane ansueir vsit the fyre, quhilk vas the seurest vay for him and sik vtheris, quha lyk parrokettis enterteneis ye auditouris be clattering tellis'.¶

* s.v. *Tyrie*. See my note at p. 395; cf. also the Bannatyne Club reprint of the *Works of John Knox*, Vol. VI, pt. 2 (1864).

† James, who had a European reputation for learning and ability, professed philosophy and theology in the Jesuit College of Clermont. – T. G. Law, op. cit.

‡ It is subscribed 'writtin at Paris the sext of December', without the year. The year may, however, be deduced from Knox's account in his *Answer*.

§ T. G. Law, loc. cit.

|| William Chrystesone was appointed minister of Dundee, 15 July 1560, and became Moderator of the General Assembly, July 1569.

¶ *Ane Catholik and Facile Traictise* (1581), sig. V4v.

VALLENGER, HENRY

fl. 1582

(see entry 9)

VAUX, LAURENCE

1519–1585

146. [*Text-title.*] A Catechisme, or a / Christian doctrine necessarie / for Chyldren and igno- / rant people. [Louvain. John Fowler. 1568.]

16°. B.L. A–R in eights+S^7. Fol. 1[A6]–135[S6]. Cw. Mg. Rt. varies. (1) (missing) [A1–5]. (2) Text-title [A6]. (3) Text of Catechism [A6–P4^v]. (4) 'To the Reader, concerning the holy Ceremonies of Gods Churche' [P5–Q1]. (5) 'The vse and meaning of the holy Ceremonies of Gods Church [Q1^v–S6^v]. (6) Imprimatur for the Catechism: Louvain. 20 April 1567 [S7]. (7) Imprimatur for the treatise of Ceremonies: Louvain. 20 April 1568 [S7^v].*

This is not the first edition of Vaux's *Catechism*, but the first to contain the treatise on Ceremonies. At the entrance of that treatise the writer says, 'Many wise and learned men haue thought it good, that I should ioyne to the Catechism (which I did lately sette foorth for the instruction of yonge children in matters of the faithe) a briefe declaratiō of certayne Ceremonies, whose signification is not so wel knowē to the ignorant people, as they should be'. These words, when taken in conjunction with those from the Address to the Reader, set down below, point conclusively to an earlier printed edition without the 'declaration of certaine Ceremonies'.† No copy of that edition seems to have survived.

Vaux, who for some time after his arrival in Louvain (*c.* 1562) kept a school, gives us in an informative and 'sympathetic' Address to the Reader an account of the origin of the Catechism, which, he says, was written for his pupils. I give the address in full.‡

'When I did inwardly consider in my minde a Decree in the seuenth Canon made at the second General Councel holden at Lateran, wherin Schoolemasters are straitly charged, vppon Sondayes and Holy dayes to instructe and teach their Scholers Christian doctrine, appertaining to Religion and good maners, as the Articles of the fayth, the Commaundements of God, & such lyke: And also to exhort and cōpell their Scholers, to be

* At the end of Chapter 4 of the Catechism occur the words 'A table of the degrees within which it is not lawful to mary', as though it had been intended to insert such a table at this point. No table follows, however.

† See Appendix IV for a full discussion of this question and others connected with Vaux's *Catechism*.

‡ This address is missing from the copy set out above. It is to be found in subsequent editions.

presente in the Churche with a reuerente deuotion, in prayer at the times of Masse, Mattins, & Euensong, the which Decree I did see diligētly obserued at Louain, & other places in Germany and Italy: These and such like considered, in myne owne conscience I did confesse a great negligence in my selfe, that I had not done my duety heretofore in bringing vppe my scollars.

'Of these thinges vppon a time I had talke with a graue godly mā,* who sometime did exercise an honorable roome in England, and much pitied the lack of instruction of youth, and the ignorāce that was amonge the simple people there, & of a godly zeale that he had toward the saluation of the souls of the simple and vnlearned, he earnestly requested me, to set foorth in writing an Instruction, what all people ought to beleue and doe, yf they will be saued.

'Whose request I was willing to satisfy for two causes, partly to recompēse my negligence, in that I had not don my duety in teaching and instructing them that were committed to my charge: (taking comfort of the parable in the Gospel, that he whiche entred into the vineyard to labour at eleeuen of the clock, receiued his pēny equally with him that entred into the vineyarde betyme in the morning to work:) partly to ioyne with the said godly man, in the intent to doe good to many, and to hurt none: trusting although I come late, that yet this my simple Myte may be receiued with the poore widowes oblation, albeit I was much afrayed to haue it put in printe, leste it should come to the hands of such learned men, as would looke for finesse of sentence, and eloquence of wordes, which are lacking ī me: by meanes whereof in the end I feared, lest any good wil and diligente labour should redound to my rebuke & reproche.

'Thus being in a great perplexitie, it chaunsed that I had conference in this matter with a learned man, whose iudgment I trusted better then mine owne, & wholy depending vpon his counsell, I did forsake mine owne fansie & will herein. And being animated and incouraged by my saied learned frend to take the matter in hand: after my simple and rude maner, I haue compiled this litle booke for yong scolers, and the vnlearned, beseching God in my daily prayers (if it be his wil and pleasure) so to geue his grace to the readers hereof, that some goodnes may come thereby in the amēdmēt of lyfe, to Gods glory, and their soules health and comfort, which is the only purpose and intent that moued me to take paynes to set furth this litle booke called A Christian Doctrine.

'And what I haue set furth in this litle booke, the grounde and substance I haue collected & translated out of the Scripture,

* T. G. Law suggests that this was possibly his friend, the Bishop of St. Asaph (Bishop Goldwell), whom he had met in Rome.

& generall Councells, out of the bookes of D. Petrus de Soto, and D. Canisius, addinge here and there some sentences of the auncient Fathers, S. Cypriã, Athanasius, Ambrose, Hierome, Damascene, & S. Bernard. God send them eares to heare which shall learne it, and them, that neede not learne it, because they knowe it, to take it quietly when they reade it, knowing that I haue made it for the simple, and ignorante, and not for the fine felowes, and learned.' [ed. 1583. *The Author to the Reader.*]

That a 'reply' to the *Catechism* was contemplated by the Protestants we learn from Fulke's lists of 'Popish Bookes either aunswered, or to be aunswered', given at Appendix V. I have, however, been unable to trace any such 'reply'.

Vaux's name appears on the title-page of all subsequent editions of the *Catechism*. The date of this edition is settled by the second imprimatur. A comparison of the printing of this work (type, ornamental caps., etc.) with other printing by Fowler's printer establishes beyond dispute this publication as his.*

VERSTEGAN, RICHARD
1548?–1641†

147. [ornament] The Post of the World. / VVherein is contayned the antiquities and / originall of the most famous Cities in Europe. With / their trade and traficke. With their wayes and distance / of myles, from country to country. With the true and / perfect knowledge of their Coynes, the places of their / Mynts: with al their Martes and Fayres. And the / Raignes of all the Kinges of England. A booke / right necessary and profitable, for all sortes of / persons, the like before this tyme not / Imprinted. / [rule] / As the Bird is prepared to flye, / So Man is ordained to labour and trauaile. / [device] / [rule] / [ornament] Imprinted at London by / Thomas East. / 1576.

[colophon on P4ᵛ] Imprinted at London by Thomas East.

8°. B.L. and roman. $*^4$+$**^4$+A–P in fours. Pag. 1[B1]–112[P4ᵛ]. Cw. Mg. No Rt. (1) Title [*1]. (2) 'An Almanack for. xvij yeares' (1572–88) [*1ᵛ]. (3) Calendar, etc. [*2–**4]. (4) Blank [**4ᵛ]. (5) New title as follows: [within a border] [ornament] The Post / For diuers partes of the world: / to trauaile from one notable / Citie vnto an other, with a descrip- / cion of the antiquitie of diuers / famous Cities in Europe. The / contents doe farther apeare / in the next leafe / folowing. / [ornament] Very necessary & profitable for / Gentlemen, Marchants, Factors, or / any other persons

* Notably a broken capital I, which occurs unbroken in Sander's *The Rocke of the Churche* (*Louanii, Apud Ioannem Foulerum.* 1567); but with the same defect in, for instance, Sander's *De Visibili Monarchia Ecclesiae* (Louvain. John Fowler, 1571).

† Verstegan, while resident in England, was known by the name of Rowland or Rowlands. On retiring to the Continent in 1582 he reassumed the family name, Verstegan.

disposed to / trauaile. The like not here- / tofore in English. / Published by Richard Rowlands. / Imprinted at London / by Thomas East, 1576 [A1]. (6) Contents [A1v]. (7) 'To the right worshipfull, Syr Thomas Greasham Knight. R. Rowlands wisheth continual encrease of renoumed worship and Vertue': ends, 'Your worshippes most bounden to commaund, Richard Rowlands' [A2–3]. (8) 'A godly prayer, very needefull to be vsed and sayde, before any Iorney to be taken in hand' [A3v–4]. (9) 'Here foloweth the varietie of myles' [A4]. (10) Address to Reader [A4v]. (11) Text [B1–P4v]. (one blank at L2v). (12) Colophon [P4v].

The original of the Itinerary, as we are told in the Address to Sir Thomas Gresham, was 'published in the high *Almaine* tongue, and the like also to be seene in the *French*, and *Italian*'. In the same Address Rowlands also informs us that he has 'set downe the antiquitie of many cities worthy of memory, & the founders of auncient monuments', which he has 'diligently collected out of sundry approued aucthors'.

148. A Declaration of the true causes of the great troubles, presupposed to be intended against the realme of England. Wherein the indifferent reader shall manifestly perceaue, by whome, and by what meanes, the realme is broughte into these pretented perills. Seene and allowed. Anno, M.D.LXXXXII.

149. A Conference about the next Succession to the Crowne of Ingland, diuided in to two partes. Whereof the first conteyneth the discourse of a ciuill Lawyer, how and in what manner propinquity of blood is to be preferred. And the second the speech of a Temporall Lawyer, about the particuler titles of all such as do or may pretende within Ingland or without, to the next succession. Wherevnto is also added a new & perfect arbor or genealogie of the discents of all the kinges and princes of Ingland, from the conquest vnto this day, whereby each mans pretence is made more plaine. Directed to the Right Honorable the earle of Essex of her Maiesties priuy councell, & of the noble order of the Garter. Published by R. Doleman. Imprinted at N. with Licence. M.D.XCIIII.*

150. The Primer, or Office of the Blessed Virgin Marie, in Latin and English: According to the reformed Latin; and vvith lyke graces Priuileged. Printed, At Antwerp by Arnold Conings. Anno M.D.XCIX.

* There is little doubt that Verstegan took a leading part in the writing and publication of this work.

151. Odes in Imitation of the Seauen Penitential Psalmes, VVith Sundry other Poemes and ditties tending to deuotion and pietie. Imprinted, Anno Domini. M.D.CI.

152. A Dialogue of Dying Wel. First written in the Italian tongue, by the Reuerend father Don Peeter of Luca, a Chanon regular, a Doctor of Diuinitie and famous preacher. VVherin is also contayned sundry profitable resolutions, vpon some doubtful questions in Diuinitie. Translated first into French, and novv into English.

you knovv not when the

by A.C. 1603.*

153. A Restitution of Decayed Intelligence: In antiquities. Concerning the most noble and renovvmed English nation. By the studie and trauaile of R.V. Dedicated vnto the Kings most excellent Maiestie. Printed at Antvverp by Robert Bruney. 1605. And to be sold at London in Paules-Churchyeard, by Iohn Norton and Iohn Bill.†

WALPOLE, HENRY, S.J.

1558–1595

154. The Song of Mary the Mother of Christ: Containing the story of his life and passion. The teares of Christ in the garden: With The description of heauenly Ierusalem. E. Allde for William Ferbrand. London, 1601.‡

WINZET, NINIAN, ABBOT, O.S.B.

1518–1592§

155. Certane tractatis for / Reformatioun of Doctryne and

* Neither of the two copies of this work (at Lambeth and at Oscott College) which I have seen is perfect.

† There are a number of other works attributed to Verstegan. There is considerable uncertainty about the authorship of some of these: others remain untraced.

‡ The three poems of the title in this Song Book have been attributed to Henry Walpole on fairly reasonable grounds. They were probably written after his imprisonment in York Castle at the end of 1593. In addition, the book contains three further poems of uncertain authorship. These include a shortened version of the well-known *Hierusalem My Happy Home*, which may possibly also be Walpole's. For other poems of this author see under Alfield above.

§ A full account of Winzet will be found in the Scottish Text Society publication: *Certain Tractates together with the Book of Four Score Three Questions and a Translation of Vincentius Lirinensis by Ninian Winzet. Edited with Introduction, Notes, and*

maneris, set / furth at the desyre, ād in ye name of ẏ afflic- / tit Catholikis, of inferiour ordour of Cler- / gie, and layit men in Scotland, be / Niniane Winzet, ane Catholike Preist / borne in Renfrevv. / [ornaments] / [ornament] Quhilkis be name this leif turnit sall schaw. / Murus aheneus, sana conscientia. / Edinburgi. 21 Maij, / 1562. / [device and ornaments] [John Scot]

Sir R.L.H.

4°. B.L. A–D in fours+E³. Not fol. No Cw. Mg. Rts – (1) The First Tractat. (2) The Secund Tractat. (3) The Thrid Tractat. (1) Title [A1]. (2) Summary of the three Tractates [A1ᵛ]. (3) First Tractate (to which is appended 'Ane cleir Mirrour for the Reformatioun of all Estatis. Ezech. 22.'): ends, 'Delyuerit to the Quenes Grace, the 15. of Fabruar. 1561' [A2–C1]. (4) Second Tractate: ends, 'Niniane vvinzet at the desyre of his brether' [C1–D1]. (5) Third Tractate, preceded by an Address to the Reader (dated 24 May 1562): ends, 'At Edinburgh ye last of Marche, be zouris M', followed by 'Quhais name ze sal knaw quhen ze sa[l] knaw zoure Errour, or quhen Iohne Knox or his Brether answeris heirto in writ' [D1ᵛ–E3ᵛ]. (6) Woodcut of the Transfiguration [E3ᵛ].*

The letter to Queen Mary of 15 February 1561–2, which forms the first Tractate, is described by Winzet in his summary (bibl. details (2) above) as 'Ane Exhortatioun to the maist excellent and gracius Souerane, Marie Quene of Scottis, &c. To the Bischoipes, and vtheris Pastores, and to al thaim of the Nobilitie within this hir graces Realme: For vnfenzeit reformation of doctrine and maneris, and for obtening of licence, to propone in wryt to the Precheours of the Protestantis certane artyculis tweching doctrine, ordour, and maneris approuin be thame'. Licence having been granted, Winzet proposed three questions to Knox relative to his lawful vocation as minister. Knox replied only from the pulpit,† which called forth a demand for a written reply from Winzet in three letters dated 3, 10 and 12 March 1561–2. These questions and letters make the second

Glossarial Index by James King Hewison, M.A. Edinburgh and London. Vol. I, 1888; Vol. II, 1890. This work includes an essay on Winzet's Life and Works and facsimile pages of Winzet's hand-writing, *Certane Tractatis*, *The Last Blast of the Trompet* and *Vincentius Lirinensis*. Full texts of the works are given. See also the Maitland Club reprint of Winzet's works (1835), with a life of Winzet by J. B. Gracie (?). Bishop Robert Keith reprinted the *Tractatis* and the *Buke of fourscoir thre Questionis* in his *History of the affairs of Church and State in Scotland* (Edinburgh, 1734), at Appendix, pp. 204–55.

* It will be evident from the date of the Address in the Third Tractate (bibl. details (5) above) that the title-page was already set up when this Address was written.

† Nicol Burne's comment is as follows: 'being demandit of the reuerend father Maister Niniane Vingzet nou Abbot of Ratinsburgh of his authoritie, he ansuerit that he vas extraordinarlie callit euin as vas S. Iohne the Baptist, And this he ansuerit in publik befoir the people: Bot priuatlie he scheu him self to be callit in ane vther maner, that is be gunnis, and pistolis' etc. *Disputation* (entry 24), sig. P6ᵛ. Cited by Hewison.

Tractate, thus described in the summary: 'Thre Questionis, tweching the lauchful vocatiōn of Iohne Knox, & his brether Precheours to the Protestantis, in Scotlande: quhilks ar in noumbre the xxxiii. xxxiiii. ād xxxv. of the four score thre questionis proponit to thaim be the saidis Catholickis, togidder with thre wryttingis deliuerit to ye said Iohne: quhairin is replyit aganis his ansueris maid to ane part of ye said thre questiōis'. The third Tractate was occasioned by the proclamation by the magistrates of the Act of 1560, which commanded Priests, Adulterers, etc. to leave Edinburgh.* The populace apparently marked with chalk the doors of suspected persons. Winzet summarizes it as follows: 'Ane declamatioun to the honorable Prouest Baillies, and Counsell of Edinburgh, for the obseruatioun of the glaid solemniteis off the blyssit Natiuitie, Circūcisioun, Epiphanie, Resurrectioun, and Ascensioun of our Saluioonr [sic], with the feist of Witsonday: haistelie maid one Pasche twisday. Anno. 1562. Quhē thair apperit ane daingerous seditioun in Edinburgh, throw calking of the durris on euery syde: as efter sall follow.'

Hewison says of the typography of this book that it is 'undoubtedly the work of the press of John Scot, printer in Edinburgh and St. Andrews, 1539–1572'.†

156. The / last blast of the trompet of / Godis vvorde aganis the vsurpit auctoritie of / Iohne Knox and his Caluiniane brether / intrudit Precheouris &c. / [ornaments] / Put furth to the Congregatioun of the / Protestantis in Scotlāde, be Ni- / niane Winzet, ane Catho- / lik preist borne in Renfrew: / [ornament] / [ornament] At the desyre and in the name of his af- / flictit Catholike brether of ye inferiour / ordoure of Clergie, and laic men. / [ornament] / Vir impius procaciter obfirmat vultum suum: qui autem / rectus est, corrigit uiam suam. / Prouerb. 21. / Edinburgi vltimo Iulij. 1562. [John Scot]

SIR R.L.H.

4°. B.L. π^1+A^4. Not fol. One cw. (at sig. A2). Mg. No Rt. (1) Title [π]. (2) 'Ane Submonitioun to the redar' [π^v–A1]. (3) 'To the Congregatioun of the Protestantis in Scotlande' [A1–A4^v]. The last leaf of this fragment breaks off abruptly in the middle of a sentence.

In the 'Submonitioun to the redar' the story of the *Tractates* is carried a step further. 'The caus quhy we haif intitulit yis tractate on the maner preceding', writes the author, 'is: that we first soundit the trompet of godis word, twiching this purpose in thre questions specialie, amangis mony ma proponit to

* Hewison, op. cit., Vol. II, p. 118.

† op. cit., Vol. I, p. lxxix; cp. also J. B. Gracie, Maitland Club reprint, p. xvi.

Iohne Knox ād his brether . . . And secundlie quhen this fornamit Iohne wes nott mouit thairby, bot erar puft vpe $\overset{t}{w}$ mair pryde, intendit to preue his vocation planelie in $\overset{e}{y}$ pulpet . . . we blew the samyn trompet againe in thre wrytingis according to his preching on sindry dayis: ād yat verray schortlie as it had bene be thre sindry sōndis blawin almast at ane tyme . . . Zit . . . thay wyll not zit descend in thaim selfis to humilitie and pennance . . . Quhairfor $\overset{t}{y}$ the blynd of thaim and thair scoleris be not impute tyll vs in ye sycht of god, for not schawing our brotherlie lufe to thaim, in admonising of thair erroure & perrell: we put furth this thrid and last blaste, to call abak the scoleris frome ye plaig of godis iustice, as we callit (as we mycht) thair techaris afore: thinkand this to be sufficiēt aduertismēt to al thaim quha hes earis to heir ye treuth, yat we neid not in this mater ony ofter to sound this trompet. *Reid and Iuge*' [π^{v}–A1].

There seems to be little doubt that this was the work 'whose passage through the press John Scot was superintending when he was apprehended'.* Bishop Leslie gives a minute account of the scene, which is thus translated by Fr. James Dalrymple: 'This mater maid Mr Ninian verie inviet with the haeretickis and verie sair quhan tha hard that he was busie with the prenter in setting furth a buik, quhairby he thocht to compleine of Knox to the Nobilitie for falsing his promis: be this onelie way he thocht he mycht prouoik thame til answer. Thay consult to hinder his labour, to tak Mr Ninian, to punise the prenter. The Magistrates with the suddartis brak in vpon the prenter: the buikes that tha fand tha tuik. Johne Scot the prenter quhen of al his gudes spoyled him tha had, tha cloised him in prisone. Bot Mr Ninian, quhom with sa gude wyl tha wald have had, met the Magistrat in the zet; bot because tha knew him nocht tha mist him, and sa he chaiped: the haeretickis war wae – the Catholickis luiche.'†

157. The buke of fourscoir- / thre questions, tueching doctrine, ordour, / and maneris proponit to ye precheouris of / ye Protestants in Scotland, be ye Catholiks / of ye inferiour ordour of clergie and layt / men yair, cruelie afflictit and dispersit, be / persuasioū of ye saidis intrusit precheours. / Seth furth be Niniane VVinzet a Catholik / Preist, at ye desyre of his faythfull

* Hewison, Vol. I, p. lxxxi; cp. also J. B. Gracie, op. cit., p. xiv, et seq.

† Leslaeus, *De Origine, Moribus, et Rebus Gestis Scotorum* (1578), p. 584, Fr. Dalrymple's translation, printed by the Scottish Text Society. Cited by Hewison, Vol. I, p. xli; cp. also Gracie, loc. cit. The latter says that 'it is highly probable that Scot's licence was taken from him, as no books printed by him for a considerable time subsequent to 1562 are to be met with'.

affli- / ctit brethir, and deliuerit to Iohne Knox / ye. xx. of Februar or yairby, in ye zere / of the blissit birth of our Saluiour. 1563. / [ornament] / Ne sis sapiens apud temetipsum. Prouerb. iij. / Sed interroga patres tuos, & annunciabunt / tibi: maiores tuos, & dicent tibi. Deu. xxxij. / [ornament] / Antuerpiae / Ex officina Aegidij Diest. M.D.lxiij. xiij. Octob. / Cum Gratia & Priuilegio.*

SIR R.L.H.

8°. Italic. A–G in eights+H4. Not fol. Cw. Mg. Rt – To the Caluiniane / Precheouris. (1) Title [A1]. (2) Privilegium: Brussels. 28 August 1563 [A1v]. (3) 'Niniane Winzet a catholik Preist to ye Christiane Reidar wisshis grace, and peace': Louvain. 7 October 1563 [A2–6v]. (4) Text in 83 Articles, with a preliminary address 'to Iohne Knox and his complices', and a concluding exhortation. Article 70 reads only: 'My copie heir wantis ane quaestioun in yis place, anentis ye signe of ye croce: quhilk ye Reidar may haif in ye writtin copiis at hem' [A7–H3v]. (5) 'To Iohne Knox. writtin. 27. Oct. 1563': ends, 'Of Antwerp. ye. 27. of October. 1563. Ninianus Winzetus Presbyter' [H4–4v].†

This work appears to have been compiled from a series of theological exercises, drawn up by Winzet when he was Rector of Linlithgow Grammar School (1552–62) and set to his pupils for translation into Latin. 'Humane childer of happy ingynis', he calls them, 'mair apt to leir than I wes to teche, to quhom I usit to propone almaist dalie sum theme, argument or sentence, of the quhilk, I wald haif thaim intending to mak orisone or epistle in Latin tong, and thocht that this mater of sedition afore namit had bene ane verray convenient theme to that purpose.'‡ These exercises appear to have been widely circulated in writing, and since many corrupt versions were abroad owing to their having been copied 'be vnleirnit writtaris', Winzet decided to print. Therefore, he says, 'we sett furth yis iust copie, without altering or eiking ony thing, sa fer as we cā remember: except onlie yat in place of yis epistill wes sum Latin to ye cunning reider, exhorting him nocht to haif respect to our ruid style, bot to ye trew catholik sentence: sen we controuertit nocht with our aduersaris for trim talk, bot for ye trying of ye trewth: nocht for deckit vanitie, bot for ye aeternall veritie. Quhilk thing we requeist the, gentill Reidar, zit anis agane, and to purge yi copie according to yis praesent: willing ye to be persaudit, yat gif it pleisit ws at yis tyme and place, to alter or eik yis tractate, yat with litill labouris, it micht be maid tueching ye style mair plesing and persuading, and in sentēce fer mair strenthy and difficill to our aduersaris to mak anssuer yairto. Zit nocht-yeles because Iohne Knox apperis to

* The errata, which is found at the end of Winzet's *Vincentius* (next entry), reads 'sett furth' for 'seth furth', and '1561' for '1563' in line 12 of the title.

† The margin of the last page reads: 'Och for mair paper or pennyis'.

‡ Cited by Hewison from Tractate III, sig. D2.

schaw yat with his fallowis he labouris to fulfill his oblising, we will eik nor alter na thing heirin, except sum illustratioũ in ye mergin, yat ye Reidar, gif ony anssuer beis maid, may syncerlie cõfer ye ane with ye wthir: and in ye mein tyme yat ye sempill beleuear may haif sufficient licht, to eschew ye dissaitful snairis of ye erroneous'. [Address to the Reader (bibl. details (3) above), B3^{v}–4^{v}.]

158. [within a compartment] Vincentius / Lirinensis of the natioun of / Gallis, for the antiquitie and / veritie of the catholik fayth, / aganis ye prophane nouationis / of al haereseis, / A richt goldin buke writtin in Latin / about. xi. C. zeris passit, and neulie / translatit in Scottis be Niniane / Winzet a catholik Preist: / Vt aedificentur muri Ierusalem. / Psal.50. / Antuerpiae / Ex officina Aegidij Diest, / 1. Decemb. 1563 / Cum Gratia & Priuilegio.

Sir R.L.H.

8°. Italic. A^{8}+a^{4}+B–H in eights+I^{4}. Fol. 1[B1]–59[I3]. Cw. Mg. Rt – Vincent Lirin. aganis / ye nouationis of al haereseis. (1) Title [A1]. (2) Royal Arms of Scotland [A1^{v}]. (3) 'To ye maist Catholik, Noble, and Gratious Souerane, Marie Quene of Scottis': Antwerp. 2 December 1563 [A2–a3^{v}]. (4) Testimonies of ancient writers to St. Vincent (two Latin quots.) [a4]. (5) 'To the Reidar' [a4^{v}]. (6) Text in 34 chapters, concluding with, 'Heir endis ye first parte. The secund Memorial is loist, and na thing yairof mair vnperisit, bot a litle of ye last parte, that is, a recapitulatioun onlie: quhilk heir also followis' [B1–I3]. (7) Latin elegiacs [I3]. (8) 'In defence of yis auctour aganis certane mockaris, the sones of Cham and mekle wors' [I3^{v}–4]. (9) 'The faltis' (includes errata from *The buke of fourscoir-thre questions*) [I4^{v}].

This work is a translation of the well-known *Commonitorium pro Catholicae fidei antiquitate et veritate, aduersus profanas omnium Haereseõn nouationes* of St. Vincent of Lerins. J. K. Hewison points out that Winzet, in his marginal notes, draws attention to the similarity or identity he marked in the heresies condemned by St. Vincent and the teachings of Luther, Calvin and other reformers.*

159. Ane Answer to ane Epistle written by Renat Benedict, the French Doctor professor of Gods word (as the translater of this Epistle calleth him) to Iohn Knox and the rest of his bretheren ministers of the word of God made by Dauid Feargussone, minister of the same word at this present in Dunfermling . . . Imprentit at Edinburgh by Robert Lekpreuik cum Priuilegio 1563.

* op. cit., Vol. I, p. xciv.

It seems highly probable that Ninian Winzet was the translator of René Benoist's Latin letter of challenge to Knox. The translation, which presumably was circulated in manuscript, is given in full, but without the postscript, in this Answer. It is distributed into four sections, occupying about three and a half pages in all, and ends 'Written at Edinburgh, in the Palaice of the most noble Quene of Scotland, 18th calend of December', etc.*

The above title is taken from the Bannatyne Club reprint: *Tracts by David Fergusson, Minister of Dunfermline. 1563–1572.* Edinburgh, 1860.†

* The original Latin letter, printed in the Bannatyne Club edition, bears the date 'xiii. calendas Decembris 1561' (i.e. 19 November 1561); 18th appears to be a mistake in transcription.

† Short notices of René Benoist, David Ferguson, etc., are given in the Introduction by the Editor, Very Rev. John Lee, D.D., LL.D.

APPENDICES

I

ALLEN'S *SCROLL OF ARTICLES*, BRISTOW'S *MOTIVES*, AND RISHTON'S *CHALLENGE*

II

JESUS PSALTER

III

STAPLETON'S *COUNTERBLAST*. FECKENHAM OR HARPSFIELD?

IV

VAUX'S *CATECHISM*

V

FULKE'S CATALOGUE OF POPISH BOOKS

VI

HAND-LIST OF PRINTERS OR PUBLISHERS OF RECUSANT WORKS, 1559–1582

VII

CHRONOLOGICAL LIST OF WORKS

I

ALLEN'S *SCROLL OF ARTICLES*, BRISTOW'S *MOTIVES*, AND RISHTON'S *CHALLENGE*

THE origin and history of Allen's 'Scroll of Articles', which William Fulke answered in his *Two Treatises written against the Papistes, the one being an answere of the Christian Protestant to the proud challenge of a Popish Catholicke* . . . (1577) can be clearly gathered from passages in Nicholas Fitzherbert's *Life of Allen* (1608) and Bristow's *Reply to Fulke* (1580). It should be clear from the context in each of these passages that Fitzherbert and Bristow are referring to the same work of Allen's.

Fitzherbert writes, in speaking of Allen's sojourn in England between 1562 and 1565:

> Translatus deinceps Alanus in Norfolciensem provinciam haud frustra in illius Ducis domo ipsa atque vicinia laboravit. Nam ad Romanam ecclesiam aliquos adjunxit, atque ut plures una eademque adjungeret opera summam quandam perbrevem rationum collegit literisque mandavit, quibus et haereseos vanitatem ac fidei catholicae praestantiam ac firmitudinem ante omnium qui videre vellent oculos clarissime proposuit. Rationes istae mox late sparsae . . .*

Bristow's statement is as follows:

> Twelue or thirteene yeres agoe M. D. Allen, hauing amongst other learned Catholikes of our time and countrey on this side the sea, opened and defended in print most perspicuously and substantially, certayne speciall articles of the Catholike faith: and beeing driuen not long after by sicknes to seeke to the ayre of his natiue soyle, did in the short space of his abode there,† deale also the other waye with many Gentlemen, confirming some, and setting vp agayne others, by most euident and vndouted rules of truth, which were alwayes common for the most part among Catholikes, but the weight of them deepely considered of very few, and the number of them as yet neither

* *Nicolai Fitzherberti De antiquitate, et continuatione, Catholicae Religionis in Anglia, et De Alani Cardinalis vita, libellus*. Rome, 1608. Cited by Knox, *Letters and Memorials of Cardinal Allen*, p. 6. See also Wood, *Ath. Oxon.*, edited Bliss (1813): I, 616, where the summary is referred to as 'Certain brief Reasons concerning Catholic Faith'.

† This would put Allen's visit to England after 1565; that is, after he had *returned* from his visit, for this Address appears to have been written in 1578 (see date referred to later in the quotation). There is abundant evidence to show that Allen did not return to England after 1565. It is possible, of course, that Bristow confused the dates purposely.

by him nor by any other bound vp together. Onely to one gentleman requesting so much, he gaue a copie of them, such a one as of extemporall and priuate writing might be looked for.

It is now nine yeres since I heard the same of his own mouth, what time I came first into his blessed familie,* and was present very often when amongst vs he discoursed familiarly vpon the said rules, to such liking of my part, that I left him not vntill I had intreated him to take his penne one morning, and out of his memorie to frame me also a copie. Which copie a friende hauing seene here with me, who afterward was sent home into our lords haruest, in a letter from thence desired instantly to be made partaker therof, affirming that he saw how medicinable it would be to many soules, I communicated the matter to the Author of it. He beeing wholly occupied him selfe in publike teaching of Diuinitie, would haue me who then had more leasure, though for skill not worthy to beare his booke, to deuise somewhat vpon those and the like rules, which might in print be published to the world: not as though the very bare rules, as in the foresaid copies, were not conuenient and sufficient, specially for men of intelligence and that willingly would be informed, but that by the declaration and confirmation of them the rude also and obstinate might be induced. And this was the occasion of my *Motiues* in the end of the yeare 1574. and also of my Demaundes in the beginning of the yeare 1576, which I made vpon the motion of certayn, who desired to haue the Motiues printed agayne, because the first impression was for the greater part taken and destroyed by the aduersaries.†

The significant facts in these two passages are: The Articles were originally formulated by Cardinal Allen during his visit to England. He left one copy with a gentleman for reproduction before he finally left England in 1565. Later he made from memory a second copy for Bristow, which no doubt varied considerably from the first. This copy served as the basis for Bristow's *Motives* and *Demands*. The Articles were never printed by Allen.

The Articles have come down to us in three versions:

(1) Bristow's elaborated version, which is quite unlike the other two.

(2) Fulke's version, set out, in customary manner, in his *Two Treatises*.

(3) The version which is known as Rishton's 'Challenge'.

These latter two resemble each other fairly closely and must be

* Bristow arrived at Douay in 1569.

† Bristow, *A Reply to Fulke*, 1580. The Address to the Reader.

copies of the original Allen left behind in England.* The most important difference between them is the additional six points ('signes') of the 'Challenge', referred to in the bibliographical note at entry 2 above. The question as to how Rishton's name came to be associated with the third version of the Articles (the *Challenge*) we shall now proceed to examine.†

When Fulke printed his answer to Allen's 'Scroll of Articles', in his *Two Treatises* referred to above, in 1577, he wrote in his preface that his answer was eight or nine years old, that he had seen written copies of the Articles in many men's hands, and that he was informed that there was a printed version. He adds that on grounds of style he suspects Allen's authorship.‡ There is no mention of Rishton's name either here or in the edition of his answer published later in the year. When, however, he refers to this work in 1579, in his Catalogue of 'Popishe Bookes', he speaks of it as an answer to 'Ristons challenge'.§

The reason for this change of view as to the authorship of the 'Articles' or 'Challenge' would appear to lie in a note in Bristow's *Demands*, which must have come to Fulke's notice after the publication of his Answer. Bristow's note runs: 'In M. Edward Rishtons *Table of the Church*, may be sene with the very eie, all wel neare that hath been saide in this Booke' [sig. F4^{v}]. Fulke refers to this note in answering Bristow's charge that his *Two Treatises* was in no sort a reply to his (Bristow's) *Motives* and *Demands*.|| He replies that he 'had alreadie made aunswere to Ryshtons challenge, which as I take it, is that table of the Church, which Bristowe confesseth to conteine all his demaundes, which demaundes are almost all conteined in his motiues'.¶ Unfortunately, the 'table of the Church' is *not*

* For example, the closest correspondence can be observed between Articles 7, 12, 13, 22, 26, 27, 28 and 29 of Fulke's version and Articles 7, 11, 12, 17, 19, 20, 21 and 22 of Rishton's 'Challenge'. Fulke sets out 29 Articles in all, Rishton 22. There is a more general agreement in the remaining Articles. Articles 10, 16, 20, 21, 23, 24 and 25 in Fulke have no counterpart in Rishton.

† Bishop Tanner, for instance, credits Rishton with the authorship of these Articles. See his *Bibliotheca Britannico-Hibernica*, 1748, p. 634. He states there that the work was published in English and began with the words, 'Firste, seeing it can not be denyed' – the first words of the 'Challenge'. Tanner is followed by Joseph Gillow, *Bibl. Dict.*, and others.

‡ Preface to the Reader, sig. *3^{v}.

§ In his *D. Heskins, D. Sanders, and M. Rastel, accounted (among their faction) three pillers*, etc., 1579. The Catalogue is given at Appendix V.

|| Bristow's actual words are quoted at pp. 393-4.

¶ Fulke, *A Retentiue, to stay good christians, in true faith and religion, against the motiues of Richard Bristow*, 1580, sig. A.

'Ryshtons challenge'. It would be a singularly ill-fitting title for that work. We may be fairly sure that it is the Table referred to in the *Douay Diaries* in the passage: [Bristow] *curavit tabulam chronographicam rerum ecclesiasticarum decem columnis distributarum per Edouardum Rishtonum unum de seminario componendam et typis imprimendam.**

A misconception on the part of Fulke, then, appears to have brought about this association of Rishton's name with the 'Challenge'. But it was only a temporary misconception in his case. With Bristow's reply in defence of Allen the matter was cleared up. It ran, *A Reply to Fulke, In defence of M. D. Allens scroll of Articles*; and Fulke in his 'Preface to the Reader' in his *Reioynder to Bristows Replie in defence of Allens scroll of Articles* begins, 'Allen the Author of the Popish challenge (as it is now confessed) . . .' It is noteworthy that both Robert Crowley and Thomas Spark in their later answers to the 'Challenge' refer to it as though it were the work of an anonymous writer.†

One difficulty remains in respect of Allen's Articles. Dodd, in his Church History, includes in his list of Allen's printed works 'Certain Brief Reasons concerning Catholick Faith. 1564'.‡ The explanation would seem to be that he was misled by a passage in a letter of Allen's to Dr. Vendeville, written in 1580 (?). Allen is writing of his sojourn in England (1562–5) and of his success as a missioner. His words are, I believe, the only personal reference he makes to the part he played in the writing of the *Motives*. They are as follows:

> Juvit etiam incredibiliter familiare colloquium quod aliquot ante annis vel mensibus in multis nobilium ac magnatum aedibus in Anglia existentes frequenter habuimus, in quo irrefragabilibus notis ac indiciis Ecclesiae et Sedis Apostolicae authoritatem vindicavimus; popularibusque argumentis sed invincibilibus demonstravimus apud alios quam nos, id est, catholicos, non posse esse veritatem: quas notas, regulas vel motiva ad fidem catholicam certo ab haeresi dignoscendam curavimus fusius postea Duaci explicari et excudi.§

* *D.D.* Appendix IX, p. 304. The table seems to have been reprinted (and perhaps extended) at Douay in 1595 under the title *Synopsis rerum ecclesiasticarum usque ad annum Christi 1577*. – *Bibl. Dict.* under Rishton.

A further reference by Bristow to 'Rishtons table' in his *Reply to Fulke* [sig. C4] supplies confirmatory evidence.

† See bibl. entry 2.

‡ C. Dodd, *The Church History of England*, 1737, Vol. II, p. 53. He is followed in this by T. F. Knox in a note in *Douay Diaries*, and by Gillow and others.

§ *Letters and Memorials of Cardinal Allen*, p. 56. The letter is dated 16. Sept. 1578 (altered to 1580).

The words 'curavimus fusius postea Duaci explicari et excudi' might, of course, be interpreted as meaning that Allen himself afterwards enlarged the Articles and had them printed at Douay. This was Dodd's reading of them. In view, however, of the express statement of Bristow to the contrary, we must interpret them more generally, viz. that the Articles were later on at Douay enlarged and were printed or published. That is to say, Allen is referring here to Bristow's version of his Articles, not to a printed version of his own. The words 'motiva ad fidem catholicam' become thus significant. They are the very words Bristow himself uses. Motives unto the Catholic Faith.

II

JESUS PSALTER

OF the two further editions of Whytford's *Psalter*, published by John Fowler in or about the year 1575, the first given below (the 'Bodleian' edition) is bound up with the 1574 edition of Vaux's *Catechism*, and, it will be observed, differs in minor points from the copy in the British Museum. For the second our sole authority is Thomas Sampson, the 'answerer' of the Psalter. Sampson's statement in regard to it has, therefore, been given at length.

The 'Bodleian' edition

Has same title as the Museum copy, but differs in the following details:

(*a*) Reverse of title-page has cut, with the words 'Miserere mei, Iesu, fili Dauid' above, and 'The Woman of Chanane ceassed not to crie. Matth. 15. Haue mercie on me, Iesu, the Sonne of Dauid. O Lord, help me' below.

(*b*) Heading at sig. D5^v runs: 'Here foloweth a holsome doctrine, howe to resist & ouercome the ghostly tentations of the Fende.'

(*c*) Appended to the *Psalter* is *Godly Contemplations for the vnlearned*, with new title, occupying sig. D8. This is repeated from the end-title of Vaux's *Catechism*.

'Sampson's' edition

Probably had the same title as the Museum copy, and is described by Thomas Sampson, in his *Warning to take heede of Fowlers Psalter* (1578), in the following passage:

> It seemeth also that the worke of this psalter did fall out shorter, then M. Fowler thought it would, and therefore he hath filled vp aboue three score leaues of his booke as in one of his copies is to be seene though it be left out in the lesser booke, with a certaine new deuised Imagerie, so y^{t} sithence wordes fayled him, he might yet fill vp his booke with some thing to feede the eyes of his simple reader, that is with a new stampe of Imagerie. This his workemanshippe of Imagerie he doth adorne with this title: *Godly contemplations for the vnlearned.* He doth also for confirmation of this his worke adde a sentence out of Basill which he turneth into English meeter.

The images are thus described: God 'in the likenes of an aged person with a crowne vpon his head' – 'before Christ on ye top of the mountaine on which he praied, a Chalice with a litle round host or cake in it, holden (as he doth graue it) in the hand of an Angell' – 'Christ Jesus [descending] into hell corporally with a long staffe in his hande, hauing a crosse and a banner cloth in the top of it, & . . . [drawing] soules by the handes out of hell, by a payre of stayres at a great gate of hewen stone' – the Virgin Mary 'personally or bodily assumpted into heauen, by the handes of Angells' – the coronation of the Virgin Mary [sig. B8].

The following editions, also printed during the sixteenth century, were either not known or *misknown* to Godwin and Sole, and are given by way of supplementation of the lists of editions given in their reprints:

1529. Referred to in the bibliography as the first printed edition.

1580 (?). *Certaine deuout and Godly petition | commonly Called. Iesus Psalter*. B.L. 16°.*

This follows Fowler's edition (Brit. Mus. copy) of 1575, though it is not necessarily a reprint of that edition. It was printed at Rouen by George L'Oyselet, the printer of the 1581 (?) edition of Vaux's *Catechism* (entry 146). With regard to the date there is less certainty. The inaccuracy of the text suggests that there was no English supervision of the printing and that the book is, therefore, earlier than the winter of 1581, when George Flinton began to supervise the printing at L'Oyselet's

* Godwin suggests 1545 as the date of this edition. He is followed by *Pollard and Redgrave*. Brit. Mus. Catalogue suggests 1570.

press for Fr. Persons.* If the *Psalter* is indeed Richard Whytford's, confirmation of the date of printing might be sought in the fact that the Brigittines of Syon settled in Rouen in mid-July 1580, and that about that time George Gilbert promised to pay for the printing of their Office and for the reprinting of the *Scale of Perfection.*†

1581 (?).

Bound up with the 1581 (?) edition of Vaux's *Catechism.* The pages of the *Psalter* are, however, missing from the (probably unique) copy in the British Muesum. The evidence for its existence is a note by some previous owner of the copy, who has written on the page where Richard Whytford's prayer occurs:

> Q. Would Rich. Whitford have published this prayer himself with such a title? Haud scio. The above, as well as title to Jesus Psalter in this book, & particularly what occurs at p. 90 – shew this catechism not to be Rich. Whitford's. Sic opinor.‡

1583. *Certaine deuout and godly petitions, commonly called. Iesus Psalter.* [cut, with the words 'Non est aliud Nomen datum hominibus. Act.4.'] *There is none other name vnder heauen geuen vnto men, in whiche we must be saued. Act.4. Cum priuilegio. Anno. 1583.*

The copy in the Bodleian Library of this duodecimo edition is bound up with the 1583 edition of *A Manual of Prayers.* It has, however, no connexion with the *Manual* beyond the binding. The two works are separate publications from the press of George L'Oyselet of Rouen.§ Appended to the *Psalter* are the

* Such inaccuracies as 'Narratiou' for 'Narration' in a section-heading, 'they' for 'thy', 'wich' for 'with', 'My spent' for 'mispent', would hardly have been overlooked by an English proof-reader. In one place (sig. B8v) the French 'Et' is substituted for 'And'.

† See *The Story of the English Bridgettines of Syon Abbey*, by J. R. Fletcher, 1933, p. 59. No edition of Hilton's *Scale*, printed about this time, is extant. Whytford's translation of the *Imitatio Christi*, on the other hand, was printed by L'Oyselet in 1585, possibly at the inspiration of the Brigittines, and the printing of a longish prayer of Whytford's by the same printer in the 1581 (?) edition of Vaux's *Catechism* (see below, and again at Appendix IV) may also have been due to 'Syon'.

‡ For the meaning of the writer's query see the title to the prayer given at Appendix IV. The reference to p. 90 is to the allusion there to Sess. 8, *anno* 1563 of the Council of Trent.

§ The name of the printer does not appear on either title-page, but each book bears unmistakable signs of L'Oyselet's press.

Golden Litany and Prayers 'made and collected by Syr Thomas Moore whyle he was Prisoner in the Tower of London'.*

1599. [within a rule, within a border] *Certaine deuout and Godly petitions, commonly called: Iesus Psalter.* [cut, between crosses and rules] *Cum Priuilegio.*

A duodecimo, printed in the 1599 edition of *A Manuall of Praiers*, with separate title-page as shown, but not a new register. Appended to the *Psalter* is the Golden Litany. Probably printed in England, although the title-page of the *Manual* has 'Printed at Calice 1599'. Gillow notes it in his monograph on the *Manual*.†

III

STAPLETON'S *COUNTERBLAST*. FECKENHAM OR HARPSFIELD?

In his Preface to the Reader in the *Counterblast*, Stapleton says that he was reluctant to undertake the task of replying to Horne on Abbot Feckenham's behalf, partly because he was insufficiently informed on certain points at issue. 'Howbeit', he goes on to say, 'afterward it so happened, that by suche as I haue good cause to credit, there came to my knowledge such Instructions . . . that I was the better willing to employ some study and paines in this behalfe.' Thus he came to *shape to* 'the whole booke, a whole and a full Reply'.‡ The providing of these 'Instructions' has been attributed to both Feckenham and Harpsfield.

Henry Holland, in his short life of Stapleton prefixed to the *Opera Omnia*,§ informs us that Feckenham supplied Stapleton with the subject-matter of his reply.|| He writes:

> Vbi autem Robertus Hornus Superintendens Vintoniensis, (cui traditus erat in custodiam *Ioannes Feckenhamus*, Reuerendissimus Abbas Westmonasteriensis) iuramentum primatus Regij in causis Ecclesiasticis ab eodem Feckenhamo exigebat, isque eleganti libro causas iustissimas cōceperat; cur tale iuramentum

* This is the edition referred to by Strype, *Annals* (1824), Vol. III. pt. 1, p. 292.

† *The Origin and History of the Manual. By Joseph Gillow.* London, 1910.

‡ Stapleton's words are quoted more fully at p. 501.

§ *T. Stapletoni . . . Opera quae extant omnia, nonnulla auctius et emendatius, quaedam iam antea Anglice scripta, nunc primum studio doctorum virorum Anglorum Latine reddita*, Paris, 1620, 4 vols. The *Counterblast* occupies pp. 817–1195 of Vol. II.

|| He is followed by T. Cooper in his article on Stapleton in the *D.N.B.*, who, n his turn, is followed by Gillow (*Bibl. Dict.*, s.v. *Stapleton*).

recusaret: Hornus inde occasionem arripuit de regio primatu Ecclesiastico scribendi, percurrens plerasque Regum & Imperatorum Historias, easque intolerabili audacia & impudentia foede nimis corrumpens. Quocirca meruit Hornus stylo aliquo dentato & aculeato pungi, vt sapere deinceps disceret. Placuit vehementer grandaeuo Feckenhamo iuuenilis Stapletoni stylus, vtpote viuus & acer, *& quasi facula ardens, verbum eius*. Venerab. ergo senex Responsionis suae contra Hornum subiectam quasi materiam ad Stapletonum transmisit, vt eam disponeret, suoque stylo exornaret, & aliunde locupletaret, suoque proprio nomine in lucem emitteret, ne illi incarcerato nouum periculum crearet. Quod pereleganter & erudite admodum praestitit Stapletonus; conuincens Hornum in hoc vnico suo de primatu libello sexcenta falsa quam impudenter deblaterasse.*

Clement Reyner, on the other hand, attributes the 'Instructions' to Harpsfield.† In his life of Feckenham in the *Apostolatus Benedictinorum in Anglia*‡ we read:

Ibi [i.e. in the Tower, where Feckenham was confined] anno 1563, cum iuramentum suprematus regii fuisset edicto parlamenti propositum, Feckenamus quaedam collegit argumenta, quibus illud ostendit illicitum fuisse: sequenti hyeme domo Horni pseudoepiscopi, pro carcere, vti iussus est, a quo inciuiliter & perfide, more ministrorum noui Euangelij tractatus fuit, & in turrim Londinensem iterum retrusus. Interea Hornus librum impium, plenumque mendacijs contra rationes Feckenami edidit: cui libro doctissimam opposuit Stapletonus responsionem; aut potius Harpsfeldius, ita enim constanter assertum a multis audiuimus, illum librum contra Hornum, quem Stapletonus edidit, reuera ab Harpsfeldio fuisse conscriptum, qui cum ipse in carcere teneretur, voluit latere, & sub amici vmbra, hostem hunc communem impugnare, sicut sub Alani Copi nomine dialogos suos contra Centuriatores Magdeburgicos euulgauit. Hoc responso pudefacti haeretici, quod hominem tot officijs de ipsis bene meritum, tam inhumaniter tractassent, iterum ex turri Londinensi liberatus est Feckenamus, & ad carcerem Mareschalli, vt vocant, aliquanto liberiorem, carcerem tamen, translatus fuit; paulo post permissa est illi potestas in priuato hospitio in suburbio Londinensi, quod Holburn vocant, habitare, vbi aquaeductum insignem condidit.§

* op. cit., Vol. I, sig. ā6v.

† He is followed by Miss E. T. Bradley in her article on Feckenham in the *D.N.B.* So, too, Dom Bede Camm (*Catholic Encyclopaedia*, s.v. *Feckenham*).

‡ *Apostolatus Benedictinorum in Anglia siue disceptatio historica, de antiquitate ordinis congregationisque monachorum nigrorum S. Benedicti in regno Angliae . . . Cum appendice* . . . Douay, 1626.

§ op. cit., Tract. I, Sect. 3, p. 235. We need have no doubt as to which of the Harpsfields is referred to here. Nicholas, the well-known controversialist, is obviously intended, not John.

If we had no more than these two conflicting statements to rely upon, we might well deem it impossible to decide which contained the truth. There is, perhaps, a little more to be said for Reyner than for Holland: there is an indifferency about his account which is absent from the other. The fact that he is writing a life of Abbot Feckenham for the 'authorized' history of the Benedictine Order in England, and that he excludes Feckenham altogether from the authorship of the 'Instructions', in spite of Holland,* and attributes them to Harpsfield, gives his statement an air of verisimilitude. This, however, would hardly of itself warrant our concluding in favour of Harpsfield's authorship.† Fortunately, corroborative evidence for Reyner's view is to be found in the *Counterblast* itself.‡ Book III of that work deals with 'the pretensed practise of Ecclesiastical gouernmēt in Emperors and Kings as wel of our own Countre of Englande, as of Fraunce and Spayne, in these later. 900. yeres'. Harpsfield's *Historia Anglicana Ecclesiastica* covers a good deal of the same ground.§ It is not surprising, therefore, to find a number of passages in the *Historia* which are closely parallel to passages in the *Counterblast*. Altogether I have reckoned up a dozen important parallels, and I have no doubt that a closer scrutiny would reveal more.|| As it is, this number is by no

* Since he is writing some six years later than Holland, it is difficult to suppose that he would be unaware of Holland's view.

† It should, perhaps, be remarked here that, in the dedication to Cardinal Bentivoglio of his *Apostolatus*, Reyner declares 'non author operis sum, sed, iussu congregationis, editor et dedicator'. This fact, of course, does not in any way prejudice the view expressed above.

‡ On the other hand, Holland's view is supported by John Bridges, the answerer of the *Counterblast*. Bridges's words, however, can hardly be taken as evidence. He writes: 'But first whatsoeuer he [i.e. Stapleton] wil set downe for master Feckenham, whom he calleth *the reuerent father my lord Abbot of Westminster*, bicause him selfe hath no knowledge hereof, but by hearesay, all that he declareth he buildeth on this groūd, *as I assuredly vnderstand*. Now who gaue him thus *assuredly to vnderstande*, a man may easily deuine, euen forsooth this *reuerent father*, who as we must *vnderstande* with all, would tell M. Stap. nothing that should be partiall to himselfe in his owne case. We must therefore beleeue that all is true that Master St. telleth of Master Feckenham, for assuredly master Feck. his own self & no worse man hath let him so to vnderstand' (*The Supremacie of Christian Princes*. London, 1573, sig. C4[v]). He admits, that is to say, that he is guessing.

§ *Nunc primum in lucem producta Studio & Opera R. P. Richardi Gibboni Angli Societatis Iesu Theologi. Duaci*, 1622.

|| There is also one sentence in the *Counterblast* which seems to derive directly from Harpsfield's *Treatise on the Divorce*. It concerns Cranmer, 'who caried about with him his prety conie in a chest full of holes, that his nobs might take the ayr' (*Counterblast*, fol. 8[b]). This echoes Harpsfield's, 'Sometime [Cranmer] carried her about with him in a great chest full of holes, that his pretty nobsey might take breath at' (*Treatise on the Divorce* (Camden), 275).

means small, seeing that only a small proportion of the 200 folios of the third book of the *Counterblast* contains matter relevant to the *Historia.** Alternatively, if we do not accept this corroborative evidence in favour of Harpsfield's authorship of the 'Instructions',† we are thrown back upon the supposition that Stapleton himself had access to a copy of the *Historia*, which he was able to use in this part of the *Counterblast.* The odds are against this. The *Historia* was, of course, in manuscript, and was still being revised by Harpsfield in the year when the *Counterblast* was published, and indeed for several years after, and it is unlikely that copies would be multiplied at this time.‡

We may reasonably conclude, then, that Reyner's view of the authorship of the 'Instructions' is the correct one. And, indeed, it might well be asked what *could* be the point of Stapleton's keeping Feckenham's name out of his Preface if he had supplied them. After all, it was Feckenham's controversy with Horne. The controversy had been carried on up to this point quite openly. Feckenham might naturally have been expected to frame a reply. On the other hand, there was good reason for keeping Harpsfield's name dark. Harpsfield was in a much worse position than Feckenham. He was looked upon, rightly or wrongly, as a much more dangerous man. And there can be no doubt that his 'butting in' on this controversy might have had serious consequences, not only for him but for his brother John as well.

It remains, finally, to call attention to these words of Reyner's: 'Harpsfield . . . wished to remain anonymous, and to attack the common enemy under cover of a friend's name, just as under Alan Cope's name he had published his own dialogues against the Centuriators of Magdeburg.' They may be taken as defining Stapleton's word 'Instructions', as it appears in his Preface, and clearly give an importance to the part played by Harpsfield in this production. We should conclude from them that the great body of the work was his.

* Since the *Counterblast* and the *Historia* are both rare books and are seldom found together in the same library, I have added as a note at the end of this appendix an example of the parallelism referred to. The reader will have no doubt, both from the expressions used and from the 'logic of events' that the same hand has been at work in the two passages quoted.

† It has never been suggested that Harpsfield and Feckenham collaborated to produce the 'Instructions'. We may, therefore, rule out Feckenham here.

‡ See R. W. Chambers's *Introduction to the Life and Works of Nicholas Harpsfield*, p. cc, in the Early English Text Society's edition of *Harpsfield's Life of More*, 1932.

Note

De eodem Thoma eiusque indigna caede

Rex audita caede Pontificis, supra modum indoluit, veritus ne, propter veteres inimicitias, illius author haberetur. Per quadraginta dies a publico, causarumque omnium cognitione, rerumque ciuilium cura; luctu, ciborumque se tenuitate macerans, abstinuit. Ad cuius postea caedis suspicionem dimouendam, publice coram *Romani* pontificis legatis, se iureiurando purgauit, neque se vnquam mandasse, neque parentum obitum ita vnquam deplorasse, atque hanc indignam caedem, contestatus. Ingenue tamen confessus est, prae irae magnitudine, quaedam sibi aliquando verba excidisse; per quae facilius carnifices illi ad eam excitabantur. Cuius suae inconsultae facilitatis, poenas se ex arbitrio legatorum, & pro ecclesiasticae disciplinae more, subire paratum affirmauit. Illi vero Regi cum alia quaedam, tum & id praeceperunt, vt peruersas illas consuetudines aboleret, quae totius huius perturbationis seminarium erant. Quibus mandatis non Rex modo, sed & filius pariturum se promisit. Triennio post Henricus filius, cum fratribus, patri adeo infestus fuit, tantumque tamque atrox bellum aduersus eum concitauit, vt ille res suas quodamodo deploratus haberet. Reges enim *Galliae* atque *Scotiae*, cum multis proceribus tam Angliae quam transmarinarum regionum, quae Anglico imperio parebant, ad eum opprimendum coiere. Et o miram Dei prouident – iam iustitiamque! vt Rex, qui tam indigne patrem suum spiritualem infestauerat, ipse quoque a filio suo, eoque praesertim, quem insolenti exemplo, singularique in eum fiducia, ad regnum admouerat, tam seditiose infestaretur. Rex in his tantis angustiis, e *Normannia* Angliam petit. Quam ingressus, *Cantuariamque* omni celeritate petens (visione quadam didicerat, nullam, nisi reconciliato Thoma martyre, pacis spem superesse) quam primum metropolitanam ecclesiam, vbi martyris monumentum est, vidit, vestibus se exuit, nudis pedibus, & nudo etiam corpore (nisi quatenus vilis quaedam illud tunica operiebat, ciuitatem ingreditur) atque ita per plateas sordidas, sepulchrum adijt, apud quod totum eum diem noctemque insequentem, in ieiunio, precibus, & lachrymis vigil perseuerauit, virga ab Episcopis quinquies, a singulis monachis (quorum numerus erat supra octoginta) ter caesus est.

Historia Anglicana Ecclesiastica. Cap. xvii. sig. Tt4v et seq.

Of Henry II and S. Thomas of Canterbury

But what shal we say to kinge Henry him selfe? what thowghte he trowe ye of this blessed mans doings and death? This parte of the story of all other is moste notable. The king being in Normandy, and hearing that S. Thomas was slayne toke the matter so heuely, that for forty dayes, he kept him selfe solitary in great mourning and lamentatiō, in great abstinence, setting a syde al the affayres of his great ād large dominiōs, for greif and sorow: And forthwith sent his ambassadours to the Pope to purge him selfe of the sayd murther. Wheruppō certayn Legats were sent to him, before whom vpō his othe he sayd, that he neither cōmaunded, nor willed that the Archbishop should be slayne, and added that he was neuer so sory for the death of his owne father or mother. Yet did he not denie, but by vnaduised words, he gaue the murtherers an occasion of theyr fowle enterprise. Wherfor he submitted him self to the Legats to enioyne him penaunce as they should thinke good. Then was yt among other thinges enioyned him, that he should breake and reuoke the foresayde statutes and ordinances, for the which al this troble rose: al the which cōditions the king by his othe promised to obserue. This done the kings son also promised on his part, to see these couenants kept. But yet see the iuste iudgement of God. As this king rebelled againste his spirituall father S. Thomas, and his spirituall mother the Churche, so did his sonne and heire, with his two other sonnes, Richard and Iohn, rebell againste him, confederating them selues with other the kinges subiects, and with the Frenche and Scottishe kinges. The king was browghte to this distresse, that he wyste not in the world, what to saye, or what to doe: and being destitute of mans helpe ranne to Gods helpe, and to the helpe of his blessed martyr S. Thomas, at whose great miracles done at Canterbury all the worlde did wonder. Wherefore forsakinge Normandy where he was in more saftie, sayled into Englande, and commynge towarde Canterbury, before he entred the city, puttinge of al his princely apparell, lyke a newe kinge Dauid, beinge persequuted of his Absolon, for his synnes, as Dauid wente out of the citie barefoted, so this newe Dauid beinge barefoted, and all hys body naked, sauinge that he was couered withe a poore and a vile cote vppon the bare, beinge nowe hym selfe fearefull and tremblyng, whom before so many nations feared and trembled, with muche sighinge and gronynge went to the Martyrs tombe, where he continued all that daye, and the nighte followinge watchfull and fastinge: where he commended hym selfe to the blessed martyrs prayers. Neither was he deceyued of his good deuotion and expectation: as we shall anon declare. Before the sayde tombe, he toke discipline with a rodde of euerie monke . . .'

Counterblast, sig. ii. 1–1ᵛ.

IV

VAUX'S *CATECHISM*

SINCE T. G. Law wrote his admirable introductory memoir to the Chetham Society reprint of Vaux's *Catechism*,* new material has come to light which enables me to implement the account of the list of early editions referred to in that reprint.

The first edition, 1567

I see no reason to doubt the evidence of Anthony à Wood, referred to by Law, that the first edition was issued in 1567. The two imprimaturs of the 1568 edition point conclusively to a first and second edition, the first being without the treatise on Ceremonies.† If any doubt has arisen on the point, it is because Fowler in his reprint of 1574 ran the two imprimaturs together and dated the result 1567, thus allotting the treatise on Ceremonies also to that year, whereas the 1567 imprimatur refers only to the Catechism and does not mention the treatise. The imprimaturs are as follows:

> Catechismus iste Anglico idiomate cōscriptus, lectus & approbatus est a viris illius linguae & sacrae Theologiae peritissimis, vt sine periculo cū populi vtilitate credā imprimi & euulgari eum posse.
>
> Sig. Cunerus Petri pastor S. Petri Loua.
> 20. Aprilis, An. 1567.
>
> Tractatus item de Ceremonijs Ecclesiae lectus & approbatus est a duobus viris Anglici idiomatis & Theologiae peritissimis, quibus iudico merito & tuto credendum esse: quare sine periculo imprimi potest.
>
> Sig. Cunerus Petri pastor S. Petri Loua.
> 20 Aprilis, An. 1568.

* *A Catechisme or Christian Doctrine by Laurence Vaux, B.D., Canon Regular and Subprior of St. Martin's Monastery, Louvain, sometime Warden of the Collegiate Church, Manchester. Reprinted from an Edition of 1583: with an introductory memoir of the author by Thomas Graves Law.* 1885.

† Law does not seem to have been aware of this edition.

(Both from the 1568 edition at sig. S7)

Catechismus iste Anglico idiomate conscriptus, cum Tractatu de Ceremonijs Ecclesiae, lectus & approbatus est a viris illius linguae & sacrae Theologiae peritissimis, vt sine periculo cum populi vtilitate credā imprimi & euulgari posse.

Cunerus Petri, Pastor S. Petri Louan.
20 Aprilis, An. 1567.

(From the 1574 edition at sig. A1^{v}. It will be noted how the words of the original 1567 imprimatur have been used with the least possible change. Also the dropping of the abbreviated 'sig.' is significant.)

The second edition, 1568

This is the edition given at entry 146.

The third edition, 1574

A Catechisme, or a Christian Doctrine, necessarie for Children & ignorant people, briefly compiled & set forth by Laurence Vaux Bacheler of Diuinitie. With an Instruction newly added of the laudable Ceremonies vsed in the Catholike Churche. S. Athanasius. Whosoeuer wil be saued, before al thinges it is necessarie, that he hold the Catholike Faith. Antuerpiae, Apud Iohannem Foulerum, Anglum. M.D.LXXIIII.

There is a copy of this edition in the Bodleian Library. With it is bound up a copy of *Jesus Psalter* of 1575.

The fourth edition, 1581 (?)

*Godly. Contemplations for the vnlearned.** [cut with 'Si quis sitit.

* The preliminary matter includes the fragment of 'A prayer verye necessarye to be sayde at all tymes by Richard withforde a brother of Shene'. Since this prayer has, in all probability, never been reprinted, I give it here.

O Blessed Lord God my maker & redemer here nowe in thy presence / I doe (for this tyme and for all the tyme of my whole life) byqueathe & bytake or rather doe frelie giue my selfe / soule & bodie / with all my harte & mynde vnto the (swete lorde) and vnto thy hādes / to be thy bounde seruaunte for euer according to the promise made in my baptisme at the font stone. And here now / I doe ratifye and newlie confirme the same and doe fullie consent in harte & mynde therto neuer here after (by the helpe of thy grace) to contrarye the same / but to contynne[w] in thy lawes (blessed lorde) vnto the ende of my life. But where thou knoweste (sweete lorde) that I am a fraile persōne infirme feble & weake & of my selfe prone & redie ī thoughte worde & dede vnto euil frō the begynninge of my life hytherto / I beseche the good lorde god & father of all puissance & power of all might & strēthe that thou wilte defende me frō all my enemies & gyue me spirituel strēgh & power that I may in the / vanquishe / & ouercome flee & auoyde all such frailitie light manners or dispositions as may be contraire to thy will & pleasure / & that accordinge vnto this will of the spirite / whiche thy goodnes hathe nowe frelie gyuē vnto me / I may destroye the will of the fleshe / and . . .

veniat ad me et bibat. Io.7.' To right and left of cut, 'Non est aliud Nomen datum hominibus. Acts.iiij.'] *D. Basilius. Homil. in xl. Martires. What Hystorie by heare say reportes to the mind: The same the silent picture doth shew in like kinde.* [G. L' Oyselet. Rouen. 1581?]

This title refers to the preliminary matter of the volume only. The book contains both Catechism and treatise on Ceremonies. Unfortunately, the (probably unique) copy in the British Museum has lost some preliminary pages and signatures A1–B1, so that the Catechism is without title.

The ornamental capitals employed in the print of this edition point certainly to the press of G. L'Oyselet, Rouen.

I suggest 1581 as the date of this edition on the strength of a letter written by Vaux to Coppage, an old colleague at St. Mary's College, Manchester, and dated 21 August 1583, in which he says: 'god be blessed as yet I have found no lacke, my friends here be manye and of myche worship, especially sith my cathechysme came forth in prynt; at my comynge out of forande contres I Leifte it w[th] A frende in lukelande to be put in prynte but it came not forth till thys last yeare, heare weare greate plentie of theim solde for xij[d] A peice but nowe is not one to be bought, A gentlemā dwellinge w[t]hin xvj[th] myles of you tolde me that he hade 300 whiche came in at the north p'ts, so that there is no wante amongest you and in these parties the Jesuytes and semynarye prestes do vse it for the Instruction of the people'.* The natural interpretation of the words in this letter 'thys last yeare' would be the year 1582,† and, remembering that Vaux had *come out* 'of forande contres' into England in July 1580, we may conclude that the *Catechism* must have been printed between those dates. Since the copy under discussion may, on printing grounds, definitely, I think, be assigned to a date earlier than 1583,‡ and since all the other

The rest is missing, as is also *Jesus Psalter* which appears to have formed part of the preliminary matter of the book. This one gathers from the words of a previous owner of the copy in the British Museum, who writes in on the page where the prayer occurs: 'The above, as well as title to Jesus Psalter in this book, and particularly what occurs at p. 90 [reference to Council of Trent, 8th Session, 1563] – shew this catechism not to be Rich. Whitford's. Sic opinor.'

* Cited by Law, op. cit., p. lxxix. Doubtless it was Vaux's reference to 'lukelande' (Liége) which misled Law as to the place of origin of the 1583 editions.

† Law suggests that Vaux must have meant by 'this last year' *this present year*, thus referring to one of the 1583 editions of the Catechism. But he did not know of the edition we are discussing.

‡ It is undoubtedly of about the same date as *Jesus Psalter* referred to at p. 524.

known editions prior to 1583 can be definitely dated, we may assume that it is an exemplar of the edition referred to by Vaux in his letter, and the year 1581 would seem a safe date to adopt for the printing.

The fifth and sixth editions, 1583

A. [within a border] *A Catechisme or Christian Doctrine necessarie for Children and ignorante people, briefly compiled by Laurence Vaux Bacheler of Diuinitie: with an other later addition of instruction of the laudable Ceremonies vsed in the Catholicke Churche. Whereunto is adioyned a briefe forme of Confession (necessary for all good Christians) according to the vse of the Catholicke Churche. S. Athanasius. Who so euer will be saued before all thinges it is necessarie, that he holde the Catholicke faith. Cum Priuilegio.* [rule] *1583.* [G. L'Oyselet. Rouen.]

There is a copy of this edition in the British Museum. The 'briefe forme of Confession' is, of course, Fowler's (see entry 43), and is set out with a new title-page at sig. a1.

B. [within a border] *A Catechisme or Christian Doctrine necessarie for Children and ignorante people, briefly compiled by Laurence Vaux Bacheler of Diuinitie: with an other later addition of instruction of the laudable Ceremonies vsed in the Catholicke Churche. Whereunto are adioyned certayne briefe notes of dyuers godly matters. S. Athanasius. Who so euer will be saued, before all thinges it is necessarie, that he holde the Catholicke faith. Cum Priuilegio. 1583.* [G. L'Oyselet. Rouen]

Two copies only of this edition appear to be extant. One is in the library of Salisbury Cathedral; the other, in the Signet Library, Edinburgh. The printer in his Address to the Reader follows the words of the 1583 A edition above, but adds in respect of the 'certayne briefe notes': 'And finding in other godly bookes, diuers briefe notes of good and godly matters in forreyne tongues not impertinent to this argument, I haue thought good to collect, compyle, translate and publishe the same as an appendant to this booke, for a further augmentation of profit and commoditie to the vnlearned: which my trauayle I desire may be accepted of all, as profitable to the readers as they may make it, and with as good a will as I offer it.' There is no clue given as to who this compiler is. If, however, one may hazard a guess, I should say that he was George Flinton, who was in charge of the English printing at L'Oyselet's press at this time.

The dearth of copies of the 1581 edition of the *Catechism* (referred to in Vaux's letter above) accounts for these two reprints. The printer himself in 'The Printer to the Reader' (both editions) refers to the want and scarcity of the *Catechism*, and states that he would have printed it before had he not had the expectation of a 'more ample discourse'. He was persuaded of the immediate need, however, 'by some good men', and so 'newly set furth this Catechisme'. (1583 B has 'put furth in printe'.)

The ornamental capital letters in both these editions are those which were in use at L'Oyselet's press. Variations in the print point to their being separate editions of the *Catechism* and not two issues of the same printing with different additions. I have been unable to establish priority of order between them.

The seventh edition, 1590

A page by page reprint of 1583 A. Copy at Lambeth Palace Library.

The eighth edition, 1605

A Catechisme or Christian Doctrine, necessary for children and ignorant people, briefly compiled by Laurence Vaux, Bacheler of Diuinitie. With an other addition of instruction of the laudable Ceremonies vsed in the Catholike Church. Whereunto is adioyned a briefe forme of Confession (necessary for all good Christians) according to the vse of the Catholike Church. S. Athanasius. Whosoeuer will be saued, before all things, it is necessarie that he hold the Catholike Faith. [cut] *Printed at Roan. 1605.*

Copy in the library of Oscott College. Fowler's 'Briefe Forme of Confession' is set out with new title (sig. H12) as in the 1583 A edition and is dated 1599.

A. J. Hawkes, in a paper read before the Bibliographical Society, 15 February 1926, says of this edition: 'This hitherto unknown edition of Vaux negatives Mr. T. J. Law's suggestion (Chetham Society's reprint of the Catechism, N.S., Vol. IV) that a reputed 1599 edition might be the one referred to in the Bishop of Chester's inventory; this, doubtless, is the edition there listed.'*

* *The Birchley Hall Secret Press*. By Arthur J. Hawkes. Hawkes is referring to Law's note (Introd., op. cit., p. xciii), which runs: 'In 1613 the Bishop of Chester forwarded to the king an inventory of books found among the effects of "one Anderton, a recusant in Lancashire, deceased". Among these books, or parcels of books, "Vaux's Catechisms" find a place.' Tanner's list of editions in the *Bibliotheca Britannico-Hibernica* includes the 1599 one, also one of 1593. Neither of these editions is known.

V

FULKE'S CATALOGUE OF POPISH BOOKS

This list of books, set out by William Fulke in three successive publications, is a valuable guide for the student of our Recusant works. The catalogue appears first in Fulke's *D. Heskins, D. Sanders, and M. Rastel, accounted (among their faction) three pillers and Archpatriarches of the Popish synagogue . . . ouerthrowne, and detected of their seuerall blasphemous heresies* (London, 1579), and it is followed by a revised and enlarged edition in his *T. Stapleton and Martiall (two Popish Heretikes) confuted . . .* (London, 1580), which in its turn was reissued with additions in his *A Retentiue, to stay good christians, in true faith and religion, against the motiues of Richard Bristow . . .* (London, 1580). The list as it appears in the second of these issues presents a more exact description of the books than in the third, although this was probably the latest of the three to be published.* I, therefore, append this list with the additional entries from the third issue as supplement. It is headed: 'A Catalogue of all such Popish Bookes either answered, or to be aunswered, which haue bene written in the Englishe tongue from beyond the Seas, or secretly dispersed here in England haue come to our handes, since the beginning of the Queenes Maiesties reigne.' The list follows:

1. Harding against the Apology of the Englishe Church, answered by M. Iewel, Bishop of Sarum.
2. Harding against M. Iewels challenge, aunswered by M. Iewel.
3. Hardings reioynder to M. Iewel, answered by M. Edward Deering.
4. Coles quarels against M. Iewell, answered by M. Iewell.
5. Rastels returne of vntruthes† answered by M. Iewel.
6. Rastell against M. Iewels challenge, answered by William Fulke.
7. Dorman against M. Iewel, answered by M. Nowel.
8. Dormans disproofe of M. Nowels reproofe, answered by M. Nowel.
9. The man of Chester,‡ aunswered by M. Pilkington Bishop of Duresme.
10. Sanders on the Sacrament in part aunswered by M. Nowell.
11. Fecknams Scruples, answered by M. Horne B. of Winchester.
12. Fecknams Apologie, answered by W. Fulke.

* Strype reprints this second revised list in his *Annals* (1824), Vol. II, pt. 2, pp. 709–11.

† Should be Stapleton.

‡ Morwen.

13. Fecknams obiections against M. Goughes sermon, answered by M. Gough, and M. Lawrence Tomson.
14. Stapletons counterblast, answered by M. Bridges.
15. Marshall his defence of the crosse, answered by M. Caulfehill.
16. Fowlers Psalter, aunswered by M. Sampson.
17. An infamous libell or letter (*incerto authore*) against the teachers of Gods diuine prouidence and predestination, answered by Maister Robert Crowley.
18. Allens defence of Purgatory, answered by W. Fulke.
19. Heskins parleament repealed by W. Fulke.
20. Ristons challeng, answered by W. Fulke, & Oliuer Carter.
21. Hosius of Gods expresse worde translated into English, answered by W. Fulke.
22. Sanders rocke of the Church, vndermined by W. Fulke.
23. Sanders defence of images answered by W. Fulke.
24. Shacklockes Pearle answered by M. Hartwell.
25. The hatchet of heresies, answered by M. Bartlet.
26. Maister Euans answered by himselfe.
27. A defence of priuate Masse answered (by coniecture) by M. Cooper Bishop of Lincolne.
28. Certeine assertions tending to mainteine the Church of Rome to be the true and catholike church, confuted by Iohn Knewstub.
29. Sander vpon the Lordes supper fully answered by D. Fulke.
30. Bristowes motiues & demaundes, answered by D. Fulke.
31. Stapletons Differences, & Fortresse of the faith, answered by D. Fulke.
32. Allens defence of Priestes authoritie to remit sinnes, & of the Popish Churches meaning concerning Indulgences, answered by D. Fulke.
33. Martials Reply to M. Calfehill, answered by D. Fulke.
34. Frarins rayling declamation, answered by D. Fulke.

These Popish treatises ensuing are in answering, If the Papistes know any not here reckoned, let them be brought to light, & they shall be examined.

1. Stapletons returne of vntruthes.*
2. Rastels replye.
3. Vaux his Catechisme.
4. Canisius his Catechisme translated.

Supplementary to these are the three following new entries in the third list:

(*a*) Iohn de Albynnes discourse against heresies, englished, with an offer of a Catholique to a learned Protestant: which offer is aunswered vnder the name of Ristons articles, by W. Fulke.†

(*b*) Gregor. Martins treatise of schisme.

(*c*) Poyntes of the Sacrament.

* See above, 5.

† cf. Riston's *Challenge*, 20 above, for the 'offer of a Catholique'.

VI

HAND-LIST OF PRINTERS OR PUBLISHERS OF RECUSANT WORKS, 1559–1582*

(Figures in brackets denote number of entry in bibliography)

BEELAERT, John (Douay)

A notable Discourse. 1575. (2)

BOGARD, John (Douay and Louvain)

An Answere to Maister Iuelles Chalenge. 1564. (48)
A Replie to M. Calfhills blasphemous Answer. 1566. (83)
Of the Expresse Worde of God. 1567. (141)
Certayne deuout Meditations. 1576. (4)
Short and absolute order of confession. 1576? (6)
Iesus Mattens. 1576? (7)
Certayne necessarie Principles. 1579? (67)

BRINKLEY, Stephen (Greenstreet Ho.)

A Consolatorie Epistle. 1580. (see 62)
A Reply to Fulke. 1580 (23)
A Briefe Discours. 1580. (92)
A Brief Censure. 1581. (93)
A Discouerie of I. Nicols. 1581. (94)

BRUMEN, Thomas (Paris)

The Refutation of Ane Ansuer. 1573. (145)
Certaine Demandes. 1580. (56)
The Disputation? 1581. (24)
Ane Admonition? 1581. (25)
Ane Catholik and Facile Traictise? 1581. (46)
Of Prayer, and Meditation. 1582. (63)

CARTER, William (London)

The Loue of the Soule? 1578. (85)
A Treatise of Schisme. 1578. (84)
The Exercise of a Christian Life? 1579. (20)
Instructions and Aduertisements. 1579. (39)

DIEST, Aegidius (Antwerp)

The buke of fourscoir-thre questions. 1563. (157)
Vincentius Lirinensis. 1563. (158)
A Confutation of a sermon. 1564. (122)
Certaine Tables. 1565. (33)
A brieue Admonition. 1565. (34)

* This list does not include printers licensed to print in England. With the single exception of John Maes short biographical references to all of the printers will be found in R. B. McKerrow's *Dictionary of Printers and Booksellers, 1557–1640* (Bibl. Soc., 1910). Additional information will be found in the chapter headed 'Publishers and Presses' of this present work.

A Briefe Answere. 1565. (52)
A Copie of a challenge. 1565. (123)
A Replie against an answer. 1565. (124)
A most excellent treatise. 1565. (134)

FOGNY, John (Rhemes)
A defence of the honour. 1569. (75)
An Apologie and true declaration. 1581. (12)
A Briefe Historie. 1582. (13)
The New Testament. 1582. (86)
A Discouerie of the Manifold Corruptions. 1582. (87)
A true report. 1583. (14)

FOWLER, John (Antwerp and Louvain)
The supper of our Lord. 1565. (128)
An Oration. 1566. (41)
A Reioindre to M. Iewels Replie. 1566. (53)
Testimonies for the Real Presence. 1566. (117)
A Treatise intitled, Beware of M. Iewel. 1566. (125)
The Third Booke . . . Beware of M. Iewel. 1566. (126)
The supper of our Lord. 1566. (129)
A Treatise made in defence. 1567. (11)
A Request to M. Iewell. 1567. (32)
A Reioindre to M. Iewels Replie. 1567. (54)
A Brief Shew. 1567. (127)
The Rocke of the Churche. 1567. (130)
A Treatise of the Images of Christ. 1567. (131)
A Counterblast to M. Hornes vayne blaste. 1567. (142)
An Edict or Ordonance. 1568. (3)
A Learned and very Eloquent Treatie. 1568. (38)
A Detection of sundrie foule errours. 1568. (55)
A Briefe Treatise of Vsurie. 1568. (132)
A Catechisme. 1568. (146)
A Treatise of Iustification. 1569. (118)
A Treatise of the Holy Sacrifice. 1570. (26)
A Treatise concerning the Defence. 1571. (77)
A Treatise of Treasons. 1572. (78)
The Copie of a Letter. 1572. (79)
A Dialogue of Cumfort. 1573. (42)
A Table. 1573. (143)
A Briefe Treatise. 1574. (21)
Vaux's Catechism. 1574. (see 146)
Iesus Psalter. 1575. (44)
A Brief Fourme of Confession. 1576. (43)
The Psalter of Sainct Hierome. 1576. (45)

HOLOST, Hubert (Bruges)
A breefe Directory. 1576.* (81)

* Holost seems also to have been the printer of the first entry above, *A notable Discourse*, published by Beelaert.

LAET, John (Antwerp)

A Proufe of Certeyne Articles. 1564. (30)
A Treatyse of the Crosse. 1564. (82)
A defense and Declaration. 1565. (10)
A Disproufe of M. Nowelles Reproufe. 1565. (31)
A Confutation of a Booke. 1565. (50)
An Epistle of . . . Osorius. 1565. (133)
The Apologie of Fridericus Staphylus. 1565. (137)
The History of the Church of Englande. 1565. (138)
A Fortresse of the Faith. 1565. (139)
A Returne of Vntruthes. 1566. (140)

LEKPREUIK, Robert (Edinburgh)

Ane Answer to ane Epistle. 1563. (159)

L'OYSELET, George (Rouen)

Iesus Psalter. 1580? (see 44)
Vaux's Catechism. 1581? (see 146)
The First Booke of the Christian Exercise. 1582. (95)
A Defence of the Censure. 1582. (96)
An Epistle of the Persecution. 1582? (144)

MAES, John (Louvain)

A Consolatorie Epistle. 1579.* (62)

PATES, John (Leiden)

The first foure bookes of Virgil. 1582. (136)

SCOT, John (Edinburgh)

Certane tractatis. 1562. (155)
The last blast of the trompet. 1562. (156)

SYLVIUS, William (Antwerp)

An Answere to Maister Iuelles chalenge. 1565. (49)
The Parliament of Chryste. 1566. (57)

VERSTEGAN, Richard (London and Paris)

A true report. 1582. (9)
A Treatyse of Christian Peregrination. 1583. (88)
A Refutation of sundry reprehensions. 1583. (120)

* Printed for John Lion, the Catholic bookseller.

VII

CHRONOLOGICAL LIST OF WORKS*

(Figures in brackets denote number of entry in bibliography)

1559 Quintin Kennedy's Letters. (70)
The Sixt Tragedie of . . . Seneca. Jasper Heywood. (58)

1560 The Seconde Tragedie of Seneca. Jasper Heywood. (59)
Cole's Letter to Jewel. (29)

1561 An addicion with an Appologie. Morwen. (91)
Lucii Annei Senecae Tragedia prima. Jasper Heywood. (60)
An Oration by Mr. Quintine Kennedy. (71)
Ane compendious Ressonyng. Kennedy. (72)

1562 Certane tractatis. Winzet. (155)
The last blast of the trompet. Winzet. (156)
An Apologie of priuate Masse. (1)
Iohn Heywoodes woorkes. (61)

1563 The buke of fourscoir-thre questions. Winzet. (157)
Vincentius Lirinensis. Winzet. (158)
Heir followeth the coppie of the ressoning . . . concerning the masse. Kennedy. (73)
Ane Answer to an Epistle. Winzet. (159)

1564 An Answere to Maister Iuelles Chalenge. Harding. (48)
A Proufe of Certeyne Articles. Dorman. (30)
A Treatyse of the Crosse. Martiall. (82)
A Confutation of a sermon. Rastell. (122)
Feckenham's Declaration, etc. (35)

1565 A Copie of a challenge. Rastell. (123)
The Apologie of Fridericus Staphylus. Stapleton. (137)
An Answere to Maister Iuelles chalenge. Harding. (49)
A Replie against an answer. Rastell. (124)
An Epistle of . . . Osorius. Shacklock. (133)
A Confutation of a Booke. Harding. (50)
A defense and Declaration. Allen. (10)
To Maister John Jeuell. Harding. (51)
Certaine Tables. Evans. (33)
A Briefe Answere. Harding. (52)
A most excellent treatise. Shacklock. (134)
A brief rehersal & discription. (8)

* The varying practice of publishers and printers on the Continent in the second half of the sixteenth century in dating their books according to O.S. or N.S., together with the frequent omission of precise dates of publication, makes it virtually impossible in many cases to establish with any certainty the exact order of the works. We have followed the practice of giving the year as it appears on the title-pages, using such additional information as the dates of the privilegia, etc., afford as a further guide to the order of the works.

Certayn and tru good nues. (5)
The History of the Churche of Englande. Stapleton. (138)
A Fortresse of the Faith. Stapleton. (139)
A Disproufe of M. Nowelles Reproufe. Dorman. (31)
The supper of our Lord. Sander. (128)
A brieue Admonition. Evans. (34)
Maister Randolphes Phantasey. Jeney. (68)

1566 The supper of our Lord. Sander. (129)
An Oration. Fowler. (41)
A Treatise intitled, Beware of M. Iewel. Rastell. (125)
A Replie to M. Calfhills blasphemous Answer. Martiall. (83)
The Parliament of Chryste. Heskyns. (57)
A Returne of Vntruthes. Stapleton. (140)
A Reioindre to M. Iewels Replie. Harding. (53)
Testimonies for the Real Presence. Pointz. (117)
The Third Booke . . . Beware of M. Iewel. Rastell. (126)

1567 Of the Expresse Worde of God. Stapleton. (141)
The Rocke of the Churche. Sander. (130)
A Treatise. Allen. (11)
Vaux's Catechisme. (see 146)
A Briefe Shew. Rastell. (127)
A Request to M. Iewell. Dorman. (32)
A Reioindre to M. Jewels Replie. Harding. (54)
A Counterblast to M. Hornes vayne blaste. Stapleton. (142)
A Treatise of the Images of Christ. Sander. (131)

1568 A Briefe Treatise of Vsurie. Sander. (132)
A Catechisme. Vaux. (146)
A Detection of sundrie foule errours. Harding. (55)
An Edict or Ordonance. (3)
A Learned and very Eloquent Treatie. Fen. (38)
A discours of the present troobles in Fraunce. Jeney. (69)

1569 A Treatise of Iustification. Pole. (118)
A defence of the honour. Leslie. (75)

1570 A Treatise of the Holy Sacrifice. Butler. (26)
Feckenham's Assertions against Gough. (36)
The Historie of Scotland. Leslie. (76)

1571 A Treatise concerning the Defence. Leslie. (77)
The Two Bookes of the Histories of Irelande. Campion. (27)
Feckenham's Apology? (37)

1572 A Treatise of Treasons. Leslie. (78)
The Copie of a Letter? Leslie. (79)

1573 The Refutation of Ane Ansuer. Tyrie. (145)
A Table. G.T. (143)
A Dialogue of Cumfort. Fowler. (42)

1574 A Briefe Treatise. Bristow. (21)
Vaux's Catechisme. (see 146)

1575 A notable Discourse. (2)
Iesus Psalter. Fowler. (44)

1576 Bristow's Demaundes. (see 22)
A Brief Fourme of Confession. Fowler. (43)
A Breefe Directory. I.M. (81)
The Psalter of Sainct Hierome. Fowler. (45)
The Post of the World. Verstegan. (147)
Iesus Mattens? (7)
Certayne deuout Meditations. (4)
A short and an absolute order of confession? (6)

1577 The Praise of Solitarinesse. Baynes. (18)
The Historie of Irelande. Stanyhurst. (135)

1578 A Treatise of Schisme. Martin. (84)
The Loue of the Soule. Martin. (85)

1579 Certayne necessarie Principles of Religion? T.I. (67)
The Exercise of a Christian Life. Brinkley. (20)
A Consolatorie Epistle. Hide. (62)
Instructions and Aduertisements? (39)

1580 Certaine Demandes. Hay. (56)
Campion's Letter to the Lords of the Council. (28)
Sixe Reasons. Pounde. (119)
A Consolatorie Epistle. Hide. (see 62)
A Brief Discours. Persons. (92)
A persuasion delivered to Mr Sheldon. Langdale. (74)
A Reply to Fulke. Bristow. (23)

1581 A Brief Censure. Persons. (93)
Ane Catholik and Facile Traictise. Hamilton. (46)
A Discouerie of I. Nicols. Persons. (94)
The Disputation. Burne. (24)
Ane Admonition. Burne. (25)
An Apologie. Allen. (12)
Vaux's Catechisme. (see 146)

1582 The New Testament. Martin. (86)
A Briefe Historie. Allen. (13)
A Discouerie of the Manifold Corruptions. Martin. (87)
Of Prayer, and Meditation. Hopkins. (63)
The first foure bookes of Virgil. Stanyhurst. (136)
A true report. Alfield. (9)
The First Booke of the Christian Exercise. Persons. (95)
A Defence of the Censure. Persons. (96)
An Epistle of the Persecution. G.T. (144)

1583 A true report. Allen. (14)
A Treatyse of Christian Peregrination. Martin. (88)
A Refutation of sundry reprehensions. Rainolds. (120)

1617 The Baynes of Aquisgrane. Baynes. (19)

INDEX

The references are to pages. When an 'n' accompanies a page reference a footnote is indicated. Principal authors and subjects are in capital and small capital letters. The index does not duplicate the information supplied in the Bibliography (Part II) and in Appendices V, VI and VII.